COMMAND MISSIONS

From a painting by Boleslaw Jan Czedekowski

LT. GENERAL L. K. TRUSCOTT, JR.

COMMAND MISSIONS

A Personal Story

by

Lt. General L. K. Truscott, Jr.

Illustrated with Maps and Charts

E. P. DUTTON AND COMPANY, INC.

NEW YORK, 1954

To

ERRATA

Page 18, line 30   *Change* ODWD *to* OPD

Page 21, line 26   Colonel (later Brigadier General) "Arch" Hamblen's christian name *is* Archelaus, *not* Archibald.

Page 28, line 36   *Change* St. Paul's *to* Westminster Abbey

Page 32, 33, 409   *Change* Somerville *to* Somervell

Page 49, line 35, page 77, line 36   Before Costobadie *insert* de

Page 55, line 13   *Change* Huges-Hallet *to* Hughes-Hallet

Page 68, line 26   *Change* Les Quartes Vents *to* Les Quatres Vents

Page 77, line 20   *Change* Karl Victor Klopet *to read* Carl Victor Clopet

Page 92, Paragraphs 1 and 2   Major Hamilton volunteered for this mission as soon as he joined me on board after arrival in the transport area.

Page 108, line 3   *Italicize* Infantry Journal

Page 121, 123, 133, 135   *Change* Mathinet *to* Mathenet

Page 135, 139, 142, 143, 145, 152, 157, 160, 166, 171, 537, 538   *Change* Robinette *to* Robinett

Page 133, 139, 158   *Change* Tulergma *to* Telergma

Page 142, last paragraph, to top of 143   *Change 1st sentence to read:* Robinett's Combat Command B had entered Corps reserve at Bou Chebka, January 28th and was moved to Maktar in Army reserve by February 2nd.

Page 145, line 9   *Delete middle initial* P in General Ward's name.

⌊*see over*⌋

ERRATA

Page 147, line 1 — *Change* January 28 *to* January 30

Page 147, line 26 — *Change* General McQuillin's middle initial *to* E

Page 148 — *Change* southwest *to* southeast

Page 149, last line — *Change* still *to* again

Page 155, 7 and 8 — *Delete* Lieutenant; *Delete* one of the battalions of

Page 155, line 17 — *Change* Tebessa *to* Sbeitla

Page 155 — *Change* four *to* six; *Delete* had

Page 167, line 28 — *Change third sentence to read*:
In the south, the Germans and Italians drove south of Combat Command B toward Bou Chebka, cutting off a battery of artillery, but a counterattack by the 2d Battalion 6th Armored Infantry supported by a company of tanks and some other elements during the afternoon recaptured the guns and all lost ground.

Page 170, line 29 — *Change* a day or so later *to read* a few days

Page 171, line 12 — *Change* Chief of Staff *to read* G-3 Operations

Page 172, line 22 — *Change* 24th *to* 25th

Page 182, 207, 252-253, 296, 320, 323, 340, 346, 352, 360, 367, 371, 400, 408, 421, 422, 428, 440, 547-548 — *Change* O'Daniels *to* O'Daniel

Page 277, 321, 323, 326-327, 332, 342, 349, 548 — *Change* Templar *to* Templer

NOTE: It is a matter of deep regret to the author that these errors have crept into this text. He can only plead that separation from personal records and pressure of other work has made the business of proofing a most difficult and unsatisfactory task.

TABLE OF CONTENTS

CONTENTS

FOREWORD

IT is with some trepidation that I add another to the long list of personal war experiences of the Second World War, and my temerity demands some explanation. Several factors led me to begin the work in the first place and to continue the onerous task to completion under conditions which have often been particularly difficult for one who has no pretensions as a professional writer.

In the first place, my war assignments, which were unique in many respects, brought me into close relationships with those responsible for the concept, planning, preparation and conduct of the war in the European Theater and afforded me some part in the various phases. This relationship spanned the entire period of American participation from the hour of decision early in 1942 to the end of the war in Italy and beyond to include the first year of the occupation. If these experiences have any historical or popular interest, there is no one else to relate them for me.

Secondly, my own war experiences are merely testimonials to the accomplishments of the American soldier who has no superior and few equals when adequately equipped, properly trained and afforded good leadership in the various echelons. Officers and men under my command—the 3rd Infantry Division in Sicily, in Italy from Salerno to Anzio, the VI Corps at Anzio and in Southern France, the Fifth Army in those final glorious 19 days from the Apennines to the Alps—established records that were not equalled by others in this war and have not been excelled in any other to my knowledge. In large measure,

9

these magnificent accomplishments of American soldiers passed without full recognition at the time because they were overshadowed by events in other areas of perhaps greater importance at the time. This book is therefore a recognition in some measure of magnificent deeds of the officers and men who served with me.

Lastly, when this war began I had never heard a shot fired in anger—I had had no battle experience. I had applied myself in military and other studies during peacetime and had formed decided opinions concerning the techniques of combat and leadership. More than most American senior commanders, I had the opportunity to apply these theories in battle in command of units varying in size from a regimental combat team to a field army. In this respect, my war experiences may have some value as an example of development in the art of command and of battle leadership.

In writing this book, I have no great controversies to pursue, no individuals to condemn, no ally to castigate. I encountered no problems during my war experience which reasonable men regardless of nationality could not consider without recrimination, and I found officers and men, superiors and juniors, ever willing to give sympathetic consideration to opposing points of view. I have not sought to write the military history of the various campaigns in which I participated nor to describe the political and economic factors which had bearing upon them. These are problems for historians who must have access to records on both sides, and this history will require research and analysis quite beyond my own capabilities. Rather, I have sought to allow the reader to follow the war with me—to know some of the atmosphere of unreality and uncertainty in which we lived and carried out our various tasks. I have taken no liberty with historical facts and any positive statement of mine is documented by records in my own possession or immediately available. If COMMAND MISSIONS accomplishes these purposes in any measure, if it affords some pleasure to those who served with me, if it adds to the recognition due the American soldier for his achievements, my object will be achieved.

While I have written this book without professional assistance, acknowledgments are due to many persons without whose advice and assistance it could not have been written, including members of my staff. In particular, acknowledgment is due to my Chief of Staff, Brigadier General Don E. Carleton for his loyal support and encouragement; to Colonel Theodore J. Conway and Colonel Ben Harrel for reading various portions of the manuscript and for valuable advice and suggestions; to Nicholas Wreden for encouragement to continue the writing after scanning only a portion; to my good friend Severence A. Millikin of Cleveland, Ohio for reading many of these chapters and for valuable advice and encouragement concerning them; to the late Frank Page of Washington, D.C. for reading a portion of the manuscript and for advice of a personal and professional nature, and to Leslie Rowe for patience in editing the manuscript. To these and many others my grateful appreciation.

L. K. TRUSCOTT, JR.
Lt. General, U.S.A.

CHAPTER ONE

COMMANDO MISSION

1. *A Mission Begins*

Luck plays a part in the life of every man. This is particularly true of the military life. It has certainly been so in my own. Had I not been transferred from the Armored Force—without my consent and rather against my will—and assigned to General Staff duty in February, 1941, it is probable that some one else would be telling the story of "Commando Mission" and that my experiences in the years that followed would have been quite different.

In June, 1940, I was a major of cavalry just completing a tour of six years as student and instructor at the Command and General Staff School at Fort Leavenworth, Kansas. The Armored Force was just being formed from the nucleus of the mechanized cavalry brigades. Like many others, I sought experience in this new arm and was assigned to it in August. During the next few months, as battalion executive and regimental S-3 in the 13th Armored Regiment at Fort Knox, my duties were interesting but normal ones for such assignments. However, I had been promoted to the rank of lieutenant colonel in October, and I was looking forward to increasing opportunities as the Armored Force expanded.

About the end of January, 1941, General Ben Lear, then beginning the organization of the Second Army at Memphis, asked the War Department if I was available for assignment to that Army staff. Some weeks later, orders came assigning me to General Staff with troops and transferring me, not to the Second Army, but, to my astonishment, to the IX Army Corps at Fort Lewis, Washington. I hated to leave the Armored Force at this time, but had always felt that an officer should accept assignments without question. Nevertheless, it was with something akin to resignation that my wife and I packed our belongings and with our younger son headed for the Pacific Northwest.

Here Fate played its first card. For the Commanding General, IX Army Corps, was Major General Kenyon A. Joyce under whom I had served as a captain before going to Leavenworth. And the Chief of Staff was Colonel Dwight D. Eisenhower, whom I met for the first time.

The duties assigned to me as Assistant G-3 involved preparing and conducting training exercises and maneuvers for the divisions of the corps, the 3rd and 41st Infantry Divisions. During the course of this summer's work, not only did I come to know and appreciate the Chief of Staff, but I came in contact with many others who were concerned with the expanding war effort and with many who would have grave responsibilities during the following years.

In November, 1941, I was assigned to command the 5th Cavalry in the 1st Cavalry Division at Fort Bliss, Texas, for which General Joyce released me from my staff assignment. Joining the regiment in the latter part of November, I found myself commanding a regiment soon to be on war-footing. After Pearl Harbor, the 1st Cavalry Division, and Fort Bliss, seethed with war-like activities.

The Border, free of dread for many years, knew again the creak of saddle leather and the sound of marching troops, the roar of motors aground and aloft, and all of the rumors and alarms so familiar to other generations. Outposts screened five hundred miles of Rio Grande and desert waste. Bridges and tunnels on transcontinental railways, power plants, magazines of ammunition and military installations all were placed under heavy guard. And, as always when activities are shrouded in secrecy and normal channels of information are interrupted, rumors and false reports spread like the seeds of cottonwood borne on desert winds. Besides these security measures, there was also preparation for war. Drill mounted and dismounted, tactical exercises, maneuvers, target practice, schools, parades, practice marches on horse and on foot, lectures, demonstrations, fire drills, combat firing, inspections, cadres for the expanding army, all these and the administrative routine of military life filled our days—and nights.

In the last week of April, 1942, the struggle on Bataan had ended, Guam and Wake had fallen, and the struggle on Corregidor was entering upon its final hopeless stage. The Japanese tide had engulfed Malaya, was overflowing into Southeastern Asia, and rolling on toward Australia where General MacArthur was only beginning his enormous task. Nazi legions, after the great victories of the preceding summer, were at the gates of Stalingrad and Moscow, and waited only the winter's end to resume their march to the east. Britain, momentarily free from the threat of invasion, had weathered a succession of costly defeats and was locked in the struggle for existence with the strangling submarine blockade. The remainder of Europe, except for the few neutral states, was helpless under the conqueror's heel. In America, the industrial, economic, social and military organization for war was developing, supported by a people united as never before by Pearl Harbor.

But to a people with sons and daughters on Bataan and Corregidor, progress seemed depressingly slow. A wave of enthusiasm swept the country at the news of Jimmie Doolittle's gallant if somewhat bootless raid on the homeland of Japan.

On a Thursday morning in April, I had ridden out over the mesa to observe squad combat exercises below the rim. I had watched several exercises and was waiting for the range to clear and another to begin, when the regimental messenger dashed up and breathlessly informed me: "Sir, Colonel, Washington's trying to get you on the phone. Sergeant Major says it's important and they want you to call right away."

There was an undercurrrent of excitement when I dismounted at regimental headquarters. Lieutenant Thomas, the regimental adjutant, informed me that I was to call General Clark, Chief of Staff, Army Ground Forces, in Washington. He placed the call. Washington was soon on the wire.

"This is Truscott."

"Clark speaking. Say, how soon can you leave there for an important assignment?"

"Why, er"—I even glanced at my watch. "Right now, I reckon, that is, as soon as I can get transportation."

"Well, it need not be that soon. Take what time you need to get ready, but you ought to be here within the next two or three days. Come to Washington and report to me. Ike knows about this. I can't tell you where you are going nor what you are going to do, but it is a whale of an important job. All I can tell you is that you are going overseas. Be prepared for extended field service in a cold, not arctic, climate. Understand?"

"Yes, sir."

Click. The connection was broken.

And so began four eventful years.

Naturally, I reported immediately to the division commander, Major General Innis P. Swift. He knew no more than I. And of course I informed my wife. During the next two days of preparations for departure, there was much speculation among family and friends as to where I might be bound. But when the clipper lifted into the pre-dawn air, I was headed into adventures that none of us could guess.

Washington seemed little changed from the beautiful and peaceful city I had known in previous years, for the migration to the Capital City was then only in its initial stages. Gas rationing had not yet restricted movements, nor had the parks yet been marred by temporary wartime construction. One noted more uniforms in evidence than in

pre-war years; for military personnel the wearing of civilian clothing
had passed with Pearl Harbor.

The Army War College, which the peace-time emergency of 1940
had suspended to make officers available for training the expanding
army, now housed Headquarters, Army Ground Forces, where I was
to report. This beautiful old post, formerly known as Washington Barracks, seemed anything but war-like in its seclusion behind its high red
brick walls on the peninsula between the Washington Channel and the
Anacostia River. Beside the quiet waters of the Washington Channel,
a long row of two-story red brick quarters with tall white pillars amid
sheltering shade trees fronted the grass-covered parade. The parade
was dotted here and there with the greens of a rather diminutive golf
course. On the opposite side, temporary frame buildings loomed.
And at the far end, the great college building stood under its glistening
dome against the Anacostia. The scene was reminiscent of some peaceful college campus rather than the nerve center of gathering hosts.

General Mark W. Clark, whom I had met the previous summer,
greeted me by asking how I would like to be one of the Commandos
whose exploits had recently been receiving such wide publicity. In
spite of my astonishment, I was able to say that I thought I would like
it very much. Then General Clark explained that the British and Americans had agreed to invade Europe the following spring, and that I was
to head a group of American officers who were to join the staff of
Lord Louis Mountbatten, whose organization was responsible for the
Commandos, and for amphibious training in the British service. I could
hardly have been more amazed, for in spite of all our speculations, this
was a possibility that had never crossed our minds. General Clark added
that I would be given my instructions by General Eisenhower, who
was now Chief of the Operations Division, War Department
(ODWD). He then telephoned General Eisenhower that I had reported. After paying my respects to General McNair, Commanding
General, Army Ground Forces, who had been Commandant at Leavenworth while I was there, I proceeded on to the Munitions Building
with, I must admit, some trepidation.

At the 20th Street entrance to the Munitions Building, all was in contrast to the peaceful seclusion of the War College. Streams of people
arrived and departed on foot, by bus, by taxicab, and by private and
official cars. Guards at the door checked the personal indentification of
all who entered. Others, strategically placed, kept all who entered under observation, until some office door closed behind them. Through
the halls passed, in ever changing streams, foreign officers on their way
to conference or committee; officers of every branch and rank bearing
important-looking cases, folders, or rolls of maps and blue prints;

clerks, stenographers, civilians with bulging brief cases; janitors, plumbers, carpenters, painters, electricians with the tools of their trades, engaged in endless remodelling and renovation. And there was everywhere the sense of urgency, of hurry, as though time were pressing; and everywhere an air of mystery as though all could tell of deep dark secrets. Threading my way with the uncertainty of the outsider, I found the Operations Division, and was soon in the office of General Eisenhower.

The General greeted me warmly, questioned me about my recent activities, asked news of mutual friends, and interrogated me at length concerning the reaction of people in the Southwest who had lost so many sons on Bataan. He listened to my answers in his characteristic intent manner.

Then he told me why I was there.

General Marshall, he said, believed that the United States and Great Britain should direct their first major offensive against Germany, and he considered continued Russian participation in the war a vital factor in the defeat of Germany. The offensive would have to be an invasion across the English Channel because only in this area could the British employ their maximum strength. Only in this area could we attain the overwhelming air support vital for successful ground operations. Further, the United States could concentrate and maintain larger forces in Britain than elsewhere. Logistical and other factors fixed the 1st of April, 1943, as the earliest date for a major invasion; but General Marshall believed that it might be possible to establish an active front on a limited scale in Western Europe during the early fall if the urgency of the situation demanded it. General Marshall had just returned from London where he had obtained British agreement to plans based on this concept. American forces would be concentrated in England as rapidly as shipping and other considerations permitted.

General Marshall, he continued, was confident that American troops would be well trained, but he was concerned that none of our soldiers would have had any battle experience whatsoever. And General Marshall considered it vital that every American assault unit have within its ranks a few men who had met the Germans in battle and who could be instructors and examples to their comrades and friends. Accordingly, he had arranged with Admiral Mountbatten to send a group of American officers to join his Combined Operations Headquarters. It was this group that I was to head. The War Department was selecting officers who would accompany me, and these officers would report shortly. General Marshall had also arranged to place other American officers in other British headquarters to assist in planning and to facilitate mutual understanding.

Our Navy, General Eisenhower went on to say, was cold toward this plan. They favored operations in the Pacific where the Navy would have the dominant role. Our naval authorities thought that commitments in the Pacific would absorb all of their resources, and they were unwilling to undertake to provide the landing craft and to organize and train the crews to operate the craft, which would be required in large numbers. Therefore, Army Ground Forces itself would organize special engineer units to operate and maintain landing craft, establish bases, and the like. No naval officer would be assigned to me until the question of naval participation had been more fully considered and developed. Meanwhile, he added, I would want to study the information available, talk to the officers who had accompanied General Marshall to London and who had participated in the conferences with British officers, and assemble data that I might need. General Marshall would want to see me within a few days.

I listened attentively while General Eisenhower unfolded this new field in my professional experience. I had had no battle experience, no practical experience in amphibious operations. Only twice in my life had I ever been in a small boat on salt water. My cavalry background had brought limited contact with the Navy, and but little more with the Air Force. True, I had studied theory in our service schools, and had even been an instructor at both the Cavalry School and the Command and General Staff School. But this assignment to a staff of battle-seasoned veterans of naval, ground and air battles, actively engaged in planning and conducting operations against the Germans, would seem to call for an expert. This I definitely was not. These facts I tried to express to General Eisenhower. He listened gravely, regarding me under lowered brows, then said: "I consider that your background as a cavalry officer, your experience with the Armored Force, your experience as an instructor at Leavenworth, your experience on a corps staff, and even your experience as a polo player especially fit you for this assignment. You know that Lord Louis wrote a book on polo. You can learn, can't you?"

Colonel John E. Hull, Chief of the European Section, and Lieutenant Colonel Albert E. Wedemeyer, of the Plans Section, Operations Division, (both were subsequently made lieutenant generals) were two of the officers who had accompanied General Marshall to London. They had participated in the staff discussions of the American proposals with British staff officers. These officers were old friends of mine. We had been classmates at the Command and General Staff School in the 1934-1936 Class. We spent many hours discussing the plans which had been agreed upon. They described various British personalities, outlined some of the differences in British organization and methods which they had observed, and suggested some of the problems which might confront us.

Colonel Wedemeyer provided me with copies of all the documents relating to the subjects considered during the London conferences. These included the original proposals for the invasion presented by General Marshall, minutes of numerous meetings, notes by British staff officers on items such as landing craft, shipping, engineer organization, concentration and training of American troops in England, Commando tables of organization, organization of various British headquarters, and many other subjects. There was more than enough to further confuse and to challenge an already well-confused cavalry colonel.

Meanwhile, the officers who were to accompany me reported one by one. Lieutenant Colonel H. B. Cleaves, Signal Corps, was brought from the Signal School at Fort Monmouth; Major Theodore J. Conway, Infantry, was brought from the faculty at West Point; one air officer, then another, was considered, until the assignment finally fell to Lieutenant Colonel Loren B. Hillsinger, Army Air Force. These officers, I think, felt almost as inadequate for the assignment as I did, and my own uncertainty could hardly be expected to imbue them with boundless confidence. However, we struggled along together trying to prepare ourselves for—we knew not what.

We studied such intelligence reports, estimates, manuals, and other data as we could obtain in the War and Navy Departments. We worked with the officers who were to join other British staffs. Colonel Arthur S. Nevins, Plans Section, was to join British Joint Staff Planners. Colonel Joseph R. Sheetz, G-3 Section, and Colonel Archibald R. Hamblen, G-4 Section, were to join British Home Forces. None of us had more than a vague idea as to what these various British headquarters were. We knew next to nothing of British organization and staff procedures. We rushed here and there consulting others who knew little more than we. Only the British officers then on duty in Washington knew much about the headquarters we were to join. Their advice was helpful but their lack of knowledge of our own organization and staff procedures placed limitations upon the value of their information. All in all these were confusing days. But it is always difficult to prepare for a new and strange experience.

General Eisenhower talked freely with me about my assignment and about the problems of the war effort in various theaters. At his suggestion, I spent much time in his office listening to the discussions of problems and studies brought to him by officers of the Operations Division, by other sections of the War Department, by naval officers, Congressmen, committees, and by the endless chain of visitors that passed through his office during his long days. His methods had not changed from those I had become familiar with the year before. Every view was considered. Each problem was carefully analyzed. There was the same extraordinary ability to place his finger at once upon the crucial fact in any problem or the weak point in any proposition .There was the same ability to arrive at quick and confident decisions. And the same charming manner and unfailing good temper. In retrospect, I think the most valuable hours of my preparation were those I spent in General Eisenhower's office. More than anything else these hours enabled me to appreciate the magnitude of our national undertaking and the vast complications involved in the direction of world-wide warfare. Viewed in this perspective, my problem, however confusing it might seem to me at the moment, did not loom so large.

Then General Marshall sent for me. Ushered into his office, I saw him for the first time. His calm and dignified personality was most impressive. He shook my hand in a quick firm grasp, indicating a chair beside his desk. Then, leaning back slightly in his chair, he gazed at me steadily. Without change in expression, he spoke slowly: "You are an older man than I wanted for this assignment. I looked you up—you are forty-seven. Mountbatten is forty-three. Most of his staff are younger. All of them are battle-experienced. They are even now engaged in planning and conducting raids against the Germans." He paused. There seemed to be nothing for me to say, which was probably just as well for my mouth was more than dry enough to make speech difficult. He continued: "But some of your friends assure me that you are younger than your years, and that your experience especially fits you for this assignment."

I tried to explain my lack of qualifications. But disregarding my attempted interruption, General Marshall went on to describe Admiral Mountbatten, the organization which he headed, the activities in which they were currently engaged, and the part they would have in preparations for the projected invasion.

Then he continued: He was gravely concerned because our soldiers would be committed to their first battle which would be one of vital concern to the nation. He had no fear that they would not be well trained, but there could be no substitute for actual battle in preparing men psychologically to meet the nervous tensions and uncertainties of combat. American soldiers would be at a disadvantage as compared with our British allies in this respect. British soldiers had met the German in battle and knew that he was only a well-trained soldier. While the nature of the proposed operations would preclude battle experience on any large scale for our divisions as was done in World War I, it still would be possible to give such experience to a limited number of men in raids. A few experienced men in every assault unit would be able to counter the fears and uncertainties which imagination and rumor always multiply in combat. These men would be able to disseminate practical information among their comrades, and thus in some measure compensate for our inability to give such experience to all.

It was primarily for this reason, he continued, that he had arranged with Admiral Mountbatten to send my group to London. Raids against the German-held continent would be increased in scope and in frequency until the time for the invasion. As many American soldiers as possible would be given an opportunity to participate in these operations. My task would be to arrange for this participation and for the dissemination of this battle experience among assault units. We would be working members of Admiral Mountbatten's staff and would assist in every way possible in the training of American troops and the preparations for the invasion. General Eisenhower would see that necessary instructions were issued and that proper facilities were provided in England. He wished me every success, and would see me later on in London.

This interview made an everlasting impression upon me. General Marshall had removed any confusion in my mind as to what was expected of me. For the rest, it was up to me—and I could not fail.

When I returned to General Eisenhower, I recounted my interview with General Marshall in detail. General Eisenhower called a stenographer and dictated a letter of instructions which was to guide the operations of my group in England. He also dictated a letter of instructions to the Commanding General, United States Army Forces in the British Isles, on the subject of War Department representation at British headquarters. My letter of instructions was as follows:

SUBJECT: Letter of Instructions

TO   : Colonel L. K. Truscott, Jr., Cavalry

   1. In accordance with orders issued, you with designated assistants, are directed to report to the CG USAFBI for attachment to the staff of the Commander of Combined Operations, British Army. You will be working members of that staff; as such, you will perform all duties allotted to you which are not clearly incompatible with your missions set forth herein.

   2. Your missions are· To study the planning, organizations, preparation, and conduct of combined operations, (especially of commando type) and to keep ODWD informed as to developments in training, technique, and equipment pertaining to these and related operations;

   To initiate plans for participation by American troops in these operations to the fullest practicable extent with a view to affording actual battle experience to maximum personnel, and to plan and coordinate training of detachments designated for such participation;

   To provide information and recommendations relative to the technique, training, and equipment involved in these and related operations, to assist

HQ AGF in planning, organizing, and conducting training in such operations within the US;

To promote in every practicable way the spirit of cooperation and team play between the Allied Forces.

3. Your official communication with the WD, AGF, AAF, and SOS will be through the CG USAFBI. You will keep the CG USAFBI and appropriate members of his staff informed of developments in your work, and will advise them in matters pertaining to training of and participation by American troops in these operations. The CG USAFBI will facilitate in every practicable way the accomplishment of your mission.

4. In carrying out the missions assigned to you, you will keep in mind at all times the desirability of retaining existing American command and administrative organization, and that new organizations and installations should be held to the minimum.

You will keep in mind at all times that the principal objective of this program must be that of providing actual battle experience for as many as practicable of our personnel.

For the Chief of Staff

(*Signature*)

DWIGHT D. EISENHOWER
Major General
Assistant Chief of Staff.

This letter, and the one addressed to the CG USAFBI, General Eisenhower handed to me for study and recommendations. While I had no occasion to recommend any changes whatever, the incident illustrated his characteristic method of dealing with subordinates, a method which I was subsequently to observe on many occasions. General Eisenhower was interested in the success of the mission; he had confidence in the personnel to whom it was assigned; he was anxious that the orders for the mission should not only be clearly understood by those concerned, but should be so carefully drawn as to facilitate the accomplishment of the task even under unforeseen circumstances. This characteristic is in my opinion one of the marks of high command ability.

Our departure was in keeping with our normal state of confusion. Several times we were notified that we should be ready to leave and then our departure would be postponed. Conway finally left on a B-24 which was being ferried over. The remainder of the party were eventually notified that we would depart on May 10th.

Fortunately for me, after I left Fort Bliss my wife had been able to see our daughter married, pack our belongings, and come on to Washington with our younger son before my departure overseas. It was a comfort to both of us that she could learn something more, although not much more, than I had been able to tell her previously. Once again she was to send me off to face an uncertain future. But there were no tears, only pride. Hers was the courage of the Roman matron.

Our route was to take us to Montreal where certain secret equipment known to us later as IFF, Identification Friend or Foe, was to be installed on the *Apache*, our Pan American Stratoliner, by British technicians, then by way of Newfoundland and Iceland to Scotland, weather permitting. We reached Montreal after a quick trip in fine weather but were delayed there three days, first by waiting for installation of the IFF, and then by weather. While all of us were anxious to be on our way, we were glad to see Montreal which had been under wartime conditions for many months. I think that we were most impressed by the warm welcome accorded our American uniforms, and by the matter-of-fact and philosophic way in which citizens accepted rationing and other restrictions as yet unknown in the United States.

We left Montreal on May 13th but bad weather forced our return to Stephensville, a new base under construction by the American Air Force on the Southwest coast of Newfoundland. On the following day, we were able to land at Gander, and that night we took off again for Iceland. The remainder of our flight, after our departure from Iceland, was over the Atlantic whose restless waves we could see only now and then. For the most part, we roared along hour after hour in bright sunlight above a carpet of clouds. As we approached the British Isles, we saw our first big convoy at sea. With seemingly hundreds of ships, and destroyers trailing great curves astern and airplanes circling overhead, it was a magnificent sight. But we had little time to enjoy it for we were forced to detour, and even then we were carefully investigated by the covering aircraft. We were approaching the end of our first transatlantic flight and all felt the excitement of it. Some time later we circled the huge air terminal at Prestwick, let down upon the runway, and rolled to a halt at the end of our flight. It was a thrilling experience.

Our journey from Prestwick to London was at night and reasonably comfortable in a sleeping car. Viscount Bowes-Lyon, a flight companion on our trip, sat with me in my compartment for several hours. He told me something of the psychological warfare activities in which he had been engaged, and discussed quite frankly some of the personalities with whom I would come in contact. Most interesting to me was his description of the effects of war upon the British people. Continual exposure to danger from bombing and battle, loss of loved ones, deprivation of all but basic necessities of life, days filled with nothing but labor, a future seemingly devoid of hope—these could be expected to affect the whole psychology of a people, although I had never considered it before. The evening passed all too quickly.

In the morning, near the end of our journey, we were awakened by the steward with the cup of tea which we were to find customary on British sleeping cars. Soon we could begin to see some of the physical effects of the bombing by which the Germans had sought to bring England to her knees. Rail lines leading into London had evidently received special attention. Most of the stations were ruins surrounded by demolished masonry. On all sides were burned-out factories, warehouses, and dwellings. Through these bombed areas trains proceeded gingerly over repaired road beds. Little of the damage appeared to be of recent origin, but the effect was stark and dismal, full evidence of the horrors through which a people had passed.

2. *Breaking In*

We arrived at St. Pancras Station on May 17th, a week almost to the hour from our departure from Bolling Field. Commodore Ellis and Colonel Archibald from Combined Operations Headquarters were at the train to welcome my group on behalf of Admiral Mountbatten, who was out of the city. Nevins was met by one of the British Joint Staff Planners, Hamblen and Sheetz by representatives of British Home Forces. On the American side there was a military police lieutenant. He informed us that he had been directed to take us to our assigned billets and to inform us that we should report to theater headquarters the following day as this was Sunday.

We were assigned billets, two to a room, in Grosvenor House, one of the swank hotels on Hyde Park. Here we remained until early June when we were able to find lodgings, with breakfast, in the home of Mrs. Gordon Leith at 1-A Manchester Square where we lived comfortably during the rest of our stay in London. For other meals, we joined the recently organized American Officers' Mess at 8 South Audley in what had been the Bachelors' Club.

This mess utilized American rations but obtained vegetables, dairy products, and some meats from local sources. The mess employed British civilians and conformed to British rationing regulations. Most of us who had meals there during the summer of 1942 will long remember the three-course meals, the heavy gray bread which many of us learned to like, the sausages compounded of very little meat and much potato meal and cereal, the endless monotony of Brussels sprouts and cabbage, and the countless ways in which Spam can be prepared and served without any change whatever in identity, or flavor.

London seemed like a great country village at first. One saw comparatively few people on the streets, and many of those were standing patiently in what the more experienced informed us were "queues". Londoners, we were told, had to wait in queues for everything from transportation and theater tickets to articles of food and clothing. Shop windows displayed little for sale, prices were high, and all essential items were strictly rationed.

We were surprised at the drab and untidy appearance of the women we saw on the streets and in the shops, for we had just come from an America in which the rough hand of war had not yet swept aside the luxuries, much less the necessities, of life. Nor did we appreciate the psychological change that results from continued exposure to danger, denial of the ordinary amenities of life, and from conditions of existence that could offer only "blood, sweat, and tears."

We were not prepared for the numbers of women in uniform and in military formations. Women manned most of the clouds of balloons which kept hostile planes far above the streets of London. They drove most of the vehicles we saw in the streets and replaced men in many other positions. While it was new to us, this mobilization of women brought home to us the strain which war had placed upon British man power.

The Commanding General, United States Army Forces in the British Isles, at this time was Major General James E. Chaney, Army Air Force. With a group of ground and air officers, he had been in London for more than a year, before we entered the war, observing British organization, equipment, methods, and techniques. After the United States entered the war and the employment of American troops in Europe became more than a possibility, General Chaney had been directed to begin the organization of the European Theater of Operations. This organization was well under way when we reported, all of the principal staff positions being occupied by members of the observers group. Theater Headquarters, or as it was more commonly called ETO or ETOUSA, was located at 20 Grosvenor Square, where the principal offices remained throughout the war.

At nine o'clock Monday morning, we reported to the Chief of Staff, Brigadier General Charles L. Bolte. Here I presented my letter of instructions and a few minutes later was taken into General Chaney's office and introduced to him. General Chaney glanced briefly at my letter of instructions, but gave no indication that he had any previous knowledge of my assignment or any interest whatever in the mission I was sent to perform. With a few perfunctory remarks, I was dismissed. The remainder of the day I spent in visiting the principal members of the staff and in calling at the American Embassy.

There was much curiosity among the staff at theater headquarters

concerning our missions, and there was among them a distinct air of disapproval of the whole idea. Comments on "running the war from
Washington", "free-wheeling missions", and "infringing upon the prerogatives" of the theater commander" were common. This attitude on
the part of the theater staff toward our assignments was to become even
more pronounced during ensuing days and was to plague us for some
time, in fact until General Eisenhower arrived to command the theater
during the latter part of June. It was obvious that the staff had not
been fully informed as to plans or consulted with reference to the assignment of American officers with British staffs. Both General Bolte
and General Dahlquist, his deputy and G-1, repeatedly expressed their
views that no American officers should be working members of any
British staff and that such contact as might be required should be done
by liaison officers from the theater headquarters. Even though the decision had been made by high authority and was beyond their power
to change, their attitude remained consistently critical. But this is not
uncommon among senior officers, surprising as it may seem. It stems
from a feeling that merits and abilities may not be sufficiently recognized, for experience undoubtedly gives a feeling of superiority over
those less fortunate. Or possibly, in this case, these attitudes can be attributed to the fact that these officers had been so long isolated from the
gathering war effort at home. But it is fortunate, I think, that these
traits tend to disappear as war creates greater opportunities, and demands increasingly unselfish and patriotic service.

Tuesday morning, Hillsinger, Cleaves, and Conway joined me at
20 Grosvenor, all of us diked out in our best and gleaming spit and polish, and no doubt endeavoring to exhibit an air of confidence. Here
Lieutenant Commander Morrison, U.S. Navy, reported to me and said
that he had been added to my party by Admiral Stark, our naval commander in London, at the request of Admiral Mountbatten. Colonel
Hart conducted us by way of Park Lane, Piccadilly, and Whitehall to
1-A Richmond Terrace where Combined Operations Headquarters
was located. This building, known as the War Office Annex, was
dwarfed by other government buildings in the vicinity. It occupied a
site on the bank of the Thames across Whitehall from Downing Street
and only a short way down stream from St. Paul's and the Houses of
Parliament.

We were met by the Flag Secretary, conducted past security guards
at the door, and shortly found ourselves in a room where Admiral
Mountbatten had assembled the principal officers of his staff to greet
us. Presentations made, there was a confusion of names and titles which
no one understood. For the rest, my impressions of this first meeting
were recorded in a letter to my wife.

I was prepared to some degree by the various accounts I have had of Admiral Mountbatten from Generals Marshall, Eisenhower, and Al Wedemeyer. His pictures do him justice. Rather tall and slender, perfectly straight but graceful, a fine face, fine dark eyes, high brow, and rather curly dark hair. Extremely easy and natural manner of speech, more personality and force apparent than in any other Britishers I have met—and much more appealing to an American.

He welcomed us gracefully, hoped that we would like them, and assured us that they were grateful for having us with them. I replied that General Marshall desired that we be working members of his staff and expressed the hope that we would not be too much in the way while we were learning. He was sure that we would not and that they would have much to learn from us.

He then informed us that the Combined Operations Command had been organized from personnel of the three services and described the functions of the organization. He said that it would have an important part in planning, training for, and carrying out the invasion agreed between the two countries. With a combined Anglo-American staff, the headquarters should be of inestimable value in solving the problems occasioned by our differences in organization, methods and doctrines, and should point the way for a joint staff which the operations would require.

Admiral Mountbatten then conducted us on a tour of the headquarters, introduced us to each section chief, and had each one explain the functions of his section. All of this was interesting but it was also confusing at the time. Afterwards there was only one of these section chiefs whose name I could recall.

Anyone who joins a large organization requires some time in which to "learn the ropes". This is especially true of military headquarters, for each one has its own peculiarities, even those organized along familiar lines. Combined Operations Headquarters, or COHQ as it was usually called, was like no other headquarters we had known. Not only were British staff organization and procedures different from those in our own service, but there were also differences resulting from combining three services in a single staff, and still others resulting from the personality of the man who was Chief of Combined Operations. To say that we found all this confusing at first would be to put it mildly. Some weeks elapsed before we became so familiar with the organization and procedures that we could go about our work with confidence.

Combined Operations Headquarters had its origin in the need for a single headquarters to direct raiding operations involving naval, ground, and air forces. Until shortly before we joined, it had been a small organization comprising about twenty-three officers responsible for raids and minor overseas operations such as the various commando raids and the Madagascar expedition, all of which had attracted considerable publicity. No doubt the success which attended these operations coupled with the fiascos made by landing operations in Norway and elsewhere had much to do with the expansion of the organization and the increase in its responsibilities. And these factors no doubt influenced the appointment of Admiral Mountbatten to be its Chief. Be that as it may, the organization had expanded from its small beginnings to more than one hundred fifty Army, Navy, and Air Force officers and more than that number of clerks and other specialists.

Figure No. 1 shows diagramatically the organization of the Combined Operations Command as it existed during the summer of 1942. British officers named on the chart are those who occupied the principal staff positions; American officers named are those who were members of the organization during this period.

The Vice, Deputy, and Assistant Chiefs of Combined Operations and the U.S. Adviser, Admiral Mountbatten designated as the Council. He usually met with us once or twice weekly when he was in London, and occasionally assembled us at other times. At these meetings, he discussed matters of policy affecting the headquarters and decisions at higher levels that had bearing upon our work. His unique associations with both the Chiefs of Staff and the Combined Commanders, not to mention his intimate personal relationship with the Prime Minister, and his own frank personality, gave to many of these meetings an unusual interest.

I shall never forget the first committee meeting which I attended with British and American officers. It was one of the first to begin detailed studies of the cross-channel operation envisaged in the American proposals. On the morning of May 20th, the day after I had reported at COHQ, as I reached 1-A Richmond Terrace I met General Haydon, Marshall Robb, and Commodore Ellis just leaving the building. They were looking for me to accompany them to Home Forces at 20 Queen Anne's Gate for a meeting of the Principal Staff Officers to begin discussions of the plan. There in a large conference room about a long table were ten or twelve British officers, Army, Navy, and Air. Besides myself, the Americans present were Nevins, Hamblen, Sheetz, and Colonel Barker from ETO. Major General Phillip Gregson-Ellis, Deputy Chief General Staff Home Forces, presided. Brigadier C.V. O'N. McNabb, Plans Section Home Forces, was the secretary.

After introductions, General Gregson-Ellis announced the purpose of the meeting—"to consider the draft of an appreciation of the situation for Operations in Northwest Europe in 1943." The secretary distributed an outline which listed the paragraph headings to be considered—object, factors affecting an invasion of western Europe, landing craft, airborne force, possible landing beaches, fighter support, limitations on assault area, maintenance requirements, naval requirements,

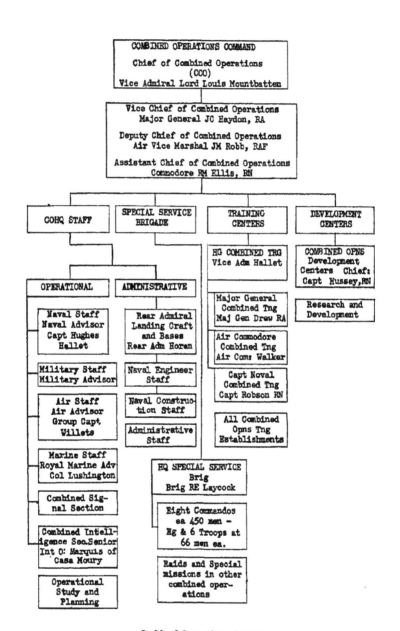

COMBINED OPERATIONS COMMAND

Chief of Combined Operations
(CCO)
Vice Admiral Lord Louis Mountbatten

Vice Chief of Combined Operations
Major General JC Haydon, RA

Deputy Chief of Combined Operations
Air Vice Marshal JM Robb, RAF

Assistant Chief of Combined Operations
Commodore RM Ellis, RN

| COHQ STAFF | SPECIAL SERVICE BRIGADE | TRAINING CENTERS | DEVELOPMENT CENTERS |

HG COMBINED TRG
Vice Adm Hallet

COMBINED OPNS
Development
Centers Chief:
Capt Hussey,RN

| OPERATIONAL | ADMINISTRATIVE |

Naval Staff
Naval Advisor
Capt Hughes
Hallet

Rear Admiral
Landing Craft
and Bases
Rear Adm Horan

Major General
Combined Tng
Maj Gen Drew RA

Research and
Development

Military Staff
Military Advisor

Naval Engineer
Staff

Air Commodore
Combined Tng
Air Com: Walker

Air Staff
Air Advisor
Group Capt.
Willets

Naval Construc-
tion Staff

Capt Noval
Combined Tng
Capt Robson RN

Marine Staff
Royal Marine Adv
Col Lushington

Administrative
Staff

All Combined
Opns Tng
Establishments

Combined Sig-
nal Section

HQ SPECIAL SERVICE
Brig
Brig RE Laycock

Combined Intell-
igence Sec.Senior
Int O: Marquis of
Casa Moury

Eight Commandos
ea 450 men -
Hg & 6 Troops at
66 men ea.

Operational
Study and
Planning

Raids and Special
missions in other
combined oper-
ations

Combined Operations Command
1942

courses open, and conclusion, and the like. For the most part the outline was blank under these various headings, although in some cases there were some brief notes. The chairman read the first paragraph. After much discussion, the statement of the object was agreed upon after a fashion. And then paragraph by paragraph the discussion went on back and forth and from side to side, for more than four and a half hours.

I found that I had difficulty in following the discussions because of the differences in the manner in which we spoke the language. And this was to plague me for some time. Not only did our British cousins always use the broad *a;* their speech was also filled with abbreviations or "short titles" with which we were not familiar; they gave many words a pronunciation not common in America and used familiar words with unfamiliar meanings. They spoke with astonishing rapidity, practically through closed teeth and with little action of the lips. All this made it very difficult for me to understand English "as she is spoke".

Most of us encountered this difficulty until we became more familiar with our surroundings and better acquainted with our associates. But it is only fair to record that the difficulties were not altogether on our own side. We evened matters to some extent for we found that our opposite number also had difficulty in understanding us. The blank expressions which greeted some of my early efforts changed later into knowing smiles after my British associates had learned that I was born in Texas.

When the conference was about to end, the secretary was directed to prepare a draft of the agreed version for discussion at another meeting before final approval for submission to the Combined Commanders for their consideration. And of course he was directed to prepare for distribution the minutes of the meeting, which we were to find an invariable practice in British committee meetings.

All of this was quite interesting and quite different from the staff procedure I had known. But then this was my first experience with "high level" planning except in a purely theoretical way. We were to find that British practice had much to commend it. I was always impressed with the care taken to insure that a final paper represented accurately the considered views of the committee, the careful selection of words to express exact shades of meaning, and the unfailing courtesy of British officers toward each other as well as toward ourselves, even when disputes were warm. Their staff papers usually had a literary quality generally superior to staff papers within my own experience in American practice.

One of the first groups of VIP's to visit London after my arrival was a party which included General Arnold, General Somerville, and General Eisenhower. Each of these officers visited COHQ on successive days. For each visit, Admiral Mountbatten assembled the Council and Advisers to meet the distinguished guest, and then led a discussion of problems involved in the projected operations.

Shortly before General Somerville's visit, the problem of relief maps or models for the entire invasion coast had been under discussion at COHQ. Constructing relief models of some hundred miles of French coastline would require several hundred model-makers for a number of months. There were only a handful of such specialists in England, and apparently no more in the United States. British experience had indicated that persons trained in the decorative aspects of the confectioner's art could be easily trained in making relief models. I was asked about the probable availability of such persons in America. While I knew nothing of the field of model-making, I thought that suitable persons might be found among the confectioners, bakers, hotels, and clubs in America. I suggested that we present the matter to General Somerville on the occasion of his visit. Accordingly, during the meeting with General Somerville at COHQ, this problem was explained to him, and he was asked whether or not such persons might be found. While he smiled at the unusual nature of the request and admitted that it was a field of which he was ignorant, he took out his note book, jotted down the reference, and undertook to send over two hundred persons if they could be found in America. He kept his promise. Model-makers began arriving in groups of about fifty early in July, and I was notified of the arrival of the last group shortly before my departure from England in late September.

One lesson was indelibly impressed upon my mind during these early days — SECURITY. Few American officers during the period between the two World Wars had access to much secret information which had to be guarded to prevent its falling into the hands of a potential enemy. As a result, American officers were not nearly so security-minded as were the British who had already been at war for more than two years. British preoccupation with security may have been due to their own success in penetrating enemy security measures as well as to unfortunate experiences resulting from breaches in security. At any rate, British authorities were security-minded to an extreme degree. Special passes were required for admission to all government buildings. Knowledge of plans and other secret information was limited to the fewest possible number of persons, and even these were given no more information than their own work required. To discuss operations with planners, one had to be on a special list indicated by a special identification card. All important telephones had "scrambling" devices, which broke up and distorted voices in transit to prevent interception or eavesdropping. Important papers were transmitted "by hand of officer only." Breaches in security were dealt with rigorously.

"Security" almost terminated my career in COHQ before it was well begun. I had attended one of my first meetings with the Council and Advisers. The projected invasion was a subject for discussion. Admiral Mountbatten had expressed some of his own views as well as some of the Prime Minister's. All in all it was a broad concept of the proposed operations. On returning to my office in the building, I made some notes of the discussion on a scratch pad for future reference. As it was past the dinner hour, I cleared and locked my desk, including, as I thought, the memorandum which I had made notes on, locked my office door and went on my way. The next morning, the Senior Intelligence Officer, the Marquis of Casa Maury, telephoned to ask if he could see me, and came to my office. I invited him to be seated, but he replied that he could transact his business standing. Taking a piece of paper from his pocket, he unfolded it and handed it to me, asking if I had written it. I acknowledged that it was a memorandum which I had made the preceding evening, and said that I did not understand how it came into his possession. He said that it had been found in the courtyard in front of the building, and went on to point out the obvious danger which could result from such a paper falling into the hands of Axis agents, who were known to be in London. He added that the CCO viewed security so seriously that, if my dereliction were known to him, he would ask General Marshall for my relief. There seemed to be nothing for me to say except to express the opinion that he should let no consideration for an American officer stand in the way of what he would consider his duty if a British officer were involved. Casa Maury replied that no harm had been done and that he thought it would be better for future allied relations if no further action were taken with regard to the incident. He expressed the opinion that I would never again be so remiss with regard to security measures. In this opinion, he was entirely correct. Never again during my stay in London did I leave secret papers except in the hands of a responsible person or securely locked in a safe. This incident I related on many subsequent occasions to impress upon officers the importance of unremitting care in all matters connected with security.

Not all of our activities during these early days were confined to London. On May 23rd, less than a week after we joined, Hillsinger and Cleaves accompanied two of the British officers in COHQ on an operation called LANCING, a small raid that was turned back by weather before touching shore. On the following day, several of my group including myself were taken to Largs in Scotland, the location of one of the combined training centers, to witness a combined training exercise. Though the exercise was cancelled on account of foul weather, we did have the opportunity of inspecting the training center, the landing craft base, signal school, and other activities.

As arrangements were being made in COHQ for us to witness this exercise at Largs, Colonel Archibald had informed me that while we were in the North Admiral Mountbatten wished me to witness a very secret development of which the British had great hopes. However, I must promise that I would not mention this development to anyone whatsoever, including the American authorities, until Admiral Mountbatten specifically authorized me to do so.

Sunday afternoon, May 25th, I accompanied Commodore Ellis and Colonel Head, both of COHQ, on a beautiful drive from Largs to Carlisle, through the heart of the "Bobby Burns country", with a stop for tea at Gretna Green, to see this secret development.

The development had been given the code name Canal Defense Lights or CDL for security reasons. Great secrecy had shrouded every phase of development. In brief, it consisted of powerful searchlights mounted on tanks. The theory was that in any attack of organized defenses, a breakthrough would not be achieved in a single day. Tanks and armored elements cannot operate effectively at night and are then most vulnerable themselves. Thus, regardless of the measure of initial success in such an attack, the enemy under the protective cover of darkness would be able to withdraw or to make changes in his dispositions which would minimize or neutralize the initial advantage. By equipping large numbers of tanks with powerful searchlights, the attack could continue day and night until the breakthrough was achieved and the enemy demoralized.

It was the intent that personnel would be trained to employ the equipment but that it would not actually be used in operations until it was available in large numbers and could be employed in mass, thus avoiding the mistake made in the first employment of tanks in World War I.

All of this was explained to us upon our arrival at Carlisle. Then the Commandant of the training center outlined for us the demonstration that had been arranged. An area of ground represented a sector in a defensive position through which the attacking force had determined to effect a breakthrough. Infantry supported by artillery was assumed to be in position and would be represented. Tanks equipped with CDL were in assembly positions where it was assumed they had concentrated secretly the previous night. We would be taken to an observation post from which we could witness the action.

The demonstration was rather amazing. In inky blackness we waited in our designated position. There was some firing of artillery and machine guns simulating normal activity for such periods on a battle field. Suddenly there was a brief period of intense artillery fire, then a flood of light illuminated the battle field. Off to our left we could hear the roar of tanks, but looking toward them we could see nothing, we were so blinded by the intense light. Then the tanks rumbled past us and we watched them roll on across the little valley toward the position of the assumed enemy, all of the foreground as light as day. Then the lights began to flicker on and off with great rapidity. This, we were told, completely blinded anyone who faced the lights without materially reducing the vision of the tank crews. After reaching the objective, the tanks turned about and displayed for us the effects of the light under various conditions. Although we were a mile from the source of light at times, with my back to the light I could read the fine print of a newspaper which I carried. Looking toward the light, I could see nothing.

I wondered what might be the result on some future battle field when many hundreds of tanks were so equipped, if the secret were kept and surprise achieved.

So far as I know, CDL was never used in battle during the course of the war, although there must have been many occasions when such equipment might have been a decisive or powerful factor. I have wondered if the great secrecy with which the development was shrouded did not prevent the commanders who might have had occasion to employ it from becoming familiar with its existence or even its potentialities. There is, I think, a point at which the value of disseminating essential information must outweigh the risk of loss of security. And I have wondered what might have been the result if, instead of training only a few tank battalions in the employment of CDL, senior commanders and staffs of the armies and corps and armored divisions had been thoroughly indoctrinated with its potentialities during this period.

Early in June, we were observers during the first rehearsal for Operation RUTTER, which was to be the Dieppe raid. The rehearsal I witnessed from a rather luxurious yacht which had been taken over by the Royal Navy and was used by COHQ for escorting visiting officials and others on tours of inspection of installations and activities. The operation did not go well and a second rehearsal was ordered. The second one, on June 23rd, we witnessed from the beaches. We also visited General Eaker's Eighth Bomber Command, then being formed at Widewing, and witnessed demonstrations by British parachute troops.

On May 26th I was notified that I had been promoted to the rank of Brigadier General. This was the occasion for a small celebration by the group I came over with, in the bar at 8 South Audley, including presentation of my first stars which they had obtained I know not where. I was to find the promotion to general officer rank to be of no small assistance in my relations with others with whom I had to deal.

When we began considering the problem of gaining battle experience for American soldiers in accordance with my directive, several factors led to the decision to organize a special unit along commando lines rather than to employ one of our regular formations as we would have preferred. First, there were few American ground troops available in the United Kingdom. The 34th Infantry Division had moved from the United States to North Ireland in three echelons starting January 15th, and it would not be complete there until the end of May. The first echelon of the 1st Armored Division had arrived in early May, and the remainder of the division was scheduled for arrival during June. Owing to requirements for the early establishment of aviation and service elements in the United Kingdom, these would be the only ground forces available for several months. It was primarily from their ranks that must come the first American soldiers to be "blooded" if we were to take advantage of such raids as were then scheduled.

A second factor was the uncertainty of raiding operations. COHQ had at this time planned only five raids for the summer months, and only one of these involved more than four hundred ground troops. Eight other operations were under consideration, but none of them had reached the actual planning stage. And, of these eight, only two as then conceived would involve more than two hundred ground troops. After September, weather conditions would make raiding operations difficult, if not impossible, except for very small Commando operations. There were already some forty-five hundred Commandos all spoiling for fights. Both Canadian forces and British regular formations were seeking some of the action which had been a commando prerogative for many months. All of these factors indicated that the numbers of American troops that could be given battle experience in raids would be far less than we had hoped and in any case would not be large.

A third factor was the fact that all raiding operations would be under the direction of COHQ, transported in British craft, and supported by British naval elements. The British Commandos had been specially organized, selected, and trained for raiding operations. Such operations differ from the more normal offensive operations in which the objective is usually to seize and hold some terrain objective. In raids, the objective is a limited one, usually to accomplish some destruction or other purpose in enemy-held territory and then withdraw. The seizing and holding of terrain is usually a temporary consideration.

Commandos were trained tactically, physically, and psychologically for enormous efforts over limited periods. The Commando organization had been designed to fit the requirements of British assault craft and British naval support. Thus, a Commando platoon was the load for one ALC or assault landing craft; a troop the load for two; and a flotilla would transport an entire Commando (battalion).

There was much opposition to the Commandos among British army officers, and some even within COHQ. Not only did British army officers resent losing their best men to the Commandos; there was a further resentment that only the Commandos had the opportunity for active operations, while the regular formations had only the monotony of defensive organization to meet a danger which was no longer imminent, or training for operations not yet in prospect. Many British officers thought the publicity accorded the Commandos adversely affected the morale of other British ground forces. Others thought that Commando operations could have been carried out by regular formations. Colonel Archibald in COHQ was one of the officers who expressed such views to me. General Haydon on the other hand held the contrary view. He believed that the organization of the Commandos had paid great dividends and that it was one of the best things that had ever happened to the British army. In general, the opinions of most American officers with whom I discussed this subject were in line with those expressed by Colonel Archibald rather than with those of General Haydon and others who had served with the Commandos.

However, our American soldiers were to be transported in British craft, supported by Naval elements, and operated under control of COHQ. It therefore seemed logical that we should form a unit organized along the lines which the British had found desirable, rather than utilize a regular formation whose organization would have to be modified for every operation. Through such a unit, personnel could be rotated as men gained battle experience, with fewer complications than would be the case if men were transferred away from old organizations.

On May 26th, I submitted to the Chief of Staff proposals that we undertake immediately the organization of an American unit along Commando lines; that we proceed with the organization on a provisional basis utilizing skeletonized tables of organization pending War Department authorization of necessary grades and ratings, and the completion of tables of organization and equipment. These proposals were approved by the theater, and War Department authorization was received in a cable on May 28th.

I also drafted a letter of instructions to the Commanding General, United States Army Forces in North Ireland, informing him of the purpose and directing him to proceed with the organization of the unit with the least practicable delay. This letter was approved by the theater on May 31st. I delivered it in person on June 1st, and then spent the following two days in North Ireland discussing details with the Commanding General, Major Russell P. Hartle, and his staff, as well as with various subordinate commanders and staffs of his command, particularly those of the 34th Infantry and 1st Armored Divisions.

General Hartle was completely cooperative from the very beginning, although I am sure that he had his tongue in his cheek with regard to the prospects of ever seeing any of this personnel again, even if his divisions should be designated as assault divisions. General Ward, commanding the 1st Armored Division, was opposed to the selection of personnel from this Division because they were "trained tankers", but he, too, was cooperative when he fully understood that the object had originated with General Marshall.

Plans called for a Headquarters Company of eight officers and sixty-nine men, and six Ranger Companies each of three officers and sixty-three men, or a total authorized strength of twenty-six officers and 447 men. To this aggregate of 473 officers and men we added ten per cent to allow for rejections and for accidents and injuries during training. Thus a total of 520 officers and men were drawn from the following sources: 34th Infantry Division, 281; 1st Armored Division, 104; Anti-aircraft Artillery Troops, 43; V Corps Special Troops, 48; North Ireland Base Section, 44.

It was General Hartle who recommended the officer who was to be the first commander of the 1st Ranger Battalion. Major William O. Darby, General Hartle's aide (and my guide during my stay in North Ireland) was a young artillery officer from the Class of 1933 at West Point. He had had experience in both pack and motorized artillery, as well as with cavalry and infantry. He had had amphibious training with one of our divisions in the United States. He was outstanding in appearance, possessed of a most attractive personality, and he was keen, intelligent, and filled with enthusiasm. General Hartle's judgment was to be fully justified, for Darby's career both with the Rangers and subsequently, up to the time of his death in battle during the last days of the war, was to be a most distinguished one.

Major Darby interviewed and selected from the many volunteers the men who were to comprise the Ranger Battalion. He completed the organization of the unit, the assembly of its equipment, and personally led and directed its early preliminary training. Major Conway of my staff remained with Major Darby during this organizational period. Brigadier Laycock of the Special Service Brigade rendered valuable assistance.

Before leaving Washington, I had discussed with General Eisenhower the organization of American units along Commando lines. In one of our discussions General Eisenhower had said: "If you do find it necessary to organize such units, I hope that you will find some other name than 'Commandos' for the glamor of that name will always remain—and properly so—British." Accordingly, when the organization of such a unit was decided upon we sought a designation more typically American. Many names were recommended. I selected "Rangers" because few words have a more glamorous connotation in American military history. In colonial days, men so designated had mastered the art of Indian warfare and were guardians of the frontier. In Revolutionary days, others so designated were noted for desperate ventures, and many military formations among the Continentals wore the name proudly. Some of the oldest units in the Regular Army were originally organized as Rangers, and have carried the tradition into every war in which the nation has been engaged. On every frontier, the name has been one of hope for those who have required protection, of fear for those who have lived outside the law. It was therefore fit that the organization destined to be the first of American ground forces to battle the Germans on the European continent in World War II should have been called Rangers, in compliment to those in American history who exemplified such high standards of individual courage, initiative, determination, ruggedness, fighting ability, and achievement.

3. *Genesis of Allied Planning*

The question as to how best to go about Allied planning and preparations for the invasion was a matter of no small moment among the various staffs in London. It was, no doubt, a matter that received much consideration at the highest levels, and it was certainly the subject of much speculation and conversation among the lower ranks in London.

One concept envisioned the assault operation as a separate and distinct phase in the invasion, for which one commander should be responsible both for planning the assault and training the assault divisions. This view was widely held in COHQ, and General Eisenhower, on the occasion of his first visit to COHQ on May 28th, lent considerable encouragement to it. According to the minutes of that meeting he stated: "that he had at a previous meeting expressed the view that the first assault echelon of six divisions should all be under one command . . . and that this view had been greeted with some astonishment; but that he was certain that it was essential for the troops in the assault divisions, whether American, British, Polish or of any other nationality, to respond to the same orders in the same way. He considered it very desirable that there should be one commander of the assault divisions who would control them and their reserves and command support, whether by naval gunfire or aircraft."

Another view held that British and American authorities should appoint commanders for their expeditionary forces, and these commanders should be responsible for planning, training, and preparations for the operations under direction of the Combined Commanders, who would in turn be responsible to the Combined Chiefs of Staff. The view had many adherents in British headquarters other than COHQ, but few among the American contingent.

Yet a third group felt that the Combined Chiefs of Staff should appoint a Supreme Allied Commander for the projected operations, provide him with an Allied staff, and place upon him the responsibility for all planning, training, and other preparations for the invasion under the immediate direction of the Combined Chiefs of Staff themselves. This was the almost unanimous view among American officers from the very first and among most British officers as well. It was realized that the appointment of such a commander would become increasingly urgent as planning progressed beyond initial stages. But it was not until July 18th that the Combined Commanders officially recommended such an appointment to the Combined Chiefs of Staff as a matter of urgency.

Thus it was that the planning organization grew rather like Topsy at first but gradually assumed a well developed form. Directives from the Chiefs of Staff or Combined Commanders initiated work on studies and plans. The Principal Staff Officers were responsible for preparing appreciations or estimates, studies, and plans for consideration by the Combined Commanders, and for preparation of such matter as the Combined Commanders approved for submission to the Combined Chiefs of Staff. Many individuals on the staff of each of the Combined Commanders as well as in other headquarters were involved in the preparation of this material, both operational and administrative. This work entailed almost endless staff and committee meetings, and it came to occupy the full time of a considerable body of the Principal Staff Officers. This body came to be known as the ROUNDUP PLANNERS.

As early as June 9th, the Combined Commanders decided to place their ROUNDUP planning staff together in one place, but it was not until July 8th that suitable accommodations could be found in Norfolk House. The planning organization remained unchanged until after the appointment of General Eisenhower as Supreme Allied Commander toward the end of July. And this appointment was made, not for ROUNDUP, but for TORCH, the invasion of French North Africa,

Joint Chiefs of Staff (Am)

Principal Administrative Officers

Combined Chiefs of Staff (Br)

Joint Movement and Transport Control

Joint Planning Staff

Joint Intelligence Committee

General Staff War Office

Air Staff Air Ministry

Naval Staff Admiralty

European Theater of operations

HQ SOS ETO

HQ US Air Forces

GG

COMMANDERS

COMBINED

Chief of Combined Operations

C in C Home Forces

C in C Fighter Command

C in C Naval Command

PRINCIPAL STAFF OFFICERS

Combined Operations

Home Forces

Fighter Command

Naval Command

US Officers

Control

Consultative

which had been decided upon by the Combined Chiefs of Staff during the last week in July.

In addition to the operational estimates, studies, and plans which were the special province of the Principal Staff Officers, numerous committees and sub-committees dealt with a vast number of special and related subjects. Beach studies, coast defenses, intelligence, smoke requirements, antiaircraft measures, deception, psychological warfare, command organization, communications, landing craft, obstacles, demolitions, underground activities, administration, training, concentration, movements, navigational aids—all of these and many other subjects were included in the investigations.

The development of this initial planning organization was not a simple task, but it did produce some excellent studies. Of even greater importance, it was a training school for Allied commanders and staffs. Few persons had then appreciated the difficulties which were to arise from different political and military organizations, from differences in national psychology, command and staff procedures, doctrines, language, and even from personal prejudices. These months were invaluable in preparing Allied Staffs to understand one another.

During all of these weeks, the question of who would finally be designated as the Supreme Allied Commander for ROUNDUP was an ever-recurring subject of conversation among staff officers concerned with this early planning. It was interesting to me that all British officers with whom I discussed the matter were outspoken and unanimous in expressing the opinion that the supreme commander should be an American. I think that most of them thought that, because of Britain's almost unbroken record of defeats on land, no British commander would win the confidence of the American forces or the American people. Most of them were hopeful that the mantle would fall upon the shoulders of General Marshall. Admiral Mountbatten expressed this hope and his great admiration for General Marshall to me on many occasions. The fact that there was no officer of recognized stature available during these early days other than General Marshall was no doubt a contributory reason for delaying the appointment of a Supreme Allied Commander and postponing the organization of an Allied headquarters. Then the TORCH decision compelled it.

It was brought home to us almost from the first that other headquarters in London, both British and American, looked with a somewhat jaundiced eye upon Combined Operations Headquarters, and more particularly, upon the man who was its chief. Admiral Mountbatten, youthful in comparison with some of the others at high levels, was already a distinguished naval officer, intimate with those in high places, and high in the councils which directed the war effort. Others viewed with some alarm the expansion of COHQ under his command from an insignificant Commando organization, subordinate to other British headquarters, into a large and coordinate organization. Tradition-bound services looked with ill-concealed disfavor upon a unified command of selected Army, Navy, and Air Force personnel equally represented with these three older services on the highest levels. And there was evidence of resentment that assault functions, which it had theretofore been usual to consider of minor importance and thus neglect, were now being accorded a degree of recognition equal with their own.

Among the British officers in COHQ there was a strong feeling that Home Forces was dominated by a defensive and defeatist attitude; that the Fighter and Bomber Commands were interested only in the air war and more particularly in its strategic bombing and defensive aspects; and that none of these other headquarters had much stomach for continental operations such as had been proposed and agreed upon. Among other British headquarters there was obviously a fear, which colored thought in our own American headquarters, that Admiral Mountbatten was building up an Anglo-American headquarters specialized in assault operations with some thought that it would dominate or even control the assault phase of ROUNDUP as well as Allied preparations therefor. Nor was there ever much doubt in my own mind that he did have some such ambition.

In one of my first meetings with the Council at COHQ, on May 22nd, Admiral Mountbatten stated that he had been under some pressure to obtain an early decision as to the place and responsibility of COHQ in the projected operations. But he had been sure that if he forced the issue before the arrival of the Americans, the decision might not give COHQ the place it rightfully deserved. He went on to say that he had talked with both General Marshall and the Prime Minister, and there was no question that they expected him to command the assault echelon. An adverse decision before the arrival of the American commander might be extremely difficult to reverse, while if the situation were left in its present state, he would be in position to take advantage of opportunities to secure for COHQ its rightful place.

Admiral Mountbatten believed that COHQ was the organization most eminently qualified by training and experience for planning the assault, conducting training for it, and actually controlling it when it should take place. He emphasized over and over again that those in COHQ were the experts and that there must never be any question of anyone else becoming as good as they were. In this he had the loyal support of all of his British officers.

It was my own view, subsequently confirmed by experience, that the assault phase of major landing operations cannot be divorced from the land operations that follow. Troops that make the assault must continue in subsequent land phases, and the whole operation must be organized and controlled in depth. A single headquarters would have difficulty in controlling an assault being made on a wide front in numerous places. A separate command for the assault phase would not only be confusing, it would be unsound, for decisions made during the assault phase might jeopardize the subsequent course of land operations for which the assault was being made. For these reasons, I felt the detailed planning for the assault and all preparations for it should be the responsibility of the commander responsible for the land operations that would follow.

On the other hand, I wholly agreed with the concept that Admiral Mountbatten as Chief of Combined Operations should be responsible for smaller assaults such as raids, and that he should actually be the Commander in Chief for such operations, which for the most part were planned in COHQ and some even were conceived there. But none of these raids undertook land operations beyond the assault area, for they were raids where the assault forces would withdraw, and in which the assault objective would accomplish the purpose of the operation.

Immediately after the decision in April to undertake the cross-channel operation—ROUNDUP—in 1943, BOLERO, which was the code name for the movement of U.S. troops to the United Kingdom, became the primary objective of the American war effort. Concentration of American forces in the United Kingdom was pressed to the uttermost of available shipping and air transportation. Early in June, Major General John C. H. Lee arrived in London to begin the organization of the Service of Supply which was to support this vast force. And Major General Ira C. Eaker at Widewing initiated the organization of the Eighth Bomber Command which was the first major headquarters of the American Air Forces in Europe. Airplanes, pilots, technicians, doctors, nurses, staff officers, ammunition, weapons, equipment, supplies —all of the vast impedimenta of war flowed into the British Isles in a never-ending and ever-increasing stream. On June 24th, General Eisenhower arrived to replace General Chaney, who had departed some four days previously, as Commanding General, European Theater of Operations. General Eisenhower was to infuse into the organization in England some of the intensity of purpose and spirit of cooperation which characterized the war effort at home. So far as American personnel was concerned, there was now no backward glance, and, for obvious reasons, there was less indulgence in that favorite American pastime known as "Monday morning quarterbacking".

With our British associates, we were to find the situation somewhat different. British experience was recent, and not altogether fortunate. Their actual experience in amphibious operations was far more extensive than our own. British officers approached the studies of ROUND-UP with some reservations. British staff officers had learned in practice to allow wide margins for error between promise and fulfillment, and broad safety factors for errors in calculations and estimates. Their experience had shown them that unless operations were thoroughly prepared and in ample strength, reverses could be most expensive and unproductive. And Britain was already feeling the pinch of the manpower shortage. That British authorities did not fully share the American enthusiasm for ROUNDUP was a fact which was recognized, I think, by the American officers who participated in the April discussions. However, it was rather startling to discover, in view of the recent date of these agreements, that on June 9th, less than three weeks after our arrival in London, the British Combined Commanders recorded their opinion of the proposed operation in a memorandum to the British Chiefs of Staff in the following terms:

> . . .we are of the opinion that unless the German morale has deteriorated by the spring of 1943 owing to another failure to defeat the Russians, such a re-entry into FRANCE will not be a feasible operation of war.

On June 15th, the Prime Minister sent one of his famous "minutes" to the British Chiefs of Staff, setting forth in masterly fashion his own conception of how ROUNDUP should be conceived and executed. The operation, he said, required the "qualities of magnitude, simultaneity, and violence". It should comprise at least six heavy assaults in the first wave, with at least half a dozen feints from Norway to Spain to mystify the enemy. At least ten armored brigades should land in the first wave "to penetrate deeply inland regardless of losses to rouse the populace and to spread confusion among the enemy". Simultaneously, four major ports should be seized. If, in two weeks, 700,000 men were ashore, air supremacy gained, the enemy in considerable confusion, and the Allies had four workable ports, "we shall have got our claws well into the job." In his concluding remarks he said: "Unless we are prepared to commit the immense forces comprised in the first three waves (i.e., 700,000) to a hostile shore with the certainty that many of our attacks will miscarry, and that if we fail the whole stake will be lost, we ought not to undertake such an extraordinary operation of war under modern conditions." Inasmuch as it was then known that shipping and other considerations would limit the forces envisaged to little more than half of the Prime Minister's minimum, this remark seemed rather significant.

The officers with whom we were associated in COHQ viewed ROUNDUP with a degree of enthusiasm, but there were many references in our discussions that led me to believe that British authorities generally approached the operation with considerable reluctance. If the American concentration in the United Kingdom continued for some months and then British authorities decided that ROUNDUP was not a "feasible operation of war", it required little imagination to see that those directing the American war effort might be seriously embarrassed in undertaking any desirable alternative operations. Such matters were beyond the scope of my responsibilities, yet I was vastly relieved when General Eisenhower arrived to command the theater and I was able to explain to him the basis for my fears, which I did without delay. General Eisenhower was reluctant to believe that British opposition was then of serious proportions, but he was fully cognizant of the effect such opposition might have on Allied plans.

The first week in July, most of the American officers in COHQ went to Cowes on the Isle of Wight to observe the sailing of the RUTTER operation for Dieppe, returning to London when the operation was finally cancelled because of bad weather. The week following our return was an interesting one for me because it was filled with evident tensions. The Council was called in frequent sessions, and judging from the scraps of information passed on to us, there were many high-level discussions during these days among those responsible for the British war effort. Even Admiral Mountbatten with all of his boundless energy and vitality was showing signs of weariness and strain.

This undercurrent of tension and uncertainty was not altogether surprising. German advances in the East, particularly the capture of Sevastopol about July 1st, made the Russian situation look very grim. In Africa, Rommel had chased the British to the doorstep of Egypt and had been stopped there by line of communication troubles rather than by effective fighting. Vital convoys at both ends of Europe were suffering staggering losses—convoys to Malta in the Mediterranean, and convoys to the Russian Murmansk past the northern coast of Norway. These were bitter days for Britain. Agitation in much of the American press for a "second front" did little to sweeten the unpalatable draught. This agitation was certainly a source of irritation among the lower British levels with whom we came in contact. It was probably so among the higher levels in London—and it may have been so in Washington.

It is possible that the Prime Minister was not wholly satisfied with the reply to his minutes of June 15th made by the Combined Commanders on July 1st. Possibly the urgency for action in 1942 to keep Russia in the war was an impelling consideration. At any rate, Admiral Mountbatten informed us on July 12th that it looked as though ROUNDUP was off for 1943 and that the Prime Minister was going to discuss some other operation with the President. This seemed to me a confirmation of my earlier impressions concerning the British attitude toward ROUNDUP. I could inform General Eisenhower of this further basis for my impressions, which I did without delay. General Eisenhower had now been meeting with the Combined Commanders since his arrival late in June. And his relationship with the British Chiefs of Staff was very close. He was of course familiar with the state of ROUNDUP planning; and he was informed at highest levels concerning the grim aspects of the general situation which then confronted the Anglo-American Allies. He listened gravely to the report of my impressions, but I do not think that he was then convinced that we would not proceed with the plans agreed upon.

On Saturday, July 18th, Admiral Mountbatten informed me that General Marshall and the American Chiefs had arrived in London that morning. That meant "high level talks", and it was my thought that they had probably come to stiffen the weakening British attitude toward ROUNDUP. But it was not my problem. We could only wait and see.

Late in the afternoon, I returned to my office in COHQ and found my adjutant, Major Embury, in a dither. The Chief of Staff at 20 Grosvenor had been trying to locate me for several hours. I telephoned at once and was informed that I was to report to General Marshall at Claridge's immediately. Needless to say, I allowed no grass to grow under my feet. And I was worried because the prospects for giving battle experience to American soldiers in any considerable numbers was rather dim to say the least.

At Claridge's I was shown to General Marshall's suite. I knocked. A voice called: "Come in." I opened the door and entered. General Marshall spoke from the bathroom. "Sit down. I am dressing. I will be with you in a few minutes." He came out shortly, greeted me, and continued with his dressing while he talked. He asked how I was. How the job was going. About each of the officers who had accompanied me. What our activities were. What I thought of Mountbatten. About British organization and methods. About other British officers. About British people. There was a knock at the door. A waiter entered. General Marshall said: "You will stay for dinner with me." I did not want to impose upon his time, but he brushed the suggestion aside. Would I have a drink? Yes. He ordered Scotch and soda for us both. And dinner. Soon he had finished dressing and dinner was ready.

I remember that it was a delicious dinner, although I cannot remember what it was. For I was being subjected to the most thorough examination and in the most charming manner that one can imagine. Every activity since my arrival, every personality, every impression, views concerning the British, their attitude toward the plans. Nothing was overlooked. I could well understand the expression "pick your brains".

General Marshall asked me what the people at COHQ thought of SLEDGEHAMMER—the operation for the fall of 1942, if necessitated by deterioration in the Russian situation, for which a maximum of six British divisions and one American might be available, and which envisaged an assault to capture Cherbourg or Le Havre. There had been much discussion of the plan in COHQ and some of the younger planners took exception to the concept that it was not possible to seize a foothold on the continent and maintain it during the winter unless there was a break in German morale. I told General Marshall that these Raid Planners believed that an operation to seize the Cherbourg peninsula was not only practicable and within our means, but that it would be a desirable operation to undertake during the fall in preparation for ROUNDUP the following spring. I also pointed out that the next higher level in COHQ—the Advisers—had disagreed with them. General Marshall was keenly interested and gave me a searching investigation of the young planners ideas. At his request, I undertook to provide him with an outline of their views the following morning.

General Eisenhower and General Clark came in about ten o'clock, Admiral King and several others a little later. General Marshall repeated to them the views I had outlined to him and indicated that all efforts were to be devoted to preparing an outline plan which he could present for discussion with the British Chiefs of Staff. The discussion carried on until well past midnight, when General Marshall dismissed us with the remark that he had expected to let us go by half-past ten but had been too much interested in the discussion.

Major Henriques, Commander Costobadie, and Wing Commander Homer, the "younger planners" whose views I had given to General Marshall, felt that they were placed in an embarrassing position. They believed enthusiastically in the plan they had proposed, but it was not the official view of COHQ or any other British headquarters. There was no disloyalty involved in their providing me with their own personal opinions even though they knew my purpose, so long as it was clearly understood that these were their own personal views and in no way represented any official viewpoint, and were in fact contrary to the expressed official views. So these officers, working with Hillsinger and Conway, prepared for me in haste the outline plan which represented their views as I had described them to General Marshall. They also provided me with copies of the replies they had made to the "ground which the proposers found unconvincing" when the Advisers at COHQ had previously rejected their proposals.

In this plan, which I produced the following morning, the strength of the assault forces was determined by the capacity of the landing craft which it was estimated would be available. These forces would consist of specially trained infantry on light scale of transport, armored forces, and airborne troops. The object was to occupy quickly a line across the base of the Cherbourg peninsula, simultaneously seizing the airdrome by airborne attack, and capturing the port by land assault by infantry, armor, and airborne troops. Four additional divisions would be brought in as rapidly as transportation permitted together with necessary supporting and service elements to maintain the defense and construct necessary landing fields.

This plan, these Raid Planners had insisted in their replies to the Advisers, was a practicable method of seizing the Cherbourg peninsula, and with the forces available it could be held throughout the winter. They believed the operation could be carried out more easily during the autumn than in spring or summer because the extra hours of darkness would enhance the chance of surprise, facilitate the problem of supply and simplify the question of air cover. They pointed out that a beachhead could not be established as cheaply at any time in the future unless the Germans substantially altered their dispositions, because the Germans had appreciated that we could not attack this year and had accordingly reduced their defenses. At the same time they were aware of the danger of ROUNDUP for next year, and whatever the position on the Russian front, the Cherbourg peninsula would be reinforced by that time. During the winter, the Germans could withdraw troops from the Russian front to refit in France in preparation for the efforts of the following spring. For these reasons, the planners thought the operation should take place by mid-November.

They pointed out that the operation could easily be mounted within twelve weeks instead of "well on into the winter" as the Advisers claimed. They showed that adequate air cover could be provided from present sources and pointed out that it might be substantially increased by October. They insisted that the operation would not interfere with ROUNDUP, but on the contrary would provide a fully trained assault force for that operation if assault troops were relieved immediately after the assault by regular formations. They showed that capture of the Channel Islands was not a necessary preliminary to the operation, but a desirable sequel thereto, and naval forces operating from the peninsula could interfere with German supply to such an extent that the Islands would in time "tend to fall by their own weight". Nor did they consider that planning the operation would require COHQ to drop everything else, because operations already under way could take place "under their own steam", small scale raids could be planned by one naval and one military planner, and the only other operation then under consideration was not a very valuable objective at this stage of the war.

During this weekend, there was much pushing of pencils, much pounding of typewriters, and much burning of midnight oil by all of the planners in General Eisenhower's headquarters, to assemble proposals in such form that General Marshall could use them as a basis for discussion with the British Chiefs of Staff.

The week following General Marshall's arrival in London was an exciting one, for there was everywhere an atmosphere of mystery and of curiosity ill-concealed. In theater headquarters, only those who had been actively engaged in ROUNDUP planning seemed to know anything of what was going on, and there was in consequence much speculation in all offices. The planners of course were busy day and night with estimates, appreciations and studies. And when one saw them now and again at mess or dashing from one place to another with bulging brief cases, there was about them something of a conspiratorial air that would have done credit to the villains of the Keystone comedies of former years.

Nor was COHQ in much better state. Here again the Principal Staff Officers were engaged at all hours with papers and plans. For Admiral Mountbatten, this must have been one of the busiest periods of his life. There were meetings with the Prime Minister, with the War Cabinet, with the British Chiefs of Staff, with the Combined Chiefs of Staff, and with the Combined Commanders, British and American. We at COHQ caught occasional glimpses of the Admiral when he came to his office to confer with members of his staff or to obtain data for one or another various meetings. At such times he often called in the Council and told us something of what was transpiring at high levels.

On July 20th, the Combined Chiefs of Staff directed the Combined Commanders to review their SLEDGEHAMMER plan with a view to establishing a foothold upon the continent, during the fall of 1942. The Combined Commanders then directed their Principal Staff Officers to prepare the appreciations and plans for their consideration. Then followed the usual flood of appreciations, outline plans, first drafts, second drafts, agendas, minutes and meetings. And almost at once there was a momentous decision. In view of the fact that SLEDGEHAM-

MER envisioned a return to the continent only under very unlikely conditions involving a collapse in German morale, the operation in 1942 to gain and maintain a foothold on the continent should not be known as SLEDGEHAMMER. It would be designated by the code name WET BOB.

WET BOB as finally produced by the planners and accepted by the Combined Commanders turned out to be little more than an amplification in some twenty-five or thirty pages with charts and maps of the "low level plan" which the Raid Planners at COHQ had urged upon the Advisers and which I had been the instrument for bringing to General Marshall's attention. In its final form, there was general agreement among the planners and among the Combined Commanders that "plan WET BOB could, if urgent considerations made it necessary, be carried out regardless of the state of German morale though such a course was not recommended since, owing to shortage in landing craft, the operation must be considered hazardous." The Commander in Chief, Home Forces, Sir Bernard Paget, however, was "not able to agree with this wording since he believed the operation militarily unsound and could therefore be justified only by urgent political considerations." But the change in name and this general agreement as to the feasibility of the operation did not insure final approval for the operation, for the planners and the Combined Commanders were already too late, and their weighty decisions were never presented to the Combined Chiefs of Staff.

On July 14th, the British Joint Staff Planners had submitted to the War Cabinet a paper dealing with the American GYMNAST plans, an operation planned for invading French Morocco under the assumption that the French would not resist the Americans and that there would be little or no opposition. This assumption the British Joint Staff Planners did not consider realistic. They also showed that an invasion of French North Africa would postpone ROUNDUP until 1944, and would require complete revision of the American plans as well. They suggested that if GYMNAST planning were left to the Americans, progress would be doubtful for American service opinion was opposed to the operation. As an alternative they suggested that the British might plan GYMNAST on comprehensive lines and then confront the Americans with the results of their investigations. When I saw this paper some days later, it seemed evident to me that British eyes were even then turned away from any cross-channel operation, and particularly from any operation during 1942.

On July 23rd, Admiral Mountbatten informed members of the Council that the British Chiefs of Staff had on the previous day refused to consider SLEDGEHAMMER and that any invasion across the channel during 1942 was definitely off. He added that the Prime Minister was proposing GYMNAST to the President, and that British planners were investigating GYMNAST although they had as yet said nothing to the Americans about their interest in it.

On July 25th, Admiral Mountbatten told us that the Combined Chiefs of Staff had the day before reached a decision as to the line of action to be adopted providing the President approved the paper sent to Washington on that day. This decision, he explained, was:

To initiate TORCH planning at once (TORCH replacing GYMNAST as the code name for the invasion of French North Africa and involving not only Casablanca but Oran, Algiers, and the whole of French North Africa). TORCH would involve at least twelve divisions with three or more landings; both British and American troops would be used, but the initial assault waves would be Americans for political reasons; planning for ROUNDUP and WET BOB was to be continued because it was felt that our own public opinion, deception of the Germans, our obligation to Russia, and the remote possibility of the Russian situation so developing as to make such operations possible, made it necessary to go on with these plans; the decision as to TORCH would be made by September 15th and perhaps before that. He emphasized that the TORCH decision would delay ROUNDUP until 1944 for it would set everything back at least twelve months.

Admiral Mountbatten, anticipating that COHQ would be responsible for continuing the ROUNDUP and SLEDGEHAMMER-WET BOB planning, directed that Air Vice Marshall Robb, Commodore Ellis, Brigadier Lushington, and I prepare an appreciation visualizing SLEDGEHAMMER-WET BOB blossoming into ROUNDUP perhaps in 1944.

So it was that when the Principal Staff Officers submitted their final revision of WET BOB to the Combined Commanders on July 31st, there was little the Commanders could do except to approve the plan and decide that it was not necessary to submit it to the Combined Chiefs of Staff at that time.

On June 29th, arrangements were made for the assignment of spectators who were to witness RUTTER, the raid then scheduled for Dieppe. Cleaves, Hillsinger, Morrison, Conway, and I were to go as the American observers. Some sixty officers and men from troops in North Ireland were to participate with British units. I was briefed on the operation at COHQ, and I asked to have other American officers briefed also. For security reasons, that was not considered desirable, they would learn the details of the operation only after the expedition sailed.

Tuesday afternoon, we proceeded to Portsmouth where Hillsinger, Wing Commander Homer, and I were assigned to HMS *Fernie*, a destroyer commanded by Lieutenant Commander Ackworth. We found that we were among a considerable body of observers, who, with the help of a military headquarters on board, crowded the *Fernie* almost to bursting. I slept on the floor of the ward room with one blanket; most of the observers had none.

Wednesday morning broke with foul weather and sailing was delayed. There was nothing to do on board and nothing was visible within the hundred yards or so that we could see. Everything was secret and spectators could not be briefed until the expedition actually sailed. During the afternoon, Admiral Baillie-Graham, who commanded the base on shore, offered me a berth on shore which I was glad to accept. On our way in we visited the tank landing craft and other vessels anchored in the roadstead. Each one was packed with personnel like sardines in a can and none were too comfortable in the inclement weather, but all seemed cheerful though disappointed at the delay in sailing.

I spent the rest of the week with Admiral Baillie-Graham and his staff at the Royal Yacht Squadron, the exclusive yacht club to which, I was told, Sir Thomas Lipton had been admitted to membership only shortly before his death. The Club had been taken over by the Royal Navy, which had greatly distressed the membership by admitting females to the premises even though only in menial capacities. Each day we hoped for an improvement in the weather. Each day the weather grew worse. While there must have been much discomfort among personnel packed in such close quarters on board the destroyers, landing craft, and assault ships, there was keen disappointment when the operation was finally cancelled.

The experience had been of little value to the troops themselves, but it was of considerable value to the commanders and staffs who had been responsible for planning the operation and making all preparations for it. Many imperfections in communications, security, coordination, planning, and administrative arrangements were disclosed, all of which could be corrected before the operation was again mounted.

When the original agreement for ROUNDUP was made in April, it was the understanding that raids would be increased in scope and frequency during the period available before the operation would be undertaken in April, 1943. During the time we were in COHQ, five raids were actually planned and mounted: one involving about sixty Commando troops, two involving about one hundred twenty, one involving about four hundred, and one (RUTTER) involving about five thousand troops. Nine others were planned in whole or in part and then abandoned for one reason or another, usually either for being too hazardous or because of shortage in naval craft. Eleven other plans were in various stages of consideration during the period. During this time only one operation—Dieppe—was actually carried out. Five operations were mounted and cancelled; nine operations were abandoned at some stage of planning; and ten others were under initial stages of consideration. One other was ready for mounting if it had been approved.

The fact that so many operations were planned, with all of the labor involved, without any coming off was a matter of much concern among the working members of the staff. At a meeting just after the cancellation of RUTTER in early July, the Naval Adviser, Captain Huges Hallet, caused considerable consternation among the higher levels by stating that he considered the failure to launch RUTTER to be a serious matter, for it indicated either a weakness on the part of the Force Commanders or the inability of COHQ to plan a practicable raid of that size. He recommended an inquiry by an impartial investigator to fix the responsibility for failure to carry out the RUTTER operation, and he recommended asking Sir Stafford Cripps to conduct the inquiry. Needless to say, the CCO took a dim view of having an inquiry by any other than a service agency, and consequently the recommendation was not favorably considered.

Outside of COHQ there was considerable opposition to raiding. In connection with ROUNDUP planning, the Naval Commander in Chief, Expeditionary Force, submitted a memorandum on the subject to the Chiefs of Staff during the latter part of July. In this memorandum he wrote:

> Within the last twelve months we have made a number of small and ineffective raids on the French coastline, South and West of Cape Gris Nez. Circumstances suggest that we are using these raids either to train our own forces or to employ our own forces. If the former, there is some justification, despite the fact that we are also training the enemy, but if the latter, there can be little justification.
>
> The Germans welcome these raids for nothing shows up weakness in the defense more than an attack with a very limited objective. Every time we find a weak spot on the enemy's coast we point out his weakness, and there is ample evidence that he has taken and is taking full advantage of this information to increase the strength of his defenses both at sea and on land. As it is our present intention at some future date to make an attack in force upon the enemy's coast, we are now doing our best to make that attack less likely to achieve success.

These were some of the reasons why my success in carrying out that part of my mission dealing with the gaining of battle experience for American personnel was limited to the dozen officers and fifty men who participated in the Dieppe Raid when it finally took place in August.

4. *TORCH*

Following the decision of the Combined Chiefs of Staff on July 24th to undertake TORCH—the invasion of French North Africa—the planning staffs had immediately turned their attention to the preparation of appreciations, estimates, and studies incidental to that operation. At the meeting in COHQ on July 25th when Admiral Mountbatten had informed us of that decision, he had also designated a syndicate to work with the TORCH planners and to brief him daily upon the state of TORCH. This syndicate was composed of Colonel Archibald, Commander Strauss of the American staff, and a British air officer who had not yet reported.

For some days after this announcement, while there was much activity among the various staffs in London, progress was in what might be termed a state of suspended animation, for transatlantic discussions with Washington were still in progress. Up to this time, the planning had been carried on by the Principal Staff Officers and the ROUND-UP planners under the Combined Commanders. British and American officers worked together, but there was no one commander or chief of staff to direct and coordinate their work. I had been away from London for a few days and when I returned Admiral Mountbatten informed me that General Eisenhower had been appointed Supreme Allied Commander for TORCH, and that the decision would not be announced for several days. Meanwhile, General Eisenhower would take over responsibility for planning TORCH and would begin the organization of an Allied staff in Norfolk House where most of the ROUNDUP planners were located by this time. He said he had promised General Eisenhower that COHQ would assist him in every possible way; accordingly, he would make a syndicate available to assist in planning the assaults. This syndicate, which he wished me to head, would be composed of the officers who had been keeping in touch with the TORCH planners, and several others.

Norfolk House has connotations in British history. Through its halls had passed many of the real and legendary figures of history. What tales its walls could tell of plot and counterplot! What tales of glory and of beauty. What pomp and ceremony had graced its floors in past days. But all was changed. An ancient doorman guarded the entrance and checked the passes of all who entered. And inside there was confusion. ROUNDUP planners had been meeting there since July 8th. Some of them had rooms which were reasonably well furnished with office equipment. But many were assigned to long, almost empty halls and empty rooms, through which others wandered in varying degrees of uncertainty. But after some searching, my syndicate found two rooms in which there were some tables and a few chairs. Here we established squatters' rights.

Then I looked for someone who might help with information. From the planners I obtained the initial drafts of their intelligence studies and appreciations. With these and the excellent British ISIS, Interservice Intelligence Studies, we set to work.

The initial plan had some points of interest. It was obviously an amplification of the original GYMNAST plans—the American plans for occupying French Morocco based on the assumption that the French would not resist. Two assaults were now envisaged with the object of securing French Morocco, occupying Spanish Morocco if that should be necessary to control the Straits of Gibraltar, and building up striking forces to occupy Algeria and Tunisia. The assault echelon of both forces would be American in the hope that the French would be less likely to oppose them than would be the case if British troops were used. One force would comprise four regimental combat teams and an armored combat team composed of American troops in the United Kingdom. The force, transported in British shipping and supported by the Royal Navy, would have the initial mission of seizing the port of Casablanca and airfields in that vicinity. The second force of similar size, composed of American troops sailing from the United States and supported by the United States Navy, would have the initial mission of seizing the port of Oran and the airfields in that vicinity. These forces would have the necessary supporting and service troops, and the forces would be built up as rapidly as shipping permitted. Such was the plan outlined as a point of departure for further study.

Meanwhile more and more officers were coming into Norfolk House to join in the planning, and more positive organization became increasingly essential. Colonel Al Gruenther, who had been Deputy Chief of Staff, Third Army, in San Antonio when General Eisenhower had been Chief of Staff there, arrived in London on August 2nd. General Eisenhower immediately designated him as Acting Chief of Staff in charge of TORCH planning. British authorities were proceeding upon the assumption that General Eisenhower's appointment as Supreme Allied Commander was firm and they were giving him complete and loyal support. But I think that he may have been embarrassed by the fact that official confirmation and announcement from Washington was delayed.

On August 7th, Admiral Mountbatten announced at COHQ: "In

order to decentralize and speed the work of preparing the outline assault plans for TORCH, I have decided to strengthen considerably the small staff lent to General Eisenhower." Accordingly, he designated four syndicates comprising a total of some twenty officers including those already working on TORCH plans. The syndicate which I headed was to be the examining committee to control and direct the work of others. These syndicates began work the following day.

By now the initial plan had been modified. In the second draft, the forces from the United Kingdom would be employed inside the Mediterranean to seize Oran, while forces from the United States were assigned to Casablanca with the understanding that surf and swell conditions might make landing there impossible, in which case the force would land behind the other at Oran and then move westward.

It was immediately obvious that landings in the Mediterranean should not be limited to Oran, but should include Algiers and go as far to the eastward as available means would permit. The plans were modified accordingly and in what might be termed the third draft the outline plan envisaged assaults at Oran, Algiers, and Bone, as well as on the Atlantic Coast of French Morocco.

We did not know in London what would comprise the forces from the United States at this stage. For the operations inside the Mediterranean the assaults were envisaged then about as follows:

At Oran, the 1st Infantry Division (less one regimental combat team) with one British Infantry Brigade group attached, as well as an American armored combat team. The 1st Division, which had had amphibious training in the United States, was just beginning to arrive in the United Kingdom.
At Algiers, the British 78th Division (less one brigade group) with two US regimental combat teams attached, one from the 1st Infantry Division, the other from the 34th Infantry Division. This force would be under command of the general commanding the British division.
At Bone, one US Ranger Battalion as assault force, the remainder of the force to consist of about one British brigade group.

This plan was designed "merely to initiate and give direction to more detailed planning." In this design it was wholly successful, for planning activity in Norfolk House was now intense at every level. It was on this plan that the planning syndicates from COHQ began their studies of the outline assault plans for Oran, Algiers, and Bone.

The changes had only begun. As more detailed investigations and estimates were made, the British side became more and more insistent that naval resources were insufficient to attack both the Atlantic Coast of Morocco and inside the Mediterranean simultaneously. They believed that greater results could be achieved by concentrating against the Mediterranean Coast to seize the whole of Algeria and Tunisia quickly. During the week following the day of August 9th, the plan was changed accordingly.

General Patton arrived in London on August 9th. I saw him in Norfolk House on the following morning, when I briefed him and General Doolittle on the outline plans. He had been selected by General Marshall to command the task force which was to sail from the United States. When he left Washington, the objective of this Western Task Force had been Casablanca.

General Patton was accompanied by only one member of his staff, Colonel Kent Lambert who had been G-3 on the staff of General Patton's I Armored Corps.

I had of course known General Patton for many years. He was interested in learning what I was doing in London. I told him. Then he said: "Dammit, Lucian, you don't want to stay on any staff job in London with a war going on. Why don't you come with me? I will give you a command." I told him that if there was to be any fighting, I certainly wanted to be in on it, and that if he could persuade General Eisenhower to release me, I would be happy to go with him. Later, he informed me that he had obtained General Eisenhower's consent.

In view of the change in objective for the Western Task Force, General Patton needed staff assistance in preparing the initial estimates and plans. My syndicate did much of the work for him.

Shortly after General Patton's arrival, I arranged a dinner in his honor at Claridge's, for I wanted him to meet Admiral Mountbatten and some of the British officers with whom I was associated in COHQ. General Haydon, Group Captain Willets, Colonel Neville and one or two others from COHQ, with General Patton, Colonel Lambert, Colonel Gruenther and myself made up the party. General Patton was always keenly interested in all that pertained to battle experience, and all of these British officers were veterans of naval, ground, and air war. He was impressed with them—"damn good fighting men" he termed them to me. On their side, they were more than interested in General Patton, and he won their respect and admiration.

After dinner, we had been conversing in groups of two and three for some time. Group Captain Willets had been deeply engrossed in conversation with General Patton and I supposed they might be discussing Willets' experiences during the invasion of Crete of which I had already told General Patton. But Willets came to me and said he had been discussing English nobility, and that General Patton had insisted there was no such thing as "typical English aristocracy." Willets had offered to show General Patton that he was wrong and had invited him to dinner for the following evening. The dinner would be a small private affair, and he wished me to bring General Patton.

So the next evening, General Patton and I presented ourselves at the given address. General Patton, with gleaming boots and spurs, riding breeches, shining buttons, rows of ribbons on his well cut blouse, was immaculate—a magnificent figure of a soldier. We entered, and Willets presented us to our hostess, Lady G. Somewhere in her thirties perhaps, simply dressed, she was most attractive and charming, a cultured woman. Then there was a commotion at the door, which Willets opened. And into the room sailed—there is no other fitting word—a majestic presence followed by another of lesser mien, like a battleship trailed by a destroyer.

The first was Lady——, a dowager of sixty-five or thereabouts with several chins seeking rest upon a more than ample bosom. Her towering coiffure quivered with her every movement. Divested of her furs, with trailing skirts, strings and strings of pearls, soft hands sparkling with numerous rings, a lorgnette through which she looked down upon us lesser creatures, she was a picture from a page in history.

She was followed by her daughter, Lady——, a colorless blonde of perhaps thirty-five, straight hair bobbed at shoulder length, frozen-faced, flat-chested, anemic-looking, simply dressed in something light in color, and almost devoid of jewels or ornamentation—like a wraith from some dark castle. And obviously more than dominated by ma mère.

Willets produced cocktails and conversation became general. Lady G had been in America; neither of the others had. They examined us with interest while General Patton and I told them about America. I think they rather expected something more barbaric.

That it was an entertaining evening was due in full measure to General Patton's conversational powers. It was an audience such as he loved for he was a master of the art of startling anecdote. After dinner he held them spellbound, for that night he was in rare form. He told of the notches on his guns and how he came by them. He talked of Mexico and Pershing and outlaws of the great Southwest. He told of the murderers he had known and where and why. Of the rare California vintage he had sampled and enjoyed only to discover, when the great cask was cleaned, it contained the body of a drowned Mexican. And similar tales from his long experience. Needless to say, his audience was duly appreciative, and registered the appropriate degrees of horror, astonishment, and doubt.

When we departed, General Patton remarked that Willets had more than kept his word, and charged me with the responsibility for sending flowers to our hostess on the following day.

About the middle of August, General Eisenhower designated General Clark, then commanding the II Corps, a headquarters without troops in England, as Deputy Commander in Chief for TORCH. He placed upon him the responsibilty for TORCH planning and the development of an allied staff for the operation. One of General Clark's first actions after familiarizing himself with the state of planning was to assemble all who were engaged in the planning work. He reviewed the events that led to the TORCH decision and then announced the decisions relative to the details of the plan which were then agreed upon. This was an important step, for planning could now proceed upon a sound basis and decisions could be obtained where previously planners could only make assumptions.

The outline plan now provided for simultaneous assaults about October 15th at Oran, Algiers, and Bone by land, sea and air forces with a view to earliest possible occupation of Tunisia and the establishment in French Morocco of striking forces which could insure control of the Straits of Gibraltar by moving rapidly into Spanish Morocco if that should become necessary.

At Oran, a force of one infantry division and one regimental combat team, amphibiously trained, plus an armored force of about one regiment, plus necessary auxiliary troops and ground echelons for the United States TORCH air forces, would make two pre-dawn landings to secure the port of Oran and the airfield at Tafaroui. In this area a total force of five infantry and two armored divisions would be built up to consolidate the position and provide striking forces to occupy Spanish Morocco if required. This force would come from the United States and would be under General Patton's command. It was designated as the Western Task Force.

At Algiers, the British 78th Division with one US regimental combat team attached would make three pre-dawn landings to secure the port of Algiers and the airfields at Maison Blanche and Hussein Dey. In this area a total of four infantry and two armored divisions would consolidate the position and prevent any enemy landings in Tunisia or to the westward. The assault waves in these landings were to be American troops for political reasons, and a senior American representative of the Allied Commander in Chief would accompany this force to treat with any French forces willing to collaborate.

At Bone, the 1st Ranger Battalion would make a pre-dawn landing to secure the port of Bone and the airfield at Dozzerville some six miles inland. The remainder of this force, about one brigade group, would be British and would be landed as rapidly as conditions permitted.

The assaults were to be supported by carrier-borne aviation and by fighters and bombers flown from Gibraltar and the United Kingdom as soon as airfields were captured. Naval forces would protect all movements and would support the assaults throughout. Protection against the Vichy and Italian fleets and from German submarines and aircraft was a matter of grave concern.

It was understood, of course, that detailed planning for the Western Task Force would have to be done in America by the commanders and staffs who would conduct the operation. But an outline plan had to be developed, not only as a basis for this further detailed planning, but to determine the practicability of the operation. It was this function that engaged the attention of my group during General Patton's stay in London.

British intelligence concerning the assault area was remarkably complete and accurate and included very good aerial photographic coverage of comparatively recent date. This intelligence included detailed information concerning terrain, weather, beaches, roads, ports, the population, obstacles, towns and villages, French air, ground, and naval forces in the area, and many other details essential for intelligent planning.

We did not know the composition of General Patton's force although we could guess the units from which the assault echelon would be drawn. We had little information as to the American naval forces which would support the Western Task Force, but our naval planners finally succeeded in obtaining lists of the American assault and cargo ships which would probably be available for the operation. These lists included the characteristics of these ships and the landing craft which they could transport. From these lists, we compiled suggested groupings of combat loaded transports which we used as a basis for calculating the strength and composition of assault forces which could be carried, rates of debarkation and landing, and similar details required in planning such an assault.

Thus, by the time General Patton left England on August 19th, he was able to carry back with him the intelligence which we had assembled, a skeletonized assault plan which would provide a basis for further planning, and outline military, naval, and air plans for all of the assaults.

5. *Operation JUBILEE—The Dieppe Raid.*

On August 20th, 1942, in a letter to my wife, I wrote: "I will have to admit that I have seen war—and have been in danger—and have seen men die on land, in the sea, in the sky."

It happened thus.

About a week or so before, Admiral Mountbatten had informed me that the operation which we had known as RUTTER, and which was now christened JUBILEE, would be mounted soon, and he wished me to make arrangements for participation in the operation by about fifty American soldiers, in addition to the observers who would be permitted to go along. Consequently, I had arranged for a detachment of six officers and forty-four men from the 1st Ranger Battalion to participate in the raid with Canadian and Commando units. These men were brought from Scotland and attached to the units which they would accompany. As American observers I designated Major Conway, Lieutenant Colonel Hillsinger, Commander Strauss, and Colonel Hart of Admiral Stark's headquarters, besides myself.

About noon on August 18th, I was warned that observers should proceed to Portsmouth by eight o'clock that evening, and I passed the word accordingly. I informed General Patton of what was in the offing. He was most enthusiastic and even wished that he could delay his departure, which was scheduled for the following day, so that he could go on the operation himself. Then, since I could not leave without authorization, I informed General Clark. He refused to allow me to go because of my part in TORCH planning. However, when I explained the matter to General Eisenhower, he gave his permission, and off I went.

On our arrival at Portsmouth, I was assigned to HMS *Fernie*, the same HUNT Class destroyer on which I had spent a night in early July, which was the alternate headquarters ship for the expedition. Other American officers were assigned to other vessels. I boarded the *Fernie* at the pier and almost at once she pulled away. Then I was told that the ship's captain, Lieutenant Commander Ackworth, had been injured the day before, and the *Fernie* was being taken on the expedition by the first officer, Lieutenant Willets. As we left the harbor, a medley of hunting songs blared forth over the "loud hailer," as the British term a loudspeaker system. These were the hunting songs of the HUNT Class destroyers.

As the *Fernie* moved on to take station in the convoy, we could see tank landing craft filled with men and tanks, infantry assault ships with landing craft at the davits and with decks crowded with men, assault landing craft loaded with commandos, motor gunboats, launches. There were other destroyers, too—all heading out into the Channel and toward the French coast. It was a novel and thrilling experience, and I hated to go below even to be briefed on the plan for the operation.

Below, a small wardroom had been converted into an operation room for the assault. Here the alternate headquarters for the raiding force had been established. The walls were covered with maps. On a table was a model in relief of that portion of the French coast where the operation would take place. All about were the radios which were to be the means of communication with troops on shore and other elements of the landing force afloat. Everything was shrouded in silence for the moment. In the ward room we found Brigadier Mann, Chief of Staff, 1st Canadian Division, with half of the staff of the landing forces which had been drawn from the First Canadian Army. Major General J. H. Roberts, the division commander and also the military force commander for the operation, was on board HMS *Calpe*, another HUNT Class destroyer, with the remainder of the staff. Brigadier Mann explained to the observers on board the plan for the operation. He asked us to try to follow the action with the least possible interference with the work of the staff, in view of the cramped quarters.

The primary purpose of raids is to harass the enemy. It was thought that a raid on a larger scale than any heretofore attempted would not only harass the enemy and destroy valuable military objectives but would also test German defenses in the west and provide the Allied staffs with valuable information concerning their effectiveness and the means for overcoming them. In addition, it was thought that an attack in broad daylight might provoke a reaction by the Luftwaffe and bring on an extensive air battle, which the Luftwaffe had for many months avoided with the Royal Air Force. This was considered especially desirable at this time because much of the German air force was concentrated against the Russians. Heavy losses over France might even divert German aircraft from the Russian front, and thus assist the Russians in their battles. This aspect—bringing on an air battle—was considered the principal objective by the higher levels, although it was not so considered by the ground and naval forces actually engaged in the operation.

Dieppe was selected as the objective for the operation because it was typical of the defenses that would be encountered in the ports along the French coast. It was a harbor used by German coastwise convoys on which the Germans were compelled to rely in ever increasing degree for supplying their far-flung garrisons. Also, it was a base for the E-Boats which had been annoying British channel shipping. At Dieppe were marshaling yards, a pharmaceutical factory, oil dumps, power stations, and an airfield—all of which it would be desirable to destroy. And Dieppe was just within the range at which the fighter aircraft based in England could provide effective fighter cover.

Dieppe is located at the mouth of the D'Arques River, which is the most important break in the high cliffs that front the sea to the east and west. Immediately in front of Dieppe there is a beach some eighteen hundred yards in length, and there is a sea wall and esplanade between the beach and town. To the east and west there are only a few other places where breaks exist in the high cliffs, offering an opportunity for possible landings, and the beaches in all these spots are small and narrow. The whole area had been strongly organized by the Germans for defense.

No. 4 Commando, about 450 strong, was to land at two places on each side of Point D'Ally to destroy a battery of 5.9 coast defense guns near Vesterival.

No. 3 Commando of similar strength was to land at two places on each side of Berneval to destroy another battery of 5.9 coast defense guns on the heights nearby.

Destruction of these batteries was essential because their fire would make it impossible for ships to remain within their range during daylight, and naval support was essential to effect the landing.

The main assault was to be delivered against the town of Dieppe itself by two landings on the main beach which fronts the esplanade. The Royal Hamilton Light Infantry was to land on the western half of the beach, the Essex Scottish Regiment on the eastern half. When these two regiments had cleared the beaches, the 14th Canadian Army Tank Battalion would be put ashore to enter the town and help the infantry to seize and hold it while the various objectives were destroyed.

To the west of the main assault, the South Saskatchewan Regiment was to land, capture Pourville, and occupy a defensive position overlooking Dieppe from the west. On their way, they were to destroy a radio location station and a battery of anti-aircraft guns. When the regiment had seized Pourville, the Queen's Own Cameron Highlanders were to land and pass through the Saskatchewans, and proceed up the valley of the Scie River to capture and destroy the airfield at St. Aubin.

To the east of the main assault, the Royal Regiment of Canada was to land at Puits, capture a coast defense battery just inland and seize the headland overlooking Dieppe from the east.

These two headlands, east and west, were the keys to the town's defenses.

The assault was to be preceded by a short and intense naval bombardment which would be followed by a concentrated attack by Spitfires and Hurricanes, firing cannon and dropping bombs. Smoke was to be laid on the eastern headland from where it was expected the heaviest fire would come.

Overhead, there would be continual air cover by British fighters.

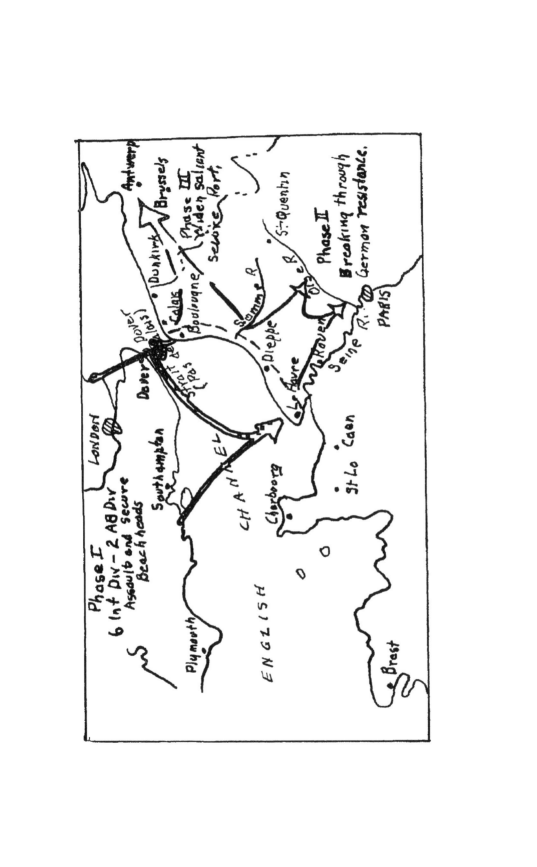

And on the airfields in England, fighters were to be alert to intercept German aircraft as radio direction finders disclosed their approach.

The naval escort included motor gunboats, motor launches, eight destroyers, a gunboat, and a sloop. All told, the expedition totalled some two hundred vessels of various kinds.

It was expected that withdrawal would begin on signal about eleven o'clock in the morning.

It had been a warm summer day, but the night was cool as the darkened armada ploughed its way toward the coast of France under a partial moon. From the decks of the *Fernie*, we saw the low, flat tank landing craft crawling along like great dark water beetles with white waves now and again splashing against their tall snout-like ramps. We passed the infantry assault ships gliding along like dark gray ghosts with moonlight reflecting like jewels in the trailing wakes. In the distance, dim shapes of other destroyers and gunboats were barely visible now and again through the slight surface haze. No lights. No noise. All was dark and still. There was only the hum of driving motors, with occasional low murmurs of voices on the *Fernie's* decks.

Far out in front, two mine-sweeping flotillas swept a channel through the German mine fields which protected the coast.

The voyage passed without incident for hours, with hopes mounting of attaining the desired surprise. Suddenly, at nearly four o'clock in the morning, off to our left front and distant some two or three miles, a star shell flared into the sky and illuminated the sea below. Then followed intense flashes and streaks of red and white and green crisscrossing in the sky like a great display of fireworks. The rumble of cannonading drifted back to us over the waves.

It was obvious that No. 3 Commando had encountered the enemy off shore, less than an hour from that prescribed for landing. There were grave faces on board the *Fernie*. Now that surprise was lost, the enemy would be waiting at his guns to greet the landing troops.

But on we went.

As the light began to gray in the eastern sky, out to the front the bombardment began. It was not nearly so heavy and impressive as I should have liked to hear. The *Fernie* was not taking part in the bombardment because of the danger to the delicate communications equipment of the headquarters on board from the concussion of firing guns. From a mile or more off shore, we could barely discern the dim outlines of the forbidding cliffs, and these were soon shrouded in the drifting smoke. It was my first sight of France. And after this day it was to be almost two years before I saw France again.

Overhead by now, squadrons of Spitfires circled and wheeled crossing and recrossing far up in the sky above us, like watchful eagles.

Suddenly, over the shore line, airplanes dived low into the smoke with flashing guns and emerged off to the eastward in steep climbs, turning toward the sea amid the great puffs of gray and black smoke of the bursting antiaircraft shells. Bright flashes appeared along the cliffs and great clouds of smoke drifted over the scene of action. These were the Spitfires and Hurricanes making their low-level attacks and dropping smoke on the eastern headland.

All of the battle area was now concealed in smoke. From the seaward side we could see only a few landing craft circling and a destroyer or two firing shoreward. So I went below to see what might be learned there.

In the operations room radios were now chattering and staff officers were busy in their cramped quarters. Brigadier Mann was talking to someone apparently on shore, and then to the Force Commander. He turned to me and said that one or two of the radios were out of order on board the *Calpe* and that the only communication with two of the landing forces was through the alternate radios on board the *Fernie*. I asked how things seemed to be going, and he remarked cheerfully that while things had not developed as well as had been hoped, they seemed to be going better than might have been expected in view of our loss of surprise.

No. 4 Commando, he said, had landed successfully at Vesterival and was now attacking its objective. At Pourville, the Saskatchewans had captured the town and were advancing toward Les Quartes Vents which was their objective. The Cameron Highlanders had landed there, and in that area the situation did not look unfavorable. No word had come from No. 3 Commando but the coast defense battery at Berneval had done little if any firing. Nor had there been any word from the Royal Regiment at Puits, but they had been very late in landing and had been subjected to heavy fire. The main assault on the beaches in front of the esplanade had encountered heavy resistance and the Essex Scottish had suffered heavily. But the Royal Hamiltons had finally breached the sea wall and were fighting in the Casino which was practically in their hands. Fire on the eastern half of the main beach had slackened and the Force Commander was sending in one of the reserves, the Fusiliers Mont Royal, to reinforce the Essex Scottish so that the eastern headland could be taken. All in all the situation looked quite hopeful.

I went back on deck. The *Fernie* was then moving shoreward. Everywhere there was firing. Nearby, the assault craft which had returned from landing the initial waves were circling—the Boat Pool—

and shells were now and again dropping into the sea among them with great splashes. Shoreward, smoke was drifting over the town and cliffs as wave after wave of Spitfires and Hurricanes dived into the attack. Overhead, other Spitfires were engaged in dogfights with German planes which were coming in by then in increasing numbers. And the antiaircraft guns of the *Fernie* and other covering ships were firing almost continuously. Now and again as we watched, an airplane burst into flames or plummeted seaward trailing smoke.

As we moved on shoreward, an airplane appeared coming towards us almost at eye level. The antiaircraft guns opened fire, then stopped. It was a wounded Spitfire, limping back toward England, almost skimming the waves.

Toward the town there was the crash of bursting bombs and shells and the distant rattle of machine gun fire. A few hundred yards from the beaches, we could see through drifting smoke a blasted tank landing craft with lowered ramp swinging to and fro with the tide and with only dead men visible within. Closer to the beach there were assault craft half sunk and aground with the ebbing tide. On the beach itself, there was a confusion of broken landing craft and burning tanks.

Standing near the companionway and watching the scene through glasses, I was thrown against the rail by a sudden crash which almost knocked me flat. The whole ship quivered. Something struck my boot and clattered to the steel deck. I picked it up. It was a nut torn loose from the *Fernie's* superstructure by a shell which had just struck aft. Sixteen men were killed or wounded. Then the *Fernie* sought the sheltering smoke to seaward laying a smokescreen as she went.

Below again to the operations room. There Brigadier Mann informed me that Lord Lovat had just reported that Commando No. 4 was re-embarking, its mission accomplished in full. The battery was totally destroyed together with some two hundred Germans. At Pourville, the Camerons were through the town which the Saskatchewans had taken. On the main beaches, the Casino on the esplanade was taken, some of the tanks were over the esplanade, and the tobacco factory and other buildings in the center of the German defenses were now on fire. The Force Commander thought there was a chance of seizing the town by employing the other reserve to assist the Royal Hamiltons in capturing the western headland. He was sending in the Royal Marine Commando to help.

It was past nine o'clock when we saw the assault craft moving in toward the beach through drifting smoke. Shortly thereafter, there was heavy firing toward the town. Later we learned that many craft were hit and few men reached the beach unhurt, for it was swept by heavy, concentrated fire. The Royal Marine commander, seeing the conditions on the beach, turned about half the craft back into the sheltering smoke.

Below in the operations room, there were grave faces and heavy hearts. The radios kept on chattering. It was obvious to the Force Commanders that the headlands could not be taken in time. Conversing with those on shore, Brigadier Mann learned that the situation on the esplanade was becoming increasingly serious. The order to withdraw was given. This was to begin at eleven o'clock under cover of a curtain of smoke laid between the headlands by aircraft. Brigadier Mann turned to me and remarked: "General, I am afraid that this operation will go down as one of the great failures of history."

Back on deck, I saw the destroyers and gunboats standing in to cover. It was a bloody business. Fire was intense. Craft were hit, yet others ploughed their way forward to the water's edge under withering fire. Some craft took on men and came away again. Others remained on the beach. Yet on and on they came, a marvellous display of courage. The final effort to bring men off was made about one o'clock. The *Fernie* was now in close to shore and well inside the sheltering smoke that shrouded the transport area, so close that machine gun bullets from guns on shore were spattering against the ship's armor. Nothing but derelicts and the wreckage of war was now visible on the beaches. Spreading smoke, the *Fernie* turned again to seaward.

I went below again to the operations room, just in time to hear a commander on shore talking to Brigadier Mann for the last time. He was saying that they were forced to surrender, then: "Goodbye, take a message to—" Then all was still.

The battle on shore was ended.

When I came on deck again, someone said that one of the destroyers had been hit. At some distance, we could see smoke rising from a destroyer around which motor gunboats and launches were clustered, apparently taking off survivors.

It was, we learned, HMS *Berkeley*. She had been hit by bombs jettisoned by a Junkers 88 when it was attacked by covering Spitfires.

Lieutenant Colonel Hillsinger was on board the *Berkeley*. British officers later reported this incident. Hillsinger was wearing a pair of Peel tank boots which he had just had made and of which he was very proud. When the bomb struck the *Berkeley*, Hillsinger lost a foot. He applied a tourniquet made of his necktie and handkerchief to his leg. Looking down, he saw his new boot with his foot inside in the water. In disgust, he took off the other boot and threw it after the first. After being taken on board the rescuing gunboat, he refused treatment until other wounded had been cared for. Then he refused to go below, remaining on deck to spot aircraft for the antiaircraft gunners.

For his heroism, he was awarded the Distinguished Service Cross, and it was my privilege later to pin it on his chest in the hospital where he recovered from his wound.

The return across the channel was a sad and wearisome journey, in contrast to our trip of the previous night, when our hearts had been filled with hope. On board the *Fernie* every nook and cranny was filled with wounded for we had taken on board from landing craft all that we could carry. The medical staff and medical supplies were totally inadequate to give more than bare first aid to those on board. It was a grim ship.

The *Fernie*, escorting the small assault landing craft, brought up the rear of the returning convoy. We were pursued almost to the English coast by German aircraft. Most of them were intercepted by our own covering aircraft, but our own antiaircraft guns were frequently in action. They accounted for at least one German airplane which fell into the water not far away. Fortunately, we were not hit again although bullets and bombs were more than once uncomfortably close.

Standing in the doorway, I saw a wardroom floor completely carpeted with wounded men. Some of the wounded were breathing the labored breath of deep unconsciousness. Others slept quietly under the effects of opiates administered by the medical staff. But a number of bright eyes were regarding me intently and in silence. Hardly aware of what I was doing, I pulled out my packet of Bull Durham and rolled and lit a cigarette. One of the men spoke: "I say, you wouldna have another un about yuh?" I gave him my cigarette and then, until my sack was empty, I rolled and lit cigarettes for the others. The only sounds were the labored breaths of grievously wounded men and the cheerful words of thanks from those who smoked.

It was nearly midnight when we berthed at Portsmouth, where the wounded men were removed to waiting hospital trains. There I said goodbye to Brigadier Mann, the Skipper, Lieutenant Willets, and others of that gallant staff. I took the train to London, a sadder and wiser man.

Few Canadians will ever consider JUBILEE as other than a costly failure, for of some 5,000 engaged, nearly 3,400 were casualties of war. Nearly 600 were either dead or died of wounds. About 600 wounded were returned to England. More than 1,900 more were prisoners of war, and many of these were wounded. Almost 300 more were missing. Twenty-eight tanks and most of the weapons and equipment used had been destroyed or left in German hands. One destroyer and many landing craft were lost and few escaped the scars of battle.

There was, however, a credit side. In the air battle, which had been hoped for, 98 German planes were shot down and there were indications that 300 were damaged, against the Allied loss of 100 aircraft, destroyed. Much was learned of German defenses in the West. And much was learned of conditions to be met in any large scale assault of a German channel port. The Allies had gained experience on how to plan and conduct large scale assaults, and what weapons and equipment such assaults would require. It gave the German General Staff cause for alarm as to where the next blow would fall, although it was not to fall on the same coast. A little more than two months later, TORCH flamed in Africa.

I am not among those who consider the Dieppe Raid a failure. It was an essential though costly lesson in modern warfare.

6. End of Mission

Before I left London for the Dieppe Raid, it was understood between General Patton and me that I would remain in London for a week or so until the overall plans were somewhat firmer and some additional intelligence was available, and then would join him in Washington.

On the day after my return from Dieppe, General Clark told me that it was necessary to have someone in London to represent General Patton, to insure complete coordination of the various assault plans and to keep General Patton informed of current decisions and developments. General Eisenhower had directed that I would remain in London for the time being as General Patton's deputy.

On August 25th, I wrote General Patton about this decision, of which he had of course been advised by General Eisenhower. At the same time I forwarded to him revised outline plans for the Oran assault by the Western Task Force together with additional intelligence which had become available. I wrote:

> All this may be love's labor lost as this headquarters has been in a whirl all day over prospective changes. As you probably know, we are thinking again of the Atlantic Coast; consequently, I shall start the boys working on Casablanca again, as well as investigating Spanish Morocco and Tangiers.

It seemed that the American Joint Chiefs of Staff were unwilling to accept an operation wholly within the Mediterranean because of the danger of having communications interrupted at the Straits of Gibraltar if Spain should permit the Nazis to strike through Spanish territory. They believed that this danger was sufficiently grave to demand an alternate plan of communications in case of need. Casablanca would provide a modern port of ample capacity on the Atlantic coast, and there were good roads and a railway line connecting Casablanca with Oran and Algiers. In consequence, the plans were again changed on September 1st.

Our syndicate turned over the outline plans which we had prepared for the Oran assault, together with intelligence and other assembled data, to the 1st Infantry Division when Major General Terry Allen and his staff arrived about this time to begin their detailed planning. Back we went to our original studies of the TORCH operation, which we still had in our files.

Our plans for the Oran and Casablanca assaults had considered each one under two contingencies: one using British assault craft and shipping, the other using American assault craft and shipping. Under the different conditions of beaches and weather which would be encountered in the two localities, these studies indicated that the decision of September 1st—diverting General Patton's Western Task Force from Oran to Casablanca and the Center Task Force from Algiers to to Oran—would necessitate the employment of both American and British assault craft and shipping under conditions least favorable to their special characteristics.

The Oran assault entailed rapid landing of armor and assault troops on beaches which had a gradient of 1 in 65. These beaches were suitable for the LCM (III) of which American assault ships each carried eight or ten. No British assault ship carried more than three and most carried only two. The beaches were not suitable for British LCM's, tank landing craft, or tank landing ships. Thus, debarkation of armor would be much more rapid with American than with British assault shipping. The employment of British tank landing craft and tank landing ships would entail landing American armor and vehicles, which could not be waterproofed, in depths which they could not wade.

In the Casablanca operation, landings were to be made in small ports and harbors for which the small British assault ships were much more suitable than the larger American ships. And British tank landing craft and tank landing ships could effect far more rapid landing of armor within these port areas than would be possible with the American LCM (III). On this exposed Atlantic coast, there was more than a fifty per cent probability that landing craft would have to be lowered outside of ports in an ocean swell of greater than five feet for the initial assaults. Since British assault landing craft were manned at the davits and lowered fully manned, these conditions favored the use of British assault ships rather than the American in which the landing craft were lowered empty and then manned by men clambering down nets over the ships' sides. Since landings in the Casablanca operation were in port areas, more opposition was to be expected than at Oran where landings were to be made at a considerable distance from the port area. This factor favored the employment of British assault landing craft which were armored rather than the American craft which were not.

These differences seemed to be of sufficient importance to warrant calling them to the attention of my superiors. Accordingly, I submitted a memorandum to the Chief of Staff on September 2nd in which I summarized these differences. I pointed out that the success of each of these operations depended upon getting armor ashore quickly, and recommended that consideration be given to leaving the Oran assault to the Patton force and assigning the Casablanca operation to the force from the United Kingdom.

General Clark sent for me. He was, I think, somewhat startled by my recommendation. He wanted to know whether or not I thought the Casablanca operation possible with American shipping. I told him that if we had a break on weather and swell conditions so that we could get ourselves established on shore, I believed that the operation was entirely practicable with American shipping. But, I said, I had no means of knowing whether or not there were other reasons for determining the allocation of forces to the two assaults, and that my purpose had only been to point out the important effect which the special characteristics of British and American assault shipping might have.

General Clark replied that he was of the opinion that under the circumstances the Combined Chiefs of Staff would take a very poor view of any more changes in plans at this time. And I agreed with him.

The Casablanca operation faced a peril that no other amphibious operation has ever faced. There were a number of beaches suitable for landing troops under favorable circumstances but most of the beaches either had no exits or were far from the desired objectives. Ports and harbors on the northwest coast of Africa were scarce. Only Casablanca, itself largely a man-made harbor, was of sufficient depth and capacity to take ocean-going shipping. All landing beaches faced the broad Atlantic. In this area, a swell in no way connected with local weather conditions could, even on fine days, cause surf conditions that made beaching of craft difficult or impossible, not to mention the difficulty of disembarking from ships at sea by means of nets, into landing craft. Statistics indicated that during the fall season we could expect no more than four or five days in a month in which swell condition would permit disembarking at sea and navigating the surf to the beaches.

We had reasonably accurate information as to the strength and composition of French forces in Morocco. In both ground forces and airplanes they were probably superior in numbers to the forces with which we would invade. However, French armament and equipment were incomplete and obsolescent. French aircraft were entirely of the outmoded types left over from the French debacle of 1940. The French air force was known to be strongly pro-British in sentiment. French ground forces were believed to be pro-Ally, if not pro-British.

But it was the French Navy which constituted a hazard. Still smarting under the British assaults at Dakar and Oran, the French Navy, was known to be very strongly anti-British. This Navy manned all coast defenses and was known to be relatively strong at Casablanca, where the modern battleship *Jean Bart* was stationed as well as cruisers, destroyers, submarines, and other naval vessels.

It was expected that the French would resist any assault landing in Morocco, but it was hoped that it would be a token resistance, sufficient only to satisfy the demands of "French honor." Yet the plans had to be based on the assumption that French resistance might be bitter, for there was known to exist in Morocco considerable Vichy—that is to say, collaborationist—sentiment.

In our initial investigations of the Casablanca operation, we had considered a direct assault upon the city, but we came to the conclusion that the seaward defenses, together with the strong French naval forces which were based there, might make such an assault costly and might result in destruction within the port area which would interfere with our subsequent use of it. Then we had considered landings immediately north and south of the city just beyond range of the defenses, seizing the city and port as well as the airfield by attack from the landward side. But when we had made detailed studies of the beaches and weather conditions in the area, we found that beaches immediately adjacent to the city were difficult and that the whole of this exposed coast was subject to those unusual conditions of swell and surf which might make landings on open beaches impossible except for a few days in each month. Such conditions might interrupt landings at any time and thus might jeopardize the whole operation.

There were a few small ports at widely separated points on this coast where landings might be effected except under the most violent conditions of weather. Such ports were Fedala, a few miles to the north of Casablanca; Port Lyautey, some 80 miles to the north; and Safi, some 130 miles to the south of Casablanca. Rabat lay about midway between Fedala and Port Lyautey, but its small port-town had fallen into disuse and was closed by sand bars. While there was a landing field near Rabat, beaches in the area were quite difficult. Besides, Rabat was the residence of the Moslem Sultan of Morocco, the spiritual and political symbol for all of the Arab tribes. Any injury to him or to his holy city might set the Arabs against us, which was a risk to be avoided.

Our outline plan therefore provided for the main landing to be made on beaches in the vicinity of Fedala to seize that port. Here one division with an armored regimental combat team would seize the port and then, assisted by naval and air forces, would capture Casablanca. A secondary landing would be made on the Atlantic coast near the mouth of the Sebou River opposite Port Lyautey to open the river and capture the airdrome located some distance inland. Air forces established on this field would assist in the attack on Casablanca. Original drafts of this outline plan General Patton had carried with him to the United States in August. Revised drafts together with assembled intelligence I forwarded to General Patton by courier on September 6th.

On the same date, General Patton sent his initial estimate and outline plan for the Casablanca operation to the Supreme Allied Commander in London where it was received several days later. This estimate analyzed the various ports on the Moroccan coast as possible assault objectives. The outline plan indicated that the main landing would be made at Fedala by a division less one regimental combat team with an armored regimental combat team attached. One secondary landing would be made at Rabat by two battalion combat teams and one armored battalion combat team with the objective of capturing and stocking one airport. A subsidiary landing would be made at Safi with one infantry battalion combat team and one armored battalion combat team to capture the port and establish a beachhead, after which a sea train (seagoing railroad ferry), if one could be obtained, would unloaded additional armor to attack Marrakech some 60 miles inland, or "should resistance to other landings prove formidable, to attack enemy in rear at points in question." One regimental combat team was to be held in floating reserve for use as circumstances indicated.

This estimate and plan was referred to me for comment. In my reply, copies of which I sent on to General Patton, I pointed out that I did not believe that an attack on Marrakech would have any effect on the early capture of Casablanca, and that it was my opinion that the success of the Western Task Force depended upon the early capture of at least one airdrome and the neutralization of French aircraft. Our studies indicated that our best chance of capturing an airdrome quickly was in the Port Lyautey area, and that neutralization of French aircraft would have to be done by carrier-based aviation, parachute troops, and sabotage.

The final plan for the assault of the Western Task Force retained the landing at Safi to provide armor to assist in the assault on Casablanca. It substituted the assault on Port Lyautey for the one proposed for Rabat.

One of the problems that caused us some concern in connection with the assault of the Western Task Force was that of intelligence. While intelligence was in most respects relatively complete, it was by no means as recent as was the case with intelligence within the Mediterranean. Aerial photographs are a most important source of military intelligence. Those available of the Atlantic coast were a year or more old, and the intelligence people were extremely reluctant to undertake new photographic missions for fear of disclosing our intentions to the enemy. Such photographic work as well as most of the intelligence immediately available had to come from British sources, and it was only by persistent efforts that I was able to obtain the photographic coverage which we considered necessary. Waiting for this photographic intelligence held me in London several weeks longer than should have been required.

One productive source of intelligence in this area was of American origin. After the fall of France, our State Department had maintained in French North Africa an unusually large number of very able consular officials. This group was under the leadership of Mr. Robert Murphy, later General Eisenhower's political adviser. From these sources and from our military attaché in Tangiers we obtained much detailed information concerning conditions in Morocco and were placed in contact with loyal Frenchmen who opposed the Vichy regime and hated the Axis with undying hatred.

Two Frenchmen who were smuggled into London during this period, and whom I sent on to General Patton, were to prove most useful to us. One, Karl Victor Klopet, had lived in Casablanca for more than twelve years. His connection with salvage operations there gave him an intimate knowledge of ports, beaches, and coast defenses along the entire Moroccan coast as well as internal conditions in French Morocco. Another was Jules Malavergne who had been for twenty years a pilot on the Sebou River at Port Lyautey. He was thoroughly familiar with every turn and bar in the river channel, knew all of the shipping which was engaged in the coastal trade, and provided important information concerning pro-Nazi political sentiment which was stronger in the Port Lyautey area than in any other section of Morocco. Malavergne was returned to America just in time to embark on the expedition. His service in piloting the destroyer *Dallas* up the river to the airfield during the action was to win for him the award of the American Silver Star.

Early in September, Admiral Mountbatten offered to General Eisenhower for loan to General Patton the services of Major Henriques, Commander Costobadie, and Wing Commander Homer to assist in planning in the United States. General Patton had formed a very high opinion of these British officers while we were working with him during his visit to London. I had recommended this because their considerable experience in raid planning would make them of enormous value to the commanders and staffs engaged in detailed planning of the assaults. General Patton was delighted to have their services, and the three of them left for the United States about the middle of September.

On September 18th, I finally obtained the photographic coverage which we had sought. Meanwhile, we had made final revisions of our outline plans, and had assembled all other available intelligence. We packed up, Conway, Hamilton and I, and were ready to depart for the United States.

It was with real regret that I said good-bye to the officers with whom I had been associated in London. This brief period had been one of the most interesting and instructive periods of my career. It had vastly enriched my life in friendships, as it had the lives of other American officers who were there with me.

The afternoon before my departure from England, on September 19th, I went in to say good-bye to General Eisenhower. While I was sitting in his office talking with him, an aide announced that a French officer was outside with a message from General De Gaulle. I started to leave but General Eisenhower told me to remain. A French officer entered and saluted smartly. It was General De Gaulle's chief of staff. General Eisenhower greeted him and offered a chair which was declined. Then in very good English, the French officer said: "Sir, I am directed by General De Gaulle to inform General Eisenhower that General De Gaulle understands that the British and Americans are planning to invade French North Africa. General De Gaulle wishes to say that in such case he expects to be designated as Commander in Chief. Any invasion of French territory that is not under French command is bound to fail." Without any change in expression, General Eisenhower merely said: "Thank you." The French officer again saluted smartly and departed.

Then General Eisenhower turned to me and remarked: "Now do you suppose there has been a breach of security somewhere?" All of this TORCH planning had taken place without any consultation with the "Free French" of whom General De Gaulle was the chief in London. For security reasons, the Combined Chiefs of Staff had decided that they should be kept in ignorance of TORCH planning. This visit might indicate that there had been some breach of security and that General De Gaulle had actually obtained information concerning the projected operation. But on second thought, it did not seem to me that that had been the case, for General De Gaulle would have used it as an excuse to protest to Allied authorities. From all of the activity in London during the preceding weeks, anyone could guess something was in the wind. It was my belief that General De Gaulle was fishing for information, but I never learned whether this was correct or not, for I left London the following morning.

CHAPTER TWO

SUB TASK FORCE GOALPOST

1. *Preparing for Battle*

When we drew the outline plans for the assault on Port Lyautey in London, we had not known what troops would be allocated to the task. Now I was informed that Sub Task Force GOALPOST, as it was called, would have as assault troops the 60th Infantry Regimental Combat Team of the 9th Infantry Division and an Armored Battalion Combat Team of the 2nd Armored Division. Besides the assault troops, the command would include all of the Air Task Force troops of the Western Task Force, except the pilots and aircraft which would be transported on carriers—from which they could fly off, but on which they could not land. Capturing and stocking the airfield at Port Lyautey was our principal mission. In all, the troop list included more than forty units of various sizes and categories including infantry, artillery, armor, aviation, antiaircraft artillery, tank destroyers, engineers, signal and medical troops, prisoner of war interrogators, counter-intelligence and military government personnel.

The infantry and armored combat teams were at Fort Bragg in North Carolina. Some of the engineers were at Fort Bragg, others in Camp Pickett and in Richmond, Virginia. Some medical troops were at Fort Bragg, others in New Jersey and California. Air Force troops were scattered from Muroc Lake in California to Langley Field in Virginia. On September 26th, a half dozen units on the troop list had not yet been located, and no one in Headquarters Western Task Force knew where they were.

The Sub Task Force organization was a temporary one for the tactical control of troops during the assault and early operations on shore. Administrative functions were to be primarily the responsibility of other headquarters. The Sub Task Force would require, therefore, only a small staff and for only a brief period. Western Task Force plans specified that the 2nd Armored Division would provide the staff of an armored regiment or combat command for this purpose, which was considered adequate.

On September 26th, there was no Naval side to Sub Task Force GOALPOST, but its designation was expected momentarily. However, I had been provided with the list of transports allocated to the force together with some information as to their performance and character-istics. Thus, with troop list and allocation of transports in hand, and with brief case bulging with intelligence and outline plans, I was ready to join my new command and get on with the detailed planning.

On Sept. 26th, Maj. Gen. E. N. Harmon flew up from Fort Bragg to attend a conference of commanders with General Patton. It was arranged that I return with him to assume my new responsibilities. We landed at Fort Bragg shortly before dark and were driven on past the permanent post and for miles through the piney woods to the camp area of the 2d Armored Division. General Harmon gave me a room in the temporary building in which he and some members of his staff had quarters and made me welcome at his mess. His chief of staff, Colonel Maurice Rose, was an old friend, and most of his staff were cavalry officers. We spent the evening reminiscing in the way of all old troopers.

When I asked about my Sub Task Force staff, it developed that there was none. General Harmon explained. Both of his brigadier generals would require their combat command staffs. One was to accompany him on the Safi operation, the other was to remain behind in command of that part of the division left at Fort Bragg. He could not leave an armored regiment without a staff; besides, his regimental staffs were not experienced and he did not think they would be suitable. His division staff was small; part of it would accompany him, and part would remain behind with the chief of staff. Further, he thought that I would want to select my own staff. While he would do anything he could to help me, he was sure that I would understand that his first responsibility was for his own command.

It had not occurred to me that with all of the divisions then in training in the United States there would be any difficulty in allocating a regimental headquarters for this purpose. I had thought that any commander would gladly seize the opportunity to have officers and men gain some degree of actual experience I had been too optimistic. I was confident that if I forced the issue General Patton would require the 2nd Armored Division to produce the staff as provided in the plans. It seemed unlikely, however, that any staff produced under such embarrassing conditions would be worth the trouble. It was better to improvise.

Conway and Hamilton, whom I had brought back from England, I had left in Headquarters Western Task Force working on plans. I called for them. From General Harmon, I obtained First Lieutenant Oliver T. Sanborn, Infantry, who began assembling essential enlisted personnel and equipment. Later, I was able to obtain from the 2nd Armored Division two other officers, Captain William Makowsky,

Infantry, and Captain Richard C. Storey, Cavalry. Then I had to look elsewhere.

My first need was for an executive officer or chief of staff. No suitable officer was available at Fort Bragg. And those officers of my acquaintance who were qualified already had commands or assignments which prevented their being available for assignment to my staff. However, an old friend had been my operations officer in the 5th Cavalry at Fort Bliss, becoming regimental executive officer upon my departure. He had recently been promoted to colonel and was surplus in that regiment. I thought I might obtain his assignment, as well as that of a junior officer whom I knew, who could serve as my aide. Accordingly, I telephoned Colonel Gay and asked to have Colonel Don E. Carleton, Cavalry, and First Lieutenant Alvin T. Netterblad, Cavalry, assigned to my command.

Conway joined me at Fort Bragg on September 28th and was for the time my whole operational staff. While assembling a staff, we set to work to become acquainted with the command and to initiate detailed assault planning. There was much to be done and all too little time for doing it.

We realized there were not sufficient berths in the port of embarkation to permit all of the Western Task Force to load and embark simultaneously. One Sub Task Force would have to load early, a full week before the date of sailing. As luck would have it, this assignment fell to my Sub Task Force, the only one with no staff whatsoever. Advance parties were to report to the port of embarkation on October 7th. Loaded transports were to clear their berths there on October 16th. Meanwhile, there were detailed plans to be prepared for the debarkation and assault in every assault echelon and all of these had to be coordinated. There were intelligence, administrative, communications, air, and naval gunfire plans to be prepared and checked; intelligence information, orders, and other data to be prepared for distribution; loading and embarkation plans to be completed; movements to the port of embarkation to be planned and made; and plans for rehearsal training to be prepared and coordinated.

The 60th Infantry Regimental Combat Team, under Colonel Frederic J. de Rohan, and the 1st Battalion Combat Team of the 66th Armored Regiment, under Lieutenant Colonel Harry Semmes, I found in excellent condition. Their staffs were well organized, units almost at full strength, and all were as well trained as could have been expected. Both had received some amphibious training.

Everyone at Fort Bragg knew that we were going overseas, but no one among subordinate commanders and troops knew where we were going nor when. For security reasons, higher headquarters had specified that no information as to our destination would be disclosed until the expedition had actually sailed. Personally, I have always felt that mutual confidence between commanders and subordinates is a fundamental basis for establishing proper command relationships. While security is served by providing those involved in military operations only with the information which their own functions require, principal commanders and staff officers can carry out plans more effectively if they know all that the commander knows. Accordingly, I took de Rohan and Semmes into my confidence with the understanding that they would pass on to subordinates only such information as I should authorize, and that they would take every possible measure to maintain security. Their knowledge of all details pertaining to the operation and to my plans enabled them to plan more intelligently, and to stop much speculation and gossip.

In nearly all of our problems, accurate Naval information and advice was essential, but no Naval advice was available closer than Norfolk during this early planning. There was no Naval staff on our level to work with us. While transports had been allocated, some were still fitting out in shipyards and none would be available until they berthed for loading. I met my opposite number, Rear Admiral Monroe Kelly, briefly at Admiral Hewitt's headquarters on October 5th, but his command had not been assembled and none of his staff was available. The Navy felt that Admiral Hewitt's Headquarters could provide us with all of the information and advice we would require in making our plans. Then we would submit them to the Naval side which would prepare their own and tell us what coordination was required. Naturally, we made many visits to Headquarters Amphibious Force Atlantic Fleet.

The Navy would provide the ships and be responsible for berthing them, and for loading all naval stores and equipment. Ship personnel would man ship loading gear, but their only responsibility for loading troops and military cargo would be to see that the operation of the ship was not interfered with nor the ship endangered. Troop units and services would furnish lists of their equipment, vehicles, and supplies with weights and measurements. Troops would be responsible for loading plans, utilizing available space and insuring that troops, supplies, and equipment were available as desired in the operation. Preparation of loading plans and supervision of loading was to be the responsibility of transport quartermasters—junior Army officers detailed for the duty after a short course of instruction. Each transport quartermaster (TQM) would ascertain the capacity of the ship to

which he was assigned, plan the stowage of vehicles, supplies, and
equipment, and supervise the actual loading. Considering that few
junior officers were familiar with ships, none too familiar with purely
military equipment, and relatively inexperienced in assault operations,
this was a rather large assignment. Army Service Forces port of embarkation authorities would receive troops, supplies, vehicles, and
stow them on board in accordance with the loading plans.

Colonel Carleton's arrival on October 5th relieved me of many
burdens. Even though he had had no amphibious training and was not
yet familiar with all details of the operation, he assumed full responsibility for completing the organization of the staff, equipping
the headquarters, organizing the communications, and coordinating the
administration.

Working day and night, we met our successive deadlines after a
fashion. By October 10th, we had completed and forwarded our
operational orders for the expedition, and had sorted and packaged
orders, maps, and aerial photographs for distribution on board, along
with intelligence and other information which would be required. We
had dispatched advance parties to the port and had issued orders for
the movement of individuals, troops units, and equipment by road or
rail in successive echelons continuing during the next five days. We
had prepared loading plans although we knew that these would require
revision during loading. Some of the smaller units had reported in the
staging areas without the necessary equipment and were in process
of being equipped. All had been done that could be accomplished at
Fort Bragg, and our scene of activities shifted to the port of embarkation in the Norfolk area.

We turned at once to the problem of coordinating debarkation and
assault plans with Commodore Gray and his staff, to planning with
them the details of rehearsal training for the week following embarkation, and to the problems of loading, which were in an immense state of
confusion. Many supplies had not yet arrived from the depots. Ammunition and bombs which should have been loaded already had not
yet reached the port. Equipment, vehicles, and weapons which we had
not expected—amphibious bantams, tractors, bazookas, boxes of pyro-
technics—were being added without warning or previous notice, some
after loading was all but complete. Others were on cars in the port, but
since no one knew where they were, they had to be found by search.
Port personnel, stevedores, transport quartermasters, and troops were
all inexperienced. Few of them knew their own jobs well, let alone
the functions of others. But in spite of defective plans, delays, and confusion, loading proceeded and troops were finally embarked by the
night of October 15th. Some last-minute loading was done the morning

of October 16th, and on that day, at 1340, we sailed for Solomon's Island in Chesapeake Bay, where we were to have our rehearsal training. One cargo ship was left behind for a day, to take on additional supplies.

In contrast to our own and other military headquarters concerned with preparations for this operation, the Naval headquarters and ships' companies with whom we came in contact were experienced and well organized. They seemed to know what they were about and proceeded with comparatively little of the disorder and confusion which was normal with us. We were properly envious. With great relief we saw the piers of the port of embarkation recede as we set our course for the rehearsal area off Solomon's Island. We were confident that the worst was over and that there would be an end to all uncertainty.

It had taken a full twenty days, but we had produced results. We had organized a Sub Task Force Headquarters of sorts. We had planned and issued orders for an operation and a rehearsal. We had assembled and loaded a diverse command of more than forty units totalling nearly 9,000 men, 800 vehicles and tanks, nearly 100 towed weapons of various kinds, and 15,000 tons of cargo including ammunition, aviation bombs, gasoline and oil, rations of all kinds, maintenance supplies, and even steel mats for air fields. It was not surprising that there had been confusion, for one learns that it is a customary adjunct of war.

On October 14th, there was a final conference of commanders with General Patton in Washington. It was called primarily as a last check on coordination after landing, but one new item emanated from it. We had neglected to provide a countersign for identification purposes during operations. We discussed the characteristics a countersign should have—it should be easy to remember, to pronounce, yet difficult for Arabs, Frenchmen, or Spaniards to repeat. Someone suggested the words "George Patton," which met with unanimous approval. The challenger would call "George"; the challenged, if a friend, would answer "Patton."

2. Off Solomon's Island in Chesapeake Bay

Rehearsals practice troops in combat formation, disclose deficiencies in organization, training, planning and technique. They are essential steps in preparing for assault landings, and particularly vital to hastily assembled and inexperienced commands. Our schedule had precluded any rehearsal prior to our actual embarkation. However, both military and naval force commanders had agreed that we would have the week, October 17th to the 24th inclusive for rehearsal training while the remainder of the Western Task Force was loading.

In planning this training, we had coordinated every detail with

Admiral Hewitt's staff, and had obtained from them all of the maps, hydrographic charts, and other information concerning the area which was necessary for planning and conducting the training. During the loading period, we had coordinated all plans with Admiral Kelly and Commodore Gray and their staffs. Commodore Gray was just as anxious for the training as I was, for half of his transports were newly joined and more than half of his landing craft were manned by inexperienced personnel. On the beaches at Solomon's there could be no test of naval gunfire or air support, but we did hope to make limited tests of communications and procedures. We would certainly be able to achieve some degree of coordination between the troops and the transports which would carry and disembark them, and between assault troops and the landing craft which would actually put them on shore.

Our purpose was to attain within the time available the maximum proficiency on the part of individuals, troop units, and boat crews in disembarking from ships into landing craft moving in proper formation to a designated point on shore, disembarking there, and testing combat formations for carrying out planned missions. One day was to be spent in boat and net work on transports to train ships' crews in lowering and handling boats and to train soldiers in disembarking by means of nets over the ships' sides. Another day would be spent in rehearsing our operation in daylight following the operational plan as closely as possible except that we would land only a few vehicles. Another day would be spent in a similar rehearsal at night as our landing was to take place in darkness. After each of these periods, there would be time for correcting deficiencies, for additional training by troop commanders and ships' captains, and for preparing for the next training. Commodore Gray was in full agreement, and was insistent that his boat crews rehearse their full operation, including traversing the full distance to shore which they would undertake in the operation. When we sailed for Solomon's Island, all subordinate commanders and their staffs were on board the *Henry T. Allen* in conference with me to coordinate all details so that no time would be lost.

Saturday morning off Solomon's Island dawned bright and clear. From the quarterdeck of the *Henry T. Allen* we could see the other transports riding at anchor like great gray geese with landing craft swarming in the water about them like goslings. On the *Allen*, men were milling about the decks and over the sides, clambering up and down nets. All seemed to be going according to plan. Then Colonel Demas T. Craw reported from one of the ships carrying aviation personnel that no training was in progress. The ship's captain had refused to hang any nets or lower any craft, giving the reason that his crew was not sufficiently trained to go on the expedition.

I appealed to Commodore Gray. He was aware of the captain's attitude, but said it was a matter that would have to be referred to Admiral Kelly when he arrived. Commodore Gray would not accompany me, but he interposed no objection to my visiting the ship in question.

With Colonel Craw and two members of my staff, I clambered down the nets for the first of what was to be many times during that and the following days, and into a landing craft. The ship's captain met us at the rail, escorted us to his cabin, and served us coffee. He knew of me through his wife, who had gone to school with my own wife and had visited us one summer while we were stationed at the Cavalry School, Fort Riley, Kansas. After some reminiscing, I asked what the trouble was. He repeated that his ship was in no condition to take part in any operation. He had been assigned to it with a skeleton crew while it was refitting and had sailed for Norfolk for loading even before all landing craft had been placed on board. His crew had been completed while loading was in progress, with half-trained men who did not even know how to lower a boat. In fact, the ship had never lowered its boats. None of his officers were experienced, and the ship was in no way fit to go on any expedition. He simply refused to be responsible for taking it out.

I related something of what I knew of the background for the operation, and pointed out that the decision to undertake it had been made on the highest levels with full knowledge of our inadequate state of preparation. There was no possibility that his refusal to take the ship out could have any effect whatever on going on with the operation; it could only jeopardize his own career, and the training of the soldiers and sailors on board his ship. So far as the ship was concerned, Navy authorities would have no difficulty in finding some officer willing to do the best he could under the circumstances. If he persisted in his attitude, it could only reflect upon him and the uniform he wore. I suggested that since the ship was not carrying assault troops, his crew would not have to be so well trained, and in any event he would have the remainder of the week in Chesapeake Bay, and the voyage over to further instruct the crew. My arguments had the desired results. Before I left the ship, landing nets were being placed and booms were busy lowering away landing craft.

Rehearsal plans contemplated landings by the assault battalions on three principal beaches, and practice by the armored battalion on still another. These plans had been approved by Admiral Hewitt and his staff and of course by Admiral Kelly and Commodore Gray. During

Admiral Hewitt's headquarters limiting the use of landing craft to one small beach. We protested, but the reply confirmed the restriction for the reason that possible underwater obstructions on other beaches might damage landing craft propellers and there were no replacement propellers to be had.

Our plans for the daylight rehearsal were entirely upset. We could only land the infantry battalions one after another on the one small beach and immediately reembark them, and we could land no vehicles. Neither troops nor boat crews did well, both showing evidence that this training was sorely needed. It seemed to me that someone on the Naval side considered landing-craft propellers more important than soldiers' lives and the success of our assault landing. What would be the use of saving propellers in Chesapeake Bay if lack of training of boat crews and soldiers was to lose the battle on the Moroccan coast? From my previous association with Admiral Hewitt, I could not believe that he had issued this order. But there was obviously no use in further protesting through our naval channels—some staff officer would only turn us down again.

While we were watching the landings, Carleton and I went ashore. In an unoccupied shack used when troops were training there, we found a telephone. We finally got General Patton in Washington. I explained our predicament and pointed out that a night rehearsal on one beach would be utterly impossible. I emphasized that I considered a night rehearsal vital in preparation for the operation. I explained that I did not believe that Admiral Hewitt knew of the change in orders, and asked him to call the Admiral and arrange for us to have our night rehearsal as planned. Then the wire almost sizzled. "Dammit, Lucian, I've already had enough trouble getting the Navy to agree to undertake this operation. All I want is to get them to sea and to take us to Africa. Don't you do a damn thing that will upset them in any way." Bang. He hung up. And that was that.

But I was still responsible for GOALPOST. No help from General Patton, but there was still Admiral Hewitt. We placed a call for him in Norfolk. How many exchanges the call went through I will never know. What security risks I was undertaking, I did not stop to consider. We finally got Admiral Hewitt on the telephone. I explained the problem and reminded him of the importance of this rehearsal training. As I had suspected, Admiral Hewitt's staff had ordered the change without consulting him because of the critical state of propeller replacement. Admiral Hewitt authorized me to use all beaches and to carry out the night rehearsals as we had planned. He would issue the necessary instructions. Both Admiral Kelly and Commodore Gray were relieved, and we proceeded with plans for the night rehearsal.

But my troubles were not yet over. About ten o'clock that same night, Commodore Gray came to me with a message which he had just received and which required him to send certain ships, including some carrying assault battalions, into Norfolk the next day for "topping off" —that is, adding last minute fuel, provisions, and supplies. Under original plans, this was to have been done in the rehearsal area so that rehearsal training would not be interrupted. This change in orders would preclude any night rehearsal, disrupt all plans for issuing final orders and prevent a final conference with commanders.

Over the side we went, Commodore Gray, Carleton, and I, and off to the *Texas* to confer with Admiral Kelly. Admiral Kelly was sympathetic and agreed to send a message to Admiral Hewitt recommending that ships lay over for a day to permit the night rehearsal. He was not optimistic that the reply would be favorable, for this topping off was a function of the Naval Service organization.

I could not believe that Admiral Hewitt was aware of this further disruption in our schedule, and I had grave doubts that he would ever see any message that Admiral Kelly might send. To have some staff officer disapprove the request at this time would be disastrous. Accordingly, Carleton and I left Commodore Gray about half-past eleven at night and once more set our course for the telephone on shore. About three o'clock in the morning, again I had Admiral Hewitt on the telephone. I apologized for disturbing him at such an hour, and explained the urgency of the situation which justified it. Once more, Admiral Hewitt had not known of the change in orders, and was somewhat irritated by it. He won my undying gratitude right there by telling me to forget it and go on with the night rehearsal as we had planned. He would see that the ships remained there for the necessary time.

On Monday, October 19th, armored and aviation units practiced landings while troops prepared for the night rehearsal. We also had our final conference on naval gunfire and air support. That night, we had the night rehearsal. It was well that we did for we learned much, both military and naval, and were able to make corrections. The exercise ended and all were back on board by noon on Tuesday, October 20th. After a final conference, we sailed for Norfolk.

October 22nd we moved out to anchorage, and other transports of the force were either at anchor or at the piers. Here we received final dispatches from General Patton, and I assembled all the assault commanders and their naval opposite numbers on board the *Allen* and explained to them in detail the operation which we were undertaking, detailed orders of which were already on board their respective ships.

When I stood at the ship's rail and watched the last of the boats carrying my subordinate commanders disappear into the gathering dusk, I experienced a solemn moment. It was borne in upon me with an awesome finality that, for better or worse, the die was cast. As our plans were drawn up, so would we fight weeks later, two thousand miles away on the shores of Africa. My own mistakes and the mistakes of others in preparing this command for battle would be paid for in the lives of the Americans for whom I was responsible. It was a sobering thought I wished we were better prepared, but there was no use now in thinking of what we might have done. Our problem was to make the plans succeed. I had learned that preparation is the first essential for success in war, and that the adequacy of preparation reflects the capacity of a commander and his staff. This lesson was to harass me and those who served with me on many occasions in the years that followed.

3. *The Voyage*

Men like Columbus, Drake, John Paul Jones, Farragut, Nelson, and Dewey had pitted their strength against the sea in high adventure. What names to stir the hearts and fire the ambitions of American youth! There are few who have not felt the majesty of the ocean and at one time or another responded in some way to the appeal of the sea. There is always something of romance about a sea voyage, and how especially is this true of a first one. For the vast majority of the 9,000 soldiers on board the transports of our division when we slipped out through Hampton Roads and past the Virginia capes onto the broad Atlantic, this was a first sea voyage. More, it was a voyage that would end for them in their first battle—and a battle on foreign soil two thousand miles from the homes they had no wish to leave. As we watched the dim outlines of the American shores dip below the western horizon, I was sobered by the thought that for many of these on board this would be their last view of our native land.

We had lived on board for a week or more, and we were more or less accustomed to the routine of life on shipboard. Our transports with their accompanying escorts plowed their way steadily eastward, but not for several days were we to see the full strength of the convoy bearing the whole of the Western Task Force. For reasons of security and to deceive possible Axis agents, each division of the convoy slipped out at different times, each one ostensibly for a routine training exercise or for some port which would conceal the purpose of our sailing. The rendezvous had been fixed for a point in the unmarked ocean several hundred miles distant from our shores. There, during the day of October 27th, other transport divisions and their accompanying escorts joined and took their assigned stations in the vast armada.

A great convoy at sea is a magnificent sight. One thinks of stately swans gliding across some park lagoon, or of waterfowl in precise formation winging their way against leaden skies, or of a great herd of cattle undulating across western plains under watchful eyes of guardian cowboys. But none of these matches the grandeur of a convoy at sea in war time. Forward of us was the battleship *Texas*, broad of beam, bristling with guns, a symbol of power. We followed at a distance of perhaps half a mile. Behind us spaced at similar distances followed other transports. Off to our right, or starboard, there was a similar column; beyond it another, another, and still another, each column of transports following the leading cruiser or battleship like a file of Indian squaws trailing an Indian warrior. To the rear as far as we could see the formation extended—transports, cargo ships, aircraft carriers, tankers—all with white waves curling back beneath their bows, and a shimmering wake trailing out behind. And everywhere the tossing of signal flags and the incessant blinking of signal lamps as the ships communicated one with another. Now and again far out across the tossing blue waves polkadotted with white caps, one caught glimpses of the sleek destroyers speeding along like outriders protecting a moving herd. No sound but that of wind and waves and the faint hum of driving motors. No smoke by day, no lights at night, and the faintest indication of either brought quick reprimand from watchful eyes.

And so we passed day after day, night after night. Our course bore far to the south as though for the Indian Ocean around Africa, then back to the northward in irregular trace to confuse scouting submarine or aircraft.

Life on board had disadvantages for soldiers preparing for battle. Men were crowded in close quarters, and all available space was occupied by the paraphernalia of war. There was little room for exercise, for recreation, or for training—and space is the soldier's medium. Continuous training was essential to perfect individual and team techniques and skills, to maintain the physical condition which combat requires, and to avoid the idleness that leads to boredom and discontent. Training programs prescribed that every available moment during the voyage was "to be devoted to an intensive training to the end that all men of the command would be conditioned mentally and physically to achieve victory regardless of hostile resistance or privation," and these had been carefully prepared. They had to be carried out with ingenuity and enthusiasm.

German submarine warfare was at its height at the time we sailed, and the "wolf packs" were taking their toll of shipping in spite of protective measures. There was the grim possibility that our own convoy might be attacked. The loss of a transport with an assault battalion would disrupt plans, for each battalion had a specific mission. If one battalion were lost, we would have to revise our plan and continue with the operation. If two were lost, the operation would not be practicable. Accordingly we prepared alternate plans for the eventuality that any of the three assault battalions should be lost at sea.

Naval officers emphasized the difficulties in navigating to a specified point off the shore of a continent more than two thousand miles away to find unerringly at a scheduled hour in darkness the point we sought. Even the charts in use noted that the Moroccan coast might be three miles west of its charted location. A scouting submarine was to locate the mouth of the Sebou River and was to lay off shore making signals which would confirm our location, but Naval officers were none too sure that something might not go amiss. Then the ships' officers were convinced that we could not land at 0400 as we planned unless we arrived in the transport area by 2300 instead of 2400 as the Naval plan provided. All in all, there was a possibility that we might have to land in daylight instead of in darkness as we wished. And there is much difference in landing secretly in darkness, to gain a foothold on shore and in landing in broad daylight under fire. Accordingly, we prepared alternate plans for a daylight landing.

Those responsible for the decision to undertake TORCH hoped that the French would not offer serious resistance to our landings, but would welcome us as friends. It was for this reason that all assault landings, even those in the Mediterranean, were to be led by American troops, and every possible measure was taken to minimize resistance when we should land. We knew that the President would broadcast a proclamation to the world at the hour of landing, and that this would be followed by a broadcast by General Eisenhower as Supreme Allied Commander in Chief. Just before we sailed we had received copies of General Eisenhower's message assuring the French that we came as friends and that we would take no offensive action unless the French first took hostile action against us. It emphasized that we wanted French help and prescribed signals by which we could recognize French willingness to welcome us as friends and allies. It ended with an appeal to the French forces to follow these instructions so that "bloodshed will be avoided and we shall welcome you as comrades in the fight against the oppressors of your country."

There was reason to hope that these appeals might be successful if heard in time, and the effort was certainly worth making. Our area was distant from any large center of population. There was a possibility that the messages might not be heard, or that local commanders would await instructions from higher authority. It seemed to me that a personal message to the French commander in our local area might reinforce these radio appeals, and some of the French-speaking officers on my staff thought that it might be even more effective. Accordingly, I prepared a letter to the French commander. Major Conway and Lieutenant Grimsley translated it into French. To lend something of ceremonial aspect, we even had the translation engrossed in fine Old English lettering on a scroll which we bound with ribbons and seals. This message I would dispatch by two officers to be selected for their knowledge of French, their military background, and personal characteristics which might be expected to add impressiveness to the mission.

This was a desperate venture, but desperate ventures never want for volunteers, and eventually, I selected two. Major Pierpont M. Hamilton of my staff had spent many years in France. He had been a pilot in World War I. He was a man of great dignity, fine appearance, and definite personal charm. He had been with me in England, and was thoroughly conversant with every detail of TORCH planning. He was a logical choice. Colonel Demas (Nick) T. Craw finally persuaded me to allow him to accompany Hamilton. I hesitated long for Craw commanded the air contingent of GOALPOST. Craw was a man of good appearance and persuasive personality. He had been in the Balkans and Greece when the Germans entered and had wide acquaintance among foreign officers including Frenchmen. His presence, background, and peculiar fitness for the assignment led me to consent to his undertaking the mission.

Thus the voyage passed with each day filled with its own activities. There were occasional reports of contacts with enemy submarines, but we saw none. There was a report of an intercepted merchantman, but it was far out beyond our field of view. There were occasional scouting airplanes, but all from our own carriers. At times it was difficult to realize that this was more than a pleasure voyage. But when the convoy separated into its three component forces on the morning of November 7th, and we bore off to the northward on our own, the ocean seemed strangely empty. We knew that our time was drawing near.

Saturday evening, November 7th, the zero hour approached. About ten o'clock word flashed over the ships that there were lights on shore. We were sliding along silently in darkness at reduced speed under a star-studded sky. Off to starboard glittered the lights of a good-sized town only a few miles distant. Lights were encouraging, for lights meant that we were not expected. But what town? Neither Commodore Gray nor any Navy officer on the quarterdeck would hazard a guess, but some thought that it was Rabat some twenty miles south of our objective area. There was a silence of intense concentration on the quarterdeck of the *Henry T. Allen* as we glided along through the calmest seas we had yet known.

A little later word came that contact had been made with the scouting submarine off the river mouth. We were then so close to shore that the outlines of the cliffs and sand dunes beyond the beaches could be dimly discerned. We turned seaward, reduced speed, and finally stopped. Then there was agitation on the quarterdeck. Naval officers were going from side to side, nervously peering off into the murky darkness, and conversing in tense tones. I asked: "Well, Commodore, where are we?" The Commodore was obviously worried when he replied: "Well, General, to be perfectly honest, I am not right sure exactly where we are." Then I was worried too.

We had been steaming northward too close to shore and had turned seaward to reach our transport area some eight miles off. Some of the ships had either not received, or had misunderstood, the signal. As a result, when we entered the transport area where everything depended upon every ship being in its prescribed location, no one ship knew the position of any other, or was certain of its own. And we were already an hour late.

Port Lyautey, a river port, lies about nine miles upstream from the mouth of the Sebou River, a broad stream with a depth ranging from thirteen feet at low to nineteen feet at high tide. Just below the town, the river forms a wide loop, a "U" open to the south, in which lies the airfield. Ignoring surf, there were beaches suitable for landing all along the coast, but exits inland were few and difficult across the commanding ridges which paralleled the coast close behind the beaches. A coast defense battery situated in the old fort on Kasbah on the south bank of the river protected the river channel and blocked the principal road from the coast to the town. Another road inland passed around the southern end of the lagoon which lay along the foot of the high ridge for three or four miles southward from the Kasbah. The road connecting Port Lyautey with Rabat some twenty miles to the south and with Casablanca some fifty or sixty miles farther on, parallels the coast, and, at the south end of the lagoon, is not more than two or three miles inland. Just below the Kasbah, the French had stretched a cable or net across the river to prevent unauthorized craft from proceeding upstream.

Besides the coastal battery in the Kasbah, we knew that the airfield was well protected by antiaircraft defenses, and that a detachment guarded the bridge north of the town. We also knew that the high ground in the river loop between the Kasbah and the airfield was honeycombed with trenches and other defensive works, although not occupied. Otherwise, the French garrison consisted of a regiment of

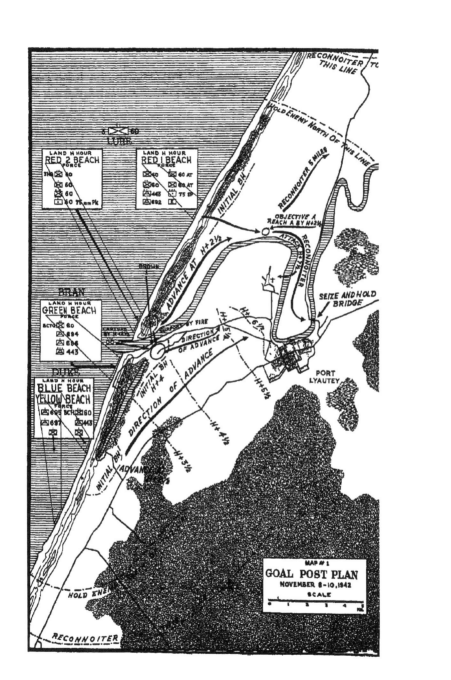

GOAL POST PLAN
NOVEMBER 8-10, 1942

infantry, several battalions of artillery, and some cavalry stationed in Port Lyautey. There were strong forces in Rabat including at least forty-five old-model tanks which could be expected to reinforce the garrison at Port Lyautey in case of need. Other reinforcements could be expected from Meknes farther on to the east where parts of the French Foreign Legion were stationed. The French were known to have a number of airplanes but all were believed to be old models which our carrier-borne aircraft would quickly eliminate.

The 2nd Battalion, 60th Infantry, commanded by Major John H. Dilley, was to land on Green Beach opposite the resort village of Mehdia at 0400, assault and capture by surprise the coast defense battery in the Kasbah by first light, about 0600. If the assault by surprise was not practicable for any reason, the battalion was to take the battery by assault in daylight following air and naval bombardment on call after 0615. A demolition party of engineers and naval technicians under Colonel Frederic A. Henny, the Sub Task Force engineer, was to accompany the battalion, locate and remove the obstruction across the river. When the battery was taken and the cable removed, the destroyer *Dallas*, carrying a Raider Detachment, a company of the 60th Infantry trained as Rangers or Commandos, was to proceed up river and land the Raiders at the airfield. The *Dallas* had on board M. Malavergne, a Sebou River pilot, whom we had smuggled out of Morocco and who had landed in America in time to sail with the expedition.

North of the river, the 3rd Battalion, 60th Infantry, under Major John Toffey, was to land on Red Beaches 1 and 2. A small force near the river with artillery pack howitzers and machine guns was to assist the 2nd Battalion in capturing the Kasbah by fire from across the river. The remainder of the battalion was to move directly inland to a point opposite the airfield, cross the river in rubber boats, and assist in capturing the airfield. It was also to seize the bridge north of the town.

To the south of Mehdia Plage, the 1st Battalion, 60th Infantry, under Major DeWitt McCarley, was to land on Blue Beach, move inland around the southern end of the lagoon, establish road blocks with machine guns and antitank guns along the Rabat Road to protect the south flank, and then advance rapidly to the northeast to block the western exists from Port Lyautey and assist in capturing the airfield.

The armored battalion combat team, under Lieutenant Colonel Harry Semmes, was to land as soon as possible after the assault battalions on Blue or Green Beaches, reconnoiter to the south toward Rabat without delay, protect the south flank, and be prepared to assist in capturing the airfield, or to advance to seize the one at Rabat.

By 1100, we hoped that all three battalions would be in position prepared for a final assault to take the airfield. Colonel de Rohan with his combat team headquarters was to land early on Green Beach, a central location which would facilitate early establishment of communications with the battalions on shore. I would remain on board with communications from the ship to the battalions on shore until landing craft returned from landing them. Then I would land on Blue or Green Beach. By 1100, I hoped to be directing the final assault to take the airfield if we did not have it by then.

The *Henry T. Allen* began lowering boats at half-past twelve. Troops were to begin disembarking at 0125. No landing craft had reported from other ships, nor had we been able positively to identify the few ships whose faint outlines we had seen. I wondered what the troops on the other ships were doing. In the confusion, would commanders wait for orders? Would they proceed with the plans for landing in darkness? With the daylight plan? Radios were still silent. I had to find out.

Leaving Carleton on the *Henry T. Allen*, my aide and I clambered down the nets and into a landing craft which Commodore Gray called to the ship's side. We found ships everywhere, but each one was reluctant to identify itself for they were suspicious of this unexpected visit. When we were finally able to identify ourselves, none could tell us in what direction to find the ships we sought. But from one to another we went until I had found and boarded each of the assault ships and had verified plans with troop commanders and ship's officers. We were late, but all hoped that with luck we could still reach the shore before daylight.

By half-past three, I was back on board the *Henry T. Allen*. Carleton met me at the rail and dragged me to the communications room saying: "Boss, just listen to this!" It was General Eisenhower's message to the French people coming over the radio. The President's proclamation to the world had started at 0300 and had been followed by General Eisenhower. It was the rebroadcast which I was now hearing. My heart sank. Our people in the Mediterranean had landed an hour before our scheduled time. If the French were not now alert and waiting at their guns we would indeed be lucky!

A few minutes later, five French ships in column, all brightly lighted, came from the river's mouth and moved slowly westward through our fleet, so close that we could read the name *Lorraine* on the leading ship. I questioned the Commodore. He assured me that the ships must certainly have prize crews on board. As the *Lorraine* passed within a few hundred yards, a signal lamp blinked a message from her deck in French. A young Naval officer standing beside me translated as he read: "Be warned. They are alert on shore. Alert for 0500." And the five ships glided slowly westward through our fleet and bore off to the south. Later, we were to learn that destroyers protecting the landings near Fedala had fired upon them whereupon the Frenchmen had run their ships ashore.

Meanwhile, debarkation proceeded and landing craft carrying the assault battalion from the *Allen* cleared away for shore. Major Hamilton reported from the *George B. Clymer*. He and Colonel Craw, clad in their best uniforms, in blouses and caps, brass and leather gleaming, with rows of ribbons and pilot's wings adding a touch of color, were ready for their mission. In the landing craft which was to carry them ashore, we had placed a radio-equipped bantam and a walkie-talkie so that they could report their progress. They were lowered into the landing craft, bearing message and scroll, and off they went into the early morning gloom.

There was a lull on board the *Henry T. Allen*, and I suppose a similar one on every transport in the fleet. Landing craft were gone with half of the ship's population. On board there was minor activity as those who were next to go made ready, but there would be three hours or more to wait. There was little talk on the quarterdeck where we waited —only the blinking of signal lamps and the chatter of the now unsilenced radios as contact was reestablished among the transports.

By radio, Carleton followed Craw and Hamilton shoreward. They could see nothing yet. Now they could see landing craft moving shoreward. They were passing the control boat. They could see the shore. They were at the jetties which marked the river's mouth.

It was 0550 and the first faint glow in the eastern sky portended our first Moroccan dawn, although land and water were still shrouded in the pre-dawn darkness. Shoreward, a red rocket flared into the air and burst in a panoply of shooting stars, and then there were flashes of guns on shore—the coastal battery was firing! Off to the southward, great chains of red balls streaked through the darkness toward the shore. Seconds later the sound of firing drifted to us across the water. Our destroyers had opened fire and the battle was on.

Then another message from Craw: "At mouth of river. Being shelled by enemy and our own Navy. Going to land on Green Beach." A little later, another message: "On Green Beach. Bantam stuck. Looking for one. Troops landed and moving inland. Proceeding on mission." And that was the last we were to hear of our special mission for two full days!

4. *First Battle*

One of the first lessons that battle impresses upon one is that no matter how large the force engaged, every battle is made up of small

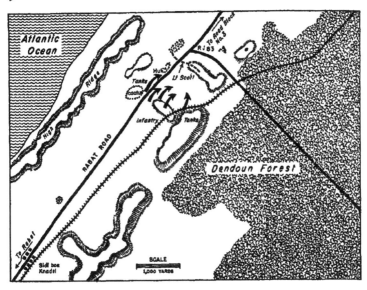

actions by individuals and small units. An incident of Lieutenant Jesse Scott's flank patrol is a case in point. It starts as follows:

"Platoon, HALT. Rest."

The 1st Platoon, Company A, 60th Infantry (less one squad) straggled to a halt and each man dropped to the ground as the light dust scuffed up by marching feet settled slowly earthward. It was the morning of November 8th, 1942. The place was Africa. Second Lieutenant Jesse Scott opened his map and walked across the road to consider the situation.

It was the Rabat Road, a two-way concrete strip. To the west some two miles or more away was the high ridge that paralleled the seacoast and blended into the great mounds of shifting sand behind the beaches where they had come ashore that morning. To the northeast on the Rabat Road beside which they had marched for the last hour was the road junction where they had left Road Block No. 3. Beyond that the road disappeared into dense woods in the distance. To the southwest, the Rabat Road followed the valley floor, almost level except for slight rises or folds in the ground which concealed some stretches. Along the road was a telephone or power line and the remnants of what were once two rows of fair-sized trees. There, a mile or so away, Lieutenant Dooley with Road Block No. 1 was disappearing over a rise on the way to Sidi bou Knadel. To the east, a strip of pavement, wide enough for only a single vehicle, led over a sandy ridge some 1200 yards away. Beyond that there should be a railroad crossing. The railroad following the ridge to the southwest crossed through a saddle and came into view to the south. Roughly paralleling the ridge and the Rabat Road, lines of poles, barely visible in the distance, traced its route to Sidi bou Knadel.

The sun, almost overhead, shone warm and clear. The stillness was broken only by the rumble of thunder to seaward—no, Lieutenant Scott told himself, not thunder, but the roar of naval guns.

Yes, this was RJ 83. Here he was to establish Road Block No. 2 to protect the right flank of the battalion which was moving north to capture the airfield.

Scott turned and considered his platoon. Two squads of nine men each. Sergeants Steinke and Augusta, squad leaders. Sergeant Taylor, platoon sergeant. Corporals Buttz and Paddock, assistant squad leaders. All watching him. How different from OCS and training back at Bragg. No horseplay now. All sitting quietly, cooling off from the hot march, smoking and talking in murmurs. Like himself, they felt a suppressed excitement at finding themselves on a foreign shore and "going for record" after all these months of confusion.

Scott turned to Sergeant Taylor who had crossed the road and joined him. Taylor had the oldtimer's slightly condescending but always correct military attitude. He was obviously anxious to get started.

"Sergeant Taylor, I believe this is the place, don't you?"

The sergeant briefly examined the map.

"Yes, sir, Lieutenant. It don't seem to have changed none in the past three weeks. How does the Lieutenant want the platoon deployed?"

"Call the squad leaders."

The squad leaders reported. Their military correctness made Scott feel a little self-conscious and reminded him of OCS.

"You all know the situation.

"Sergeant Augusta, you take four men of your squad. Follow this road to the southeast over that ridge about a mile and a half and you will come to a railroad. Take a position there where you can block anything approaching from that direction.

"Corporal Paddock, you take the other men of the first squad and reconnoiter to the front. Move out across country to the south toward that low ridge where those telephone poles come into view. Follow generally along the railroad observing to both sides. About four miles down this Rabat Road the railroad comes into a little town. You will find Lieutenant Dooley there with Road Block No. 1. Let me know at once if you see any enemy.

"Sergeant Steinke, you put the rocket guns in position somewhere along the road this side of that native hut down the road there. Better put the BAR over in that cactus patch to cover them. Be sure to get good fields of fire.

"Sergeant Taylor, you put the rest of the platoon in position along this little rise to the front. Better have everybody clean weapons and check ammunition before they start digging. All that salt water and sand we went through won't do them any good. Send me a messenger. I'm going to send back to the beach to see if they've got that weapon carrier out of the sand yet.

"It's now eleven thirty-two. Check your watches. Any questions?"

Sergeant Steinke saluted. "Yes, sir, Lootenant. Them rocket guns was only put aboard the day we sailed from Norfolk. We ain't had but one chanst to try 'em out, and that was on ship, and them rockets wouldn't explode when they hit the water. Why don't we put the AT grenade launchers over there and hold these rocket guns back. They ain't no good."

"No sergeant. That rocket gun is supposed to have more range and more power than the antitank grenades. They wouldn't have issued them to us if they were not good. That's the main avenue of approach. We'll put the rocket guns over there."

No more questions. Good reason, thought Scott. They had been living, eating, sleeping this problem for the last three weeks on shipboard. After hours of studying that model, he felt he had been here before.

Scott watched the patrols move out on their missions. Blankowitz, the platoon butt, short and stubby, looking like anything but a soldier, trailing along behind Sergeant Augusta's patrol. Blankowitz, good natured and willing, but always a problem. Can't shoot, can't march. Loses equipment. Can't talk. And there's Hart. The platoon musician. Always an accordion or a harmonica. Hill billy songs. Ballads about everything. He'll be making up one about the "First Platoon of Company A, hit went over to Africa-a-a." Just like maneuvers back at Bragg —and OCS—and before. That thunder—that's not thunder—nor artillery on maneuvers, firing blanks! That's naval gunfire at an enemy on shore—a real enemy. We are actually in battle in a foreign land!

Private Blank broke in upon Scott's reverie. "Sir, does the Lieutenant want me?"

Scott collected his thoughts, finished the message he was writing and said: "Yes, Blank. Take this message back to the battalion CP at the south end of the lake we passed after we crossed the sand dunes. Then go on to the beach. Find that weapons carrier. If they have got it out of the sand and can get it over the sand dunes, guide it over here. We need it."

The messenger departed. Scott seated himself in the slight shade afforded by a telegraph pole by the roadside and produced a well-oiled rag from his belt. Glancing over to where Taylor and Steinke were cleaning their own weapons and chatting with the men around them, Scott removed the salt stains and sand from his tommy gun and clips, wiped his ammunition, and reloaded. Scott wondered how the battalion was getting on, and whether or not it had reached the airfield.

Several hundred yards across the foreground a small group appeared. A native clad in turban and flowing robes sat sidewise on the rear end of a small, patient donkey, and belabored it with a stick. Following in Indian file were several women and children who plodded along under burdens seemingly as great as that of the diminutive donkey. All the soldiers were watching. The Arabs crossed the road and approached the cactus hedge surrounding the native hut. The mounted native gesticulated violently with his stick. A woman ran forward. The sound of unintelligible words. The woman opened a gate. All passed within. A noble Sheik!

Scott suddenly realized that the men were through cleaning their weapons. He crossed the low swale and joined Sergeant Taylor. He inspected the arms.

"Ferber, this is no time for goldbricking. Unload those magazines, clean out the salt and sand, wipe off that ammunition.

"Hart, where are your grenades?—Lost them? Well, I notice that you have not lost that damned harmonica. Sergeant Taylor, see if you can get grenades from the rocket gunners for him.

"Polka, where's your helmet?—Dropped it overboard? You'd lose your head if it wasn't tied on.

"McCoy, your rifle, as usual, is the best in the platoon.—You ain't aiming to miss no Frog? Well, any man that shoots like you do I'm sure won't miss."

And so on from one to another. The same old strong points. The same old weak ones. Just like maneuvers at Bragg—or OCS. They don't realize yet that this is war. After all, why should they? They don't hate the French, or anybody else. Sand, cactus, sunshine, donkeys, dirty natives, heat, dust— might as well be any place on the Border back home. Might at least get a good meal. . . .

Scott realized that he was hungry. Long time since sandwiches and coffee on the transport at 0100. His watch said twelve-thirty.

"Sergeant, better have the men eat a K-ration before they finish digging."

"Yes, sir." Then to the platoon: "OK, you gents, mess call, and make it snappy."

Scott and Taylor sat down on the low rise facing off to the south and shared a K-ration. Scott wondered how Dooley was getting on at Road Block No. 1. No word yet from Paddock.

"Hey, Lieutenant, just look at this. Crummy cheese, sweet crackers, a chocolate bar, a sugar lump, and lemonade powder! Ain't that a helluva mess to feed a soldier?"

"But, Sergeant, that has been worked out by scientists as the perfectly balanced ration in the most compact, edible, and imperishable form. That's supposed to be the cat's whiskers."

"Crap! Mebbe so. But give me a can of corn willy, a can of tomatoes, and a box of hard tack anytime, and a little strong coffee to wash it down. Lookie here! Two cigarettes in a regular carton! 'Nutsies'. Now I ask you, ain't that somethin'?"

A call from farther along the small rise interrupted.

"Hey, Lieutenant, here comes Blankowitz with a coupla Frogs."

Scott and Taylor walked back across the low swale to meet Blankowitz. Blankowitz reports:

"Sir, Lieutenant, Sergeant Augusta he send dese Frogs. Say me tell you he got de truck and got de seventy-five."

Scott looked at the Frenchmen, obviously officers, although he cannot remember to save his soul what the insignia of rank means.

"Can you speak English?"

"Non parlez—" A stream of unintelligible words accompanied by much shrugging of shoulders, waving of hands, and pointing to the east and northeast.

"Damn, sergeant. I sure wish we had someone who could speak French. We might find out something that would be useful. Send them back to the beach under guard."

Scott turned to Blankowitz as Sergeant Taylor moved off with the prisoners.

"Did Sergeant Augusta send me a field message?"

"Sure, he say me tell you he got de men, got de truck, got de seventy-five."

"You mean he has captured a truck and a seventy-five?"

"Nah, nah. He say tell you."

"Did you see a truck and a seventy-five?"

"Nah. I'm a fox hole. Dig lak hell. Sergeant he kick me lak dat. Say take de Frogs, tell you."

"Did you see any enemy?"

"Nah. Sergeant he say take de Frogs, tell you."

Damn Augusta, thought Scott. Why does everybody in the Army always try to get rid of goldbricks even if only temporarily?

"O.K., Blankowitz, you wait right here. I will send a message to Sergeant Augusta directly."

Nearly 1300. Taking too much time. Must check those positions. Moving across the swale toward the native hut, Scott joined Sergeant Steinke at the position of one of the rocket gunners. Private Tomah, an Indian from New Mexico, with all the stolidity of his race, was prone in a fox hole with the four-foot tube across his shoulders trying out the position.

"Now, Heliker, you lay down," Tomah was saying. "See can you poke them rockets in that gun."

Heliker went down, wiggling around on the ground, searching for a position.

"Heliker, you keep them rockets off that dirt. We don't want to have no misfires. I aim to get me a tank."

Heliker inserted a rocket into the rear end of the tube.

Tomah spoke: "O.K., now we dig you in there."

"Tomah, can you fire that thing?" Scott asked.

"Yes, sir, Lieutenant, I fired it twice on ship. Paper says it's good for five hundred yards. I measured to that white road marker. It's three hundred. Ought to be able to hit one there."

Scott and Steinke inspected the other rocket gun and then the BAR position in the edge of the cactus. Scott tried the BAR position and saw that he could only see fifty or sixty yards to the front. He moved the position forward to a better location. Finding a grenade rifleman along the road near the rocket gunners, he sent him over to the left flank where there would be better visibility for anything approaching along the road from the southwest.

He must hurry, Scott told himself. Wasting too much time. Crossing the road, Scott started up the low rise toward Sergeant Taylor over on the left flank. A voice halted him, a runner from the south, breathless.

"Lieutenant, sir—we're being attacked by infantry and tanks. Lieutenant Dooley sent me to say that he needs ammunition and tank granades."

"How many enemy are there?"

"Sir, I don't know. But there's an awful lot of shooting. We've had several men hit already."

Scott looked toward the beach. No truck there. He remembered Blankowitz.

"Sergeant Taylor, Augusta sent word by Blankowitz something about a truck and a seventy-five. I can't make heads or tails of what Blankowitz says. Send a non-com over there with him on the double to see if Augusta really has a truck. If so, bring it over here quick. Dooley is in trouble and needs help quick.

"Sergeant Steinke, you get that rocket gun team and a grenade launcher. Collect some ammunition and get it ready to send Lieutenant Dooley right away."

Taking his field glasses, Scott searched the horizon to the southwest, cursing the slight haze that interfered with clear visibility. Is that dust? Is it moving? God, it's tanks! Dooley is in for it now. Scott looked to the east. Nothing in sight. Suddenly from the rear, a roar—the weapons carrier! Scott ran across the swale calling to Taylor and Steinke to bring those men.

Scott looked into the truck. Loaded with packs. Ammunition probably underneath. And rations. And water. No time to unload.

"Climb aboard. Cartwright, Lieutenant Dooley's road block is being attacked down there. I can see tanks beyond them. They need ammunition and antitank grenades. Drive like hell and get to them."

"Yes, sir."

The four men piled in. Private Blank was still sitting beside the driver. Gears ground and the weapons carrier lurched forward. It gathered speed. Scott ran back to the low rise and with Sergeant Taylor watched to the southwest through field glasses. The truck passed the kilometer stone beyond Tomah and picked up speed. Trailing smoke and dust it roared on down the road, one kilometer—and another. Momentarily lost to view over a rise, then it appeared again travelling as though the devils of hell were behind it. Another swale. Another ridge. Must be almost there. What's that? A sudden puff of smoke from the truck. It lurched wildly, came to a stop, and burst into flame. Two small figures dashed from the truck and plunged headlong into the green patch to the west of the road—probably cactus, thought Scott. And the distant sound of fire like a shotgun—or a 37—came faintly back up the valley. Scott looked at his watch. It was 1450.

Scott's mouth was dry. His heart pounded. He tried to swallow. He was breathless—like finishing that obstacle course at OCS. Wetting dry lips, he turned to Sergeant Taylor. Something, maybe sweat trickled slowly down the sergeant's weather-beaten cheeks. He muttered to himself: "The goddam sonsabitches! Never gave 'em a chance. Good men—"

"Sergeant, what the hell do we do now?"

"Well, Lieutenant, even if we had a truck," Taylor brushed a hand quickly across his face and turned away, "we couldn't help Dooley now. No use sending good money after bad. Better get ourselves set, cause we're sure going to catch hell before dark."

Scott looked along the low rise and toward the road. There was much activity now. No need to urge them to dig. "Hey, Butch, lemme that shovel, will ya?"—"To hell with you. Use your pick."—"Wish to God I had one of them engineer shovels they was so free passing out on them fatigue details at Bragg instead of this damn toy."—"Hey, Joe, how about to the PX for a beer?"

"Sergeant, caution the men to remain quiet and not to expose themselves."

"Yes, sir." A roar. "Pipe down and stay down, you gents."

Scott watched through his field glasses. A great plume of smoke rose from the burning truck and drifted slowly westward, waving to and fro like a great plume fan—grandmother's ostrich feather fan. Near the burning truck a tank stood. No sign of movement. Yes, there is! There's another tank beyond the road advancing slowly! And another this side of the burning truck moving slowly along the road. God, there's more to the east of the road—one, two, three—coming over that low ridge east of the town. Poor Dooley!

"Tomah," Scott called. Tomah, lying quietly in his fox hole with the tube of the rocket gun over his shoulder, turned his head. "Tanks are coming up the road down there quite a ways off yet. Watch them. Hold your fire until they are so close that you will be sure not to miss."

"Yes, sir, Lieutenant."

Scott remembered that he himself had no fox hole. Why don't they issue intrenching tools to officers? Going to have one next time. He found a slight depression behind a bunch of grass. He tried it. Cover from observation—OCS—can see Tomah, and Breitkreitz with the BAR. And just to the rear, Steinke. This side of the road near Tomah, two riflemen, Polka and McCoy. To the left farther up the low rise, Sergeant Taylor—beyond him, two riflemen,—can't see who they are. Lifting himself up on his hands—like push-ups in physical training at OCS Scott could see the grenade rifleman. It must be Antonio, he thought. There was another rifleman beyond. Wish we had a 37 with some of that new armor-piercing ammunition. A crashing roar in the woods to the north, and off to seaward, the distant thunder-like rumble of naval guns. And all was suddenly quiet. Wish to hell it was dark, thought Scott. It was 1510.

He picked up his field glasses. The truck was still burning. But no tanks were in sight. Yes, there they are. God, how did they get there so quickly? There's one on the road at that bend beyond Tomah. It's stopped. There's another a little way behind it. It's stopping too. There's another back by that cactus patch, still moving—no, it stopped. Wonder why they stopped? Do they see anything? Where are the others? Scott searched. There was dust back of the rise toward the railroad. The dust was moving—a tank! There's another, and another! A rifle cracked off to his left and then another. Then there was firing all along the line.

"CEASE FIRING, you goddam fools!" Sergeant Taylor roared.

"Do you want to get the whole gang blown right plumb to hell?"

There was a crash on the road to the front. Antitank grenades burst off the road a hundred yards or more in front of the leading tank. No hits. Tomah was quiet in his fox hole. Scott looked around toward Sergeant Taylor. He was sprawled on the ground, his helmet off. There it was beyond him. And beyond that the helmet liner with a broken strap dangling. Scott looked at Taylor again and caught his breath. A great gaping wound in Taylor's head from which blood and brains slowly oozed. Taylor's sightless eyes were open.

Scott suddenly realized that the spat and whine were bullets. All the enemy tanks were firing now. Bullets spat into the tuft of grass before him and filled his eyes and mouth with dirt. Bullets struck the hard ground and ricocheted off to the rear with the characteristic whine. Sounds like duty in the pits at Bragg—or OCS—only there is no parapet here. OCS—wonder what they would do now?—As suddenly as it began, all was quiet. Scott could hear his watch ticking. It was 1525.

Minutes passed. Scott could see Tomah and Heliker lying quietly in their fox holes. And McCoy and Polka. Something wrong with Polka, hit maybe. Can't see Breitkreitz and the BAR but they must be there. There's Steinke to the left rear. Scott turned his head slowly. No one visible. Only foxholes—and Taylor.

Lifting his head slowly, inch by inch, Scott forced himself to look through the thin screen of the grass tuft. There was the leading tank in the same position on the road. Another to its left beside the cactus hedge near the native hut—wonder what the Sheik is doing now? Another tank under a tree to the east of the road. Two more over near the railroad cut in the ridge a thousand yards to the south. All quiet. No! There's some movement! On the road beyond the tanks. One, two, three, four—trucks!

The trucks halted beyond the last tank, and infantry tumbled out. Must be a company. God, what now? Should we withdraw? No way for those men along the road or for us to withdraw. Over on the left, some might get back to the road and the woods. But we got to hold till dark to protect the battalion. What would OCS do now?

Scott watched the infantry detruck and deploy to the east of the road. Slowly, they moved forward. Looks like squad or platoon columns—like OCS. Then the noise of grinding gears and the clank-clank of iron treads. The tanks were advancing! Off to the rear a faint clatter of machine gun bursts. And one, two, three faint shots—like an M-1. Scott looked at Tomah and Heliker still quiet in their fox holes.

There was a blinding flash and a roar like escaping steam. Whitish-blue smoke shrouded Tomah and Heliker. Tomah had fired the rocket gun! A crash! He had hit the first tank! No! A tree toppled and slowly fell across the leading tank. Tomah had missed! He had hit a tree! Then all hell broke loose. The tanks were firing. Everyone was firing. That infantry got closer and closer! Four hundred—three hundred yards! Advance by platoon rushes. One falls—another—they're hit! Just like OCS—and maneuvers! There, an officer—throws out his hands and pitches forward. They kept coming. Scott joined in with his tommy gun. Got one—no, can't tell—hope so for Dooley. Bullets spat into the dirt around him and ricochets whined overhead. Scott hugged the dirt. There's the clatter of the BAR across the road—and the plunk, plunk, plunk of M-1's to his left. Crash, crash—the antitank grenades!

Tomah's voice came clear and distinct: "Heliker! Heliker! Put in another one! Heliker, what hell's matter with you! Put in another one."

Scott could see Tomah, still lying quietly in his fox hole. He could not see Heliker. Roaring motors and clanking treads! The tanks were still moving. They advanced slowly toward Tomah. One circled to his right and rear. They've got him! Oh, God!

"Hey, Lieutenant." It was Corporal Buttz. He pointed to the front. The infantry! Can see their dark faces—not Frenchmen! Everybody firing! Scott tried his tommy gun. God, it's jammed! Rolling over on his side, he removed the magazine and struggled to clear the jam! Damn! Too many thumbs! Oh God, got to get—

"Hah."

Dark faces, two, three, five, six looked down at him over gleaming rifle barrels. French infantry! Arabs!

A French officer approached. He spoke. Scott did not understand. They took his tommy gun, the French officer took his map and field glasses. They moved toward the road. Heliker and McCoy were dead. There was Tomah and Sergeant Steinke and Corporal Buttz, Buttz with blood streaming from a wounded arm. And Breitkreitz severely wounded.

Private Tomah spoke: "Sir Lieutenant, I hollered for Heliker to put in another one, but I looked around and Heliker didn't have no head."

The French were collecting their dead and wounded. Several bodies like cordwood beside the road. More coming. The French hurried the prisoners to a waiting truck.

"Sergeant, we didn't hold out. It is only 1700."

This story is a reconstruction of the action of Lieutenant Scott's patrol based upon the stenographic report of an investigation, by a

Board of the senior officers of the command, into the circumstances of Lieutenant Scott's surrender to the French. The essentials of this story were published in the Infantry Journal of January, 1950. Most of the personnel, all that had not been killed or wounded, were available for interrogation on the actual scene of the action. There the actual fox holes and places where men had lain were clearly visible, as were the tracks of tanks, of men both friend and foe, and even the scars left by bullets. The burned out and wrecked truck and the demolished tree were there. Even many of the cartridge cases had escaped the pilfering fingers of those scavengers of the battle field—the Arabs.

Every incident took place as described, though I have pictured it through the eyes of Lieutenant Scott. The wording is of course my own. Where the record does not indicate the names, I have employed fictitious ones to designate the individuals who were present. Tomah's remark at the end of the story may have been made to Lieutenant Scott at that time, as he said—the record does not show. He did make it to me when this magnificent American soldier was describing and demonstrating to the Board of officers at the identical fox hole he had occupied what took place in this action, which was probably the first instance in which a bazooka was fired at an enemy tank in battle.

I restored Lieutenant Scott to duty.

5. The Battle on Shore.

Daylight had come and the morning sun was shining on a sea like glass. We had expected to follow events on shore by radio reports, by observation, and by reports from aircraft. This was not to be. In spite of planning and preparations, our communications with shore were almost nonexistent. Conway was writing messages to report to General Patton every two hours what we knew, but naval radio channels were now so crowded that none of them were ever received. Naval aircraft were flying over the battle area and others were flying inland on bombing missions, but nothing of what they saw ever came to us.

Confused and fragmentary reports indicated that McCarley's and Dilley's battalions had landed by dawn and had moved inland, and there was even a report that Dilley's battalion was in the fort. There was no word from Toffey's battalion until late in the morning when returning landing craft reported that he had landed on Red Beach 2. Just after sunrise, five or six French airplanes appeared from the north and flew southward along the beaches strafing. Meanwhile, guns on shore were firing now and then, and the destroyers in close were returning the fire with interest. Every radio in the control room was chattering, but interference was general, and we could learn but little.

When the first waves of landing craft returned to the ships, the coxswains' reports were sketchy and conflicting. Some said we had captured the fort, and there were other reports that Green Beach was calling for help. What help, whether for troops or shore party, none could tell. Then, when the next waves were disembarking, a few stray shots from a gun on shore struck the water some hundreds of yards away. And Commodore Gray's voice blared out over the loud speaker: "Cease unloading. Clear away landing craft. Stand by to move out to sea." Both Carleton and I protested. Our operations on shore required these men —they might be vital even now. We had to take chances. The Commodore saw the point, and unloading continued for the moment.

There were several air alerts, but no airplanes had flown over the transport area. About mid-morning, a bi-motored airplane appeared from the north sweeping low toward us. From every ship within range a hail of steel swept into the air about it. As the airplane approached the *Allen,* Carleton recognized its allied markings and shouted to officers and gunners alike: "Cease fire! That's a British airplane!" Too late. Within a stone's throw of the *Allen,* the airplane turned, caught fire, and plunged into the sea. Landing craft went at once to the spot, but there were no survivors. Later, we were to learn that it was an airplane sent from General Eisenhower's headquarters at Gibraltar to report the progress of the western landings.

I took about half of our small staff—Conway, Bond, Southworth, Sanborn, the surgeon, my aide, and a dozen enlisted men—and with a command half-track and several bantams set off for Blue Beach about half-past twelve.

Swell had been increasing during the day, and we landed about 1500 in a pounding surf. My jeep was embedded in heavy sand within a few yards of the water's edge, and there it was to remain all night. There was much confusion on the beach for craft destined for Green Beach were also landing on Blue. The soft, powdery sand, much worse than we had anticipated, was causing trouble. The wire netting and burlap roadways on the sand across the dunes were already ruined by traffic, but the engineers were building others and reconnoitering for better routes. Some landing craft had broached to in the surf and had been abandoned by their crews. Some weapons and equipment had been dumped into the surf, but everywhere men were working.

At the beach command post, marked only by a staff displaying the Blue Beach flag and lantern and the antenna of the beachmaster's radio, little was known of the situation inland and nothing of the situation on other beaches. There were rumors of heavy fighting inland, and a noncommissioned officer from McCarley's battalion was somewhere

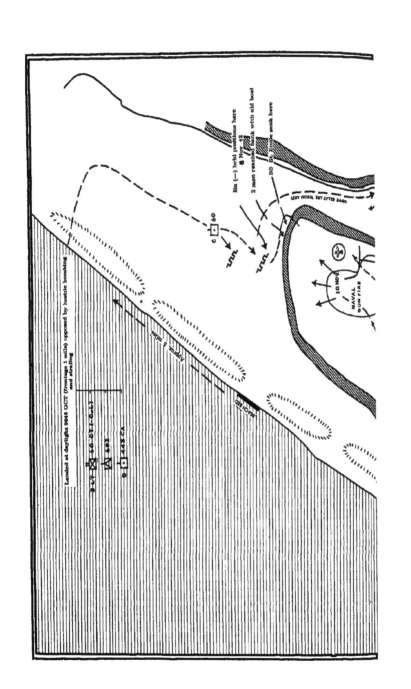

Landed at daylight 0845 GCT (frontage 1 mile) opposed by hostile bombing and strafing

3 LT ⊠ 1-8-3-173-60
△ 683
D ⊡ 148 CA

Approx 8 rods

BEACH RED

10 NOV
NAVAL
GUN FIRE

SENT PATROL OUT AFTER DARK

Bn (→) held positions here
6 Nov 42
2 men reached hunk with old boat
BB 55 mile sunk here

c ⊡ 60

on the beach looking for tanks. We could barely see the transports at sea. They were beyond the range of the beachmaster's signal lamps and even his radio. However, I wrote a message to be sent off to Carleton and the Commodore when it might be possible, and went inland to learn how things were going.

In the staff half-track, we followed the trace of the 1st Battalion. Passing two light tanks and a tank destroyer on the way, we took them along. One of the tank gunners almost ended my career right then and there. When I told them to load and follow me, one of the gunners fired an accidental burst from a machine gun that missed my head by a hair's breath. On the ridge just east of the southern end of the lagoon, we found McCarley's rear command post with his executive officer, Major Otto Koch, in charge. There, also, was part of Company A and part of the Regimental antitank company, which had established the road blocks along the Rabat Road to protect the flank. There had been fighting along the Rabat Road during the afternoon— French infantry and tanks had overrun our road blocks. Some few men had straggled in, but the company commander was missing. However, most of the company were there and in position with antitank guns, and Major Koch had sent to the beach for tanks. I left the two light tanks and the tank destroyer with him, and set off to find McCarley.

Leaving Bond and Netterblad with the command half-track struggling to establish radio communication with the ship and with the other battalions, Conway, Southworth and I set off on foot along McCarley's telephone line. After an hour's rugged going through the dense woods along the ridge east of the lagoon, with naval gunfire cracking overhead and the distant crash of bursting shells and clatter of machine guns to keep us company, we found McCarley. He had not reached the south end of the lagoon until 1100, and his progress northward had been slow. He had been held up by machine gun fire from along the road to the east, and had only located the source a short while before. A skirmish was in progress in that direction, and artillery shells were crashing in the woods beyond.

McCarley had not yet made contact with the 2nd Battalion, but we could hear sounds of firing along the ridge to the north not more than a mile distant. It was now almost six o'clock and the day was nearly done. I told McCarley to make contact with the 2nd Battalion during the night and to advance at daylight the next morning on the airfield. Company A would have to remain where it was to protect the south flank until I could get Semmes and his armor there, but I would send the Provisional Assault Company up to him during the night so that he would have some reserve at least. McCarley and others whom I had encountered were all in good spirits even though our plans were behind schedule.

It was nearly dark when we had retraced our steps and reached the staff car. Our radio had not been able to contact anyone. French infantry and tanks were still in the woods along the Rabat Road, and I was fearful of an attack from that direction. Stopping only to send the Provisional Assault Company to join McCarley, and to warn Major Koch of the danger, we went on to the beach. Our half-track could not negotiate the steep slope of the sand dunes in the darkness. Leaving it with Bond in charge, Conway, Netterbald, and I set off on foot once more.

At the beach command post, all was dark and silent. There was only a sleepy operator listening for radio signals which he could not hear. No officers were about, but all around men were sleeping the profound sleep of exhaustion. Figures were stumbling about the beach and sand dunes in the darkness. There were shouts and oaths and calls of "George" and "Patton". And there was roaring surf. But I had to find Semmes and his tanks. Sending Conway to the north and Netterbald to the south to find him, I sat down on the sand dune to wait.   ·

When their figures disappeared into the gloom, it came to me that even with hundreds all around me, I was utterly alone. And I had to stay just where I was, or they would never find me when they returned with Semmes. Out to sea, much closer than when we had come ashore, signal lamps were flashing among the ships. As far as I could see along the beach, there was chaos. Landing craft were beaching in the pounding surf, broaching to the waves, and spilling men and equipment into the water. Men wandered about aimlessly, hopelessly lost, calling to each other and for their units, swearing at each other and at nothing. There was no beach party or shore party anywhere in sight. And I was chilled. Not a light could I see on shore except the dim blue lantern under which I sat. I was lonely. More than anything else right then I wanted a cigarette. There had been no enemy aircraft since early morning. A cigarette on shore could be no more dangerous than those flashing lights at sea. I lit one. In a matter of moments, I was glad when other glows appeared as other lonely and uncertain men sought the comfort of tobacco. They would have been surprised to know that the Commanding General had been the first to violate the blackout order.

I was sitting there with my cigarette half smoked wondering what I was going to do next and how, when out of the gloom from the shore appeared a strange looking figure, approaching with uncertain steps, and peering nervously from side to side. He stopped in front of me and in alien accents addressed me: "Heyyuh, gimme a cigarette." I handed him one from the package I held. He spoke again: "Goddam.

All Wet. Gimme a light too." I extended the lighted end of my cigarette. As he put it to his face, Conway appeared on one side, Semmes on the other, both thrust tommy guns into his midriff, and Conway challenged "George." And the response was instantaneous: "George? George, hell. Me no George. My name Lee, Cook, Company C, 540th Engineers."

Lee had just come ashore and was seeking his company which was the shore party on the beach. I was to remember this incident after the battle had ended, when I needed a cook. We installed Lee as cook for my headquarters mess. When General Patton visited us first at Port Lyautey and had lunch with us, I told him the story. When I left the Western Task Force at Christmas time, Lee was not allowed to accompany me. He was to be General Patton's cook for the rest of the war.

But Semmes had been found. Semmes had assembled four tanks and thought there were others on the beach. He went off to find them, promising to be in position on the ridge at the south end of the lagoon before daylight.

While I was talking to Semmes, Carleton appeared. He had heard nothing from me after I left the ship, and knew little more of the situation on shore than we had known then. He had left the G-4, Colonel Libby, in charge of directing unloading, and had come ashore to look for me. Then Netterblad returned and shortly Bond and Sanborn appeared. Soon we found Captain Meunier, the shore party commander, and set officers and men to work to clear the chaotic conditions on the beach before daylight should expose us to possible air attack.

Some time during the night, a wire crew connected Blue Beach with the regimental switchboard of the 60th Infantry at Mehdia, and I was able to talk with Colonel de Rohan. Dilley's battalion had been stopped by naval gunfire before it reached the Kasbah. The battalion was somewhat disorganized but had crossed the lagoon, captured the lighthouse, and cleared the area around the coastal battery. It had been counterattacked by French infantry and artillery and had been in danger of being cut off from the beach, but de Rohan had gathered reinforcements which had enabled it to hold on. Colonel de Rohan had had no word from Toffey's battalion. I told de Rohan of the orders I had given McCarley and ordered him to renew the assault on the Kasbah at daylight.

It had been a grim and lonely night for me, but with returning daylight, my spirits rose. We could now see to work, and we were hopeful.

Before dawn, Semmes was off with seven tanks and others would follow as they came ashore. Shortly after daylight, Carleton set off with part of our minuscule staff to see what the conditions were on the beaches and to establish a command post at Mehdia adjacent to the command post of the 60th Infantry. He was to communicate with Commodore Gray and our staff on board the *Allen*. I set off with Conway and Netterblad to tour my threatened south flank.

The sun was little more than an hour high when I found Semmes out near the Rabat Road a mile or so east of the lagoon. We had heard the crash of naval gunfire and the sound of firing soon after we left the beach, but the noise of battle had died away when we arrived. Still, the dust had barely settled, smoke trailed upward from four French tanks in the foreground, and a number of bodies were sprawled about in the various postures of sudden death—the first enemy killed by American soldiers I had yet seen. Semmes, standing in his open turret, his brown face under his tanker's helmet with the battle flush still upon it, was looking out over the scene when my bantam stopped alongside his tank.

Semmes had the pride of a halfback who had just plunged through the opposing line for a touchdown. He pointed out the destroyed French tanks, light tanks of old types, two or more of which he had accounted for in person, and showed me where his own and other tanks had been struck repeatedly without damage. Two armor-piercing projectiles slightly smaller than 37mm were still embedded in the armor of Semmes' tank. Just after six o'clock, Semmes had attacked a company of French infantry along the Rabat Road and had dispersed them into the woods to the east. Then he had attacked a column of French tanks which approached from the south and had dispersed them destroying the four we saw. Semmes had the situation well in hand, so I turned north to find McCarley again.

Going back over our route of the afternoon before, but this time by bantam, at 0800 I found McCarley where I had left him the evening before. McCarley's leading companies were just clearing the ridge several hundred yards to the northeast, and McCarley was about to follow with his reserve company, the Provisional Assault Company which I had sent up to him during the night. He had not made contact with the 2nd Battalion, for his patrols had returned at daylight without having found it. Obviously the patrols had not ventured far from their own lines during the darkness, for we could hear rifle and machine gun fire less than a mile away, where I was confident that Dilley was renewing his assault to take the Kasbah. I told McCarley to press his advance with the utmost vigor for it was essential to capture the airfield during the day. We watched him move out with his reserve and follow his leading companies over the ridge. Then hearing the sound of firing to the south, we hurried back to Semmes.

It was 0930 when we reached the ridge just south of the lagoon to find Semmes engaged with French tanks which had returned to the attack. Off to the southeast a thousand yards or so, French tanks were firing, and in groups of two and three were crawling about like ants in a disturbed ant hill in the midst of smoke and dust raised by salvos of naval gunfire and artillery crashing about them. On a ridge in the foreground, seven or eight of our own tanks moved jerkily forward, stopping now and again to fire. We could see the muzzle blast of their 37's and their sharp reports were welcome sounds. Not far away, a 105 fired now and then, and smoke drifted lazily seaward. There was a lull when French tanks disappeared from view beyond a distant ridge still pursued by the naval guns. On the ridge where I stood with Semmes, men were moving about quite casually. Nearby a young Naval officer was talking by radio to the ships at sea. Overhead sunlight sparkled on the wings of a naval spotting plane. The scene might have been one in any peace-time training exercise—but it was war.

Just then a message from Colonel de Rohan informed me that the French in the Kasbah wanted to talk about surrender. That was thrilling news. Near the south end of the lagoon, I met de Rohan coming in search of me. A French officer had come from the Kasbah to Green Beach to arrange a meeting between the French commandant and the American commander with a view to ending the fighting. Colonel de Rohan had sent him back in company of an American officer to arrange a meeting for noon. It was 1100 when we reached Mehdia Plage.

Mehdia, a seaside resort village of summer cottages with cabanas along the beach, was unoccupied at the time of our landing. Colonel de Rohan's command post was in a ramshackle frame building which a weatherbeaten sign proclaimed to be the Casino. Carleton had arrived a short while before. We were excited, of course, but we sat down and talked over plans for the meeting. We decided that our terms would be generous. My preparations for the impending parley were complete after I had shaved with a borrowed razor and had shaken the worst of the dust and grime from my boots and clothing.

Noon came, but no French. It was some time before we learned that the American escort had been fired on near the Kasbah and that nothing more had been seen of the French officer. I was in a quandary. There was something peculiar about the incident. The French proposal had not been made in writing, nor had the French stopped firing while we were waiting. However, there seemed to be no good reason to doubt that the offer had been made in good faith. I thought there might be some dissension among French officers within the fort, and that a proposal from us might turn the scales. Accordingly, I wrote a letter to the French commandant expressing regret that "circumstances beyond our control prevented the emissary requested by you from arriving within your garrison," and our distress that "Americans and Frenchmen, friends of long standing, should be involved in needless waste of life." I reminded him of the President's proclamation and indicated my willingness to meet him at any time during daylight hours to discuss cessation of hostilities. This letter we dispatched under a flag of truce, but the bearers were fired upon and the letter could not be delivered. There was nothing to do but continue the battle. All that we had accomplished was to lose valuable time.

After the battle was over, we were to learn that no such offer was ever made by the French commandant within the Kasbah. The whole incident was invented by an English-speaking French lieutenant who was about to be captured near Green Beach and who used it as a means of making his escape. We had been gullible enough to send him back to his own lines with better information concerning us than he could have obtained by even a successful reconnaissance. We had allowed our wishes to father our thoughts, a dangerous practice in war.

Meanwhile, I learned from Colonel de Rohan and his staff something more of the situation of Dilley's battalion, and what I learned was none too pleasant. According to de Rohan, Dilley's battalion had been in desperate straits the afternoon before and he had saved it only by sending Company L, which was a regimental Sub Tank Force reserve at Mehdia, to reinforce Dilley. Dilley had tried to reorganize during the night, but his losses had been very heavy. His companies were down to forty and fifty men. Colonel de Rohan had ordered Dilley to renew the attack at daylight, but the French had tried to attack Green Beach. Dilley had cleared the French off the ridges west of the lagoon, and then the French officer had arrived to talk about surrender. Colonel de Rohan was worried over Dilley's losses and doubted that his battalion would be strong enough to take the fort.

Surf conditions had grown steadily worse during the day, and the loss of landing craft was causing grave concern. In fact, landing on the open beaches had to be suspended early in the afternoon. One look at the mounting surf was more than enough to show that we had to take the fort and open the river or we were lost, and we had to do it with what forces we had for there were no more reserves.

It did not seem to me that the action had been so severe as to cause the losses which de Rohan described. Nor were the numbers of wounded on the beach excessive. We had taken many prisoners. Casual inspection of the beach and village showed an unduly large number of soldiers wandering about. The obvious conclusion was that most of Dilley's losses were due to straggling, for confusion and disorder always lead to straggling even in maneuvers. Accordingly, I had Colonel de Rohan, with officers and men from his headquarters company and staff, search every house in the village from ground to roof and comb the wooded areas between the village and the lagoon. The search turned up more than two hundred men.

Early in the afternoon, McCarley requested tanks to support his final drive for the airfield. There was a vague report that Toffey's battalion was on the river opposite the airfield. Leaving Colonel de Rohan to finish his search for stragglers and to reorganize Dilley's battalion, and Carleton to arrange for the demolition party to remove the river cable during the night, I set off for Blue Beach to see what help I could find for McCarley.

At Blue Beach, I learned that more tanks had come ashore during the day and had gone on inland. Surf had caused trouble and there was some confusion, but the beaches were reasonably clear of equipment and the organization of supplies was proceeding. Near the south end of the lagoon, I found Captain Edwards with Company C, 70th Tank Battalion. Most of his tanks were now on shore but some of them were still with Semmes. Semmes had been fighting earlier in the afternoon, but the French tanks had again drawn off to the south. I detached Edwards' tanks from Semmes, and sent him on at his best speed to join McCarley with orders for McCarley to get on to the airfield by dark. Edwards moved off about 1600 and I turned back over the beaches to Mehdia.

Our second night on shore was not a cheerful one, although for me it was less grim and dismal than the night before. Someone produced K rations and an alcohol stove and made coffee, my first food on shore. Soon after dark, Colonel Henny set off with his engineer detail to meet the naval demolition party at the cannery below the Kasbah and remove the cable. Men collected during the afternoon had been organized by units and sent up to Dilley along with a platoon of self-propelled guns of the Cannon Company which had come ashore. Colonel Teece, the regimental executive, was up with Dilley assisting in his reorganization. Edwards and his tanks joined McCarley about 1630, but I learned after dark that McCarley had not gone on. I ordered him then by telephone to continue his advance during the night. I sent a message to General Patton informing him of our situation and plans and said that if we failed to take the fort next morning, we would have to be reinforced for we would have no troops left. Snipers were active all through the area between Green Beach and the Kasbah and around the village during the night. Shortly before midnight, Colonel Henny returned in a state of considerable agitation. He had not reached the cannery where he was to meet the naval demolition party. His party had been fired upon by snipers and an officer at his side had been killed. However, the naval demolition party persisted and removed the cable under fire about 0200. Heavy rain after midnight did nothing to improve our spirits, our comfort, or our communications.

During the night, we had our first news of Craw and Hamilton. Loyal Frenchmen who would cooperate with the Allies were to make themselves known to us by the word "Bordeaux" carried on a slip of paper within the sweat bands of their hats. Two of the "Bordeaux Boys", as we called them, came into our lines and to my command post at Mehdia during the night. They informed us that the American colonel had been killed before the party reached the town and that the American major was being held at the French garrison in town. The French were afraid to release him because they feared our reaction to the killing of an officer under a flag of truce. That was sad news for us. These "Bordeaux Boys" proposed that I send a battalion through the woods south of the town to seize it, and offered to guide such a force. As we had no battalion to send, we sent them on back through the lines to obtain more detailed information of French dispositions.

So the night passed.

I had told Colonel de Rohan that he was to supervise the assault of Dilley's battalion in person. Finding him still in his command post at dawn, I sent him on to join Dilley. There was the sound of heavy firing around the Kasbah. Seaward, we watched the *Dallas* enter the river between the jetties and move upstream. When she disappeared below the fort, we could hear the sound of her guns. There was no word from McCarley for the storm during the night had wrecked both radio and telephone communication with him. Toffey we knew to be on the river opposite the airfield.

During this time Captain Forte, regimental S-3 of the 60th Infantry, at my direction had collected a motley group of seventy or eighty men from along the beach—air force mechanics, cooks, clerks, and chauffeurs. These he had organized into squads. With them he was to clear snipers from the brush-covered area between Mehdia and the Kasbah. I had come up to watch the group move out, when one of the air force soldiers armed with a submachine gun addressed me: "General, we have never shot these things. Couldn't we try them out to see how they work before we have to fight?" That seemed reasonable. Captain Forte had them face about toward a sand bank. Then by command, he had them load and fire several volleys into the bank. Satisfied, the group moved out, deployed in line of skirmishers, and set off toward the Kasbah.

Then word came from Dilley. He had reached the walls of the Kasbah and had been stopped by heavy mortar and machine gun fire from within. He asked for air support. There was a forward control group on the beach, a young Naval aviator with a radio mounted in a bantam. Carleton asked how long it would take to obtain a mission to attack the fort. There was a mission of eight dive bombers in the air en route to attack some point inland near Meknes. In a few minutes, the controller had called them from that mission and had brought them overhead. Carleton stood by and described the target, the controller repeated directions to the circling airplanes until they knew where the bombs were wanted. Meanwhile, I had arranged for Dilley to withdraw his men to a distance three hundred yards from the walls, prepared to assault when the last bomb fell.

While these preparations were under way, Major General John K. Cannon, General Patton's air commander, arrived at my command post. He had been sent by General Patton to learn how things were going with us. Taking General Cannon along, I set off in my bantam to follow Captain Forte's skirmishers to be on hand when the assault was made.

We were a few hundred yards from the cannery below the fort when the first airplane peeled lazily off, turned slowly, and dived toward the Kasbah, followed in turn by the others. Then explosions inside rocked the ground above us and sent great clouds of smoke and dust rolling upward. It was a beautiful sight for a soldier's eyes. A few minutes later when we reached the main gate of the Kasbah, the battle was all but over. Dilley had brought his self-propelled 105's to point-blank range and had breached the gate and wall. When the last bomb fell, infantry rushed in with bayonets. French officers and native soldiers were appearing in all directions with upraised hands.

I left de Rohan with a detachment to clear out the Kasbah and collect the prisoners. Dilley I sent on at once toward the airfield. Cannon and I accompanied him until his advance was well under way, then we turned back to call the P-40's in to land.

It was just 1000 when we saw the first P-40's overhead, and General Cannon wanted to go on to the airfield. As there was still fighting between the Kasbah and the airfield, we put him on board a landing craft at the cannery and sent him up the river. Already landing craft were coming up the river and beginning to unload at Brown Beach, and others with aviation personnel and equipment were moving on upstream. We had collected hundreds of prisoners, and more were coming in from every side. Then Carleton found me with a report that French cavalry were moving in on our right flank and that an infantry regiment with tanks was approaching from the south toward Rabat. This, in the moment of victory!

Leaving Carleton to arrange for aircraft and naval gunfire to help repel the threat, I set off again for the south end of the lagoon, and Semmes. Semmes was not alarmed and was confident that with his naval gunfire support he could take care of the threat from the south.

I warned Major Koch of Mc Carley's battalion, who was still in position along the ridge, and then with four light tanks I set off along the ridge to the north to locate the cavalry threat. The tanks I sent off toward the Rabat Road to find the enemy, but they found none. The cavalry threat turned out to be no more than four nondescript troopers who had come into our lines and had surrendered to a lineman who was repairing McCarley's telephone line.

It was now well past noon, and I continued on north to find Dilley and McCarley. There had been fighting all along on the high ground between the Kasbah and the airfield where the whole area was honeycombed with French defenses. But the fighting was almost over and the French were surrendering in ever increasing numbers. Edwards' tanks were on the airfield along with part of Toffey's battalion, the Raider Detachment, and a part of McCarley's battalion. McCarley and the rest of his battalion I could not find. I left Toffey to organize the security of the airfield and Dilley to assemble his own battalion. Then I turned back to Mehdia.

It was late in the afternoon when I stopped at the command post of the 60th Field Artillery Battalion at the Kasbah. There Carleton telephoned that McCarley's battalion had captured the French commander and most of his men, and that the French colonel wanted to arrange an armistice. I told Carleton that I would not talk to the French commander until Major Hamilton was released. It was well after dark when the French brought Hamilton to the airfield where he was able to talk to us by radio. Through him we arranged for the French commander to meet me at 0800 the following morning at the main gate of the Kasbah.

Meanwhile, we had alerted Semmes with his tanks, the 60th Field Artillery Battalion, and all of Dilley's battalion that we could find trucks to move. They were to be ready to move at daylight to seize the airfield at Rabat. While the staff worked on these preparations, Carleton, Conway, and I made plans for another parley.

Some time after midnight, a group of French officers arrived at my command post brought in by Semmes. They had approached one of his outposts in an open car with lights on and a bugler standing on the running board sounding the French bugle call for "cease fire". They were somewhat perturbed because our outpost had fired upon them, but fortunately with damage only to their car. They informed us that General Mathinet had arrived in Port Lyautey from Meknes during the evening with instructions from Admiral Darlan to cease all opposition as an armistice had been agreed upon. General Mathinet wanted to meet me the following morning to arrange for cessation of hostilities in the local area. We sent them back through the lines accompanied by an American officer to inform General Mathinet that a meeting was arranged for 0800 the following morning and that I would meet him then.

Then we received a message from General Patton saying that French resistance had ceased all through North Africa and that American troops would remain in place prepared for further action.

Our first battle was ended.

I had hoped that I would receive instructions during the night from General Patton which would guide me in the meeting with the French commander, but there was no word beyond that first brief message. We were well informed, however, as to the general policy which should govern our relations with the French, and we had these in mind as we formulated plans for our parley.

The next morning, escorted by a company of Semmes' tanks to lend something of military display to the event, we proceeded to the appointed place. I was accompanied by General Cannon who had stayed over for the meeting, and by the principal commanders and staff officers. There under the high walls of the Kasbah and just in front of the main gate through which we had blasted our way was the French general and his party. General Mathinet, somewhat apart, his blue cape thrown back over one shoulder with its scarlet lining gleaming in the sun, and seven or eight other French officers in trim uniforms with gleaming belts and boots, were in contrast to our own battle-stained appearance.

I approached with Conway to interpret, and my party arranged themselves behind me. Mathinet and I exchanged salutes with stiff military correctness as did our respective groups. General Mathinet said that he had received orders to cease all opposition by direction of Admiral Darlan and that he desired to arrange details for terminating hostilities in the local area pending decision by higher authority. I replied that so far as we were concerned there was no question of French surrender. We desired French cooperation and had sought it by every means. Our single purpose was to strike the common enemy and all who stood with them. General Mathinet protested that he was powerless to agree on any terms without reference to higher authority. I informed him that there was no question of terms—I would indicate what would be done pending further instructions from General Patton. French troops not now prisoners could retain their arms and could return to barracks in areas not occupied by American troops, pledging only that they would not fight again against us. American prisoners in French hands would be returned to us at once. When this was done, we would release the large number of French prisoners then in our hands. We would occupy the port area in Port Lyautey, but otherwise American troops would remain generally in their present areas which no French troops would enter. French civil officials would continue their normal functions but would take no action prejudicial to American forces. We would not interfere with the civil economy of the area, and whatever we found it necessary to requisition would be paid for at fair prices. Unarmed French parties would be permitted to search the battle area for their dead, and I would provide American soldiers to see that they were not molested.

One amusing incident occurred during this conversation which we carried on through Major Conway. We were discussing the collection and burial of the dead, and Conway translated one of General Mathinet's remarks. Seemingly, he made an error in translating the word for "shroud" for General Mathinet corrected his translation. The General spoke English as well as any of us.

Our parley ended with another interchange of stiff salutes.

•

CHAPTER THREE

COMMAND POST FOR IKE

1. *Looking For Trouble*

American soldiers who survived the bitter months of January and February, 1943, in Tunisia will never forget them—or forget Tunisia. For it was during this period in the deserts and mountains of that ancient land, amid the ruins of a long dead Roman civilization, that American forces first crossed swords with veteran German legions and learned of war from them—the hard way. There, American soldiers, suffering from faults in leadership, from their own ignorance, from inferior equipment, reeled in defeat and yet rose to victory. Ousseltia, Fondouk, Faid Pass, Sidi bou Zid, Sened Station, Sbeitla, Kasserine Pass—these are names we will long remember. They are indelibly inscribed in the blood of comrades.

I was closely associated with the stirring events of these two months.

General Patton had no berth for me in the Western Task Force, but he had no objection to my going to Algiers to learn whether General Eisenhower intended for me to remain in the theater, or to return to the United States for assignment. I was hopeful that I would remain in the theater, but even more, I wanted an active assignment.

I arrived in Algiers late Christmas Eve with Major T. J. Conway of my staff, driving overland in a car borrowed from the II Corps at Oran where our airplane had been grounded by bad weather. Algiers we found in a state of intense excitement. Admiral Darlan had been assassinated that day. We made our way to Allied Force Headquarters in the St. George Hotel with some difficulty, after repeated challenges by French, British, and American patrols. At AFHQ we learned from a secretary on duty in the office of the Chief of Staff that General Eisenhower was on his was back from the front and was expected some time the following day. What was left of that cheerless Christmas Eve, Conway and I spent in the Alletti Hotel in Algiers.

Christmas Day we spent in AFHQ renewing associations with the many officers whom we had known in London and learning what we could of happenings in Algiers and Tunisia. Neither Major General Mark W. Clark, General Eisenhower's Deputy at the time, nor Major General W. B. Smith, General Eisenhower's Chief of Staff, knew what General Eisenhower would have in mind for me. From them and others in AFHQ, I learned much of what had happened along the Mediterranean front, and told them about conditions in Morocco.

General Eisenhower returned late Christmas Day. I saw him briefly the following morning. Burdened with care and responsibility as he was, he greeted me in his usual warm, cheerful manner. When I told him why I had come to Algiers, he said he was glad I had done so. He wanted me to wait around a few days. He was considering an operation, and if it materialized, he would have a job for me. The staff was studying the problem, but it would be several days before there would be any decision. Meanwhile, this Darlan business was going to occupy all of his time. While I was waiting around, I could occupy my time making a study of his headquarters. He turned to General Smith, and reminded him of his concern about the size of his headquarters. It was growing much too large. General Smith should have me investigate while I was waiting. Perhaps I could suggest something that might help.

On December 29th, I saw General Eisenhower again. He had been terribly disappointed that the Allied drive had been stopped before capturing Tunis. All during the month of December, General Anderson had tried to mount an attack, but weather conditions had all but prevented movements except on roads. On his recent visit to the front, General Eisenhower had postponed the attack indefinitely, for they would have to wait for better weather. While at the front, he had discussed with commanders there the feasibility of an operation farther to the south where the country was more arid and weather conditions would permit operations. The idea was to employ our 1st Armored Division and a Regimental Combat Team of our 1st Infantry Division to cut Rommel's line of communication with Tunis. Staff studies indicated that the plan was practicable, and that the forces could be assembled in the vicinity of Tebessa by January 22nd. My job would be in connection with this operation. The British First Army had been created to control all operations in Tunisia, but unfortunately the French forces, who now occupied a wide sector of the front and on whom we would have to depend, would not serve under British command. To overcome this obstacle, General Eisenhower would have to exercise control of British, French, and American forces in his capacity as Commander in Chief. For this purpose, he would establish a small command group in Constantine adjacent to Headquarters First Army where he could be when the situation required his presence. I was to organize this advanced command post. I would be in charge there as Deputy Chief of Staff, and would keep in touch with those who were developing the plans for the operation.

I telephoned General Patton at Casablanca, informed him of my new assignment, and asked him to have Carleton and the rest of my party sent on to me by air. They arrived the following day.

The operation which General Eisenhower had outlined came to be

known under the code name SATIN, and it was preparations for
SATIN that were to set the stage for the dramatic episodes of the next
two months. To appreciate how these episodes came about, one must
know something of the situation which confronted Allied forces in
North Africa during the last days of the year 1942. Out in Morocco,
we had known little of the course of events along the Mediterranean
coast beyond the fact that the Allied drive on Tunis had been turned
back at the end of November when almost within sight of the city, and
that British forces from Egypt were driving Rommel westward through
Libya toward Tripoli. These were still the salient features of the situation as I was to learn it in AFHQ during these days.

Immediately after French resistance ceased on November 11th,
British forces under Lieutenant General Sir Kenneth A. N. Anderson
advanced eastward from Algiers with the objective of capturing
Tunis some five hundred miles distant. Because of shipping limitations
for TORCH, General Anderson's forces comprised little more than an

infantry division and an armored brigade with obsolescent tanks, and these were short of much of their organic transportation. To bolster General Anderson's small force, a Combat Command of the 1st Armored Division and a Regimental Combat Team of the 1st Infantry Division had been moved up from Oran as rapidly as the single road and rail line permitted. French forces in Algiers joined in the drive to liberate Tunisia, and some French forces had been brought up from Morocco. While these French forces were inadequately armed and equipped, some of them fought bravely in the earlier operations. However, their refusal to serve under British command was a complicating factor in this early drive for Tunis. Beset by supply difficulties, troubled with French allies, and hampered almost from the outset by unseasonal rains which made movement off roads almost impossible, General Anderson's forces had nevertheless pushed boldly on toward Tunis. Against increasing German opposition on the ground and in the air, leading elements had reached Djedeida on November 28th. There they had been stopped and turned back to Medjez el Bab some thirty or forty miles from Tunis. There, the front had literally bogged down in a sea of mud, and on December 24th, General Eisenhower had finally postponed the attack for Tunis indefinitely.

Thus, at the end of 1942, the Allied front in Tunisia extended from the Mediterranean coast west of Bizerte southward some 250 miles to the edge of the desert at Gafsa. The British V Corps, with three or four infantry brigades and an armored brigade, occupied the northern sector from Cap Serrat southward through Medjez el Bab to the vicinity of Pont du Fahs. The 26th Infantry Regimental Combat Team of the 1st Division and Combat Command B of the 1st Armored Division had just been relieved in this sector and were reorganizing. General Juin's French XIX Corps, with some four or five inadequately armed and equipped divisions, held the mountain passes around Pont du Fahs, Pichon, Fondouk, and Faid and the mountain passes to the westward. At Gafsa on the southern extremity of this long front was Task Force Raff, so named from its American commander, Colonel Edson D. Raff. This force comprised a detachment of American paratroopers that had seized airfields in the Tebessa area during the earlier operations, some French irregulars, and a detachment of the French Constantine division.

The rugged nature of the country, reinforced by bad weather in the northern sector, restricted military operations to areas where the relatively small number of roads crossed this extensive front. These were areas where troops were concentrated; the remainder of the front was covered by patrols.

Most of the German strength was centered in the northern area to block the approaches to Tunis, although there was contact at other points along the front. German reinforcements were continuing to arrive in Tunisia by air and sea in spite of interference by British naval power and Allied air power.

Far to the east beyond Tripoli, Rommel faced Montgomery's British Eighth Army which was even then preparing to renew its drive for Tripoli. The overland route from Tunis through Sfax, Gabes, and Tripoli, paralleling the Allied front in Tunisia and only a few miles distant from it, was becoming increasingly important as Rommel's line of communications. Once Tripoli was taken, it would be his only line of communications and withdrawal.

Supply was the absorbing problem in every headquarters in North Africa. There was still a dearth of service troops and transportation. Few units in North Africa yet had their full scale of motor transportation. The single rail line eastward from Oran and Algiers had suffered from neglect, and there was a shortage of locomotives and rolling stock. The two principal roads east from Algiers, one along the coast and the principal highway farther inland, although paved were not in good repair; and both traversed rugged, mountainous terrain with steep grades and turns and many bridges. British supplies and equipment destined for Tunisia came for the most part from Algiers and the small ports of Bone and Philippeville. Oran was the principal American port and base. French supplies and equipment came in part from local sources, the remainder from British and American stocks. So critical was the problem of supply that the loss of a single truck was almost a tragedy, the destruction of a bridge or locomotive a catastrophe of concern even to the high command. And the Germans were employing agents already in the country and others dropped by parachute to sabotage this tenuous line of communications.

Reinforcements in men and materiel were arriving as rapidly as shipping permitted, but the only troops immediately available to reinforce the front were the American 1st Armored and 1st and 34th Infantry Divisions. Both of the latter were for the most part scattered in small detachments protecting airfields and critical points on the line of communications.

This disposition provided the background for the SATIN plan.

The purpose of the operation was to create a situation which would permit the resumption of the attack to capture Tunis as soon as weather and logistical considerations permitted. In brief, the American 1st Armored Division and one Regimental Combat Team of the 1st Infantry Division were to assemble, together with certain auxiliary and supporting troops, in the Tebessa area as rapidly as possible. This force, supported by American aircraft on the airfields at Tebessa, Feriana, Thelepte and elsewhere, was to advance rapidly to the east, capture

Gabes or Sfax or both, cut Rommel's line of communications with Tunis, and destroy supplies, bridges, rail lines, and port facilities. If compelled to withdraw it would pull back to the Feriana-Tebessa area. This action, it was hoped, would draw German forces from the northern part of the front and thus permit General Anderson to renew the attack to capture Tunis when weather conditions were more favorable in that area. Meanwhile, every effort would be made to build up the power of the British First Army in men and materiel for this offensive.

To command the SATIN force, Major General L. F. Fredendall and Headquarters II Corps moved from Oran to Constantine. Overall command of American, British and French forces would be exercised by General Eisenhower through the advanced command post which I was to establish in Constantine.

This bold concept appealed to almost everyone with whom I talked in AFHQ. Most officers would have liked to see the SATIN force in greater strength, but the factors which limited its size were the logistical considerations. The administrative staff in AFHQ was dominated by British influence, and the logistical organization in Algiers and Tunisia was essentially British in organization and in methods. The administrative planners insisted that the single railway, narrow gauge from Constantine to the Tebessa area, and the one hard road that paralleled it would not permit maintaining a larger force than the one Armored Division and Regimental Combat Team in addition to the air forces which would be required.

AFHQ was then, as afterwards during the war, an Allied headquarters combining American and British ground, sea, and air elements. Basically, the headquarters was organized along American General and Special Staff lines, although the British retained their own staff organization and procedures for administration and control of British forces. American officers headed the chief of staff and operations sections with British officers as their principal deputies. A British officer headed the combined intelligence sections with an American officer as deputy. The administrative sections G-1 and G-4 were under a British Chief Administrative Officer. The General Staff sections were composed of approximately equal proportions of British and American officers. Each side maintained its own Special Staff sections.

The Allied nature of the headquarters was one of the principal reasons for the ponderous size of the headquarters which was causing General Eisenhower so much concern. Differences in organization, equipment, procedures, and national characteristics between British and American forces resulted in much duplication of effort. Had all forces been either British or American, the size of the headquarters could have been reduced by half. Most staff officers like to be close to the throne, and many of them are empire builders at heart. There is more prestige in belonging to the top headquarters than to a lower one even though the duties may be identical. And assignments always seem more important when one commands the services of assistants. Thus every staff always tends to increase in size. Few ever decrease in size through staff volition.

The Advanced Command Post was actually part of AFHQ. Our plan was to have it contain only enough personnel to provide the Commander in Chief with the information and service which he would require for control during the proposed operations. Essentially, the purpose was to furnish General Eisenhower with an office closer to the front than AFHQ so that all information concerning the situation would be available and where his personal contact with subordinate commanders would be more convenient than in Algiers. The same information would be available to him in either place. Only a small group would be required, and the personnel would be drawn from staff sections in AFHQ and would be rotated now and then to give others experience with conditions at the front and to insure complete coordination between the Advanced CP and the staff sections in AFHQ.

The Advanced CP consisted of G-2 (Intelligence), G-4 (Supply) G-3 (Operations), and Air and Communications sections. Normally there were two officers in each of these sections. In addition, there were several liaison officers who could be dispatched to any area to report information direct to the Advanced CP by radio. There was a 'War Room" where sections kept a combined operations map and all the data pertaining to their respective functions that might be required. Communication with each of the commanders on the front and with AFHQ was by telephone, telegraph, radio, and courier. A mechanized cavalry troop provided security for the Advanced CP and for General Eisenhower when he should visit the front.

Immediately after New Year's Day, Carleton and I went to Constantine to select suitable accomodations for the Advanced CP and for General Eisenhower when he should be there. Constantine, one of the principal cities of Algeria, we found to be crowded almost beyond capacity. The main headquarters of the British First Army was located there, as well as both British and French area or line of communications commands. Both British and American air forces had establishments there. And Constantine was filled to overflowing with refugees from the battle zone and from Tunisia. After many conferences with representatives of the First Army and the local French and British line of communications commands, we finally selected the almost empty American Orphanage as a suitable location for the Advanced CP, and a villa next door as suitable quarters for General Eisenhower. Billets for other personnel of the Advanced CP we found in adjacent buildings and in local residences nearby.

During the second week in January, there were many conferences with the various staff sections concerning the organization of the Advanced CP and the SATIN plans. While some of the section chiefs in AFHQ were fearful that the Advanced CP might trespass upon their prerogatives, they were cooperative on the whole. Our arrangements proceeded, and on January 11th, I departed for Constantine accompanied by General Eisenhower's aide, Major Tex Lee, who was to pass judgment on the suitability of the living accomodations we had selected for the Chief.

By January 14th, all arrangements were complete, and the Advanced CP was open for business.

General Fredendall with Headquarters II Corps was still in Constantine, completing detailed plans for SATIN, although they were preparing to move to the Tebessa area. General Ward with Headquarters 1st Armored Division was at Guelma a few miles to the east. On January 12th and 13th, I conferred with these officers and their staffs concerning their plans and preparations, as well as with General Anderson and others in the British First Army.

General Fredendall's plan was to strike eastward from the Feriana-Gafsa area with the 1st Armored Division and one Regimental Combat Team of the 1st Infantry Division, to seize the bottleneck on Rommel's line·of communications at Gabes. Sowing mine fields to protect his right flank against any reaction by Rommel, he would turn north to capture Sfax and destroy the German base there. These operations would be closely supported by American tactical aviation operating from air fields at Tebessa, Feriana, Thelepte, and elsewhere in Algeria and Tunisia. General Fredendall hoped to accomplish the operation in about ten days if all went well.

Supply was the principal concern in all SATIN planning. In addition to the heavy requirements of the British and American air forces in the forward areas for gasoline, oils, bombs, ammunition, and other supplies, reserves of ammunition and supplies of all kinds had to be provided for the build up of the First Army for its projected offensive as well as for the SATIN force. General Fredendall and his staff estimated that a reserve of 11,000 tons in the Tebessa area was essential before the operation began, and that maintenance thereafter would require 500 tons daily. General Fredendall feared that French forces on his left would not be able to protect his line of communications east of Tebessa against a German attack from the north. For this reason, he wanted an additional Regimental Combat Team of the 1st Infantry Division which could be held in the vicinity of Feriana. This would increase the tonnage requirements.

I summarized the problem in a memorandum to the Chief of Staff AFHQ, on January 13th:

> . . . As Hamblen (G-4 AFHQ and Advanced CP) outlined to me late this afternoon, the situation is about as follows:
>
> *a.* It is barely possible to build up the reserve of 9 or 10 thousand tons required for the II Corps by January 23 (this approximates the 11 thousand ton requirement).
>
> *b.* It is barely possible to provide the 450 to 500 ton daily maintenance requirement thereafter and this possibility depends upon no interruption of rail traffic by bombing, no destruction of engines, rolling stock, etc.
>
> *c.* To add CT 16 will require about 100 tons daily, which can only be pro-provided at the expense of the First Army. If the First Army is to undertake operations in mid-March, it will require a reserve of about 8 thousand tons. To take this 100 tons daily from the First Army would reduce this possible reserve by some 6 thousand tons and thus reduce reserves to a point where General Anderson will be unwilling to undertake offensive operations.
>
> . . . In general, I think Hamblen's point of view is this: That the operation contemplated by II Corps is a knife edge proposition which is logistically sound if everything is one hundred percent. If trucks are destroyed, supplies lost, railroads interrupted, there seems to be no answer. As to giving CT 16 to the II Corps, Hamblen's investigation indicated that this cannot be done unless you are willing to delay offensive operations by the First Army beyond mid-March proportionately. You will understand that these investigations are not complete, but this seems to be the picture at the moment. I might add that General Anderson will not consent to alloting this 100-tons a day without a command decision on this point.

Logistical estimates affect tactical decisions, and staff officers who make these estimates are usually conservative. Within less than two months, the course of events was to compel us to concentrate and supply more than four American divisions from the Tebessa area along with other requirements not then foreseen!

However, preparations for SATIN continued apace. Headquarters II Corps moved to the Tebessa area and established a command post at Djebel Roumaine just east of the town. The 1st Armored Division, the 26th Regimental Combat Team of the 1st Infantry Division, several tank destroyer, artillery, engineer, and other auxiliary units were concentrating in the forward areas. Airfields at Tebessa, Feriana, Thelepte, and elsewhere in North Africa bristled with aircraft. Liaison officers were dispatched from the Advanced CP to various areas to report on the progress of preparations. Supplies were moving into the

Tebessa area on schedule, and there seemed to be every prospect that SATIN could begin on January 30th which was now the scheduled date. Combat Team 16 of the 1st Infantry Division was moving into the forward area, but it was not to be released to the II Corps. It would be held in AFHQ reserve at Guelma. On Sunday, January 17th, all seemed to be going as well as could be expected. Two incidents that day caused a flurry of activity in the Advanced CP: the Germans attacked French forces near Pont du Fahs just outside the British sector; and we were advised that General Eisenhower would arrive the following morning for a conference with commanders.

First reports from British sources indicated that the German attack was only a local one, although both infantry and tanks were used. Weather was still unfavorable in the forward areas and General Anderson thought that assistance by adjacent British units with artillery and antitank guns would bring the Germans to a halt. General Anderson was concerned about the danger to the British right flank and the Medjez el Bab area if the Germans advanced much farther. He thought that we might have to employ Combat Command B of the 1st Armored Division for an attack from the south toward Pont du Fahs to restore the situation.

French forces in the area of the German attack were commanded by General Mathinet whom I remembered from our armistice meeting in Port Lyautey. And I knew from personal experience the inadequate state of French organization, armament, and equipment. I fully agreed with General Anderson that French forces alone would not be capable of restoring the situation. But the employment of Combat Command B would have repercussions on the SATIN plan.

General Eisenhower arrived at Tulergma, our airfield, where I met him with the mechanized cavalry escort. He was accompanied by Major General Spaatz and Brigadier General Kuter of American Air Forces, Air Vice Marshall Walsh, RAF, and Commander Butcher, his Naval aide. I had assembled Generals Anderson, Juin, Fredendall, and Cannon at the Advanced CP.

General Anderson explained the situation along the front as it was known to us, and outlined his view that a counterattack employing Combat Command B might be necessary to restore the situation if the Germans penetrated much farther. General Juin emphasized the French need for arms and equipment, particularly for antitank guns of which the French had practically none.

Then General Eisenhower explained that recent information from General Alexander's Middle East Command indicated that the Eighth Army expected to capture Tripoli within ten days and to be assaulting Rommel on the Mareth Line near the southern border of Tunisia by the first of March. In view of this accelerated rate of Rommel's retreat, SATIN would be premature for it would expose Fredendall's force to attack in flank from both the north and south and in superior strength. Fredendall's force should therefore be concentrated as a mobile reserve in the Tebessa area, prepared to attack when the Eighth Army should be assaulting Rommel on the Mareth Line. From now on the battle to drive the Axis from Africa was one big battle, and our operations would have to be closely coordinated with those of the Eighth Army. This coordination General Eisenhower had arranged with General Alexander. Meanwhile we would concentrate upon building up our power and improving our positions. Fredendall's force should not remain inactive, but should conduct operations with limited objectives to seize advantageous terrain and to confuse the enemy. It should not, however, expose itself to undue risk. It could attack Pont du Fahs if that were desirable, but it should not attempt to take either Sfax or Gabes.

So far as the French were concerned, we would do our utmost to rearm and equip them as rapidly as the means available in the theater permitted. Both General Anderson and I were to give this matter our personal attention. He would like to have French forces more active in protecting the line of communications and rear areas against sabotage and German paratroopers.

I think that everyone present at this conference agreed that General Eisenhower's decision concerning SATIN was sound. General Anderson and his staff had looked upon SATIN with somewhat jaundiced eyes, for any buildup of the SATIN force they considered as being at the expense of the buildup of the First Army's offensive power. Most of us at the Advanced CP considered that SATIN was merely postponed for some weeks until it could be coordinated with the attack of the Eighth Army when its effect would be more immediate and conclusive.

But the German attacks at Pont du Fahs precipitated a series of events which, like a powder train, exploded in unexpected places during the next few weeks and had us dancing to German tunes—with no inconsiderable discomfiture to the Allied command and particularly to American troops on the Tunisian front.

All our plans so far were based upon the assumption that French forces would be able to hold the mountainous region between the American and British forces. Even with their inferior armament, some of the French units had fought gallantly in the earlier advances. There were few roads in the area, and the terrain was not thought to be suitable for the employment of armor. In this mountainous region, French weakness in antitank weapons should be no great disadvantage.

But German estimates of French capabilities and German appreciation of what constitutes suitable tank terrain were better than our own. The German attack had struck the weakest link in our chain with infantry, artillery and tanks—and with tanks more powerful than any we then possessed. It was in this area that British antitank guns first knocked out and captured the first of the monster Mark VI "Tiger" tanks. We should have been prepared for what transpired but we were not.

The German advance continued, and General Anderson was becoming increasingly concerned over the danger to the British right. It was obvious that in spite of support by British artillery and antitank guns, General Mathinet's French forces were having a rough time. Reports from British and American liaison officers at General Juin's headquarters were more and more discouraging. The continuing German attacks, striking chiefly in the French sector, forced repeated withdrawals with resulting heavy losses in men and materiel. This caused a lowering of morale and loss of combat value which affected even the French high command. On January 19th, it was decided to employ Combat Command B, 1st Armored Division, Brigadier General P. M. Robinette commanding, for an attack to restore the situation as proposed by General Anderson.

Generals Anderson, Fredendall, and Cannon met with me at the Advanced CP on the morning of January 20th to discuss the situation and to arrange coordination of Robinette's attack with French and British forces. General Juin was represented by his American liaison officer, Colonel William S. Biddle, as the situation required General Juin's presence at his headquarters. Robinette was placed under General Juin's command for the proposed operation but General Juin was instructed "to employ General Robinette's force as a unit" and advised that "the Commander in Chief desires to avoid having the striking power of this force dissipated by numerous detachments. He desires to avoid the risk of expending General Robinette's force in any operation, the results of which would not justify the sacrifice." Following this conference, I dispatched Colonel Carleton to join Robinette and keep the Advanced CP posted on developments in the situation.

Reports from the front were discouraging for the German advance continued. General Anderson conferred with me again during the afternoon. It was his opinion now that no reliance could be placed on French troops to hold any part of the Front unless they were strongly supported by British or American troops, an opinion in which I concurred. General Anderson now believed that it would not be practicable for Robinette to restore the situation on the French front as it had existed prior to the German attack. In view of General Eisenhower's recent directive, further review of the situation along the front by General

Eisenhower would be desirable. This proposal I transmitted to General Eisenhower, and he agreed to come to the Advanced CP the following morning for another meeting with commanders.

General Eisenhower was accompanied by Generals Spaatz and Kuter. Again I had assembled Generals Anderson, Fredendall, Cannon and Juin. The results of the conference are summarized in a memorandum which General Eisenhower dictated to a stenographer in my office immediately after the conference ended, copies of which I sent to the various persons concerned.

1. The tactical situation was explained by General Anderson and General Truscott.

2. The collapse of the French forces in the mountainous regions south and southwest of Pont du Fahs made it evident that the American forces in the south and the British in the north must operate toward a common boundary, in order to cover this gap.

3. It was evident also that collaboration by air forces was faulty to date, due particularly to the absence of an air Advanced Headquarters.

4. *a.* The general plan agreed upon was that British forces would continue to operate to the south and southeast to cut the road leading from Pont du Fahs to the southwest and hold it.

b. That Combat Team B, under General Robinette, would continue operations, probably starting today, to the north from the general area of Ousseltia.

c. That General Fredendall would immediately constitute a force approximately equal to Combat Team B to attack Fondouk on Saturday morning the 23rd.

d. General Fredendall is to hold a strong mobile reserve in the general area of Tebessa-Sbeitla and to operate his forces so as to permit rapid concentration for operations in any direction.

e. The battalion and Regimental Headquarters of the 16th Infantry now at Guelma comes under the orders of General Fredendall and will be used by him to hold the line gained by Robinette's attack of today. The British are making available one battalion on that line and Fredendall is sending forward one battalion of the 26th Infantry to operate in the same region.

f. The remainder of the 16th Infantry comes under General Fredendall's orders when it reaches the forward areas.

5. To insure coordination of the British and American forces, General Anderson has been directed to act in an executive capacity for these purposes. He is to operate within the general scope of the plan described above and is not authorized to transfer forces from one sector to the other. He is

charged with informing General Juin of the arrangements made and to request General Juin to direct cooperation by remaining French forces with the British on the north, and the Americans on the south. He is also to request General Juin to employ the maximum number of troops possible on the line of communications. General Robinette's attack today is under French direction, and the plans for the Fondouk attack for the 23rd have been drawn up under French command. Nevertheless, these forces will remain part of General Fredendall's command and upon completion of these specific movements will be subject completely to his direction.

6. General Fredendall retains responsibility for the general protection of the right flank of the Allied forces.

7. The Commanding General, Allied Air Force, is being directed to place at Advanced Headquarters immediately an officer who will be in executive control (in command of) the air forces supporting General Fredendall and General Anderson. This officer will receive his instructions for battle from General Anderson so far as they affect all air forces alloted to the support of ground Armies. He will be in communication with the headquarters of the Air Forces at Algiers and will secure assistance of the strategic air arm upon specific request. This air officer will report at Advanced Headquarters tomorrow, the 22nd.

General Eisenhower and his party returned to Algiers after this conference, and I sent off a letter to Colonel Biddle, our liaison officer with General Juin, to inform him of the details of General Eisenhower's memorandum. He was to inform General Juin that General Anderson would visit him the following day to discuss the matters with him. Biddle was to inform Colonel Carleton who was with Robinette at Ousseltia, concerning whose operations we were anxiously awaiting information.

The next afternoon, January 22nd, General Spaatz, General Kuter, and Colonel Barker of General Spaatz' staff, arrived to establish the air support coordination which General Eisenhower had directed. There was a lengthy conference at the Advanced CP that evening with these officers, General Anderson and his chief of staff, and the commanders of the British and American bomber commands in Constantine, to discuss the problems of air support and the organization which would be required. General Kuter remained in Constantine to command this air support.

Meanwhile General Fredenall was encountering obstacles in carrying out the assignments which General Eisenhower had alloted to him. At 1045 that morning General Fredendall telephoned me as follows:

Relative to the attack to be pulled at Fondouk scheduled for tomorrow, I do not think it can be pulled because the French do not feel they can. My head man who has been running the show down there (General Porter) spent the night arguing with them but without result. States they have no intention of doing anything and that even if they are ordered to do it, they will accept the orders but do nothing about it.

Relative to that force at Ousseltia (Robinette), it has been passed down from the head Frenchman to a second Frenchman and now to a division commander. There is now some enemy between our outfit and the French. Am informed the Division C. G. intends to pull out the French this AM which will leave our people in a bad way. Carleton requested infantry to hold ground gained but we do not have the infantry. Get this word to First Army and let me have your reactions.

Shortly after noon, Fredendall telephoned me again. He had just talked with his chief of staff who was at the French command post. Everything north of Pichon had been withdrawn or collapsed leaving three weak battalions near Pichon and three weaker ones at Fondouk. He repeated that he did not think the attack planned for Fondouk the following day could be done. And I agreed with him.

Robinette attacked a German force near Ousseltia on January 22nd and drove it eastward toward Kairouan. At the Advanced CP we were elated by their report of more than four hundred German prisoners taken. This report, however, turned out to be somewhat exaggerated as subsequent verification was never able to account for even a tenth of that number. There was further fighting near Ousseltia during January 23rd which Carleton described in a note sent to me by courier during the evening.

We had our first controlled air action today. It took a lot of hell raising with everyone from General Craig down, but it worked after a fashion. Attack was planned last night, request sent in and finally after repeated signals for confirmation was OK'd at 1000 today. We wanted it set for 1100 but air finally agreed to put it on at 1230. Fortunately Jerry felt pretty secure as he had been taking all the artillery we had to offer and feeling little the worse for it. At 1230 the planes came over, headed for the target, and as they approached, artillery put one smoke shell on the target, and without hesitation the planes moved in and dropped their loads well on the target. They hit and blew up two ammunition trucks and did other damage. Our artillery started pounding the position with everything as soon as the bombs dropped. A truck load of American prisoners broke and ran and are just now drifting in here. They report that the Germans there are being supplied from Kairouan. Though that road is covered by a battalion of French, they have only light rifles and seem unable or unwilling to interrupt traffic. Unfortunately, our troops were not close enough to take advantage of the bombardment and move in and seize the area. I was disappointed as I had been assured they were all set to do this. However, this is the first successful air mission and I suppose they lacked confidence that it would come over—or hit the target if it did.

In the same note, Carleton informed me that staff officers from General Fredendall had informed Robinette that Colonel Fechet was to join him with the 16th Regimental Combat Team to take over ground that Robinette's command captured. They were developing plans for a general attack at 0800 the following day, January 24th, in which one battalion of the 16th Infantry with one artillery battalion would "have a go at the pass to Kairouan if it is not already in our hands," while Combat Command B attacked to the north to join with the British who had been asked to advance at the same time.

Every report from the front emphasized the continuing demoralization of French forces. On January 23rd, I sent General Eisenhower a memorandum recommending that we review the problem to determine how French forces could best be employed to contribute to the immediate common effort. I suggested that French troops should be withdrawn to training areas to protect lines of communications while they were being rearmed and reequipped. However, I pointed out that I did not believe that "any level lower than the Commander in Chief has any prospect of effecting the program" and that if it was to be accomplished "there can be no better chance to convince French authorities than now, while the recollection of their recent collapse is still fresh in their minds."

General Anderson had directed Fredendall to attach Colonel Fechet's 16th Regimental Combat Team to Robinette's command, which Fredendall had done. General Fredendall was laboring under the impression that Robinette was already on the objective in the north end of the Ousseltia valley and had ordered Fechet to fight his way up the valley to join Robinette. When General Anderson heard of this order, he was concerned for fear that Fechet would become entangled in fighting in the valley and be unable to reach the objective which could be occupied without fighting by approaching it from the west. At General Anderson's request, I transmitted these instructions to General Fredendall.

General Anderson was now concerned because British and American forces would be spread so thin to hold the extensive front that there would be no possibility of building up offensive power for the eventual drive for Tunis. He thought the situation should be presented to General Eisenhower once more with a view to finding additional forces. I agreed with General Anderson and so informed General Eisenhower, who arranged to meet us at Tulergma the following morning.

General Anderson and his chief of staff, Brigadier McNabb, and I were waiting at the airfield when General Eisenhower arrived. He was accompanied by Major General Jock Whitely, his British deputy chief of staff, and Major General Lowell Rooks, the American officer who was AFHQ G-3. There on a map spread over the hood of a jeep, we reviewed the situation. General Anderson explained that General Fredendall agreed with us that no reliance could be placed upon the French and emphasized the importance of withdrawing these badly shaken troops and replacing them with British and American units. He explained his plan for defending the French sector and expressed the opinion that at least four more American Regimental Combat Teams should be found. General Rooks discussed bringing up the American 34th Infantry Division then scattered along the line of communications from Constantine back to Oran, as well as bringing the 9th Infantry Division on from Morocco. General Eisenhower outlined a possible disposition of American forces and indicated his determination to place the whole front under General Anderson's command. My minutes of this meeting record the decisions made:

> The C. in C. directed General Truscott to issue orders attaching II Corps to the British First Army. He directed General Anderson to confer with Juin and explain to him that the urgency of the situation had compelled him to place American units in this area under his (Anderson's) command; to convince Juin that it was necessary to withdraw the bulk of his tired French troops for rest and refitting, that the political situation made it desirable to retain a French sector, but this could be done by placing selected French elements on the Western Dorsal and leaving the Constantine Division in the south; that Anderson should invite Juin to establish his headquarters with Anderson to supervise French troops and protect French interests.
>
> Further discussion as to the distribution of American units indicated that the 34th Division (less one CT) should eventually take over the French sector with such French units as could be made available; that the 1st Division Headquarters could be used by First Army now; if necessary; but that these details were to follow the conference between Anderson and Juin.
>
> The final disposition of American troops suggested by General Rooks is as follows·
>
> *a.* The 1st Division Headquarters is available to First Army now on request to AFHQ.
>
> *b.* Eventually, the 34th Division (less one CT) should relieve British units on the Western Dorsal.
>
> *c.* The 1st Division should be assembled at Guelma, eventually for use with the V Corps (British).
>
> *d.* One CT 34th Division to replace the 26th now with Fredendall. It was felt that the 34th Division should be retained under First Army control rather than being attached to either V Corps or to II Corps.
>
> *e.* The 9th Division to be brought forward to Algiers in reserve.

Immediately after General Eisenhower's departure, General Anderson suggested that I call General Juin in to the Advanced CP, and that together we tackle him with the Commander in Chief's proposals. He thought that General Juin might listen more receptively if these proposals were presented with the backing of an American officer. We met with General Juin that afternoon, and that evening I sent a memorandum by courier to General Eisenhower.

> 1. I have been in conference with General Anderson and General Juin since 5:30. I am enclosing some notes that General Anderson prepared prior to the conference which were followed rather closely. Anderson presented the picture much better than the paper reads.

> 2. Juin is agreeable to everything, except that he insists he must have a French sector, preferably the least active. In discussing the command set-up, Anderson finally suggested the following:

> In the North, the V Corps, British—with certain French units under Barre—under Awlfrey.

> In the South, Fredendall, with certain French units, the Constantine Division under Welvert under him.

> In the center, in the northern part a small French sector under French command and in addition to that on the south, to include the Pichon-Fondouk area, an American sector (the 1st Division or the 34th Division with two RCT's), with any French units they desire; both of these sectors, French and American, to be under a French corps commander.

> 3. I believe that this solution can be made to work. It will be necessary to place selected American officers with the French corps headquarters as working members, and it will probably be necessary for British and Americans to supplement communications. This seems to be the only feasible solution to this problem.

> 4. General Juin is perfectly willing to withdraw from the lines any French troops we want withdrawn. So far, I have not mentioned the protection of the lines of communication because I feel that if French units can be withdrawn to training areas, that is a question that can be solved without rubbing salt in open wounds.

The morning of January 24th General Fredendall had sent an improvised Combat Command from Gafsa to attack a small German force some miles to the east at Sened Station. At half-past three that afternoon General Fredendall telephoned me again:

> "Remember that force I sent toward Maknassy looking for trouble? They ran into some stuff and smeared it. I can't give you the details. There were some tanks and infantry out around a place called Sened. They were very cheerful about what they had done—our trouble is to get them back. They

are coming back tonight. As soon as I get the details I will give them to you. Whatever it was, they smacked the hell out of them. I thought you might like to have a little cheerful information from down here."

About half-past nine o'clock that night, General Fredendall telephoned me again.

"I've got a little dope for you. Yesterday we received a note from the Axis forces wanting to know why the Americans did not come out and fight. This morning I sent a command consisting of a battalion of infantry, a little reconnaissance, company of medium tanks, and a battalion of artillery with the object of hitting some people we thought were at Sened. When we got to Sened they were gone. I told them to go on and get contact. They got contact at Maknassy. They ran them all out of town. We lost no prisoners. One man wounded. All the men including the tanks got back. We took 80 prisoners, 60 Italians and 20 Germans, including one officer, and we think we got some of Rommel's Afrika Korps among the Germans. Trump that if you can, damn it! . . . This is just a primary report. Get word to the C. in C. there is a splendid note of cheer down here. We must have killed a hell of a lot but could not stay to find out. . . ."

And that was to be the last "splendid note of cheer" we were to have from II Corps after a fight for some time to come.

There was a lull on the front that lasted nearly a week. Robinette's operations in the Ousseltia valley together with the support which British troops had given the French southwest of Pont du Fahs had brought the German advance in the area to a halt. Or perhaps the Germans had already achieved far more from this local operation than they had expected and did not fully appreciate the full extent of the demoralization which their operations had caused. At any rate, pressure on the French was relieved and General Anderson was able to establish the defense on suitable terrain. Then it was a question of reorganizing the front along the lines now planned.

Major General Terry Allen arrived with Headquarters 1st Infantry Division and was assigned to relieve French and British troops in the central part of the French sector. Two regiments of the division, the 16th and 18th Regimental Combat Teams, were immediately available, and the 26th Regimental Combat Team would be released by II Corps as soon as the 168th Regimental Combat Team could be collected from the line of communications and could join—within the next few days. Robinette remained in the vicinity of Ousseltia until the 1st Division took over its part of the French sector, and was then withdrawn to Maktar under First Army control. The remainder of the 34th Infantry Division began its movement from near Oran on January 30th, the 9th Infantry Division from Morocco about the same time.

Thus, on January 28th, the 1st Infantry Division was not yet complete in the French sector, but Robinette's Combat Command B was behind it and the French forces at Maktar. The 168th Regimental Combat Team was just assembling at Tebessa. Parts of the 1st Armored Division were at Sbeitla and near Tebessa, with another improvised Combat Command D at Gafsa preparing for another raid toward Maknassy. Gafsa was still held by Task Force Raff and part of the Constantine Division of Welvert's. Some thirty miles to the east of Sbeitla at Faid, a detachment of the French Constantine Division under General Schwartz held the passes leading toward Sfax. Still farther to the north around Fondouk and near Pichon, there were a few more weak battalions of French troops. Nowhere on the front was there a reserve of any size, nor could there be one until the movements then under way could be completed. Such was the situation on the southern portion of the Tunisian front when the Germans lifted the curtain on the opening scene of the next act in this drama.

2. *Personality Problems*

Not all of our troubles in Tunisia were of German—or even French —origin. Some were traceable to differences in organization, methods, interests, and national characteristics among the nationalities involved on the Allied side. Still others were to arise from conflicting personalities among the nationalities involved, and even among the personalities within each one. Some of these problems had been evident from the first. Others were to develop under the ambitions and tensions and strains of combat. To comprehend the events which were to follow in this Tunisian campaign, one should appreciate something of the problems of personality as we were to learn them during troublous days.

Tunisia had been planned as a British area of responsibility. Essentially, the line of communications for administration and supply was British in organization and control. British armament, organization, equipment, and even rations were different from the American. There were even differences in language and in military and other terminology. American and British soldiers always got on well together whenever they came in contact. The troubles occurred at higher levels—among the commanders and staff officers. British officers knew no more of American organization and methods than Americans knew of theirs, yet British officers usually impressed Americans as being both supercilious and conceited. American officers were less reserved and more outspoken in their criticisms than were their British comrades.

American units employed with British forces during the earlier operations had encountered difficulties in supply and communications which for them were not normal. That these British methods and procedures were those which had been found best suited to British problems and procedures, was not understood by the Americans. There was a feeling among American officers and men that the British command had not respected the integrity of American units, but had employed them piecemeal intermixed with British units to their disadvantage. American officers came to feel that British troops were being favored over them in missions, equipment, supplies—and that American units were being employed to "pull British chestnuts from the fire". General Eisenhower had early recognized the dangers of such attitudes to Allied cooperation, and had been positive in his instructions to all American personnel concerning it. But there is perhaps no field in which personalities play a more important part than in that of Allied realationships in war.

General Anderson was a soldier of distinguished appearance, tall, trim, and dignified. A cultured gentleman, charming in manner and quiet in speech, he was reserved and reticent. Personally bold and fearless, he nevertheless usually took a pessimistic view of military operations Although stubborn in his opinions, he was always completely loyal to General Eisenhower. All in all, General Anderson was not easy for American officers to know and understand, nor was his personality one to inspire them with confidence. Unfortunately, Brigadier C. V. O'N. McNabb, General Anderson's chief of staff, suffered the same disadvantages from the American point of view. McNabb, with whom I had worked much in London during the ROUNDUP and TORCH planning, was a dour, silent, kilt-clad Scotsman, whose great personal charm and rare military abilities were never apparent to American officers on short acquaintance, and few American officers in Tunisia ever came to know him well. Like most British officers, McNabb took the pessimistic view in planning. He believed in wide margins for error. His consistent view was that everything given to Fredendall's force in the south was at the expense of the more important task, that is, the buildup of the First Army for the eventual drive on Tunis. McNabb was reticent almost to the point of secretiveness and difficult for Americans to approach. It is not surprising that American officers with Fredendall should come to feel that their problems were not always well understood in First Army Headquarters.

Nor was General Fredendall endowed by nature or training with those qualities which would have simplified the problems of inter-Allied cooperation and command relationships. In appearance and in personality, he was almost the exact opposite of General Anderson. Small in stature, loud and rough in speech, he was outspoken in his opinions and critical of superiors and subordinates alike. He was inclined to jump at conclusions which were not always well founded. He rarely left his command post for personal visits and reconnaissance, yet he was impatient with the recommendations of subordinates more familiar with the terrain and other conditions than was he. General Fredendall had no confidence in the French, no liking for the British in general and for General Anderson in particular, and little more for some of his own subordinate commanders.

The 1st Armored Division, the principal element of General Fredendall's command during this period, was commanded by Major General Orlando P. Ward. General Ward was quiet in speech and manner, well trained, and methodical and thorough in all that he did. His division was well organized, had great esprit, and held General Ward in high esteem. Between General Fredendall and General Ward there developed an antipathy most unusual in my experience. General Ward came to believe that General Fredendall knew nothing about the employment of armor and was motivated by personal animus in disregarding the division commander and his recommendations. General Fredendall, on the other hand, thought that General Ward was incompetent and personally disloyal to him.

Another personality that complicated command and staff relationships during this period was General Ward's principal subordinate, Brigadier General P. M. Robinette of Combat Command B. Robinette had taken part in some of the earlier fighting in Tunisia and felt that he had had more actual combat experience than either General Fredendall or General Ward. Robinette disliked his subordinate position. He liked having Combat Command B separated from the rest of the 1st Armored Division so that he could deal with higher headquarters on the same level as the division or corps commander. Robinette was an egotist. He was sure that he had a better grasp of the situation in Tunisia, both tactical and strategic, than anyone in the division, corps, or higher headquarters. In consequence, he bombarded higher headquarters with tactical and strategic studies and recommendations relative to the conduct of operations. His tendency to neglect General Ward and staff of the 1st Armored Division except for essential administration and supply was not calculated to pour oil on the troubled waters of command and staff relationships.

I have mentioned the understandable lack of confidence among both British and Americans toward the French forces. This lack of confidence was accentuated by the barrier of language. General Juin himself was a distinguished soldier whose past reputation was well known to the British and American command. He was a man of great personal charm and undoubted military ability. General Juin was always cooperative and loyal in his dealings with Allied headquarters, but there was a general feeling among both British and American headquarters that his control over subordinates was far from complete. And there was some doubt as to the extent of the authority permitted him by his own superiors. The only accurate source of information about conditions among French forces was always personal observation.

I will never forget my first visit to General Fredendall's command post a few days after it had opened in the Tebessa area. A command post is usually placed near a road and adjacent to existing communications facilities, but his was far up in a canyon accessible only by a difficult road constructed by the corps engineers. Although it was sheltered by towering mountains and concealed among trees, the corps engineers were blasting away at the mountainside to build underground shelters for the operational staff—and this a good sixty or seventy miles from any point where there was contact with the enemy! General Fredendall explained to me that German aircraft were still active in the area and that Germans always made special efforts to destroy command posts. He had no intention of having his command post disrupted for it was the vital center in control of the corps operations. As he would exercise control by means of communications, he did not need to be any closer to the front!

This command post remained in this location for some weeks, until later German attacks caused a reorganization of the front. However, it was never necessary to occupy the underground shelters for the command post was never attacked. Most American officers who saw this command post for the first time were somewhat embarrassed, and their comments were usually caustic. Among subordinate commanders and staffs, there was an impression that "Corps" was looking out for itself first and never understood the situation as it was known to the "troops"—and there was some basis for this reaction. No matter how perfect the communications and how adequate the maps, there can be no substitute in command for personal visits and reconnaissance by commanders and staff officers alike. The actual sight of soldiers, guns, ground, and sky will often erase the pessimism created by the pictures drawn in grease pencil upon maps.

From Tebessa, one of the main roads leading toward Sfax on the Tunisian plain passed through the easternmost mountain chain at the village of Faid. Faid Pass was important. It was essential for any Allied advance toward the German line of communications at Sfax. In German hands, it would expose forward airfields at Feriana and Thelepte to attack by German ground forces, and would facilitate a German advance toward Tebessa and to the northwest. Faid Pass was guarded by a detachment of the French Constantine Division commanded by a General Schwartz.

On January 28th, while every allied headquarters in North Africa was struggling to reinforce and reorganize the front, the Germans struck General Schwartz' command with a well coordinated attack by infantry, armor and aircraft and almost annihilated it. General Schwartz, who narrowly escaped capture himself, fled with the remnants of his command back across the desert to Sbeitla where Combat Command A, 1st Armored Division, was then stationed. Then General Anderson directed General Fredendall to "restore the situation at Faid", and General Fredendall assigned the task to Combat Command A.

I spent the night of January 29th with the II Corps at Tebessa, talking with General Fredendall and members of his staff. They were assembling a force at Gafsa for another raid toward Sened and Maknassy, and I had intended to go on to that area the following day. Learning that Combat Command A would begin its advance from the vicinity of Sbeitla the following day, I went there instead, accompanied only by my aide, Captain Grimsley, and my driver, Sergeant Barna.

The next morning I visited General Ward and members of his staff at the command post of the 1st Armored Division not far from Tebessa. During the afternoon, we drove on past the airfields at Feriana and Thelepte to Sbeitla, a distance of some eighty miles through sparsely settled desert country reminiscent of our own New Mexico and Arizona borders. At Sbietla, a small native town whose most notable features were nearby Roman ruins, I found the command post of Combat Command A and that of the remnants of the French forces from Faid.

Brigadier General R. A. McQuillin, who commanded Combat Command A, was an old friend. I had served with him on the faculty of the Cavalry School at Fort Riley, and during my service with the Armored Force at Fort Knox in 1940 I had been operations officer of the 13th Armored Regiment under his command. Many of his staff and subordinate commanders were cavalry officers whom I had known for years. The occasion was for me, therefore, one of more than usual interest. General McQuillin I found in conference with the French commander, General Schwartz. From General Schwartz, I learned some of the details of the German attack and the extent of French losses. Caught by surprise, without air support, tanks, antitank weapons and almost without motor transport, the French were incapable of effective resistance against the well armed and equipped Germans. More than 1500 men had been lost and only a few hundred had reached Sbeitla where occasional stragglers were still arriving. General Schwartz told us that even if General McQuillin drove the Germans from Faid, he had nothing left with which to hold the position. His immediate task was to confer with General Juin about the reorganization of his command.

At McQuillin's command post on the eastern outskirts of Sbeitla, he told me of his own plans. Screened by reconnaissance elements, two columns each with a battalion of tanks, a company or so of armored infantry, artillery, tank destroyers, and engineers, would move during the night to positions near Sidi bou Zid about thirty miles to the east. He would follow with his reserve column when the others had reached their designated positions. At daylight, the two columns would attack, one from the northwest, one from the west, to capture Faid and drive the Germans from the pass.

That night I sat with General McQuillin in his command car—a half-track fitted with an enclosed body to shelter the radios, map boards, and work tables, with barely room for an operator, a clerk, and the two of us. All through the night the radios chattered—with little regard for codes—as elements of the force moved eastward. Commanders reporting locations, contact with German patrols, German tanks reported here, antitank guns reported there, reports of obstacles encountered, of delays and lost units, requests for information, and for instructions—all through the night McQuillin was kept busy. All night long we plotted locations and followed the progress of columns just as we had done in many peacetime training exercises. The advance continued and the columns reached their destinations well before dawn. Then we moved forward to a new spot near Sidi bou Zid.

Sidi bou Zid, an oasis in the desert about five miles southwest of Faid, was a cluster of native huts with scattered trees and a few small irrigated plots enclosed by the ever-present cactus prickly pear. A mile or so to the north and just across the main road leading from Sbeitla to Faid, a rugged butte, the Djebel Lessouda, rose steeply from the desert floor. There I went soon after daylight to watch the course of the battle. Almost due east of Djebel Lessouda and distant about five miles was the village of Faid nestled within the pass which was the objective. To the north and south of the pass as far as one could see were the rugged, barren mountains which bordered the Tunisian plain. Two miles or so to the southwest of Sidi bou Zid, and opposite a break in the mountain chain, there was another butte, the Djebel Ksaira. From where I stood on the eastern slopes of Djebel Lessouda, the flat brush-covered desert rose gradually and then more steeply over rocky and irregular talus slopes to the mountains which marked the pass. Westward toward Sbeitla, whence we had come, all was flat desert.

Just east of Sidi bou Zid half hidden among the trees and cactus, I could see some of the reserve tanks and an artillery battalion firing. On the slopes below me, another battery of armored artillery was in position and firing while a forward observer not far from where I stood adjusted the fire. Off to the east, the flash and smoke of bursting shells marked the entrance to the pass. Well out on the desert along both sides of the road leading eastward, deployed tanks were lumbering along like giant beetles, stopping now and again to fire. It was difficult to follow them through the filmy haze of dust and smoke. Off to the northwest, I could see the dust of movement southward toward Faid, which I took to be the northern column. Now and again a salvo of German shells burst somewhere out on the desert before us, but seemingly did no harm. For the most part the firing was all our own. It was like watching a training exercise at Fort Knox.

Then, for the first time, I saw German airplanes attack American troops. High up over the Djebel Ksaira to the south appeared five Stukas. One after another they turned lazily over, plummeted earthward, and then pulled up in steep climbs. We watched the flash and towering columns of smoke, and seconds later heard the muffled explosions of bursting bombs. They were attacking artillery and tanks around Sidi bou Zid, but we learned later that only one truck was damaged. Then four ME 109's appeared low against the mountains and strafed the troops attacking toward Faid. It was with keen satisfaction that we watched one crash in flames, shot down by antiaircraft fire.

It was nine o'clock. The battle had moved on toward the Pass where we could hear the sound of firing but could see little but dust and smoke. Hoping that our forces were about to take Faid, Grimsley and I climbed into my jeep and followed the route the tanks had taken. We had not gone far when we came up to the rearmost tanks deployed along a ridge. Nearby, one of our Sherman tanks had been disabled by a direct hit on the turret from a German 88. On another ridge to the front there were more tanks, most of them firing. We could hear the rattle of machine gun fire off to the front and flanks, the continuing crash of artillery, and now and then the whine of a shell passing overhead. It looked as though our attack was stalled.

Back at the command post, General McQuillin informed me that our tanks were stopped by rough terrain and that the German defenses around Faid were too strong to be overcome by his one small infantry battalion. He was reporting to Corps that he would have to be reinforced before he could take Faid and restore the situation. In the meantime, he would take position to block any German advance westward from Faid.

Leaving McQuillin before noon, I returned to the Corps Command Post. General Fredendall and his staff were disappointed that McQuillin had not been able to take Faid, but they were encouraged by optimistic reports from Combat Command D which had captured Sened Station against considerable German opposition. General Fredendall was concerned because General Anderson was still holding Combat Command B, a good part of the combat power of the 1st Armored Division, under Army control at Maktar. The 168th Infantry was just beginning to arrive in the area, and the only reserves available within the II Corps were a battalion of tanks, some artillery, tank destroyers, and the corps engineers.

By six o'clock the evening of January 31st I was back at the Advanced CP. General Anderson was disturbed because conditions on the front were preventing him from carrying out General Eisenhower's orders to build up offensive power for an onslaught in the north. He thought the matter should be discussed once more with General Eisenhower, and we met him at the airfield at Tulergma the following morning.

General Anderson explained that he had been conferring with General Juin. The French had lost more than 2,500 men in this recent German attack at Faid and about twenty battalions since the German attacks began in the Pont du Fahs area. French combat value had been reduced to a point where no reliance whatever could be placed upon them, and British and American troops had to be employed to hold our extensive front. General Anderson went on to say that General Fredendall had a force trying to take Maknassy and had reported that he expected to capture the place during the day. I described McQuillin's unsuccessful attempt to take Faid, and the substance of conversations I had had with General Fredendall the day before. General Anderson expressed the opinion that we were spreading ourselves too thin and that we were not accomplishing the Commander in Chief's directive to build up power in the north for a drive on Tunis. He proposed that we should withdraw from exposed places like Gafsa, Maknassy, and Faid in order to shorten our lines. I pointed out that such withdrawal might jeopardize our forward airfields and that giving up Gafsa might have political repercussions.

General Eisenhower, noting that Fredendall's force was broken up into many detachments, was fearful that Fredendall might be too rash and expend men and materiel in unproductive operations. He emphasized to General Anderson the importance of maintaining Fredendall's command as a mobile striking force on the south flank, prepared to strike in any direction when the time came. He authorized General Anderson to withdraw from Gafsa, Maknassy and other exposed points if that would permit the desired concentration of force on the south flank.

General Eisenhower explained that the Eighth Army had driven Rommel fifty miles west of Tripoli and was continuing the pursuit. General Alexander was coming on from the Middle East Command to be his deputy in actual command of the Eighth and First Armies when they were close enough for their operations to be controlled by one headquarters. He thought that operations were approaching that point, and had asked that General Alexander and his staff come on as soon as possible.

Later, General Eisenhower interrogated me at length about the relationship between General Anderson and General Fredendall and about British and American relations throughout the command. He directed me to see General Fredendall and explain to him in person the views he had expressed about the employment of his command, and to stress the importance of complete cooperation with General Anderson. After that, I was to come to Algiers to discuss the future of the Advanced CP once General Alexander had established his Army Group Headquarters in the forward area and had assumed command.

I saw General Fredendall on February 2nd, flew to Algiers the afternoon of February 3rd, and returned to the Advanced CP the afternoon of February 4th. In Algiers, General Eisenhower gave me the welcome news that as soon as General Alexander arrived and assumed command, he was going to assign me to command the 3rd Infantry Division in Morocco to prepare it for the invasion of Sicily which would take place as soon as possible after the Germans were defeated in North Africa.

So far as the Advanced CP was concerned, there had been some feeling among the staff of the First Army, after General Anderson was placed in command of the Tunisian front that there was no longer any necessity for maintaining it. And to some extent, this feeling was reflected among the staff sections in AFHQ. Few subordinates ever look with much favor upon inspectors and observers who represent superior headquarters and most staff officers are inclined to be somewhat jealous of their prerogatives. It is perhaps only human for subordinates to feel that reports on their activities may not always present them in the most favorable light. Such attitudes are rarely justified because subordinates should welcome any measure which will provide their superiors with complete and timely information. Such was General Eisenhower's view for he decided that he would maintain the Advanced CP for closer liaison with General Alexander's headquarters after he had assumed command. It was decided that Brigadier General Ray Porter, who had been with General Fredendall in the II Corps, would relieve me.

When I returned to the Advanced CP, I learned that Combat Command D had not reached Maknassy. It had captured Sened Station and a strongly held ridge five miles farther on to the east. A few prisoners had been taken and a number of German tanks, trucks, and artillery pieces had been captured. German dive bombers had inflicted rather severe casualties on an American infantry battalion which was moving forward in trucks in broad daylight, but otherwise casualties had not been severe. However, with the Germans in strength at Faid, General Anderson thought the force too exposed and ordered it withdrawn. The force withdrew the night of February 4th after destroying the captured materiel.

For the next ten days there was a lull in combat activities along the front. In the north, adverse weather continued, there was little activity beyond the occasional interchange of artillery fire. In the central sector, where the 34th Infantry Division (less one Regimental Combat Team) was joining the 1st Infantry Division in relieving the badly shaken French forces, there was a flurry or so of patrol activity, but no action of any importance. In the southern sector, the 168th Regimental Combat Team of the 34th Infantry Division had joined and two of its battalions had been sent on to reinforce McQuillin's Combat Command A at Sidi bou Zid along with a battalion of artillery. The Corps held Gafsa, Feriana and Sbeitla, but there was contact only in the vicinity of Sidi bou Zid where McQuillin had been formulating plans to recapture Faid. Meanwhile, troops, supplies, and equipment were rolling into the forward areas as rapidly as the line of communications permitted.

During the second week in February, intercepted radio messages indicated that the Germans were planning another attack on the Tunisian front in greater strength than their previous ones. As the intelligence officers at AFHQ and First Army interpreted the area and direction indicated for this attack, it would come through the passes around Fondouk in the direction of Maktar and the flank of the British Army. General Anderson based his dispositions upon this conclusion. Plans for offensive operations were dropped and the front alerted for defense. Gafsa was to be evacuated in the face of any threatened attack. Feriana and Sbeitla were to be held, Combat Command A was to remain at Sidi bou Zid, and Robinette with Combat Command B was held at Maktar to back up the 1st and 34th Infantry Divisions and such French as remained on what was considered the most threatened portion of the front. On February 11th, General Fredendall issued detailed instructions to General Ward prescribing exactly how McQuillin's Combat Command A was to be disposed for defense at Sidi bou Zid.

So far as I could see from my access to this same intelligence, there was nothing to substantiate this alarm over the possibility of a German attack from the Fondouk area toward Maktar. I had no grounds for doubting this source of intelligence, which heretofore had been almost infallible, but there were no other factors in the situation as we knew it to support this conclusion of the intelligence sections. There had been little or no German air activity of any kind. It is true that we were taking almost no prisoners, but neither were the Germans. There was little activity even among patrols along the front. Neither ground observation nor aerial reconnaissance, or for that matter any other source of intelligence, indicated any significant change in German dispositions along the front, or any significant change in the pattern of Montgomery's Eighth Army. There was no indication of danger in any great strength immediately, but there was also no doubt that the Germans had the capability of attacking at some point along our front if we did nothing to prevent it. I was of the opinion that the advantage in combat strength, ground, air, and sea, lay with us, and that Axis supply difficulties were as great as, if not greater, than our own.

The most damaging blow that the Axis could strike us would be to take from us forward air fields in the southern area. It seemed to me that we should hold Gafsa and Faid to protect these air fields, to facilitate subsequent operations, minimize losses, and insure early termination of the campaign. It was my view that we should destroy Rommel's army before it escaped into the Tunisian bridgehead. Some of these thoughts I expressed to General Eisenhower, when he came to the Advanced CP on February 12th for his first visit to troops in the American sector. In this memorandum, I wrote:

> In one respect only have Axis forces demonstrated superiority, the ability to concentrate superior means in local areas and to retain the initiative. This fact may be attributed to shorter lines of communications and perhaps to more experienced leadership.

Little did we realize how soon the Boche was to underscore my remark as a masterpiece of understatement and to demonstrate how faulty our intelligence was.

We left the Advanced CP the morning of February 13th for Tebessa and the front. At this period, occasional German planes strafed roads in the forward areas, and they were still dropping occasional parachutists to destroy bridges and harass communications. There were among the Arabs and French colonials Axis sympathizers who were not above sabotage and occasional sniping. To protect the Commander in Chief when he visited the forward areas, we had provided and trained a mechanized cavalry platoon for escort duty. Thus, our cavalcade included a total of eleven vehicles. One section of bantams and a scout car led off, the bantams scouting the road ahead. General Eisenhower, his aide, Major Lee, and I followed in General Eisenhower's sedan, driven by his British chauffeur, Miss Kay Summersby. General Rooks, Major Conway, and Captain Grimsley followed in another sedan, trailed by two bantams. Another section of scout cars and bantams brought up the rear.

We stopped at an RAF airfield at Canrobert and at an American air base at Youks les Bains. There General Eisenhower talked with commanders and airmen and inspected the installations. These airmen were living and operating under rigorous field conditions—dug in like front-line infantrymen, living on K and C rations, and experiencing the dangers and discomforts of front line troops. German airplanes had visited them many times, but their morale was high. We reached the II Corps Command Post in the canyon east of Tebessa shortly after noon. Although I had warned General Eisenhower what to expect, his reaction to the location and to the tunneling which was still in progress was that of nearly everyone who saw it for the first time. There were some acid comments.

During the afternoon, General Eisenhower discussed the situation and plans with General Anderson who had come to the Command Post to meet him, and with General Fredendall. Shortly before dark, we left II Corps to visit General Ward of the 1st Armored Division and other forward elements.

For night travel, we reduced the size of our party. One bantam armed with a machine gun and carrying Lieutenant Colonel R. F. Akers, Assistant Corps G-3, and Colonel Conway of my staff led off. General Eisenhower's sedan followed with my driver, Sergeant Barna, substituting for Miss Summersby who remained at the Corps Command Post. General Rooks followed in another sedan. Another bantam from the mechanized cavalry platoon brought up the rear.

Our route took us past the airfields at Thelepte to Feriana and northward to Sbeitla. There General Eisenhower conferred at length with General Ward and some of his subordinate commanders and General Ward showed how his division was dispersed. Combat Command A was at Sidi bou Zid opposite Faid. A detachment called Combat Command C, a battalion of infantry and a company of tanks, was some twenty miles to the north of Combat Command A. Combat Command B was still at Maktar under First Army control. Ward had in division reserve a battalion of light tanks, a company of engineers, and two guns of an antiaircraft battery. Back at Bou Chebka near the Corps Command Post in corps reserve was another battalion of tanks, some artillery, tank destroyers and engineers. General Ward joined our party, and we proceeded on to Sidi bou Zid thirty miles to the east to visit Combat Command A, where we arrived soon after midnight.

McQuillin's Command Post was concealed amid the cactus and scattered trees near the village not far from where I had left it just two weeks before. McQuillin explained his dispositions. One battalion, 168th Infantry, dug in behind wire on Djebel Ksaira. Another battalion, 168th Infantry, with a battery of artillery and a company of tanks dug in on Djebel Lessouda. A battalion of armored artillery and one of corps artillery in position generally east of the village to support both. A battalion of armored infantry and a battalion of tanks in reserve around Sidi bou Zid, prepared to counterattack. Reconnaissance elements reconnoitering to the north and to the south with occasional contact with German patrols. There had been no changes observed in German dispositions and the Germans had not been very active.

General McQuillin brought into the Command Post Lieutenant Colonel Drake who commanded one of the battalions of the 168th Infantry. Drake had been cited for gallantry in an earlier action. There in the dim light of McQuillin's blacked-out Command Post tent, General Eisenhower pinned the Distinguished Service Cross upon the breast of this gallant officer, a ceremony we were long to remember. Shortly thereafter, we departed for our return trip. It was just at two o'clock in the morning that we turned off at Djebel Lessouda onto the main road leading westward toward Sbeitla.

The monotony of our long cold drive in utter darkness was enlivened by two small incidents. On the outskirts of Tebessa, a flurry of shots and the flash of small arms brought us up in grave concern for the moment. However, Akers and Conway scouted ahead and could find nothing. It turned out to be no more than trigger-happy sentries firing at sounds in the night, prowling Arabs perhaps, or burros. Later on, as we climbed the winding road into the hills above Feriana, we stopped with a sudden jar that brought us wide awake. Sergeant Barna, intent upon following the blue black-out light on the bantam ahead, had dozed, and had dropped the right front wheel into the road side ditch. Fortunately, no damage was done, and we soon continued on our way. We reached the Corps Command Post just at half-past five.

At the Corps Command Post there was news. At four o'clock the Germans had attacked McQuillin's Combat Command A. And the main attack had apparently come down from the north on both sides of the Djebel Lessouda which we had passed with the Supreme Allied Commander in Chief barely two hours before! There was little information available beyond the fact that the infantry battalions were intact upon the two Djebels and that McQuillin was preparing to counterattack. No action was reported elsewhere on the front. Seemingly it was another local attack, and there was no reason to think that McQuillin would not be able to hold his own. Nor was there much more information available when, after a few hours rest, we left II Corps to return to Constantine.

We started out at half-past eleven that Valentine's Day with our original cavalry escort. We lost it before we had gone many miles. At Ain Beda, we turned off the main road to visit the famous Roman ruins at Timgad which General Eisenhower was anxious to see. The escort missed the turn, and did not find us again for an hour or so. Unlike most Roman cities which had once dotted all North Africa, Timgad had never been other than a Roman city. Whatever the causes that led to the abandonment of this once populous city, those who followed the Romans had never lived there. Timgad and its outlines had not been changed by the successive civilizations. Aside from wandering shepherds who may have sought the shelter of its walls, Timgad's last inhabitants had been those who held this Roman outpost some fifteen hundred years before. We walked through the narrow, well paved streets where Roman life had passed, looked into the dwellings where Roman families once had lived, gathered in the Forum where Roman orators once had spent their eloquence, and stood on the walls where Roman soldiers had once stood guard. We were not unmindful of the fact that not so many miles away, American soldiers were fighting on ground where Roman legions had once borne their victorious eagles.

We reached the Advanced CP about midafternoon, and at once sought news of the action at Sidi bou Zid. It was difficult to learn just what had happened. Reports indicated that McQuillin's counterattack had failed and that there still was fighting around Sidi bou Zid. By night, we learned that McQuillin's reserve tank battalion had been destroyed, a battalion of corps artillery had been overrun, and the remainder of McQuillin's force had been driven toward Sbeitla, leaving the two infantry battalions surrounded upon the Djebels. General Fredendall had appealed to General Anderson for Combat Command B and was planning to counterattack the following day to relieve the infantry battalions. That was bitter news. It was obvious that this German attack had been made in much greater strength than we had thought from first reports.

These were anxious hours at the Advanced CP. General Anderson was forward in the XIX Corps sector where he was expecting the major German attack to come. He and his staff persisted in the belief that the action at Sidi bou Zid was a diversion and that the major German attack was still to come through the passes around Fondouk in the direction of Maktar. He withdrew elements of the 34th Infantry Division, which had just relieved French forces between Fondouk and Pichon, to a new defense position twenty-five miles to the west near Sbiba. He was reluctant to release any part of Combat Command B which he was holding at Maktar to meet the expected main attack. He finally did release one medium tank battalion, which moved down from Maktar to Sbeitla during the night of February 14th to join with Combat Command C in a counterattack to relieve the beleaguered infantry battalions. General Anderson also directed General Fredendall to evacuate Gafsa during the night.

There were many long faces in the Advanced CP all during the day of February 15th. Information was slow in reaching us and it was usually incomplete and conflicting. There was delay in organizing the counterattack force at Sbeitla, and it was slow in starting. All during the day, there were reports of fighting between Sbeitla and Sidi bou Zid but our advance seemed to be making slow progress. Our aircraft were active over the area and there were occasional radio contacts with the infantry battalions surrounded on the Djebels. As detachments and individuals, overrun in the previous day's onslaught, straggled in, there was increasing evidence of German strength in armor, infantry, artillery and aircraft. There was still no action elsewhere along the front, but we were hopeful that the counterattack would succeed in rescuing the infantry battalions. It was night before we learned that the effort had failed, and not until the following morning did we learn the extent of this further disaster.

General Fredendall telephoned me at 0800, February 16th, to say:

> The picture this morning does not look too good. The counterattack force —Colonel Stack with two battalions of infantry, some artillery, and a battalion of medium tanks under Colonel Alger—got into the fight at Sidi bou Zid just before dark. Then their radio went out and there was no news until they phoned at three A.M. and recommended that the railhead be moved back from Sbeitla. Information is confused but G-3 has them on the phone now getting the latest information. I will have a full report and will call you back in a few minutes. It does not look good. The worst will be the loss of two battalions of tanks.

A little later, General Fredendall telephoned me again:

> At dark last night, Alger's tank battalion and its supporting artillery were hit in the flank. They ran into two battalions of German tanks in concealed positions. Stack had infantry and artillery on Djebel Hamra behind them, but he could not continue the attack without support. There has been no contact with Alger's battalion since dark last night, and we fear that it is lost. There is a possibility that it has gone on to join Drake's battalion on Djebel Ksaira, but I doubt it. . . . The first day's losses will include sixty-two officers and 1536 enlisted men, about half killed and missing.

In reply to my question, General Fredendall informed me that General Anderson had finally released Combat Command B and that Robinette had joined Ward at Sbeitla. He had told Ward to get his division straightened out and to hold defensively east of Sbeitla. The infantry battalion on Djebel Lessouda had started to fight its way out during the counterattack, but there had been no further word from it.

That was the bitter picture, at 1000 hour the morning of February 16th, which I had to convey to General Eisenhower. More than one hundred American tanks destroyed in two days, along with two battalions of artillery overrun, and two battalions of infantry lost, and no one knew how much more!

General Eisenhower decided that his best contribution would be to return at once to AFHQ and put impetus behind the measures to make good our losses. On arrival at the airfield at Tulergma, he found that his plane was out of order and decided to continue on to Algiers by road. He sent me two notes in long hand, one written at the airfield, the other on his way back to the highway. In the first one he wrote:

TRUSCOTT   Feb. 16—11:15

I have been thinking over the latest news phoned in by CG II Corps.

There seems to be little that A. (General Anderson) can do in the north to relieve the southern situation. On the other hand he cannot be subjected to any heavy tank attack.

Consequently, A. should support II Corps by direct help—infantry and A. T. guns would appear to be the best immediate means, also extra transport and, if possible, some tanks to go in reserve.

Movements should begin quickly—no later than dusk this evening.

Tell CG II Corps, again, that every position to be held must be organized to the max. extent—at once—mines, etc. *Emphasize reconnaissance.*

Discuss above with McCreery and get it to Anderson as quickly as possible.

Wire me at my hq. that you have received this; and action taken by Anderson.

In the other he said:

TRUSCOTT   Feb. 16

Please phone Whiteley as follows:

I expect to be in my office between 8.00 and 9:00 PM today.

I want Whitely, Rooks, Gale there.

He is to phone (*sic*) notify Giraud (who wants to see me) that I will phone him (Giraud) as soon as I get in and he can come to my office then if he so desires.

Above is written in galloping auto but believe you can read it.

DE

Be sure to wire in Anderson's plans (see my other note) as soon as you know them.

DE

General McCreery was General Alexander's Chief of Staff. He had arrived in Constantine the day before for preliminary conferences and reconnaissance prior to establishing General Alexander's Headquarters 18th Army Group in the forward area. I discussed General Eisenhower's memorandum with him and telephoned the instructions to Brigadier McNabb at First Army to be relayed to General Anderson when he could talk with him. I also dispatched a courier to find General Anderson and deliver a confirming letter. All of this information I repeated to General Fredendall.

I dispatched Colonel Carleton to join the 1st Armored Division at Sbeitla, and Lieutenant Colonel Conway to join our forces at Feriana. This time, both of them had radios with sufficient range to report directly back to the Advanced CP. Then there were conferences to orient members of the 18th Army Group Staff on the situation and conditions in Tunisia, telephone conversations with the staff at AFHQ and with II Corps relative to replacements in men and materiel, conversations with First Army, II Corps, and others relative to the situation and their various requirements, conferences with officers arriving to establish an American supply base near Constantine, and reports to keep General Eisenhower and AFHQ informed of the situation. All in all, it was a busy day at the Advanced CP.

Late in the afternoon, General Fredendall telephoned to report "a tank battle coming up at Djebel Hamra east of Sbeitla. They are coming in with sixty tanks," and another German force advancing north from Gafsa being delayed by mechanized cavalry about thirty miles south of Feriana. He had requested the British about ten o'clock that morning to send a regiment of tanks and a battalion of artillery to Sbiba. General Anderson was to call him from XIX Corps where he was at the time, but more than six hours had passed with no reply. Fredendall said: "Here is the danger: if we are run out of Sbeitla with our armor, that exposes the Maktar Valley. I wanted them to send something down to block so I could withdraw my armor back on the supply line and also block that pass up to the new air field. If we get rocked loose from that place, it is going to expose the Maktar Valley."

I asked General Fredendall if there was any further information on developments around Sidi bou Zid. Yes, he had a report from a patrol, which they believed to be accurate. When night fell, Alger had only eight tanks left in his battalion. Alger's tank was seen to be hit and burst into flames. No one got out. That would leave the battalion with about six tanks. (Actually, as we learned later, only four tanks and a few dismounted men escaped.) General Fredendall went on to say that most of the battalion which had been on Djebel Lessouda had gotten out, but there had been no word from the rest. He thought they would lay low until German tanks cleared out north of the road, and then make their way back. He went on: "As for Drake over to the east, I have sent him word that he will have to cut his way out. You can't give him much help. The air mission we laid on today could not be flown."

I asked about Robinette. He was at Sbeitla. Combat Command B was "getting set in behind so if they come through they can take them."

This was the picture which I reported to AFHQ at nightfall on February 16th.

The command post of any higher headquarters is a trying place in which to follow the course of a battle. Far removed from the battle scene, there is no opportunity for personal observation, and the orderly array of military symbols on the situation maps can never depict the scene as it actually exists. Reports are frequently vague, conflicting, incomplete, and often missing altogether. They are subject to delays in transmission, and all too often they are colored by the personalities of the individuals who pass them on. Following the course of a battle thus, it is difficult to avoid the extremes of optimism and pessimism until one learns that in war the situation is almost never as good as the first optimistic reports and rarely as bad as the first pessimistic ones. During the next few days, most of the reports that came into the Advanced CP were to be on the pessimistic side.

Carleton and Conway reported their arrival at their destinations. There had been fighting east of Sbeitla during the afternoon. Ward was organizing his defenses, and Carleton would report dispositions as soon as he could obtain them. At Feriana, there had been no contact and everything was quiet, but the force was ready.

About half-past ten that night, I telephoned the Corps G-3 to ask if there was any further information about the tank battle which had been reported as imminent shortly before dark. I was told that it had apparently been only a reconnaissance as the German tanks had withdrawn to the east.

All seemed relatively quiet, so I turned in about half-past eleven. But I was not to sleep for long. At one o'clock in the morning, General Fredendall telephoned, and my records show:

> Fredendall reported that German tanks were fighting on edge of Sbeitla; estimates gave them 89 tanks—80 Mark IV's and 9 Mark VI's. Apparently had pierced covering position 5 kilometers east of Sbeitla, which had been established along the line: Djebel Koumin (?)—south slope Djebel Mrhila, and had attacked in the moonlight. Considered situation extremely grave, and uncertain of ability to hold. If kicked off Sbeitla, the Thelepte-Feriana position exposed as well as valley toward Maktar. Said he had talked to McNabb earlier and had asked to be allowed to withdraw to high ground

but had been refused. Said he had not reported present situation to McNabb yet.

Directed him to report situation to McNabb and let me know result.

Said Ward had just reported situation in person. Ward considered situation grave—but was doing best he could.

I had barely finished talking with General Fredendall when a message from Carleton reported that tanks were fighting in the moonlight in Sbeitla, and were all around Ward's command post. Ward was determined to fight it out there. He was uncertain of the outcome, but could not withdraw then if he wanted to do so.

At half-past one General Fredendall telephoned again:

Fredendall reported that McNabb had authorized him to withdraw. Orders had been sent as follows:

To Colonel Moore at Kasserine with one battalion 26th Infantry, four companies 19th Engineers, four 37 mm guns, two 75 mm guns of Cannon Company, reinforced by one company of medium tanks and 805th Tank Destroyer Battalion (less Company) from Stark's command, to hold at all costs along the Oued east of Kasserine for a minimum of at least 12 hours. When forced to withdraw, to withdraw to the north and hold Kasserine Pass.

Armored Division to move north through Kasserine Pass in direction of Thala.

Stark to pull in covering force to hold main ridge line at Feriana, leave covering force of one company infantry, one battery artillery, one company light tanks. Take remainder of command including French to ridge north of Thelepte airdrome.

Williams (Air Support Commander) informed of situation making arrangements to remove aircraft from Thelepte at daylight.

Ward reported tank battle east edge of Sbeitla himself. Uncertain of ability to hold. Was not breaking off battle at Sbeitla because he could not if he would. He fears we have lost 1st Armored Division.

Fredendall feels that First Army has not given credit to his reports as to gravity of situation.

Towards morning, there was another message from Carleton. The German attack had apparently been beaten off at Sbeitla, but there was still firing. He would report when he could find what the situation actually was.

And a message from Conway at Feriana. His radio operator had roused him from sleep to inform him that everyone had pulled out of Feriana. The headquarters was gone. He would follow and report when he could find it.

Just at daylight another message from Conway reported that our people on the airfield at Thelepte were destroying airplanes and burning gasoline and other supplies. Roads were crowded with vehicles but the troops were establishing themselves on the ridge north of the airfield.

Those early hours of February 17th had been anxious hours at the Advanced CP—and elsewhere.

By now it was obvious even to General Anderson that this was the German offensive which intelligence officers had been so certain was to come through the passes around Fondouk farther to the north. We knew that some of Rommel's Panzer divisions were involved, and there had still been no action anywhere else on the front.

At half-past nine the morning of February 17th, Brigadier McNabb telephoned to say that one brigade of the British 6th Armored Division with artillery and antitank guns had been ordered from the northern sector to Thala, and that the 34th Infantry Division on the right of what had been the French sector was to hold the high ground east of Sbiba.

At 1045, General Fredendall called to report that our troops had withdrawn from Feriana to the ridge north of the airfield at Thelepte, and that our forces were already withdrawing through Kasserine Pass. Ward was to start west at 1100 to come through Kasserine Pass and take position south of Tebessa. McQuillin was to start at 1100 but was to delay en route and reach Sbiba at nightfall in order to insure protection of Ryder's (34th Infantry Division) south flank. Fredendall said: "There is some confusion, but we are getting along pretty well. We are acting offensively in the air and have air cover over them."

Fredendall had had another big argument with General Anderson. He said: "He wanted me to hold all day at Sbeitla, but if I had, it (the armored division) would have been tangled up in another dog fight. Finally I got him to agree to let me go ahead. They not only want to tell you what to do, but how to do it. Anyway, I think we are going to get our tail out of the door all right."

Fredendall wanted a battalion of the 18th Field Artillery to replace the one that had lost its guns at Sidi bou Zid and all but some three hundred of its personnel. In answer to my question as to what else he would need, he replied that he was going to survey the situation and take inventory and would let me know. He had already asked for a battalion of tanks. Then he added: "We are going to have to write

Drake and his battalion off. I am going to get a plane over him and tell him to give in. There is no out. He is completely surrounded. He had two days' ammunition and two days' rations. He had been out for twenty-four hours. There is no use prolonging the agony. We have got to write him off."

That was bitter news.

I sent messages to Carleton to report General Ward's plan in full, and to AFHQ reporting the situation and the sad news about Drake's battalion. More of General Alexander's 18th Army Group were in to inform themselves of the situation. And about noon, a staff officer called from Tebessa to say·

"Hello, General Truscott. This is Colonel Arnold. Got a little point. The French railroad people in Tebessa are packing up and evacuating —apparently on orders from their higher headquarters. I wonder if something could be done to cancel this and make them stay here. They are sort of panicking the population here."

I was hard put to answer that one. I telephoned Whitely at AFHQ. He said he would find someone in authority there to deal with it, and suggested that I get after the line of communications people, both British and French, in Constantine, which I did. Then I reported the matter to Brigadier McNabb at First Army, and he replied:

"Yes, we have heard the rumor. I think it is fairly a rumor. I am sorry to say that I think it was started by the British Town Major in the place. I am not quite sure about the French civil. The whole thing has been started by some blasted rumor. I am after the bloke who did it. I think we have got it in hand, but I will make sure again."

We were in almost continuous communication with AFHQ concerning the situation and the reinforcements and replacement materiel which General Eisenhower was straining every resource to send to the front. General Rooks telephoned me at 1100 to say that twenty-two M-4 tanks would leave Casablanca February 18th and arrive at Kroub (our supply base near Constantine) on February 24th. Twelve would leave Oran February 17th by sea and arrive in Philippeville on February 19th. Sixteen more would leave Oran by February 24th. Aside from tanks in the 2nd Armored Division in Morocco, the only other tanks in all the theater which might be used as replacements for the 1st Armored Division were some fifty-four M-4 diesel powered tanks which had just been delivered to First Army for reequipping the 6th Armored Division. General Eisenhower was considering taking these tanks for the 1st Armored Division. There were problems of maintenance and it might not be the best or most practicable solution, but the only alternate course would be to ship tanks from the 2nd Armored Divison by sea. General Eisenhower wished me to investigate, but an early decision was necessary as the ships were about ready to leave Casablanca.

General Rooks also informed me that he was sending on the artillery and regimental cannon companies of the 9th Infantry Division as I had recommended, and was assigning an officer to keep track of their movements and report locations daily. The rest of this Division would follow as rapidly as transportaton could be provided. A GHQ tank battalion equipped with obsolete M-3 tanks and another tank destroyer battalion were arriving in the theater and we could expect them in the forward area about February 28th.

General Eisenhower had AFHQ actually scraping the bottom of the barrel, but there was little there which would help our hard-pressed troops in the battles then in progress.

General Fredendall telephoned again at half-past one that afternoon (Feb. 17th) to appeal for another regimental combat team. As he expressed it:

"I am holding a lot of mountain passes against armor with three and one-half battalions of infantry. If they get together any place a couple of infantry battalions, they might smoke me out. . . . I haven't got a damn bit of reserve. I need a combat team of infantry worse than hell. All I have got are three and one-half battalions of infantry. They are not enough. And we just got a little dope from First Army that indications are the enemy is going to continue the attack from Feriana with the objective of taking Tebessa."

I explained to General Fredendall that the artillery and cannon companies of the 9th Infantry Division were on their way, but that even they could not be expected for several days. The rest of the Division was moving, although it would be some time before any of its infantry regiments could reach the forward area. I suggested that he appeal to General Anderson again for infantry to help meet the emergency.

About mid-afternoon, Carleton reported heavy fighting at Sbeitla where our troops had just been attacked by twelve ME 109's. Our people were blowing up ammuniton dumps and destroying supplies in preparation for withdrawing. And we had thought the withdrawal was already well under way!

There was a period during the afternoon when the Advanced CP had no contact with II Corps as the command post was moving from its canyon haven to a new location north of Tebessa. Not until six o'clock that evening was I able to call General Fredendall for an answer to the problems of the diesel tanks and about the situation at Sbeitla. He thought he would be able to answer the first "when I can get the 1st Armored together and count noses and see about the crews," which would be late the following day. He had heard nothing from Sbeitla.

He said that McQuillin was where he was supposed to be and he thought the Germans might have jumped his tail. As it turned out later, Ward had held Sbeitla until three o'clock in the afternoon to cover the withdrawal, and had then withdrawn through Kasserine Pass.

We did succeed in "getting our tail out of the door" during February 17th, and we were hopeful that the doors—Kasserine Pass and the Feriana Gap—were shut and barred so that we could lick our wounds and repair some of the damage.

The morning of February 18th, General Fredendall telephoned to say that he wanted one hundred twenty M-4 tanks, including the fifty-four diesels which were to come from the British, and which McNabb had already informed me the British had made arrangements to turn over to the II Corps. Fredendall concluded:

"We are a little thin but if they will just reconnoiter for awhile, we'll be all set. The longer they let us alone, the better we'll be set. The air is working fine. The 1st Armored will not have its tail in until noon, so I am giving them air cover."

So far, we could only guess at the extent of our losses, and what would be needed to make them good. And I was becoming doubtful of obtaining any prompt or exact report from the Corps staff. Accordingly, I charged Carleton to check with every element of the 1st Armored Division to obtain an accurate account of requirements. Carleton's report telephoned in the evening of February 18th, and confirmed in writing the following morning, summarized what defeat in battle can mean to an armored division. He wrote:

Since the start of the Sbeitla battle the morning of 15 February until its close at dark 17 February, the 1st Armored Division suffered the following losses:

Medium tanks	112
Light tanks (81 Recon Sq)	5
Half tracks	80
Self propelled 105's	11
Assault 75 mm howitzer self propelled	5
Half tracks 81 mm mortar mounts	5
Scout cars	15
Wreckers	7
Tank destroyer 75 mm self propelled gun	10

These losses are the best information available. Scattered portions of units were still putting in their appearance and vehicles of various types that had been abandoned on the field of battle and considered lost were appearing.

Though the loss in personnel in the division has been considerable, it has in no way been commensurate with the losses in vehicles, and trained replacements are available and are being made promptly.

The reverses suffered by this unit in the past few days and the magnification of losses in conversation between soldiers would normally indicate a decided lowering of morale and consequent effect upon efficiency. However in the case of this division, I do not believe this to be true. A very fine spirit still exists . . . and I am convinced that they can always carry more than their own weight against the Boche under any circumstances.

There is a definite feeling in the 1st Armored Division which it is very difficult to argue against and which I have made every effort to explain logically—that our Allies are being given A-1 modern American equipment while they must be content to fight with obsolete Mark III tanks. I do not believe this has a detrimental effect upon the morale, as might appear in stating it; however, the feeling is there. The Mark III tanks have a 34 degree traverse of its only effective gun—the 75 mm. In a withdrawal, it is helpless. The tank crews and the officers who man the Mark III tanks have a definite inferiority complex when opposed to the German Mark IV's. . . .

It is to be noted that Colonel Carleton's summary of losses applied only to the 1st Armored Division. It did not include the guns and half the personnel of the 2nd Battalion, 17th Field Artillery; all of one infantry battalion and most of another one lost on the Djebels at Sidi bou Zid; the numerous half-tracks mounting the light 75 mm guns with which the tank destroyer battalions and companies had challenged the superior German armor and armament; nor any losses in the 1st or 34th Infantry Divisions or among the Corps troops. There were plenty of holes in the dikes and all too few boys' fingers with which to plug them.

On the 19th of February, we were "getting set" as General Fredendall expressed it. Holding Kasserine Pass was Colonel Moore's force, the 19th Engineers, a battalion of the 39th Infantry, a chemical mortar company, a company of medium tanks, and the 805th Tank Destroyer Battalion (less one company). West of Kasserine, in the valley leading toward Tebessa, was Robinette with Combat Command B—one battalion and one company of medium tanks, 13th Armored Regiment, the 27th Field Artillery Battalion, the 601st Tank Destroyer Battalion, and the 2nd Battalion, 6th Armored Infantry Regiment. To the north around Thala, was the remnant of Combat Command A, and in this area the "Nick Force"—so called from its British commander, Brigadier Nicholson, 6th Armored Division—was gathering. Nick Force included an armored brigade of the 6th Armored Division equipped with obsolete Crusader and Valentine tanks, a reconnaissance squadron, three batteries of artillery with twenty-four 25-pounder guns, several anti-tank detachments with forty-eight 6-pounder and eight 17-pounder antitank guns, a battalion of infantry, and the Cannon Company of the 39th US Infantry. To the east defending the Sbiba Gap was the 34th Infantry Division (less one regimental combat team and one infantry battalion) with the 18th Regimental Combat Team of the 1st Infantry Division attached.

During the day, the Germans reconnoitered along the front from Feriana to Sbiba, and on February 20th, the German Panzer divisions struck through our poorly organized defenses at Kasserine Pass. Infiltrating around the small infantry forces placed too far out in front, and onto the heights behind them, and avoiding the mine fields and obstacles which had been carefully marked off with tape and flags to avoid casualties among our own troops during the withdrawal, Rommel's Panzer divisions struck through the pass and then fanned out in two columns: one of Germans and Italians heading west toward Tebessa, the other stronger column northward toward Thala and Maktar. During these hours, we had little information at the Advanced CP, and most of that discouraging. To us, it seemed almost touch and go. If we had not been able to hold the strong position at Kasserine Pass, how could we hope to hold the weaker ones of the wide front between Thala and Tebessa?

From all along the front and from the rear, every gun and tank which could be brought to bear upon the enemy was being rushed to the critical area. And the whole weight of Allied Air Power in North Africa, including the mighty B-17's, was brought in to support our hard-pressed troops. At nightfall, no one knew what would happen next.

That night the enemy was reported withdrawing, but he was only regrouping himself for battle. At dawn on the 21st, he renewed the attacks. In the south, the Germans and Italians drove Combat Command B back to a point only eight miles from Tebessa, but a counterattack by the 2nd Battalion, 6th Armored Infantry, supported by a company of tanks, in the late afternoon regained all lost ground. In the north, the Germans were stopped just short of Thala by the fires of massed artillery and the pounding of the Allied Air Forces.

This was not the end of the Kasserine battle, but it was to be the highwater mark in the tide of the German storm. And it was while the storm was raging that I saw for the first time operations instructions issued by the headquarters of a group of armies during combat.

General Alexander had arrived in Constantine on February 18th. On February 20th he assumed command of the First and Eighth Armies, hence the typically British designation of the Army Group in the instructions. HQ 18 ARMY GROUP OPERATION INSTRUCTION NO. 1 was addressed to Lieutenant General K. A. N. Anderson, Commander First Army, with copies to General Eisenhower, General Montgomery, and others. It read:

1. Your immediate Task is·

    (a) To stabilize the front in the southern sector.
    (b) To reorganize and regroup your forces in order to allot separate sectors to:—

British
Americans
French.

We must regain the initiative at the first available opportunity and then keep it.

2. Positions must be held to cover the following vital areas:—

    (a) Landing Grounds in the Tebessa area.
    (b) The plain with its Landing Grounds between LE KEF AND THÁLA.
    (c) The "gap" between SBIBA and MAKTAR.
    (d) The BOU ARADA valley.
    (e) MEDJEZ-EL-BAB and the MEDJERDA valley.

To cover these key positions the general line at present occupied by your forces will be held. There will be no further withdrawal except for local adjustments to improve your positions.

Between inclusive BOU ARADA and inclusive MEDJEZ it is essential to retain the approaches to the TUNIS plain.

3. Troops will be reorganized into their proper formations and regrouped as early as possible to allot separate sectors to the American troops, French troops, and British troops, under their own commanders. In the case of the French sector you may allot certain British supporting arms, such as field and Anti-Tank artillery, if you consider these essential.

4. A general reserve must be formed as soon as possible. This reserve will consist chiefly of the armoured formations. To facilitate forming of this reserve and to enable intensive training to be carried out, the important areas on the general line of your present positions must be decided and held strongly. The wide intervals between these areas, in most cases in mountainous country, can only be lightly held, or covered by active patrolling, and by the moves of reserves if a threat develops. Training must be carried out intensively by all troops. The fighting spirit of all must be raised to the highest possible pitch. Training with a definite "aim" is a great help in this.

5. Battle experience for those without it must be gained, starting with small raids and leading up to bigger operations. Such operations must be successful, this is important.

s   H. R. ALEXANDER
General.

20 Feb. 43   Commander 18th Army Group.

In a message on the same date, PERSONAL TO GENERAL EISENHOWER FROM GENERAL ALEXANDER, copy of which came to me at the Advanced CP, General Alexander wrote:

> Consider it most important to have 9 U.S. Inf. Div. up in CONSTAN- TINE area as soon as possible. This Div. is our only central reserve. Hope you will take all possible measures to expedite move.

I have often wondered what General Anderson's reaction was to this operations instruction. In view of the crucial situation existing on the front at the time it was issued, and the strenuous efforts both General Eisenhower and General Anderson had been making for weeks to accomplish its specific intent, it has always seemed to me to have been most untimely—rather like telling a man who has a bear by the tail to "hold on".

Since the start of the battle at Sbeitla, relations between General Fredendall and General Ward had grown steadily worse. They had long since passed any normal stage in command relationships, and were barely upon strictly "official" terms. Neither had any confidence whatsoever in the other, and every conversation with either of them, every report from the front, emphasized this unfortunate fact.

On February 19th, General Fredendall called me to say that Ward simply had to be relieved, and he wanted me to put the matter up to General Eisenhower. It was my opinion that both of them were at fault, but it was obvious that the two could never work together without detriment to the whole command. Something had to be done. I relayed General Fredendall's request to General Eisenhower. We had previous- ly discussed the possibility of bringing Major General E. N. Harmon on from Morocco where he was in command of the 2nd Armored Di- vision. This General Eisenhower now decided to do. I was to inform General Fredendall that Harmon would be sent to him to use in any way that he desired. Carleton and I made a special trip to the II Corps on the following day to inform General Fredendall of this decision.

On February 22nd, General Eisenhower arrived at the Advanced CP accompanied by General Harmon and his aide, Major Rooney, Brigadier Whitely, and Commander Butcher. I briefed General Har- mon on the situation and conditions as I knew them, and he then de- parted for the II Corps.

During the afternoon General Eisenhower discussed with General Alexander the reorganization of the front and future operations. And in the evening, he talked with General Fredendall by telephone. There had been a lull on the front during the day with only minor fighting. Some thought that Rommel was regrouping for another and more powerful thrust. General Eisenhower thought the German attack had lost its momentum and that General Fredendall should counterattack at once. Fredendall believed that he should wait at least one more day.

After his conference with General Alexander, General Eisenhower told me that he wanted an American aide for General Alexander—the best American officer he could find, one with combat and staff experience who would be invaluable to General Alexander in his dealings with American troops. His eye had fallen upon Conway of my staff. Much as I hated to lose Conway, I concurred in General Eisenhower's appreciation of this outstanding officer, and regretfully released him for the assignment.

The morning of February 23rd, our lines were still holding and the situation looked better. That afternoon, General Eisenhower, Brigadier Whiteley, Captain Grimsley and I drove to Tebessa where General Fredendall and Major General Terry Allen met us for a conference. All along the front, conditions were vastly improved and there was a distinct note of optimism. General Eisenhower insisted that every effort should be made to destroy the Germans before they could escape.

We left Tebessa late in the afternoon. During the meeting, General Eisenhower had directed me to have his sedan come down from Constantine to meet us at dark in order to avoid the long drive back in open bantams which we had used because of the danger of air attack. I sent the message but told Carleton to leave Miss Summersby behind as I doubted that General Eisenhower would want her in the forward area under the circumstances. I made a mistake. It was the only time in all of our associations that General Eisenhower showed irritation with me. Miss Summersby was the only driver in whom General Eisenhower had complete confidence for black-out driving at night.

February 23rd brought to an end the Kasserine battle. When General Harmon returned to the Advanced CP a day or so later, he showed me the order which had been handed to him on his arrival—not placing him in command of the 1st Armored Division, but in command of the battle then in progress. Harmon, pacing up and down the room, smoking one cigarette after another, eyes sparkling in his flushed face, described his experiences, in his characteristically hoarse voice, while Carleton transcribed:

> I never had such a time in my life. It was dark as hell and we found ourselves sometimes on the left of the road with these big damn trucks roaring by on the right side of the road. Several times, I seriously considered pulling over to the right side of the road and waiting for daylight. But I was worried about what was ahead and decided to keep on.
>
> When I got near Tebessa, I tried to find the Corps G-4 (located there at the time). No one seemed to know where it was, and those I talked to told me that the G-4 and the Corps Command Post had moved to the rear; that

everything was moving to the rear. Someone took me to the place where the G-4 had been and I got Corps Headquarters on the wire, and asked them if they were moving to the rear and if so where were they going.

They told me they had not moved to the rear and were waiting for me to come up before they made that decision. I kept on to the Corp CP and arrived there about 3:00 AM.

As I walked in the Headquarters, Fredendall and his staff were sitting around looking very glum, and they handed me an envelope saying, "Here it is. The party is yours."

I was rather startled and did not quite know what to do next. Fredendall was on the phone asking Ward to hurry up those 33 diesel tanks he was putting in shape. He was apparently talking to Howze (Ward's chief of staff), and Fredendall looked up at me and said he could not do a damn thing with Ward. I said: "Am I in command?" and he said, "Yes," and I said, "Well, here give me that phone." I told Howze to get those tanks to Thala by daylight, that that was an order. Howze said he would issue the order, but that it was wrong. I told him I did not give a damn whether it was wrong or not, the tanks were doing no good if the Germans got to Thala; that I wanted those tanks there by daylight.

I then got in my bantam with my aide and we went to see Robinette. Robinette had 48 tanks running. He said that was all he had, but he seemed to have his outfit well in hand and felt he could hold where he was without question. I told Robinette we were not only going to hold but we were going to drive the damn bastards back.

I then drove in the bantam over to Thala to have a meeting with the Brigadier there. The general commanding the 6th Armored was supposed to be there but he did not show up. The Brigadier said he thought he could hold with the force he had, but they had ordered the 9th Division Artillery withdrawn. He said First Army had ordered it, and I told him to hell with that. I would take responsibility with the First Army and the 9th Division Artillery would stay there. I told him we were going to stay and stop the Germans if it was the last thing we did and we knew we could do it.

I described my plan to the Brigadier: that it was to hold that day and that night, to move infantry along the ridges supported by all the artillery we could throw in from both Robinette and his force to seize the shoulders of the pass. The attack was to be made by infantry and artillery only, and that attack to take place the coming night and following morning. Robinette agreed to it, as did Brigadier Nicholson.

I then looked over the artillery positions and reconnoitered around Thala and prayed for the 1st Armored tanks to get there. They arrived about 10:00 AM. Of course, they did not get there at daylight, but I guess they got there as quickly as they could. I disposed the tanks just in rear of the line of hills south of Thala and told them to reconnoiter and be prepared to counter-attack to the southeast as I expected that if the Germans did attack they would attempt to turn our left flank around a small pass in the hills south-east of Thala. Of course, as it happened, they did not attack. I believe if they had we would have chewed them up.

That afternoon, I received a half-track with a radio and a signal officer. That with my aide constituted my total staff during that action.

Of course, our follow-up was slow and we let them get away, although they did abandon much equipment and we took some prisoners. Our slowness in following them up was mainly because of the mines they left behind in the road. We lost some men and vehicles when trying to follow them up.

I think that if this plan had taken place 24 hours earlier, that if the infantry had been pushed along the ridges to seize the shoulders overlooking the passes, we would have been able to cut him off and make it cost him a hell of a lot more than it did.

When I returned to Corps Headquarters, they were all very jovial and happy and seemed to be very pleased about everything. I don't know whether I did Fredendall any good or not, but I believe that at least he did go to bed and get some rest as soon as I got there.

Now I would like to go back to my Division and teach then some of the lessons I have learned. Of course, if the Army needs me again, I would be very glad to do so. I got here in 24 hours the first time and could do the same thing again.

Rommel, pounded by our vastly superior air forces and confronted by superior strength in front, had actually begun his withdrawal the night of February 22nd. Attacking troops on February 23rd received only light artillery fire. On the 24th, there was no opposition at all—the bird had flown. We reoccupied Feriana and Sbeitla and within a few days the Germans were back on the ground from which they had begun operations the morning of February 14th. Rommel had accomplished little in the way of gaining elbow room in Tunisia and he had sustained losses which could not be replaced. He had thrown a scare into every headquarters in North Africa, and he had taught us much. More than enough to pay the cost in men and materiel which had fallen so heavily upon the American troops of the II Corps.

Rommel's withdrawal through Kasserine Pass and General Alexander's almost simultaneous assumption of command of the operations in Tunisia almost marked the end of my mission with the "Command Post for Ike". Brigadier General Ray Porter had already been designated to succeed me, and had been working with me in the Advanced CP for some time. Plans had been made for its continuation in close relations with General Alexander's Headquarters 18th Army Group.

On February 24th, Carleton and I rode out to Ain Mlila to meet the first regiment of the 9th Infantry Division arriving in the forward area to join II Corps. This regiment, the 60th Infantry, had been in my command for the initial landings in North Africa at Port Lyautey. It had been only a few weeks since I had left them for this assignment, but so much had happened since then that it seemed much longer. Now they were to join in the fighting here, and I was to go back to the place where we had started the war together—to another command.

The following day, Carleton, Grimsley and I left to visit American troops who had taken part in the recent fighting, to talk with the officers and men who had fought, to see for ourselves the actual scenes of the battles which I had watched so intently upon maps. We visited every American unit, talked with commanders and staffs, walked over the positions and battle fields with officers and men who had been there and who could describe what had taken place. From their descriptions, examination of the ground, the still fresh marks of the fighting, and our own knowledge of the enemy, it was not difficult to reconstruct the various actions. And the evidence was often contrary to the reports that were then being given credence, for the legends which characterize battle were already beginning.

We were back at the Advanced CP on March 1st to meet Mr. John J. McCloy, then Assistant Secretary of War, and to send him on to visit American troops, escorted by General Porter. There was a final conference with General Alexander's staff on the reorganization and rearmament of the 1st Armored Division, some odds and ends to clear up before we were ready to depart for our new assignment.

I spent the nights of March 3rd and 4th with General Smith in Algiers, and the day of the 4th in conferences with General Eisenhower and members of the staff at AFHQ. General Eisenhower, General Smith, and I discussed the reorganization of the II Corps and its employment in forthcoming operations under British command, General Anderson and General Alexander. Asked for an opinion, I replied that General Fredendall had lost the confidence of his subordinates and that I did not believe the Corps would ever fight well under his command. I also believed that General Fredendall disliked and distrusted the British and would never get on well under British command. I recommended that General Eisenhower assign General Patton to the command with Brigadier General Hugh J. Gaffey from the 2nd Armored Division as his chief of staff. This was General Eisenhower's decision. The following morning General Eisenhower left Maison Blanche for Tebessa, and we climbed on board our airplane and headed west for our new assignment. General Patton was to arrive at Maison Blanche that same afternoon, and remain in command of the II Corps until the Eighth and First Armies joined forces in Tunisia. General Bradley, who had arrived in Constantine a few days before my departure, was General Patton's deputy commander, and he inherited the command when General Patton returned to Rabat to begin preparations for the invasion of Sicily.

CHAPTER FOUR

INVASION OF SICILY
HUSKY AND JOSS

1. *HUSKY*

When I left the Advanced CP and AFHQ, I had known for some time that the 3rd Infantry Division to which I was now assigned was to have an important part in HUSKY—the invasion of Sicily. President Roosevelt and Prime Minister Churchill at their meeting in Casablanca in January had determined that the next objective in Allied strategy was to be that of knocking Italy out of the war, and that the first step would be the invasion of Sicily. It was thought then the Tunisian campaign would be finished by the end of April. HUSKY was to take place as soon thereafter as possible, and early July was indicated as the target date.

The forces to be employed, Ground, Naval, and Air, were to be under the command of General Eisenhower as Supreme Allied Commander in Chief. Ground forces were to be commanded by General Alexander and were to consist of a British Field Army under General Montgomery and an American Task Force commanded by General Patton. For security reasons during the planning phase, General Alexander's planning headquarters was designated Force 141; the British Field Army, Force 545; the American Task Force, Force 343. Force 141, established in Algiers adjacent to AFHQ, began initial studies of the operation early in February.

Because of the time element involved in planning and preparations, and some uncertainty as to the availability and condition of divisions then fighting in Tunisia, other divisions were to be employed for the assault. I had known that the 3rd Infantry Division was to be one of these. When I left Algiers, I knew that plans under consideration by Force 141 envisaged landing the British Forces in the southeastern corner of Sicily and the American Task Force in the northwestern corner with the capture of Palermo as its immediate objective. It was not expected that outline plans would be ready for issue to Force commanders until the middle of March, but AFHQ had just designated the units which were to be assigned to Force 343. These were: Headquarters I Armored Corps, Headquarters VI Corps, one Combat Command 2nd Armored Division, the 3rd Infantry Division to which I was now assigned, 36th Infantry Division, the 45th Infantry Division which was to train in the United States and arrive combat-loaded for the operation, and either the 1st or 9th Infantry Divisions from those now fighting in Tunisia.

Every person who is given a new task takes stock, and measures himself against its requirements as best he can. When my small party boarded our C-47 at Maison Blanche that morning of March 5th and headed westward toward Morocco, I was on the way to a new command with increased responsibilities. It was only natural that we should ponder over the problem and plan to profit by our experiences.

I had known the 3rd Infantry Division while I was a member of the IX Army Corps Staff at Fort Lewis, Washington, in 1941. I had prepared and conducted the training exercises and tests which had been given to the divisions of the Corps that summer, and I had come to know the Division well. There would have been many changes. Only recently, it had been upon my recommendation that AFHQ had called upon the Division to provide 3,500 men—almost one-fourth of its strength—to fill the ranks of the 1st and 34th Infantry Divisions for the fighting in Tunisia. There is a tradition and spirit in all good organizations that carries on through periods of adversity, and the 3rd Infantry Division had been recognized as one of the best. I was fortunate to be assigned to command this fine regular division which was already in an active theater, had experienced one landing operation, and was destined to have an important part in another one forthcoming.

I was a cavalry officer as was Carleton, my Chief of Staff. Few of the command would ever have had much experience with cavalrymen. There has always been a measure of Branch jealousy in the Army, and few men are ever predisposed to like things they do not know or understand. Both brigadier generals in the Division, two of the three regimental commanders, and perhaps other officers as well, had been senior to me until my temporary war-time promotion. It was to be expected that we would be viewed with some reserve. These factors I did not consider to be of any importance other than as an indication that I should proceed carefully in establishing that complete mutual understanding and respect which is the only proper basis for command relationships.

I had formed strong views concerning the standards which should be expected of American infantry divisions in war. From my previous military training and experience, particularly at the Command and General Staff School, I believed that I was as familiar with the theory of the organization and employment of an infantry division as any other American officer, and more so than most. I had long felt that our standards for marching and fighting in the infantry were too low, not up to those of the Roman legions nor countless examples from our own frontier history, nor even to those of Stonewall Jackson's "Foot Cavalry" of Civil War fame. My experiences during the past year had confirmed me in these opinions. I had observed modern war at Dieppe, I had experienced it in command at Port Lyautey, and I had just been closely associated with American troops in the first battles against the veteran Germans. Not least in importance, I had acquired an intimate knowledge of plans and personalities involved in the conduct of the war in Europe that few division commanders could hope to have.

In my experience with the Rangers and Commando training, I had seen what could be accomplished in the physical and psychological preparation of men for battle. While the Rangers and Commandos had been selected according to relatively high standards, it had not seemed to me that they had been markedly superior in physique to the average of our infantry battalions. What I did not know was whether the average American soldier, even though free from physical defect or weakness, would bear the rigorous training required in the physical and psychological preparation of Rangers and Commandos. Most young Americans of that generation had been born during and immediately after World War I. They had gone to school during the time when pacifism was rife in the schools and colleges of the world. They had grown to manhood during the period of post-war depression and "peace in our time" appeasement. Their lives had been far easier in the way of physical comforts and conveniences than had been those of any preceding generation. For the most part, their feet were far more at home in sport shoes on the way to a game or dance than in combat boots lugging the impedimenta of war along the road to battle.

On the other hand, I had known many of this generation as soldiers, and my own children were part of it. Only recently I had seen them "swap punches with the champ", and if they had "lost the decision on points", they were supremely confident that another time they would "take him." So while I believed the average American soldier should be able to approximate these Ranger and Commando standards in preperation for battle, to prescribe such standards for an entire infantry division and then fail to attain them would cause lack of confidence, affect command relations, and be generally harmful. A wise commander does not demand results which are beyond the capabilities of his troops, or issue orders which he cannot enforce or can only enforce by that tyrannical and arbitary authority which is so repugnant to Americans.

From my observation and experience, I was convinced that our tactical principles and training methods were sound. Most of our difficulties had been due to faulty execution and inadequate standards. Throughout my service, I had heard "you young officers" blamed for everything that went wrong, and combat had been no exception. I believed that the blame was wrongly placed. Junior officers were usually willing and enthusiastic. Generally speaking, most of them were better trained than their superiors. If they did not respond with initiative and ingenuity, the fault was not wholly their own. Either, we had not trained them properly, or we had held the reins so tight that the horse could not use his head. And these were faults of command. Rank carries with it certain prerogatives, but more important, it carries also certain responsibilities. I thought then, as now, that no officer should expect to retain rank or assignment unless he fulfilled his responsibilities, or if another could fulfill them better.

Most soldiers have their own private superstitions and symbols of luck even though they may not admit complete belief in them. I always dressed for battle as I was dressed for my first one, and the three or four coins and a key which I had in my pocket, I carried throughout the war. There seemed something symbolic in returning to Port Lyautey, the place of my first battle command, to begin the preparations for my next one. It was as though the chain of experience had there been broken, and there had to be repaired. We passed over our first battle field on our short flight from Rabat, and we picked out the landmarks of that first battle with keen interest. But it was with far different emotions than those which had filled us when we beheld it first—it now seemed ages ago. There, where we had left off our first battle mission we would begin our next one.

March 8th, I signed the order assuming command of the 3rd Infantry Division. Immediately thereafter, I had my first conference with the Division staff: Lieutenant Colonel Albert Connor, G-1; Major Grover Wilson, G-2; Lieutenant Colonel Ben Harrel, G-3; Colonel Charles Johnson, G-4; Lieutenant Colonel Karl Glos, Inspector General; and Colonel Matthew Pugsley, Surgeon. Other members of the staff were temporarily absent as was Brigadier General William W. Eagles, the Assistant Division Commander. I was favorably impressed with these officers, although their constraint was apparent. Little did we realize, as we talked together that morning under the cork trees in the Forest of Mamora, the close bonds of mutual respect, comradeship, and friendship which the fires of war were to forge between us in the months that followed.

During the afternoon, I met the subordinate commanders and their immediate staffs. General Campbell I had known before. We had been instructors together in the same section at the Command and General Staff School. Between us there was already the basis of mutual respect and friendship. Colonel Thomas H. Monroe, 15th Infantry, and Lieutenant Colonel Harry B. Sherman I met for the first time. Colonel Arthur H. Rogers, 30th Infantry, was detached from the Division and under Fifth Army control at Oujda. Monroe was a very large man, considerably overweight at the time and obviously soft, although a man of real intelligence and great personal charm. I was to be very sorry to lose him a few weeks later. Sherman had only recently been transferred to command the 7th Infantry from an assignment as Executive Officer 15th Infantry, and had been recommended for promotion by the former division commander, General Anderson, as one of his last official actions. Sherman impressed me as being a dour, sarcastic type, perhaps soreheaded because others of his age and rank were already colonels. I was not favorably impressed, but first impressions are often misleading. Sherman was to be one of the best regimental and assistant division commanders I was to know in combat, and a loyal friend as well.

The loss of so many trained men as replacements for divisions fighting in Tunisia—and the 3rd Division had sent the best—together with the relative inactivity of duty in Morocco had resulted in a sort of "rear area" feeling among those left behind. In consequence, disciplinary standards had suffered and the attitude toward training lacked the fire and intensity which I had hoped to find in a division which might be called upon to fight at any time. It was far less rigorous than the training which I had observed in the division that summer at Fort Lewis. The proverb, "The devil finds work for idle hands," was peculiarly applicable and I think every officer and man looked forward with anticipation to the end of inactivity.

In most divisions at the time, the division commander and staff messed together in a headquarters mess operated by the headquarters commandant, as was contemplated in the tables of organization then in effect. This was the practice in the 3rd Infantry Division when I joined. The practice had certain disadvantages for both the commander and staff. The commander had to adjust his hours to those prescribed for general mess or cause inconvenience to both staff and mess personnel. Then, too, the presence of the division commander at meals naturally imposed some constraint upon juniors, and this was accentuated whenever the division commander entertained senior officers as it was necessary to do on many occasions. I decided to establish a separate mess for the division commander, chief of staff and aides. After a little search, Carleton found another Chinese cook, also named Lee, and three orderlies, Hong, Dare, and Wong. These splendid men were to remain with us throughout the war and were to become well known to the many officers who visited my headquarters. My mess was dubbed by them the "Canton Restaurant".

On March 10th, Carleton and I described our experiences in Tunisia to the officers of Division Headquarters and Special Troops. On subsequent days, we repeated the conference with officers of each of the infantry regiments and the Division Artillery. In these conferences we described what had happened to American troops in their first battle with the Germans, and we pulled no punches in pointing out the weaknesses in our equipment, training, leadership, and will to fight. I found every officer intensely interested in these first-hand accounts, for it was obvious to them that if we made the same mistakes we would fare no better. These conferences gave me an ideal opportunity to make myself known to every officer in the division and to tell them something of my views on training for combat, on fighting, and on the responsibilities of leadership.

I was out daily inspecting training in progress, visiting troops on outposts or observing demonstrations for French troops being trained with our equipment. I saw much, but said little, and that little usually only to officers on the subject of standards. While the movement of the 15th Regimental Combat Team to Arzew presented no problem, the training that it would have there was a vital concern to me, for my views on such training had to be known to the staff, to the regiment, and to the Invasion Training Center. All this necessitated many conferences and a visit to the Invasion Training Center. Along with this, frequent trips to Rabat were necessary to confer with the Corps concerning our preparations, and there were occasional officials and dignitaries to greet. There were interchanges of courtesies with French and native officials, both civil and military, to repair relations which had become somewhat ruffled during the previous weeks. Included was a ceremonial visit, along with French officials and other senior American officers in Morocco, to the Sultan of Morocco on the feast day celebrating the birth of Mohammed. My days were busy ones.

I had been in command for about a week when there came an opportunity for which I was waiting. A battalion on outpost about ten miles north of Port Lyautey was to be relieved within the next few days, and I had indicated that the relief was to be done by marching. Colonel Harrel came to me with the order for the relief, which I approved, and then I added: "Colonel, have that battalion march out at four miles an hour and the other return at the same rate."

Colonel Harrel looked rather startled, as though wondering whether he heard me right. "But General, infantry marches at two and a half miles an hour."

I was patient. "Yes, Colonel, I know. But I want those battalions to march at four miles an hour."

Colonel Harrel departed, obviously still concerned. In a little while he returned. In his hand he held a mimeographed pamphlet and a field manual. "Sir, I want to show you in the Field Manual and in this order where infantry is required to march at the rate of two and a half miles an hour."

This time, I was less patient, but I still spoke quietly. "Colonel, you can throw that Field Manual and that order, too, in that wastebasket there. Will you issue that order or shall I detail someone else to issue it?"

Ben issued the order of course, but he did not know that he was beginning the experiment to determine whether the average of American soldiers would bear up under rigorous physical training. When the time came, I went out toward the end of the march to inspect the battalion. All along the road were men who had fallen out, and the first aid party which followed the column was busy with cotton and adhesive tape. More than a hundred of the thousand in the battalion had fallen by the wayside. Both running and walking, the battalion had made four miles during the first hour, but had averaged less than three miles an hour for the entire march.

On the following day, the relief was effected, and next day the relieved battalion marched in. Again I went out to observe. Only twelve men had fallen out, and the battalion, of about the same strength, had averaged just under four miles an hour for the march. This battalion had been in the field for two weeks, and had been training daily over rugged sand dunes. The difference was simply a matter of physical condition. I was confident then that an average infantry battalion could approximate Ranger and Commando standards for marching, but I realized that I would have to approach the objective gradually. Officers and men would have to be imbued with the importance of such preparation and with confidence in their ability to attain it. It would be some time before each battalion could be required to attain a marching speed of five miles in one hour, four miles an hour for twenty miles, and three and a half miles an hour for distances up to thirty miles. But each battalion would attain it.

A few days after I joined the Division, General Keyes called me to Rabat concerning amphibious training. A message from AFHQ indicated that the Navy now wished to assume responsibility for amphibious training and that AFHQ was disposed to approve. I believed strongly that the Navy should be responsible for providing, maintaining, and operating all landing craft and giving Naval support of such operations, but my experience with the Navy in training for GOALPOST was too fresh in my mind for me to believe that the primary responsibility for control of training should be vested elsewhere than in the command of the troops that would fight on shore. I drafted a recommendation for accepting the proposal with reservations which would limit Navy responsibility for amphibious training to responsibility for Navy matters. It seems to have had the desired effect for it was the policy which remained in force throughout the war in the Mediterranean Theater, with eminently satisfactory results.

People at home often form conclusions which differ widely from those of soldiers engaged in combat, for opinions depend upon points of view. Archbishop Spellman visited us. He had just come from Rome by way of Spain on his way to Algiers on some high-level mission. He had visited the American cemetery at Port Lyautey where I had bowed with him in prayer for our dead and had accompanied him as he visited each grave and noted the names of Catholic soldiers so that he could write to the next of kin. At a dinner in his honor that night in Rabat, the Archbishop was seated beside General Keyes and directly across the table from me. Conversation turned to the subject of war production at home and the Archbishop held forth on the wonders of our industrial organization and the superiority of American weapons and materiel. He was surprised when I commented that our soldiers at the front would question the statement that our weapons and equipment were superior to any in the world. I pointed out that we had no weapon in Tunisia comparable to the German 88 and that the Germans had many weapons superior to ours in caliber and range. German tanks had been better armored and better armed, and Tunisian fields were littered with the improvised half-track "tank destroyers" which had been little better than death traps. I repeated the statement I had heard so often at the front "out-gunned, out-armored, out-maneuvered". The Archbishop was impressed. After dinner, we discussed the subject at length. He was scheduled to make a radio address the following day in Algiers and had been requested to mention our "superior equipment" as one his principal points. I never learned whether or not he did.

The 15th Regimental Combat Team departed for Arzew on March 13th, but I was advised that the beginning of training would be delayed for two weeks because of shortage of equipment in the Invasion Training Center.

We had been anxiously awaiting the outline plans for the invasion so that we could plan our training more effectively. On March 18th, representatives of Force 343 and Force 545 attended a meeting at Force 141 at which the outline plan was presented. General Montgomery's representatives promptly interposed objections. General Montgomery wanted a greater proportion of effort in the southwestern corner of the island. For some days there was talk of assigning the 3rd Infantry Division to the British command, although General Keyes assured me that every possible effort would be made to keep the division in Force 343. And that was the state of affairs on March 29th when my headquarters departed for Arzew.

2. *Invasion Training Center*

Training of the 3rd Infantry Division under my command actually got under way with the move to the Invasion Training Center at Arzew. We were to learn much about the capabilities of American soldiers and of an infantry division in the months that followed. The Center had been organized by Brigadier General John W. (Mike) O'Daniels whom I had known the summer before in England. O'Daniels was later to become my Assistant Division Commander, and eventually was to follow me in command of the 3rd Infantry Division when I left it the following year.

The area adjacent to the Bay of Arzew looking out over the blue Mediterranean was an almost ideal setting for such a training center. The small port of Arzew provided ample facilities for the landing craft, amphibious vehicles, and other naval support utilized in training. Other naval support was available in Oran only twenty miles away. The broad bay offered plenty of beaches for training under varied conditions, from small rocky beaches leading on to rugged mountain heights to broad flat beaches with access to open country. Inland, there was space for marching and maneuver and for facilities for training with all division weapons. The only serious drawback was in suitable impact areas for adequate training with naval gunfire.

General O'Daniels had his headquarters in the village of Port aux Poules a few miles to the east of Arzew and adjacent to one of the principal training beaches. Besides facilities for training with landing craft and with the Navy, General O'Daniels had provided all of the varied aids for training which we had observed in Commando exercises—obstacle courses, for street fighting, and the like, as well as facilities for training in the waterproofing of vehicles and equipment. Two companies of the 30th Infantry provided the School and Demonstration Troops that furnished specialists to assist in training and simulated the enemy in opposed landings and maneuvers.

The Naval command at Oran was headed by Rear Admiral John F. Hall. With him was Rear Admiral Richard L. Conolly who was destined to be my opposite number for the projected operation. Naval cooperation in every phase of training and planning was always wholehearted and complete under these distinguished officers.

General Keyes and some members of his staff came to Arzew on April 5th, just after we had begun our invasion training, and brought with them the initial HUSKY plan and the directive which was to guide my force. This, I was surprised to find, followed the initial concept for HUSKY, but the Force 343 planners assured me that General Montgomery was still bitterly opposing it.

My force was to be known by the code name ENSA. It was to consist of my own Division, one armored combat command, two regiments of paratroopers, and one Ranger battalion together with auxiliary and supporting troops. We were allotted landing craft for a shore-to-shore operation. Our mission was to land in the Mazana del Vacco-Sciacca area, capture the airfield at Castelvetrano and a landing field northwest of Sciacca and make them secure for our air forces by the evening of D Day plus 3 so that fighter and bomber aircraft could support the landing of the remainder of the command and the assault on Palermo by D Day plus five. Plans were to be submitted to the Force Commander for approval by April 30th.

Most of the Division staff and all subordinate commanders were fully occupied with training at this period, and I had no wish to distract their attention from this important function in order to plan this operation. Accordingly, I established a Planning Board much on the order of the planning syndicates we had utilized in Combined Operations Headquarters in London for this kind of initial planning and relieved this Board of all other responsibilities. It was headed by Lieutenant Colonel Albert O. Connor as Deputy Chief of Staff, and consisted of the principal assistants in each of the General Staff sections with representatives of the Division Artillery, the armored combat command, the engineer beach group, the Ranger Battalion, the airborne troops, and the Navy.

We established the Planning Board in a "War Room"—a hospital tent surrounded by wire and under constant guard—located within the Command Post where others of the staff could be kept informed of progress and where I could supervise preparation of plans. There we assembled intelligence and other information, prepared estimates and studies, and formulated plans for the operation. When the time came to produce loading and landing plans, regimental and subordinate staff officers were added to the Planning Board to assist in the work of preparation and to keep their respective commanders informed. This board was an innovation, for on the division level, division staff and subordinate commanders and their staffs had normally done such planning. But it was effective because it insured the utmost in cooperation among all of the branches and services involved and the careful and coordinated planning of an infinite number of details.

I was convinced that "speed marching", asking as it did the utmost in determination on the part of individuals to sustain the enormous

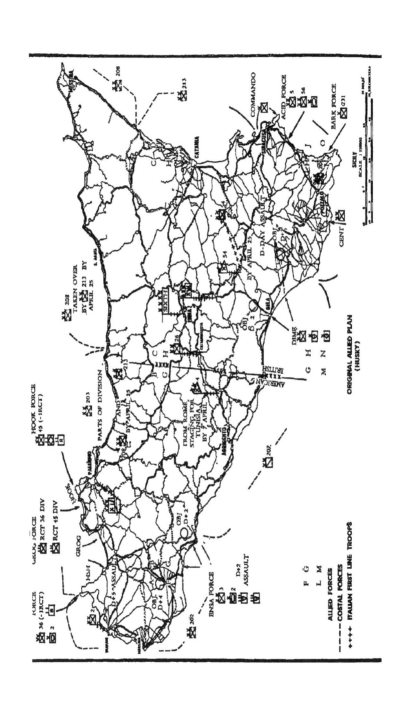

ORIGINAL ALLIED PLAN
(HUSKY)

ALLIED FORCES
— — — COSTAL FORCES
+ + + ITALIAN FIRST LINE TROOPS

SICILY
SCALE 1:250000

physical exertions, was one of the most important aids in physical and psychological preparation of men for battle. My initial experiment had indicated that our infantry battalions could approximate Ranger and Commando marching standards, but it was important that those undergoing training should have objectives which were within their capabilities. It was important, too, that those undergoing training should not consider the requirement as an unreasonable demand, but should be presented with a challenge to the competitive instinct so strong in Americans. Thus, part of the training scheduled during the two weeks at the Invasion Training Center prescribed:

Marching.

a. Full advantage will be taken of movements to and from training areas, and exercises and other opportunities to train individuals and units in *speed marching*—i.e., traversing given distances at maximum rates and arriving fit for combat. Officers and men will be instructed in techniques of speed marching and in methods of pace setting and checking for various rates of march.

> 104 steps (30″) per minutes—3 mph
> 123 steps (34″) per minute —4 mph
> 146 steps (36″) per minutes—5 mph

b. The purpose of this training is two-fold: first, development of physical condition and stamina; second, determination of standards of which units are capable.

c. As a minimum standard, every officer and man will march five miles in one hour twice each week, and 8 miles in two hours once each week. Material improvement in these standards by any company or battalion will be reported to the division commander.

Attaining these standards presented no difficulty and almost every battalion reported greater speeds during its first two weeks, reaching eventually five miles in one hour, four miles an hour for twenty miles, and three and a half miles an hour for distances up to thirty miles. It is true that some men, an average of less than four per cent, were unable to make the grade because of physical weaknesses or defects, and these were reassigned to other posts so as not to jeopardize the combat efficiency of the units or the lives of fellow comrades.

Besides speed marching, physical training included obstacle courses, log tossing, calisthenics, rope climbing, bayonet and battle courses, individual combat, and the like.

Other training at the Invasion Training Center stressed cooperation with the Navy in practice landings, both day and night, for companies and battalions. Every type of landing craft and vehicle then available, from LST's and LCT's to amphibious trucks and rubber boats, was thoroughly tested until every soldier felt completely at home on the water and in disembarking on a beach to seize an objective inland. There were schools for transport quartermasters, for Army and Navy communications personnel, for waterproofing of vehicles and equipment, in beach organization, maintenance and supply.

There was one-half hour's close-order drill daily to practice company officers in command, and men, in response. And training in antiaircraft and antitank firing, in reduction of pill boxes, in removal and passage of obstacles, in mines and booby traps which had caused so much trouble in Tunisia, and in all the countless details incident to preparation of men for battle. Other exercises stressed the coordination of all arms and the development of mutual confidence between arms, between units, and between leaders and men. Infantry worked more closely with its supporting artillery than ever before and learned to follow artillery concentrations closely, sometimes within one hundred yards, under battle conditions involving the employment of all divisional weapons. The few casualties which occurred during this training were more than justified by the mutual confidence engendered. There is no doubt that this training saved many lives in the months that followed.

The graduation exercise for each regimental combat team was a landing exercise, RAINBOW, which duplicated as closely as possible the operation allotted to the unit under the outline plans which we were developing. This exercise tested every detail of our invasion training.

To develop a sense of leadership responsibility, I never addressed any assembled unit during the training period, but I missed no opportunity to talk to groups of officers and noncommissioned officers. Over and over, I told them that fighting was a simple business in which all of their problems could be solved by common sense. We must know our weapons and tools, we must be physically conditioned, we must be disciplined to the determination to achieve, and we must know how to live and work together in the field. Over and over I told them that leaders must assume responsibility—must "stick their necks out"—and that I would permit senior officers to correct mistakes of junior officers but not to punish for honest errors of judgment. I would encourage the punishment of any leader who failed to assume responsibility.

A psychological change developed within the Division as this rugged training progressed. There was an obvious pride in attaining standards which had theretofore been considered practicable only for selected individuals, standards which a few of their own comrades had not been able to attain. Development of this individual and mutual confidence resulted in an *elan* and *esprit* which was to distinguish the 3rd Infantry Division throughout the war.

While this invasion training was going on, we selected an area for mountain warfare training in the Pont du Cheliff area, and planned a two-week course to be given to each Regimental Combat Team. It was designed to train the command in operations in mountainous terrain—not in the technique of fighting in high mountains which involves the use of specialized techniques and equipment. A representative of the Mountain Training Center in the United States assisted in preparing the program and in supervising its execution. Physical fitness remained an important consideration, and each unit was required to run one mile daily as a special conditioning exercise. Other techniques included mountain walking and marching, tactical formations for mountain fighting, combat firing for all weapons for mountainous terrain, and night and day combat exercises for operations in mountains.

It so happened that only one regiment was to complete the program of mountain training. The 15th Infantry had just completed it, the 17th Infantry was just beginning, and the 30th Infantry was still in its period of training at the Invasion Center, when there was an interruption.

On the last day of April, I was about to leave the Command Post to visit the 30th Infantry when I was called to the telephone—"Algiers calling". It was General Rooks, G-3 at AFHQ. General Alexander needed another infantry division to provide fresh reinforcements to insure the rapid destruction of the Axis forces in the final assault which was then under way in Tunisia. Was the 3rd Infantry Division in condition to go and would I like to take it there? It was and I would.

General Patton's I Armored Corps Headquarters had just moved to Mostaganem about twenty miles east of Arzew a few days before. I went there at once to inform him of this new development. He already knew it. He had just talked with AFHQ and had been directed to issue warning orders which he did forthwith and in few words.

The outline plan for ENSA had been completed only that day. To keep plans up to date, we arranged to leave my Planning Board at Mostaganem with General Patton's planners. We received the AFHQ movement orders at 2200 that night. Five hours later the 15th Regimental Combat Team was on the road.

The word "movements" had almost magical and fearful significance in British practice, and all movements of troops and supplies were closely controlled by a special staff organization known as "Q-Movements". British planners always took an extremely pessimistic view of road and rail capabilities, partly because of the nature of their equipment, and partly the nature of the road nets in their own islands. British officers were never so "motor" or "movement" minded as were Americans. And movements in North Africa were dominated by the British administrative side in AFHQ.

I had informed General Rooks that all elements of the Division would be on the road by 0900, May 2nd, and that the Division could be concentrated in an area east of Constantine by the morning of May 5th. We reckoned without "Q-Movements". Hardly was the 15th Infantry on the road when "Q-Movements" became alarmed over the possible density of our movement and fearful that we might interfere with the transportation of other troops or supplies. We were told that not more than 800 vehicles of the 3rd Infantry Division could pass any given point during any one day. I protested, but "Q-Movements" had its way, thus doubling the time required to place the Division on the road. Nevertheless, by Friday afternoon, May 7th, the Division was concentrated east of Ghardimau inside the Tunisian border.

With Carleton and my aides, I left Port aux Poules the afternoon of May 2nd, passing the 30th Infantry along the road, and reached Algiers about ten o'clock that night. The next morning I saw General Eisenhower. He told me that he had turned my Division over to General Alexander without strings, except that the Division was to be employed as a unit. The night of May 3rd we spent in the Villa Lepeca in Constantine where we had spent the months of January and February. My successor in the Advanced CP was there, Brigadier General Ray Porter, and we listened with interest to his account of events which had followed our departure. May 4th, we inspected the 7th Infantry along the road and found they were progressing according to schedule with little on the road other than our moving column. That night we spent in Headquarters 15th Army Group near Le Kef, where I reported to General Alexander.

General Alexander informed me he was attaching the Division to the American II Corps as he thought that best for reasons of morale and supply. He also told me that the HUSKY plan had now been changed, as we had feared earlier. All the effort was to be made in the southeast, but General Patton was to command the Western Task Force and my Division was to remain under his command. The change in plan had been approved by General Eisenhower and wanted only the approval of the Joint Chiefs of Staff which he was confident would be forthcoming. General Alexander wished me to send a G-3 and G-4 planner to Force 141 where his planning staff could assist in drafting my assault, but I told him I had left my Planning Board in General Patton's headquarters.

We reached the concentration area east of Ghardimau about ten o'clock the next morning. Leaving Carleton and the staff to see to the concentration of the Division, I set off to report to General Bradley, and found him about five o'clock that afternoon. General Bradley had not been warned by the First Army of the arrival of the Division and was uncertain as to his authority to employ it, but was somewhat reassured by the instructions which I had from General Alexander. We were too late for the attack scheduled for the following day, but General Bradley said he would like to relieve the 1st Infantry Division which was in his words "depleted and battle worn". With his approval, I set off at once for Ghardimau to send regimental and battalion commanders to join the 1st Division and prepare for the relief when he directed it.

The following day, May 6th, I spent inspecting elements of the Division and bringing subordinates up to date on the situation as we knew it. Next morning, as the last elements of the Division were arriving in the concentration area, I set off again for the Corps to see what could be learned. At the Corps Command Post there were reports of heavy fighting by the 1st Armored Division around Mateur. I accompanied General Bradley and his Chief of Staff, Colonel William B. Kean, forward to General Harmon's Command Post. Harmon was tired but had plenty of energy left, was driving his Division hard, and his attack was making progress. General Bradley returned to his Command Post, but I arranged to spend the night with Harmon to watch the progress of the battle.

It was then late in the afternoon. Harmon's Command Post was on an open plain north of Mateur entirely without cover. A mile or so to the east, his division engineers under heavy shelling, were struggling to repair a bridge. The running comments between Harmon and his Commanders—one combat command fighting north toward Ferryville, the other far off to the eastward, and both heavily engaged—was an exciting show well worth hearing. Harmon's language was rarely suitable for drawing room conversation.

About half-past ten that night, General Bradley telephoned me at Harmon's Command Post. He wanted to know if I could move a combat team forward at once to relieve one in the 1st Infantry Division. I told him that preparations were all made and that all we needed was to get a message through to my Command Post at Ghardimau. General Bradley undertook to have the message relayed by his staff, and I started back immediately for Corps Headquarters. I reached there about 0100 and was informed that the message had been relayed to Carleton, so I continued on to Ghardimau. I reached there about 0400, found no one moving, and wakened Carleton to find the reason. Corps had postponed the move until 0900 the following morning.

The 15th Regimental Combat Team moved out at 0900. I arranged for the Command Group to join the 15th Infantry forward and set off for the Corps Command Post and the 1st Infantry Division. An hour later, I found the most appalling traffic jam which I had ever seen. Besides the 15th Infantry which had been given priority on the road, there were battalions of French heavy artillery—GPF's—bound for I know not where. There were British engineers, British supply trucks, detachments of British troops, and even a hundred huge British trucks loaded with long sections of 6-inch or 8-inch cast iron pipe. All movement was stopped and passage even for my bantam almost hopelessly blocked. A British officer informed me that the pipe was destined for a British Naval Base at Bizerte (which was not captured for another three days). All of this was within the combat area controlled by the American II Corps. It was obvious that "Q-Movements" had slipped somewhere. Eventually I found the Corps Provost Marshal, and we located a road by which we could pass the 15th Infantry forward. All the rest he held in place on the road.

Although I visited Terry Allen at the 1st Division Command Post that afternoon and arranged details for the relief, another change was to intervene. I returned to the Corps Command Post for the night. About half-past ten, General Bradley called me. He had just talked to Harmon. Harmon believed the Boche would defend the rugged peninsula east of Bizerte, and tanks would not be able to get at them there. Infantry would be required. General Bradley wanted to know if I had enough staff with which to operate. I said yes. I was to move the 15th Infantry on forward to the vicinity of Ferryville. Corps would attach the 39th Infantry of the 9th Infantry Division then west of Mateur, the 5th Armored Artillery Group with two battalions of 105's, one battalion of antiaircraft artillery, a reconnaissance troop and some corps artillery. I was to attack as soon as possible the following morning.

I arranged for Eagles to move the 15th Regimental Combat Team forward, ordered the Command Post forward by infiltration, and arranged to have commanders, artillery commander and signal officer meet me in an olive grove south of Ferryville at 0800. My aide I sent off with a message confirming arrangements. Then I roused my driver, Barna, and set off to find Harmon.

At 0530, I found his Command Post southeast of Ferryville, waked Harmon, had breakfast with him, and found him optimistic. Then we set off to find how far forward I could assemble troops for the attack.

We went eastward along the southern edge of Lake Bizerte. A clear day, marred only by the haze of previous fighting. Across the lake to the northward, Bizerte was barely visible, still in German hands, we thought. Around the lake, the flat plain was covered with olive groves amid which tank crews and others were stirring about the business of K Rations and coffee. To our right, butte-like hills rose steeply from the road. East of the lake, a long rugged ridge extended southeastward from opposite Bizerte. This ridge—the sensitive area—was barren along the crest and upper slopes, but covered with olive trees along the lower as far as we could see. At the eastern end, we turned northward, drove on, past occasional tanks halted under the olive trees, to a point almost opposite Bizerte, then turned and retraced our route, and continued on to the southeast toward Porto Farino. Harmon's tanks were everywhere in possession of the whole peninsula except this high ridge which overlooked the sea. All was deathly still. No shot or sound disturbed the quiet of that May morning. It seemed obvious that the battle in Tunisia was all but done and that no large force would be required to clear the ridge. Before many hours had passed, we were to learn that more than fifty thousand German eyes had watched our slow reconnaissance.

Back at Harmon's Command Post I telephoned General Bradley our estimate of the situation and recommended that only the 15th Infantry continue the movement into the forward area. General Bradley approved. At my Command Post, I found the commanders waiting, informed them of the situation, and dismissed all except the antiaircraft. By noon, Harmon was receiving the surrender of the German commanders. And this about ended the active participation of the 3rd Infantry Division in the final phase of the Tunisian campaign.

One must see to believe the disintegration of a proud and mighty army following defeat in battle. Before nightfall, endless streams of once arrogant Germans were streaming past on their way to the Prisoner of War Enclosure on the plain north of Mateur where Harmon's Command Post had stood just two days before. There were no guards, only occasional soldiers posted to point them on their way like policemen directing traffic. Hour after hour all through the night and most of the following morning the movement continued. Most were on foot. Some were on horseback. Some were in automobiles and trucks. Others were in horse-drawn carts and other vehicles obviously looted from natives with whom they had come in contact. Among them, some still had an arrogant and defiant air; others seemed sullen; but for the most part there was only an air of dejection and weariness. I was glad that the soldiers of my Division could witness the results of defeat in battle.

We were assigned to guard prisoners of war and to salvage the battle field. Corps had made preparations for an estimated 10,000 prisoners of war, there were nearly 40,000. Salvage presented no great problem for the Germans had done an effective job in destroying their equipment before it could fall into our hands. There were no serviceable tanks, guns, trucks, or cars. Troops and natives had looted the area of small articles. For the most part, salvage consisted of quantities of ammunition and stocks of rations used primarily by the prisoners of war.

On May 11th, I saw General Bradley to discuss future plans, as I was becoming concerned about renewing my interrupted preparations. He informed me that the Division was to move to the Bone-Philppeville area within the next few days, just as soon as the 1st Infantry Division cleared the roads. On the following day, I attended a conference at II Corps—a meeting of all commanders down to regiments and separate battalions for orientation as to future plans and to discuss the lessons learned in Tunisia. My notes of that conference are interesting in retrospect:

> Bradley's staff summarized the lessons learned (so he said). "Stay out of natural avenues of approach; pick key terrain and concentrate, eliminate tendency to surrender; hate—teach to kill; discipline—hats, uniforms, saluting." Was not impressive from a command that has just won a glorious victory. There seem to be none of these commanders who are "telling the truth" even though it hurts—too much satisfaction with a mediocre performance. Bradley told me only yesterday that campaign showed American soldiers unwilling to close with enemy—and that was his greatest worry. It is also obvious that elements never maintained contact with Boche—that reconnaissance was defective throughout. Why not at least be honest with ourselves.

The 30th Infantry moved out on May 14th. That day I turned my back once more on Tunisia.

3. JOSS

Inasmuch as other divisions had borne the brunt of the fighting in Tunisia, it was most natural that the II Corps should have assigned to the 3rd Infantry Division the after-battle chores of guarding prisoners and battlefield salvage. On the other hand, the Division was to have an assault mission in the coming invasion, and its training had been interrupted by this movement to the front—unnecessarily, as it had turned out. While Bizerte was an ideal spot for invasion training, I welcomed the move to the Bone-Philippeville area where battle-field chores would not interfere with training. Or at least I did until I had inspected the area which had been designated for us.

It would have been difficult to find in all of North Africa an area more unsuitable for our invasion training than the area which AFHQ had selected. Located near the village of Jemmapes, midway between

Bone and Philippeville, it was back some miles from the coast along which there were no suitable beaches, only rocky ledges. Inland, the area was covered by a cork forest with a dense undergrowth of almost impenetrable brush. There were few roads and trails, and few clearings adequate for drills or training of any kind. The area might have been suitable for training in jungle warfare; it was entirely unsuited for training in landing operations, or for the kind of warfare which we might expect to encounter in Sicily. I was confident that there had been some error, and that when I explained matters to the authorities at AFHQ, we would be permitted to return to Bizerte or be assigned to a suitable area. But I reckoned without considering an important factor: staff officers have a human dislike for admitting errors and they are usually reluctant to change arrangements which they have once approved.

I protested to AFHQ. General Rooks discussed my proposal to assemble the Division in the Bizerte area, where most of it was at the time, with General Gale and his supply sections in AFHQ. They insisted that they could not supply the Division in the Bizerte area because every truck and rail ton was needed to build up supplies for the air offensive preliminary to the invasion. General Rooks said flatly that the Division would get no more amphibious training until the rehearsal for the operation. I doubted the calculations of the Chief Administrative Officer and pointed out that back in January these same officers had held that we could supply only four divisions in Tunisia, but we had ended up with twentyone. I pointed out that if the operation depended for success upon the small margin of aviation supplies represented by my 200-ton a day requirement for two or three weeks, the plan was unsound and probably impracticable. But the refusal stood, at least for the time.

Meanwhile, I had met Admiral Connally in Constantine on his way to Bizerte to reconnoiter for mounting and rehearsal areas, and had arranged to leave General Eagles in Bizerte to accompany him. Admiral Connally was anxious to establish his Naval force there as soon as possible, by June 1st if the channel between the harbor, the lake and the sea was open, as it turned out to be. It was obvious that it would be ideal to have both the Army and the Navy assault forces working together in the Bizerte area. Persistent protests, like drops of water falling upon hard stones, eventually wore down the staff resistance. On June 1st, we were ordered back.

The new HUSKY plan changed the entire assault area of Force 343 from the western end of Sicily to the northern coast in the southeastern corner of the island. None of the assault areas which had been previous-

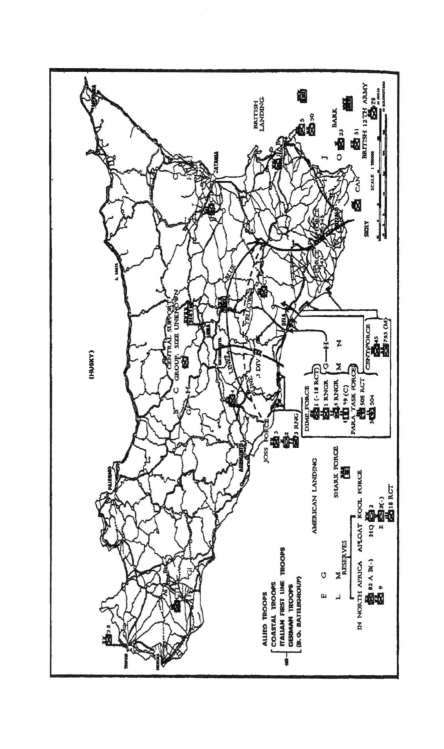

ly assigned to Force 343 were included in the new plan. Two of the areas, CENT and DIME, had been British areas in the original plan, and intelligence concerning them, including recent aerial photographs, had been assembled. The new plan included an assault area which had not been an objective area for either British or Americans in the original plan. This area, designated by the code name JOSS, had not been photographed and intelligence concerning it was extremely limited. These changes in HUSKY, brought about by General Montgomery's bitter opposition to the original plan, not only permitted the British Force to concentrate its full strength on a smaller front, but placed almost the full weight of the American assault beside it, in an area which had been considered within the capabilities of the British forces in the original plan.

General Patton's mission was to assault the southeastern portion of Sicily in conjunction with the British Eighth Army and capture it as a base for further operations. The Patton command—which was to become the Seventh Army after it had embarked for the operation—was to land and operate west of the line Pozallo-Ragusa-Vizzini, capture airfields and landing grounds and the small port of Licata, and prepare for further operations under direction of General Alexander. General Patton's plan was to make simultaneous assaults under cover of darkness on D Day in the Sampieri, Gela, and Licata areas to capture and secure the airfields and the port of Licata by D plus two, extend the beachhead to Line Yellow and establish contact with the British forces in the vicinity of Ragusa, then to Line Blue to include the high ground around Aidone and Piazza Amerina to prevent hostile interference from the Northwest.

The CENT-DIME assaults, under command of General Bradley, II Corps, were to capture and secure the airfield at Ponte Olivo by daylight D plus one, the airfield near Comiso by daylight D plus two, the airfield near Biscari by dark D plus two, extend to Line Yellow and make contact with the 3rd Infantry Division on the left.

The JOSS assault, under my command, was to capture the port and airfield at Licata by dark of D Day, extend the beachhead to Line Yellow, protect the left flank of the operation against interference from the northwest, and make contact with the II Corps on the right.

Since there were no major ports suitable for ocean-going shipping in the Force 343 area, the force was to be supplied and maintained over beaches and through the small ports for a period of at least thirty days. The II Corps was to have no administrative and supply functions other than for its own Corps troops. Supply and maintenance during this period was to be the responsibility of the CENT, DIME, and JOSS Sub Task Force Commanders.

The U. S. Amphibious Force operating procedure in effect at this time was a ship-to-shore technique based upon the employment of large ships to transport troops and equipment to an objective area. In this technique each regimental combat team was embarked in five AP (personnel) and AK (cargo) ships with each infantry battalion embarked upon one ship. Since no ship carried sufficient landing craft to disembark an entire infantry battalion at one time, craft from other ships had to be assembled so that assaulting infantry could be put ashore with sufficient rapidity. Thus, landing craft had to grope their way from one ship to another in darkness and in strange surroundings before assault battalions could go in to land. Further, all tanks, artillery, and transport had to be hoisted over the ships' sides and into landing craft for transportation to the beach. It was this procedure which had caused much of the trouble we had experienced in GOALPOST.

The proposed cross-channel invasion which we had studied in England during 1942 had been based largely upon a shore-to-shore rather than a ship-to-shore technique. The shore-to-shore operation envisaged the utilization of specially designed landing craft and smaller shipping which could lift men, weapons, and transport from one shore and disembark them on the hostile shore prepared to fight without the necessity of assembling craft from other vessels to assist in the disembarkation. This technique would permit landing troops, weapons, transport, and supplies far more rapidly and far better organized for fighting than the ship-to-shore procedure, wherever over-water distances permitted its use as was the case in the invasion of Sicily.

While specially designed landing craft and ships were in production and had been built in some quantity, they were not available in sufficient numbers to equip all of the assault forces of Force 343 for shore-to-shore operation. Nor, for that matter, were there sufficient ships to have equipped all of them for ship-to-shore. Thus it was that the 45th Infantry Division was combat-loaded in the United States even before the outline plan was known. Its tactics for the assault had to be designed to fit a landing plan which had been made before actual requirements of the situation were known. The 1st Infantry Division, embarking in North Africa for what was essentially a shore-to-shore operation, was provided for the most part with ship-to-shore ships and craft with the bulk of its vehicles loaded into AK ships.

Only JOSS Force was provided with an adequate number of craft entirely suitable for a shore-to-shore operation. Thus, the JOSS operation became the first real test of shore-to-shore operations under actual conditions of war with adequate equipment.

While I was familiar with the theories of shore-to-shore assault and had observed one at Dieppe, none of my staff had ever studied such operations until we began the HUSKY planning, for all American literature on landing operations dealt with ship-to-shore operations. For this invasion, we were planning with equipment which had never been tried under operational conditions, some of which had never been seen by the Army and Navy staffs involved. There were many problems which could only be resolved by joint study and experiment with the Naval staffs concerned. For example, LST's (Landing Ship Tank) were designed to transport tanks and other vehicles to a beach where they could drive off under their own power. LCI's (Landing Craft Infantry) were designed to transport and disembark an entire company directly upon a beach after the assault waves had landed from smaller craft. Both had been designed for use on beaches with steeper gradients than those which we would encounter, and thus would beach so far out that neither men nor vehicles could wade ashore.

There were other problems which resulted from our own inadequate study of the technique of assault landings. Personnel and equipment provided for in Tables of Organization and Tables of Basic Allowances were designed for normal operations incident to land warfare and included both personnel and equipment beyond the needs for the relatively brief period of an assault landing. Yet we had never drawn up agreed "light" or "assault" scales of personnel and equipment required for such operations, and such tables had to be devised for each individual operation.

I returned to Mostaganem on May 16th and was briefed on the outline plan and directive. My small Planning Board had been working with members of Admiral Connolly's staff and the staff of Force 343 since the change in HUSKY, and had assembled intelligence and other information then available. On May 11th, they had received the troop list for JOSS Force and the allocation of craft for transporting it, and had begun studies on the administrative and logistical organization of the force, preparation of assault scales of personnel and equipment, and, in conjunction with members of Admiral Connolly's staff, on the problems of loading and unloading the LST's and LCI's which were to carry a large portion of the force.

The troop list of JOSS Force totalled nearly 50,000 men, three times the strength of my Division, and included many units which I had never seen and which were scattered all over North Africa. Based upon a rough calculation of assault scales of personnel and equipment, less than half of this force could be lifted in the D Day assault convoy. As a basis for further planning, an order of battle for the assault had to be determined, and the order of battle in turn depended upon the tactical plan for accomplishing the mission.

Intelligence was scanty, maps old and inaccurate, and aerial photographs were poor even for the beaches in the western portion of the JOSS area which was the only one covered. From our previous studies, we knew that Sicily was prepared for defense and that beaches were protected by coast defense guns, pill boxes, wire, and other obstructions. The island was garrisoned by the Italian Sixth Army consisting of eight or ten divisions of which four or five were second class troops (Coastal Divisions), the others being rated first line Italian troops. In addition there were some 40,000 German troops on the island, chiefly around Palermo and on the major airfields. However, this enemy strength might change for better or worse during the six weeks that must elapse before we sailed on the expedition. Our plan had to accomplish the mission regardless of enemy resistance.

Information showed that there were four beaches in the Licata area but beach intelligence was too scanty to indicate that all would be practicable for landing. About five miles inland, surrounding the Licata plain, there was a range of hills ranging in height from 1,200 to 1,600 feet. The rapid capture of four critical areas in this range of hills would permit us to disembark the force and develop our full strength for the next step toward our objective. The keynote of the operation was therefore speed and momentum, and the key to speed was simplicity. Therefore, I determined to land all the infantry of the Division, with some tanks for close support, as rapidly as possible—within sixty or seventy minutes—and to hold the powerful Armored Combat Command in reserve to be landed and exploit any success attained by the initial assault as soon as it was apparent. Thus, we would use all four beaches if they were found to be practicable; if not, we would adjust our plans accordingly.

To expedite the seizure of key areas inland, each regiment was to select and train one battalion as the beach assault battalion. These battalions were to fight in the small detachments made up of infantry and engineer demolition experts which could be carried in a single craft. They were to work like hunting dogs, seeking out and engaging the beach defenses while the other battalions by-passed beach resistance and proceeded inland at top speed to seize their objectives. The Ranger Battalion, similarly trained, would land with the beach assault battalions to destroy the coast defense battery which protected the town, and then seize the port. One company of medium tanks would be landed immediately after the last battalion in each regiment, but no wheel vehicles would land until the shore parties had a full two hours for construction of beach roadway.

Such was the broad outline of the plan which I submitted to General Patton on May 19th, which he approved. We proceeded on the assumption that we would be able to use all four beaches and developed the order of battle for the assault accordingly, but we were forced to develop alternate plans, each with its order of battle, and keep these plans up to date until intelligence confirmed the practicability of all four beaches. On May 20th, I returned to Jemmapes to get on with the specialized training. The Planning Board followed two days later, and we were again established in a "War Room" tent within the Command Post, surrounded by wire, and under constant guard, similar to those precautions taken originally for the ENSA plan.

I made several important additions to the Planning Board at this time, and not the least important was the addition of a British officer. Major Robert D. Henriques, with whom I had worked in Combined Operations Headquarters in London and who had assisted General Patton's staff in the TORCH planning, had joined Force 343. With General Patton's permission, he now joined my staff. This brilliant and accomplished officer was thoroughly conversant with British shore-to-shore techniques, had wide experience in operational planning, and actual experience in assault operations from his service with British Commandos. His knowledge, enthusiasm, and cooperative spirit were invaluable to me and to the American officers with whom he worked in all of our JOSS planning.

Back in the Jemmapes area, we made the best of a bad situation. While the Planning Board continued its work on preparation of assault scales, order of battle, and the outline plan, intensive training went on. We moved the beach assault battalions to areas adjacent to such beaches as there were, constructed typical beach obstacles and defenses, and instituted exercises in the technique of engaging and reducing them, under the personal supervision of General Eagles, the Assistant Division Commander. Other units were moved about to find practicable areas for speed marching, individual combat, and combat firing. These were rigorous days for everyone.

One amusing incident illustrates the fact that the efforts of a higher headquarters to help in training may sometimes be misdirected. The British had always endeavored to rescue every flier shot down in enemy terrain and had gone to lengths in indoctrinating every soldier and airman with the will to escape if captured. Every flier was provided with an escape kit, a pocket-size affair in a plastic case containing a map printed on cloth, a compass, concentrated food, first aid materials, and even saw blades for sawing through iron bars. Some staff officer in AFHQ decided that this would be good training for all troops and teams of specialists were formed to instruct troops in such escape methods. One such team arrived at my headquarters at Jemmapes with orders from AFHQ to give such instructions to my battalions. I announced that the team could give the instruction to me first. These young officers put on their show, described how easy it was to be captured, how important it was to escape, and how to use each item of the escape kit. I then told them that I had no desire to have my men instructed in how to escape, but if they had another spiel on how not to get captured and could do it better than the Division officers, I would consider allowing them to talk to my battalions. Otherwise, they could return to AFHQ and report that I would not permit them to accomplish their mission. One of these young officers gave me a silk map of Sicily which I carried from that time on.

Meanwhile, our planning was proceeding under difficulties. My headquarters at Jemmapes was more than 600 miles, two and one-half days by road, distant from General Patton's Force 343 in Mostaganem. Force 141 was between us in Algiers, 250 miles distant from Force 343. Intelligence, information, and orders circulated from Algiers to Mostaganem, back again through Algiers and Constantine to reach the users in Jemmapes. Admiral Connolly's Naval staff was another 250 miles farther on to the east in Bizerte. Communications were slow and unreliable. Message after message went astray. We had only the intelligence and the other information we had brought from Force 343, which I described in a letter to Bedell Smith at AFHQ thus. "When the change was made from ENSA to JOSS, it so happened that British photographic intelligence covered the beaches only in the western half of my area. Outside of two copies of small-scale maps, the only map we have had is a 1:25,000 dated 1883. Beyond the ISIS (Inter Service Intelligence Studies) reports and the so-called black book furnished by Force 343, which is essentially a compilation of appropriate ISIS sections, we have received only two terrain studies, chiefly of value in confirming studies already made."

I had requested aerial photographic coverage of the area and the assignment of an aerial photographic interpreter before leaving Mostaganem. None came. I repeated the request almost daily. Eventually I was informed that the Senior Intelligence Officer (G-2) at AFHQ would not permit the photographic missions to be flown for fear of jeopardizing security and disclosing our intentions to the enemy. Then I was desperate. This photographic intelligence was essential to our planning. I remembered the Eighth Bomber Command in Constantine. I knew that they were engaged in the pre-invasion air offensive, bombing Sicilian targets almost daily; they might have aerial photographs of our particular area.

I went to see Jimmie Doolittle, then commanding the 8th Bomber Command, and explained my predicament. He called in his Chief of Staff and G-2 to listen to my tale of woe. The G-2 thought I might need help and suggested that he accompany me back to Jemmapes to see just what we had. Leaving the pilot of the Cub plane in which I had come from Jemmapes, this young bomber pilot flew me back, and spent the night in the War Room with my planners. Next morning he told me that I really did need assistance, and that he thought they could help me. They did. Photographic missions were flown by British planes based on Malta. Eighth Bomber Command requested the mission, it was flown and delivered to them within a matter of hours after its completion. Eighth Bomber Command also lent me an aerial photographic interpreter who remained with us until shortly before we sailed, when one was assigned to us by Force 141. Thus, we were able to request photographic intelligence by telephone and receive it within twenty-four hours. JOSS Force had far superior photographic intelligence for this operation than any other Sub Task Force—far better than I was ever to have again. However, it was not any better than any unit should have when preparing for such operations. We will always be grateful to Jimmie Doolittle and his Eighth Bomber Command for their contribution to our success.

With this intelligence we were soon able to complete the outline plan, prepare the order of battle, and get on with the preparation of landing and loading. Normally, the work of drafting landing and loading plans devolves upon the combat team commanders and their staffs, but time was pressing, there was a shortage of craft, and these staffs were not as experienced as the military and naval officers of the Planning Board. After consulting combat team commanders, I determined to have the landing and loading plans prepared by the Planning Board, adding to it for this purpose staff officers of the combat teams. The procedure had the advantage of producing a universal time-landing program for the Force, insuring the most efficient methods of landing on each beach, and vastly simplifying the Naval plan, not to mention freeing the combat team commanders for the more important work of training. It was eminently satisfactory to everyone concerned.

Scale diagrams were prepared for each craft assigned to the Force. Scale templets were prepared for each type of vehicle and gun to be loaded. As vehicles were fitted into craft allocated to each beach, each one was sketched in on the diagram and listed on the side of the sheet. A master landing table showed all beaches and the waves of craft allocated to land upon them together with the time of landing and the units to which they pertained. All of these were in a constant state of change until the landing plan took form, for the addition of any unit to a beach, such as a company of tanks or a battalion of artillery or a hospital, necessitated working over the diagrams and models to determine graphically how the change could be made. Along with the vehicles, the planners simultaneously provided for personnel. Thus, we were able to determine at any moment the exact state of the loading and landing plan for every craft and ship allocated to the force.

During the first week in June, we moved back to the Bizerte area, where other elements of JOSS Force soon began concentrating. We wished to have mortars in the landing craft fire grapnels as they approached the beach to remove beach and underwater wire and obstacles that might interfere with landing. We also wished to have the tanks in LCT's following the assault waves fire from the craft if the landing should be discovered during the approach. Neither had ever been done before, but joint tests during this period showed that both were praticable. Our requirements for loading personnel vastly exceeded the rated personnel carrying capacity of LST's. To find out the maximum load, we embarked eighteen officers and 450 men, with all their equipment and a complete load of 94 vehicles, on an LST together with its Navy complement, and ran a test for forty-eight hours in Lake Bizerte. We found this overload feasible without any addition to the existing mess and sanitation facilities. The soldiers rather welcomed the brief vacation from rigorous training.

We knew from experience how difficult it was to obtain information about the progress of assaults on shore. For this reason, I was determined to land a specially selected officer with a radio-equipped bantam with each beach assault battalion so that he could report progress on shore. Then Colonel Carleton, my Chief of Staff, suggested that we build a runway on an LST from which two cub planes could fly off. They would not be able to land on the LST but could land on shore behind the assault elements when their fuel compelled it. With Naval cooperation, we constructed a ramp on an LST and carried out tests in Lake Bizerte which were highly successful. Time prevented building more than one such Cub carrier, but these two planes were to play an important part in the assault.

One of my regiments, the 30th Infantry, had, with my approval, obtained about forty Arab donkeys or burros for each battalion that was to pass through the Beach Assault Battalions to seize objectives inland. The thought, which tests on land confirmed, was that having burros to carry the load of ammunition would expedite their rate of progress and free men for fighting. This regiment which loaded at Bizerte for its regimental night landing exercises, included its burros in its loading exercise, eight or ten on each LCI. This operation was completed about nightfall. While the flotilla was anchored in Lake Bizerte, Admiral Conolly visited the fleet at anchor. I learned of his visit when Admiral Conolly telephoned me in my Command Post in the olive groves just south of the lake. The conversation—over a wire that was almost sizzling when I picked up the telephone—was about as follows:

"General"—the Admiral's voice was choking with anger. "I am astounded to find that you have taken advantage of me. I thought that we were working together. Now what do I find? You have loaded a bunch of damn mules on my ships. And you have done it without saying a word to me!"

I was rather taken aback. I tried to explain.

"Admiral, with all of our discussions of these plans and with the joint staffs working together in your headquarters, it had never occurred to me that you were not thoroughly familiar with this detail. I know that your planners are familiar with it, and if Rogers' opposite number had not approved, he could not have loaded them. If I have failed to mention it to you, it is simply an oversight which I deeply regret."

The Admiral was in no whit mollified, for I had violated the tradition of livestock on Navy ships.

"General, you have taken advantage of my spirit of cooperation. You are making a cavalry stable out of my ships. I will be the laughing stock of the Navy. The unsanitary mess will endanger your soldiers as well as the sailors. I am surprised at you. I won't stand for it."

I thought hard—and fast.

"All right, Admiral. I certainly had no intention of taking advantage of you, for no two men have ever worked together better than we have done so far. I regret more than I can say that I have not discussed this detail with you, but I can only assure you that it has been an oversight. You command the ships. You don't want to carry the burros, so I will have them unloaded."

The Admiral was most formal.

"Very well, General. I am glad that you agree."

"But, Admiral, I don't agree. I have assumed that you were to land us complete with all of our weapons prepared to fight. Those 'mules' as you call them are actually weapons which we think we need to accomplish this assault. You don't want them on your ships. I am going to have them off. But what I am wondering now is what I shall do tomorrow if you should object to carrying infantry mortars, or tanks, or any other item of equipment which the Navy does not usually transport."

There was silence for a full minute. I could almost hear the Admiral thinking. Then he spoke again, all anger now gone from his voice.

"Dammit, General, you are right. We will carry the goddam mules and anything else you want carried."

Admiral Conolly was more than as good as his word. This was the only approach to a rift that ever occurred in our relations. No Army commander ever had a Navy opposite number more able than Admiral Connolly. "Push 'em up Closer," the 3rd Division dubbed him, and this same spirit permeated every Army and Navy echelon.

JOSS Force was more than three times the size of the infantry division, and it was responsible for its own supply and maintenance for at least thirty days. It was obvious therefore that a rear area supply depot, maintenance unit, and administrative organization far beyond that of an infantry division and comparable to that of a Field Army, but on lesser scale, would be required. All of this had to be improvised, and this work fell upon the capable shoulders of Colonel Charles E. Johnson, the Division G-4.

The organization that evolved comprised a Force Depot, the Beach Group, and an Administrative Headquarters which we termed Near Shore Control. The Force Depot consisted of all personnel, supplies and equipment required to maintain the force for the designated period. It was assembled initially in the Bizerte area and moved over after the assault in accordance with our plans. The Beach Group unloaded craft over the beaches and established the initial supply dumps which were expended into the Force Depot on the Sicilian shore. The Near Shore Control exercised authority over the movement of personnel, supplies, and equipment from the Bizerte area after the Division was established in Sicily. Under Colonel Richard L. Creed, whom I had obtained from England, it worked closely with the Eastern Base Section and with the Naval Base at Bizerte. We established excellent radio communications between the Division and the Near Shore Control at Bizerte so that changes in priority of loading, notifications of sailing, and requests for supplies and equipment were handled quickly and effectively. I was to learn much later that this channel also provided AFHQ with most of its information during the early stages of the assault—but that is another story.

Cooperation between Army and Navy staffs was a model of unified team work but there was one important omission—the complete lack of participation by the Air Forces on our level and almost complete lack of participation at any level below that of the high command. I had requested over and over again an air planner to assist and advise us. None ever came, nor did any air officer or adviser ever visit my headquarters with the exception of those 8th Bomber Command officers who helped us out with photographic intelligence. Considering that our supply convoys were scheduled to sail every four days, and that no air planner was available to work with us during this period, it is a tribute to Colonel Johnson and his able assistants that the air force supplies and materials were ever moved at all.

A pre-D Day bombing schedule for targets within the assault areas was eventually evolved by the higher levels and we were informed of targets which were to receive attention. But when we sailed for the operation, we had no information as to what, if any, air support we could expect on D Day. We had no knowledge of the extent of fighter protection we would have. We sailed ignorant of when, where, in what numbers, or under what circumstances we would ever see our fighter protection. There was a statement in the Air Plan submitted for HUSKY that after D Day commanders could put forward requests for air support to a Target Committee in North Africa but that none would be considered on less than twelve hours' notice.

It was fortunate for HUSKY that the Allied Air Forces had achieved almost complete air superiority in the battle area and that our casualties from enemy air action were relatively light during the assault and following operations. But there is no doubt that this lack of air participation in the joint planning at every level was inexcusable. And it is probable that it was a factor in the unfortunate misunderstanding which led on D Day to the shooting down off Gela and Sampieri of transports bearing paratroops of the airborne division.

Early in June, the Division was still more than a thousand men under strength as replacements had not been available to fill the places of men transferred to the 1st and 34th Infantry Divisions some months earlier. AFHQ finally decided to have the 34th Infantry Division, which was not destined to take part in HUSKY, provide replacements to fill the assault divisions. General Charles W. (Doc) Ryder visited me to arrange this transfer. He was loud in his praise of the 1,500 men he had received from the 3rd Infantry Division and assured me that he would permit all former 3rd Infantry Division men to return to the Division if they wished, but he pointed out that a great many of them had received one or more promotions. Some might wish to remain in their assignments; others we might not be able to utilize in their increased ranks. Both turned out to be the case, although several hundred old Division men did elect to return.

At the end of the Tunisian campaign, there was an inexplicable rumor, started no one knew how or when, which spread the word like wildfire through the 1st and 34th Infantry Divisions that these divisions had done their share of fighting in the Tunisian battles and were to be sent back to the United States while other divisions took their places. It had been rife during the days we had spent in the Bizerte area immediately following the Tunisian campaign. Among these men who had survived the tensions and dangers of these long hard months, there was a feeling of relief and anticipation that beggars description —as though for them the war was over. And this belief persisted in spite of every effort on the part of every responsible headquarters to disabuse their minds. When these divisions found that one of them was to take part in HUSKY as an assault division and that the other would furnish men as replacements to other divisions which would take part—that they were not going "home"—there was an intense reaction among them that required stringent measures to control.

Most of the replacements assigned to the 3rd Infantry Division at the time were of this category. Few wanted to take part in any operation whatever. More than half of them had no wish to join the 3rd Infantry Division. All of them wanted to go home. A few days after the transfer had been effected and the men absorbed into our own units, Colonel Pugsley, the Division Surgeon, reported to me a case of self-maiming. One of the replacements had "accidentally" shot himself through the hand while cleaning his weapons, but there were of course no witnesses. Next day, two or three such cases were reported, each one among the replacements and each one occurring with no witnesses to prove that it was other than accidental. I became alarmed.

Men who have fought as long and bravely as these men had done were not necessarily cowards. They had been subjected to the physical and psychological strain of exposure to danger in a long campaign. The emotional strain caused by their recent disappointment had brought them to a point of mental unbalance where they had temporarily lost all sense of moral values. I was confident that most of them regretted the act as soon as committed. On the other hand, there were thousands of other men under my command who had been subjected to the same intense physical and psychological strains and were now keyed to a high point of battle tension. Incidents like these can infect a command like a contagious disease, and I was alarmed that this epidemic of self-maiming might spread—even among the older men of the Division. Drastic measures were necessary.

I called a conference of subordinate commanders with my judge advocate present. Each officer was already doing everything possible to prevent recurrence. It seemed to me that the surest measure of control would be to convict one case and publish a long sentence to the entire command with appropriate ceremony. I directed that every effort be made to make the next incident a court martial case. One occurred that same night. Charges were prepared by the judge advocate. A selected general court martial was convened at once. The case was tried without delay, and a sentence of fifty years in prison imposed. Within a matter of hours after trial, I had approved the sentence and it was read with due formality to every member of the command that same day. Personally, I had no doubt that the sentence might be reduced by higher headquarters, but it had served my purpose. There were no more cases of self-maiming in the command. I am confident that by this rapid application of military justice, we had prevented many fine young American men from a disgraceful deed which they would regret so long as they lived, even if they should escape punishment for it.

During the final weeks of preparation, there was a constant flow of high-level visitors, to inspect troops, training, plans and preparations. When General Eisenhower visited me, he thought that I might need another general officer. I suggested that Brigadier General John W. O'Daniels from the Invasion Training Center be attached for the operation, and discussed with General Eisenhower how he would be utilized within the command. General O'Daniels arrived a week or so later with orders from AFHQ indicating that he was to be second in command. In a letter to General Smith concerning this matter I wrote:

> That would be a slap in the face for Campbell and Eagles which I certainly do not believe is warranted. I discussed the matter with the Chief when he was with me. He told me he had sent O'Daniels to me because he thought I needed another general officer and that I was to use him as I saw fit. Accordingly, I shall use him for the assault phase but I shall not change the order of rank in command succession at this time. O'Daniels' rugged qualities will be of the utmost value in this operation. If anything should happen to me, I would recommend that a major general, such as Keyes, Harmon, Eddy, or Ryder, be sent on as soon as possible. Such action will cause far less disruption in organization. I have a good staff, well organized, and with the general officers remaining, they should be able to put such a commander into the picture without difficulty and without jeopardizing the operation.

> "I discussed all this with General Keyes, who informed General Patton. I also informed him that I had discussed the matter with the Chief. I think that you should know about it.

Our final three weeks of rigorous training culminated in the full-scale dress rehearsal: Operation COPYBOOK, which was so realistic that most of the soldiers actually believed the invasion was under way until morning found them still landing on North African beaches. It brought to light some faults which we were able to correct, and it generated full confidence among the soldiers in the ability of their Navy comrades to land them on proper beaches according to plan. Afterwards intensive training ended, drill hours were shortened, and more time was allowed for recreation, although speed marching and physical conditioning were continued to maintain the high physical standards which we had now attained.

Never was any division more fit for combat and more in readiness to close with the enemy than the 3rd Infantry Division when we embarked for the invasion of Sicily. On the evening of July 3rd, just at sunset, I addressed the assembled officers of the command, reviewed with them the results of our preparations, our readiness for our great adventure, and emphasized once more that the degree of our success depended upon their leadership. It was a solemn moment and few speakers have ever had a more attentive audience. The following day, July 4th, I addressed every member of the command in seven different formations. That evening, we boarded the *Biscayne*, the headquarters ship for the Force, from which we watched the progress of embarkation. The first element of the Force sailed on the morning of July 6th. The following afternoon, the *Biscayne* sailed out through the channel to take her place in the formation for our great adventure.

The question of command is always a delicate one where more than one service is concerned, and it is even more so when all services of several nations are involved. Most of the concern, however, occurs at the higher levels. At lower levels commanders are usually too preoccupied with common problems to worry very much about who gets credit for commanding this or that. During all the preceding weeks neither Admiral Connolly nor I had ever referred to the command question. Both of us were determined that we would work together smoothly and without friction and that every echelon of our respective commands should do likewise. It was not until we had weighed anchor and taken our station in the convoy that the subject was brought up. I had just joined Admiral Connolly on the quarterdeck, when he turned to me and said:

"General, you are in command of this expedition. I know what the orders say, but so far as I am concerned, you are in command. Our job is to help you in every way we can. I will carry out any order you issue, and I will continue to do so until you notify me that you do not require us any longer."

To say that I was surprised by this gallant and selfless remark would be an understatement. My reply was inadequate.

"Admiral, I can't tell you how deeply I appreciate your spirit of cooperation. So far as I am concerned, there will never be any question of command between us. You are in command at sea, and I know that you will stay with us until the assault succeeds. We have worked together in harmony so far, and we will continue to do so."

We shook hands, and the subject was never again referred to between us. It has always seemed obvious to me that landing operations which are a step in a land campaign should be the responsibility of the commander who must fight on shore. But this incident illustrates that the personalities of commanders concerned and their ability to work together toward the common end is far more important than the phraseology contained in any order.

Our three types of craft, LCI's, LST's, and LCT's, each had a different sailing speed. In consequence, each group sailed with its naval escort by different routes, all routes initially leading off to the southeast for purposes of deception. The first convoy of LCI's sailed the morning of July 6th and stopped over briefly at Sousse where soldiers disembarked and stretched their legs in a speed march. The other two convoys sailed the morning of July 8th from the anchorage at Bizerte, the LCT convoy taking a shorter course which would permit them to rendezvous with the others during the late afternoon of July 9th off Gozo Island near Malta.

Our first day was clear and the blue Mediterranean was peaceful and serene. On the *Biscayne*, we held a short command post exercise during the morning, but for the most part, we rather enjoyed relaxing after our weeks of strenuous work.

At 0315 the morning of July 9th, "general quarters" sounded. I dressed hurriedly and joined the Admiral on the quarterdeck. Seemingly, there had been an air alert of sorts, but nothing happened. However, there was another cause for alarm. The wind was rising and the seas were becoming rougher by the hour. This unseasonal storm worried everyone, for the landing craft which were carrying 60,000 or more soldiers and sailors to battle had never been tested under such conditions. As the day wore on, the wind increased in force and the seas became higher and higher. The flat-bottomed, broadnosed landing craft were buffeted about; breaking waves drenched everyone and everything on board. We wondered whether or not the craft could withstand the storm. For the Admiral and me, there was an additional cause for worry. The storm caused a reduction in speed, and this was of grave concern to the LCT's. At their best speed, they could barely make the rendezvous on their prescribed course. At half speed there was doubt that they could even reach the assault area in time for the assault.

But Admiral Connolly was equal to the occasion. Calling in a destroyer, he directed a change in course for the LCT's. Then as the seas increased and further reduced their speed, he changed their course again until they were sailing direct for the objective area. Reduced at times to no more than two and a half knots, these great flat-bottomed open craft plowed steadily on and arrived in the transport area only just in time to continue on to the beaches. The other flotillas made the rendezvous off Gozo Island late in the afternoon and headed on for the transport area off the Licata beaches. And every craft was loaded with sea sick, sea weary, and thoroughly drenched soldiers who asked no more than a beach on which to land! Fortunately, as night came on the wind abated and the sea subsided, although it was still rougher than we would have liked to see.

Our mission depended upon the early capture of Campobello and Palma di Montechiaro. The approaches to both lay to the west of the Salso River which bisected the Licata plain, as did the airfield which we were to capture. Other dominant features in the landing area were the semi-circular range of hills several miles inland which encircled the plain, and a rugged hill—Monte Sole—several miles in length just west of the town on which there was a fortification and a coastal battery. East of the town the beaches were broad, and except for shallow gradients, excellent for landing. West of the town, the single beach was narrow and backed by almost vertical cliffs which were not of excessive height but through which there were only two rather indifferent exits inland.

If we landed the entire force on the good beaches east of the town and opposition was effective, there was danger that the enemy might defend the river line and delay our capture of the port and airfield as well as our advance toward Campobello and Palma di Montechiaro. Consequently, our plan was to land two Regimental Combat Teams (less one battalion) on the good beaches east of the river; one RCT on the indifferent beach west of the river; and the Ranger Battalion and one infantry battalion in two small rock-bound coves near the western end of Monte Sole.

The 30th RCT was to land on Blue Beach, advance rapidly inland and seize the hills overlooking the plain from the Salso River to the sea on the east side.

The 15th RCT (less one battalion) was to land on Yellow Beach, seize the bridge and the hills overlooking the Salso River, and assist in capturing the town and port.

The Ranger Battalion and the 2nd Battalion 15th Infantry were to land on Green Beach, capture Monte Sole including the fort and coastal battery, and seize the port and town.

The 7th RCT was to land on Red Beach, advance rapidly inland and seize the hills overlooking the plain which covered the approaches to Campobello and Palma di Montechiaro. After the capture of the port and airfield, the 15th Infantry was to take the route to Campobello, the 7th RCT that toward Palma.

Combat Command A, in floating reserve, would land as soon as possible on the first available beach in readiness to advance to the northwest.

Every possible provision had been made for naval support. Support Groups of cruisers and destroyers were ready to fire on call on prearranged targets and on targets of opportunity. Support landing craft accompanied the landing waves to fire on targets of opportunity and to fire grapnels across wire to open up passage. Every possible infantry

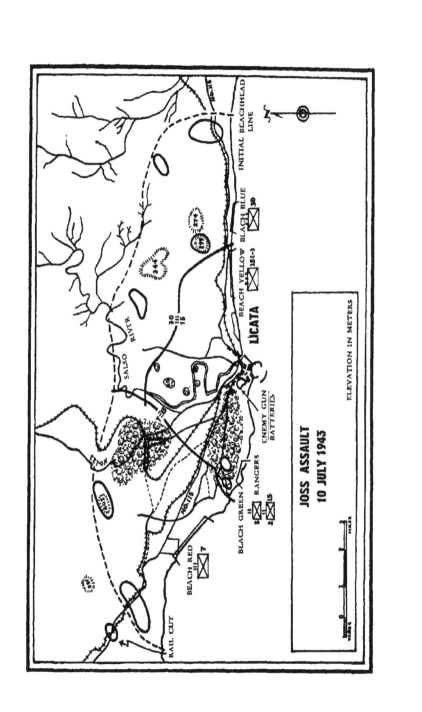

JOSS ASSAULT
10 JULY 1943

ELEVATION IN METERS

weapon in the assault battalions was prepared to fire as the battalions approached the beaches, as were all tanks and self-propelled artillery. Every possible antiaircraft weapon—40 mm, 37 mm, 20 mm, and machine guns—had been mounted on the upper decks for antiaircraft fire. These battalions were prepared to fight their way ashore.

At 0135, that morning of July 10th, the *Biscayne* dropped anchor a few thousand yards off shore between Yellow and Green Beaches. We could see little, but we assumed that our flotillas were in their areas and preparing to disembark, otherwise commanders would have broken radio silence to report. All was quiet on the quarterdeck of the *Biscayne*, for each one was concerned with his own thoughts. Mine turned back to other transport areas in the final moments before assault —to Dieppe and French Morocco. In GOALPOST, our plans had been hastily prepared, our troops inexperienced, and confusion had surrounded all of our preparations. Here we had planned carefully, troops were experienced and in a high state of training, and cooperation had been complete with most everybody concerned. What was to be the result?

Just at 0200, off to the east in the direction of Gela where DIME Force would soon be landing, there was a flash of guns, the flare of bursting shells, and streaks of light as searchlights swept the sky. Later, we were to learn that this activity was for the most part enemy antiaircraft searching for the airplanes which were carrying our paratroopers inland. At the time, we thought the battle was on and that surprise was lost.

Suddenly, two searchlights on Monte Sole flared and swept seaward in a wide arc, joined almost at once by two others behind the eastern beaches. All swept slowly inward and came to rest with the *Biscayne* focused in their beams—four great searchlights and the distance less than 7,000 yards. A command rang out over the *Biscayne's* loudspeaker.

"Stand by to shoot out searchlights!"

And there was a clatter of activity about the *Biscayne's* guns. I protested to Admiral Connolly that we should wait until enemy guns actually fired, for the support craft off the beaches and landing craft moving shoreward were clearly visible but had not been fired on. Admiral Connolly agreed, and rescinded the order. And there we stood silhouetted in the searchlight beams, so bright on deck that one could read a book. It was an uncomfortable period—momentarily expecting the blast of coastal guns. But no shots came. Then one by one the lights went out and only one remained. It shifted shoreward and focused upon a guide boat just off Green Beach. Still no shots came, and the last light flickered out. Once more the coast was dark. Unbelievable as it seemed, we had stood focused in their beams for twenty minutes!

Then off to the westward, the thunder of naval guns broke the silence. It was the cruisers *Brooklyn* and *Birmingham* and their accompanying destroyers bombarding the coast off Agrigento in a diversion planned for deception.

H Hour—0245—came and passed. Off to the east toward Gela, antiaircraft guns still flashed now and then as enemy aircraft dropped flares over the fleet off shore. Where we were all was darkness. We knew that the Licata area was prepared for defense. Every beach was organized with pill boxes, beach obstacles, barbed wire entanglements, trenches, fortified blockhouses, antitank ditches and mines. There were rifle pits, machine gun positions, antiaircraft guns, and emplaced artillery. Would the garrison be standing by their guns awaiting our approaching craft? These were trying moments for commanders who could only wait!

Then the flotillas reported that all were present and the battalions on their way to the beaches. More waiting. Then came the characteristic flash of rifle and machine gun fire along the beaches and the flash of bursting shells. The assault battalions were on shore and about their work. Soon reports were in from all except Green Beach; no word came from there nor could we contact either the commander or liaison officer by radio. But at 0440, we reported to General Patton that our battalions were all on shore.

About 0500, when the shore line was barely visible through the haze of a breaking dawn, there had still been no report from Lieutenant Colonel Brady at Green Beach, except the Naval report that troops had landed. Then we ordered off one of the Cub airplanes from our improvised LST carrier to locate the Rangers and the infantry battalion on Monte Sole. Through a misunderstanding, both airplanes took off. Shortly one pilot reported that he could see troops climbing the hill and approaching the fort. For more than two hours, these two pilots, First Lieutenants Oliver P. Soard and Julian W. Cummings, flew back and forth over the battle area reporting the locations of our own troops and spotting artillery positions which were soon silenced by naval gunfire.

Soon after daylight, the *Biscayne* got under way and stood in close to shore so that we could see the beaches. All was quiet on the Blue and Yellow Beaches, craft were discharging cargoes, and those on shore seemed to be going about their business. As we approached Red Beach, the flotilla of LCT's was standing out to sea with their load of tanks and guns still on board. When Admiral Connolly signalled the flotilla to halt, the commander reported that he had been turned back by the beachmaster because the beach was still under artillery fire and it was not safe to land. Needless to say, we received this reason with ill grace. Admiral Conolly soon ordered them in to unload, sending craft in to screen the beach with smoke. We lay off shore until the tanks were landing and then turned back to Yellow Beach where I went ashore with my command group.

With the exception of a slight delay in the hour of landing occasioned by bad weather, the JOSS assault had gone almost exactly as we had planned it. Careful planning and preparation, rigorous and thorough training, determination and speed in execution, had paid dividends in success. In spite of searchlights and all the activity along the coast, our assault battalions had landed before they were discovered and had quickly cleared the beaches of all resistance. In little more than an hour, ten infantry battalions including the Rangers with supporting tanks had landed and were about their business. In seven hours, these ten battalions with their supporting tanks and artillery had seized their first day's objectives and were pushing reconnaisance far out to the front. In seven hours, the airfield, town and port were in our hands, beaches and port were organized, and additional troops and supplies were flowing ashore in steady streams. All beach resistance had been smothered by the speed and violence of the assault and more than 2,000 prisoners were taken. Our own casualties were little more than a hundred. With evident pride, more than one officer and man remarked to me that "fighting the battle was a damn sight easier than training for it."

But there was never a pause. By noon, July 11th, within thirty hours of our landing, we were everywhere on the Yellow Line, our D plus three objective. The 15th had taken Campobello, the 7th Palma di Montechiaro, both after brisk fights in which organized German resistance was first encountered. A battalion of the 30th was advancing cross-country to Riesi, and an armored column from the 30th was fighting its way along the coastal road to make contact with the II Corps at Gela, which it did about 1400, reporting to General Patton in person. This armored patrol, consisting of a platoon of tanks, two platoons of the Regimental Cannon Company, and a platoon of infantry led by Major Lynn D. Fargo, fought its way through three enemy positions, destroyed three batteries of artillery, and took more than 550 prisoners. Combat Command A had occupied Naro and had assembled northeast of the town. By nightfall, contact had been established between all elements along our fifty mile front and every unit was pressing reconnaissance to the front to maintain contact with the withdrawing enemy.

Other than "protecting the left flank of the operation against interference from the northwest", my instructions did not extend beyond the Yellow Line, nor, for that matter, did General Patton's. We had established a firm base. The next phase under General Alexander's

Force 141 (15th Army Group) overall plan was "to conduct operations for the capture of Augusta and Caltanisetta and the Gerbini group of airfields", after which the final phase would be "the reduction of the island." But no orders had been issued for these operations. Caltanisetta and Enna are the important communications centers that dominate the center of the island and control the approaches leading on to the Catania plain. It seemed likely that General Patton would be ordered to seize them, in which case that might be our direction of advance. During the afternoon of July 11th, I had directed General Rose to make reconnaissances and preparations to capture Canicatti. General Keyes, General Patton's deputy, visited us during the morning of July 12th. He had no further information, but he was sure that General Patton would approve our taking Canicatti. Accordingly, I telephoned Rose to get on with the attack.

General Rose set the hour for 1330. General Keyes, Major Henriques, and several others went out to watch the operation. The Germans held a ridge along the southwestern outskirts of the town with infantry, about forty tanks, and artillery. Rose had three battalions of artillery in position within a few thousand yards of the German position. Rapidly deploying his battalion of armored infantry and two battalions of tanks, he launched his assault under heavy fire and quickly drove the Germans off to the north of the town. Henriques and I, seeking a better observation post, had a narrow escape when we were caught in the impact area of a salvo of German artillery. Rose occupied the town about three o'clock, General Keyes and I following him in. I had already directed the 15th Infantry to relieve CCA when the town was taken, whereupon CCA was to assemble in reserve at Campobello, reconnoiter toward Caltanisetta, and be prepared to advance in that direction, all of which was completed by the following day.

By nightfall, July 12th our third day ashore, all vehicles were ashore, all units reorganized, more than 7,000 tons of supplies unloaded, the Force Depot in full operation, and more than 4,000 prisoners had been evacuated to North Africa.

My pride in this 3rd Infantry Division knew no bounds, but even the best troops need some prodding. During the second day ashore when the 15th Infantry was advancing toward Campobello, I went forward to see how things were going. I found Colonel Johnson along the road waiting for reports from a battalion he had sent to attack Campobello from the east. There had been two delaying actions during the morning in which several German and Italian tanks and self-propelled guns had been destroyed, but the advance was continuing. Leaving Colonel Johnson, I proceeded on forward along the column. I had not gone more than a mile when I made a turn in the road and found the column halted and men prone in the roadside ditches. I asked the first noncommissioned officer I saw: "Why are you hiding in the ditch?" His rather sheepish reply was: "Sir, I don't know." I soon found a company commander and repeated the question. He informed me that they had been fired on from the woods off to the right and were taking cover. How much firing? Well sir, not very much, we heard three or four shots. No, he had not sent out patrols to see what was there. Why wasn't he advancing? Sir, he was waiting for orders. He was very quickly impressed with the fact that battles are not won by lying in ditches. He soon had a patrol on the way to scout the woods, and was under way again.

A mile farther on almost on the outskirts of Campobello, I came up with the advance party, perhaps a dozen men. Some hundred yards off to the left, where the rest of the company had deployed to clear out some resistance, firing was rather brisk. Over to the east, there was an open field between the town and the woods to the south, broken only by a few scattered trees. While I was looking across this field rather hoping to see Johnson's battalion emerge and attack Campobello, a column of about seventy soldiers emerged from the woods to the south advancing toward the town. No one paid much attention to them; at the distance of a few hundred yards, I took them at first glance to be Americans. The whole group was in the open and the head of the column was approaching the first building, when I looked through my field glasses and saw that they were not Americans. Others noted it at the same time, and the machine gun opened fire. Soon everyone was firing. Colonel Johnson, who had joined me, seized a rifle from a soldier, and joined in. Men fell, others started to run, then plunged forward, others scattered and sought cover, all very much like a startled covey of quail. Those nearest the buildings reached the cover of the town and the action was over as quickly as it had begun. It was not until the action was almost over that Sergeant Barna called my attention to the fact that the Germans were firing at us too. I had stood in the middle of the road absorbed in watching the brief action.

Later, when Colonel Johnson resumed the advance and moved on into the town, I went over to look at the scene of action. A dozen or more Germans lay dead, a number of wounded were being cared for by American aid men, and several prisoners were being marched off. It was the first time I had seen Germans killed by infantry fire in front line action.

During the day of July 13th, CCA assembled near Campobello and began reconnaissance to the outskirts of Caltanisetta. The 7th Infantry reconnoitered northward toward Serra di Falco, and the 30th Infantry moved from the east flank to the vicinity of Naro.

Several days before sailing we had been informed that a few correspondents were to be attached to the Division for the operation, but at the time we sailed none had reported to my headquarters. After we were under way I learned that several were on board, attached to Admiral Connolly's Headquarters to cover the Naval aspects of the landing. During the voyage, I briefed these gentlemen on our assault plans. When I went ashore, there were, so far as I knew, no correspondents with any part of the JOSS Force on land.

We had been fighting on shore for three days when Carleton told me he had a report that a correspondent was wandering around the 7th Infantry area. We had no instructions from Army concerning this correspondent. He had not checked in at Division Headquarters. We did not even know who he was. I sent the Division Provost Marshal out to arrest him and bring him in for an accounting. Then I had a surprise.

General Eagles, my assistant division commander, brought him in to me and introduced him. He was Michael Chinigo, INS correspondent. He was properly accredited to the Division, but had not reported to Division Headquarters because he wished to land with a combat unit and was afraid that we would not permit it. He had therefore gone to the loading pier and had climbed on board an LCI, finding himself with Colonel Sherman's 7th Infantry.

Eagles and Sherman both reported that Chinigo had landed with the 7th Infantry under fire and had distinguished himself during the action on the beach and the advance inland. When the 7th Headquarters reached the railroad station a kilometer or so inland, the telephone was ringing. Chinigo, speaking perfect Italian, answered. Agents at some inland town had heard that the Allies were landing, but Chinigo assured them that conditions in the area were entirely normal. Subsequently, Colonel Sherman recommended that Chinigo be awarded the Silver Star for his gallantry during this landing. This was approved in Washington. Several months later, I was to have the pleasure of pinning the decoration on him.

Chinigo accompanied the division throughout the Sicilian campaign. He was the first correspondent to enter both Palermo and Messina. His early dispatches, cleared at AFHQ, were a principal source of information there as to the progress of the campaign during the early days of the landing. We became close friends. His intimate knowledge of Italians and of Italy was to be invaluable to me.

General Patton paid us his first visit, after the landings, just before noon, July 14th, and told us something of future plans. All landings, both British and American, had been successful; the only serious threat had been the German counterattack in the Gela area on D plus one and

D plus two in which German tanks had approached to within 1,000 yards of the 1st Division beaches. These counterattacks had been repelled and considerable numbers of German tanks had been destroyed, whereupon the II Corps had resumed its advance and had taken its objectives on schedule. On the right, General Montgomery's Eighth Army had taken Augusta and was advancing against moderate resistance. For the next phase in the operation, the effort of the Seventh Army was to be shifted to the north toward Palermo, which pleased General Patton very much for he had long been preoccupied with Palermo, the largest city and most important port in Sicily. However, until the Eighth Army reached the line of Catania-Enna, the Seventh Army was to conform to its movements, securing the line Caltanisetta —Palma di Montechiaro to protect Montgomery's left flank, a passive mission which did not appeal to General Patton.

General Patton remarked to me that the Army would need the port of Porto Empedocle for the drive toward Palermo. He would like to establish a base there now, but he had orders not to attack Agrigento, which protected the port, for fear of becoming involved in a heavy battle and risking exposure of the flank of the Eighth Army. I told General Patton I was confident that we could take Agrigento without too much trouble if he gave the word. He reminded me that he had specific orders not to attack the place, but was "extremely anxious to have that port." I suggested that the high command would probably have no objection to my making a reconnaissance in force toward Agrigento on my own responsibility. General Patton, with something of the air of the cat that had swallowed the canary, agreed that he thought they would not. General Patton departed immediately after lunch, and I set the wheels in motion.

> Reconnaissance is the operation carried out by troops in the field for the purpose of gaining information relative to the enemy or the terrain and the resources of the theatre of operations. . . .

> Reconnaissance in force sometimes constitutes the best means of clearing up an uncertain situation. . . . For the troops engaged in the operation, reconnaissance in force usually consists of a local attack with a limited objective. (Field Service Regulations)

The operation I had in mind was to be a "reconnaissance in force" for the object was "to clear up an uncertain situation," and for the troops engaged it would consist of "local attacks with a limited objective." However, I hoped to maneuver these troops into a position in which their "local attacks with a limited objective" would "clear up the situation" by bringing about the capture of the places in question. If we were successful, no one would then object. If not, we would have gained valuable information.

Accordingly, the mission was assigned to Colonel Sherman and his 7th Infantry, with the 10th Field Artillery, one battalion of the 77th Field Artillery Regiment, and the 3rd Ranger Battalion attached. Next day, as units could be moved into position, we attached the remainder of the 77th Field Artillery Regiment, and two battalions of Armored Field Artillery, the 58th and 65th. This was the "force." Sherman was to move to an assembly area in the vicinity of Favara and develop the situation near Agrigento. It was my thought that the battalions of the 7th Infantry would surround Agrigento with as little fighting as possible while the 3rd Ranger Battalion worked its way into the port. Since the operation was called a "reconnaissance in force", Sherman, to his distress, had orders not to become involved in any action from which he could not withdraw.

Sherman moved the night of the 14th to the designated assembly area, a night march across very difficult country. Next morning the 1st and 2nd Battalions occupied the high ground west of the Naro River between Favara and the coastal road, on which the enemy had destroyed the bridge. Then both battalions reconnoitered to the front, locating enemy in strength in organized positions west of the bridge and between the Naro and Agrigento. This was the situation when I joined Sherman at his observation post on a bluff overlooking the Naro during the latter part of the morning and looked over the situation.

The problem looked more formidable on the ground than it had looked on the maps and photographs on which we had planned it. The Naro River was a dry stream bed running south through rugged hills to the sea some six miles east of Porto Empedocle. From the bluff where we stood, we looked west across barren and rocky parallel ridges to Agrigento about four miles away. Agrigento, like most ancient Sicilian towns, was perched on the top of a craggy hill, of which the sides visible to us appeared to be sheer cliffs. The town overlooked all of the intervening terrain. North of where we stood was the village of Favara. From Favara, a rugged and rocky tree-clad ridge led due west to the north side of Agrigento where a prominent hill dominated all roads leading into Agrigento from the north and west. The road from Favara to Agrigento was visible in most places along the southern slopes of this ridge. Porto Empedocle, about five miles south of Agrigento, was barely visible across sand dunes and undulating ridges sparsely clad with vegetation.

During the day, Sherman had the 1st Battalion attack across the Naro north of the coastal highway and seize the ridge just west of the river, developing the enemy positions. During the afternoon, the 3rd Battalion occupied the high ground west of Favara. This seemed to set the stage. Our plan was to have the Ranger Battalion avoid all resistance, circle around Agrigento during the night, and seize the port. The 1st Battalion would keep the enemy occupied in front, while the 2nd Battalion advanced westward along the ridge from Favara and seized the high ground just north of Agrigento. The 3rd Battalion in reserve would be used as required. When I left Sherman at nightfall, I was confident that we would have Agrigento and the port by noon next day.

However, the terrain was extraordinarily rough and difficult to traverse. Communications with the 2nd Battalion were slow and difficult at best and non-existent for much of the time when enemy patrols cut our wires. And enemy patrols were active. The Regimental Executive, Lieutenant Colonel John O. Williams, was killed on his way from the Regimental Command Post to the 2nd Battalion, we were to learn later. Nevertheless, the advance got under way according to plan.

Shortly after noon, we could see the 2nd Battalion approaching its objective. Then came a report of a large motor column of enemy reinforcements moving south from Aragona toward Agrigento. Almost every gun in seven battalions of field artillery (148 guns) was brought to bear. When the first salvos crashed into the crowded column, clouds of smoke and dust blanketed the column from view. We saw men fleeing in all directions. It was an artilleryman's dream! When firing stopped, columns of black smoke were rising from burning vehicles, and the remnants of the column were disappearing in the direction whence they had come. Later we learned that more than fifty vehicles had been destroyed and more than one hundred enemy killed.

Meanwhile, the 1st Battalion had worked its way forward to the southwestern edge of the town. Then about half-past two, the 3rd Battalion attacked across the Naro immediately north of the destroyed bridge in the direction of Porto Empedocle. I went to an observation post overlooking the Naro to see Lieutenant Colonel Heintges form his battalion and cross his line of departure. There was a short artillery preparation, then the leading companies crossed the river in deployed formation and advanced up the farther slopes. Almost at once, small white patches began to appear all about them. Then men arose as though from underground with hands uplifted. I clambered into my bantam and followed. On this hill which I had searched repeatedly during this day and the day before without ever seeing one single enemy, more than four hundred prisoners were taken. Colonel Heintges left a detachment to collect the prisoners and pressed on to Porto Empedocle for we had heard nothing from the Rangers all during the day, nor from a patrol I had sent in search of them the evening before.

By mid-afternoon, the 1st Battalion had fought its way into the city from the southeast and the 2nd Battalion had blocked all northern and western exists. After some street fighting, Agrigento surrendered. Heintges' 3rd Battalion and the Rangers reached Porto Empedocle about five o'clock in the afternoon. We had "cleared up the situation."

That evening I was advised that General Patton had received instructions to begin the next phase of the campaign. General Alexander's plan was now to have the Eighth Army drive the enemy into the Messina peninsula, while the Seventh Army protected its rear in two phases: first, by establishing a secure base in the Enna-Caltanisetta area; and second, by thrusting northward to hold the road centers at Petralia and Resuttano. The message added: "If it entails heavy fighting, the capture of Agrigento and Porto Empedocle will be undertaken on completion of the above task. If the port can be occupied without getting committed seriously, it should be secured early as it will be required for maintenance in the future."

The next morning, July 17th, I was on the scene of action of the patrol I had sent in search of the Rangers. First Lieutenant David C. Waybur with a patrol of three bantams, seeking a way across the Drago River, had come upon a destroyed bridge almost under the northern walls of the city. There the patrol was attacked by four Italian tanks and most of its members wounded. Waybur, although himself wounded, stood with his tommy gun on the road immediately in front of the leading tank and killed two of its crew by firing through the ports, whereupon the driverless tank plunged into the chasm beneath the destroyed bridge. There, Waybur and his gallant patrol held off the remaining tanks until elements of the 2nd Battalion arrived some hours later. For this heroic action, Waybur received the Medal of Honor.

Besides heavy casualties inflicted upon the enemy in killed and wounded and in destroyed vehicles and equipment, the reconnaissance in force yielded more than 6,000 prisoners (rather to my surprise, I must admit), more than a hundred vehicles and tanks, and more than fifty pieces of artillery 75 mm or larger, together with considerable stores of other weapons and supplies.

Army orders dissolved JOSS Force as of 1800 July 18th, at which time the Army was to take over operation of the ports and beaches, and placed the 3rd Infantry Division in a Provisional Corps for the advance on Palermo. Meanwhile we were to secure Highway 122 between Serra di Falco and Agrigento and be prepared for further effort by dark July 17th.

During the 17th, the 7th Combat Team cleared the area about

Agrigento as far as Raffadali and was concentrated there by noon July 18th. During the night, the 15th CT occupied Serra di Falco and San Cataldo, and moved next day to Milena. The 30th CT remained in the vicinity of Castrofillippo, reconnoitering actively to the north. Patrols from CCA seized Caltanisetta early on the morning of July 18th, and CCA reverted to Army Reserve along with the remainder of the 2nd Armored Division.

4. Capture of Palermo

General Patton disliked the idea of playing second fiddle to Montgomery with the secondary mission of protecting Montgomery's flank and rear while Montgomery was adding fresh laurels to those of his recent victories over Rommel. And Palermo drew General Patton like a lode star. It was General Patton's view that he could split the enemy's forces and protect Montgomery's flank and rear by capturing Palermo. Accordingly, General Patton conferred with General Alexander on July 17th and proposed that the Seventh Army mission be changed to read: "The Seventh Army will drive rapidly to the northwest and north, capture Palermo, and split the enemy's forces." Inasmuch as we now held Agrigento and the port, General Alexander agreed. This change was the basis for the orders for the drive on Palermo which we received during the afternoon of July 18th in Field Orders No. 1 Provisional Corps.

The Army plan was to have the II Corps, with the 1st and 45th Infantry Divisions, "secure strong base in rear of British Eighth Army" in the Enna-Caltanisetta-San Caterina area, and "advance within its zone to the North and Northwest, cut Highways 121, 120, and 113, and be prepared to attack Palermo from the East." The Provisional Corps, under General Patton's Deputy, General Keyes, with the 3rd Infantry Division and 82nd Airborne Division, was to "advance within its zone to the northwest, prepared to attack Palermo from the south and southwest. A powerful armored striking force"—the 2nd Armored Division—was "initially to follow the advance of the Provisional Corps prepared to exploit a breakthrough or extend envelopment to the west." Red, White, and Blue phase lines were designated to coordinate the advance, but we were not to stop on any phase line except Blue on which "the final assault on Palermo will be coordinated by Seventh Army."

What General Patton had in mind was to break through the mountainous region immediately to the north of us, whereupon he would commit the 2nd Armored Division in a spectacular sweep to capture Palermo, which would be touted as the first great exploit by American armor. We knew by this time that most of the German forces in Sicily

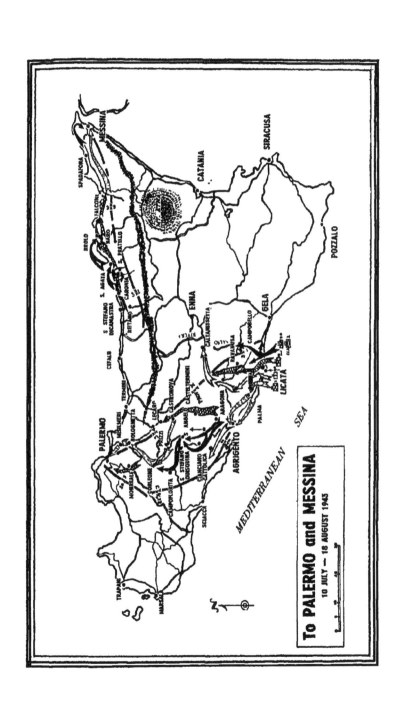

To PALERMO and MESSINA

10 JULY — 18 AUGUST 1943

were now opposing the Eighth Army, and that most of the enemy forces remaining in the western end of the island would be found on the main route between Agrigento and Palermo in the 3rd Infantry Division zone. When General Keyes discussed the plan with me I remarked to him that there would be little for the armor to exploit except demolitions. General Keyes admitted as much, but thought that even so it would be a good buildup for American armor. Personally, I had some reservations, for I was commanding an infantry division of which I was justifiably proud.

Palermo was a hundred miles to the north and west. Our first forty or so miles led through rugged mountains which rose to a height of more than 4,000 feet around Cammaratta and San Stefano di Quisquina. Our three tortuous roads northward had steep grades, numerous hairpin turns, and many bridges which would be rendered more difficult by enemy demolitions and delaying actions. Once through the mountainous belt at Prizzi, there would be easier going for another forty miles across the central plateau, bringing us to the range of rugged hills which encircled Palermo, marked for us by the Blue Line which we were not to cross. Since demolitions would constitute our greatest obstacle, it seemed to me that the faster we could traverse the distance, the less time the enemy would have for demolitions and destruction. I explained the problem to the combat team commanders at our last conference of July 18th. I told them I expected them to be in Palermo in five days and be the first to arrive. We broke out a bottle of Scotch from our slender stock and toasted the "American Doughboy." Then at 0500, July 19th, the drive for Palermo was on.

The 15th RCT had the eastern road with an attached Tabor of Goums (Morrocan irregulars under French command) paralleling the route on their right. CT 30 was to advance on the central route and capture San Stefano and Prizzi at the northern exit from the mountainous belt. The Ranger Battalion followed the western road in contact with the 82nd Airborne Division on the coastal road, while the 7th CT remained in division reserve at Raffadali. In the stifling heat and choking dust of Sicilian July, the interesting feature of this drive on Palermo was the marching power of American infantry.

We knew that the enemy was in sizable numbers in strong positions at San Stefano di Quisquina, and that we would encounter demolitions and delaying detachments along the principal route. Colonel Rogers ordered Lieutenant Colonel Edgar C. Doleman and his 3rd Battalion to move across country from Aragona and seize the hill mass Cerro Stagnatoro northeast of the town. The battalion moved out about midnight in what was to be a record-breaking march. Over mountainous trails and without resupply of water or rations, the battalion covered fifty-four heartbreaking miles in thirty-three hours and reached the designated objective. Meanwhile, the other battalions fought their way through demolitions and delaying detachments into position for a coordinated attack on the town. This attack got under way early in the afternoon of the 20th and ended with the capture of San Stefano just before dark, along with nearly 1,000 prisoners, a large number of vehicles, and many other weapons and equipment.

While this battle at San Stefano was under way, I was over on the eastern road with the 15th Infantry near Cammaratta. Fearing that Rogers would be delayed in taking San Stefano and Prizzi, I decided to make what Leavenworth, in my days, would have called a "wide envelopment." I decided to move the 7th by motor during the night to the vicinity of Castronova, attacking westward at daylight next morning to capture Prizzi in conjunction with the attack of the 30th from the south. The 15th was to continue its advance to Lercara Fridi and Castronova and protect the movement. Warning Carleton by radio to alert the 7th for movement and to provide the trucks, as well as to have Sherman at the Command Post for orders, I made my way back, arriving shortly before five o'clock. All was in readiness. Sherman soon had his orders. And the movement was underway before dark.

I would have gotten a "U" at Leavenworth for that "wide envelopment," for the night move of more than fifty miles was on a road that had never been better than second class and which enemy demolitions and obstructions had rendered all but impassable. However, the division engineers had repaired bridges and constructed bypasses and the road was in use by the 15th CT. The move was made and two battalions of the 7th, the 1st and 3rd, were ready to attack westward before six o'clock next morning.

Meanwhile, we learned that the 30th had captured San Stefano and got off instructions to Rogers for the attack on Prizzi next morning. Then we sent the forward echelon of the Division CP to San Stefano, and at 0330 I was on my way there to be on hand for the battle.

Lieutenant Colonel Lyle W. Bernard's 2nd Battalion advanced north from San Stefano, while the remaining battalions of the 30th held positions north and west of the town. The 7th attacked west from Castronova at 0550 with the 3rd and 1st Battalions abreast, although the 2nd Battalion had not yet closed in the assembly area. As soon as the road to the north was clear, I made my way forward through the confusion of vehicles, soldiers, streams of prisoners, and even cheering natives to the outskirts of the town, where I conferred briefly with Generals Campbell and Eagles, and with Carleton, Harrel, and Wilson. There was to be no pause. As soon as the battalions of the 7th could reorganize they were to press on to Corleone, while the 30th turned

west and north on a parallel road through Palazzo, Bisaquino, and Roccamena. The 15th was to remain in the Castronova area in readiness to
follow the route of the 7th CT. A brief period for reorganization, and
the 3rd Battalion of the 7th led off.

Early in the afternoon I went forward to the head of the column
where I spoke briefly with Heintges whose battalion was leading. Then
I stood by the road and watched both battalions pass. In blistering heat
and stifling dust, these soldiers plowed their way forward like waves
beating on an ocean beach and at a rate which Roman legions never
excelled. At the tail of each battalion I stopped the battalion surgeon
and chaplain and asked how many men had fallen out so far. In both
cases, the answer was none. Both battalions had moved by motor all
night, had attacked cross-country soon after daylight, and both had
already covered twenty-five miles on foot since morning. For both
there was another ten miles before halting.

About five o'clock General Keyes arrived at my temporary Command Post near Prizzi. The 82nd Airborne had kept pace along the
coastal road, and the stage was now set for the big armored push. The
Rangers had fallen behind and complained of exhaustion. Keyes relieved them from my command and placed them under Corps control.
His only other instruction was that no elements would cross the Blue
Line except on order.

The 3rd Battalion of the 7th occupied Corleone shortly before dark
and by 2100 the whole of the 7th was concentrated in an area north
of the town, where the 2nd Battalion, brought forward from Castronova by motor, detrucked and began the advance northward. Meanwhile, the 15th CT was following in trace of the 7th by marching and
motor shuttling with such transportation as it had.

We had moved the Command Post forward to Corleone. There at
two o'clock in the morning, I had a conference with my staff and the
regimental commanders to outline plans for occupying objectives on
the Blue Line. The 7th was to press on at top speed shuttling its rear
battalions forward to block the eastern exits from Palermo north of
Misilimeri. The 15th was to take a secondary road west of the principal route through Piana del Greci and occupy the heights overlooking Palermo on the south. I had intended to have the 30th advance
from Roccamena and occupy the heights west of Altofonte and south
of Monreale, but an order from Provisional Corps changed our western
boundary, giving this road to troops on our left. Consequently, the
30th was ordered to assemble in reserve south of Corleone.

Before noon, the 7th had reached the Blue Line near Misilimeri and
the 15th at Piana del Greci, near which I had my first view of Palermo.
Both had encountered scattered opposition but Italians were surrender-

ing in such large numbers as to be embarrassing. Explosions could be seen in the city and it was evident that the Germans were about their work of destruction. Repeated requests for permission to send troops into the city to prevent destruction met refusal and a final order at 1400 from Seventh Army that no one would cross the line Villabete-Belmonte-Montreale until further orders. About six o'clock, civilians representing Palermo offered to surrender the city to General Eagles who was with Sherman at Villabete. Repeated requests eventually brought permission from General Keyes to send reconnaissance parties into the town to protect the port. Thus it was that when Generals Patton and Keyes entered the city about half-past ten that night at the head of the armored column, 3rd Infantry Division soldiers of two infantry battalions were already patrolling the streets. The drive for Palermo was over.

I was ordered into the city next morning to report to General Patton and his greeting was: "Well, the Truscott Trot sure got us here in a damn hurry."

In a letter to my wife a day or so later I wrote:

> You will have guessed where I am and what I have been doing. . . . The censor will permit me to say that I am now in Sicily, and you will guess that the division has been in the forefront It has done well. I do not believe that the equal of these men has ever existed in our Army—though I will admit that I may be somewhat prejudiced! Anyway, it has been a grand experience and we have opened lots of eyes.

In the same letter I gave her my first impressions of Sicily:

> This is a most interesting island—and in ways unexpected to me. I have never seen so much poverty and filth. Natives are obviously but a jump ahead of starvation. Seeing this, I can understand the growth of our slum districts in cities like New York, Chicago and the like. The country seems to be predominantly agricultural, but at least 95% of the population lives in the towns and villages. These towns nearly all date from medieval days, houses are usually of stone, close packed beside narrow streets, and filled with unwashed women, children and men living and playing in the filth of the barnyards which are the streets. The mules and donkeys are the primary beasts of burden and they add their litter to that of chickens and goats which share the streets and dwellings with the natives. Most of the towns and villages are built upon hill tops accessible by steep rocky roads. Usually there is a castle or the ruins of one perched atop a nearby crag. All of this may have seemed romantic—and may have been in Sir Walter Scott's pages—but now it stands as a living monument to the cause of war—and social unrest. Believe me, when I am once more home again I shall never have any desire to leave the feel and smell of good clean American air.

The Sicilians were weary of war and they hated the Germans. We had in our ranks many soldiers of Sicilian origin. Thus the greater part of the population welcomed us and the welcome grew warmer as the invasion progressed. There were many defections in the ranks of Italian troops and their resistance had never been bitter or determined. But every unit encountered resistance on every road and our advance had not been without its cost in killed and wounded. There is little doubt it would have been more so had not the speed of our advance spread confusion and allowed them no time for reorganization.

On July 20th, even before the capture of Palermo, 15th Army Group had informed General Patton the Eighth Army was meeting heavy resistance in the Catania plain, and had directed him to push reconnaissance eastward along the coast road and the road east from Nicosia as soon as Seventh Army reached the coast north of Petralia. On July 23rd, the day after the capture of Palermo, another message from 15th Army Group directed General Patton to leave sufficient forces to mop up remaining enemy elements in western Sicily and to employ the maximum strength that could be maintained in a drive eastward along the coast road and the road Nicosa-Troina-Cesaro to drive the enemy out of the Messina peninsula in conjunction with the attack of the Eighth Army. General Patton assigned this mission to General Bradley's II Corps, to which all non-divisional artillery was immediately sent.

I was anxious for the 3rd Infantry Division to have part in this eastward drive, but General Bradley planned to have the 45th Infantry Division continue the advance along the coastal road. My division would be held on police and line of communications duty for an indefinite period. For a few days, we were occupied with the collection and evacuation of thousands of prisoners and with guard and police duties about the city. These were gradually taken over by Army troops and the Division settled down in bivouac areas to refit and refurbish in preparation for whatever might come next. My Headquarters settled down in a "castle by the sea"—a beautifully romantic place belonging to a Princess di Gangi, a lady-in-waiting to the Queen of Italy—to enjoy a respite from our labors. But not for long.

On July 26th, the afternoon we moved into the "castello", I visited General Patton in the Royal Palace. Over a highball, talk turned to the course of the campaign then in progress. General Patton remarked that he "would certainly like to beat Montgomery into Messina." With some brashness, and doubtless a measure of conceit—I was never modest where the 3rd Infantry Division was concerned—I replied half seriously that putting the 3rd Infantry Division in the fight was one way to insure that. General Patton said that it might come to that, and there was some talk of employing the Division to relieve the 1st Infantry Division which had then been in action longer than any other American division. The following day, I sent staff officers to visit General Bradley's staff and the staff of the 1st Infantry Division, to look over the situation.

On the morning of July 30th, General Keyes came to the "castello" and informed me that we were to relieve the 45th Infantry Division near San Stefano di Camastra some miles to the east, the relief to begin the following day. We alerted the Division, then Carleton and I set off at once for the 45th Command Post where we completed arrangements for the relief with General Troy H. Middleton and his staff. The 45th Infantry Division had made a record of which any division could well be proud. This was its first campaign. The Division had planned and prepared under great disadvantages. For three weeks before the landing, while other divisions were training, this division had been at sea. Yet it had taken every objective and in the long drive across Sicily had kept pace with the veteran divisions. General Middleton and his staff, I think, welcomed a break, just as we had done.

The 30th Infantry relieved elements of the 179th and 157th Infantry Regiments west of San Stefano di Camastra during July 31st. By midnight, August 1st, the 3rd Infantry Division was concentrated in the area, and the race for Messina was on.

5. Race for Messina.

From Aragona to Palermo, the distance by our central road was 157 kilometers, or approximately 98 miles. From San Stefano di Camastra to Messina by Highway 113, the distance was 169 kilometers or approximately 105 miles. Thus, the distances involved in the two operations were about the same, but there any resemblance ended. The first we had made in just three days; the latter was to take seventeen.

Heretofore in all of our operations there had been space for maneuver. When resistance was encountered, leading elements could fix the enemy in front while others swung wide to attack in flank and rear. Also, there had been plenty of roads so that artillery could keep forward with its infantry, ammunition, water and rations could reach troops as required, and reserves could be moved rapidly by motor and by marching. If one road was blocked, there was always an alternative. Furthermore, the enemy had for the most part been Italians whose hearts were not in the war and who had little stomach for fighting. Now all was changed.

The Nebrodi Mountains parallel the north coast of Sicily from San Stefano di Camastra eastward to Messina. This rugged chain, averaging in elevation between four and five thousand feet, lies only twelve or fifteen miles inland from the coast. Centuries of rainfall on long denuded slopes have cut channels northward to the sea which, in their upper reaches, are deep gorges with sheer rocky walls down which there are only occasional footpaths. Between these channels, for the most part dry at this season, long ridges thrust finger-like toward the sea, some pitching off steeply onto the narrow coastal plain, others jutting into the sea in rocky headlands. The coastal plain was in most places no more than a few hundred yards in width. The only road, Highway 113, was a first class concrete strip which followed the shore line closely, crossed over the stream beds on concrete or stone bridges, clung precariously to cliffs overhanging the sea in places, in others passed through the headlands in tunnels. The lower slopes of the ridges, the narrow valleys, and the coastal plain were usually covered with olive groves. Off the road to the south, there were few lateral roads and these were for the most part dead-end roads that led along the ridges to end against the mountains. South of the road the terrain forward was passable only for men on foot and for mules, and for them with unusual difficulty. The weather was hot. Each day dawned clear and bright, and the blazing sun was merciless. There was no wind but an occasional sirocco which seared like an oven blast. Every plodding footstep and turning wheel raised clouds of powdery dust which soon enshrouded all in a stifling pall and brought thirst for which there was all too little water. In ordinary times, the distance to Messina would be a few hours drive of great scenic beauty. Now it was an area in which a determined enemy had every advantage for defense and delay. And the enemy was almost wholly German.

In our earlier operations around Agrigento and during the drive for Palermo we had captured many mules and a number of horses which we had utilized to transport water, ammunition and rations in areas where vehicles could not go. Immediately after the capture of Palermo, we had turned these animals over to the 45th Infantry Division. Now they were returned to us. We organized them into a Provisional Pack Train and a Provisional Mounted Troop under command of Major Robert W. Crandall, a cavalry officer who had formerly commanded the Division Reconnaissance Troop, and who had served under me when I had commanded the 5th Cavalry at Fort Bliss, Texas. All told we were to use more than 400 mules and more than 100 horses during this advance. We did not always employ them economically and efficiently, for we lacked trained personnel and had to improvise much equipment. Nevertheless, without these Provisional units, the drive for Messina would have been much slower and far more costly.

The drive entailed attacking successive delaying positions organized along the naturally strong defensive terrain at Caronia, San Fratello,

Cape Orlando, Cape Calava, Fernari, Spadafora, and the mountain heights overlooking Messina. Each position was so strong that frontal attack would have been slow and costly. On our one road forward, bridges were destroyed, areas which could be used to bypass were mined; and demolitions and mine fields, so located that no vehicles could pass without engineer assistance, were invariably covered by fire of artillery, machine guns, and small arms.

Our rate of advance depended upon the speed with which we could clear hostile fire from the demolitions and obstructions and construct by-passes over which our artillery and transport could move forward. The slower we advanced, the more time the enemy had to prepare demolitions and defenses in succeeding positions.

Our plan of advance was to have one element thrust along the main axis to clear the spurs overlooking the main road, and protect the engineers clearing demolitions and mine fields so that artillery and supplies could move forward. Meanwhile, other elements with mule transport would be working their way forward over tortuous mountain trails to the south to strike the enemy in flank and rear. The scanty water supply was delivered in water cans carried on mules, as were ammunition and rations. The mountain trails were often so precipitous that mules could not negotiate them, and water and rations had to be carried forward on the backs of men. Our effort was always to encircle the enemy and prevent his escape, but in such terrain the advantage was all with the Boche. Our maneuver required days of laborious struggling under the blistering Sicilian sun and enemy fire, to reach positions from which we could strike. The enemy could hold to the last minute and then withdraw by motor while we could only follow up on foot.

On August 3rd, General Keyes, still doubling as General Patton's Deputy and Commander of the Provisional Corps, informed me that General Patton had arranged with the Navy for landing craft and naval support to lift one reinforced battalion in a landing operation behind German lines. Preliminary studies indicated several places where such a force might be landed. It was my thought that any such landing should be coordinated closely with the advance of the Division for such a small force could not be expected to maintain itself for many hours against German attacks without suffering excessive losses. General Keyes agreed that the force would be employed entirely under my command. I selected Lieutenant Colonel Lyle W. Bernard's 2nd Battalion, 30th Infantry, and attached to it Batteries A and B, 58th Field Artillery Battalion, one platoon Company C, 753rd Tank Battalion, and one platoon Company C, 10th Engineer Battalion. Placing General Eagles to supervise planning and preparations, we established the planners in a tent in the division command post, and set them to work planning a landing at Sant' Agata di Militello, some miles east of Monte Fratello where we expected to encounter the enemy in a strong position.

The 30th Infantry advanced eastward the morning of August 1st, two battalions with mule transport, by mountain trails to the south with the objective of cutting the road east of Caronia, the other, on the main axis clearing the spurs overlooking the main road. The regiment encountered mines and demolitions along the stream bed a mile and a half west of San Stefano, and around each of the numerous bridges to the east. The road east of San Stefano was under continuous artillery fire; in fact, San Stefano was shelled for several days by long range guns which we could not reach. I had expected to take Caronia during the day, but the enveloping battalions could not reach the objective until the following morning. Caronia was taken after a sharp fight the morning of August 2nd, the Germans employing tanks to cover their withdrawal. We had bagged less than one hundred fifty prisoners.

We passed the 15th Infantry through to take up the drive eastward. During August 3rd, the 15th made contact with the Germans in strength along the Furiano River in front of Monte Fratello in the most formidable defensive position we had yet encountered.

Monte Fratello is a rugged flat-topped peak of 2,200 feet, a mile and a half from the sea at the northern end of the divide between the Furiano and Ignanno Rivers. The crest of the mountain is a rugged, rocky escarpment, and the lower slopes talus formations, which on the western side are broken by numerous ravines and ridges. One of the few lateral roads from the north coast to the central Sicilian plain winds its way up the northern and western slopes of this mountain across a saddle in which lies the village of San Fratello, and through a pass in the Nebrodi Mountains just west of the 5,700 foot Mount Toro only ten miles to the south to Cesaro which was still in German hands. Water falling on the northern slopes through past ages has cut two deep, rocky gorges which unite just above Monte Fratello to form the Furiano River. The Furiano, a broad, boulder-strewn stream bed, almost dry in August, with high steep banks, passes along the foot of Monte Fratello and for some three miles on to the sea. Just west of the Furiano, the coast road passes around a prominent spur, less than a third the height of the mountain, and crosses over the Furiano on a high concrete bridge. From Monte Fratello, the road and railroad and all of the narrow coastal plain is clearly visible as far west as Caronia.

On August 4th, the 15th Infantry launched a strong attack to develop the enemy position. The attack made little progress but developed the enemy in strength identifying three German battalions and several Italian units. The Germans were dug in along the east bank of the Furiano, on the slopes of Monte Fratello, and around the village of San Fratello. Our attacks encountered heavy fire from artillery, mortars, machine guns, and small arms. The Germans had destroyed the bridge, mined the approaches, and laid an extensive mine field with anti-tank and antipersonnel mines from above the bridge on down to the sea.

The German position was so dominating that we had difficulty in repairing demolitions, displacing artillery forward, and making dispositions for our attack. Every move on the coast road was exposed to German observation, and German artillery fire was accurate. We solved the problem by shrouding the mountain top in smoke, employing artillery and chemical mortars, and instituting a rigid traffic control. During the 4th and 5th, we extended reconnaissance to the south, and Division engineers built a road more than three miles in length up the side of a mountain ridge so that we could emplace artillery to support an attack from the south. The night of the 5th, we moved the 30th Infantry (less its 2nd Battalion) to the vicinity of the junction of the two gorges where the 3rd Battalion of the 15th was in concealed positions. The plan was to have these three battalions gain the ridge south of the mountain next day in an attack which was to follow air and artillery preparation. The air attack was late and not very effective. The terrain was even more difficult than I had anticipated, and the attack of the 30th could not be coordinated with the attack of the 3rd Battalion 15th Infantry. In consequence only the latter made any progress, and it had to be withdrawn at nightfall.

During the day I was to realize sharply the difficulties of the terrain. I had gone to an observation post overlooking the gorges west of San Fratello where the battalions of the 30th were supposed to be advancing. I had sent General Eagles to join Colonel Rogers and push the advance, but they seemed to be making no progress so far as I could see, and I had no communication with them. I could see a command post about a mile distant, and almost straight down. However, a path led downward along the cliff side up which Major Crandall with a train of pack mules was returning for new loads. I had decided that I would go down there to see if I could speed up the attack. When Major Crandall emerged from the trail, I asked: "Crandall, how long will it take me to get down there where General Eagles and Colonel Rogers are?" Crandall squinted downward toward the distant group, then looked at me and replied: "Well, sir, I made it in a little over an hour." "Well," I remarked, "I think I'll go on down there and see them." Crandall looked at me quizzically and dryly replied: "Well, General, it has taken me just three and a half hours to come back from there hanging onto the tail of a mule."

Six hours for me! I decided that General Eagles could fight that part of the battle.

During the afternoon of August 6th, we mounted Bernard's landing force to land the following morning in conjunction with a renewal of the attack by the Division. However, a German air attack sank an LST while loading was in progress, and we had to delay the operation for a day until another could be brought up from Palermo.

During the day of the 7th, the 30th Infantry and the 3rd Battalion of the 15th fought their way onto the ridge south of Monte Fratello and during the night captured the village. At daylight the 7th Infantry attacked through the 15th along the coastal road, Bernard's landing force landed before daylight at Sant' Agata, and the 30th Infantry attacked the mountain from the south. The battle was soon over. Our losses had been relatively heavy, but we collected more than 1,600 prisoners, several batteries of artillery, destroyed a number of tanks, and much other material. It had been the toughest fight we had had so far.

At Sant' Agata, the 7th Infantry again took up the advance while Bernard and his battalion, who had contributed so much to the Battle at Fratello, made ready for another landing. The 7th pushed on against increasing resistance and gained a foothold east of the Zoppulo River. Once more we encountered great difficulty in repairing demolitions and displacing artillery forward because of artillery fire, some of it from long range guns on Cape Orlando. And German observation was spread too wide to enable us to screen with smoke. Besides, we were running low on smoke shells.

The night of August 9th, we started the 15th Infantry with mule transport south through San Marco di Lunzo to gain the ridge south of Naso and attack the morning of the 11th in conjunction with the landing of Bernard's force at Brolo. All during that night and the following day we struggled to make preparations for the attack. Late in the afternoon, we had not been able to get artillery in position to support the attack of the 15th adequately, nor had the 15th been able yet to reach the Naso ridge. I decided to postpone Bernard's landing for a day because I did not think we could reach Brolo in time to support him. General Keyes arrived about this time, and I informed him of my decision. General Keyes said that General Patton would want the operation to go on. Arrangements had already been made for a large number of correspondents to accompany it, and there would be criticism if the operation were postponed. We telephoned General Bradley, under whose immediate command I was. General Bradley agreed with me that the

landing should not go on unless it was properly timed with the operations of the remainder of the Division. Then General Keyes telephoned
General Patton saying that I did not want to carry out the landing
operation. I took the phone and tried to explain my reasons. Needless
to say, General Patton would not listen. He sputtered and said:
"Dammit, that operation will go on," and banged down the receiver.
I issued orders for Bernard, whose force was standing by at the loading
place, to load for the operation.

An hour later, General Patton came storming into my Command
Post giving everybody hell from the Military Police at the entrance
right on through until he came to me. He was screamingly angry as
only he could be. "Goddammit, Lucian, what's the matter with you?
Are you afraid to fight?" I bristled right back: "General, you know
that's ridiculous and insulting. You have ordered the operation and it
is now loading. If you don't think I can carry out orders, you can give
the Division to anyone you please. But I will tell you one thing, you will
not find anyone who can carry out orders which they do not approve
as well as I can."

General Patton changed instantly, the anger all gone. Throwing his
arm about my shoulder he said: "Dammit Lucian, I know that. Come
on, let's have a drink—of your liquor." We did. General Patton departed soon after in his usual good spirits. We turned to the problem of
getting through to support Bernard.

That day of August 11th I will never forget. Bernard's battalion was
already somewhat reduced in strength from previous losses, and probably did not number more than 650 men. We knew that the beach at
Brolo was none too good, and that the exits inland were difficult,
through an olive grove and up steep banks onto the coastal highway.
Bernard's objective was Mount Cipolla, a steep spur that overlooked
the coastal highway and the town of Brolo a short distance to the east.
This objective was not far behind the German lines from Cape Orlando
south through Naso, and it was to be expected that the German reaction
would be even more violent than in the previous landing at Sant' Agata,
for the Germans' one route of escape was along the foot of Mt. Cipolla
where Bernard was to pull the drawstring in the bag.

No other battalion was within ten miles of Bernard's objective, and
those miles were across inconceivably difficult terrain with a bitterly
defending enemy. We knew that Bernard's battalion would be hard
pressed to maintain itself for many hours. We committed every element
in the Division, including a Ranger Battalion just recently attached, to
fight their way through to Bernard's battalion. The 15th Infantry was
to continue on across the Naso ridge to the spurs overlooking Brolo on
the south. The 7th Infantry attacking south of the highway was to cap-

ture Naso and the spurs overlooking Brolo from the west. Between
them, the Ranger Battalion was to infiltrate through the German positions to link up with Bernard. The rest of Bernard's own regiment was
to fight its way along the coastal road past Cape Orlando and down the
highway to reach their comrades. Every gun and tank was emplaced
as far forward as we could get them. The aim was not merely to defeat
an enemy and take an objective; it was to aid comrades who were in
danger. The urgency of the situation was impressed on all, and by daylight the whole Division was in movement.

I sent a liaison officer, Captain Walter K. Millar, General Eagle's
aide, to land with Colonel Bernard. He had a jeep which was equipped
with an SCR 193 radio. His mission was to keep me informed of the
course of the action, for commanders in such cases are usually too busy
to make adequate reports or too intimately concerned to be objective
in their reports. It was fortunate that I did. Bernard's radios failed, and
Millar's radio was the only means of communication with Bernard's
battalion throughout the fateful day.

My Command Post was located in an olive oil factory, a rather exposed location on the eastern edge of Terranova. Long before Bernard's
H-Hour of 0400, we were tensely waiting. We had listened to the roar of
our own guns as the attack began, and had the first reports from the
regiments that the attack was under way. We had shot the works. We
could only wait. Day dawned clear and hot, and with daylight, shells
from a long range gun of large caliber screamed past our factory Command Post to burst on the road and in the town just behind. Millar's
first message brought a note of cheer.

Time: 0600
BLUE (Bernard's force) ALL IN. LIGHT RESISTANCE. ATTACK PRO-
GRESSING. JEEP BROKEN DOWN.

We supposed that Millar's jeep had drowned-out on landing and that
it would probably not leave the beach. I was irritated but we were glad
to know that the force had landed on schedule. We still had miles of
difficult country held by Germans before we could link up with them.
With Bartash, my aide, I made a trip to the regimental commanders to
check with them and to spur them on. Our airplanes were overhead
providing cover for the operation. We watched a squadron of A-36's
bomb the Cape and hoped that they were after that long range German
gun. But they did not get it for the shells were still screeching by when
we returned. Millar's next message continued optimistic.

Time: 0830
BLUE AS PLANNED. ENEMY REINFORCEMENTS STOPPED BY

ARTILLERY. MANY ENEMY TRUCKS HIT. CASUALTIES LIGHT.
ENEMY PLANES BOMBED OUR POSITION.

That was encouraging. Bernard, we thought, was off the beach and
on his objective. So long as his ammunition held out, he should be all
right. The next message rather confirmed us in this opinion.

Time. 0905
ONE COMPANY ITALIANS ATTACKING FROM THE WEST. WE
ARE ON THE BEAM.

By this time, no one worried much about Italians. In this Command
Post there was relief; we were beginning to think that everything would
be all right. The next report was even better.

Time: 0930
APPROXIMATELY FIVE ENEMY TANKS APPROACHING FROM
WEST. SHERMANS (our tanks) OUT AFTER THEM.

Now it was obvious that the German reaction was getting under
way. A few minutes later, came the first shades of doubt.

Time: 0945
WHERE IS DOC AND HARRY?

The 15th Infantry was commanded by Colonel "Doc" Johnson, the
7th by Colonel "Harry" Sherman, the 30th by Colonel "Art" Rogers.
Bernard was asking where the battalions of the 15th and 7th were, and
it was only just mid-morning! They were still many hours away! But
a half-hour later things looked better.

Time: 1010
TO SIX (Division Commander) INITIAL COUNTERATTACK RE-
PULSED. RECONNAISSANCE EVIDENT BOTH FLANKS. JEEP
NOW OK.

It was obvious now that the Germans were building up for a power-
ful attack from both east and west against Bernard. We were urging
"Doc", "Harry", and "Art" on, but progress seemed agonizingly slow.
Then came a desperate appeal.

Time: 1140
ENEMY COUNTERATTACK MASSING EAST BROLO 1000 YARDS.
REQUEST AIR MISSION ON THAT POSITION AND 753513 AND
729511. URGENT. ALSO NAVY.

What had happened to Bernard's shore fire control party? Why could not he direct the fire of the Navy off shore? Obviously there was something wrong. Carleton, Harrel and Connor were on the phones with urgent requests for the Navy and Air missions requested. But there was no way for us to know whether or not the missions were fired and flown. We had barely gotten off the requests when there was another appeal.

> Time: 1200
> REQUEST ALL POSSIBLE ARTILLERY SUPPORT ON BROLO EAST 1000 YARDS.

That was maximum range for our Long Toms—155 mm guns—but we turned them on, and got off new requests for Navy and Air support.

> Time: 1230
> MOTOR VEHICLES AND M-6 TANKS 3000 YARDS EAST AND IN BROLO. MUST HAVE EVERYTHING.

There was not much conversation in the olive oil factory where we gathered about the situation map and watched our slow progress toward Bernard. Men spoke in whispers and moved about on tiptoe, though the German shells screeched by at frequent intervals. The air mission was on but we did not know when. And Bernard's situation was growing worse.

> Time: 1305
> NAVY SAYS THEY CAN'T FIRE UNTIL 1630. MUST HAVE IT NOW. AIR NOT HERE. SITUATION CRITICAL.

There had been an arrangement by which we would have naval gunfire support in our operations along the coast for certain hours of the morning and afternoon during which the Air Force would provide fighter cover for the ships off shore. There was some misunderstanding here which we soon cleared up, although not as quickly as Bernard would have liked.

> Time: 1340
> ENEMY COUNTERATTACKING FIERCELY. DO SOMETHING.

All of us felt a sense of desperation. Our nearest battalions were hours away, but those of the 7th Infantry were fighting around Naso. The 7th Infantry code name was CUSTER. Carleton sent off a message "BOYS FROM LITTLE BIG HORN ON THE WAY." Before that got off came another one from Millar:

Time: 1425
REPEAT AIR AND NAVY IMMEDIATELY. ALSO ON CAPE HOW
ABOUT OTHER DOGFACES. CAN TOMS REACH CAPE. ALSO
NAVY AND AIR. SITUATION STILL CRITICAL. MUST BE CON-
STANT.

I left Carleton and the staff to lay on the Navy and Air, and took off
for the front to see what I could do. Because of demolitions, I was able
to reach only one Regimental Command Post. I found Colonel Rogers
there with a telephone in each hand directing artillery fire, with his
staff, artillery liaison officer, and others standing around idle. I asked
Major Byrnes, the artillery liaison officer, if he did not think that he
could direct the artillery fire. He assured me that he could. I soon
had Colonel Rogers on the way to join his 1st and 3rd Battalions then
making slow progress along the coast road toward Cape Orlando. His
appearance seemed to have had the desired effect, for it turned out
later that the regiment was one of the first to reach the beleaguered
battalion. Back at the Command Post, there was another message.

Time: 1610
WHERE IS REINFORCING INFANTRY. NEED DOUGHBOYS
BADLY. ANOTHER COUNTERATTACK ON. AMMO VERY
SHORT. HAVE LITTLE YELLOW SMOKE LEFT.

The yellow smoke was the means to mark positions for our airplanes.
There was no way we could get ammunition to them, and the battal-
ions still had miles to go. We sent off a message that help was on the way.
Then came another desperate message.

Time: 1725
BEING COUNTERATTACKED BY BATTALION FROM WEST.
MUST HAVE NAVY AND AIR ON 702504 IMMEDIATELY OR WE
ARE LOST.

This coordinate was immediately under the western brow of Mount
Cipolla where the battalion was. It was obvious that the Germans were
preparing a final assault. Then came a query.

Time: 1745
WHITE SIX (That was Bernard) MUST HAVE PREVIOUS MESSAGE
OF APPROXIMATELY 1700 IN CLEAR.

This was the message we had sent saying that the "BOYS FROM
LITTLE BIG HORN ON THE WAY." We repeated the message
in clear with location and then came Millar's final message.

Time: 1850
GIVE NAVY PRIORITY AND LET THEM—

The radio was silent. Nor were we able to contact Millar again. We knew that our leading battalions were still some distance away, and we pictured the final German assault swarming over our gallant comrades. There were long faces in our Command Post then and more than one moist eye. We had done all that we could, and it had not been enough.

At ten o'clock that night, there was still no word. Nor did we know where our leading battalions were. They had outrun communications with the Regimental Command Posts.

Later we were to learn that the end of the final message was "LET THEM FIRE EAST SIDE OF NASO." It was fortunate that we did not for it would have been on the leading battalions of the 7th making their way down the spurs to the rescue. Simultaneously, the leading battalion of the 30th was doing a speed march down the road from Cape Orlando, and the 15th was on the spurs just above Mount Cipolla. We rescued the battalion, but the enemy escaped.

Bernard had not been able to get his artillery and tanks up the steep embankment and onto the hill with his infantry battalion, and they were almost destroyed. We lost seven of the eight guns we put ashore and three of the four tanks which landed, although two were later recovered. We took only a handful of prisoners, but the roads were littered with German dead and with destroyed tanks and vehicles. Our losses from this small force totaled 167.

Early the next morning, I saw Bernard when he came down off the mountain which his little force had held so gallantly. I could only say, "Thank God, Bernard, for I am certainly glad to see you." Bernard's reply was even more heartful· "General, you just don't know how glad I am to see you."

Had we delayed a day, we might have captured most of the German force. Nevertheless, we had gained important time.

Just east of Brolo, two rugged spurs jut northward for six or seven miles toward the sea from the 3,500-foot Mount Fossa Del Neve on the main divide. The westernmost spur ends in a cone-shaped peak of some 1,500 feet about two miles east of Brolo up which a winding mule path leads to the mountaintop village of Piriano. The easternmost spur juts into the sea in a rugged headland which is Cape Calava. East of Brolo, Highway 113 crosses the San Angelo River, an almost dry stream bed of several hundred feet, just below Piriano, clings precariously to the northern side of the cone-shaped peak on overhanging cliffs, continues along the rocky shore for perhaps four miles, and disappears into a tunnel below Cape Calava. Southward, a dead-end cart road follows the San Angelo to the village of San Angelo di Brolo perched against the mountainside near the head of the San Angelo canyon. Eastward from San Angelo men and mules can follow the mountain crests to the village of Patti, a dozen miles to the east as the crow flies, on the coast road five miles beyond the tunnel.

Leaving Bernard and his gallant band for a well-earned rest, the remainder of the 30th pressed eastward and drove the Germans from the heights overlooking Brolo from the east. That night, the 15th Infantry, once more with mule transport, moved south to San Angelo di Brolo, to cross over the mountains the following day and capture Patti.

Late in the afternoon of the 12th, Sergeant Barna drove Bartash and me to the top of the cone-shaped peak by the winding mule path which our jeep could barely make. Piriano is a medieval village, stone buildings clustered around a small square dominated by the church, with streets so narrow that even our jeep could not pass through. We went on foot to an observation post beyond from which we could see the battalions working their way toward the cape and tunnel.

When I returned Sergeant Barna met me, saying: "General, there's an Italian here who speaks English. He wants to see you." I was impatient of the delay, but said. "Well, bring him on, and make it snappy." In the village square, several hundred persons were now assembled. From among them stepped a figure with well-waxed mustachios, clad in an ancient but well preserved double breasted blue serge suit on which were five campaign medals of World War I, blue shirt, red tie, yellow shoes with pointed toes, and a soft straw hat with a red band. Saluting smartly, then sweeping off the hat in a bow, he spoke in rather rusty English: "My General, I too am an American soldier." Producing from an inner pocket a packet of papers, he handed to me a discharge from Company D 30th Infantry, dated 1919 in Germany. He had been discharged from the 30th Infantry in Europe following World War I. Returning to Sicily to visit his parents, he had never been able to leave. It was a coincidence that the company from which he had been discharged was then engaged on the peak just east of the town. I am told the wine flowed freely during the short time they were to remain there.

The Germans had mined the tunnel at Cape Calava, but they had withdrawn in such haste that they had not been able to complete the demolitions. However, they had done something even more effective. Just beyond the tunnel they had blown one hundred fifty feet of the roadway from the cliff side into the sea a hundred feet below. Days would have been required to blast another road from the cliff, and building one passable for motors over the mountains would have required many weeks. Already the 15th Infantry and the Ranger Battalion were beyond the Cape without artillery or tanks, and with only infantry weapons. We had to cross. Colonel Bingham and his engineers solved the problem by erecting a trestle bridge across the gap. It was this bridging operation which Ernie Pyle, who was with the 3rd Engineers at the time, made known to millions in his graphic description. I spent most of the night at the bridge site and talked much with Ernie Pyle during those hours of waiting. Ernie's account was in error in only one respect. He thought that I "couldn't help any". But I had given the engineers until noon next day to get jeeps across and First Sergeant Adilard Levesque had assured me that he would see it done. I had only to wait right there and act impatient until the job was finished. Mine was the first jeep to cross with just minutes to spare before noon. By mid-afternoon, artillery was crossing. By midnight, our heaviest loads were crossing.

East of Patti, the costal plain was wider, there were fewer bottlenecks to impede our progress, and German advantage in observation was no longer so pronounced. We pressed on relentlessly. During August 14th, the 15th Infantry made contact along the high ground around Fernari and by dark had driven the Germans east of the last lateral road leading southward to the Sicilian plain. During the night, the 30th Infantry blocked roads leading to the south and the 7th Infantry passed through the 15th after the retreating Boche. So close upon them were we that the Germans had no time to destroy supplies on Cape Milazzo where we took a huge ammunition dump, several batteries of artillery, more than one hundred fifty undamaged vehicles, several thousand gallons of gasoline and oil, huge stocks of lumber, several long-wave transmitters and a complete radio direction finder. During the afternoon of the 15th, the 7th Infantry was approaching Spadafora. I ordered the advance continued on during the night, and started Colonel William O. Darby, that night, with his Ranger Battalion and a battery of pack artillery to climb the mountain heights above Messina overlooking it from the west. I expected then to be in Messina the following day, the 16th.

Back at my Command Post in a farm house near Falcone, General Keyes appeared about mid-afternoon. He informed me that the 157th Regimental Combat Team of the 45th Infantry Division, which had been preparing for another sea borne envelopment since the Brolo landing, was to land before daylight next morning on beaches east of Cape Milazzo. I was astounded. We were already beyond the landing beaches, and the landing would take place in the midst of my Division now pressing on after the retreating Germans. With troops coming in from the sea for an assault landing and expecting to fight their way ashore if need be, one could easily imagine the possibilities of conflict and confusion. Such a landing could serve no useful military purpose and was almost certain to have dire and unfortunate consequences. All this I pointed out to General Keyes. He was reluctant to cancel the landing, for General Patton was not averse to profiting from such a spectacular operation. It was not until I offered to stop the pursuit and withdraw the Division to the west of Cape Milazzo, that General Keyes finally agreed that the landing was not practical. Even then he insisted that the force would land, but behind us on beaches west of Cape Milazzo. It fell to the lot of Lieutenant Colonels Ben Harrel and Bert Connor of my staff to meet the incoming waves at the water's edge to inform them that the beach was already in friendly hands.

During the 16th, the 7th Infantry overcame the last resistance and by nightfall was on the heights overlooking Messina. About dark we emplaced a Long Tom well forward and had the pleasure of unloading the first one hundred rounds of American artillery on the mainland of Europe. Patrols entered the city during the night as the last Germans made their escape across the Straits of Messina.

Early the next morning, I was on the heights above Messina looking down into the town and across the toe of Italy. At 0700, one patrol brought out the Podesta and several civil functionaries to make the civil submission of the city. At 0800, another patrol brought the senior Italian military authority to surrender the city. Colonel Michele Tomaselle presented to me the Beretta pistol which he carried. I sent him back to Messina to make the formal surrender there.

General Keyes had directed me to await the arrival of General Patton before entering the town, and had notified General Patton that arrangements were complete. We had arranged transportation with motorcycle and scout car escorts for a considerable party. General Patton finally arrived about 1000 with his characteristic flurry: "What in the hell are you all standing around for." I assured him that we were only awaiting his arrival. We took our places in the waiting cars and the cavalcade moved off down the winding road into Messina. In plain view of the mainland across the Straits, we were accompanied all the way down the hill by German artillery. Colonel Walters, riding with General Keyes in the car behind that in which General Patton and I were riding, was wounded by a shell fragment. Otherwise, there was no damage.

Just after we arrived in the city, a British armored patrol entered it from the west. General Montgomery had no doubt been anxious to beat General Patton into Messina for he had landed a patrol a few miles down the coast for the purpose of being there before us.

The race to Messina was ended.

We remained in Messina for only a brief period—long enough for General Patton to receive the formal surrender from the civil and military officials in the square and for a few photographs. Then leaving General Eagles to supervise the establishment of military government there, we wended our way back up the winding road and over the mountain. This time, the Boche guns across the Straits, which had fired the salute for our entry into Messina, were fortunately silent. Back at the Command Post at Rometta, there was a victory luncheon. Then there was a day of rest, and once more the Division was in movement, this time for a rest and training area near Trapani in the extreme western end of Sicily.

At half-past eight the morning of August 20th, Carleton and I left Rometta in a light sedan, with the aides and the rest of our party following. Just before noon, we stopped for lunch at the "castello by the sea" which we had occupied so briefly. We had required sixteen laborious days to reach Messina; we had returned in just three hours. A brief stop at Army Headquarters in Palermo, and we continued on to Trapani where the entire division was assembled two days later. Here we were to rest and refit and prepare for whatever was next to come.

•

CHAPTER FIVE

SOUTHERN ITALY

1. Mountains and Mud

Mussolini had fallen from power on July 25th, just after the capture of Palermo, and the Badoglio government had taken over in Italy. Even before the end of the Sicilian campaign, plans were afoot for the invasion of the Italian mainland to complete the elimination of Italy from the war. While I was not, at the time, familiar with the details of higher level planning, I was aware by the time we had captured Messina that the broad concept was to have the British Eighth Army cross over the Straits of Messina, seize the Italian naval base at Taranto, and advance northward up the Italian boot in conjunction with a later assault somewhere in the vicinity of Naples, by a combined British-American Force under the newly organized Fifth Army.

We also knew that the cross-channel invasion was to take place the following spring and that certain American divisions were to be sent from Sicily to England as soon as the campaign was over to begin preparations. I had rather thought that the 3rd Infantry Division would be one of these, partly because of its assault training, and partly because of my experience in Combined Operations Headquarters in London during the preceding year. I was relieved, however, when I learned that we were to remain in the Mediterranean theater, for there was promise of early action. England would have meant many months of relative inactivity. Later, General Eisenhower told me that General Clark had persuaded him to leave the Division in the theater.

I was rather disappointed to learn, just as the Sicilian campaign was ending, that the 45th Infantry Division was to be the first one to be taken by the Fifth Army from Sicily, and that one regiment of that Division would accompany the assault force in floating reserve.

And no sooner had Messina fallen than Sicily was rife with rumors of high level diplomatic dickerings looking toward an Italian surrender.

One of my first assignments after the Division reached Trapani was to select and organize a staging area where two British divisions coming from England could land, rest for a day, and have some good meals before joining in the Fifth Army invasion of Italy. Needless to say all of this was to be done with great secrecy, and the staging troops were to be isolated from all contact with natives and from troops in Sicily except those actually operating the staging area. Even under the best of conditions, however, such preparations always result in gossip.

On August 29th, I accompanied Generals Patton, Keyes, and Gay on a visit to General Montgomery's Headquarters in Catania to be present when General Eisenhower decorated General Montgomery with the highest order of the American Legion of Merit. On our return, we landed on the airfield near Palermo. We had scarcely rolled to a halt when a huge black Italian bomber swooped low over the field, leveled off over the runway, landed, and taxied off to one side of the field. Then General Patton told me that the airplane was expected, and that our antiaircraft had been warned not to fire upon it. I was to go about my business and make no mention of what I had seen. I did so. But when I reached my headquarters in Trapani, several members of my staff asked me if I had seen the Italian plane, and told me that it was rumored that General Eisenhower was conferring with high Italian officials near Palermo. He may have been, but neither he nor anyone else had mentioned it to me during the hours we spent together that day. The rumors had spread through the airfields, doubtless because of the measures which were necessary to prevent firing upon or attacking the Italian airplane.

On September 2nd, I inspected the staging area at Castellamare which had been established by Lieutenant Colonel E. C. Doleman and his 3rd Battalion, 30th Infantry, and found all in readiness to receive the British divisions which were expected within the next few days. The following day, we learned that General Montgomery's Eighth Army had crossed over the Straits of Messina against only slight opposition, and the invasion of the Italian mainland was on. On September 4th, I was ordered to proceed to Algiers with certain key members of my staff to confer with General Clark and members of the Fifth Army staff concerning future employment of the 3rd Infantry Division in Italy.

Accompanied by Carleton, Lieutenant Colonel Walters, G-2, Lieutenant Colonel Johnson, G-4, and Lieutenant Colonel Kerwin, Division Artillery, I arrived in Algiers about noon, September 5th. We found General Clark and his immediate staff on board the *Ancon* in Algiers harbor with Admiral Hewitt and the Naval staff. Brigadier General Don Brann, Fifth Army G-3, briefed us on the plans for AVALANCHE—the assault landing at Salerno—and plans for the capture of Naples. Members of my staff conferred with their corresponding sections on the Army staff concerning staff details incident to the employment of the Division in the Fifth Army. Carleton and I talked at length with Generals Clark, and Brann, concerning plans for the landing and possible future missions for the Division.

The assault plan envisaged landing the American 36th Infantry Division, fresh from the United States, on the beaches at Paestum, while the British X Corps landed two divisions on beaches farther to the north opposite Salerno. The port of Naples was to be the first objective. General Clark informed me that the Italians had already surrendered, but the announcement was to coincide with the landing of his force at Salerno, where the Italians had agreed there would be no opposition. Neither General Clark nor General Brann seemed to think that there would be much opposition, or any necessity for landing the 3rd Infantry Division there at all. General Clark told me to be prepared for landing farther north, and said that he might even have it land as far north as Rome, which was already looming large as an objective with General Clark and others. However, I had already had enough experience with the Boche to believe that the landing at Salerno would bring a violent reaction of some sort even though the landing itself might be unopposed.

The *Ancon* sailed on the expedition during the night of September 5th, and we returned to Trapani to prepare for whatever was to come. One of the first things that I did was to have the Division Signal Officer established a radio intercept net on wave lengths of the Fifth Army and Naval Task Force nets in an endeavor to obtain some knowledge of events during the actual landings on the 9th of September. On the morning of September 8th I was called to Palermo for a conference with General Patton and Corps and Division commanders. General Patton had been advised that the announcement of the Italian surrender was to be made that night. Among the conditions stipulated, the Italians were to fly their Air Force to our Sicilian fields and sail their Navy to Allied ports. My division was to guard six airfields in western Sicily, to prevent any trickery on the part of the Italians, or in case the Italians should be followed in by German airplanes. We reinforced our guards on each of the six airfields and held a strong reserve in readiness. Late that evening, the radio announced the Italian surrender, but no airplanes arrived to land upon our airfields or upon any other airfields in Sicily. It was obvious that the Germans had interfered with the Italian plans. Early on the morning of September 9th, the landing of Allied forces at Salerno was announced.

In the three weeks that had elapsed since the capture of Messina, we had done all that we could to prepare the Division for further action. The Division was still some 2,000 officers and men under its authorized strength, but except for this shortage it was fit and ready. Colonel William H. Ritter had replaced Colonel Charles Johnson in command of the 15th Infantry. Because of shortage of officers, I had sent Colonel Ben Harrel, Division G-3 to Colonel Ritter as Executive Officer, Lieu-

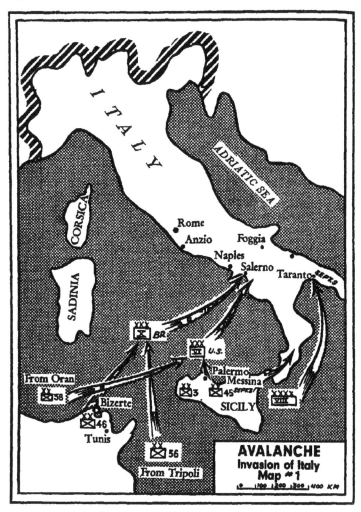

AVALANCHE
Invasion of Italy
Map #1

tenant Colonel Bert Connor taking over the duties of Division G-3. Colonel Walters, lent to me by General Lucas, left to join the II Corps. Otherwise command and staff positions were about as they were when we landed in Sicily.

We waited with intense interest for news from Salerno. First announcements were that the landings were successful. Then, during the day, there were fragmentary messages intercepted by my improvised and incomplete radio intercept system that indicated that all might not be well. There were indications that some of the beaches were under fire and that one or more could not be used for landing. Appeals for help, for naval gunfire, and the like, came over the ether but we never received enough information to permit us to know what was taking place on shore. During the afternoon of September 11th, General Keyes came to Trapani and told me that the situation at Salerno was desperate. However, we still knew little or nothing of the tactical situation on shore. The Eighth Army was advancing northward from the toe of the Italian boot, although it did not appear to us that it was making very rapid progress.

About nine o'clock the evening of September 13th, General Patton telephoned from Palermo. I was to proceed there by boat the following day to confer with General Clark. I notified the key members of my staff to be ready to leave early the next morning. Then just before midnight a message came from 15th Army Group saying the 3rd Infantry Division was to be moved to Salerno as soon as possible to meet the urgent situation there. We issued orders at once for the movement of the Division to the staging area in Palermo, where it would be brought to strength by transfers from the 1st and 9th Infantry Divisions. At five o'clock the next morning, I conferred with Generals Eagles and Campbell and the Division staff on final details, then, leaving them to supervise the movement of the Division to the staging area, Carleton and I departed for Palermo. We conferred briefly with General Patton, and then boarded a British PT boat for the run across to Salerno.

Our first sight of AVALANCHE in the gathering dusk was a ring of fire that flamed and glowed and sparkled in the distance with occasional flares streaking through the heavens like great sky rockets, and occasional bursts of flame which mushroomed and fell in showers of fire. It was a beautiful, although not a comforting, view. Approaching closer, the rumble of guns like thunder drifted across the waves. As we drew near, it seemed as though the whole sea off shore was filled with ships of every size and type. Reducing speed, we approached warily blinking prescribed recognition signals. Hailing one vessel after another, we eventually found the flagship and found that it was the *Biscayne* which had borne us to our landing in Sicily. On board, we found my comrade, Admiral Connally, and others of our Navy friends, and learned that Admiral Hewitt had departed with the *Ancon* soon after command had passed to General Clark on shore.

On board, we had supper and gathered what news there was. So far as news of the tactical situation on shore was concerned, there was little enough, for the troops had not been able to keep those on board abreast of developments. General Clark and his Headquarters were established on shore. There had been desperate fighting; it was obvious that things were not going too well, because General Clark had requested that the *Ancon* be recalled in case it became necessary to reembark. No one knew where the Army Command Post was located on shore, but since only one beach was in use in the American sector, it should not be hard to find. I sent off a message to General Clark saying that I was coming ashore and requesting that a guide meet us at the beach with transportation. Then, arranging with the skipper of the PT boat to stand by to return us to Palermo, we went ashore in a landing craft provided by Admiral Conolly.

Approaching the beach from the *Biscayne* anchored some four or five miles out, we saw the shore line stretched before us in a wide semi-circle. still marked by the flare of bursting shells. Most of the cannonading seemed to be off to the north in the British area, but there were occasional bursts in the mountains behind the beach toward which we were heading. All of these bursts seemed terribly close to the beaches as we drew closer. Knowing little or nothing of what had transpired on shore, we were prepared for the worst.

There was little activity on the beach where we landed. No craft were beaching, nor was there any congestion of men, vehicles or supplies as we were prepared to expect. There was no one to meet us, but we found the Shore Party Command Post, where we obtained transportation to take us to the Army Command Post, which we found about a mile inland well concealed in a dense thicket, ensconced in vans, trailers and tents, well dispersed.

There I found General Gruenther, Chief of Staff, and learned that General Clark was absent on a visit to the British X Corps, a trip which enemy activity had compelled him to make by sea. General Gruenther outlined for us the events of these harrowing days. It had been a near thing—one AVALANCHE almost overwhelmed by another. And the danger was not yet past. Instead of Italians, the German 16th Panzer Division had met them on the beaches so that they had literally to fight their way ashore. And this Division had been reinforced by other elements, notably by the 29th Panzer Division and elements of the Herman Goering. Striking in the gap between the British and Americans, the Germans had the day before overrun one battalion of the 36th Infantry Division near Persano, had surrounded another at Altavilla, forced back a regiment of the 45th Infantry Division, and had been almost through the defenses on their way to the Paestum beaches. Desperate measures had been necessary to establish a new defense line along which the renewed German attacks had been turned back only during the day.

Map #2
SALERNO BEACHHEAD
12 SEPTEMBER 1943

GULF OF SALERNO

In the British sector, the X Corps had not been able to clear the heights back of Salerno and Battipaglia and secure the Montecorvino airfield which was their objective. During the German counterattacks, the situation on the front of the X Corps had been so grave that General Clark had ordered the drop of a parachute battalion in the mountain passes to the north to interrupt communications of German forces opposing the X Corps. This drop had been planned for the previous night, but was actually taking place during the present night.

Still farther to the north, Colonel Bill Darby and his Rangers had seized the mountain passes leading from Salerno toward Naples, but General Clark had been forced to send a battalion from the hard pressed 36th Infantry Division to reinforce the Rangers and tighten their grip on these passes to prevent their use by German troops approaching from the north.

The afternoon had been relatively quiet on the front of the VI Corps. The arrival of the last Regimental Combat Team of the 45th Infantry Division during the day had provided a much needed reserve. And while General Gruenther thought then that the Germans would renew their attacks, the situation looked more hopeful.

It had been expected that the Eighth Army would advance more rapidly than it had done and that its approach would have reduced the threat to the beachhead. As a matter of fact, the advance of the Eighth Army probably had this effect, albeit a somewhat tardy one, for the hard pressed AVALANCHE forces. While we were talking with General Gruenther, two correspondents were brought into him. They had made the trip overland from the Eighth Army then some forty miles to the south by the coastal road. They had encountered no enemy and had had only slight delay avoiding a few scattered demolitions. It was obvious then that the worst was over even though the Germans renewed their attacks on the following day.

The next morning, September 15th, I saw General Clark. He was encouraged although still expecting a renewal of the German attacks. I explained that my Division was in Palermo, ready to load as soon as craft were available. He was anxious that the Division arrive as soon as possible, and told me that it would be assigned to the VI Corps under General Dawley. I proposed to depart at once to expedite this move, but General Clark suggested that I visit the front to see what the country was like before starting back. Which I did.

Carleton and I set forth in a jeep. Our first visit was to the left of the 36th Infantry Division sector along the high ground just west of La Cosa Creek and just south of its junction with the Calore River. Here we found Brigadier General Mike O'Daniels. Mike had been in charge of the beach organization in the American sector. In the desperate hours of the German counterattacks, General Clark had sent him to this area with an engineer battalion and a few tank destroyers to organize the defense. Mike took us over his position and showed us the scenes of the action of the preceding days. Looking east three or four miles, he pointed out the high hill and the town of Altavilla where one battalion had been surrounded and from which only a few stragglers had as yet come in. Off to the left in the angle between the Calore and Sele Rivers, he pointed out the position where another battalion had been overrun. Mike had been hard put to hold his position against the German attacks of the day before. While we were forward looking out toward Altavilla, Mike saw three soldiers moving back across the hill toward the rear. Running toward them he called out: "Here, you men. Where do you think you are going?" They stopped, and one replied: "Sir, we are going back for rations which they told us had just been brought up." Mike answered: "Well, I can't spare all three of you for that purpose. Two of you go back to your fox holes, and let one man go for the rations." It was a dramatic underscoring of how desperate had been the need for men.

I visited both General Dawley, the VI Corps commander, and General Fred Walker, commanding the 36th Infantry Division. General Dawley had not expected to assume command of operations on shore until after the beachhead was established. He had not been prepared when he was ordered on D Day to assume command. His staff scattered, his headquarters and communications scheduled for later unloading, he had been compelled to impose his needs upon those of the 36th Infantry Division, and the communications organization of the 36th Infantry Division was already strained. Neither Dawley nor Walker were very happy about the situation, and both attributed much of the early confusion to the disorganization of Command.

Carleton and I made our way back to the Army Command Post shortly after noon, where we found increasing optimism. Later, we made our way out to the *Biscayne*, found our PT boat, and were on our way back to Palermo. The trip was uneventful except for one minor thrill. Just before sunset, one lone German airplane came suddenly out of the sun barely skimming the waves and dropped a single bomb which struck the water just a few yards off our starboard bow. Fortunately for us, it skipped on the water like a flat rock, barely cleared the deck where we were standing, and sank harmlessly a few yards off the other side. It must have been the only bomb that the airplane was carrying for it did not return to the attack but was gone into the gathering haze before our antiaircraft gunners could even open fire.

We were back in Palermo before midnight. During the day the Division had been brought almost up to strength by the transfer of about

2,000 men from the 1st and 9th Infantry Divisions, both of which were departing soon for England. Loading began the next morning as soon as the LST's were ready to receive us. By nightfall, Division Headquarters, Division Artillery, the 30th Infantry and part of the service troops were loaded. Early the morning of September 17th, the first convoy sailed, and the next began loading. Once more I boarded a PT boat to return to Salerno, this time accompanied by several members of the Division staff, to arrange for unloading and assembly of the Division. The first convoy began unloading at 0900 September 18th, and moved to assembly areas north of the Sele River. The 7th Infantry disembarked during the next night, the 15th Infantry during the day of September 20th. Except for the Administration Center left in Sicily, the entire Division was now in Italy and ready for its new mission.

Late in the afternoon of September 18th, I attended a conference at Army headquarters at which future plans were discussed. The situation was vastly improved by the advance of the 45th Infantry Division in the area north of the Sele River. It was known then that the Germans were withdrawing, but it was expected that they would hold the difficult mountain terrain as long as possible in order to give them time to wreck the port of Naples thoroughly and to make our advance as costly as possible. Already there were indications that the Germans were preparing defenses along the line of the Volturno River still farther north.

From the Army point of view, Naples and the airfields on the Neapolitan plain were the next objectives. The Army plan, dictated largely by the availability of roads, was simple enough. The VI Corps, with the 45th and 3rd Infantry Division abreast on the two available roads, was to advance north through the mountains to secure the line Avellino-Teora, prepared to continue the advance on order. The Eighth Army had not yet come up abreast of the beachhead forces, so the right flank of the VI Corps was to advance northward beyond Teora as the Eighth Army advanced on its right. Meanwhile, the British X Corps was to attack northward from Salerno through the two passes where the Rangers had been maintaining a foothold, gain the Naples plain, then pass an armored division through to capture Naples and drive the enemy north of the Volturno.

Army orders for the advance were issued during September 19th. About nine o'clock that night I was called to the VI Corps Command Post to confer with General Dawley about plans for the Corps advance. Carleton and I arrived at the headquarters, located in a huge building known as the Tobacco Factory. On the way there, driving the jeep in the blackout with only the small blue lights, I was stopped by a Corps M. P. who, in rather forceful language ordered me to "douse" the cigarette I was smoking. Inside the building, all was darkness although one could make out figures clustered about in the gloom. We were escorted to a distant corner where we found General Dawley seated in darkness with two or three staff officers about him facing what I eventually identified as a map board leaning against the wall. There were many huge windows in the Tobacco Factory which could not be covered. No lights were permitted inside, not even the glow of cigarettes. There was some discussion of plans for the Corps order for the advance, before General Dawley, using a flashlight a little larger than a pencil to illuminate the map pointed out the routes of the 45th and 3rd Infantry Divisions and the phase lines upon which we could maintain contact with each other and with the British on our left. It was an eerie and not altogether inspiring experience. Although German aircraft had been active over the beachhead from the beginning, the danger from air attack at night hardly seemed sufficient to warrant such extreme protective measures as to preclude normal and efficient functioning of command and staff.

At 0700 the morning of September 20th, we received the Corps order for the advance which was to begin at 1100. I had, the evening before, directed Colonel Rogers to send reconnaissance out to gain contact with the enemy on the road leading toward Acerno. Captain Richard Savaresy with the I and R Platoon, 30th Infantry, moved out at midnight. A few hours later, near a road fork where one road leads west to Montecorvino, the platoon attacked and defeated a German detachment, and so was the first of the Division to "draw blood" in the Italian campaign.

The 3rd Infantry Division, fresh from its experience in Sicily, was as well prepared for the task that lay ahead as any division could hope to be. We had learned much of German delaying methods and how to overcome them; the term "superman" applied to the Germans was now a term of derision. We had learned much of the technique of moving and fighting in mountains, and we were to learn a great deal more. We had provided ourselves with a pack train to supply infantry operating in difficult mountain terrain; a pack battery to provide some artillery support; and a troop of mounted infantrymen to expedite reconnaissance of difficult mountainous areas as well as communications between the Division and elements in inaccessible terrain. While we had just absorbed 2,000 replacements to make up for our Sicilian losses, all of these men had the experience of the Sicilian campaign behind them. It was not with the careless curiosity of tyros that the men of this Division set about their tasks, but with the almost detached confidence and determination of veterans, which they were.

Our one road forward entered the craggy Apennines right at Battipaglia, following generally the course of a mountain stream, Tuscania Creek, northward to Acerno. A few miles north of Acerno, it passed

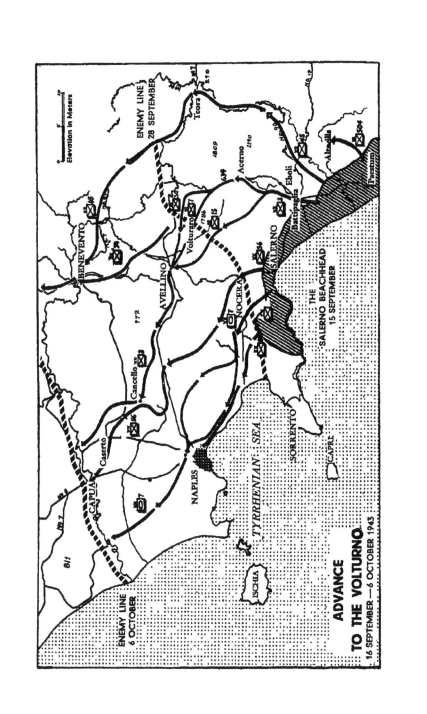

ADVANCE
TO THE VOLTURNO.
16 SEPTEMBER — 6 OCTOBER 1943

over a divide into the drainage net of the Volturno River, about fifty miles farther on to the north. About twenty miles north of Acerno, the road joined Highway 7, near the town of Montemarano, which our route followed northwest over another divide for a dozen miles to Avellino, an important road center on the Corps' initial objective. From Avellino, one road led westward over another divide to the Naples plain, then northward along the mountains to the Volturno River at Caserta. Another road led northward from Avellino through the mountain towns of Montesarchio and Airola to the junction of the Calore and Volturno Rivers a few miles above Caserta. This was to be the zone of the Division's operations.

The terrain was enormously difficult. Narrow valleys were broken by intensely cultivated plots. Rugged mountains rose to elevations of more than 5,000 feet. Our road wound its way through defile after defile, crossed over numerous bridges, and clung precariously to precipitous cliffs in many places. Off the roads, occasional cart trails led to villages nestled among the mountains, and a few mule paths led to the mountain tops, and along the mountain ridges. Off these roads and tracks, the country was passable only for men on foot and for mules. We were to find many places that pack mules could not climb where supplies had to be carried on the backs of men.

Some miles north of Battipaglia, a road led off westward through Montecorvino to the mountain village of Curticelle. Thence, a mule path led over the mountain ridge and beyond into the valley of the Sabato River leading toward Avellino, but it was passable only for men and mules. Our only way to move artillery and supplies forward was by the one road leading northward through Acerno, and this road offered the resourceful enemy all too many opportunities for effective demolitions to delay our advance and add to the difficulties of our problems. And these difficulties were vastly increased by the rains which began on September 26th and increased in frequency until they were of almost daily occurrence.

When lines of action are limited, military decisions are not difficult, and the formulation of operational plans is relatively easy. So it was in this case. Our plans followed the general pattern of our Sicilian operation. It was the execution which was difficult. One regiment with the bare minimum of vehicles required for transport of weapons, ammunition, and for communications, advanced along the main route brushing aside light enemy resistance. When the advance was stopped by enemy demolitions defended by the enemy, one battalion remained on the axis of movement to maintain contact and protect the deployment of the Division artillery, while other battalions took to the mountains on either side to outflank the enemy positions, the whole operation being supported by Division artillery emplaced as far forward as positions could be found. When enemy fire had been cleared from the demolitions, the Division engineers cleared the obstruction, constructed bypasses, or built bridges, and the operation was then repeated, usually with another regiment leading. This general plan was followed throughout the next two months.

The 30th Infantry with its attached tanks, tank destroyers, and engineers advanced north from Battipaglia at 1100, September 20th, and our Italian campaign was on. I was not to see General Dawley again, shortly before the advance began I received from him this handwritten message: "Dear Truscott—Sorry I will not be with you. I am leaving. best of luck always, Sincerely, Dawley." That was the first intimation that I had that Dawley was being relieved. A little later I met General Clark who confirmed it and told me that my old friend, Major General John W. Lucas, was being brought over from the II Corps in Sicily to command the VI Corps.

The 30th Infantry encountered only slight opposition during the afternoon, and halted for the night with its leading battalion a dozen miles north of Battipaglia. Moving out at daylight the morning of Sept. 21st under sporadic artillery fire, the battalion soon met the first of the effective German demolitions. About two miles south of Acerno, a deep gorge, the Isca della Serra, joins Tuscania Creek. Our road forward passed around a mountain spur and crossed this deep gorge on what had been a beautiful stone arch bridge, but now only parts of the abutments remained. The Germans had destroyed the bridge leaving a yawning abyss more than sixty feet across. From a hill just to the east, German riflemen, machine guns and mortars supported by artillery in the town behind, were firing on the bridge site and all approaches leading to it. The Germans soon made it evident that they would not give up Acerno without a fight.

It was nearly dark before Colonel Doleman's 3rd Battalion was able to make its way over the mountains to the west and across the Isca della Serra to clear the enemy from the eastern bank. During the night, Colonel Rogers passed the 2nd Battalion over the mountains to the west of the gorge to cut the road leading north from Acerno, and a company went through the mountains east of Tuscania Creek to positions from which to attack Acerno from the south, while Doleman's 3rd Battalion attacked from the west. About noon, the regiment launched an attack supported by three battalions of the Division artillery and cleared the town.

I reached the scene of action around the town just after the fight was over and while prisoners were still being collected. Accompanied by my aide, Lieutenant Bartash, I had left my jeep at the bridge where Division engineers were already hard at work, and had proceeded on foot. Doleman's battalion had encountered determined opposition in a grove just west of the town and had finally assaulted with bayonets and hand grenades, led by Doleman himself.

The previous afternoon I had started one battalion of the 7th Infantry into the mountains above Montemarano with mule transport, to follow by-paths across the mountain ridges and cut the road some six miles north of Acerno in the hope of cutting off the retreat of the Germans defending the town. While I did not know just where the battalion was when the 30th Infantry cleared the Germans from Acerno, it was later apparent that the German discovery of this threat to their rear had led to their precipitate withdrawal from the divide north of Acerno where we had expected them to stand and fight again.

While Acerno was in our hands, our rate of advance was limited to the speed with which our engineers could repair German demolitions or construct by-passes around them. No by-pass was possible over the Isca della Serra; a bridge was necessary. Working night and day, Captain Stanley E. Larsen and his Company C, 10th Engineers, spanned the gap with a two-storey, two-bent trestle bridge. The bridge was passable for jeeps early in the afternoon of September 23rd; by nightfall it was ready for all Division loads.

North of Acerno, between the town and the crest of the divide, the Germans had blown five bridges. A few miles north of the divide where the road spanned another canyon on a stone arch bridge, the Germans had destroyed the bridge and blasted more than a hundred feet of cliff-side, dropping the road into the canyon below. It was reminiscent of the demolition at Cape Calava back in Sicily. This was to be our first experience with the Bailey Bridge, a knock-down steel bridge which is put together like a boy's Erector Set and is then pushed out across the span to be bridged, counterbalanced by its own weight. Captain Edwin H. Swift's Company A spanned the bridge and cut out a new road from the cliff-side in just two days.

All in all, the story of the advance during these fifty-nine days is an epic of engineering feats. Building bridges, constructing by-passes, building roads and trails, sweeping roads and bivouac areas for mines, removing mine fields, constructing landing strips for artillery observation airplanes, operating water points, providing the engineer supplies for troops, and occasionally taking their weapons in hand and fighting as infantry: these were the missions performed by the 10th Engineer Battalion and the Corps Engineers which supported them. There was no weapon more valuable than the engineer bulldozer, no soldiers more effective than the engineers who moved us forward.

After Acerno, Avellino was our next important objective. Avellino was about forty miles to the northwest by a road across a mountain chain and in the valley of the Sabato River. It was safe to assume that there would be as many demolitions as the enemy had time to prepare. It was my plan to have the 7th Infantry lead the advance north from Acerno, cross over the mountains along Highway 7 and by trails through the mountains to the south, if such trails could be found, and attack Avellino from the east. At the same time, the 15th Infantry would advance northward down the valley leading from Curticelle and attack Avellino from the south. The final marches would be made under cover of darkness the night of September 27th, with the final attack at dawn the following morning. However, I reckoned without the elements.

The 7th Infantry passed forward during September 24th on the heels of the retreating Germans, and were soon beyond the range of their own supporting artillery. Early in the afternoon I went forward to see how the advance was going. Standing with Colonel Sherman and several members of his staff on the northern slopes of the divide north of Acerno, we could see several batteries of German artillery displacing little more than a mile away. Not a single gun in our Division artillery was within range, although one battalion was then displacing forward.

By the 27th, the 7th Infantry had cleared the enemy north to Highway 7 and had found one trail across the mountains to the south which, with some engineers' work, could be made possible for jeeps. The 30th Infantry had occupied Montemarano on Highway 7 and was prepared to follow the 7th toward Avellino. The leading regiment of the newly arrived 34th Infantry Division had moved up alongside the 30th Infantry.

Rain had begun falling late in the afternoon of September 26th. It developed into a terrific downpour which lasted all through the night. This rain washed out all the road repairs which we had so laboriously constructed, made movement of vehicles off roads almost impossible and movement of men enormously difficult and slow. Hardly were essential repairs effected, when another torrential all-night downpour washed them out again. It was not until the night of September 29th that the final advance on Avellino got under way, and each one of seven infantry battalions headed into the foggy darkness for an assigned objective about the town.

I will never forget my view of the Avellino valley the following morning. With Bartash, I had gone forward along Highway 7 to a point on the eastern slope, where I found Colonel Sherman and his command group waiting for the engineers to construct a by-pass around the first of several blown bridges. Westward across the valley in which Avellino lay, there was a sea of fog above which the sun shone brightly and distant mountains were clearly visible. And from this vast sea of fog, there were the sounds of firing, of scattered actions in a dozen places—rifles, machine guns, mortars, the characteristic sound of the German machine pistol, occasional salvos of artillery. Our infantry battalions, moving through darkness and fog, had by-passed enemy resistance and had so completely infiltrated German defenses that small fights were in progress over a wide area as the German delaying forces tried desperately to escape.

I watched while Sherman and his command group set off on foot down the highway toward the town, disappearing into the fog. I waited while the sounds of firing grew less and less, until there was only an occasional shot off to the northwest, and finally none at all. I knew then that Avellino was in our hands.

Most panics in war are caused by rumors, for the tensions of war render men especially susceptible to rumors, no matter how unfounded. The day before our entry into Avellino, a rumor spread through part of the Division that might well have resulted in panic and seriously interfered with our operations. There had come an electrifying report that the Germans were using gas. A wire-laying party had sustained severe burns from contact with wet bushes along the road, and containers nearby led them to believe that the Germans were using mustard gas. Without protective clothing, men cannot enter an area drenched with mustard gas unharmed, and we had no protective clothing. I did not believe that the Germans would dare to employ gas under the circumstances, but little imagination was required to picture the harm which would result from the spreading of such a rumor. Accordingly, I issued strict orders to isolate the casualties and to stop all talk of the incident while we verified the reports. At the place where the casualties occurred, we found several empty containers which had obviously contained gas, as well as several full ones. These we sent back at once for analysis which showed the contents to be only a relatively harmless form of tear gas. It seems likely that the Germans had carried this gas for control of refractory mobs, and had cast these containers aside in their flight. The casualties recovered quickly and were back at their assigned tasks within a day or so. So ended the only gas scare which I was to encounter throughout the war.

In the mountains north of Acerno, the Division made contact with several detachments of the 2nd Battalion, 509th Parachute Infantry Regiment, which had been dropped in the mountainous areas south of Avellino the night of September 14th to interfere with German movements toward the British X Corps front. These gallant men had maintained themselves in rear of the German lines for two weeks, with some assistance from friendly Italians. According to their reports, the Germans had made some effort to hunt them down during the first days. Since the paratroopers had not been in sufficient strength to do very much damage, the Germans had soon gone on about their business. The paratroopers reported that the Germans were systematically withdrawing to the north of the Volturno River.

Avellino presented a spectacle that was to become increasingly familiar to us in Italy. The town had suffered heavy damage, first from our own bombers during the effort to prevent German reinforcements from reaching the Salerno beachhead during its dark days, and more recently from German demolitions. All about were damaged buildings, bomb craters, shell holes, and other marks of devastation, and the whole town reeked of putrefying bodies buried in the debris. It seemed strangely sad to me that the townsfolk who had suffered so should greet us with cheers and flowers, fruit and wine.

Army orders had directed the VI Corps to shift the bulk of its troops to the westward, as soon as Avellino was taken, prepared either to attack westward through Avello on the edge of the Campanian plain to assist the British X Corps in taking Naples, or to turn northward and capture Benevento. When my Command Post moved to Avellino early on October 1st, all combat elements of the Division were in the Avellino area. I had no wish to allow the Germans more time for demolitions than we could help; accordingly, the 15th Infantry immediately started westward by Highway toward Avello, while the 30th Infantry turned northward toward Montesarchio. During the morning I learned by radio that the British had entered Naples at half-past nine that morning without opposition. That night, orders came directing the VI Corps northward toward Benevento with the Volturno as the next objective.

The following day, October 2nd, I was called back to the Corps Command Post for a conference with General Lucas and the other division commanders, Major Generals Troy H. Middleton, of the 45th, and Charles R. Ryder of the 34th. General Clark had issued a new Operations Instruction outlining the plan for future operations. General Alexander's 15th Army Group had prescribed that future operations of the Eighth and Fifth Armies were to be conducted in two phases. The first phase was to be the advance to seize a line from Termoli on the Adriatic coast through Iserna and Venafro to Sezza near the Mediterranean coast. When the armies were established on this line, the second phase was to be the advance to a line well to the north of Rome. General Clark's instructions assigned a boundary between the two corps and directed the British X Corps to "push its attack to the Volturno, force the crossings of that river, and continue the advance to the first phase line. Due to the present location of the VI Corps, the advance of the X Corps will not await the arrival of the VI Corps abreast of it, but will advance as rapidly as the situation permits."

The VI Corps was to "capture Benevento, and secure the crossings of the Calore River in that area using initially not to exceed one division. As soon as the crossings are secured, this division, moving by roads northwest of Benevento, will advance to the first phase line. The remainder of the corps, moving northwest by road between Benevento and the corps boundary, will move forward with all speed in the Corps zone of action."

The 34th Infantry Division had begun arriving in the line at Montemarano on September 27th, as the 3rd Division turned westward toward Avellino. The 45th was still farther to the east. General Lucas decided that the 34th Infantry Division would continue the advance to seize the crossings at Benevento, whereupon the 45th would be passed through to continue the advance to the first phase line. The 3rd meanwhile would continue its advance to the Volturno by the roads we were already using—the 15th Infantry advancing northward along the edge of the Campanian plain from Avello through Cancello to the mountains above Caserta, with the 30th Infantry following the mountain roads through Montesarchio and Airola toward the junction of the Calore and Volturno Rivers.

Incessant rains did more to delay our advance than either German demolitions, which were bad enough, or German delaying action. Along the main highways there were piles of fine big trees which the Germans felled to interlock across a road, in places where there was no way round. Booby trapped and mined, these were formidable obstacles which required much time and labor to remove. In many places in the mountains, the road passed through the narrow streets of ancient towns. Here the Germans demolished the fronts of whole blocks of old stone buildings, completely blocking the narrow streets. By-passes were rarely possible, and removal of the rubble was impossible. Our one way forward was to bulldoze new tracks across the rubble heaps often at the level of the second storeys of the gaping buildings. There was an encouraging sign, however, that the enemy might be running short of demolitions. In many places artillery shells and antitank mines were used for demolition purposes, and many structures prepared for demolitions lacked demolition charges. One rather unusual delaying measure which the Germans employed during this period was that of destroying mules in the countryside to prevent their falling into our hands. Obviously, the Germans had not liked our pack trains and mounted men.

On the right of the VI Corps, the 34th Infantry Division occupied

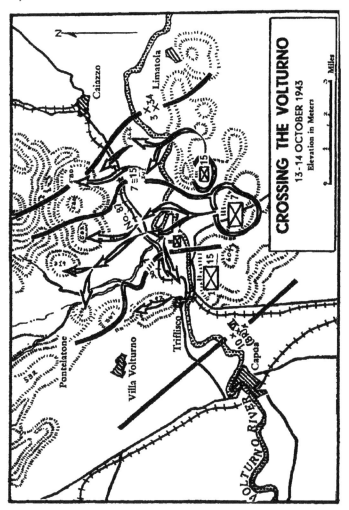

Benevento and secured a crossing over the Calore River there on October 3rd. The following day, the 45th Infantry Division began passing through the 34th and advancing northwest toward Mt. Acero and Amerosi. The 3rd Infantry Division, with the 30th Infantry on the right and the 15th Infantry on the left, reached the Volturno on October 6th on a front of about fifteen miles extending from its junction

with the Calore south of Amerosi to Mt. Tifata on the edge of the
Campanian plain opposite the Triflisco Gap. On our left, the British 7th
Armored Division had reached the river line below Capua on October
5th, and the British 56th Division was moving up to the river line in the
vicinity of Capua. During the afternoon of October 6th, I visited the
2nd Battalion, 15th Infantry, on the heights overlooking the river south
of Caiazzo and found Lieutenant Colonel Jack Toffey and his artillery
liaison officers cursing their luck. Much enemy activity was plainly
visible on the north side of the river, but rain and mud had delayed the
displacement of our artillery so that none of it was within range of
these excellent targets.

Up to this time, neither General Clark nor General Lucas had anticipated much delay in crossing the Volturno and continuing the advance. Nor had I. Orders issued on October 2nd had directed the British X Corps to push its attack to the Volturno, force the crossings of
that river and continue the advance to the first phase line without waiting for the VI Corps which was advancing through the mountains and
had a longer distance to traverse. The VI Corps was to cross one division over the Calore River at Benevento to advance to the first phase
line by roads northwest of that place, while the remainder of the Corps
moved northwest by roads between Benevento and the Corps boundary "with all speed". Since this latter provision referred to the part of
the Corps zone in which the 3rd Infantry Division was operating, I
expected to clear German patrols from the south bank of the Volturno
during October 7th, make necessary reconnaissance and preparations,
and cross over the following day if dispositions could be completed in
time. But it was not to be.

Lieutenant General Richard L. McCreery, who commanded the
British X Corps, came to see me about noon on October 6th, and told
me that his troops could not be ready to cross the river for several days.
He was planning to make his main crossing in the vicinity of Capua
with the 56th Division, with others crossing farther down toward the
coast. He was concerned because the area around Capua was dominated by German observation on the heights north of Triflisco and there
was a mass of German artillery north of Capua. He thought that the
VI Corps should cross first and seize those heights before his troops
began to cross. These heights were in the sector of the 3rd Infantry Division. Since this procedure would have left the Germans free to concentrate against it, it seemed to me that it would be better for all concerned if the two divisions crossed the river at the same time.

General Lucas came to see me not long after General McCreery's
visit, and I related to him the substance of our discussion. General Lucas
and I were confident that the Division could cross the river without too

much trouble, but we were also of the opinion that the Germans would be able to concentrate sufficient strength against one division to make progress slow and costly; for that reason both Corps should cross at the same time. It seems, however, that General McCreery's proposal met with initial favor at the Army level, for it was the essence of Operations Instructions No. 6 issued by General Clark the following day.

During October 7th, the 15th and 30th Infantry Regiments cleared the last German patrols from the south bank of the river and began intensive reconnaissance for crossing sites. Meanwhile, the staff developed plans for the operation and all elements of the Division continued preparations for crossing. That evening General Lucas informed me that General Clark's Operations Instructions No. 6 ordered the VI Corps to cross during the night, October 9th-10th, while the British were to cross the following night. The VI Corps was to concentrate one division along the river, another in the vicinity of Montesarchio, force a crossing in the vicinity of Triflisco and attack northwest along the high ground running northwest from Triflisco. The X Corps was to cross within its zone the following night and attack northwest to seize the heights above Mondragone. However, General Lucas then proposed to General Clark that the VI Corps be permitted to cross with two divisions abreast instead of one, employing the 34th Infantry Division on the right of the 3rd Division, and this proposal was approved.

The morning of October 8th, I spent at the corps Command Post in Avellino discussing plans for the crossing with General Lucas and General Ryder, returning to the Division at noon with the draft of the new plans for the crossing. These provided that the 34th Infantry Division would relieve the 30th Infantry in the right half of the Division sector from the junction of the Calore River to a point south of Caiazzo. Both divisions were to cross simultaneously beginning about 0200 the morning of October 10th.

But there were still more delays and changes. Incessant rains had created appalling road conditions along the entire front. The 34th Infantry Division required an additional day to move in adequate supplies, so the attack was delayed for a day. The same conditions had delayed British preparations so that General McCreery required more time to complete his preparations. At a final conference at Army Headquarters in Naples on the morning of October 10th, General Clark designated the night October 12th-13th for the crossing of both corps.

The two corps faced different terrain problems in the crossing. The X Corps was in the intensely cultivated flat Campanian plain, partly reclaimed from the sea, and crossed by many drainage canals, on a front of sixteen miles where the river was wide and deep between steep banks backed by dikes. The VI Corps had a similar frontage but within the mountains, for the flat river valley, never wider than three or four miles, was bordered by rugged, barren mountains which rose steeply from the valley to heights of nearly 2,000 feet.

While the VI Corps crossed two divisions above Triflisco, the X Corps was to cross two divisions below. General McCreery's plan now was to have his 46th Division make the main crossing near the sea, the 7th Armored Division was to make a demonstration near Grazzanise, while the 56th Division making the secondary attack crossed one battalion at Capua assisted by a demonstration force in the hills to the east. LCT's were to land forty tanks north of the mouth of the Volturno. All attacks were to be preceded by intense artillery preparation. General Clark had alerted one parachute battalion of the 82nd Airborne Division to be dropped on the objective of the British Corps, but when no German strength was drawn from the area during the attack, the drop was cancelled.

The problem in forcing a river crossing is to put infantry across in sufficient numbers and with adequate supporting weapons to clear crossing sites so that combat power can be built up on the enemy side of the river, to attain the objective regardless of enemy opposition. Assault boats, rafts, swimming, wading, foot bridges—all are means for crossing men with the weapons they carry under appropriate conditions. More difficult is the problem of crossing tanks and antitank weapons to support infantry in the early fighting, and crossing artillery so that it will be within effective range to support its infantry closely, and crossing trucks and heavy equipment to transport ammunition, supplies, communications, materials and equipment for repair of roads, bridges and the like. Properly waterproofed for assault landings, tanks and tank destroyers can wade depths of six feet or more if banks are in such condition that vehicles can enter and leave the water. But to cross artillery, armor and heavy equipment in quantity and to maintain adequate supplies, bridges are essential and must be constructed early. Ferrying is much too slow.

Under ordinary conditions, the Volturno was fordable at many places, but the incessant rains had transformed it into a major obstacle. We had been preparing to cross the river even before we reached it on October 6th. Few assault boats were available—not nearly enough to lift the assault battalions—so we had to improvise. We obtained life rafts from the Navy in Naples, extra water and gas cans from our own and captured stocks, a large quantity of Italian life jackets found in storage in Naples, and other material from which we improvised rafts and ferries for crossing men, mortars, and machine guns, and even a few light vehicles. As reconnaissance indicated some places where men could wade the stream, we found miles of rope for use as guide ropes to aid in fording. There was a limited amount of waterproofing material left over from the Salerno landing. This we obtained and used to waterproof tanks, and tank destroyers, and communications vehicles for early infantry support.

Division engineers had sufficient pontoon equipment for one ten-ton bridge, capable of division loads, but not for tanks, heavy artillery or heavy engineer equipment. Provision of heavier bridges is a Corps and Army responsibility which Corps solved in this instance by attaching to the Division Company B, 16th Armored Engineer Battalion, with pontoon equipment for a bridge capable of carrying thirty tons. Besides these two bridges, we improvised another bridge from a few extra pontoons, floats, railroad iron, and matting used for landing fields, which was capable of carrying light vehicles. Because of time required for construction, the light "jeep" bridge was to be ready first, and over it would pass the light vehicles with heavy weapons, communications, and supplies for the infantry battalions. Several hours later, the Division bridge would be ready for trucks and Division artillery. Still later, the thirty ton bridge would be ready for crossing tanks, heavy artillery and heavy engineer equipment.

While these preparations were under way, the regiments were conducting intensive reconnaissance night and day to find the best crossing places and to locate every enemy machine gun, gun emplacement, and defensive position along the river line. Night after night, men waded and swam the cold river, often under fire, to obtain the vital information. Meanwhile commanders and staffs worked night and day to complete and perfect all plans and preparations.

In the 3rd Division sector, which was seven and a half miles wide, the Volturno ranged from two hundred to three hundred feet in width and was more than six feet deep except in a few places we had found possible for fording. Here, the depth averaged about four feet. Banks were steep, ten feet or more in height except in a few places where changes of course had left low banks. Two bridges, which had crossed the river in the Division sector, had been destroyed.

To the left of the Division sector at the edge of the Campanian plain, the 1st Battalion, 15th Infantry, occupied Mt. Tifata, a rugged mountain more than 1,800 feet high, which overlooked the Volturno with barely room along its foot for the road and railroad which had crossed the river to the village of Triflisco on the northern bank.

On the right of the Division sector, the remainder of the 15th Infantry occupied Mt. Castellone, another rugged mountain of some 1,200 feet which overlooked the valley southwest of the town of Caiazzo. To the east, the river swung back to the south in the zone of the 34th Infantry Division.

Between Mt. Tifata and Mt. Castellone, there was a small valley about two miles long and somewhat wider at its lower end along the river. The upper end of the valley was broken by scrub-covered spurs; the lower end along the river consisted of cultivated fields. At the upper end of this valley, in an abandoned monastery, we had an excellent observation post which overlooked most of the Division zone of action, and which was to be a mecca for numerous visitors during these days.

These were the positions which the 15th Infantry had seized on October 6th. While we were making plans for crossing, I had maintained the battalions in their original positions to avoid disclosing information of our intentions to the enemy. When the 30th Infantry was relieved by the 34th Infantry Division, I had attached its 3rd Battalion to the 15th Infantry for the crossing, and had moved the remainder of the regiment to Mt. Tifata to cross the Triflisco area. The 7th Infantry was in concealed positions near the upper end of the valley between the two mountains.

On the enemy side of the river, opposite Mt. Tifata and immediately above the village of Triflisco, was the spur which marked the southern end of the long ridge leading northwest toward Teano along which the Division was to attack. This spur rose steeply to a height of more than 800 feet and the ridge extended northwest to Mt. Grande and a series of higher hills. From the sides open to us, the spur could be scaled by infantry; it was not practicable for vehicles, although vehicles could come down the crest from the north.

Immediately east of this ridge, a small stream, which rose in the mountains north of Pontelatone, paralleled the ridge and entered the Volturno at an ox-bow loop almost in the center of the Division sector. Surrounding mountains formed a horseshoe-shaped valley about five miles long and nearly as wide at its lower end. On the eastern side of the valley stood Mt. Majulo rising 1,500 feet from the valley. Thence, the mountains curved back to the east more than two miles from the river leaving a flat cultivated valley along which lay the road and railroad from Triflisco to Caiazzo onto the east and north. The flat Volturno valley was broken only by two small hills, of 800 and 500 feet, which stood almost on the river bank about two miles southwest of Caiazzo and directly opposite Mt. Castellone.

We knew that we were opposed by the Mauke Battle Group, at least half of the German Goering Division, one of Germany's best. The Germans had fortified the two small hills opposite Mt. Castellone, the line of the road and railroad, and the heights beyond. Knowing that the Triflisco area was the only suitable site for a heavy bridge, the Germans held the ridge above Triflisco in strength. Mobile reserves including tanks were in readiness in the northern end of the valley to oppose our crossing.

Our plan was simple, as all good tactical plans must be. Our aim was to clear enemy fire from the river line to permit building bridges so that the entire Division could cross over in the shortest possible period of time. We would first cross the infantry battalions with tanks and tank destroyers supported by the fire of the Division artillery emplaced south of the river. Opposite Triflisco, where the Germans expected an attack in force, we would make a full scale feint, which timed and coordinated with the British crossing at Capua and their demonstration in the area, would lead the Germans to believe that it was our main attack. While the Germans were preparing to meet this attack, we would cross the 7th and 15th Infantry Regiments in the flat valley to the east to advance rapidly to the north and gain the heights in the rear of German defenses.

The 30th Infantry was to employ the 1st Battalion, 15th Infantry, and the regimental heavy weapons companies, coordinated with the British on the left, to make the feint attack; fire was to begin at midnight and continue thereafter shrouding the heights in smoke until they were finally cleared. The 2nd Battalion, 30th Infantry, was to be held in readiness to cross immediately if there was any sign of German withdrawal.

The 7th Infantry, making the main attack of the Division, would cross on both sides of the ox-bow loop in the center of the Division sector, employ one battalion to protect its left flank, while the other two advanced to the north, captured Mt. Majullo and gained a foothold on the western ridge. Simultaneously, the 15th Infantry would cross opposite Mt. Castellone, capture the two small hills on the north bank which dominated the site we had selected for the Division bridge, and then drive northward, capture Piana di Caiazzo, and the mountain heights east of Mt. Majullo.

The feint attack was to begin at midnight. The main crossings would begin at 0200, preceded by an hour-long artillery preparation on all known enemy positions and observation points by Division and attached artillery and the 84th Chemical Battalion. Five minutes before the crossings began, these positions and the river bank on the enemy side would be shrouded in smoke and this smoke screen would be maintained thereafter.

Every officer and man knew the part he was to play. All preparations had been completed with great secrecy. All bridging, ferrying, and fording materials were in readiness in concealed positions near the river banks. During the early hours of the night of October 12th, all guns were laid, and the battalions moved silently to their assembly positions to begin the crossing.

Fortunately, the weather had cleared that day. The night was clear and cold.

Promptly at midnight, the fireworks began, marked by the flash and rumble of guns as the feint attack and the mass of British artillery on the left opened fire. Accompanied by Major General Geoffrey Keyes, now commanding the II Corps soon to arrive in Italy, who had come up to see the show, I went to the observation post in the old monastery to see the attack get under way. Promptly at 0100, our Division and attached artillery began their preparation fire. On the enemy side of the river the whole area seemed filled with the flash of bursting shells, and the guns in the valley below us rumbled and roared against the surrounding mountains, drowning out all other sounds. The night was clear but we could see little more than the flash of bursting shells as we watched and shivered in the chill night air. Five minutes before the zero hour of 0200, white phosphorus, intermingled with the high explosive, shrouded the whole valley with a heavy pall that blotted out the landscape. Then came word that the battalions were crossing.

The crossing had just begun when Carleton telephoned that the British crossing at Capua had failed. The 56th Division had crossed one company but it had encountered heavy resistance and had to be withdrawn. All further attempts to cross there were cancelled. I was not surprised for had the British intended to make a serious effort to cross at Capua, the attempt would have been made in greater strength. Nevertheless, that left only British artillery to interfere with enemy movements on our western flank.

I went at once to the Mt. Tifata area to see Colonel Rogers for the crossing of his 2nd Battalion there depended to some extent on German reaction to the British attack at Capua. Patrols had crossed the river but had found the enemy in strength on the far bank. The demonstration was continuing in full force and the 2nd Battalion was in readiness near the river if the opportunity came to cross. There in dim candlelight in Colonel Rogers' Command Post, I pinned upon his battle jacket the Legion of Merit which had been awarded to him for outstanding work during the Sicilian campaign, and which we had just received.

Back at the Command Post in the Royal Gardens, there was word about 0530 that all battalions of the 7th and two battalions of the 15th were across the river, and that two battalions of the 34th Division had crossed over on our right. More disturbing was word that tanks and tank destroyers had not been able to enter the river and cross with the battalions of the 7th Infantry. I could picture those fine battalions in the flat fields north of the river being overrun by tanks when daylight came, and I was worried.

At the observation post in the old monastery soon after daylight, I talked the situation over with Bill Campbell, the Division artillery commander. He was prepared to lay down the mass of the Division artillery on any threat which developed. Near the crossing site of the 7th Infantry perhaps an hour later, a few tanks and tank destroyers were standing about in an open field and occasional enemy shells were falling in the neighborhood but doing no damage. Across the river there were sounds of battle in the valley beyond, but all was concealed from view by the smoke. Unarmored bulldozers had been prevented from breaking down the banks so that tanks could enter, although several operators had become casualties in trying to do so.

On my way from Sherman's Command Post, I found an engineer platoon on its way to the site of the Division bridge. In a few brief words I painted for them the urgent need for courageous engineers who could level off the river bank even under fire so that tanks could cross and prevent our infantry battalions being overrun by the enemy. Their response was immediate and inspiring. I left them double-timing toward the river half a mile away to level off the bank with picks and shovels—which they did, while tanks and tank destroyers neutralized enemy fire from the opposite bank.

Sherman's Command Post was still on the south side of the river in cover afforded by a small ravine. It was here I pinned the Legion of Merit on Sherman's breast. His 2nd Battalion was at the foot of Mt. Majullo, its objective north of the river. The 3rd Battalion was engaged with German strong points along the road and railroad, which the 2nd Battalion had by-passed in the darkness. The 1st Battalion was off to the west protecting the flank along the road and railroad. Leaving Sherman to get on down to the river and get tanks across to support his infantry battalion, I turned back to the Command Post to see how the battle was going elsewhere.

It was then mid-morning. The 2nd and 3rd Battalions of the 15th had captured the hills on the north bank of the river, and were reorganizing under heavy fire to continue their advance. On our right, the 34th Infantry Division was making slow progress. On the left, the 2nd Battalion, 30th Infantry, had still not been able to cross the river but the demonstration fire and smoke screen were being maintained. But there was word that tanks were fording the river in rear of the 7th Infantry.

Major General Matt Ridgway arrived to see how the battle was going. Leaving him at the observation post with General Campbell, I continued on to see how the bridges were coming. The jeep bridge was almost finished. At the bridge site southwest of Caiazzo, work on the

Division bridge was well under way but had stopped because of artillery fire which had damaged several pontoons, trucks and jeeps, and caused some casualties. When I explained to the engineers that the bridge had to be finished in spite of enemy fire, that gallant company returned to work as nonchalantly as though on some engineer demonstration. In spite of artillery fire which caused a number of casualties and continued until the 15th Infantry advance captured the guns which were causing the trouble, the bridge was completed during the afternoon.

Not far from this point I found General Eagles, temporarily commanding the 15th Infantry. Colonel Ritter had been injured in an accident on October 6th. There on a mountain spur, we watched German tanks approaching the flank of the 7th Infantry in the valley across the river. Eight or ten German tanks drove down the valley from the north and turned eastward well north of the road and railroad. Three or four of our own tanks were making their way northward from the river toward the road. Then concentrations of artillery landed among the German tanks. When the dust and smoke cleared so that we could see, the remaining German tanks were making off to the north still pursued by bursting shells. It was a grand sight, and I felt better. Later I was to learn that a forward observer, Lieutenant Jenkin R. Jones, 10th Field Artillery, had spotted the approaching tanks. Setting up his radio in an exposed location, he called for artillery fire and continued to direct it, under fire from the approaching tanks. When the attack was stopped, the leading German tank was within fifty yards of his position.

This was the critical point in the battle, for the Germans did not attempt another counterattack with tanks. Shortly after noon, I directed Colonel Rogers to cross over in the sector of the 7th Infantry and attack the heights above Triflisco from the east. The 1st Battalion, 30th Infantry, crossed the jeep bridge late in the afternoon and during the night scaled the heights and cleared them of German defenders. The other battalions followed, and the morning of October 14th, the 30th Infantry advanced northward along the ridge toward Mt. Grande. Meanwhile the 7th Infantry seized Mt. Fallano and was engaged with the enemy toward Pontelatone. The 15th Infantry held the heights east of Majullo and protected the east flank of the division.

Work began on the thirty-ton bridge as soon as we had cleared the enemy from the heights above Triflisco. Enemy artillery fire from the British sector opposite Capua hampered the work, causing casualties among the engineers and damaging pontoons that had to be repaired while work was in progress. During the day, the enemy made several attempts to destroy the bridge by air attack, but the 441st Antiaircraft Automatic Weapons Battalion discouraged these attempts by shooting down seven of the attacking planes. When I visited the bridge shortly after noon, it was nearing completion, and was ready for traffic some hours later.

Thus, the VI Corps was in much better position to continue the advance than was the X Corps. To expedite the crossing of the X Corps, General Clark decided to change the boundary between the two Corps in order to give the British 56th Division the bridge which we had built at Triflisco. Both General Lucas and I agreed that this was a logical measure. However, we thought that the British should be responsible for the long ridge running northwest to Teano, which had been the objective of the 3rd Infantry Division. After some discussion, both General Clark and General McCreery agreed, and General Clark thereupon issued oral orders directing the change in boundary.

Since the objective of the 3rd Infantry Division was now assigned to the British, General Lucas issued orders directing the 3rd Infantry Division to turn northeast toward Dragoni prepared to continue the advance northward to Mt. Delli Angelli and Pietramelara. The 34th Infantry Division was to advance up the valley of the Volturno, cross over east of Dragoni and continue the advance northward to Raviscanina. The 45th Division would revert to Corps reserve when it reached Piedmonte d'Alife.

That same afternoon, I turned the 7th Infantry to the northeast toward Dragoni, hoping to take the town of Liberi a few miles to the north by dark. Although we did not accomplish this, we had begun the drive from the Volturno that was to take us into the Germans' so called "Winter Line" south of Casino a few weeks later.

2. *The Winter Line*

We had been fighting continuously now for a month in incredibly difficult terrain against a stubborn enemy who knew how to make our advance both slow and costly. Rain was now almost continuous. Mud rendered all movements difficult and frequently made movements of vehicles off roads impossible. Heavy rains washed out by-passes, often made them impassable, and bridging operations became a major problem. Cold and wet caused extreme discomfort, and it was beginning to affect the health of the command. Respiratory diseases, fevers of undetermined origin, and jaundice were beginning to take their toll, imposing burdens on the Division medical service and filling the Corps and Army hospitals. Our heaviest days' loss in killed and

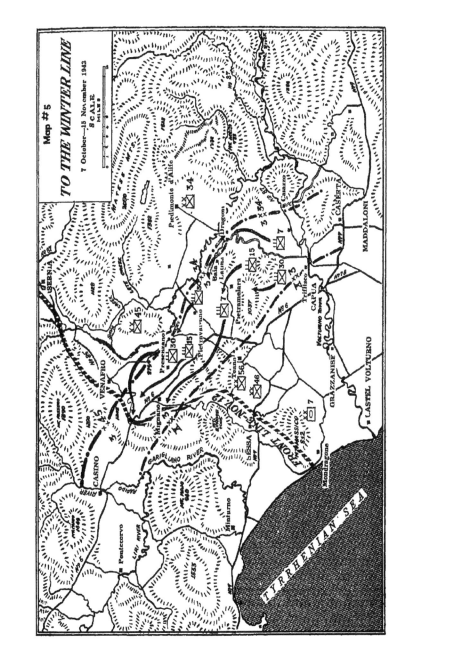

Map #5

TO THE WINTER LINE

7 October—15 November 1943

SCALE

MILES

wounded had been 314 officers and men during October 13th, the day of the Volturno crossing, compared with 230 for the other divisions of the Corps. While our losses in battle had not been excessive, the daily total was beginning to mount, and losses from non-battle causes such as sickness and injury were even larger and were affecting the combat effectiveness of every battalion.

My men were clad in woolen clothing as they had been for the Sicilian campaign, but the barracks bags and squad rolls were still in Palermo. Except for what men could carry, there were no changes in clothing, no heavy underwear, no extra shoes, no overcoats, and far from enough blankets to keep men comfortable. On October 4th, I wrote to General Gruenther, Army Chief of Staff, as follows:

> Numerous requests have been made to your headquarters to have the Third Division Administration Center and baggage shipped from Sicily, a situation that is now becoming critical both from the standpoint of essential administration and the health of the command. Morning report extracts have been accumulating since September 18, also Graves Registration reports. However, no battle casualty reports have been submitted nor can they be prepared until the Administration Center arrives with the individual records and necessary information for proper processing. The losses to the Division through casualties and sickness are averaging 130 men per day and a terrific back log of work is piling up.
>
> The Division APO, an integral part of the Administration Center, is badly needed to handle and process mail, which is arriving daily. Properly handled and efficient mail service is a decided morale factor for these troops.
>
> The Division baggage consisting of bed rolls, clothing and equipment, is essential to the successful operation of this command. The lack of sleeping rolls and shelter halves contained in this baggage has not only caused actual suffering among the men concerned, but it is jeopardizing the health of the Division.

Army and theater service and supply agencies were making strenuous efforts to obtain the winter clothing and equipment which the troops required, but many weeks would pass before anything like adequate supplies were available. Lack of shipping was the principal reason given for this delay and for the delay in sending over the Division baggage from Palermo. I think perhaps a more important reason for the critical shortage is that the requirement of such supplies for the Italian campaign had not been foreseen in time. Adequate stocks of some essential items such as overshoes did not even exist.

The 7th Infantry ran into determined resistance from the 29th and 115th Panzer Grenadier Regiments in the rugged terrain about Liberi. Two days and nights of heavy fighting were required to drive the Germans from the town. On the morning of the 17th, as the 7th Infantry continued its advance toward Dragoni, I turned the 15th Infantry (still under temporary command of General Eagles) north across the mountain trails to seize the heights north of Pietramelara, while the 7th Infantry advanced northward from Dragoni to seize Mt. Delli Angelli north of Baja e Latina. When British elements relieved the 30th Infantry on Mt. Grande on October 15th, that regiment assembled east of Formicola in division reserve.

On October 16th, we moved the Division Command Post from the Royal Gardens at Caserta to a point along the road just south of Liberi where the 7th Infantry was still engaged. I returned to the Command Post about mid-afternoon and found it situated in the open immediately adjacent to a well-marked cross roads. I had hardly finished pointing out this fact to the Headquarters Commandant and Signal Officer, when General Gerald Templar, who had just assumed command of the British 56th Division on my left, arrived with a staff officer, to discuss coordination between our divisions in the advance to the north. We had just started discussions in our War Room tent, when German artillery fire began screaming into the Command Post. Exploding shells shook the War Room tent, fragments whined about overhead, and several passed through the tent while we were talking. General Templar seemed to pay no attention; and I was determined not to be outdone. When we finished our discussion, he asked to see our Command Post set-up. We sauntered about while I showed it to him with a nonchalance I was far from feeling. Fortunately many of the shells that screamed into the Command Post were duds, but fragments whistled about—one even cut the side seam on the riding breeches I was wearing. Returning to the War Room tent, we found my staff standing about, with a British officer lying on his back under shelter of a small bank about a foot in height. We thought at first he was wounded, but he quickly reassured us. "I say," he said as he scrambled to his feet, "it's no good getting shot at unless one jolly well has to. One should take advantage of whatever cover there is." I pointed out that this artillery fire was observed fire coming from Mt. Grande on which the British had relieved the 30th Infantry the day before. General Templar and his party then left. During a lull in the enemy firing, I had the War Room and staff tents moved to the shelter of a bank a few yards away where they would not be subjected to a direct hit. Three men had been wounded by fragments in the first salvo, but there were no further casualties. Intermittent shelling continued until the following afternoon. We noticed, however, that our frequent visitors never tarried very long.

On the morning of the 18th, the 7th Infantry was on the heights overlooking Dragoni. Since the regiment had been fighting continuously day and night for six days, I ordered Sherman to halt for a day to rest men and animals, for both were approaching a state of exhaustion. Meanwhile the 15th Infantry had encountered determined resistance at Roccoromana and Pietramelara and was having difficulties with supply, evacuation of casualties, and artillery support. There was no road across the mountains on the route of the 15th Infantry, only a trail which Division engineers gradually widened to make passable for jeeps, and the incessant rains often made even their passage impossible. Company L, 15th Infantry, held an exposed position on the mountains west of Bajae Latina for eight days, under almost continuous counter-attacks by German detachments, and for three days and two nights of this period was without either water or food. Such were the arduous conditions under which men fought. By October 25th, both regiments had cleared the enemy from Mt. Delli Angelli, Mt. Monaco Pietramelara and Roccoromano, and we faced the last barrier south of the Mignano Gap where we would, as we thought, come up against the German "Winter Line."

There was a constant stream of visitors to my Command Post all during this period. General Lucas, I saw almost daily. General Clark, General Brann, and General Keyes, whose II Corps was to assume command of part of the front when we came up to the Winter Line, were frequent visitors, as was General Ridgeway. Corps staff officers and other observers also came often. On October 20th, General Clark and General Lucas, accompanied by a number of staff officers, brought Secretary Morgenthau and his party to my Command Post, where they were briefed. Afterwards I conducted them through my area to Dragoni, stopping on the way to see Lieutenant Colonel Heintges and his 3rd Battalion, 7th Infantry, the only one we could reach by motor. Heintges explained the battalion commanders' problems and emphasized the urgent need for replacements. At Dragoni, which had only been taken the day before, we met General Ryder who took the party on a tour of his sector.

Two days later, General Clark arrived with a similar party; this time it was headed by General Eisenhower. After the same briefing, another tour of the Division sector ensued, taking in a battalion of the 15th Infantry in which General Eisenhower had served just before the war, the Command Post of the 7th Infantry, and several artillery battalions. I was always glad to hear these important officers praise the Division, but I was more pleased to have them see the conditions under which American soldiers were fighting, for one personal inspection is worth a thousand reports.

So far in the Italian campaign there had been little direct air support for the divisions. It is true that the fighter planes of the Twelfth Air Support Command were attacking enemy troops and other targets which assisted the advance of the ground forces, but there was little or no coordination between the air and ground effort at the division level. A division selected targets which it wished to have attacked and submitted the list to the Army G-3. A Committee of Army and Air Force staff officers coordinated these requests with requests of other divisions and determined which were to be accepted. Then, the Twelfth Air Support Command allocated the missions to the air squadrons which were to fly them. The division rarely knew whether its requests had been accepted, and never knew whether or not the missions would be flown. Since the requests for air support always had to be made twelve hours or more before they were to be flown, there was no way to obtain air support quickly in case of need.

This problem was the subject of much discussion all during this period. Carleton and I harked back to the splendid air support we had from the Naval air squadron in the final attack on the Kasbah at Port Lyautey, and to the relative ineffectiveness of direct air support in Tunisia which had resulted from lack of ground control. We constantly urged that air support parties be provided to accompany infantry and direct air attacks on specific targets as the airplanes arrived over the division area. Air Force officers were extremely reluctant to establish this ground control, and would never permit a ground officer to direct any aircraft to a target. Eventually, however reluctantly, General House, who commanded the Twelfth Air Support Command, agreed to try the forward ground control, and provided a party consisting of two young pilots with air-ground communications to test it out in my sector. In a conference at my Command Post near Dragoni on October 23rd, General Lucas, General House, Carleton and I arranged the details. I later described the results of this test in the Division after Action Report in these terms:

> One very outstanding example (of the Division use of the XII Air Sup-Support Command) was in the attack on the hill mass in the Pietrovairona sector. For this attack, the XII Air Support Command sent forward a control party which was established on the Observation Post from which they could observe the planes in the air and the targets. This proved to be the most effective air support we have ever received. The bombing was accurate and effective. It was placed comparatively close to our own advancing troops and contributed greatly to their ability to seize their objective on schedule and with light losses against an experienced, alert enemy in well prepared positions.

Nevertheless, this was the only instance in which we ever had direct air support with forward ground control during this entire campaign. Requested missions sometimes did not arrive, and were never as closely coordinated as would have been the case with forward controllers directing airplanes onto selected targets. As a matter of fact, more than a year would elapse before I was to see the Air Force in Italy employ the system of forward ground controllers effectively.

From the Army Group and Fifth Army point of view, the tactics of our operations were simple enough. In accordance with Operations Instructions No. 8, 20th October, the "Fifth Army continues its attack to the northwest to seize the line: Isernia-M. Passero-Garigliano River from G 9011 to the sea." The VI Corps was to make its main effort on its left and seize the mountain heights north of the Volturno while the X Corps making its main effort on the right seized the mountain heights west of Highway 6.

These heights were booby trapped with trip wire demolitions, and strongly defended by the Germans. Rain and dense brush precluded effective observation so that the mountain had to be cleared with small arms and hand grenades. The first two mountains were cleared after two days fighting, the last peak, Mt. San Angelo, on the following day. Then the way was clear to attack the Mignano Gap.

Meanwhile, the 34th Infantry Division had been fighting its way up the east side of the Volturno which General Lucas planned to cross opposite Venafro to seize the mountain heights northwest of the river. The 56th Division on the right of the X Corps was approaching Teano, the 46th Division was at Sparanise, and the 7th Division had reached the vicinity of Mondragone near the sea.

The two Corps commanders, General Lucas and General McCreery, had agreed upon October 31st as the date for beginning this last coordinated drive in accordance with Operations Instructions No. 8.

General Lucas planned to have the 45th Infantry Division, which had been in Corps reserve, cross the Volturno just east of Presenzano and advance northward west of the river to seize the heights above Venafro, while the 3rd Infantry Division cleared the Mignano Gap. Meanwhile, the 34th Infantry Division and the 504th Parachute Regiment would cross the Volturno above Venafro.

The 3rd Division was to seize the heights north of Presenzano and assist the crossing of the 45th Division, simultaneously making a demonstraton to the west toward Terro Corpo to assist the advance of the British 56th Division which was attacking toward Roccamonfina and Mt. San Croce, west of Highway 6.

On October 30th, General Clark had lunch with me at my Command Post, and discussed my plans for this operation, which he approved. Shortly after noon, General Alexander arrived with General Lemnitzer, his American Deputy Chief of Staff. I took the entire group to an OP above Pietravairano where General Alexander and General Clark had their first sight of the Mignano Gap on the road to Rome toward which their attention was directed, in addition to the mountain area which still lay ahead of the X Corps west of Highway 6. While we were there, four German airplanes passed directly overhead, and attacked our artillery area just in rear, fortunately without material damage. One of General Clark's photographers caught a very fine picture of General Alexander watching the show through my field glasses. Both General Alexander and General Clark were optimistic that our progress would now be rapid. Both were wrong.

This last operation, which began on October 31st, was to be a heartbreak for me. The Mignano Gap is a narrow valley several miles wide and about twice as long. To the east the mountain mass of Mt. Cesima north of Presenzano rises to an elevation of more than 2,500 feet. To the west lie the masses of Mt. Difensa, Mt. Maggiore, and Mt. Camino, all with an elevation of more than 2,800 feet. At the north end of the valley, blocking passage onto the Rapido plain and dominating the valley to the south, were two smaller mountains, Mt. Rotundo, a conical, brush-covered peak, and Mt. Lungo, a ridge several miles in length, both having an elevation of more than a thousand feet. Highway 6 passed between the southern end of Mt. Lungo and Mt. Rotundo and continued on to the Rapido at Cassino, a dozen miles away. We knew that the Germans would mine the Mignano valley and otherwise obstruct it with demolitions, and that an attack northward along heights would be out of the question. South of Presenzano, Highway 6 and all the valley to the east was dominated by the mountain heights in the zone of the X Corps.

It was my plan to have the 7th Infantry make the demonstration toward Terro Corpo to assist the British 56th Division in its attack on Roccamonfina, and then push forward west of Highway 6 and clear the spurs overlooking the Mignano Valley on the west. Meanwhile, the 15th Infantry was to attack northward across the valley from Pietraviarano toward Presenzano, capture Mt. Cesima to assist the crossing of the 45th Infantry Division immediately to the east, and then clear the heights overlooking the Mignano valley on the east. Battle operation would have so worn these regiments and further reduced their depleted strength by then, that further effort would require troops that had been rested and prepared. Accordingly, when we controlled the spurs overlooking the northern end of the valley, I proposed to move the 30th Infantry, which would have had several day's rest, to a position in the north end of this valley from which it could attack with the whole power of the Division behind it, either to capture Rotundo or Lungo, or northward to capture the village of San Pietro and the heights behind to cut communications. I discussed this plan many times with both General Lucas and General Clark, the last time on November 2nd. It had their hearty approval.

Our attack got off to a good start and went along as planned, about as well as could be expected under the appalling conditions of weather, terrain, and weary men. The 7th Infantry began its demonstration toward Terro Corpo, to assist the 56th Division which was attacking toward Roccamonfina on its left, and then worked its way northward along the west side of the valley clearing the spurs east of Mt. Camino of a bitterly defending enemy. On one small hill, which was a battalion objective, engineers lifted more than 3,000 mines On November 5th, it had reached a point just south of the village of Mignano but had not yet cleared Mt. Difensa, the spur which overlooked Mt. Lungo at the northern end of the valley.

The 15th Infantry attacked northward across the flat valley and captured Presenzano the morning of November 1st, and Mt. Cesima to the north to assist the crossing of the Volturno by the 45th Infantry Division on the night of November 3rd. The regiment then worked its way northward clearing the mountain and the spurs which overlooked the valley on the eastern side. On November 5th, one battalion had occupied Mignano and was approaching the southern end of Mt. Lungo; others were working their way down the northwestern slopes of Mt. Cesima toward Mt. Rotundo.

Conditions on the mountain tops were appalling. All supply was by man and mules, much of it by man. Casualties had to be carried out on litters, which required hours in many cases. Hot food was out of the question. Incessant cold rain not only added to discomfort, it reduced visibility almost to nothing, interfered with the scheduled air support, and vastly increased the difficulties of the attacking troops. Companies were becoming seriously reduced in strength by casualties and sickness. It was during this period that trench foot, which was to plague us thereafter, first began taking its toll.

Morale suffers under long-continued exposure to battle and the exertion of campaign. The Air Force had been able to combat this by rotating men home to the States after a certain number of missions or a certain length of time. No such policy was considered practicable for ground forces on any large scale, but the theater had arranged to rotate limited numbers of men on a quota basis. This policy, even with the limited numbers which could be rotated, was an important morale factor, for even with only a few men being rotated, there was always an element of hope that one's turn might come. On November 2nd, while the battle was in progress, I wrote General Gruenther:

Dear Al:

I am forwarding to your headquarters through normal AG channels recommendations for rotation of Officers and Enlisted Men of this command for the months of August, September, and October. My Adjutant General informs me that there is some question as to whether the recommendations for the months of August and September will be considered under the Fifth Army quota, (whatever that may mean). I hope that you will look these over and see that my outfit receives due consideration.

You are familiar with the difficulties incident to getting my Administration Center over here, which accounts for the delay in submitting these recommendations.

If for any reason the allotment for August cannot be arranged by you, I would greatly appreciate it if you would mail it direct to Everett Hughes (CG Natousa) and ask him to adjust it for me.

We are still plugging away and apparently getting on all right. I wish you would come up and have dinner with me and see how a field soldier lives.

Some such rotation policy should always be devised for ground forces under long continued exposures to the strains of battle. A limited number of men do not materially reduce the combat effectiveness of a division for their places can be taken by replacements if the replacement system is adequate. Such battle-experienced personnel disseminated among divisions in training at home should be of inestimable value in preparing them for combat.

We had recognized for some time the urgent need for affording men in combat an opportunity to rest, completely removed from the battle area. General Clark had finally authorized a rest center program for the Fifth Army, with centers established in the Naples area to which divisions could send quotas of men for periods of five full days. The first quota of 800 men left the division area for Naples on November 5th. In spite of our urgent need for replacements, I had required each organization in the Division to fill its prescribed quota with the men who needed rest. When the group assembled for departure, I went out to address them. Haggard, dirty, bedraggled, long-haired, unshaven, clothing in tatters, worn out boots, their appearance was appalling. I outlined briefly the purpose of the program and how they were to be treated, urged them to enjoy themselves to the fullest but to uphold the honor of the Division, and to return determined to make the Germans pay for their hardships.

I saw this same group when they returned a week later. The difference was almost unbelievable. Rested, clean, shaven and trimmed, and cleanly clad in new uniforms. Some of them said: "General, I had forgotten that people could live like that. I just did not believe that anything could be so good." The effect of this rest camp program on the morale of the battle-weary men of the command was of inestimable value, and saved many men who would otherwise have broken under the strain. Since that time, I have always been a staunch advocate of a properly organized and conducted rest center program for troops in campaign.

General Al Gruenther, Army Chief of Staff, came up on November 5th to spend a night with me and visit the front. On that day our going was slow, but we were still making progress. I was still optimistic that we would clear the Mignano Gap, for I had the 30th Infantry in readiness to use when conditions were right. The regiment had now been resting almost a week. We had just finished dinner that evening, when I was called to the telephone.

"This is Truscott."

"Lucian, this is Johnny Lucas." I knew from the nervous tone of his voice that something was wrong. "You are to move the 30th Infantry by motor tonight through the zone of the 45th Infantry Division to Rocca Pipirozzi and attack northwest early tomorrow morning to capture Mt. Lungo."

I was astounded. A sudden move of about twenty miles. No reconnaissance of assembly areas. Attack without reconnaissance, and inadequate artillery support, and difficult terrain to capture an objective so far away. My plans were all shot.

"But, General, we can't do that. We have not yet cleared the spurs at the north end of the valley. It is not time to use the 30th yet. That ruins my plans and you have agreed to them—"

"Yes, Lucian. I know it. But I can't help it. This is the Army Commander's order. He's been trying to get the British to move on Camino and he told McCreery this afternoon that you could do this. McCreery didn't think you could. I tried to explain to him that this is not the time or place yet. But he wants it done."

"Well, General, let me talk to General Clark. Maybe I can—"

"No, Lucian. Dammit, you know the position I'm in with him. That would only make it worse, and put me in a helluva hole. You have just got to do it."

"O.K. General, if that's the case, we will do the best we can. I still think it's wrong. It will take the 30th two days to get across those mountains to reach Lungo. There will be no surprise. I think our chances of taking it are damn slim. And with no chance of resting another regiment, we will have shot our wad."

"Yes, Lucian. I know all that. I agree with you. But do the best you can."

"Yes, sir."

That just about marked the end of the 3rd Infantry Division's effort in the campaign in southern Italy. Some way or other, we got the 30th Infantry around to Rocca Pipirozzi that night, and the attack got under

way at half-past five the following morning. Fighting their way across
the spurs along the northern slopes on Mt. Cesima, only one battalion
came in sight of Rotundo the first day. It was not until the afternoon of
November 7th that the 2nd and 3rd Battalions were in position to make
any coordinated effort, and that without properly organized artillery
and other supporting fires. That effort was unsuccessful. In a final effort
with the entire Division coordinated the following day, the 30th again
attacked Rotundo, the 15th Infantry attacked the southern end of Mt.
Lungo from the Mignano area and the 7th Infantry renewed its attack
against Mt. Difensa. We laid on an artillery preparation with nearly
one hundred pieces of Division and Corps artillery and supported the
attacks closely. After bitter fighting, Doleman's 3rd Battalion, 30th
Infantry, captured Mt. Rotundo, and Kirtley's 3rd Battalion of the 15th
gained a foothold on the southern end of Mt. Lungo, and both held
their positions against strong counterattacks. But there we stopped, and
there we were when we were relieved by the 36th Infantry Division
about ten days later, to rest and refit in preparation for another operation.

Major Kenneth W. Kirtley was killed during the attack on Mt.
Lungo. His troops had reached the top of the southern spur. Kirtley's
Command Post was on the terraced slope below them. A German airplane flying northward up the valley after attacking our artillery area
was shot down by antiaircraft artillery just over Kirtley's position.
The engine from the plane struck the terrace above where Kirtley was
lying in a fox hole, bounded to the one below, falling upon Kirtley,
killing him instantly. The loss of this brilliant young officer was keenly
felt throughout the Division.

Every other Division in the line both British and American was in a
condition comparable to that of my Division. The British had been unable to clear the Germans from Mt. Camino on our left and were compelled to give up some of the gains made. Nor had the 34th and 45th Divisions been able to do more than gain a good foothold on the heights
north and west of Venafro. It was obvious now that there would be no
further progress until the divisions had an opportunity to rest, absorb
replacements, and refit. Accordingly, on November 15th, General
Alexander called a halt, and General Clark set about regrouping the
the Army and affording the divisions an opportunity to rest and refit.
That same day, the 36th Infantry Division began relieving the 3rd Division, which was withdrawn to the Bajae Latina-Pietravairano-Pietra-
melara area, where the Division was assembled by November 17th.

So ended our fifty-nine days of Mountains and Mud.

CHAPTER SIX

ANZIO

1. *Operation SHINGLE*

Few geographical names relating to military operation in World War II became known to more people than the name "Anzio", and few operations in World War II have occasioned more controversy. No person was more closely associated with the entire Anzio operation than I was, and there is no place that I know more intimately than the terrain of the Anzio Beachhead. Few persons, I think, are better qualified to describe how the Anzio decision was made, or to describe what actually took place in the Anzio Beachhead. I find it difficult at times to remember that there was ever a time when the name Anzio was unknown to me, but as a matter of record I heard the name for the first time on November 13th, 1943, at a conference which General Clark had called at the VI corps Command Post to discuss future plans with Generals Lucas, Ryder, Middleton, and myself.

Our advance had now spent its force. Both Armies were almost at a standstill. The Eighth Army faced the German LXXVI Panzer Corps along the Sangro River from the crest of the Apennines near Iserna to the Adriatic Sea. In the Fifth Army, we were into the "Winter Line"— so called because the Germans expected to hold it throughout the Winter—but we were making almost no progress. The VI Corps with the 504th Parachute Regiment, three Ranger Battalions, and the 34th, 45th, and 3rd Infantry Divisions, held the heights overlooking the upper Volturno above Venafro and on both sides of the Mignano Gap. On the left, the British X Corps with the 46th and 56th Divisions and the 7th Armored Division, held a foothold on the mountain masses overlooking the lower Volturno plain. A dozen miles of rugged mountain terrain and a stubbornly defending enemy lay between our battle-worn and depleted divisions and the line of the Garigliano and Rapido Rivers—the Gustav Line, which the Germans were even then busily engaged in fortifying. The 36th Infantry Division had been refitting since Salerno and was once more ready for action. The 1st Armored Division, just arriving from North Africa, was assembling in Army reserve north of Caserta.

We had long been aware that the Italian campaign was secondary to the cross-channel invasion which was to take place in the spring. We

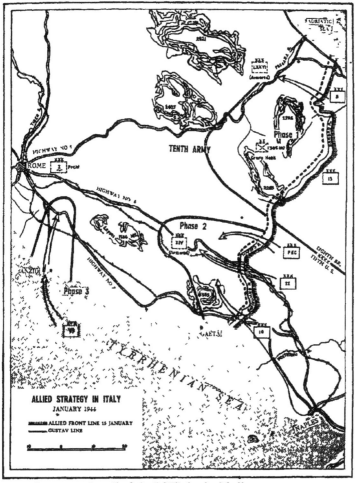

ALLIED STRATEGY IN ITALY
JANUARY 1944

ALLIED FRONT LINE 15 JANUARY
GUSTAV LINE

were also aware that all of the LST's in the Mediterranean area except
the few required for transportation of supplies, especially supplies relating to the build-up of the Mediterranean Air Forces, were already
scheduled for departure to England to begin preparations for the cross-
channel invasion. General Clark now informed us that General Alexander had conferred with General Eisenhower and the AFHQ
staff regarding the campaign in Italy. At a recent conference in Bari,
he had been assured that LST's would delay their departure until De-

cember 15th in order to bring over from Africa another division for the Eighth Army and General Juin's French Corps for the Fifth Army. General Alexander had issued a directive on November 8th which outlined plans for continuing the offensive, providing for operations in three successive phases. In the first phase, beginning about November 20th, the Eighth Army was to cross the Sangro River near the Adriatic coast, drive northward across Highway 5 leading from Pescara to Rome, and threaten communication of German forces opposing the Fifth Army. In the second phase, beginning about the end of November, the Fifth Army was to cross the Rapido River and drive up the Liri and Sacco valleys toward Frosinone and Rome. The third phase was to be a landing south of Rome, possibly supported by an airborne regimental combat team, to be made when the main forces of the fifth Army were within supporting distance to assist those forces in opening the road to Rome. My 3rd Infantry Division would be designated for this landing operation, and would be put ashore at Anzio with seven days ammunition and supply. Some doubt existed that landing craft would be available, but General Alexander was hopeful that departure of craft for England could be further delayed and that the operation could take place soon after mid-December. Meanwhile, the 36th Infantry Division would relieve us so that we could refit and prepare for the operation. And this was the first I heard of Anzio.

The Anzio strategy was sound—a landing in force within supporting distance to aid in exploiting a breakthrough already made on the main front. However, the main forces were not to break through into the Liri Valley for a long time to come, and this initial concept was to be modified by the course of events.

On November 16th, when General Clark announced his plans for regrouping and renewing the assault, the 36th Infantry Division was in the process of relieving the 3rd Infantry Division on the central portion of the Fifth Army front astride the Mignano Gap. The 3rd Infantry Division was to be withdrawn to an area near Pietravairano a few miles to the rear, where it was to come under Major General Geoffrey Keyes' II Corps, now entering action in Italy for the first time. The II Corps was to assume command of the central portion of the Fifth Army front with the 3rd and 36th Infantry Divisions under command. All three corps were to attack simultaneously about November 30th. The VI Corps would attack westward through the mountains between Iserna and Venafro to capture the mountain heights north and west of Cassino. The II Corps would breach the Mignano Gap and establish a bridgehead over the Liri River below Cassino through which the 1st Armored Division would drive up the Liri and Sacco valleys toward Frosinone and Rome. The X Corps was to assist the attack of the II

Corps and then force a crossing over the Garigliano River in readiness for further operations to the north and northwest.

A worse plan would be difficult to conceive. There was no concentration to obtain superiority at any point. It was to be a simultaneous attack across the entire Army front, and with the same worn divisions (substituting the inexperienced 36th for the veteran 3rd) that German defenses had stopped. These divisions would have had only a breathing spell which could hardly be called a rest, and they would encounter worse conditions of weather and terrain than we had yet experienced. Meanwhile, the enemy was increasing in strength and his defensive works were daily becoming more formidable. No deception. No massing of artillery. No overwhelming air support. None of us who had been fighting the Germans in that difficult Italian terrain believed that such an attack had even a remote chance of success. And after the first assault, we would be worse off than before the attack began. Our pessimism was not without effect.

On November 24th, General Clark issued a new directive, providing for successive concentration of force against three objectives, each one to be supported by a mass of artillery and the whole weight of the Mediterranean Allied Air Forces. In the first phase, the British X Corps and the II Corps were to capture the mountain masses west of Highway 6 and south of the Rapido and Garigliano Rivers—Mts. Camino, Difensa, and Maggiore—after which the X Corps would relieve elements of the II Corps in that area. The VI Corps was to make harrassing attacks to hold the enemy on its front. In the second phase, the II and VI Corps were to clear the Mignano Gap by capturing Mt. Lungo and the heights east of Highway 6—Mt. Sammucro. The X Corps was to assist the II Corps by fire, and continue offensive action along the Garigliano River. The third phase would constitute the main push into the Liri Valley. The II Corps was to attack northwest along Highway 6 and develop the defenses in front of Cassino, after which it would employ additional troops to force a crossing over the Rapido River below Cassino through which the 1st Armored Division could initiate its drive up the Liri Valley toward Frosinone. As the attack of the II Corps progressed, the X Corps was to force a crossing over the Garigliano and advance northwest to protect the left flank, while the II and VI Corps continued their attacks to seize the heights north and northwest of Cassino. If craft were available, the landing of the 3rd Infantry Division would follow in due course; if not, the Division would receive some other mission.

This plan was basically sound. However, it was to prove overly optimistic—a not uncommon failing among inexperienced higher commanders and staffs. Before the second phase was completed, it was to become obvious that the third phase, as planned, would not be possible—a fact which was to have its effect on the strategy of Anzio.

Under General Alexander's directive of November 8th, the landing operation south of Rome was a joint responsibility of the Army, Navy, and Air Forces under direction of the Commanding General, Fifth Army. Accordingly, a Planning Board, established in Army Headquarters in the Royal Palace at Caseta about the middle of November, set about assembling intelligence and other information and developing outline plans for the operation. Back in our training area near Pietravairano, the 3rd Infantry Division was busily engaged in absorbing replacements, rehabilitating our equipment, instituting a vigorous training program, and watching preparations for the offensive with deep interest. When the attacks began, we followed their progress intently.

The Fifth Army received one important reinforcement—the 1st Special Service Force commanded by Colonel Robert T. Frederick. This fine organization, roughly equivalent to a regimental combat team in strength, was composed of Americans and Canadians in equal numbers who had been specially selected and trained for hazardous missions in mountains, arctic snows and swamps, and other highly arduous conditions. Attached to the II Corps a week or so before the offensive the Force was to distinguish itself in one of the most difficult operations of the campaign.

The attack got under way on schedule supported by the whole weight of the Mediterranean Allied Air Forces, and some five hundred pieces of artillery. The X Corps led off on December 1st with its assault on the Camino Hill mass. On the same day, the VI Corps began its probing attacks in the mountains above Venafro. On the night of December 2nd, the II Corps launched its attack with the 1st Special Service Force attacking Mt. Difensa and the 143rd Infantry of the 36th Infantry Division attacking Mt. Maggiore. The attack had hardly gathered any momentum before the weather took a turn for the worse. Continuous cold rain rendered supply almost impossible, reduced the effectiveness of air and artillery support almost to zero, and caused untold hardships among the troops. Nevertheless, four or five days of bitter fighting drove the Germans from their mountain positions and cleared them from the south bank of the Garigliano. The first phase of the attack was complete when the X Corps relieved the II Corps troops on Mt. Difensa and Mt. Maggiore on December 9th.

The second phase had already begun on December 7th. General Keyes' plan was to have the 143rd Infantry Regiment of the 36th Infantry Division and one Ranger Battalion capture Mt. Sammucro and the village of San Pietro on the eastern side of the Mignano Gap, while the 1st Motorized Brigade—an Italian unit only recently changed over from the German side and used in this attack for political reasons—was to capture Mt. Lungo, the same objective which the 15th and 30th Infantry Regiments of my own 3rd Infantry Division had been unable to take a month earlier.

The 1st Battalion, 143rd Infantry, and the 3rd Ranger Battalion captured the crest of Mt. Sammucro on December 8 and held it against enemy counterattacks during the following days. The 2nd and 3rd Battalions, 143rd Infantry, attacked San Pietro on December 8th and again on December 9th, but with no success. The attack of the Italians on Mt. Lungo on December 8th failed completely and only the massed fires of supporting artillery kept the Italians from being driven entirely off the mountain. General Keyes now decided to have the 142nd Infantry cross over from Mt. Maggiore and attack the northern end of Mt. Lungo while the Italian Brigade renewed its pressure on the southern point and the remainder of the 36th Infantry Division resumed its attack on Mt. Lungo. This was approximately the situation on December 13th, when I was called to the Army Headquarters to discuss the proposed landing operation.

I found that there had been a change. General Alexander's directive had assumed that the landing operation would not take place until the main Fifth Army forces were within supporting distance, that is, in the vicinity of Frosinone. Now it was based on the assumption that the main forces would be along the Rapido and Garigliano Rivers. In conjunction with the attack to cross the Rapido and drive up the Liri Valley, the 3rd Infantry Division was to be put ashore at Anzio to threaten the German line of communication south of Rome and thus cause a German withdrawal in front of the Fifth Army in the Liri Valley. There would be craft available to lift only one division with seven days' ammunition and supply, and there would be no craft available for resupply or reinforcement. The Air Forces were to interrupt all roads leading to the battle area and prevent movement of German reserves from the north. Within seven days, the main forces would fight their way up the Liri and Sacco valleys to join up with the 3rd Infantry Division.

General Clark remarked to me that if the Division merely held a beachhead at Anzio, he believed that it would cause the Germans so much concern that they would withdraw from the southern front. My reaction was rather pessimistic, but I informed him we would study the plans carefully before expressing a firm opinion.

No Division ever had an abler staff than the 3rd Infantry Division at this time. Basila, Wilson, Harrel, Connor, Johnson, of the Division staff, Davis and Kerwin of Campbell's Division Artillery, these and most of their assistants had been on the staff when Carleton and I joined the Division back in Port Lyautey. Keen and enthusiastic, they were experienced and battle-wise—far more so than any Corps or Army staff under whom we served. I called them together, gave them the outline plan, and told them that it would be our task to find ways to do the operation, not reasons. why it should not be done. And we set to work.

We had, in the Division, light machine guns and mortars to substitute for the heavier guns in mountain fighting where guns had to be carried by hand, as well as extra field pieces and other armament. We could take with us into the landing almost twice the normal complement of fire power, and the Division staff devised special methods of loading and stowing the available craft which would enable us to take nearly twice the seven days' supply proposed. We analyzed intelligence and developed estimates. We modified our organization to increase our fire power, developed plans for landing, for establishing ourselves on shore, for loading and unloading, for naval gunfire support, air support, communications, and many other innumerable details. All of us were sure that we could land and maintain ourselves as long as our ammunition lasted. But not one of us believed that there was even a remote possibility that the main forces could cross the Rapido and drive up the Liri valley to join us within a month. There were some serious faces among the staff when I told them to get on with the preparations, and departed for Army Headquarters to express my views.

Informing General Clark of these conditions, I pointed out that the rate of advance of the main forces up the Liri and Sacco valleys would depend upon the rapidity with which German demolitions could be cleared of resistance and repaired to permit the displacement of supporting weapons, ammunition and supplies, tanks and artillery. In Sicily and in Italy, with better troops and against lighter opposition than could be expected here, the 3rd Infantry Division had averaged only about two miles a day. Then I added: "We are perfectly willing to undertake the operation if we are ordered to do so and we will maintain ourselves to the last round of ammunition. But if we do undertake it, you are going to destroy the best damned division in the United States Army for there will be no survivors."

General Clark was silent for a moment. Then he remarked: "Well, we can't make any decision until this second phase of the attack is completed, and right now it is not going any too well. We will wait and see what happens."

A day or so later, on December 20th, the plan was finally abandoned.

The II Corps had, on December 15th, renewed its attack to clear the Mignano Gap. On the right, the 143rd Infantry of the 36th Infantry Division made another attempt to capture San Pietro and clear Mt. Sammucro, but without much success. On the left, however, the 142nd Infantry crossed over from Mt. Maggiore and attacked the northern end of Mt. Lungo while the Italian brigade again battled the southern part. The 142nd Infantry was wholly successful and the Germans were driven from Mt. Lungo, after which they abandoned San Pietro. Further to the right, the VI Corps, with a French Division replacing the worn 34th Infantry Division, was making slow progress in the mountains west of Venafro.

On December 16th, after the capture of Mt. Lungo, General Clark issued instructions for the third phase of the Army attack. It was to begin on Army order after December 20th when it was estimated that the second phase would have been substantially completed. The II Corps was to capture Mt. Porchia and Mt. Trocchio, the last enemy-held hills south of the Rapido below Cassino, and then employ the 1st Armored Division to pass through the bridgehead and drive northward up the Liri Valley to the Melfa River. The VI Corps was to continue its attack to capture the heights north and northwest of Cassino. The X Corps was to establish a bridgehead over the Garigliano River and protect the left flank of the II Corps as it drove northward up the Liri valley. On December 19th the 15th Infantry Regiment of my Division relieved the 143rd Infantry on Mt. Lungo and the spurs of Mt. Maggiore so that regiment could join the 36th Infantry Division in the attacks.

On Christmas Day, I was called to the II Corps Command Post to confer with General Clark and General Keyes. The II Corps was now ready to assault Mt. Porchia and Mt. Trocchio. The next step would be the break through into the Liri valley and the advance on Rome. Now that the plan for landing the 3rd Infantry Division at Anzio had been abandoned, General Clark proposed to release the Division to the II Corps to force the Rapido crossing and General Keyes staff had prepared outline plans for the operation. In conjunction with the attack of the II and VI Corps to take Cassino and the surrounding heights, the 3rd Infantry Division was to establish a bridgehead over the Rapido River, near the village of San Angelo below Cassino through which the 1st Armored Division would drive up the Liri valley to the Melfa River.

We were enthusiastic over the prospects for action for we had been out of the lines now more than a month. We had been brought up to strength, had carried on an intensive training program, and were fit, ready, and eager. We took the problem in hand.

We had excellent information concerning the river and local terrain, together with first class maps and aerial photographs. Although the Rapido was swollen from recent rains, the problem looked much easier than our Volturno crossing. We could not reconnoiter the actual river while the Germans held Mts. Porchia and Trocchio, but from Mt. Lungo we could look over approaches to the crossing area and the surrounding terrain. Leaving the staff to begin their studies and plans,

Carleton, Harrel, and I set off for the 15th Infantry Command Post on Mt. Lungo.

We were favored by a beautifully clear day with excellent visibility. Colonel Ashton Manhart led us to an observation post in our front lines on the northern end of Mt. Lungo. From there, we could see far up the Liri valley. This farmland valley, about six miles wide at its southern end, was flanked on either side by rugged barren mountains. The Liri River lay close against the foot of the mountains on the western side. The Rapido River, almost inundating its banks, flowed from the mountains above Cassino, meandered across the valley's southern end and joined with the Liri to form the Garigliano, which carried the waters on to the Tyrrhenian Sea below Minturno. The town of Cassino and two or three miles of the river line were screened from our view by the long rugged ridge, Mt. Trocchio, but the heights above Cassino and the mountains beyond were clearly visible. Conical shaped Mt. Porchia was little more than a mile away from where we stood. In the intervening valley, Colonel Manhart assured us that both his own and German patrols were active every night. We could see where the crossing was to be made and the low ridge beyond San Angelo which was to be the bridgehead objective. Crossing the infantry battalions would not be difficult, but we would require bridges for crossing artillery, tanks, tank destroyers, and supplies. Therein was the problem.

The heights above Cassino and the mountain masses opposite the junction of the Liri and Garigliano Rivers dominated the bridging sites from both flanks and were within easy artillery range. From past experience, there was no reason to believe that the few regiments available to the II Corps would be able to storm the Cassino heights even if they were able to take the town. There was no plan for attacking the heights on the western flank. In these rough areas, German artillery could be concealed from our observation and find relative safety from our own artillery and aircraft. At such ranges, German 88's could destroy our bridges faster than we could build them. Without bridges, we could not cross armor, artillery, and antitank guns to support the infantry battalions, nor could we supply them adequately. My fine infantry battalions would eventually be whittled away by German armor, artillery, and infantry. And the 1st Armored Division would still be south of Rapido. Viewed this way, the plan was unsound, so the following day I informed General Clark of these conclusions, to which he agreed, and the plan was abandoned.

On December 28th, General Clark notified me that the high command had revived the Anzio plan. General Alexander had finally obtained authority to undertake the landing with two divisions instead of one, my 3rd Infantry Division and the British 1st Division, under command of the VI Corps. We were to move immediately to a ing area near Naples. But reverting to crossing the Rapido whi had discussed previously, General Clarke asked: "Would you be ing to undertake that Rapido crossing if those heights on either were under attack although not actually in our possession?" After some deliberation, I replied: "Yes, but those attacks should be so powerful that every German gun would be required to oppose them, for only two or three concealed 88's would be able to destroy our bridges. I doubt our capability for making any such attacks." The General agreed and there our conversation ended. However, these conditions were not fulfilled when the 36th Infantry Division made the attempt to cross the Rapido a few weeks later, and the attempt was a costly failure.

It had long been impressed upon me that American soldiers in World War II did not sing as their fathers had done in World War I. For them, war was a deadly serious business, and there was no inclination to lighten burdens with a song. There were no war songs, no new catchy tunes going the rounds in the bivouacs of American soldiers although British soldiers were now singing the captured "Lili Marlene." I have never thought much of mass singing for soldiers, and I had no wish to hear American soldiers sing as they tramped along. However, I have always thought that good ballads are healthy for morale and for the souls of men, and had often expressed the wish that we could have some appropriate Division song which men would instinctively hum, whistle or sing.

One night in my Command Post at San Felice in the Pietravairano area, three soldiers from the 7th Infantry Band entertained us with music after dinner—violin, accordion, and guitar. One catchy little tune they sang for us caught my ear at once, and I had them sing it over and over again. Private Lackey told me that the song had never been published; it had been written by two soldiers, whom he did not know, shortly before the Division sailed for the invasion of North Africa.

At the time, we were in the process of combining the regimental bands to form a Division band. I had Lackey and his group play this little song for the band leaders who reduced it to music for the Division band. When we moved to Pozzuoli near Naples just at the beginning of the New Year, the Division band was ready to try out the new tune for me. Their first effort did not sound quite right. Knowing nothing of music, I had some difficulty in making those fine musicians understand just what I was seeking. They were vastly amused, I think, when I sang the ditty for them and with them, as I did each morning for several days. Eventually we got it right. Then, with those words and music, the 3rd Infantry Division made "Dog Face Soldier" famous all over Europe and elsewhere, for wherever men of the Division fore-gathered, one always heard the song.

One of the greatest thrills I had throughout the war was the after-noon we embarked for Anzio. At the port, we drove up onto the pier, climbed over a passageway built over a sunken hull at the rock side, and onto the headquarters ship, the *Biscayne*. As I came in sight over the passageway, there on the docks below the stern of the *Biscayne*, with Vesuvius in the background across the city of Naples, the 3rd Infantry Division Band broke into "Dog Face Soldier." They played it through in march time, then one hundred twenty voices roared out the words across the beautiful Bay of Naples. It may not have been in the best tradition from a security point of view in this spy-ridden city of Naples, but it was one of the most inspiring things that ever hap-pened to me. Few who heard will ever forget it.

The eventual decision to undertake SHINGLE was made at a high level conference in Tunis on Christmas Day in which General Alex-ander discussed the prosecution of the war in Italy with Prime Min-ister Churchill and General Eisenhower. At this conference it was decided that the early capture of Rome would require the landing of at least two divisions to turn the German right flank and cause a with-drawal on the southern front. The necessary landing craft would be provided by delaying their departure for England until February 5th. January 20th was set as the target date for the operation. Craft would be available to lift two divisions for the assault convoy, but thereafter only six would be available for maintenance of the landing forces, and this number might well be reduced by losses during the assault.

Members of my staff joined the VI Corps staff and the Army Plan-ning Board in Caserta on December 28th and began developing de-tailed plans for the operation. On the same day, the 3rd Division began movement to a training area at Pozzuoli near Naples for intensive assault training. We were glad that the period of waiting was over. General Eagles left the 3rd Infantry Division about the middle of November to assume command of the 45th Infantry Division, when General Middleton departed for a Corps command in England. We were sorry to lose General Eagles, but we welcomed the merited pro-motion which came to him in the new assignment. An old friend who had been with us in the Sicilian landing was, however, a fine replace-ment for General Eagles as Assistant Division Commander—Brigadier General John W. O'Daniels. Another change had taken place in my

THE DOGFACE SOLDIER

Moderato

I WOULD-N'T GIVE A BEAN TO BE A FAN-CY PANTS MAR-INE

I'D RA-THER BE A DOG-FACE SOL-DIER LIKE

I AM——: I WOULD-N'T TRADE MY OLD-O D S FOR

ALL THE NA-VY'S DUN-GA-REES FOR I'M THE WALK-ING

PRIDE OF UN-CLE SAM——: ON ALL THE POST-ERS THAT

READ IT SAYS THE AR-MY BUILDS MEN—— SO THEY'RE

TEAR-ING ME DOWN TO BUILD ME O-VER A-GAIN—— I'M

JUST A DOG-FACE SOL-DIER WITH A RI-FLE ON MY

SHOUL-DER AND I EAT A KRAUT FOR BREAK-FAST EV'RY DAY

——. SO FEED ME AM—MUN-I-TION. KEEP ME

IN THE THIRD DIV-I-SION , YOUR DOG-FACE SOL-DIER

BOY'S O———KAY

personal staff. Late in October, I released Captain Grimsley to be General Alexander's aide. Soon after we reached Pozzuoli, Captain James M. Wilson replaced him. Wilson and Bartash were to remain with me throughout the war.

As our planning progressed during the first week in January we came to two important conclusions. First the employment of one American and one British division unnecessarily complicated supply, communications and control. General Lucas and I recommended to General Clark that two American divisions be used instead, but he informed us that the decision to make the landing an Allied effort had been made "on the very highest level" and that there was no chance whatever of making any change. Secondly, we thought the operation was not practicable without continued maintenance after the initial convoy. No one below Army level believed that the landing of two divisions at Anzio would cause a German withdrawal on the Southern front, or that there was more than a remote chance that the remainder of the Fifth Army would be able to cross the Rapido River and fight its way up the Liri and Sacco valleys to join us within a month. We foresaw that we would have to maintain ourselves against superior enemy forces for an indefinite period of time. We finally convinced General Clark that plans should envisage continued maintenance as well as possible reinforcements. Consequently there was some doubt during the first week of January that the operation would take place in spite of the Christmas Day decision.

General Eisenhower had departed for his new assignment in London. General Sir Henry Maitland Wilson was now the Supreme Allied Commander in Chief in the Mediterranean with Lieutenant General Jacob L. Devers as his Deputy and American Theater Commander. Since Mr. Churchill was still in Africa, resting at Marrakech, another high level conference was arranged to discuss the SHINGLE operation. Colonel E. J. O'Neill and Colonel William H. Hill, VI Corps G-4 and G-3 respectively, were the Fifth Army representatives who attended this conference. Later on, these two officers gave me the following description of the meetings at which the SHINGLE decision was finally confirmed.

We arrived in Marrakech on the afternoon of Friday, 7th January, and were billeted at the La Mamouila Hotel. Immediately after we arrived, we were called to a conference with General Alexander and his Chief of Staff, General Harding. We were first questioned about the tactical plan. Colonel Hill gave General Harding an overlay showing the outline plan. General Alexander asked about details of the plan including:

Number of battalions of each division to be landed in the assault.
Number and type of assault craft available
Plan for unloading the remainder of the force and
Plan for operation to secure the beachhead after landing.

He mentioned the advisability of reducing the number of vehicles to be taken to the minimum. Then we were questioned as to maintenance and Colonel O'Neill stated it was impossible to go into the operation with only seven days maintenance. This appeared to be a radical change in plans, but the necessity for it was seen by General Alexander and General Harding. The question of the amount of daily maintenance for the contemplated force was discussed at great length and Colonel O'Neill insisted that this be figured as a minimum of 1500 tons a day. This figure appeared high to General

Alexander but he finally accepted same. Colonel Hill then stated that General Clark considered the minimum requirement in shipping to execute the operation, in addition to the initial allotment, to be 24 LST's for follow-ups.

Shortly after the conference with General Alexander, we were summoned to a conference with Admiral Cunningham whose main concern was the supply of craft for the operation and the maintenance of the force. He had based all his plans on the initial force landing with 7 days maintenance and no resupply, and was very much surprised at our insistence that it could not be done under these conditions. However, he appeared to accept the fact that continued maintenance had to be planned. He, likewise, thought 1500 tons a day maintenance high but did not question the figure too extensively.

At 1830 we attended a conference at the Villa Taylor at which the following people were present: Prime Minister Churchill, Lord Beaverbrook, Generals Wilson, Devers, Smith, Alexander, Harding and Robertson, Admiral Cunningham, Brigadier Strong, Captain Lewis USN, Captain Powers, Royal Navy, Colonel William H. Hill, Colonel E. J. O'Neill, Lt. Colonel Williams, Lt. Colonel Duncan, and 2 Naval Officers on the staff of Admiral Cunningham. The Prime Minister directed the conference and started off by saying that originally it had been planned to land one division south of Rome, but for various reasons this had been discarded and now the plan was to land a larger force in the vicinity of Anzio, with possible small diversionary efforts near the mouth of the Tiber and north of Rome. He had Brigadier Strong give an estimate of the enemy situation and then stated that the plan had been based on only 7 days maintenance with the rest of the Fifth Army joining forces with the SHINGLE force within that period. He then said that he understood that this plan was not now acceptable to the people who were to do it, and asked "Why." General Alexander explained the tactical plan and stated he concurred in the fact that it could not be launched unless with continued maintenance. The Prime Minister appeared to accept this explanation after some questioning of Colonel Hill as to the tactical plan and Colonel O'Neill as to the supply plan.

With the changed conception of the plan, the Prime Minister then proceeded to the question of the craft necessary for the operation and had Captain Powers explain what craft he believed would be available. This explanation was to the effect that not more than 88 and not less than 80 LST's would be available for the operation for the initial assault. There was considerable discussion as to whether or not these craft would actually be available. Then followed some additional discussion, reference to how the force could be maintained, and Admiral Cunningham stated he could not guarantee to maintain such a force over the beaches at that time of year. He felt both Peter and X-Ray beaches could be used in good weather but that with only 2 days good weather each week this was not sufficient for maintenance of this force. He stated he felt that the Port of Anzio could not be used as all indications were the Germans had been unable to use it and had sunk a vessel or two across the channel.

The discussion then turned to the date which the Prime Minister originally planned and Colonel Hill and Colonel O'Neill said it would have to be not earlier than the 25th. A number of inquiries were made as to the reason for this and it finally hinged on the question of a rehearsal, with Colonel Hill maintaining a rehearsal was absolutely necessary because of past experience and the Prime Minister maintaining that all troops were trained troops and needed no rehearsal. Colonel Hill called attention to the turn over in the 3rd Division and the small number of personnel therein who had been in other landing operations. The Prime Minister insisted that one experienced officer or non-commissioned officer in a platoon was sufficient.

The question of maintenance of the force was then brought up and Colonel O'Neill presented his plan for supplying by trucks loaded on LST's with the empty trucks being returned to Naples for resupply. This plan was completely disapproved by the Prime Minister, Admiral Cunningham, and General Smith, and a prohibition against reloading any trucks into LST's was given. There was then discussed the question of beaching two Liberty ships so that supplies therein could be constantly available. Admiral Cunningham gave permission for not to exceed two Liberty ships to be so used but warned against the results which might be obtained due to damage in beaching the Liberties and the effects of rough weather after beaching.

The Prime Minister then directed that a conference be held after dinner at which an attempt would be made to settle the obstacles which appeared to confront the plan and that another conference would be held at 0930 in the morning.

After dinner all the personnel except the Prime Minister, Lord Beaverbrook and General Wilson assembled at the La Mamouila Hotel and were in conference until about 0130. General Smith presided at this conference. Once again the enemy situation and the tactical plans were discussed and also the availablity of craft. A final agreement was made that between 80 and 88 LST's would be available for the assault and for continued use up until the 3rd of February. From the 3rd to the 13th of February, 25 would be available, and thereafter 14. Colonel O'Neill asked what would happen if these LST's were loaded and off the beaches February 2nd with rough weather preventing their landing and Admiral Cunningham said they would have to be returned to Naples and unloaded as they would definitely have to sail on February 3rd for Great Britain regardless of the condition of SHINGLE.

The question of supply trucks on LST's was discussed and once again a plan to ship empty trucks back to Naples was opposed. Colonel O'Neill was asked how many trucks would be needed if none were shipped back and he stated that 2,000 American 2½ ton trucks each loaded to 5 ton capacity would be necessary. General Robertson said he would furnish this number. The question was raised as to the figure of 1500 tons per day maintenance and Colonel O'Neill insisted this figure could not be lowered though General Smith and General Robertson said they would have their experts study it. Colonel O'Neill stated his figures were based on the type of operation and the necessity of having a heavy reserve of ammunition and that 60% of the maintenance would be ammunition. Admiral Cunningham reiterated that the Navy could not guarantee to supply this force over the beaches at this time of year. The question of a rehearsal was again discussed with Colonel Hill and Colonel O'Neill insisting on the necessity therefore but a decision was finally made that the date would have to be advanced to the 22nd instead of the 25th in order to take advantage of the possibility of 3 extra days of good weather, even if it meant cancelling the rehearsal. This conference ended about 0130.

All personnel reassembled at Villa Taylor at 0930 Saturday morning at which General Smith reported to the Prime Minister the final decision that from 80 to 88 LST's would be available up until February 3rd, 25 LST's from the 3rd to the 13th, and 14 thereafter; that the date would be advanced to the 22nd; and that 2,000 supply trucks would be furnished by General Robertson. The Prime Minister appeared to feel this was a good solution and stated that SHINGLE would be launched under these conditions.

In a talk after the conference with General Devers, he told us that he would see that we got to keep the LST's that were necessary, and that we would be fully supported.

It is interesting to note that the "high level" conferees disapproved the proposal which actually made the maintenance of the Anzio beachhead possible—Colonel O'Neill's proposal to employ loaded trucks for resupply. Loading and unloading of supplies in bulk on LST's is a time and labor consuming procedure, during which the craft must stand idle. Realizing that LST's for maintenance would be few in number, Colonel O'Neill contrived to vastly reduce the time required for loading and unloading and thus increase the number of trips which the LST's could make. He would overload trucks in the supply dumps at Naples with five tons of supplies, and drive them onto the LST's at the piers. At Anzio, the loaded supply trucks would drive off the LST's and proceed to the supply dumps, while empty trucks previously unloaded would drive onto the LST's for the return trip to Naples. Thus, the LST's would be held at Anzio and Naples for no more than an hour or so, instead of from twelve to twenty-four hours which would be required for handling bulk supplies by hand. However, in spite of this disapproval, the technique was adopted; without it, the maintenance of the forces eventually assembled at Anzio would have been impossible.

2. A Beachhead Established

The plan which finally evolved from the frenzied studies and counterstudies—the agreements and conferences at every level from high to low—was somewhat different from the original proposal to land the 3rd Infantry Division at Anzio with seven days supply. The assault force, under Major General John W. Lucas' VI Corps Headquarters, consisted of my 3rd Infantry Division, Major General W. R. C. Penney's 1st Division (British), the 1st, 2nd and 3rd Ranger Battalions under Colonel William O. Darby, the 83rd Chemical Battalion, the 504th Parachute Infantry under Colonel Tucker, and two British Commandos. If necessary, one Regimental Combat Team of the 45th Infantry Division would join the beachhead forces on the first turn around of craft, within about three days, and would be followed by the 1st Armored Division (less one combat command) as rapidly as craft could be made available.

The Naval Force, Task Force 81, commanded by Rear Admiral

Frank W. Lowry, USN, was actually divided into two task forces, Task Force Peter for the British beaches, and Task Force X Ray for the American beaches. The Naval Force included 84 LST's, 8 LSI's, 96 LCI's, 50 LCT's, 4 Liberty ships loaded with ten days of supplies, and 2 command ships, as well as supporting cruisers, destroyers and smaller vessels, and a support group to make a feint attack for deception purposes north of the Tiber. Thus, Admiral Lowry was General Lucas's opposite number for the SHINGLE Force, but he was also my opposite number for the 3rd Infantry Division assault.

Military preparations presented no special difficulties for staff and units as experienced as those of the 3rd Infantry Division. Such obstacles as delays in assembling the Naval Force and some inexperience on the Naval side were surmounted without too much trouble. The most serious problem resulted from Admiral Lowry's dual position as overall Naval commander and commander of Task Force X Ray for the 3rd Infantry Division assault. Initial plans assigned VI Corps Headquarters to the *Biscayne* with Admiral Lowry and assigned my 3rd Division Headquarters to an LCI with the Naval commander of the LCI flotilla. Thus, during the assault—the most critical phase of the landing operation—I was to be separated from my Naval opposite number, and without communications except the LCI's rather tenuous radio channel to the *Biscayne*. My protest met a cool reception, for the limited military space on board the *Biscayne* had been preempted by Corps Headquarters. There the matter stood until our rehearsal.

Landing operations depend upon complete mutual understanding and whole-hearted cooperation between the Military and Naval forces involved. Mr. Churchill to the contrary, full scale rehearsal is the only way in which this understanding and cooperation can be tested, and it is even more important for the Naval component than for the Military, for the assault may depend entirely upon Naval ability to put troops ashore exactly as planned. Both General Lucas and I insisted that a rehearsal was an absolute essential and our views eventually prevailed. With some difficulty a date was arranged, with barely time remaining for loading. Results were to justify our insistence.

The Division loaded out for the rehearsal—operation WEBFOOT —at Pozzuoli and Naples after which the fleet put out to sea to gain sufficient distance to approach the rehearsal beaches at Salerno in proper formation and in time for the first waves to touch down at 0200 in accordance with our plans. Admiral Lowry sailed on the *Biscayne*, but General Lucas elected to wait on the beach in order to see the troops come ashore. I sailed on the LCI which had been designated as my Headquarters ship.

Some miles off shore that night, the Mediterranean was rough and choppy, although close in to the beaches the sea was calm. It was a rough night for men packed on board the flat-bottomed light craft. Even when we came into the transport area, we could see nothing, and had no means of knowing whether or not the assault waves were disembarking and proceeding toward the beaches in accordance with landing plans. At daybreak we were a dozen miles off shore, and we learned from returning craft that the assault battalion had gone into the beaches and had landed.

On the beach, I found that the battalions had already gone inland toward their initial objectives, although not without confusion. They had been disembarked so far at sea that few had landed on their proper beaches, and all had landed late. No artillery tanks or tank destroyers were yet on shore at 0800, although all should have been ashore by daylight with the infantry battalions. Then in fragments came the appalling news. Through some error in navigation, the transport area had been many more miles farther from the shore than it should have been. In darkness, the LST'S had opened their doors, lowered their ramps, discharged the DUKW's which carried the artillery into the rough seas, where twenty or more had swamped and sunk. Incomplete reports indicated that the artillery pieces and communication equipment of perhaps two battalions had been dumped into the sea. Some few pieces straggled ashore during the latter part of the morning as did a few tanks and tank destroyers. Beaches were in a chaotic condition, and the whole landing plan was completely disrupted. Only the infantry battalions were on their initial objectives, and then only because of the energy and experience of the regimental and battalion commanders. Against opposition, the landing would have been a disaster.

I sought General Lucas but he had returned to Caserta after watching the infantry battalions land, and had informed General Clark that the rehearsal was entirely successful. When we had done everything to reorganize the command and return units to their bivouac areas at Pozzuoli, I returned to my Command Post and prepared a report based on personal information submitted before the full details of the disaster could be determined.

I recounted all that had gone wrong during the rehearsal—no battalion landed on time or in proper formation or even on its proper beach; no artillery tanks or tank destroyers ashore by daylight; loss of DUKW's with much of the Division artillery; lack of communications; obvious lack of control and lack of training on the Naval side as well as lack of Naval preparation. I remarked that to land my Division at Anzio as it was landed during the rehearsal would invite disaster if the Germans counterattacked with tanks soon after daylight, and urgently recommended another rehearsal for further training. These reports I sent off by officer courier to General Clark and Admiral Lowry, and set off at once to deliver the report to General Lucas in person. Then came the flap.

General Lucas and I had been in complete agreement on every detail of preparations and planning for SHINGLE. He agreed to the desirability for another rehearsal. However, he felt himself to be in a difficult position with regard to General Clark, and he was unwilling to protest further although he had no objection to my doing so.

I found General Clark with my report in front of him. He was obviously disturbed, but his first remark was: "Well, Lucian, I've got your report here, and it's bad. But you won't get another rehearsal. The date has been set at the very highest level. There is no possibility of delaying it even for a day. You have got to do it." I remarked that I was not unwilling to do the operation—I asked only for another rehearsal. Certainly if the delay of one day or two meant the difference between success or failure, the high authorities would certainly grant it if the problem were presented to them. According to General Clark this was not so; we had been expected to do the operation without rehearsal, and there had been trouble enough arranging one. Any further delay would be flatly refused. As for my lost artillery and equipment, he would replace it from divisions then in line if necessary. I was to let him know the full extent of the losses as soon as possible. And that was that.

When I left General Clark and returned to Pozzuoli, I went at once to see Admiral Lowry and found him in very low spirits, too. The extent of the debacle was growing as craft which returned to berth were inspected and losses verified. Admiral Lowry was deeply chagrined and would have liked another rehearsal. However, when I told him of my conversation with General Clark, he assured me that the Navy would do its utmost to set matters straight, and to put us ashore exactly as we wished.

Late in the afternoon of January 21st the expedition sailed.

The second phase of the Fifth Army attack to clear the Germans from the south bank of the Rapido River was completed on January 15th when the II Corps captured Mt. Trocchio, almost a month later than General Clark's original estimate. Plans for continuing the attack in conjunction with the landing at Anzio necessitated that the French Expeditionary Corps, which had taken over the mission of the VI Corps in the mountains above Venafro, continue its attack begun on January 12th to seize the heights northwest of Cassino. On January 17th, the British X Corps was to force a crossing over the Garigliano, establish a bridgehead, and then attack northward to protect the flank of the II Corps. On January 20th, about forty-eight hours before the landing at Anzio, the II Corps was to establish a bridgehead over the Rapido River in the vicinity of San Angelo, and then employ the maximum amount of armor to exploit northward up the Liri Valley. These attacks were expected to prevent any withdrawal of forces to oppose the landing of the VI Corps at Anzio on January 22nd, and then threat to the enemy's rear and line of communications. This was expected to cause a German withdrawal on the southern front.

There has been much criticism of the Anzio decision, as there usually is when a military operation fails to fulfill popular hopes or the hopes of the military commanders responsible for it. Likewise, there has been a tendency to blame the initial failure on poor intelligence, or poor leadership, on failure to understand the enemy, and on poor planning. I suppose that all of these may have been contributing factors for there are few military operations in which these criticisms cannot be adduced in some measure, but these explanations do not enable one to understand the Anzio operation. When operations fulfill optimistic estimates they are rated as great successes and receive popular acclaim. On the other hand, sound planning ensures against the contingency that one may accomplish less, and the enemy more, than hoped. When an operation turns out according to this more pessimistic view, there is a tendency among the uninformed to condemn the plan and criticize all concerned with its execution. Anzio belongs in this latter category.

The information available when the Anzio decision was made and when the operation was launched was adequate—far more complete, accurate, and comprehensive than is usually the case. Locations of every German division in Italy and others capable of interfering were known up to the time of mounting the operation. Intelligence agencies cannot be blamed for failure to discover that the Germans had just relieved a division on the coast south of the Tiber and had reduced the strength of the garrison in the sector where the landing was to take place, for that information would not have been available until a day or so later. Except for this, the Fifth Army G-2 estimate of the strength which could oppose the landing at Anzio was not far wrong, at least as far as the first few days were concerned: on D Day, one division on the coast, a tank battalion, an antitank battalion, four parachute battalions from Rome, and miscellaneous coast defense units, or a total of some 14,000 men; by D plus 1, another division, an SS regiment from north of Rome, a Regimental Combat Team from the XIV Panzer Corps facing the Fifth Army on the Cassino front; by D plus 2 or 3, another Panzer division from the Eighth Army front.

Where the G-2 estimates erred—although the G-2's were not wholly chargeable—was in underestimating German ingenuity for moving troops from northern Italy, France and elsewhere to intervene against the beachhead, and in overestimating the effect of the combined attacks of the landing operation on the southern front of the German command. But some blame is due to our own Air Forces who overrated their ability to prevent such movements. They had been concentrating for weeks on Operation STRANGLE, to disrupt all rail and road communications in Italy in order to prevent the movement of German troops and supplies—to "isolate the battlefield." There was a tendency on the part of Air officers to believe this action would be far more effective than was demonstrated. The Fifth Army G-2 summary on January 16th overestimated the effect of the combined attacks in these words:

> Within the past few days there have been increasing indications that enemy strength on the front of the Fifth Army is ebbing due to casualties, exhaustion, and possibly lowering of morale. One of the causes of this condition, no doubt, has been the recent, continuous Allied attacks. From this it can be deduced that he has no fresh reserves and very few tired ones. His entire strength will probably be needed to defend his organized defensive positions.
>
> In view of the weakening of enemy strength on the front as indicated above, it would appear doubtful if the enemy can hold the organized defensive line through Cassino against a coordinated army attack. Since this attack is to be launched before SHINGLE it is considered likely that this additional threat will cause him to withdraw from his defensive position once he has appreciated the magnitude of that operation.

General Lucas and I, and our staffs, thought there was little chance of any breakthrough on the southern front, or any joining up with the beachhead, under a matter of weeks. There had been no change on the Cassino front even after the capture of Mt. Trocchio to make the crossing of the Rapido River more feasible in January than when we had studied it in December. While both General Alexander and General Clark were optimistic that the two attacks would compel a German withdrawal and lead to the early capture of Rome, they fully appreciated that events might turn out otherwise and had provided for that contingency by insuring the continued maintenance and, if necessary, the buildup of the SHINGLE force, and by charging General Lucas with establishing a firm beachhead before initiating any advance toward the Colli Laziali.

There was another factor which had not been appreciated by intelligence officers or by any of us engaged in planning the Anzio operation. We knew of course that the Germans would have plans for opposing a landing at any place on the Italian coast. What we did not know and failed to appreciate was the technique which the German command had developed for rapid concentration against, and the sealing off of, any such landing. Later we were to learn that the German command had developed a comprehensive plan by which—in spite of our air attacks—the reconnaissance battalions and other mobile elements of almost every division in Italy could be started almost instantly to oppose such an Allied landing and could intervene in a matter of hours to gain time for the intervention of larger forces moved from northern Italy, from France, and from other parts of the front.

We sailed from Naples in the early morning hours of January 21st on a devious course designed to avoid German mines and to deceive the enemy as to our destination. At the time, we knew that the British X Corps had established a bridgehead across the lower Carigliano and was making good progress. The Corps had launched its attack across the Rapido River the preceding day, but we knew little of its progress beyond the fact that no bridges were across during the first day. We spent a quiet day in a calm sea in balmy weather, but I think few among the commanders and staffs—Corps, Division and Navy—crowded aboard the *Biscayne* were in any frame of mind to enjoy the beauties of a Mediterranean cruise. During the evening I wrote to my wife as I always did on the eve of dangerous operations and had barely finished when we reached the transport area at four minutes past midnight, just four minutes behind our schedule.

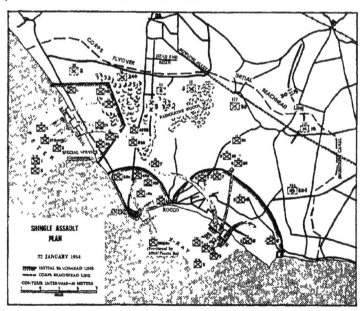

Anzio, a small port, and Nettuno, about two miles to the east, are small resort towns on the coast about thirty miles south of Rome, once favored, it was said, by the Roman emperors. A good road and railroad lead practically due north along a flat, almost imperceptible ridge through Aprilia and Campoleone to Albano eighteen miles inland on the slopes of Colli Laziali. There the road joins Highway 7, the coastal road from the south to Rome. Another road follows the coast northwest to Ostia and thence along the south bank of the Tiber to Rome. North of Anzio adjacent to the Albano road, the country is broken by numerous deep ravines—"wadi country" our British comrades termed it. A few miles inland this area was covered with dense pine woods of a reforestation project. About eight miles north of Anzio, ravines or "wadis" lead off westward from the Albano Road and into the Moletta River, flowing westward to the sea and marking the Corps Beachhead Line in the sector of the British 1st Division.

Five miles east of Nettuno is a creek known as the Asturia River which had once drained from the southern slopes of Colli Laziali to the sea. There were patches of woods along this stream near the coast, but for the most part the whole area to the north and east of Nettuno was farm land reclaimed from the Pontine Marshes in one of Mussolini's early reclamation projects. The main drainage canal began near Padiglione about six miles north of Nettuno and cut west between high dikes across the natural drainage lines to a point near the village of Sessano where it joined with an eastern tributary and flowed south to the sea nine miles east of Nettuno. This was the Mussolini Canal. The main canal and its western tributary marked the Corps Beachhead Line in the sector of the 3rd Infantry Division, with the boundary between divisions lying just east of the Albano Road. At the mouth of the Mussolini Canal, a pumping station emptied the waters into the sea.

This whole area of reclaimed marshland was passable enough in dry weather. The water line, however, was usually within two feet of the surface. When rains fell or the pumps stopped working, the area became so marshy that movement off roads was almost impossible, and fox holes filled with water. One road followed the coast eastward from Nettuno through Littoria and joined Highway 7 farther on down the coast. Still another road led northeast from Nettuno through Cisterna and Cori to Artena and Valmontone on Highway 6, the main road from Cassino to Rome. The whole area was dotted by two-storey farm houses or *poderi*, usually of plastered stone. The Beachhead area was an area roughly seven miles in depth and fifteen miles in width at its widest part.

The British 1st Division was to land over Peter beaches, the 2nd and 24th Guards Brigade Groups, six infantry battalions, were to establish an initial beachhead, and two Commando outfits of the 2nd Special Service Brigade were to block the Albano Road north of Anzio. Three Ranger Battalions and the 509th Parachute Battalion were to capture the port and the town of Anzio. The 509th Parachute Battalion was to follow the Rangers and capture the town of Nettuno. The 3rd Infantry Division was to land over X-Ray beaches and seize an initial beachhead line. Our plan was to land all three regiments simultaneously, in order to put the combat elements of the entire Division ashore as rapidly as possible. The 3rd Reconnaissance Troop, and the Provisional Mounted Troop dismounted for the purpose, both under command of Major Bob Crandall, were organized into mobile detachments with machine guns and antitank weapons. These were to land with the assault battalions and move rapidly inland to seize all crossings over the Mussolini Canal, prepare them for demolition, and hold them until the arrival of the infantry battalions. The remainder of the 1st British Division and the 50th Parachute Regiment in corps reserve were to land after the assault echelon.

We expected to encounter heavy opposition on the beaches and to be counterattacked with armor within a few hours after landing. Our plans emphasized establishing ourselves securely to repel such counterattacks even as we advanced to, and established ourselves firmly on, the Corps Beachhead Line. One Regimental Combat Team of the 45th Infantry Division was to follow on the first turn-around convoy, in about three days, to be followed—should the situation require it—by one Combat Command 1st Armored Division, and the remainder of the 45th Infantry Division as rapidly as transportation permitted.

The poor performance during the rehearsal had obviously put the Navy on their mettle. Immediately upon arrival in the transport area, craft were lowered away on schedule and headed for the beaches already marked by Naval scouts, exactly as planned. On schedule, at 0150, ten minutes before H Hour, Navy rocket craft launched a short but terrific rocket barrage on the beaches where the battalions were to land; then at 0200, the assault battalions touched down on the beaches, and the others followed in regular order and on schedule according to the landing plan. By daylight, all infantry antitank weapons were all on shore, and the unloading was progressing. After the almost disastrous performance during the rehearsal, our Navy comrades gave us one which was almost unbelievably smooth and accurate.

I went ashore with my staff soon after six o'clock. Roads were congested with armor and vehicles, but everything was moving. There had been almost no opposition. The only elements encountered were two depleted battalions of the 29th Panzer Grenadier Division which had just been relieved from hard fighting on the Cassino front and assigned to this quiet sector for rest. More than two hundred men were captured, many of them still in bed. By 0900, we were firmly established on the initial beachhead line. The most serious enemy reaction up to this time had been an air raid as we were leaving the beach, but fortunately no damage was done.

In a landing operation, one never knows too much of what is taking place even in his own sector, and all too little about what is happening in adjacent sectors. Information concerning other parts of the beachhead, the Rangers, and the British, was slow in reaching us. It was past mid-morning. I had sent the 1st Battalion, 7th Infantry, to occupy the ground just north of Nettuno, when the 509th Parachute Battalion arrived in the town and made contact with us. It was much later before we knew that the 1st Division, which had been delayed in landing by mines and beach conditions, was finally established on its initial objective.

About 1000, I returned to my Command Post which had been established in a wood a few hundred yards inland from the beach, after visiting the regiments and inspecting conditions on the beach. My orderly, Private Hong, knowing that I had had no breakfast before leaving the *Biscayne*, had breakfast waiting for me—bacon and fresh eggs and toast made over an open fire as only Hong could make it. Fresh eggs were hard to come by in Italy but by means known only to an astute Chinese, he had acquired about three dozen with which he expected to see Carleton and me through until the supply channel with Naples was fully established. Needless to say, I enjoyed this first Anzio breakfast, with the hood of my jeep for a table.

I had barely finished when General Clark, accompanied by General Brann and several others, arrived to congratulate us on the success of the landing. Yes, they would love to have some breakfast, so Hong produced more bacon, eggs, and toast. Before they had finished, General Lucas and his Chief of Staff arrived, and they, too expressed a desire for breakfast. More of Hong's bacon and eggs. One after another, visitors arrived, and of course, all wanted some breakfast. More of Hong's bacon, eggs, and toast. As the last of the visitors left, about half-past twelve, and I was preparing to leave the Command Post, I overheard Hong remark to Sergeant Barna, in a tone of exasperation most unusual with him: "Goddam, Sergeant, General's fresh eggs all gone to hell."

Major Bob Crandall's mobile cavalry detachments had seized all crossings over Mussolini Canal during the morning and had prepared the bridges for demolition. By dark, advance detachments of the 30th Infantry had seized all crossings over the West Branch from Padiglione eastward. Meanwhile, transports, ammunition, and equipment joined to augment our installations, wire lines were laid and communications established in readiness for battle. Holding ourselves organized to meet any German attack, we were now ready to secure the Corps Beachhead Line. But we were to have some trouble.

Major Crandall saw me late in the afternoon. I warned him that the detachments should be especially watchful during the night because a German reaction was almost certain. Crandall left me to inspect his road blocks. It was to be more than a year before I saw him again. German armored detachments from the Herman Goering Panzer Division drove the cavalry detachment from the bridge west of Sessano and the advance detachments of the 30th Infantry from the crossings over the West Branch during the night. Crandall, arriving to inspect his bridge guard, drove into the midst of the German battalion and was captured. The German detachments reached La Ferriere, and destroyed the bridge there just as the leading battalion of the 30th Infantry reached the spot early the second morning. Later that day we drove the Germans back across the Canal with considerable losses, and by nightfall we were established on the Corps Beachhead Line. On the 24th the 1st Division reached the Moletta River, so that by dark the Corps had occupied the Corps Beachhead Line.

I suppose that arm chair strategists will always labor under the delusion that there was a "fleeting opportunity" at Anzio during which some Napoleonic figure would have charged over the Colli Laziali, played havoc with the German line of communications, and galloped on into Rome. Any such concept betrays lack of comprehension of the military problem involved. It was necessary to occupy the Corps Beachhead line to prevent the enemy from interfering with the beaches. Otherwise, enemy artillery and armored detachments, operating against the flanks, could have cut us off from the beach and prevented the unloading of troops, supplies, and equipment. As it was, the Corps Beachhead line was barely distant enough to prevent direct artillery fire upon the beaches.

On January 24th, my Division, with three Ranger Battalions and the 504th Parachute Regiment, which had been in Corps reserve, attached, was extended on the Corps Beachhead Line from the mouth of the Mussolini Canal to the First Passover on the Albano Road— a front of twenty miles. Each regiment had one battalion in reserve; the Division had two, the 7th Infantry less one battalion. Two brigade groups of the British 1st Division held a front of more than seven miles. One brigade group of the 1st Division, was in Corps reserve. Corps artillery engineers, corps and division transport and equipment, ammunition and supplies were still coming ashore.

We were in contact with German detachments with tanks and self-propelled artillery everywhere along the front. We knew that there had been a German division south of Rome and at least one other in easy reach behind the southern front. And we knew that the II Corps attempt to cross the Rapido River had ended in failure. Under such conditions, any reckless drive to seize the Colli Laziali with means then available in the beachhead could only have ended in disaster and might well have resulted in destruction of the entire force.

We did not remain inactive. It was desirable that the Corps hold the road centers at Cisterna and Campoleone in preparation for further advance from the beachhead, or for defense if further advance should not be possible. The 179th Regimental Combat Team of the 45th Infantry Division reached the beachhead on January 24th and was placed in Corps reserve, General Lucas releasing the remainder of the 1st Division to General Penney. Both divisions then continued their thrusts toward Cisterna and Campoleone. In my sector, both the 15th and 30th Infantry attacked with one battalion each on January 25th but made little progress. The following day, we reorganized and both attacked with two battalions each supported by tanks and the mass of the Division artillery. In two days of heavy fighting against bitter German resistance, the attack made some progress, but both were still three miles from Cisterna. More power was needed.

My staff and I were convinced we could take Cisterna if arrangements were made to employ the whole Division; accordingly we worked out plans for such an attack. On January 26th, I proposed to General Lucas that the 179th Regimental Combat Team and elements of the 1st Division be used to release my Division for an all-out attack, after which we could take over defense while the 1st Division concentrated to seize Campoleone. However, General Lucas was not yet ready. Reconnaissance elements of the 1st Division had reached Campoleone and the 1st Division had seized the Factory at Aprilia. The Combat Command of the 1st Armored Division was expected to arrive in the beachhead within the next day or so. He would wait their arrival before making any all-out attack.

I was injured the afternoon of January 24th when a shell exploded beside my foot during an air raid. Had it not been for the cavalry breeches and boots which I always wore during battle, the wound would have been far more serious than it was, which was bad enough by the time the surgeon had finished cutting out the fragments and had encased my leg in an adhesive cast. Added to the laryngitis which had plagued me ever since our rehearsal and had reduced my voice to little more than a whisper, I was having troubles enough.

January 27th, General Lucas called a conference to discuss plans for the coordinated attack from the beachhead which General Clark was now urging upon him. Both General Penney and I were present with our staffs, as well as General Harmon whose Armored Combat Command A was expected to reach the beachhead the following day. The plan finally decided upon was to have the 1st Division, with General Harmon's Combat Command A attached, make the main effort along the Albano Road and seize the road center at Campoleone whereupon the Armored Combat Command would pass through, swing wide to the left and attack Colli Laziali from the west. The 3rd Division with Colonel Darby's Ranger Battalions and the 504th Parachute Regiment was to make the secondary effort, capture Cisterna and cut Highway 7 and be prepared to continue the advance toward Velletri. Elements of the 45th Infantry Division and the Corps Engineers were to relieve elements of the 1st and 3rd Divisions on the flanks of the beachhead so that both divisions would have the maximum strength available for the attack, which was set for January 29th.

The Herman Goering Panzer Division which faced the 3rd Infantry Division was extended over a wide front which it held with organized strong points supported by mobile armored detachments. Both Colonel William O. Darby and I believed two of his Ranger Battalions could infiltrate between these strong points under cover of darkness and enter the town of Cisterna. Trained for such night infiltration and for street fighting, they could be expected to cause much confusion in the German lines. Meanwhile, the 15th Infantry and the remaining Ranger Battalion would attack one hour later to break through the German defenses and support the Rangers. On the right of the 15th Infantry, the 504th Parachute Regiment would make a diversionary attack up the east branch of the Mussolini Canal. On the left, the 7th Infantry would attack northward along the Feminamorta Creek to break through the German main line of resistance along the railroad west of Cisterna and cut Highway 7 just north of the town. All attacks would be accompanied by tanks and tank destroyers, and all would be supported by the mass of the Division artillery.

We were ready on January 29th, but General Lucas found it necessary to delay the attack for a day to give General Penney and General Harmon time to complete their preparations. As it turned out, this delay was most unfortunate for us, for without our knowledge, during the night of January 29th, the German 26th Panzer Grenadier Division, brought from the Eighth Army front, relieved elements of the Herman Goering Division along that part of the front from Cisterna westward, over which we were pressing. Thus, we encountered not one division extended over a wide front, but two on fronts capable of defense.

Our attack got under way at 0100 the morning of January 30th as planned. The 1st and 3rd Ranger Battalions infiltrated through the

German lines and reached a point within a half mile of the town when they ran into trouble just at daylight. One battalion commander was killed, the other wounded, but the Rangers took to the ditches and houses along the road and fought back gallantly. Colonel Darby was in radio communication with the sergeant major of the 1st Ranger Battalion—he had been sergeant major when we had organized the Rangers back in Northern Ireland— and through him was directing artillery fire to support the beleagured battalions.

Meanwhile, the attack of the 4th Ranger Battalion with tanks along the main road from Conca to Cisterna had been stopped almost immediately by strong German resistance. All three battalions of the 15th Infantry attempted to break through to join up with the Rangers. At noon, Major Frederick W. Boye's 3rd Battalion had cleared Isola Bella and was little more than a mile away. But too late. At 1215, Colonel Darby was talking by radio with his old sergeant major when the end came—the Rangers, their ammunition exhausted, were finally overrun by German tanks and infantry. Most of the more than 750 men who entered the action were captured. Less than a dozen escaped. It was a sad blow to all of us, and particularly to Colonel Darby and me. He had organized the 1st Ranger Battalion under my direction in North Ireland, and had fought with them in North Africa, Tunisia, Sicily, and southern Italy.

There was quite a flap when I reported to General Clark by telephone that night the loss of the Rangers. He came to see me the next morning and implied that they were unsuitable for such missions. I reminded him that I had been responsible for organizing the original Ranger battalion and that Colonel Darby and I perhaps understood their capabilities better than other American officers. He said no more. However General Clark feared unfavorable publicity, for he ordered an investigation to fix the responsibility. That was wholly unnecessary for the responsibility was entirely my own, especially since both Colonel Darby and I considered the mission a proper one, which should have been well within the capabilities of these fine soldiers. That ended the matter. The remnants of the Ranger Force was returned to the United States a few weeks later.

Our attack had gotten off to a bad start, and we had not made very much progress during this first day. That night, we reorganized. The next morning we laid on an intense artillery preparation to beat down the German defenses, and then followed up with tanks and infantry pressing closely behind heavy artillery concentration. But the Boche was still there and holding stubbornly. In two days of heavy fighting, the 1st Battalion, 7th Infantry, had fought its way to the railroad line west of Cisterna capturing more than 200 prisoners; the 1st Battalion, 30th Infantry, under 7th Infantry command had reached the stream line a mile west of Cisterna, the 2nd Battalion, 15th Infantry, was little more than a thousand yards south of Cisterna and requesting permission to fight its way into the town after dark. But it was not to be. There were no more reserves. We had lost more than 3000 battle casualties since the day of the landing, and more than a third of our tanks and tank destroyers. We had discovered by now the presence of the whole of the 26th Panzer Grenadier Division, and knew that we were facing more than two German divisions. It seemed wise to adjust our front along ground which we could hold while we cleared out pockets of resistance which had been by-passed during the attack, and reorganized the Division to meet the counterattack which I thought was almost certain to come.

The 1st Division had fared little better in its attack to capture Campoleone than we had done in our effort to capture Cisterna. Encountering heavy German resistance from the beginning, it had fought its way to Campoleone but had never been able to clear and hold the road center there. During the evening of February 1st, General Lucas visited me at Conca. After reviewing the situation in both division sectors, he informed me that the Corps would consolidate the ground gained in the attacks and regroup in preparation for renewing the attack when reinforcements were available. Early the following morning, General Lucas called me to say that the Army had just informed him it had secret intelligence that the Germans were in far greater strength than we had thought, and were preparing to launch a counteroffensive to drive the beachhead into the sea. We were to stop all attacks, dig in for defense, and hold the Corps Beachhead Line at all costs.

The Corps plan was to hold the ground we had gained, but at the same time to organize the Corps Beachhead Line. Our front line, stretching for the most part across flat open fields, had few of the natural terrain features usually considered necessary in defensive positions. I rather doubted we would be able to hold it against any determined enemy attack, and decided to organize an intermediate line in order to afford depth to our position. My idea was to have each regiment develop the organization of the three lines in their respective sectors simultaneously, so each regiment would be disposed in depth from the front line back to include the Corps Beachhead Line. In theory, this seemed to be a good solution for developing the defense in the shortest possible period of time. In practice, as I was to learn very soon, it was not the best arrangement.

German attacks on February 3rd and 4th pinched off the Campoleone salient north of the Factory and inflicted heavy losses on the British 1st Division. Then on February 5th, the Germans turned their attention to the front of the 3rd Infantry Division. Shortly after dark, the Germans laid down an intense concentration of artillery, mortar, and tank fire on the front rather thinly held by the 2nd Battalion, 7th Infantry, west of Ponte Rotto, and then attacked with tanks and infantry making extensive use of flares, machine pistols, and various noise-making devices. The action had all the ear-marks of the full scale attack which we were expecting, and we watched developments tensely. About ten o'clock, Carleton talked by telephone with Colonel Sherman and with the battalion commander, Major Elterich, on a party line. Major Elterich asked permission to withdraw, so Carleton called me to the telephone. Major Elterich painted a dismal picture, saying that his battalion had suffered heavily, was in danger of being cut off and surrounded, and could not hold out much longer. He wanted permission to withdraw to the intermediate defense line where the 3rd Battalion was then assembling. At that moment, not being able to think of any other solution, I authorized Major Elterich to withdraw, which also resulted in the withdrawl of the 2nd Battalion, 30th Infantry, on his left, so that on a front of more than four miles we were back on the intermediate defense line and not far in advance of our final position on the Corps Beachhead line. And the battle had barely begun!

As I had time to study the action more closely it was evident that the German attack was a limited one and that I had made a mistake in authorizing the withdrawal. Accordingly, I called the regimental commanders and told them to get back on their original positions at once. Both regiments counterattacked and by daylight the positions had been restored. Except for some losses in the 2nd Battalion, 7th Infantry, little damage had been done. This action showed very clearly that our defense plan had a fundamental weakness, and we were fortunate that the Boche had not been in position to follow up his initial advantage. Our preoccupation with organizing three defense lines had unduly weakened our front lines, and had left troops in no frame of mind to defend there stubbornly. Our preoccupation with the organization of the Corps Beachhead Line had indicated to them that it was the strongest position and that the main defense would be made there. We set about correcting this attitude at once.

We would hold the front line as the main line of resistance. The 504th Parachute Infantry and the 30th Infantry occupied their forward areas with two battalions each, and each one had one battalion in reserve. Organizing the Corps Beachhead Line was left to the 7th Infantry in Division Reserve, and the Division engineers. We made extensive use of mines, wire, and obstacles as is usual. One unusual measure was to place tanks and tank destroyers well forward with the front line bat-of the tankers objected to this employment of armor at first, but the psychological effect on the infantry more than justified it, and it was not long before the armored experts were in hearty agreement.

The mass of our Division artillery, totalling seven battalions, could always be directed against any part of the front by forward observers, artillery liaison officers, or infantry commanders who could observe the targets. To provide for the contingency that communications might fail or observers might become casualties, we planned concentrations for every possible avenue of approach, assembly area, and possible artillery or tank support area. These concentrations could be called down by observers, but if communications failed at any time, specified concentrations were to be fired and repeated until communications were reestablished or the situation otherwise clarified. This procedure proved most effective, for German activity on any part of our front by day or night brought almost instant reaction from a mass of well placed and directed artillery. Never again during the entire beachhead period was any German attack to endanger the front of the 3rd Infantry Division.

Beginning with converging thrusts on the night of February 7th, the Germans continued whittling away at the 1st Division in the Carroceto area. In these days of heavy fighting, the 1st Division again suffered heavy losses and was driven from the Factory area. On February 11th, General Lucas ordered the 45th Infantry Division to counterattack to retake the Factory area, but efforts on that and the following days failed and the Germans were left in possession. Later, I learned that General Eagles had used only one battalion, 179th Infantry, and two companies of tanks in these counterattacks. But since the Germans had taken the Factory from a force several times that strength and were obviously holding the area in strength, this contingent was, of course, wholly inadequate. No less than a regiment should have been employed.

After the failure to retake the Factory, an uneasy lull settled over the forward areas, although the Germans increased their attacks by air and heavy artillery on the beach and port areas. Both General Lucas and General Penney were gravely concerned over the condition of the British 1st Division which had now been fighting almost day and night for ten days or more and had suffered heavily. General Lucas was struggling desperately to strengthen the weakened central sector which the timely arrival of the major portion of the British 56th Division permitted him to do. He divided the 1st Division sector between the American 45th Infantry Division and the British 56th Division, and withdrew the battered 1st Division into Corps reserve for much needed rest.

Intelligence indicated that the Germans were reorganizing for a renewed effort to eliminate the beachhead, and we knew that six or eight German divisions would be available. Bad weather hampered air observation. German preparations were so well and carefully made that we could not tell just when and where the attack would fall. There had been a build-up of German armor back of Cisterna and large increases in enemy artillery areas west of Cisterna and around Campoleone. Yet while we were on the alert on the front of the 3rd Infantry Division, we believed that the main German attack was more likely to continue along the Albano Road. The relief of the 1st Division by the 56th was actually completed during the night of February 15th with no evidence an offensive was imminent although German patrols were very active along the front of the 3rd Infantry Division during the night.

When the Germans began their major effort on the morning of February 16th to "lance the abscess south of Rome," our situation map showed the VI Corps disposed as follows: The 1st Special Service Force held a front of about six miles along the Mussolini Canal on the eastern flank. The 3rd Infantry Division, with the 504th Parachute Regiment and the 509th Parachute Battalion attached, held a front of more than ten miles from the bridge just west of Sessano through Isola Bella and Ponte Rotto to Carano. The 45th Infantry Division occupied a sector about five miles wide from Carano westward to include the Albano Road just south of Carroceto. The 56th Division had just relieved the 1st Division on a front of about three miles in the "wadis" west of the Albano Road. The 36th Engineers held a front of about three miles along to Moletta River near the coast. In Corps reserve, there were the battered 1st Division, reduced in strength and badly in need of rest, and General Harmon's 1st Armored Division, (less Combat Command B which was still on the southern front.) Considering that the Corps disposed more than 400 pieces of artillery not counting the guns of the infantry cannon companies, more than 300 tanks, more than 300 tank destroyers and antitank guns, and more than 400 artillery guns and machine guns, there was no cause for undue pessimism on the eve of the German offensive. The previous day General Lucas had told me the Army had ordered him to plan an attack to capture Cisterna, and we discussed the strategy we had in mind. We were agreed, however, that everything would have to wait until we had definitely stopped the German offensive.

Early on the morning of February 16th, German guns opened with a heavy bombardment all along the front of the beachhead. It was soon obvious that the heaviest concentrations were not in the sector of the 3rd Infantry Division, but were farther to the west along the Albano Road. After half an hour of this, the German artillery undertook to counterbattery our own artillery—a practice which our superiority in artillery usually induced them to avoid. Then they attacked with tanks and infantry.

On the front of the 3rd Infantry Division, there were no fewer than six separate thrusts varying in size from company to battalion in strength. While these occupied our attention during the day, we recognized that the Germans were merely probing. All attacks were easily beaten off, largely by the massed fire power of our own artillery. In the largest one just west of Ponte Rotto, the 30th Infantry annihilated one German battalion, capturing more than two hundred prisoners. As night came on, we expected the Germans to renew their assaults the following morning, but we were now confident we could beat them off.

There had been similar activity along all parts of the Corps front except in the sector of the 45th Infantry Division where the heaviest fighting of the day had taken place in the vicinity of Carroceto and the Factory. Even in these areas, the Germans had made only small gains. While General Lucas and some of the Corps staff betrayed anxiety, the situation appeared to be well in hand as night came on. I expected the next day to begin early and to be a full one, so I turned in early that evening. But my last rest as a Division commander was a short one.

3. *A Change in Assignment*

Shortly after midnight, Colonel Carleton came into my room at Conca and woke me, saying: "Boss, I hate to do this, but you would give me hell if I held this until morning." He handed me a message. I read:

> ORDERS ISSUED THIS DATE AS FOLLOWS X MAJOR GENERAL TRUSCOTT RELIEVED FROM COMMAND OF THIRD DIVISION AND ASSIGNED AS DEPUTY COMMANDER SIXTH CORPS X BRIGADIER GENERAL O'DANIELS TO COMMAND THIRD DIVISION X COLONEL DARBY TRANSFERRED FROM RANGER FORCE TO THIRD DIVISION X ALL ASSIGNMENTS TO TAKE EFFECT SEVENTEEN FEBRUARY X I DESIRE THAT COLONEL SHERMAN BE DESIGNATED AS ACTING ASSISTANT DIVISION COMMANDER AND THAT DARBY BE PLACED IN COMMAND OF SHERMAN'S REGIMENT X ACKNOWLEDGE.

It was a message from General Clark to General Lucas signed a few minutes before eight o'clock that evening.

My first reaction was one of resentment because no one had mentioned this change in assignment was being considered. It was not that I objected to serving under General Lucas. We were old friends. Our relations both personal and official had always been close and frank, and I had served under him in action since Salerno. He had always sought and received my advice and recommendations, and had treated me with the utmost consideration. Nevertheless, our methods of command were different. I was not blind to the fact that General Lucas lacked some of the qualities of positive leadership that engender confidence, and that he leaned heavily upon his staff and trusted subordinates in difficult decisons. His was a lovable personality, although his appearance invited the less respectful among his juniors to refer to him as "Foxy Grandpa". I was also aware that General Lucas had little confidence in the British troops of his command, and that his British commanders had even less confidence in him. There was even some feeling that perhaps I was being used to "pull someone else's chestnuts from the fire".

I had been commanding the 3rd Infantry Division for nearly a year during which period the Division's record was a proud one. I had no desire whatever to leave an assignment in which I had both command authority and responsibility for one in which I should have neither. The first reactions were rather human, I think, but passed with sober reflection. This was certainly no time to consider personal preferences. The order had no doubt been issued after all factors had been thoughtfully weighed. There was a job to be done, and I was a soldier. I could only carry the order out loyally. But it was not easy to leave the 3rd Infantry Division.

Next morning, there was some activity along the front of the Division, but the main German attack fell on the front of the 45th Infantry Division on our left just east of the Albano Road. During the morning the attacking Germans were clearly visible to Lieutenant Colonel William P. Yarborough whose 504th Parachute Battalion was on the extreme left of the Division sector near Carano. From the roof of the house where his Command Post was located, Yarborough reported that he could see the Germans advancing in close column. From there he directed repeated missions by all of the Division artillery within range.

I spent some time in conferences with General O'Daniels, the regimental commanders, and the Division staff. Immediately after noon, I sent Captain Bartash to reopen my trailer in the spot where we had spent our first days on the beach, and then with Captain Wilson, I set off for the Corps Command Post in Nettuno to begin the new assignment. Not with unmixed feelings, for just before I left the 3rd Infantry Division Command Post, General Keiser, the Corps Chief of Staff, had telephoned Carleton to ask when I was going to report. He had terminated the conversation with the observation that he did not know whether or not there would be any Corps Headquarters by the following morning for they would probably be driven into the sea. It was somewhat in this frame of mind that I found General Lucas and some of his immediate staff about half-past one that afternoon of February 17th.

General Lucas, Keiser, the Chief of Staff, Langevin, the G-2 and Hill, the G-3, were waiting for me. Lucas welcomed me to the Corps. There had been extremely heavy fighting in the zone of the 45th Infantry Division and in that of the 56th Division—on both sides of the Albano Road. Flying Fortresses and medium and fighter bombers of the Mediterranean Allied Air Forces had bombed Carroceto, the Factory and Campoleone heavily during the morning. Information was indefinite and confused, but it was clear enough that the situation was far graver than we had realized in the 3rd Infantry Division. The 179th Infantry had suffered heavily and had been driven back to the vicinity of the Corps Beachhead Line between Padiglione and the Flyover, and no one knew whether it would be able to hold there or not. The 180th Infantry had been forced back to a north-south line generally along Spaccacassi Creek north of Padiglione. German tanks had reached the Flyover and at least two had been destroyed by antitank guns after passing through this key terrain feature on the Corps Beachhead Line. The enemy had penetrated the front of the 56th Division in the broken terrain—the "wadi country"—west of the Albano Road, but General Templar thought he had checked the German advance in that area. The 2nd Battalion, 157th Infantry, was still holding part of its original position south of Carroceto, but it was under heavy attack and was asking for help.

Early in the day, General Lucas had ordered General Penney to occupy the Corps Beachhead Line on both sides of the Flyover to prevent a German breakthrough and to assist the 179th Infantry. When German tanks were reported at the Flyover, he had ordered Harmon to counterattack with one tank battalion north from the Flyover to relieve the pressure on the 179th Infantry. Then, just before I reported to Corps, he had ordered General Eagles to counterattack with his Division reserve to "restore the situation on the front of the 179th Infantry". There was a feeling of desperation, of hopelessness, since no reports had been received from Penney or Harmon, and no one knew what Eagles would be able to do. My optimistic assurance that nothing ever looked as bad on the ground as it did on a map at Headquarters did little to dispel the pall-like gloom. I set off about mid-afternoon to see what I could learn.

I found Harmon and Eagles in good spirits. They realized that the situation was grave, but neither of them seemed to be unduly worried. From Harmon, I found out his tank attack had started about noon but had been stopped by antitank fire after losing several tanks. It had not recaptured any ground, but it had stopped the German tanks, and the battalion was now supporting Penney's brigades in the vicinity of the Flyover. From Eagles I learned that communication with the battalions of the 179th Infantry had been interrupted most of the day. Eagles thought that when communication with the battalions was reestablished, we would find their position better than had been pictured. Eagles was confident that the Division would hold, and had issued orders for a counterattack by one battalion of the 157th Infantry at daylight the following morning to assist the 179th Infantry. By the time I had arranged with Harmon for tanks to support this counterattack, it was dark. I returned to Corps to report and then made my way to my trailer camp near the beach where I had spent my first night. That night General Lucas called another conference with all commanders, but no solution to our problems was reached. The conference ended about midnight on that note.

News the following morning was scarce, for the divisions were still having difficulty communicating with their battalions. Eagle's counterattack seemed to be making little progress, but we hoped it would disrupt German preparations. It was encouraging to know there had been no further penetrations of the Corps Beachhead Line. The disheartening fact was that on a front of four miles the Germans had driven a salient nearly four miles deep into the center of our lines and six German divisions had been identified within this salient. From Padiglione to the front of the 56th Division west of the Flyover we were back on the Corps Beachhead Line with no organized defenses between that line and the port and beaches. The 180th Infantry held the eastern flank of the salient along Spaccacassi Creek north of Padiglione. The 2nd Battalion, 157th Infantry, still held the western shoulder of the salient south of Carroceto, but it was cut off from ground contact with its own Division and with the 56th Division on its left. Along the base of the salient were the battered battalions of the 179th Infantry and the two weak British brigades and not much more. Behind them, Eagles had one battalion, 157th Infantry, in Division reserve, Harmon had his 6th Armored Infantry and tanks, and in Corps reserve was the remaining brigade of the 1st Division. Before leaving the 3rd Infantry Division, I had withdrawn the 30th Infantry from the lines. The regiment was not concentrated in the area around Campomorto. The 169th Brigade of the 56th Division, just arrived from Naples, was due to begin unloading at Anzio during the morning. We still had assets and I advocated a counterattack.

While we were discussing our difficulties, General Clark joined us, wanted to know what General Lucas proposed to do, and was soon brought up to date. I thought we should counterattack with everything we had. Clark wanted to know what we had to counterattack with.

We mentioned Harmon's 6th Armored Infantry and tanks, the 30th Infantry, and the British brigade which was just arriving. Clark wanted to know how soon we could organize such an attack. I thought we could launch one by the following morning. General Clark placed his fingers on the shoulders of the salient on the map which lay before us. Then in a somewhat pontifical manner rather reminiscent of an instructor at a service school, he remarked: "You should hold these shoulders firmly, and then counterattack against the flanks of the salient."

General Lucas had opposed the counterattack for he had always been reluctant to commit his Corps reserve. Now that General Clark favored the counterattack, Lucas reluctantly agreed, and we set to work. We called in Harmon and Templar, and soon concurred upon a concerted plan. It was simple enough. We would make a converging attack. Force H, under Harmon, would have the 30th Infantry and Harmon's 6th Armored Infantry and tanks. It would attack with regiments abreast northwest along the Diagonal Road to seize the ground just north of the Dead End Road. Force T, under Templar, would consist of the 169th Brigade which was just arriving in the beachhead. Force T was to strike north from the Flyover to seize the western end of the Dead End Road and establish contact with the 2nd Battalion 157th Infantry, on the western shoulder of the salient. These forces would be supported by all the artillery we could muster. General Clark undertook to arrange a maximum air effort to assist us. Orders were complete before noon, and Harmon and Templar set about their tasks.

When their preparations were under way, General Clark asked me to accompany him to Eagles' Command Post. We set off with Sergeant Barna driving. On the way, Clark told me that I would probably replace Lucas within the next four or five days. I replied that I had no desire whatever to relieve Lucas, who was a personal friend, and I had not wanted to leave the 3rd Infantry Division for this assignment. I had done so without protest because I realized that some of the command, especially on the British side, had lost confidence in Lucas. I thought we could overcome our difficulties, and I was perfectly willing to continue as Lucas' deputy as long as might be necessary. Clark said that he appreciated my reaction because he did not want to hurt Lucas either. In any case there would be no change for the present.

At the 45th Infantry Division, Eagles informed General Clark he wanted to relieve the commanding officer of the 179th Infantry and needed someone to replace him. Clark decided to give him Colonel Darby whom he had placed in command of the 7th Infantry only the day before. I went on out to the 3rd Infantry Division at Conca to inform O'Daniels and Darby and to have Sherman returned to the 7th

Infantry. I returned to the Corps about one o'clock to check the progress of preparations.

Langevin had intelligence which indicated that the Germans might employ parachute troops against the beachhead in conjunction with ground attacks. With all combat engaged along the perimeter of the beachhead and no reserves available, a few hundred parachute troops could wreck our communications, disrupt our artillery support, and create panic throughout the beachhead. We immediately formulated an antiairborne plan. Our order divided the beachhead into zones for defense against airborne troops. The forward areas were the responsibility of units holding the Corps Beachhead Line. Rear areas were divided among antiaircraft troops, the Corps artillery brigade, the Corps engineers, and reconnaissance companies of the tank destroyer battalions. In each zone, one company was held on the alert in mobile reserve and mechanized patrols equipped for antiaircraft fire patrolled all roads continuously during the hours of darkness. Any airborne landing during that or any subsequent night at Anzio would receive a warm welcome. Fortunately, none was attempted.

Early in the morning, before leaving the beachhead for Caserta, General Clark came in and approved the plans. He said that he was optimistic about prospects for a breakthrough at Cassino where the New Zealand Corps had begun its attack on February 15th with the bombing of Cassino and the Benedictine Monastery by the Allied Air Forces. We hoped that his optimism was well founded.

After he left, I went on to verify preparations. German aircraft had dropped mines in the port during the morning which delayed unloading the equipment of the 169th Brigade. Force T would not be ready, but we decided to go on with Harmon's attack as planned. I went to Harmon's Command Post and remained with him while he issued his orders to his assembled commanders, and then in the gathering dusk made my way back to my trailer camp near the beach.

During my first day and a half as Deputy Corps Commander, I had been wondering why we had not been able to stop the German thrust which had been made over flat open fields almost devoid of cover. They had been supported by more artillery than we had yet encountered, but it was still far inferior to our own. The Germans had employed tanks, but they had used them in very small groups and never in very large numbers. The Luftwaffe had provided direct air support for their ground forces, but compared with our air support their effort was almost insignificant. I was confident that on the 3rd Infantry Division sector our artillery and infantry weapons would have broken up these attacks in their early stages. Why then had we failed on this more open terrain?

Carleton joined me for supper that night and we discussed the problem. Checking over ammunition expenditure reports of the heavy fighting of the previous day, we found one battalion of the 3rd Infantry Division artillery had fired more rounds than had the artillery of the 45th Infantry Division which was bearing the brunt of the German attack. The reason seemed obvious. Enemy fire had destroyed communications; forward observers, artillery liaison officers and company officers had become casualties; and there had been no plan for insuring continued artillery support in this event. But the problem was how to achieve this organization in a single night and before tomorrow's battle. We finally concluded I should have a staff officer who knew what was required to verify artillery plans and issue whatever instructions might be necessary to insure essential coordination. General Baehr, the Corps Artillery Officer, had joined us only a few days previously. I hardly knew him, and he was certainly not familiar with some of my views on artillery coordination. Finally, I had Carleton telephone Major Walter T. ("Dutch") Kerwin, S-3 Division Artillery, and General Baehr. They were to report to me at the Corps Commander's office at ten o'clock, prepared for an all-night mission.

None of us will ever forget our meeting in the dark caverns beneath Nettuno. Most of the offices—wine storage spaces chiseled from the soft rock—were empty except for a few sleeping men and an occasional clerk on duty. Here and there dim lights flickered in the darkness and gave a ghostly aspect to surroundings already eerie. Very briefly, I informed them of my conclusions and explained my views. Then I turned to General Baehr and said: "General, I am confident that if we had two or three days I could handle this through normal artillery channels, but it has to be done tonight."

Turning to Major Kerwin, I asked: "Major, do you know what I mean when I say that I want all of the artillery fires of the Corps organized and coordinated just as they are on the front of the 3rd Division?"

"Yes, sir."

"If you had the authority, could you insure that these fires are so organized tonight—before daylight tomorrow?"

"Yes, sir."

"Well, Major, you have that authority. You are to go to the Corps artillery and to each division. You are to examine their plans. You are to issue any orders necessary to insure that these artillery fires are organized and coordinated as I want them to be."

Turning to General Baehr, I said: "General, your sole duty tonight is to accompany this young officer. If anyone questions his authority or any order that he may issue, you are to say: 'That is the Corps Commander's order.' Do you understand?" General Baehr did. They departed.

Just at daybreak, the telephone woke me. It was General Baehr who wanted to report that the mission I had assigned was completed. He told me that I would not have to worry about the organization and coordination of the artillery any more. I then wanted to know why Kerwin had not called me as I had directed. General Baehr replied: "I told Major Kerwin that I would report to you. I wanted to tell you that I have had the best lesson in artillery that I have had in thirty-five years service in the artillery." I felt better.

General Harmon's Force H attacked on schedule at 0630 the morning of February 19th, after a half-hour artillery softening up by more than 400 guns, including 90 mm antiaircraft guns within range and guns of the fleet off shore, concentrated on enemy front lines, assembly, and artillery areas. This barrage lifted in successive concentrations as the attack progressed. More than 200 medium and fighter bombers blasted enemy artillery and concentration areas and communications. Harmon's advance made fair progress against intense enemy resistance during the morning. Then mud restricted tank support, and flooded creeks prevented tanks from accompanying the infantry until bridges were built. By early afternoon Harmon's infantry had reached the eastern end of the Dead End Road.

Meanwhile, Templar had ordered tanks up the Albano Road from the Flyover in an attempt to reach the western end of the Dead End Road. Several tanks were knocked out by antitank guns and the rest were compelled to withdraw. Harmon's infantry was left in an exposed location on poor defensive terrain. I talked the situation over with Harmon on the ground during the afternoon. We believed we had broken the back of the German offensive, and would avoid unnecessary losses by withdrawing his infantry to an area west of Padiglione where the forces could remain in reserve while we reorganized the defenses. When I returned to Corps, General Lucas approved this decision. We reported to General Clark by radio and obtained his immediate approval.

One of the most dramatic and heroic episodes of the long Anzio struggle was to occupy our attention while we were struggling to reorganize our defenses—the Battle of the Caves. At the beginning of the German offensive on February 16th, the 2nd Battalion, 157th Infantry, under the command of Lieutenant Colonel Laurence C. Brown, 157 Infantry, had a front of some 1500 yards astride the Albano Road twelve hundred yards or so south of Carroceto. The German onslaught east of the Albano Road overran the right flank of the battalion position, and

German attacks to the west cut off the battalion from contact with the 56th Division on its left. Taking advantage of the broken terrain and a series of caves in the western part of its position, the battalion converted the area into a veritable fortress. Isolated from its own division and adjoining troops, its supply route interrupted, and under heavy and continuous attack, this gallant battalion fought off every German attack and held grimly on to its position in spite of heavy losses. Harmon's action on the 19th had created a sufficient diversion to enable supplies to be brought up and casualties evacuated during the night. Thereafter, the battalion was completely isolated. Efforts to reach it during the 20th failed. On the night of February 21st, General Templar laid on a carefully planned operation employing the 2/7 Queens. Unfortunately, the effort coincided with a renewed German attack. The 2/7 Queens suffered nearly a hundred casualties, lost its supply train, and thus reached the Caves without mortars, antitank guns, and supporting weapons. Both battalions beat off German attacks during the day of February 22nd. That night, the American battalion turned over its mortars and supporting weapons to the British battalion, and the remnants made their way back with great difficulty to our own lines. Of more than 800 men who had entered the action on February 16th, only 225 remained and more than a hundred of these were hospital cases. In the annals of American wars there are few deeds more gallant than the defense by this gallant battalion, and no unit has ever received a more richly merited Presidential citation.

An effort by the 2/6 Queens to get weapons and supplies to the 2/7 Queens in the Caves during the night of February 22nd failed, and bad weather prevented an airdrop the next day. On February 23rd, the Germans overran two companies, the commander divided the remainder into groups of a dozen or so and directed them to make their way back to the British lines as best they could. Less than half succeeded.

In eight days of bitter fighting, we had paid a heavy price for our unsuccessful effort to hold the western shoulder of the salient—almost three full battalions. But the operation had not been a failure, for aside from the heavy losses we had inflicted, we had disrupted German plans for the offensive and had engaged strong forces which otherwise might have followed German tanks through the Corps Beachhead Line at the Flyover. No action during the long struggle at Anzio was more crucial than this Battle of the Caves, which ended on the day I assumed command of the beachhead.

General Clark returned to the beachhead February 22nd. In the evening he called me to his quarters in the cellars of the Villa Borghese

where the Fifth Army Advanced Command Post was located. There
he informed me that I was to relieve General Lucas the following
morning. I reminded him of my previous statement that I had no desire
to relieve General Lucas, and again recommended no change be made
in command. I pointed out that relieving General Lucas now when
the situation was more stable might have an unfortunate reaction on
morale and undermine confidence among other officers. Lucas had a
host of friends and was personally popular among American officers.
There was a grave danger others might feel he was being sacrificed to
British influence; they might well come to think that whenever they
got into difficulty they, too, would be thrown to the wolves. While I
had not wanted to leave the 3rd Infantry Division, I now believed that
assigning me as Deputy had been, perhaps the best thing to do. Lucas
and I understood each other. I was perfectly willing to continue as
his Deputy, and I felt Lucas was more than willing to have me remain
so.

General Clark listened to my objections and then remarked that the
decision had already been made. He went on to say that Johnny Lucas
was also a friend of his and he would see to it Lucas was not hurt. He
intended to designate him as Deputy Army Commander for the time
being. He had sent for Lucas and would break the news to him. Since
it seemed obvious that the decision had already been approved by General Marshall, there was nothing for me to do but return to my quarters
to break the news to Carleton and the aides.

Later, when General Lucas had returned from his bitter interview,
I went to see him to express my regrets. While Lucas was deeply hurt,
he had no ill feeling toward me, and our friendship was unbroken up
to the time of his death. But he was bitter toward General Clark and
blamed his relief upon British influence. It was one of my saddest experiences of the war.

When I returned to my quarters after my last visit to General Lucas
at Anzio, Carleton and I set down to review the problems I had now
inherited, the nature and cause of which I was well aware of. The
beachhead had come close to disaster. Unnecessarily so, since we had
demonstrated that we had sufficient means to stop the German offensive much earlier had we adequately organized, properly coordinated,
and effectively employed our resources. Consequently our narrow escape had caused a general lack of confidence throughout—between
some of the divisions, especially on the British side, and the Corps command; within the Corps Headquarters; and particularly among the
numerous rear echelon service detachments and installations where
discipline is never so firm as among combat troops, and where men are
too often exposed to wild and exaggerated rumors.

Many factors had doubtless contributed, and Army, Corps and Division Headquarters all shared in the blame for existing conditions. Nevertheless, some of these elements seemed particularly important to guide me in exercising command functions.

Perhaps most important, Corps headquarters had never been positive and confident either in planning or in directing operations. Although the Corps staff comprised exceptionally able officers, operational proposals were often made without adequate staff analysis, and evolved in conferences which often resembled debating societies. Decisions agreed upon in these meetings were usually accepted with reluctance by the Corps, and rarely supported in a way to inspire confidence in a command. Operational orders were all too frequently based upon a more or less cursory map study and intelligence, and few in Corps Headquarters were bothered much about reconnaissance before or during tactical operations.

There was a lack of understanding between British and American commanders and staffs, particularly between the Corps Headquarters and the British divisions. General Lucas put little trust in the British commanders or their troops, and the British commanders returned the compliment. None of the staff had ever worked much with British units. They were not familiar with British organization, staff procedures, or tactical methods. Some failed to appreciate the differences in national characteristics. Few comprehended the effect that Britain's ordeal and British manpower shortages had upon their tactical methods. There was a tendency among American officers, by no means restricted to the Corps Headquarters, to be unduly critical of all things British and to be impatient with methods that differed from those familiar to them. I mention the American side, for it is the one I was able to fully observe. I have no doubt that our British comrades returned the criticism in full measure.

Also, numerous rear echelon service detachments and organizations jeopardized both the security and morale of the beachhead. Fifth Army Headquarters had taken over operation of the ports and beaches on February 6th, presumably to free the Corps of responsibility for supply and evacuation and thus leave them free for the business of fighting. As a result, there were in the beachhead a very large number of service troops and detachments—port troops, engineers, medical units, quartermaster, ordnance, signal units and installations and the like—which were not under Corps command. It was good in theory, but most unsound in practice. In the congested beachhead, no line could be drawn delimiting the respective responsibilities of the Corps and the Army. The Corps' "rear boundary" was actually the water's edge; common sense indicated that the whole supervision and control within the beachhead should have rested with the Corps Commander. Actually, there was no centralized agency responsible for these numerous Army service agencies short of the Army Command Post at Caserta, a hundred miles away. Except for General Clark's infrequent visits, the senior Army representative at the beachhead was a Lieutenant Colonel, Assistant G-4, with no command authority, and it was Army policy to replace him with another every week or ten days. Cut off from effective command, discipline deteriorated among these detachments and, during the tense days of the German assault, morale among them reached a low ebb. Having no reliable sources of information, rumors spread among them like wildfire, and even from them to the combat troops where such rumors served no useful purpose.

Furthermore, enemy air attacks, in considerable strength, came at frequent intervals both day and night. Concentrated for the most part against the shipping, the port areas, and rear installations, these raids caused material damage and had a serious impact upon morale that only those who have known continued air bombings can appreciate. This was most marked among the rear area installations. Weather over our own air bases often interfered with our fighter cover while enemy aircraft were able to fly over the beachhead. The few fighter aircraft allotted could not prevent the enemy air activity. During enemy air raids, our antiaircraft guns darkened the skies with their bursts, but we knocked down few aircraft. Improved antiaircraft defense was a matter of urgency.

In addition, the effect of German artillery was second only to enemy air attacks in its deleterious morale effect and was the cause, probably, of more actual damage. The rear areas of the beachhead were subjected to shelling by long range guns of heavy caliber which none of our artillery could reach, and worse, by guns of lesser caliber such as the German 88's which we should have been able to silence. We had never given this problem the attention it deserved.

Finally, both the Corps Headquarters and the Fifth Army Advanced Command Post had sought shelter underground. The Corps Command Post was situated to some extent in wine cellars carved in past ages from the soft volcanic rock which underlaid Nettuno. The Fifth Army Advanced Command Post was housed in the cellars of the palace of the Prince Borghese, the most palatial establishment within the beachhead, and Army Engineers had taken over a nearby railway tunnel and were carving out additional caverns beneath the Prince's palace. Both locations were entirely proper for protection of communications upon which control depended, and for permitting staffs to function under the almost incessant bombing and shelling. However, no division command post in the entire beachhead was below ground at that time.

General Penny's Headquarters was in a caravan above ground no more than a mile away; the 3rd Infantry Division was on the second floor of a factory building at Conca in plain view of the front lines and with a flag pole in front which German artillery used daily as a registration point. Hospitals, beach installations, and other rear establishments were all above ground and all carried on their activities under conditions little different from those which confronted the command posts. Considering the attitude of American soldiers toward higher headquarters, it would have been surprising if the lower echelons had not entertained some feeling that "Corps" and "Army" were perhaps unduly concerned for their own safety. And it was my own opinion that they were.

My aide's journal records my first days activities as Beachhead Commander—and they were not unlike the days that followed.

> General at CP at 0800. Conference with Gens. Clark and Eveleigh. Latter to remain as Deputy Corps Commander. Gen. Harmon in to see new Corps Comdr. and stays for morning conference. First full scale air meeting with groundwork laid for further support development. Gen. Templar also in and the four generals get together on situation and plans. Decision to pull 2/7 Queens out tonight coupled with limited action by 2/6 Queens. Gen. Lucas and aides leave by PT boat for Caserta Bartash spends morning rearranging the villa. Afternoon trip with Gen. Eveleigh to see Gen. Penney. He will plan action and relief with 3rd Bde. Back to CP for talk with Gen. Keiser and Cols. Carleton, Galloway, and Hill. Out to 45th; Gen. Eagles out but Gen. Paschal given situation. Then to 3rd, where General talks to Gen. O'Daniel and Col. Sherman. Arrive back at CP for talk with members of general and special staffs. Further coordination of party support plan and antiparachute defense. Paperwork keeps General in CP until 1930. Home to late supper, and Gen. Eveleigh and aide in with wire from Gen. Alexander. They stay for drink.

General Clark came in for a final discussion before leaving the beachhead. The New Zealand Corps was to press its attack on the southern front to capture the heights above Cassino and establish a bridgehead over the Rapido River. Clark was going to regroup the remainder of the front to free the II Corps for refitting. In the beachhead, we were to continue operations to restore our forward positions and be ready to resume the offensive with maximum strength either toward Velletri or toward Albano in coordination with the main advance.

We talked frankly about conditions in the beachhead with particular reference to Allied relationships. Clark expressed a confidence in my ability to set things straight that I was far from sharing. He assured me, however, that my authority in the beachhead would be complete and that he would support me in every possible way.

General Clark had brought with him Major General Evelyn Eveleigh, British Army, whom General Alexander had sent to the beachhead to investigate conditions among British troops. General Alexander offered General Eveleigh's services, which I gladly accepted, as a British Deputy to assist in coordinating the operations of British troops.

My own experience in Combined Operations Headquarters and with British staffs and troops was to stand me in good stead and enable me to advise and direct the Corps staff in their relationships with British troops. However, it was General Eveleigh who was primarily responsible for removing all previous causes of friction. This distinguished officer's knowledge, boundless energy, and rare personal charm quickly endeared him to the Corps staff and to the American commanders. His indefatigable efforts in organizing and supervising British activities were of inestimable value in establishing command relationships which were thenceforth to be a model for every Allied command. We saw General Eveleigh depart a month later for a divisional command with deep regret.

Immediately after Clark's departure, General Templar came in to confer about the plight of the 56th Division, and particularly that of the 2/7 Queens which had relieved the 2nd Battalion, 157th Infantry, in the Caves two nights before. Efforts to resupply the battalion had failed, and it was in desperate straits. Templar's division had suffered heavily in the recent fighting and he had been forced to press all "B Echelon" personnel—cooks, clerks, drivers, mechanics—into service as riflemen to enable his depleted battalions to hold their ground. No attack to restore the line on the western shoulder of the salient was possible. Regretfully, I authorized General Templar to withdraw the battalion that same night—my first decision as Beachhead Commander and not a very good omen.

My conference with Eveleigh, Harmon, and Templar had to do with reorganizing the front to improve the effectiveness of the British divisions and the now depleted 45th Infantry Division. I reassigned boundaries to increase the sector of the 3rd Infantry Division, reduce the frontage of the 45th Infantry Division by half, and strengthen the front of the British divisions. To accomplish this, I released one battalion, 30th Infantry, to the 3rd Infantry Division to take over a part of the sector west of Carano held by the 180th Infantry, and released the 3rd Brigade to the 1st Division to take over an additional sector east of the Flyover. The remainder of the day I spent coordinating this reorganization with the division commanders. Late in the afternoon, I called my first staff conference with the Corps Staff.

Commanders are rather like old garments; the well-worn ones are usually the more comfortable. Commanders differ in personality and methods of command and few staffs welcome the disruption of accustomed and established procedures. However, a few officers who are thoroughly familiar with a commander and his methods can alleviate the pains of transition to a new command to some extent. With this in mind, I brought with me from the 3rd Infantry Division Carleton, who had been my Chief of Staff since Goal Post, Ben Harrel to be Corps G-3, Major William R. Rosson, to be Assistant Corps G-3, and Colonel Kermit Davis to be Executive Officer, Corps Artillery. A little later, we brought in Colonel Richard J. Myers from the Corps Signal Battalion to be Corps Signal Officer. Otherwise, I made no change in the Corps staff. The remaining months in the beachhead, the campaign to Rome and beyond, and the campaign in southern France, were to demonstrate that no Corps Commander was ever better served.

I made no attempt to remove the staff offices from their underground caverns. However, Carleton and I established our offices in a small wine shop over the entrance to the caverns. It provided us with a War Room where the staff sections posted maps and other pertinent data. On the wall behind my desk, we hung an enlargement of one of Bill Mauldin's cartoons. Later he was to present me with the original drawing, which I now treasure. It showed Willie and Joe resting in water-filled fox holes at Anzio, both looking at headlines in the *Stars and Stripes* which heralded the forthcoming crosschannel invasion as the *major* battle front. The caption was "The hell this ain't the best hole in the world. I'm in it."

Our War Room arrangements, however, were in an embryonic stage when I called my first conference with all the chiefs of the general and special staff sections late in the afternoon of my first day of command. I called for a report from the chief of each general and special staff section on their activities and found only two or three of them fully informed, as I had more or less expected. I explained to them gently but *firmly* that I would expect full and accurate reports at eight o'clock the following morning and every day thereafter. We weighed measures of improving our antiparachute defenses which we had instituted only a day or so earlier, and ended with a lengthy debate on air support plans which I shall go into later.

These staff conferences were attended every morning by the chief of every general and special staff section and by certain commanders of the supporting troops. Division commanders and some of their staffs often dropped in and were always welcome. Each chief of a general staff section reviewed for me in detail the conditions at the front, the operations of the preceeding twenty-four hours, and described the plans under consideration. Each chief of a special staff section reported in detail on the activities for which his section was responsible.

All were encouraged to present problems for coordination and decision and to recommend improvements in their own and other fields. Thus I was able to keep myself informed of every activity in the beachhead, and what was even more important perhaps, I was able to insure that every staff section was thoroughly familiar with our situation, informed of my decisions, and active in their functions.

More than a few of our briefings were held to the accompaniment of shells crashing in the square outside, the rumble of bombs bursting along the nearby waterfront, or the deafening clatter of antiaircraft fire. Vehicles were damaged, and there were a number of casualties in the streets about our wine shop Command Post. One shell from the "Anzio Express" crashed through several adjoining buildings and buried itself a dozen feet almost directly under Carleton's desk. Fortunately it was a dud, and was subsequently removed by one of the bomb disposal squads. Our War Room and offices escaped damage.

Not more than a hundred yards or so from the War Room, on a narrow street, there was a house which contained two small apartments, one above the other, each with a living-room, kitchen, and two or three bedrooms. This was our Villa. There Carleton, the aides, Wilson and Bartash, and I settled down in the capable hands of Sergeant Barna and the "Canton Restaurant" of Lee, Hong, and Dare. There all of us lived and slept above ground during the three months which we were to remain at the beachhead. Shells passed overhead several times each day. Several exploded in the small garden just in the rear. Adjoining buildings and those across the street were struck repeatedly. Although windows were invariably broken in the Villa, and it was struck by fragments, it escaped any serious damage. We learned to sleep through the nightly cannonading. But there were some narrow escapes.

Lee, the cook, was standing one morning in the small garden just outside his kitchen door. He was holding in his hands one of the cloth dolls dressed in feminine clothes which some of our soldiers had found in Italian shops. Talking with Hong and Barna, he was making the doll salute when a shell exploded in an adjoining lot. That was not unusual. But one jagged, razor-edged fragment whizzed through the air and severed the head from the doll which Lee was holding as neatly as though done by a razor. Lee was untouched, but he returned to his kitchen, and no one ever saw him with the doll again.

Prior to Anzio, the German air forces had never been a serious threat to Allied ground operations in Africa, Sicily or Italy. German aircraft had attacked our ground troops in Tunisia and had been very active during the periods of the landings in Sicily, and at Salerno. Thereafter, no more than half a dozen enemy aircraft were seen in any one day, and attacks on ground troops were relatively rare. For the most part, the German air effort—only a fraction of our own—was directed at the major ports like Algiers, Naples, and Bari. This relative security from air attack we owed, of course, to our own Allied Air Forces for they had almost swept the Luftwaffe from Italian skies.

At Anzio this changed. The mass of shipping off shore and the congestion of troops, vehicles and supplies within the beachhead were ideal targets, and the Luftwaffe joined full measure in the effort to destroy the beachhead. Our own air bases were more than one hundred miles away. We had no fighter protection during the first and last hours of the day, nor when bad weather kept our own fighters on the ground. German air attacks increased in scope and frequency after D Day. On January 29th, while we were still expanding the beachhead, two separate attacks by about sixty bombers each, sank a cruiser, a Liberty ship, damaged a number of LST's, and caused other damage. During the major German offensive—which coincided with my week as Deputy—there were at least ninety separate attacks and in one day more than two hundred aircraft were involved. While this effort fell short of the "thousand plane raids" with which Allied aircraft were laying waste German industry, they were by far the heaviest we had known in the Mediterranean area. To add to our troubles, about the time I reported to Corps, the Germans established a ground station north of the beachhead and jammed our radar—almost eliminating our early warning and greatly reducing the effectiveness of our antiaircraft artillery.

I was not an expert in antiaircraft artillery techniques, but like most everyone else in the beachhead, I thought that I was "expert" in the need for improved antiaircraft defenses. I turned my attention to this matter as soon as I reported to Corps. After the change in command, I pursued the job relentlessly. Brigadier General Aaron A. Bradshaw was the Antiaircraft Officer and it was he who bore the brunt of what no doubt often seemed unreasonable demands. He was a man of boundless energy, thoroughly proficient, and ever willing to entertain new concepts and try new methods. More than any other individual, he was responsible for organizing and developing the defenses which made Anzio into a most effectively defended and protected area.

We had complete support from higher headquarters, both Army and Theater. When the Germans jammed our radar, Bradshaw informed me that the newly developed SCR 584 equipment, which was almost impervious to jamming, had recently reached the theater and was in use at Algiers. We submitted an urgent request for the equipment and it was sent to us at once. It was installed under trying conditions and crews were trained in its operation in record time—and none too soon.

Some sixty-four radar-directed and radar-controlled rapid-firing 90 mm antiaircraft guns formed the backbone of the antiaircraft defenses, and these were supplemented by hundreds of guns of lesser caliber, 40 mm, 37 mm, 20 mm, and .50 mm caliber machine guns and the like for protection against low flying aircraft, as well as by the guns of the fleet off shore. The defense owed its effectiveness to careful planning and organization, and particularly to a highly centralized system of control. The central gun operations room was the brain of the complex organization. Radar discovered the approach of enemy air planes, tracked their flight, laid the guns, and fired them when the enemy came within range. On many occasions German aircraft were destroyed and attacks were broken up at maximum range long before the enemy aircraft reached the beachhead. On more than one occasion, surviving aircraft jettisoned their bombs and fled. By early March, the defense had become so effective that the Germans almost abandoned high level bombing.

The enemy had discovered, however, that at elevations under a thousand feet they were relatively safe from our 90 mm guns. They now began low level atacks with single aircraft approaching simultaneously from many different directions. Since the smaller caliber guns were visually controlled, their fire at night was relatively ineffective. Bradshaw and his staff were worried. After listening to a number of reasons why this fire could not be effective, I remarked that a competent staff should be able to deploy our hundreds of smaller guns about the beachhead so that the whole area could be covered by a standing barrage. As enemy aircraft approached, the guns in a particular spot would fire a prescribed number of rounds on a predetermined barrage, and this procedure be repeated as long as the aircraft remained within range. I thought that at least this might have a discouraging effect upon the enemy. Bradshaw accepted the idea at once and developed the organization.

He divided the beachhead into five sectors, three covering the forward area and two covering the rear installations. The smaller guns were deployed and laid to maintain a standing barrage. While they were not radar-controlled, their barrages were carefully calculated and the fire was directed by telephone and radio from the Central Gun Operations Room. When aircraft approached, all sectors were alerted. When aircraft entered any sector, the guns in the sector were ordered to fire. Each gun fired six rounds at a prescribed rate, and repeated on order as long as enemy aircraft remained. These barrages became so effective that by the end of March the Germans all but abandoned any important air efforts against the beachhead.

While our antiaircraft artillery carried the heavy burden in protecting the beachhead against enemy aircraft, our own Air Forces made an important contribution with fighter cover during daylight when weather conditions permitted. And these aircraft intercepted many attacks before they reached the beachhead. Also, the sight of our own aircraft was always an important factor in maintaining the morale of ground forces. To coordinate the fire of the antiaircraft artillery with our fighters and prevent firing upon our own aircraft, an area with a radius of 12,000 yards from the port area was made a restricted area. Within it our guns fired upon any aircraft; beyond it, aircraft had to be identified as hostile.

Out of approximately two thousand five hundred sorties flown by German aircraft, our antiaircraft guns destroyed over two hundred and probably destroyed or damaged another one hundred and fifty. We became enormously proud of our antiaircraft defense at Anzio.

No sooner had we stopped the German offensive than German artillery concentrated its effort upon our vulnerable beach and port areas, our congested supply dumps, and our restricted road net. Losses mounted daily. General Baehr and his staff, headed by Colonel Kermit Davis, rapidly developed a superior counterbattery system. Like the antiaircraft defense, it was highly centralized. All artillery was tied into the Corps Fire Direction Center. Enemy artillery positions—located by observation, sound and flash ranging, aerial reconnaissance, and study of aerial photographs—were systematically neutralized by successively concentrating on each one all guns within range. This was known as TOT, that is, data computed so that every shell landed on the target at the same instant. It was most effective against the mass of German artillery, but did not silence the long range guns, and moreover, led to another problem.

When I took command of the beachhead, our longest range artillery were the 155 mm guns—the Long Toms with an effective range of about 17,000 yards. The Germans employed 170 mm rifles with a range of 32,000 yards, as well as the 210 mm and 280 mm railway guns which came to be known as the "Anzio Express." Our only means of attacking these guns was by air. Our efforts to destroy them were unremitting, but not too successful. We damaged one or two and caused several changes of position, but concealed usually in tunnels except when firing, they were relatively safe from our air attacks. The "Anzio Express" continued to arrive almost daily on schedule throughout the beachhead.

To materially reduce the effectiveness of this long range fire, two chemical companies were utilized to establish a ring of smoke generators in a wide semicircle about the beach and port area, midway between the beaches and the front lines. This screen, maintained continuously throughout daylight hours, interfered with German observations. But railway guns continued to fire almost to the very end.

To avoid our counterbattery, the Germans began employing self-propelled guns, usually 88's, for their harassing fires. With an accurate range of about 18,000 yards they could reach any part of the beachhead from positions near the front lines. Occupying previously reconnoitered positions under cover of darkness and utilizing previously prepared data, these guns could fire twenty or thirty rounds in about ten minutes, and then withdraw before the Fire Direction Center could bring effective counterbattery fire to bear upon them. Employed at various places around the perimeter of the beachhead, they caused much damage in our congested installations.

I pressed General Baehr and his staff for a solution, and after listening to a lengthy explanation one morning I asked: "How many guns do you actually control—how many are there in the beachhead?" I was assured that, including tanks and tank destroyers being used as artillery, the number was well over a thousand. Then I remarked: "It looks to me like a competent artillery staff, by studying the road nets and the terrain on maps, aerial photographs and the like, and by actual observation, should be able to select the positions from which these self-propelled guns would be likely to fire." All agreed that this should be practicable. So I replied: "Why not have a single gun laid on every one of these likely locations, loaded and ready to fire with a gunner standing by with lanyard in hand. At the first shot in any sector, every gunner in the sector would pull the lanyard, reload, and fire again. By that time the remainder of the gun crew should join him and the Fire Direction Center should soon be able to assume control. We would waste a few rounds but it should discourage the German gunners if shells begin to land in their neighborhood before they get off their second round. Besides, we might hit something."

This rather unorthodox proposal was followed by profound silence. General Baehr cleared his throat and began: "Well, General, that is not the way we do it in the Artillery. Now at the Artillery School—"

I interrupted. "General, I heard that spiel the first time about twenty years ago. I don't give a damn what the Artillery School teaches. I want this problem solved and I want it solved right now. I have suggested a possible solution. You have until dark tonight to find a better one." That ended the conference. I never bothered to ascertain what modifications the artillerymen made to my suggestion, for within the next few nights we had discouraged this German use of self-propelled 88's.

Late in March we received two 8-inch guns and a battalion of 8-inch howitzers which had a range of some 35,000 yards. The first mission fired by the howitzers completely demolished a tower in Littoria which had provided the Germans with some of their most useful observation over the port and beaches. These newly developed guns put us on better than an even footing.

The new SCR 584 radar had been so effective in tracking aircraft that I thought we might be able to track the flight of the projectiles of the "Anzio Express." If we could plot enough of the trajectory, we might be able to pin-point the gun location and destroy it by air attack. After extensive tests, we found that our equipment was not quite adequate. We could plot a part of the trajectory, but not enough to enable the experts to plot its point of origin. In my report on these tests I pointed out that our experiments indicated the need for "slightly different" radar equipment, something between the "wide and narrow beams now in use" and recommended that "every effort be made to obtain radar experts to be put upon this subject and every attempt be made to develop the type of equipment required. If this proves successful, it will make obsolete all sound and flash equipment, and it will enable us to instantly counterbattery enemy artillery as soon as it opens fire."

During my first week in command, I had become even more concerned over the deplorable conditions in the supply dumps, particularly those containing ammunitions and gasoline where German artillery and bombs were causing havoc. In one ammunition dump about a mile east of Nettuno, enormous amounts of ammunition of all kinds were piled in close-ranked stacks over a wide and exposed area with no attempt whatever at dispersion, concealment, or other protection. After discussing conditions with Colonel O'Neill, the Corps G-4, and a representative of the Army G-4 in the beachhead, I sent a memorandum to the Army staff representative directing specific measures to correct conditions among the dumps and to establish effective control over the numerous service units and detachments.

The Army staff representative acknowledged receipt of the memorandum, but the next day I received a radio from General Clark peremptorily ordering me to rescind my instructions forthwith and forbidding me to issue any orders whatever to Army troops. In view of Clark's assurance to me that I had full authority in the beachhead, I was amazed. When Clark came to the beachhead a day or so later, I raised the question. He responded that he could not have me issuing orders to his Army troops; it would ruin their morale to take orders from anyone but the Army staff. They were there to relieve the Corps of the administrative burden. If I wanted anything done, I should notify his Headquarters and his staff would issue the necessary orders.

I pointed out that it was utterly impossible for his Headquarters to control these detachmens from a distance of more than a hundred miles with only radio and sea communications, and it was impossible to have separate areas of responsibility in the congested area of the beachhead. Lack of control among these detachments jeopardized the security of the beachhead, and I could not accept responsibility under such conditions. I suggested that the detachments be attached to the Corps for operational control, but Clark refused. Then I suggested that I be authorized to control them as his deputy. Again Clark refused, but he finally did agree to place a senior officer in the Advanced Command Post who would command these units under my control.

This arrangement at first imposed an unnecessary burden upon the beachhead Command. But it worked very well when Colonel L. K. Ladue arrived to fill the post, to be replaced later on by Colonel John L. Hines. These able officers, both of outstanding ability, made themselves integral parts of the Command and staff team at Anzio. They attended all staff conferences and worked in close harmony with the Corps staff and Division commanders at all times. I considered them both to be two of my most loyal subordinates.

Supplies were dispersed in smaller dumps. Bulldozers and Italian laborers dug pits for ammunition and gasoline, heaping the soil around the edges for added protection. Since we had not yet developed an armored bull-dozer, Harmon's engineers improvised one by mounting a bull-dozer blade upon a medium tank. When a dump caught fire, this armored bull-dozer proceeded to the scene and smothered the fire by covering it with soil from the revetments. This bull-dozer was one of the most important factors in reducing our losses in ammunition and gasoline.

My first six days in command were busy ones for they immediately preceded the last German effort to destroy the beachhead. We were working day and night to reorganize our defenses, and formulate plans for meeting the expected assault. In the right half of the beachhead, where the fronts of the 1st Special Service Force and the 3rd Infantry Division were located, Frederick and O'Daniels had things well in hand. They were well organized, troops in good condition, and reserves were available for any emergency. The 30th Infantry (less one battalion) was in Corps reserve near Campomorto where it could be released for use by the 3rd Infantry Division or employed to support the 45th Infantry Division in case of need.

Reducing the front of the 45th Infantry Division enabled Eagles to reorganize his sector with four battalions occupying centers of resistance in the forward areas and two battalions immediately available in Regimental reserve. Eagles was thus able to rest some of his battered battalions while they absorbed replacements and completed their reorganization and reequipment. Harmon's 6th Armored Infantry (less one battalion) was in Corps reserve to support the central portion of the front.

Penney's 1st Division occupied a narrow sector astride the Albano Road in the vicinity of the Flyover; and Templar's 56th London Division, a slightly wider zone in the difficult "wadi country" along the upper reaches of the Moletta River. Both divisions had three brigades, but both had suffered heavy losses, and there had been few British replacements to make their losses good.

The 36th Engineer Regiment, Corps Engineers, occupied the sector along the lower Moletta River adjacent to the coast.

Reorganization of the front and strengthening of defenses progressed satisfactorily except in the British sectors where the weak strength of British units and continued limited-objective attacks against them caused us some concern. Integration of the Corps artillery was improving daily. The Corps Fire Direction Center could instantly bring to bear upon any part of the front an overwhelming mass of artillery far superior to any at German command. Our antiaircraft defenses, although not yet perfect, were daily taking a greater toll of German aircraft. We had not yet restored confidence among the service echelons on the eve of the German onslaught; but among the combat troops the American units and the Corps Command faced the future with confidence. The British units may not have shared in full the confidence of the Americans, but they faced the problem with that determination which makes the British soldier so admirable in defense.

The Germans had suffered heavy losses in their first major offensive against the beachhead, and none of the six divisions employed in that assault were in condition to continue the attack without complete overhauling. I did not believe that the German Command would make another attempt to breast the storm of our massed artillery in the open fields on the central portion of our front, without first trying to draw our attention elsewhere. Most of the German pressure during these days was directed against the British front, and particularly the 56th Division. All attacks had limited objectives and were made by combat groups rarely stronger than one or two battalions. But these attacks were annoying, and they whittled away our British front. Almost every day we lost a company position, and all too often the company with it. Some of my messages to Clark during these days reflect rather vividly our grave concern for the condition of these British divisions and the efforts that we made to help them.

February 24: Arrival 18 Brigade will help enormously but lack of replacements for British units is matter grave concern. Without adequate replacements building any offensive strength in either British division will be impossible. Most battalions are so depleted now as to have limited defensive power. Please do what you can to alleviate replacement problem. Am pressing reorganization of units and work on defenses.

February 25: I am concerned about British positions immediately west of Anzio Road. Previous message outlined intentions for tonight and tomorrow night which I hope will improve conditions materially and gain time for improving defenses of main and reserve lines which inspection today shows to be defective. Low strength of British units is my principal worry. Have released 3rd Brigade to Penney for operations referred to in previous message and to provide one battalion in local reserve in forward area hitherto not available. Thus, both 1st and 56th Divisions will have one battalion in good strength for reserve in forward area, with very weak Guards Brigade available to either. I am also releasing one battalion 18th Brigade to Penney to relieve two badly depleted battalions left of Flyover. Penney hopes to rebuild depleted battalions quickly. Meanwhile, they occupy reserve positions in rear of Flyover. Templar says that he is reasonably happy with his situation, although the country is difficult. I am pressing Penney to expedite work on defenses his area. Please do all you can to increase strength British units in this area.

February 25: I am making strong effort with artillery on front of 56th Division. Have requested cruiser gunfire support. Some delay owing to mines. Please do what you can to expedite availability of cruiser for this purpose.

Later the same day: Principal enemy activity yesterday against 2/6 Queens, London Scots, in front of 56th Division. 2/6 Queens beat off strong attack late yesterday. One advanced company London Scots driven out by surprise attack. Templar has ordered brigade commander to reestablish situation today. Enemy patrols active on remainder 56th Division front. Need for British replacements immediate action. Remainder front relatively quiet except for intermittent heavy shelling of front lines areas, especially on British front and in vicinity Carano. Enemy air active during night from 2300 to 0100, dropping antipersonnel bombs on forward troops areas First British Division and First Armored Division. Casualties reported slight.

February 26: Reference your 3412 (a message saying that British Command wished to withdraw the 24th Guards Brigade which had lost heavily in earlier fighting for reorganization) Eveleigh, Penney, and Templar believe that 24th Guards Brigade should be relieved because further operations will result in loss of key personnel who cannot be replaced. In my opinion this brigade is so weak as to have little value for any other than stop-gap purposes. Brigade commander has received orders direct concerning his relief. British units, particularly 56th Division, are so reduced in strength that the loss of this brigade will of course be felt. I believe we can expect entire 56th Division to be in similar state very soon unless drastic measures are taken with regard to replacements. There is an urgent need for a full brigade group or an American infantry regiment immediately.

Clark requested a specific report of shortages in infantry and artillery in the British Divisions. I replied on February 27th:

> Deficiencies infantry and artillery British Divisions as of 26 February. 1st Division (less 18th Brigade) 2486, 56th Division 2520. Great bulk these deficiencies in fighting infantry soldiers. In the case of 56th Division, each battalion consists of not more than two weak companies, mostly replacements. Few have any experienced junior officers and NCO's remaining. Estimate present combat efficiency 56th Division at approximately 25 per cent.

This brought a proposal the same day to replace the 56th Division with the 5th Division from the southern front. I replied:

> I do not believe that exchange of 56th Division for 5th Division would solve problem here. 5th Division would be able to do little more than relieve the 56th Division. I need an infantry division strong enough to relieve 56th Division and 36th Engineers and consolidate that front. When this has been done, the 56th Division can be withdrawn and refitted here or in Naples. Your suggestion to return them by LCI seems workable, if other troops not available. However, consider American division with its higher infantry strength preferable.

> *February 28:* Situation on front of 56th Division critical because weak strength of units renders them unable to stop enemy infiltration and loss of ground little by little. The condition is a matter of concern to Generals Eveleigh and Templar as well as myself. While I consider situation critical, I cannot alleviate it without grave risk by committing two battalions 18th Brigade which is my only British reserve. Committing these battalions now would be only a stop-gap and would seriously impair my capabilities for counterattack against a major German effort.

> Substitution of 5th Division for the 56th Division will not correct the condition because the 700 British replacements allotted weekly will not cover the attrition from casualties and I shall be faced with a similar problem for both divisions within two or three weeks. Therefore, I recommend that you send one brigade of the 5th Division without vehicles at once, to reinforce the 56th Division in the present critical situation. Instead of sending the remainder of the 5th Division, I recommend sending our 88th Division or other full-strength American division at the earliest possible time for the following reasons: (1) American units are larger and capable of longer sustained effort without replacements; (2) our replacement situation, while bad itself, is still better than the British; (3) on that section of the front the crying need is more men; (4) unless such a solution is adopted, I see little hope of collecting troops for a counterattack when the Boche attack is stopped.

> Eveleigh concurs in these recommendations. This situation is so critical that urgent and immediate action is essential.

While these attacks continued on the British front, it became obvious the Germans were covering up the massing for the main assault. A shift in German artillery to the east of Campoleone and the vicinity of Cisterna with concentration of tanks in wooded areas near Cisterna indicated a large effort in that section, where the ridges leading into our positions could be expected to offer better going for enemy armor, and where a relatively short advance west of Feminamorto Creek would jeopardize our eastern flank. We watched dispositions as closely as we could by observation and by aggressive reconnaissance, but bad weather severely restricted our aerial reconnaissance. On February 27th, I reported to General Clark:

> Enemy undoubtedly preparing to renew attack here. I believe attack will come from divergent directions to disperse our artillery effort. I cannot estimate when the Boche will attack but he has had ample time for preparation. I believe that he now awaits favorable weather and ground conditions. If the weather does not deteriorate, conditions will possibly be favorable by 29 February or 1 March at the latest.

Clark replied that he had personally informed General Alexander of the critical situation. They had alerted the British 5th Division which would be sent to the beachhead and would take over the equipment of the 56th Division which would return to Naples without it. The first Brigade Group was to leave Naples on March 4th. Clark notified me in the same message that the 34th Infantry Division would also be sent to the beachhead by Regimental Combat Team between March 15th and March 20th. He suggested that I thin out the defenses on the eastern flank to strengthen the 56th Division front. On February 28th, I replied:

> I believe the next attack will develop from two principal directions in order to cause dispersion of our artillery effort. In addition, I expect relatively strong diversionary attacks against both the 15th Infantry and Special Service Force sectors. I am holding two battalions 30th Infantry in Corps reserve now. I believe that any further weakening of east part of 3rd Division and Special Service Force Sectors would be hazardous at this time. Urgent need for immediate shipment of brigade of 5th Division as recommended in previous message.

I was about to leave the Command Post about half-past six the evening of February 28th when Colonel Langevin came in with late intelligence. Radio intercepts showed the German command had set the morning of February 29th to begin the assault. I felt the German command might delay for another day hoping ground conditions would be more favorable for the employment of armor. Although this intelligence was no conclusive proof of German intentions, it warranted positive action, and we alerted the command.

We expected the major German offensive to fall upon the front of the 3rd Infantry Division west of Cisterna in an effort to break through the Corps Beachhead Line near Campomorto. However, we expected the Germans would try to lead us to believe their main effort would be somewhere along the Albano Road where they achieved their first success. I was confident that strong attempts would be made on the eastern flank for deception and to disperse our efforts. We had, of course, studied the terrain on every part of the front, and we had selected the areas in which troops would assemble preparatory to attack, in which reserves might be expected to wait; and we had plotted location of gun positions, command posts, tank concentrations, supply dumps and the like. I now decided we should surprise the enemy before the assault began. Accordingly, I called General Baehr and directed him to lay on a counterpreparation. We would have every gun in the beachhead pound these troop assembly areas, reserve positions, artillery locations, and tank concentrations for a full hour before they could begin their attack. It was possible, I thought, we might completely disrupt the German strategy. This countermeasure was to begin at 0430 which we thought would be a full hour before German artillery started up, and probably a half hour before the beginning of the infantry assault. Carleton, Langevin, and Colonel Mack, the air support officer set to work to plan air missions for the following day, after which I sent off another message to Clark:

> In view indications of impending attack here, request all out air efforts stand by for tomorrow. Targets direct by radio after first light. Request maximum Tac/R (aerial reconnaissance) over beachhead at first light. Priority Cisterna west.

These arrangements made, we had a very late supper and then turned in to await the events portended by the shadows of the past six days.

The roar of our own guns broke my slumber the next morning—a welcome sound as they battered the German lines for the next hour. Then there was a lull. We wondered whether the German attack would come, or whether we had wasted this vast artillery effort. Gradually, our guns began to fire again, almost sporadically, as first one battalion and then another responded to calls for fire, which gradually increased in intensity. By daylight, smoke shrouded the beachhead like a fog. We knew the attack was on.

I had my staff conference as usual at half-past eight. By the time the meeting ended in mid-morning, enough information had sifted back so that I could report what was taking place, in another Truscott to Clark message:

> Anticipating possible attack this morning, we fired an intense counter-

preparation starting at 0430. Attack began developing on front of 3rd Division in 509 and 2nd Battalion 7th Infantry Sectors about 0800. Action seems to be general along 3rd Division front as far east as Conca-Cisterna Road Tank battle in progress north of Feminamorto with fifteen enemy tanks reported. Enemy tanks reported south of railroad on Tenuta del Castel-Tenuta di San Clemente and east of Fosso di Carano. Front of 509 penetrated to some extent. I believe this is the beginning of the Boche attack. Enemy probably hopes to draw my reserves eastward to facilitate a main attack down the Anzio Road. Believe all air effort should be laid on tomorrow. Will keep you posted.

Before setting off for a tour of the 3rd Infantry Division front, late that afternoon I sent off another message to Clark:

Strong enemy attacks all along front between 93 and 03 eastings. 3rd Infantry Division heavily engaged by entire 362 and Herman Goering Divisions. Elements 715 Division and 1028 Regiment also identified. Intense fighting in progress. Tac/R reports 50 tanks in Cisterna and 20 additional tanks entering town. It is most essential that heavy air bombardment be placed on this target tonight.

Our arrival on the 3rd Division front was timed beautifully with an Allied air mission over Cisterna as a hundred or more medium bombers soared over the town and released bombs which fell fair and square on the target and shrouded the whole place in a cloud of dust and smoke. Our thrill watching it was marred by seeing one B-26 fall in flames from a direct hit by German antiaircraft. Seeing the loss of this aircraft and a half dozen men had a saddening effect upon all who witnessed it, which was surprising, since we knew we had already lost many hundreds in the ground fighting still in progress. I found O'Daniels confident. Except where the 509th Parachute Battalion battled near Carano, his front lines were still intact. Several hundred German prisoners had been taken. I released the 30th Infantry to O'Daniels and told him to reestablish the front in the sector of the 509th Parachute Battalion, and made my way back to Corps. After a round-up of news from other sectors, I sent off another dispatch to Clark:

Air missions this afternoon appeared very effective and covered the area where the tanks were reported. 509 Parachute Battalion, while forced to give some ground, took 50 prisoners and destroyed many Boche. Counterattack by Battalion 30th Infantry at 1730 hours tonight to restore that situation. No results at this time. Other attacks on front of 3rd Division have been beaten off. However, attacks are continuing tonight. Four divisions have thus far been identified on the front of the 3rd Infantry Division—Herman Goering, 26th, 362, and 715. Also elements of SS Brigade. Total number of tanks located by Tac/R and our own troops 72 plus. We are asking for the dive bombers on likely areas in front of them just after daylight tomorrow. The maximum air effort you have allotted will be of great assistance. So far I feel that the situation is well in hand. 24 Guards Brigade in reserve for 56th Division. I intend to send them south on the first craft that reports with leading elements of 5th Division. 157 and 179 Regiments (45th Infantry Division) in good condition. They have reallocated older men where units were seriously thinned out, and have taken on their replacements. Will keep you informed as attack develops later in the evening. For 12th Air Support missions tomorrow, I desire to control with my air officer direct with 12th Air Support Command.

Actually, that was the high tide of the German assault. The counterattack of the 30th Infantry reestablished the front of the 509th Parachute Battalion the following morning. Heavy attacks by German Infantry and tanks were beaten off on the front of the 7th Infantry near Ponto Rotto and on the front of the 15th Infantry south of Cisterna. Lighter thrusts were put down on the fronts of the 1st Special Service Force and the 56th Division. Half of the German tanks employed in the action were destroyed. We took more than a thousand prisoners, who testified to the casualties we had inflicted upon the Germans and the particularly devastating effect of our artillery. By nightfall the second day we knew the battle was won. The following morning, clear weather permitted the Mediterranean Allied Air Forces to fly the missions that had been planned to support us the preceding day. Three hundred and fifty heavy bombers, Fortresses and Liberators, and an equal number of medium, light and fighter bombers blasted enemy concentrations tanks, artillery and communication. Watching the scene as the dust settled after the last bombs fell and the bombers disappeared in the distance, we noted that the beachhead was strangely still. Jimmie Wilson, my aide, turned to me and remarked: "Christ, General, that's hitting a guy when he's down." It was.

On March 2nd, General Clark returned for his first visit since I assumed command. He informed me that the 5th Division (British) would arrive within the next few days to relieve the 56th Division, and that plans were afoot to renew the assault on the Cassino front. We discussed the coordination of beachhead operations with those on the southern front.

The attempt of the New Zealand Corps to capture the heights above Cassino, which began with the bombing of the Benedictine Monastery on February 15th had failed after three or four days of heavy fighting. Plans for a renewed effort had been delayed by weather and then by this last German offensive at Anzio. The time had been spent in reliefs and reorganization. It was now decided to initiate the new assault about March 10th, although its exact date would depend upon several consecutive days of clear weather to insure favorable ground conditions for the use of armor as well as for maximum air effort and artillery support. Clark wanted to know my views as to our capabilities for an attack from the beachhead in conjunction with the Cassino offensive.

I pointed out that we had stopped the latest German assault with heavy losses and with no loss of ground whatever, and that we were confident we could hold the beachhead. Since the Germans had failed to destroy us in two massive assaults employing five or six divisions, I thought they were unlikely to renew the effort with less. While we could not dismiss the possibility of another all-out attack if the Germans could find the necessary troops I thought it more likely the enemy would seek to contain us and would lose no opportunity to improve his own position by local attack. We could expect German divisions to be withdrawn from our front for rest and reorganization, but the German command would doubtless hold sufficient reserves within reach to prevent any major breakout, for they, of course, had full knowledge of our strength. However, I thought that by regrouping the beachhead forces, and with the arrival of the 5th Division, we should be able to launch a limited objective attack, if we were assured adequate air support, and thus reduce the Carroceto salient in order to provide more depth in that critical area.

General Clark agreed. It was decided that I should plan such an operation for the earliest practicable date. If our minor offensive could precede the Cassino attack, we might hold badly needed German reserves. If it should follow a successful onslaught on the Cassino front, Clark thought we might even achieve a breakout. Thus I set the planners to work on the initial studies for Operation PANTHER.

I spent the next few days in a continuous round of conferences with the staff and subordinate commanders on estimates, plans and preparations. March 6th, we issued the outline of Operation PANTHER for study and further recommendation by the division commanders, and sent off copies to Army. We envisioned making a converging attack in two phases. The 1st Division, assisted by the 5th Division, would attack northward along the Albano Road while the 45th Infantry Division and Harmon's 1st Armored Division (less Combat Command B) would sweep northwest from the eastern side of the salient. The first objective was a line generally north of the Dead End Road. When we were firmly established and reorganized on that line, we would renew the assault. The 1st Division was to seize the caves in the Carroceto area; the 45th Infantry Division and Harmon's Armored command was to seize Aprilia, the Factory, and a hill to the east. The entire engagement would be supported by a maximum effort by the Allied Air Forces and all the artillery we could bring to bear.

Clark visited the beachhead again on March 9th and explained the details of the Cassino attack to take place on the following day. A massive air assault by the heavy bombers of the Allied Air Forces was to blast the town of Cassino, and hundreds of fighter bombers were to support the infantry. There would be the most impressive concentration of artillery yet employed on the southern front. Clark was optimistic. If the attack succeeded in driving up the Liri Valley, he thought that our attempt to reduce the Carroceo salient might even develop into a breakout. Unfortunately it was not to be. The general left the beachhead about mid-afternoon and about eight o'clock that evening I had a message from him.

On my return found Cassino attack scheduled for tomorrow postponed one day on account of weather.

We continued our preparations. Two brigades of the 5th Division, commanded by Major General Gregson-Ellis whom I had known in London, now arrived and replaced Templar's weak 56th Division. On March 10th I saw General Templar depart, with deep regret for he was the ablest British division commander to serve under my command at Anzio. The next day another radio message from Clark advised me that the Cassino attack was again postponed because of bad weather, and was scheduled for March 13th. Our own plans were now complete except for an assurance of air support which I considered essential. On March 12th, I notified Clark:

My attack plans now firm. I can attack 15 March weather permitting, providing all-out air effort available 14 March and continuing during attack. I am prepared to launch attack prior to Cassino effort if that attack further delayed by weather. If that is approved, can air support be made available? I am sending Butler (my assistant) to you with air plan tomorrow. He will present my views as to air requirements. Cover plan working out well. Enemy has shelled areas east of Mussolini canal heavily all afternoon.

Clark replied the same night:

Attack on Cassino for 13th cancelled because of weather and ground conditions. . . . Shall be glad to see Butler tomorrow. Weather forecast and expected ground conditions for March 14 unfavorable. I am willing to have you attack March 15 and I desire that you prepare plans on that basis. Weather permitting, all-out air effort will be given your front on March 14. However, it should be understood by you that Cassino attack has top priority and must take place as soon as weather permits. This means that if weather prediction at 1800 hours any day indicates favorable weather for Cassino attack on following day air effort will support Cassino attack even though your attack still in progress. Moreover, bulk of air will probably be needed for Cassino attack for two days after Cassino D Day.

This reply amazed me. We had never entertained any thought of undertaking this venture without adequate air support. Under the conditions indicated in Clark's message, we might begin the attack and then find all the air support diverted to the Cassino front. The next morning I sent off a protest and late that afternoon I had a message from Butler saying the tentative date for the Cassino operation was now March 14th and that our attack in the beachhead was postponed to March 18th at the earliest. We thought now that our sights were adjusted but events were to prove us wrong.

On the night of March 14th, General Penney launched a limited-objective attack near the Flyover to seize a line of departure which he desired to use for the main attack later. The effort was unsuccessful and almost three full companies of infantry were lost. Penney was greatly depressed and doubted that his Division would be able to carry out the mission assigned to it in our PANTHER plan. After examining the situation, I came to the conclusion that the original mission was not within the capabilities of the 1st Division. Accordingly, I modified the plan to place the main burden of the attack on the 45th Infantry Division and Harmon's 1st Armored Division (less one Combat Command), and I advised Clark of the changes.

The Cassino attack got underway on March 15th. A radio from Clark late that night informed me progress was generally satisfactory although slower than had been anticipated since tanks had not been able to pass through the town because of debris from the bombing. He also advised me that the earliest date for my attack would be March 19th. We continued our preparations on that basis.

We received no further word from the southern front until the night of March 16th, when two messages from Clark arrived almost simultaneously:

Date for your attack is March 19th. Extra heavy air effort will be provided for 18th as well as 19th. Confirm that your attack will be made on 19th.

The second read:

Progress in Cassino area today has been slow. Tanks are having difficulty getting through city. Hill 435 captured. Attack on Monastery Hill will be resumed tonight.

At 0800 the morning of March 17th I was asked to:

Advise immediately whether or not you plan to attack on 19th.

I replied at once:

I will attack 19 March. Since air superiority is the single factor that justifies my attack, I will require the air effort 18 March continuing during attack. Extra heavy air effort required March 18, 19, and 20. After regrouping, a period of probably two days, extra heavy air effort will be required for an additional two days. There is no change in air plan for D minus 1. Corrections for air plan D and D plus 1 by radio today. Am sorry about progress of Cassino attack. Hope you are not expecting my attack to affect situation there. I do not believe that it can have any effect on that situation. Detailed plans by courier today.

March 18th we were ready and the entire command looked forward to the attack with confidence. Early that morning I sent a message to Clark saying it was essential that I should be able to notify troops of the time that close-in air missions would be flown during the following day.

Then we learned that the "extra heavy" air mission for the 18th consisted of only nineteen missions instead of the fifty-six we had requested and that with few exceptions, they were not on the targets we had requested. I was concerned over this but was still hopeful that we could set the matter right when Don Brann, the Army G-3, arrived during the morning. However, Brann brought appalling news: no promise whatever of maximum air support, strategic or otherwise. Only one third of the air effort by fighter bombers, light and medium bombers. And no assurance of continued air support after D Day. I was appalled. I thought we could still reduce the salient, but without adequate air support our losses would be extremely heavy. The objective to be gained, particularly in view of the lack of progress on the Cassino front, was not worth the cost. Brann finally agreed, and sent off a message to General Clark recommending we cancel the attack. Late that afternoon a dispatch arrived granting our request.

To our keen disappointment, that was the end of Operation PANTHER. While we had not reduced the salient, I think that our time in preparing PANTHER had been well spent. We had eliminated a defeatist attitude and had imbued the command with an offensive spirit which was never lost. Our labors had developed our planning methods and had created a spirit of mutual understanding and confidence within the command that was thenceforth to mark all command and staff relations.

General Clark visited the beachhead again on March 19th. The Cassino attack had made very slow progress and had just about spent its force. General Alexander had decided to employ the bulk of the Eighth Army as well as the Fifth Army west of the Apennines. The Eighth Army was to take over the Cassino front while the Fifth Army was to be assigned the sector generally between the Liri River and the coast. A major assault was contemplated for about the middle of April. Meanwhile, the beachhead would regroup, reorganize, rest and train troops in preparation for renewing the assault in connection with the major attack on the southern front. The 34th Infantry Division was already under orders for movement to the beachhead. Clark said he would send on the remainder of the 1st Armored Division and perhaps another American infantry division, possibly the 88th.

4. *On the Road to Rome*

Besides the exchange of the 5th Division for the 56th on the British side, other changes among the combat echelons were taking place on the American side. The first Regimental Combat Team and Division Headquarters of the 34th Infantry Division landed at Anzio on March 19th, and the remainder was to follow within a week. But offsetting this gain in some measure, we were to lose Tucker's 504th Parachute Regiment, Yarborough's 509th Parachute Battalion, and Darby's Ranger Force, all of whom had fought so gallantly from the day of landing.

General Alexander had reviewed the problem of allocation of British infantry reinforcements and had come to the conclusion that even with arrivals expected during the next month it would not be possible to maintain the infantry battalions of the British 1st and 5th Divisions at a strength greater than six officers and 700 other ranks—less than three-fourths the strength of American infantry battalions. And none of the British battalions were at even this strength on March 19th. This relative weakness of British divisions, with its psychological effect, upon British leadership and tactical methods placed serious limitations upon the ability of British units to undertake offensive operations. I concluded therefore that American divisions should bear the burden in any assault to break out of the beachhead. Naturally I selected the divisions in which I had the most confidence: the 3rd Infantry Division and Harmon's Armored command. With this in mind I set about reorganizing our front.

As the 34th Infantry Division arrived, it relieved the 504th Parachute Regiment and the 3rd Infantry Division, which was then withdrawn to a wooded area along the beach east of Nettuno to train for its mission. The 45th Infantry Division relieved one battalion of the 3rd Infantry Division on its right flank and a portion of the 1st Division near the Flyover. The 5th Division replaced the 36th Engineers in the sector along the Moletta River near the coast, and divided the front from the Flyover to the sea with the 1st Division. Each division had two regiments in line, each with a battalion in reserve in the forward area, and one regiment or brigade group in Division reserve. Thus front line battalions could be rotated frequently to maintain morale, and regiments could be withdrawn to the rear for training. O'Daniels' 3rd Infantry Division and Harmon's Armor, in Corps reserve, set about training for the forthcoming attack.

These dispositions, which were completed about the end of March, stayed that way for the remainder of the beachhead phase. Later, when plans for the breakout were delayed, the 3rd Infantry Division relieved the 45th Infantry Division in the lines for a period of about three weeks, while Harmon's 6th Armored Infantry relieved some elements of the 1st Division for a similar period.

On the enemy side, the German command was following a similar procedure: withdrawing units for rest and reorganization. Both sides realized no major attack was forthcoming for the time being, and both confined their offensive operations to small patrol activity, occasional company and battalion attacks, air attacks and extensive employment of artillery.

One would think that after a year and a half of active operations, we should have solved the problem of air support for ground operations, but we had not. Air support was—and continued to be—the weak point in all beachhead operations. It was not until I joined the Corps and complained about the lack of liaison that an air officer was assigned to work with the beachhead staff—a month after the landing. Air support was the subject of many stormy conferences among representatives of the Army G-3, Brigadier General Gordon Saville's Twelfth Tactical Air Command Staff, and ourselves. It is true that air attacks had inflicted heavy losses upon the enemy in both personnel and materiel during the trying days of the beachhead, but this air support had never been closely coordinated with the operations of the ground forces, and consequently had lost much of its effectiveness.

Basically, the controversy arose from two opposed concepts as to what constitutes air support for ground forces. The Air Force concept was that aside from aerial reconnaissance, aircraft should support ground forces by attacking objectives beyond the battle area—bridges, trains, convoys, troop concentrations, supply dumps, and the like. "Isolation of the battlefield" they called it, and they had made valiant efforts to "isolate the battlefield" in preparation for Operation SHINGLE. They wished to designate a bomb support line (BSL) beyond the reach of beachhead weapons where the aircraft would be free to attack any target they might elect. They disliked attacking any objective close to our own front lines or within the bomb support line. Such missions the Air Force accepted only with great reluctance, insisting that pilots be carefully briefed upon each one which the Tactical Air Command would accept.

Our concept did not deny that the effort expended in "isolation of the battlefield" was of value. We did, however, believe that the Air Forces overestimated their ability to interrupt German movements, as evidenced by the German concentration to oppose the beachhead. We also believed that close air support was essential for targets that we could not reach effectively with our own artillery, for concentrated targets upon which air attack would be particularly devastating, and for its morale effect both upon our own troops and the enemy—one of its most important attributes. Nothing elates troops more than seeing their own aircraft attack enemy ground forces; nothing depresses them more than being attacked by enemy aircraft.

Air support for the beachhead was controlled by Army Headquarters. To obtain it, we sent each day to the Army, by radio, a specified list of targets, recommended by the divisions, by our own Corps Artillery Headquarters, and other intelligence sources, asking for air attacks on the following or subsequent days.

In the Army Command Post, an Air Target Committee, consisting of representatives of the Army G-3 Section and of Saville's staff, considered our requests with those submitted by other Army elements. Presumably, the committee set up priorities and then accepted targets within the air effort allotted to our front. Saville's Headquarters then decided whether or not the targets were suitable for air attack and sent out orders for attack on such targets as were approved.

At best, this was a cumbersome procedure which precluded any attack upon a target of opportunity we might select, and it almost ruled out the employment of aircraft for the close-in support of ground forces in the beachhead. With more than a hundred miles separating the Army Command Post and the beachhead, coordination was difficult. The procedure was rendered still more cumbersome and inefficient because the Army committee as often as not disregarded our targets for those of their own choice, and, moreover, usually failed to notify us as to which if any, of our targets would be attacked. Even after such notification, Saville's Headquarters frequently made changes on their own account.

Carleton and I had utilized the effective Navy air support procedure in the attack upon the Kasbah at Port Lyautey in November, 1942; and we had conducted a most successful experiment utilizing an almost identical procedure with our own Twelfth Tactical Air Command in our drive northward from the Volturno during the previous October. We wanted to use this system for coordinating air support within the beachhead. We wanted to know what air support would be allotted to us and when it would be available. We agreed that the Air Forces should refuse targets which were unsuitable or beyond the scope of the aircraft. However, we wanted the aircraft which were assigned missions on the beachhead front to check in with a forward air-ground support control party so that the air attack could be coordinated with the action of the ground forces. We wished to be able to switch the aircraft from a mission upon which it had previously been briefed to a target of opportunity if one should present itself. We fought a losing battle, for the Air Force attitude continued to dominate air support procedures in the Fifth Army.

When our PANTHER attack was cancelled, Clark and Saville proposed to withdraw all air support from the beachhead to permit the Tactical Air Command to concentrate its effort on Operation STRANGLE which was committed to disrupting German lines of communications in Italy in preparation for the major offensive. I protested. I did not think that the beachhead needed very much air support during the defensive period, but I did feel we should have six or eight missions daily, for two reasons: first, we could deal with German guns beyond the range of our own artillery only with aircraft; and second, it was important for the morale of the beachhead forces that they should see occasionally some of their own aircraft engaged with them in the beachhead battle. Clark and Saville finally agreed. These few missions during the remainder of our time within the beachhead were usually briefed upon German long-range artillery positions.

This lack of coordination was to cause trouble during our breakout operations later. On several occasions, our own aircraft strafed and bombed our own troops. While the damage was slight in a physical sense, the damage to ground force morale was enormous. Some of the division commanders, Harmon among them, irately announced that they preferred to continue the attack without air support rather than risk being bombed by our own aircraft.

Saville came to see me on May 29th while we were in the midst of our final assault before the capture of Rome. He was angry and upset, because he had received some very disagreeable messages from Clark concerning these incidents, including a peremptory one ordering him to cease attacking our own troops. Saville informed me that he intended to designate a bomb support line far in advance of our ground troops and that no missions would be accepted within that line. This meant that none of our own aircraft would be over our own troops or attacking the enemy in contact with us. We would lose all air support, and the Germans would become bolder when they found our own aircraft were not attacking them. I tried to reason with Saville, but without success. Realizing that Saville's anger was directed primarily at Clark, I later wrote Saville two letters.

In one long letter I expressed my regret if reports of bombing our own troops had caused any pilot or air commander to feel that their work was not appreciated by the ground forces. Personally, I thought it so valuable that we should not permit personal irritations to jeopardise use of this valuable weapon. I pointed out that we had taken losses in learning to use artillery and machine gun fire, but that such losses had not been in vain because we had thereby perfected a technique that enabled us to inflict terrific casualties upon the enemy. It was the same with air support: we would learn only by correcting our mistakes. It was my opinion that most of the attacks on our ground forces had been done by enthusiastic young pilots returning from armed reconnaissance or other missions not briefed for missions in the beachhead area. I proposed that the bomb support line be considered a fence to keep from our area all armed reconnaissance and other flights not briefed for missions in our area. In the second letter, which I hoped Saville would distribute to the commanders and pilots of his command, I wrote:

> I desire to express my appreciation for the magnificent work of the Commanders and pilots of the XII Tactical Air Command during the operations of breaking out of the beachhead beginning May 23rd. As you know, breaking out of this beachhead has presented a very difficult problem. The struggle has been long and bitter. For months the enemy has prepared and improved his defenses. I am confident that our success in breaking through these defenses during the first three days of the operation is due in no small measure to the commanders and pilots of the XII Tactical Air Command. In my opinion, to those gallant soldiers, and to the ground crews who kept their planes flying, is due at least 50% of the credit for the success of the operation. Every officer and man in the VI Corps has admired and appreciated their valiant work.
>
> As you know, we have had a few cases where our ground troops have been bombed by our own aircraft. I believe that every officer and man realizes that such mistakes will occur. These incidents were reported in order to minimize such incidents. I sincerely trust that no member of your command will feel that, because of such reports, the magnificent work you have done has not been fully and completely appreciated by the ground forces. For any one who might have any doubt of the destructive effect you have had upon the enemy, I recommend a trip along the road from Cori to Artena, where more than 220 German vehicles and guns of all descriptions litter the road with their wreckage.
>
> I am an ardent advocate of the forward controller. I feel that with continued practice in technique we can develop a team that will function smoothly and efficiently in all phases of combat. It has required many years to develop our infantry-artillery team. We lost many lives in the process. As a matter of fact, we have suffered more loss of life from our own artillery in this operation than we have suffered from bombing by our own planes.

These letters seemed to have had the desired effect, for our air support continued.

When I returned to Italy in December to command the Fifth Army,

Carleton and I were interested to find that the forward air-ground support control system which we had advocated for so long was finally in use.

At my staff conference on the morning of March 22nd, just three days after cancellation of our PANTHER attack, the Corps surgeon reported that German artillery had shelled the hospital area early that morning causing a number of casualties among medical personnel and patients. This had caused a general state of alarm. Accompanied by General Baehr, the Corps artillery officer, I went at once to the hospital area to inspect damage, and see what might be done to restore order.

We had at this time four evacuation hospitals, several field hospitals, and the clearing companies of the division medical battalions in a tent camp—several hundred tents of all sizes equipped with two thousand five hundred beds—in an open field about a mile east of Nettuno. The British hospital installation, about half the size of the American, was situated in an open field about a mile north of Anzio. During the early days of the beachhead, the operating room of one hospital then located near the beach had been struck by bombs jettisoned by a German bomber under attack by our own fighters. Several doctors, nurses, and patients had been killed and so much essential equipment destroyed that the hospital had to be replaced by another. Since there was no spot within the beachhead where hospitals could be placed beyond the range of German artillery, the Army surgeon had selected these open locations where the Red Cross symbols would be clearly visible to German air and ground observers with the expectation that the Geneva Conventions would protect them. While shells had at times passed overhead and fallen in the general vicinity, this was the first time in the several weeks since the hospitals had been moved that they had actually been fired upon.

We found that about sixty rounds of high-explosive antipersonnel type projectiles of 88 mm caliber, fired from an extreme range, had fallen in the hospital area. One shell, striking a stove in a ward tent occupied by fifty wounded men, had exploded with great fragmentation at about the level of the beds, killing five patients and wounding eleven others. One nurse had been killed, several doctors, nurses, and hospital personnel had been wounded, and dozens of tents showed the jagged holes left by shell fragments. One irate chief nurse approached me holding a huge fragment in each hand. Thrusting them in my face, she stormed: "General, these came through my tent while I was in bed. We can't take care of our patients properly unless we can get some rest. I want to know what you are going to do about it." Passing through the wards where wounded men lay, more than one said to me: "General, get us out of here. Let us go back to the front. We are better off there than here."

More than ever before, I realized the importance of hospitals and medical care in maintaining the morale and fighting spirit of troops. These wounded men had seen comrades die. They had narrowly escaped death themselves. It was natural that they should desire some relief from the tension of battle. And it was natural that they should expect safety and understanding care while their broken bodies were on the mend. It was this relationship between patients and hospital personnel that had made the hospitals such fertile fields for the origin and dissemination of wild rumors. A wounded man necessarily saw the bad side of any battle, made worse by the human tendency to exaggerate as the wounded exchanged stories and passed them on. Wild stories found ready listeners among the patients, and the hospital personnel were the principal sources of information about the front line fighting.

After careful examination, we decided the shelling had not been accidental, and that we could expect a repetition. I sent a message to Clark recommending that this violation of the Geneva Convention be brought to the attention of the theater commander and protested. Baehr set the Fire Direction Center to counterbattery every possible artillery position which could open fire upon the hospitals. I directed the hospital commander to telephone me immediately if any shell landed in the hospital area, for I wanted them to know that their protection was receiving my personal attention. Then I returned to the Command Post and directed the Corps Engineer to dig the hospitals in.

The 5th Division was just beginning to take the place of the 36th Engineers on the western flank. As the 36th Engineers were relieved, we put them to work in the hospital area and later reinforced them with details from the 3rd Infantry Division. Because of the water level in the area, we could not dig deeper than about two feet. However, we filled sand bags with the spoil, and used them to raise the walls to a height of nearly four feet. We sought unsuccessfully to obtain Nissen huts to house operating rooms. In lieu of these, we constructed an overhead cover of timber reinforced with sandbags and revetted the walls. There was no other overhead protection in the area, but patients on cots were below ground level and safe from anything except a direct hit by a bomb or shells. In less than two weeks, we had the hospitals well shielded. Intermittent shelling continued, but there were no more serious casualties.

No one who served at Anzio will ever forget the gallantry of the medical personnel there, particularly the Army nurses. None of them had expected to work under artillery fire or air bombardment, for they were protected by the Geneva Convention. Hospitals were usually established in areas well beyond the range of German artillery. At Anzio, there were no safe regions; every part was within the range of German guns. Because the beach and port were the primary targets for German air and long range artillery, the forward positions were usually quieter and safer than rear areas except during periods of actual offensive operations. Thus, doctors, nurses, and Corps men worked under the tensions of battle and suffered the same hardships as did the front line troop. Their contribution to the defense cannot be overestimated.

On March 25th, an order from Army limited our use of artillery ammunition to less than one fourth of what we had been expending daily; reserves of ammunition had to be built up for renewal of the offensive. As Clark's message expressed it:

> The number of LCT's and LST's now available for landing supplies appears to be the maximum we can expect. The tonnage now being landed is barely sufficient to maintain your forces. This is a matter of simple arithmetic. Since ammunition constitutes about fifty percent of the tonnage landed, it is evident that we can only build up a reserve of supplies by keeping expenditures to the minimum consistent with tactical needs.

There had been an increase in enemy shelling during the past few days, probably because there had been no air effort available. We feared that, if the increased volume of enemy shelling continued, the lack of retaliation would have an adverse effect upon morale. And our fears changed to alarm when the British guns at Anzio were further restricted to less than a fourth of the reduced allowance. Losses of ammunition ships in convoy had resulted in a critical shortage in British artillery ammunition throughout the theater. Penney and Gregson-Ellis were afraid their divisions would take increasingly heavy losses, suffer in morale, and might not even be able to hold their lines.

We moved two American battalions to increase their artillery support, and then turned to putting our reduced allotments to the best possible use to prevent the enemy from discovering our predicament. Penney said that he would like to designate the target on his front he considered most dangerous to his division, and then, on a given day, have every gun in the beachhead fire two or three rounds on it. Several hundred guns so firing would let the Germans know that we still disposed an enormous amount of artillery and would help the morale of his division. This suggestion was the basis of our solution.

Each division selected the most profitable target on its front. At specific times, every gun within range was brought to bear for three rounds of TOT, for which firing data had been computed so that all projectiles exploded on the target at the same instant. These TOT's were most successful. We maintained an effective counterbattery and even effected a saving of our reduced allowances to permit artillery support for our raids and limited-objective attacks.

During the lull in activity each division was required to patrol, to make frequent raids to learn what the enemy was doing, and to identify the units on its front by capturing prisoners. In addition, we selected objectives for minor attacks which would improve our position and inflict casualties upon the enemy. Each division was required to plan and conduct one such limited-objective attack. Two most successful attacks were conducted by Frederick's 1st Special Service Force and by the 3rd Infantry Division after that Division had relieved the 45th Infantry Division.

By the end of March, our regrouping was complete. We now instituted an intensive training program in the attack techniques needed to break through the German defenses in the final assault. Harmon and O'Daniels were especially charged with developing new equipment and methods, for passing through mine fields, reducing pill boxes, and overcoming obstacles which we could expect to encounter. The training was most realistic.

Harmon's engineers devised a treadway bridge that could be lowered by a tank across tank ditches and similar obstacles, and a Bailey bridge which could be towed by a tank to the brink of a wider obstacle, whereupon the tank would disengage, move to the rear and punch the bridge across the obstacle. Exercises were carried out with "snakes"—several hundred feet of 4-inch pipe filled with explosive. These were pushed across a mine field in front of a tank and then exploded to clear a path through the mines. Another improvisation was to mount a mortar upon a tank and fire a grapnel with cable attached, across enemy wire, whereupon the tank would back away clearing a path through the wire.

O'Daniels invented a battle sled—half of a wing tank which would hold one soldier lying prone. One tank towed sleds holding an infantry squad. The theory was the sleds would protect men from antipersonnel mines, enable the squad to approach the enemy, so that the squad and tank could team up to destroy antitank guns, machine guns nests, and the like. In practice, when it was used in battle, the tank was not protected against antitank mines and often lost tracks before the squad was close enough. Battle patrols composed of specially selected men in each regiment were trained in commando tactics and reconnaissance.

All units conducted special training for snipers. At its completion, we conducted a competition to determine how useful the training had been. The range selected was only a few hundred yards from the front lines in the Littoria sector. A realistic course had been devised with all firing to seaward to prevent firing among our own troops. In peace time on ranges in America, a huge red flag is always flown when firing is in progress to warn individuals to avoid the danger zone. I was greatly amused when I went out to watch the matches to find that the range officer had complied strictly with the regulations: a huge red range flag was flying in the wind. Before the competition ended, the Germans dropped a few rounds into the area no doubt thinking that the flag indicated some activity in progress there.

Life at Anzio was never dull, easy or quiet. German artillery and aircraft continued to strike almost daily. While mass raids of fifty or more aircraft practically ceased during April, hit and run raids by one or more planes persisted. Nor was there any part free from the daily scream of artillery projectiles in flight, the crash of bursting shells, or the thud of bursting bombs.

Life was tense as it always is when men live close to death. But we learned how to survive. The men found some means of making life more comfortable, and even discovered precarious forms of entertainment to relieve the tedium of congested living and battle tensions.

Living accomodations were, for the most part, extremely primitive: caves hollowed from canal banks, shelter halves stretched over a bit of defilade, the interior of tanks, trucks, or other vehicles. In the forward areas, a few "poderis"—plastered stone farm houses of the Mussolini Reclamation project—remained standing. Here were housed regimental and battalion command posts, and aid stations where men from the front line companies could occasionally obtain a hot meal and dry out their clothing. There were a few tents but not many, under cover in areas adjacent to the beaches. Division commanders for the most part had caravans or trailers to house their offices, but none of them were protected by more than a makeshift camouflage. Few of the buildings in Anzio or Nettuno had escaped damage, although the lower floors of those along the water front were protected to some extent by the cliff that rose behind them, and it was here the port engineers, various service installations, and the presscamp (never very large), were accommodated. The only concentration of tentage was in the hospital area which I have described. Even under these conditions, men displayed rare ingenuity in making themselves more comfortable and their humor lightened their loads. All over the beachhead signs indicated that you were approaching "42nd and Broadway", the "Good Eats Cafe", "4719¼ miles to the Golden Gate", "Beach Head Hotel, Special Rates to New Arrivals", and such forms of soldier wit.

Division, regimental and other unit commanders had their own messes. Luncheon parties became a favorite form of social intercourse, usually interspersed with business. Each one sought to outdo the others in both fare and appointments. However, the fare, except for occasional steaks or roasts from a butchered cow or pig, was usually limited to what ingenious cooks could do with rations. A lively trade went on between Americans and British—our "10 in 1" for British "bully beef" and hard bread. Appointments normally were limited to white table cloths, usually sheets pilfered from the Navy or a hospital, an assortment of china and crockery accumulated from bombed-out buildings, and the silverware issued with the Army mess kits. Flowers, in profusion as spring came on, were used for magnificent center pieces; none on other luncheon tables ever approached those produced by my Corporal Hong, arranged as divisional crests or other insigne of a guest of honor.

Springtime saw the Americans seeking relaxation in the time-honored fashion, as far as the congested area, limitations of duty, ingenuity, and enemy activity permitted. Baseball and soft ball were favorites, and it was not unusual to see soft ball games in progress with German artillery shells landing within five or six hundred yards. There were devotees of volleyball and badminton, and bridge and poker were played a great deal. Swimming in the blue Tyrrhenian Sea was increasingly popular as weather became warmer and the engineers cleared mines from the better beaches. And warm weather, aided no doubt by a desire for a change in diet, brought the followers of Izaak Walton out in force, employing some rather unorthodox fishing methods. They had found that German teller mines exploded beneath the water brought the stunned fish to the surface where bare hands readily substituted for the nets which we did not have.

By the nature of their duties, and for reasons of safety, most hospital personnel were not allowed to leave the hospital area. Each group, however, devised its own forms of entertainment and amusement. Musical instruments, radios, phonographs, informal song fests, all helped to lighten off-duty hours. There were even occasional dances with tight-stretched canvas providing a none too perfect dancing floor.

The climbing roses growing in the small garden of our "Villa" were especially beautiful. I had them cut and sent in large baskets to the hospitals. Among my much-treasured mementoes of Anzio are the notes of appreciation sent to me by the chief nurses.

No one group contributed more to uplifting the spirits of the men during these weeks than did our bands. When our PANTHER attack was cancelled, and we realized we were to be on the defensive for some weeks, the division commanders asked to have their bands brought up from Naples. They played concerts in the hospital and in the rear division areas. They played at decoration ceremonies in the square at Nettuno. Breaking up into smaller groups, they played for every unit they could reach. It was during this period that the 3rd Infantry Division Band made the whole beachhead familiar with "Dog Face Soldier". Perhaps the music of the Scotch bagpipes was the most favored. The combined pipers of the Cameronians, the Royal Scots Fusiliers, the Seaforth Highlanders, and the Gordon Highlanders, immaculate in kilts and tartans, perfect in drill and discipline, paraded for the hospitals and every American division. None who heard them will ever forget their martial, stirring strains, which were never more appropriate.

Hundreds of radio-equipped vehicles within the beachhead and many other radios were used in communications. We also obtained a few receiving sets for the hospitals and elsewhere. Soldiers displayed typical Yankee ingenuity in improvising receiving sets from cans and bits of wire and batteries. But our only source of radio entertainment were the Axis broadcasts, particularly one featuring Axis Sally and George with "Lili Marlene" as their theme song. This brought forth another letter from me to Clark:

> For several months German radio has been presenting a program featuring "Sally and George", together with recordings of the latest American dance music. This program, naturally, is designed to appeal to Allied troops, and while it has a certain entertainment value, it is primarily used to disseminate enemy propaganda.
>
> This propaganda, on the whole, is crude and ineffective; however, the psychiatrist with the 3rd Infantry Division contends that the program does have a positive morale effect on men of limited intelligence He recalled one case where a man, passed back as an exhaustion case, made remarks that obviously came from the propaganda lines on that program. He felt, as I do, that the program should be countered by one that would, first, offset the value of the propaganda by ridicule; and second, provide a high class program which our troops would listen to in preference to the German broadcast.
>
> Such a program should feature the newest recordings from "name" orchestras, humorous broadcasts such as Jack Benny and Charlie McCarthy, as well as world news items and latest sports flashes. In addition to being extremely high class entertainment, it is essential that the broadcast insure good volume and clear reception on both Signal Corps and commerical receiving sets. Furthermore, periods of broadcasts should be timed to coincide with Sally's programs.

At the time, we had no broadcast within the beachhead, nor could we hear any Allied broadcast from Naples or elsewhere in Italy. Only occasionally could some of the better sets tune in to BBC from London.

It was to be several weeks before my suggestions were carried out.

I do not wish to leave any impression that Anzio was any continuous round of pleasure. Far from it. But I shall always admire the trait in the men and women who served there which prompted them always to seek relaxation in the normal pastimes of peacetime living, reminding them of home. Without this I do not see how men could have survived the terrific nervous tensions under which they lived at Anzio.

When General Clark visited the beachhead on March 19th, General Alexander had already announced plans for regrouping the Allied Armies in Italy, and the changes were then in progress. The Eighth Army, leaving the V Corps on the Adriatic front, was to take over the Cassino sector from the Apennines to the Liri River, with the X, XIII, Polish and New Zealand Corps. The Fifth Army, with the American II Corps and General Juin's French Expeditionary Corps, was to take over the Garigliano sector, a front of about fifteen miles extending from the mouth of the Liri River to the coast. Nothing had yet been announced about the forthcoming offensive but it was apparent that General Alexander proposed to drive northward on Rome, with the Eighth Army making its main effort in the Liri and Sacco valleys while the Fifth Army fought along the coast. Clark explained that our mission was to hold the beachhead firmly and to prepare for offensive action in conjunction with the main attack by the Fifth and Eighth Armies about the middle of April. He promised to send the remaining combat command of the 1st Armored Division to the beachhead as soon as possible. He thought that an additional infantry division might be made available but this was by no means certain.

Enemy dispositions by this time were entirely defensive. We knew that the Herman Goering, 26th and 29th Panzer Grenadier Divisions and the 114th Light Division had now been withdrawn from the beachhead front. We did not expect any renewed effort to destroy our forces unless there was some radical change. It seemed evident that the German command considered six or seven divisions sufficient to contain us, as well as to attack limited objectives to improve their positions. We were much better organized and much stronger in reserves than when we had stopped the major German offensives; and we had no doubt that we could counter any German assault. Our regrouping provided the minimum strength to hold the front—local reserves for immediate support, and a sizeable reserve for division commanders to permit strengthening of their front lines and to facilitate rotation of units for rest and refitting. In Corps reserve were the 3rd Infantry Division and the 1st Armored Division (less Combat Command B), which, with possibly one regiment from the 34th or 45th Infantry Divisions, would be the maximum available for offensive operations.

An offensive action would have one of two purposes, either to improve our position by extending the beachhead, or as a major offensive in conjunction with the remainder of the Fifth and Eighth Armies to destroy the German forces. When we began our investigations to determine what we might accomplish with the forces at hand, we found four possible alternates: to reduce the Carroceto salient, recapture lost ground, improve our positions, and facilitate deployment for future action toward Albano or Cisterna; to capture Cisterna, seize an important locality which would provide more depth within the beachhead, divide the enemy forces in preparation for future operations toward Cori or Artena; to capture Littoria on the east flank which would deny the Germans observation, reduce artillery fire on the port area, and provide more space; to seize the Ardea area which would accomplish on the western flank the same results as the attack on Littoria in the east with the further advantage, perhaps, of threatening the German right.

Every major headquarters in the beachhead worked day and night during the last ten days in March preparing detailed studies, estimates and plans for each of these operations. As our investigations progressed, it became more and more obvious that the only operation which would inflict damage upon the enemy and produce worthwhile results would be one aimed at reducing the Carroceto salient or capturing Cisterna. Owing to the nature of the German defensive organization, we could expect heavy losses in men and material, and we had learned from experience that after such an assault we would require at least a month to absorb replacements and refit before they would again be ready to take the initiative. Rather regretfully, I came to the conclusion that none of these attacks would be worth the cost, and that we should limit our offensive operations to patrol actions and small scale attacks until we were ready to make an all-out effort in conjunction with the main assault.

General Clark returned to the beachhead on March 29th, and I informed him of these conclusions. He agreed, although it now appeared the Eighth Army could not be ready, so that the major offensive would not begin until after the 1st of May. This meant a month of waiting for us in our present positions—a none too pleasing prospect. He thought information of the Army plans would be forthcoming during the following week; meanwhile we could continue our studies.

Clark provided the maximum space in the rest centers for our troops and promised replacements to bring the divisions up to strength. He would see that the remainder of the 1st Armored Division came on to the beachhead, and possibly an additional division in time for the final assault. Meanwhile, we would concentrate on building up reserves of ammunition and supplies and on putting our troops into the best possible conditions for the final effort.

This date, March 29th, happened to be my twenty-fifth wedding anniversary. Just after I saw the General off in his plane that afternoon, the Germans provided the noisiest serenade in my twenty-five years of wedded life: a late afternoon air raid involving more than forty German bombers. It was quite a show.

During the first week in April, General Alexander had outlined his intentions in a conference with the Army commanders. On May 10th the Fifth and Eighth Armies were to attack simultaneously, the Eighth Army was to break through the Cassino defenses and drive up the Liri Valley, while the Fifth Army broke through the mountainous areas west of the Garigliano River to turn the flank of German forces opposing the Eighth Army in the Liri Valley. The beachhead forces were to be prepared to attack on twenty-four hours notice in the direction of Cisterna-Valmontone to cut Highway 6 in the rear of the German main forces. These operations were to destroy the German forces and drive the remnant far north of Rome. The capture of Rome was the important immediate objective.

The plan for the employment of the beachhead forces could bring decisive results if it was properly coordinated with the advance of the main forces, and launched at the proper time to cut the German line of communication delaying the advance of our main forces. In addition, as Clark and I discussed it, we thought we should also be prepared to exploit our position on the flank and the rear of the German forces. This would make possible—in the event the Germans withdrew rapidly from in front of our Eighth and Fifth to defend a line south of Rome through the Alban Hills—an attack in the Carroceto area passing to the west of the Colli Laziali, which might be the quickest way to turn the German position and to capture Rome. Moreover, if the offensive on the southern front was not marked with success—as had previously been the case—then an attack from the beachhead might be desirable to unite it with the rest of the Fifth Army and thus reduce the logistical and naval burden of maintaining the beachhead.

Our four plans previously referred to came to be known by the code names GRASSHOPPER, BUFFALO, TURTLE and CRAWDAD, and designated attacks in the directions Littoria-Sezze; Cisterna-Cori-Valmontone; Carroceto-Campoleone-Rome; and Ardea-Rome. Because of continuing British reinforcement problems and the weak strength of British divisions—about 600 men per battalion as compared with the American 1000—I had decided that the burden of our assault force would fall upon O'Daniels' 3rd Infantry Division and Harmon's 1st Armored Division. Since Harmon's Armored Division had only one regiment of infantry, the 135th Infantry Regimental Combat Team of the 34th Infantry Division would be attached. Other divisions had limited assignments to assist the assault of the two bearing the main burden of breaking through the German defenses. If the additional division materialized, it would be employed to maintain momentum when the initial effort had spent its force.

Complete orders with annexes were produced for each of these four plans. Detailed reconnaissances in preparation for the attacks were made so that during the last two nights movements could go on during the hours of darkness. All of these details were worked out with the greatest secrecy. Hundreds of gun emplacements were dug for artillery and other supporting weapons. Many thousands of rounds of ammunition (600 rounds per gun for the artillery) of all kinds were deposited at positions concealed against hostile observations. Miles of telephone lines were laid. Assembly areas were selected, routes reconnoitered, and orders were in readiness for the movement of troops, tanks and supporting weapons over our congested road net. This would have been a difficult problem under any circumstances; but in the confined area of the beachhead with its restricted road net it was a staggering one.

We discovered we would not be able to attack on twenty-four hours notice, since we would require the darkness of two nights to move troops and supporting weapons into their final positions. Without the traffic control system we had in effect, we would never have completed these movements. Our road net was extremely limited: one hard-surface road that paralleled the coast passing through the towns of Anzio and Nettuno; one north-south road leading from Anzio northward through the Flyover toward Albano; one good road that led from Nettuno to Conca and Cisterna, with a fork leading off toward Compomorto and Carano; and one road parallel to and within easy rifle shot of the Mussolini Canal from Conca to the sea. The Corps Engineers had scraped out, with bulldozers, a lateral road that connected the Albano and Conca Roads and joined a trail leading north of Nettuno. This road was little more than a mile from the front lines, exposed to enemy observation over much of it; and it always puzzled me why the engineers placed signs proclaiming this road "Truscott Boulevard."

In order to lessen vulnerability to German artillery fire, all traffic was strictly controlled by Corps Headquarters. Only the division commanders, and corps and division principal staff officers, were authorized to move as freely as their duties required. Each of their vehicles bore a special windshield sticker. Other vehicles were permitted to use certain roads for special purposes, such as the supervision of supply. They bore a special sticker of another kind. No other transport was permitted to leave the guarded parks except for specific trips authorized by regimental or division commanders, in which event a sticker was necessary. Corps and division staff officers and military police continuously checked and supervised this traffic control.

Troop movements were carefully plotted to insure that each road was used to full capacity. Each column was required to enter a road at a designated time, to maintain prescribed distances and speeds, and to clear the road at certain hours calculated according to the time-length of the column. Strictly supervised by commanders, staffs, and military police, the system worked well. Without it, we could never have concentrated for battle, and our casualties from German artillery fire would have been much greater.

We had many visitors during the month of April, but neither General Alexander nor General Clark were among them. I spent the last four days in April "resting" in Naples, and while I was there I obtained from the Army Command Post approval of our plans. Also, along with General Clark, Harmon, and several others, I had the honor of receiving from General Alexander the Order of the Bath in recognition for services in Tunisia.

General Alexander visited the beachhead on May 5th. With some measure of pride, I explained to him the details of our plans, and the extent of our preparations. General Alexander, charming gentleman and magnificent soldier that he was, let me know very quietly and firmly that there was only one direction in which the attack should or would be launched, and that was from Cisterna to cut Highway 6 in the vicinity of Valmontone in the rear of the German main forces. He had, he said, reserved to himself the decision as to when he proposed to initiate it. After he left that afternoon, I reported our conversation to General Clark:

> General Alexander arrived this morning. When I informed him of the four plans on which I am working, he stated that I was paying too much attention to alternate plans. He said that the only attack that he envisages from the beachhead is the Cisterna-Cori-Artena attack and that he does not consider that any other attack will attain worthwhile results. He advised me to concentrate on plans for that attack and said that if and when he ordered the attack he would give me every support that I considered necessary. He also said that he was most anxious to give me the 36th Division.
>
> I stated to General Alexander that my greatest concern was the timing of the attack from the beachhead and the object to be accomplished with means now existing in the beachhead or with the additional division. He informed me that he had reserved to himself the decision as to the time of launching the

attack from the beachhead. Since I believe that there is a possibility that the Sezze operation may be desirable, I am continuing all-out preparation for that operation. In view of General Alexander's statement, I am concentrating as first priority preparation for the Cisterna-Cori attack.

Please advise me if this meets your approval. I assume that you are fully cognizant of General Alexander's ideas on this subject, but I want you to know what he has told me today. If you desire any action on my part other than indicated here please advise me.

Clark came to the beachhead the following day. He was irked at General Alexander's "interference" in his American chain of command. He remarked that "the capture of Rome is the only important objective," and was fearful that the British were laying devious plans to be first in Rome. While he agreed that the Cisterna-Valmontone assault would probably be the most decisive, he also thought that the quickest way into Rome might be via Carroceto-Campoleone passing west of the Colli Laziali. Clark was determined that the British were not going to be the first in Rome. I was to be as fully prepared to fight in this direction as in the other. Also, since it was still possible that the southern attack might bog down, I was also to be prepared to lay the attack in the direction Littoria-Sezze.

D Day for this operation on the southern front was set for May 11th in orders published by both General Alexander's and General Clark's Headquarters on March 6th. Beachhead forces were to be prepared to attack on forty-eight hours notice at any time after D plus 4, or May 15th. Under General Clark's instructions, we were to employ any one of our four plans. On May 7th I sent Clark a letter of confirmation:

1. I am prepared to do the BUFFALO operation under conditions now existing in the beachhead on 7 days notice.
  a. Plans have been drawn and preparations are now under way. Upon completion of these preparatory steps everything will be set up and ready to go except those things that can be accomplished only in the last 48 hours prior to D Day here.

2. When present work has been finished, I will be prepared to launch not only BUFFALO but either GRASSHOPPER or TURTLE within 48 hours. However, if definite preparatory commitment is made to either GRASS-HOPPER or BUFFALO, and I am then required to launch TURTLE, I will need 72 hours in which to make the necessary shift and launch the attack.

One important and rather unorthodox deceptive measure was our employment of the beachhead artillery during this period. We planned to begin our assault with an intense forty-five minute preparation fired by every gun in the beachhead. In order to prevent the Germans from recognizing the preparation for what it was when D Day came, we fired a series of barrages each morning from different parts of the beachhead, varying the hours of firing as well as the length and method. During the first few nights, it alerted the Germans and brought forth large-scale defensive fires. Then they apparently concluded that these salvos were just part of the American's wasteful methods of using artillery and paid no special attention to them. This was to be a great asset to us on the morning of D Day.

The offensive on the southern front began at 2300 hours the night of May 11th. During the following days, we followed the brief reports of its progress with intense interest and mounting excitement as we pressed forward with our own affairs. The Eighth Army had slow going in the Cassino area. Cassino and the Monastery were not taken until the night of May 17th by Anders' Polish Corps. Meanwhile, the advance of the French Corps and Keyes' II Corps was off to a good start, the French Corps in particular was beginning to outflank the Germans in the Liri Valley. The Eighth Army now had three bridges across the Rapido River, and we expected the drive up the Liri Valley in full force. The question now was: would the Germans be able to stop the advance in front of the "Adolf Hitler Line"—their defensive position across the Sacco River south of Frosinone.

On May 18th, I had word from Clark that he wished me to be at Army Command Post in Teano the following morning for a conference—"prepared to discuss feasibility of following operation as an alternative plan: BUFFALO attack to be launched as now planned to include capture of objectives 1 and 2 (Cisterna and Cori). Special Service Force would continue toward Artena and Valmontone. After capture of objectives 1 and 2, regrouping would take place and new attack launched northwest from Cisterna area." Clark was obviously still fearful that the British might beat him into Rome.

At the meeting he indicated we were to launch BUFFALO on Monday morning, May 21st. The 36th Infantry Division was to close in the beachhead by Tuesday morning. He thought that he might even bring the II Corps with the 85th Infantry Division up later. He proposed to establish his Advanced Command Post at Anzio Sunday night, and would then relieve me of responsibility for the two British divisions on the west flank of the beachhead. Clark abandoned the alternative plan when we pointed out that the 1st Special Service Force would not be strong enough to seize Artena and cut Highway 6 at Valmontone. By one o'clock that afternoon, we were back in the beachhead to begin our final preparations.

But at four o'clock Sunday afternoon a message from Clark advised:

Attack from beachhead postponed 24 hours. There is a strong possibility that it may be postponed an additional 24 hours. I shall advise you further on this point by 1700 hours May 21.

We stopped all preparatory movements scheduled for that night. Then at 1715 hours, May 21st, the final words came:

Operation BUFFALO will be launched at 0630 hours on morning May 23rd. I will arrive at Advanced Command Post about noon on Monday.

In the hour before dawn on the morning of May 23rd, Clark and I, with several members of my staff, were waiting in one of the Corps artillery observation posts just in the rear of the line of departure on which O'Daniels' and Harmon's Divisions were poised for battle. Light rain had fallen during the night, but occasional stars now gave promise of a clear day. Beachhead artillery had carried out one of its deceptive tactics, earlier in the night without provoking any enemy reaction, and after some further harassing fires, the guns had fallen silent. We thought we could discern the faint outlines of the Colli Laziali against the northern sky, but we could not be sure. Around us, we could see nothing. There was no sight or sound to indicate that more than 150,000 men were tensely alert and waiting. All was strangely quiet, and in the darkness that precedes the dawn, the whole forward area seemed almost empty. There was tenseness in the air and little talk among us. For better or worse, the die was cast as the minute hands of watches moved slowly toward the zero hour.

0545! There was a crash of thunder and bright lightning flashes against the sky behind us as more than a thousand guns, infantry cannon, mortars, tanks, and tank destroyers opened fire. That first crash settled into a continuous rumbling roar. Some distance ahead, a wall of fire appeared as our first salvos crashed into the enemy front lines, then tracers wove eerie patterns in streaks of light as hundreds of machine guns of every caliber poured a hail of steel into the enemy positions. Where we stood watching, the ground quivered and trembled. Day was now breaking, but a pall of smoke and dust shrouded the battle area. At the end of forty minutes, the guns fell silent. Then, from the southeast appeared three groups of fighters, and light bombers, their silvery wings glinting in the morning light. Towering clouds of smoke and dust broke through the pall about Cisterna as their bombs crashed into the town and enemy positions. Five minutes, and the planes were gone. The artillery began anew. H hour had come and the battle was on.

Cisterna was a key locality in the German plan for containing the beachhead. We knew its strength from bitter experience, for we had

twice failed in efforts to take the town. It was an ancient town standing on a slight eminence on the edge of the Pontine Marshes and flat
farm lands. Its stone buildings and narrow streets were formidable
obstacles to any attacking force. In the three and a half months since
our last attempt, the Germans had converted the environs into a veritable fortress. Deep ravines and canals on either side of the town afforded defilade from our fires, and numerous irrigation ditches were
barriers to tank attack. Extensive caverns underneath the town protected the defenders from our heaviest artillery and air bombardments.
To the west of Cisterna, the German main line of resistance followed
the railroad line which, with its deep ditches and steep embankments,
was an antitank barrier that required special means for crossing. To the
southwest, branches of the Mussolini Canal and the numerous plastered
stone houses had been transformed into enormously strong tactical localities. Back of the German lines, broken terrain rose steadily toward
the steep mountains, with Velletri, on the edge of the Colli Laziali, and
Cori, on the side of Mt. Arestino, both about seven miles away. Between these two, a broken rugged valley almost devoid of roads led
toward Valmontone and Highway 6 about fifteen miles away.

Basically, our plan was divided into two phases. We would first
isolate and reduce Cisterna and establish a firm base on the X-Y Line,
encircling Cisterna at a distance of about two miles. Once established
there, we would then drive on to capture Cori, and push on to seize
Artena and cut Highway 6 at Valmontone. To start with, the 1st Armored Division, with the 135th Infantry of the 34th Infantry Division
attached, was to break through the German defenses west of Feminamorto Creek and cut Highway 7 between Cisterna and Velletri. The
3rd Infantry Division, in a two-pronged attack, was to encircle Cisterna from both sides and then reduce the town. On the right, Frederick's 1st Special Service Force was to attack northeast along the
northern side of the East Branch Mussolini Canal and cut Highway 7
southeast of Cisterna to protect the right flank of the Corps' attack.
To the west, the 45th Infantry Division had a limited objective to expand the breakthrough as far west as Carano. The British divisions and
the 36th Engineers were to carry on aggressive patrolling to deceive
the enemy and prevent withdrawals on their fronts. The 34th Infantry
Division was to hold the front and cover assembly for the assault. After
the assault it would assemble in Corps reserve. The 36th Infantry Division was to be prepared to pass through the 3rd Infantry Division for
the advance on Cori during the second phase.

Some five and a half German divisions opposed the beachhead when
the assault began. The German command had been compelled to strip
their forces of reserves to oppose the Allied advance on the southern

front. The 715th Infantry Division held the eastern flank of the beach-head along the Mussolini Canal. In the Cisterna region, there was the 362nd Division with the 1028th Panzer Grenadier Regiment and some miscellaneous units. The 3rd Panzer Grenadier Division faced the 45th Infantry Division, while on the British front, the 65th Division was astride the Albano Road in the Carroceto area. The 4th Parachute Division held the lower Moletta River.

Fighting was intense all day. A smoke and dust haze overhung the battle area. Late in the afternoon, Harmon's attack crossed the railroad west of Feminamorta Creek. On the right, Frederick's 1st Special Service Force had reached its objective on Highway 7 and had then been thrown back half a mile by a German counterattack with Mark VI (Tiger) tanks. The 3rd Infantry Division had heavy going and its losses had been severe, but it was on the first day's objectives as night came on. But we had inflicted heavy losses upon the enemy and more than 1500 prisoners were in our cages. The attack was going well.

The battle continued during the second day, and our fighter bombers were active over enemy areas. Strong German counterattack against the 45th Infantry Division, as well as against the forces making the main attack, were repulsed with innumerable losses. By nightfall, we were firm on the X-Y Line and Harmon's armor was probing toward Velletri. But remnants of the German garrison in Cisterna were resisting stubbornly, and O'Daniels was preparing to have the 7th Infantry storm the place the following morning. It was clear we were through the main German defenses, so we decided to have the 3rd Division continue into the second phase, and to hold the 36th Division in Corps reserve.

Late that afternoon, I returned to the Command Post at Conca to meet General Clark. He wanted to know whether or not I had considered changing the direction of the attack to the northwest, toward Rome. I replied that it had occurred to me that continuing our attack might alarm the German command to the danger to their line of communications and cause them to concentrate all available reserves in the Valmontone Gap to oppose us. I thought that we should certainly find the Herman Goering Division, which was then en route from northern Italy, in that area; and it was possible that the German command might withdraw the 3rd Panzer Grenadier Division, or the 4th Parachute Division, or both, from the beachhead front, to oppose us there. Any such concentration might delay us at Valmontone long enough to permit the German main forces to escape. If there was any withdrawal from the western part of the beachhead, I thought that an attack to the northwest might be the best way to cut off the enemy withdrawal north of the Alban Hills. My staff was already preparing plans to meet this contingency. Clark agreed with my analysis and asked that I keep the plans up to date.

On May 25th, the 3rd Infantry Division captured Cisterna and pushed on to Cori. A task force from the 1st Armored Division under Colonel Hamilton Howze crossed the valley east of Velletri to the road leading from Cori to Artena and pushed on toward Artena followed by elements of the 3rd Infantry Division. On the right, Frederick's 1st Special Service Force was making its way across the mountains to protect the right flank of the 3rd Infantry Division and to strike the road south of Artena. By the following morning, we would be astride the German Line of withdrawal through Valmontone.

Late that afternoon, I returned to the Command Post feeling rather jubilant—but not for long. Don Brann, the Army G-3, was waiting for me. Brann said: "The Boss wants you to leave the 3rd Infantry Division and the Special Force to block Highway 6 and mount that assault you discussed with him to the northwest as soon as you can." I was dumfounded. I protested that the conditions were not right. There was no evidence of any withdrawal from the western part of the beachhead, nor was there evidence of any concentration in the Valmontone area except light reconnaissance elements of the Herman Goering Division. This was no time to drive to the northwest where the enemy was still strong; we should pour our maximum power into the Valmontone Gap to insure the destruction of the retreating German army. I would not comply with the order without first talking to General Clark in person. Brann informed me that he was not in the beachhead and could not be reached even by radio, and that General Clark ordered the attack to the northwest. There was nothing to do except to begin preparations.

Such was the order that turned the main effort of the beachhead forces from the Valmontone Gap and prevented the destruction of the German X Army.

Our plan was to concentrate the 34th Infantry Division southwest of Velletri, and then move northwest with the 34th and 45th Infantry Divisions abreast to seize the line Lanuvio-Campoleone. While this was under way, we could relieve the 1st Armored Division with the 36th Infantry Division opposite Velletri, then move the 1st Armored Division across the rear of the 34th and 45th Infantry Divisions to the Carano-Padiglione area in readiness to join with the 45th Infantry Division in the drive from Campoleone. Meanwhile, the 3rd Infantry Division, with the 1st Special Service Force and Task Force Howze attached, would block Highway 6 in the vicinity of Valmontone.

This plan necessitated extensive shifts in troop dispositions, assembly of scattered elements of the 34th Infantry Division, on the right of the 45th; relief of the 1st Armored Division south and east of Velletri by the 36th Division; movement of the 1st Armored across the rear of the 34th and 45th Divisions, as well as the supply lines of the 3rd to assembly areas in the Carana-Padiglione area; displacement of practically all of the Corps and Division artillery, and all command posts and communications. Considering the congested area and restricted road net available for these preparations, a more complicated plan

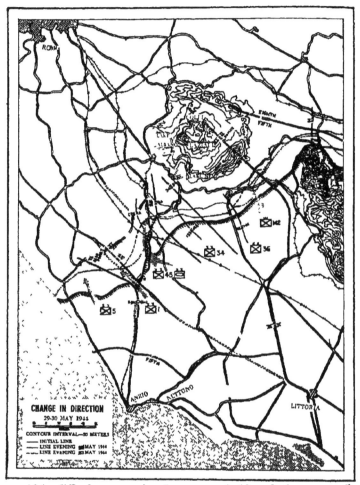

CHANGE IN DIRECTION
29-30 MAY 1944

CONTOUR INTERVAL—50 METERS
—— INITIAL LINE
—— LINE EVENING 29 MAY 1944
---- LINE EVENING 30 MAY 1944

would be difficult to conceive. It was practicable only because staff preparation was thorough and complete and it was carried out by well trained, and disciplined troops; and because enemy capabilities for interference were limited.

Two German divisions, the 3rd Panzer Grenadier Division and the 65th Division, along with elements of the 4th Parachute Division, opposed this drive, which got under way the next afternoon, May 26th. Enemy resistance was stubborn during the next two days, and at nightfall on May 28th, the 34th Division had still not been able to take Lanuvio. Nevertheless, the next morning we attacked northwest through Campoleone with the 45th Infantry Division and Harmon's 1st Armored Division abreast, supported by the whole weight of the Corps artillery. Progress was slow and losses were heavy. In two days we had made only slight advances, the Germans were still intact on our front, and the 34th Infantry Division had still not taken Lanuvio. I decided that we would continue the attack the following day, but would have the 34th Division pass around to the west of Lanuvio. Meanwhile, we would leave the Corps engineers opposite Velletri, and move the 36th Infantry Division up behind the 34th Division to climb the Colli Laziali and encircle Lanuvio from the east.

The morning of May 30th, I discussed this plan with General Walker at his Command Post about midway between Cisterna and Valletri. Walker told me his reconnaissance had just found a gap in the enemy lines east of Velletri through which his engineers were sure troops could reach the crest of Colli Laziali back of Velletri. With some engineer work on the trail, even tanks would be able to accompany the infantry. After talking with the engineer who had made this reconnaissance, I told Walker to go on with the effort and authorized him to use the Corps engineers to assist in preparing the way. This was the turning point in our "drive to the northwest".

By daylight, June 1st, the 143rd Infantry had reached the crest of the Colli Laziali back of Velletri and was advancing westward to cut the road leading from Velletri northward across the hills. The 142nd Infantry had cut the road west of Velletri, and the 141st Infantry was closing in on the town from the south and east. On the Campoleone front, our attack was at a standstill, and we withdrew Harmon's tanks for rest and maintenance in preparation for another effort. During the afternoon, I found Walker on the edge of Velletri directing the final assault which cleared the town. Leaving him with instructions to push on across the Colli Laziali by roads east of Lakes Nemi and Albano, I returned to the Command Post to see what might be done on the other front.

The 85th Infantry Division had now reached the Artena area to reinforce the 3rd Infantry Division; General Keyes II Corps Headquarters had assumed command of operations there. Heavy fighting was reported in the Valmontone sector.

During the next two days, the infantry attack in the Campoleone area made little headway but the advance of the 36th Infantry Division across the Colli Laziali was forging ahead though slowly, and by the afternoon of June 3rd was approaching Lake Albano. Reports now indicated that the Germans were withdrawing from Valmontone and that the II Corps was advancing rapidly along the northern side of the Colli Laziali. I ordered Harmon's tanks back into the action for the final effort to break through Campoleone. That night we received the Army plan allocating sectors for the advance which was to secure the bridges over the Tiber and continue the pursuit beyond.

Chinigo, the correspondent, who had been with the Corps Headquarters since the beginning of the breakout operations, came back to the Command Post at Conca about eleven o'clock that night. He had attended a press conference at the Army Advanced CP at Anzio. There, the correspondents were told that the II Corps would enter Rome the following morning and the Army Commander was going over to join the II Corps to make his triumphal entry into Rome. Chinigo was getting ready to leave when I remarked that if he wanted to be the first correspondent in Rome, he had better stay where he was. Chinigo, no doubt influenced sentimentally by recollections of Palermo and Messina, elected to stay, and he was the only correspondent with the VI Corps on the morning of June 4th.

Our assault in the morning encountered stubborn German rear guard action protecting their flight north. While the 34th and 45th Infantry Divisions cleared out the last resistance around Lanuvio, Genzano, and Albano, Walker's 36th Infantry Division was pushing down the northern slopes of the Colli Laziali, and Harmon's tanks were driving down Highway 7 and a parallel road to the south, all headed for Rome.

Around noon, I made my way down Highway 7 through the all but abandoned villages and past the ruined Roman aqueduct, passing a column of tanks halted on the road. At an intersection on the edge of the city, I found the head of the armored column, as well as one of Walker's regiments. A regiment of the 85th Division came up shortly thereafter, and all had arrived by different roads from the east and southeast.

Walker and a crowd of staff officers were bustling about trying to decide what to do next. He was supposed to have been on another road about a half mile to the east, so I soon had him straight, and on his way. Then I turned to Colonel Hightower who commanded the armored advance and asked if he knew what his orders were. He assured me he was to secure the bridges over the Tiber. I asked: "Well Colonel, what are you waiting for?" He saluted and without a word turned and signaled: "Forward, march," then ran for his own vehicle. There was a grinding of gears, a roar of motors, and clouds of dust and smoke and the column roared off down the street toward the Tiber.

I turned to Chinigo. "Mike, if you want to be the first correspondent in Rome, you had better follow that leading tank." Chinigo climbed into his jeep and disappeared with the column. It was several days before I saw Chinigo again and heard his story. Thinking to make better time when they reached downtown Rome, he had turned off into a parallel street and encountered a column of Germans withdrawing in the direction our troops were moving. After passing the word to Hightower's formation, Chinigo headed for the Excelsior Hotel where he signed the register to show that "Chinigo was there". Finding no other Americans, he visited several other of the principal hotels and repeated the procedure. Early the next morning he made his way out Highway 6 until he reached the press camp where he filed his story and so set off a rush for Rome.

Harmon joined me while I was watching Hightower's column pass. German snipers, who had taken cover in a building near the road junction, opened fire. Although they did no damage, there was a flurry of excitement until we turned a tank platoon aside to work over their places of concealment. This was the last action south of Rome.

Meanwhile, Harmon's other armored column, Combat Command A, had entered Rome from the south. I turned back to my Command Post to get on with the crossing of the Tiber and the pursuit to the north of Rome.

Bridges over the Tiber were seized intact by the 1st Armored Division which began crossing during the night and moving on to the north. South of Rome, the 45th Infantry Division reached the Tiber and the Engineers were hard at work on a partially demolished bridge while Corps engineers were commencing to build a pontoon bridge. The following morning, in the midst of these activities, and just as I was trying to get my scattered Corps in hand again, I received orders to report to General Clark on Capitoline Hill for orders. Neither my Italian-speaking aide, Captain Bartash, nor I had ever been in Rome, and we hadn't the slightest idea where the Capitoline Hill might be. But with Sergeant Barna driving the jeep we set off to find the place. It turned out to be quite an experience.

A few blocks beyond the crossroad where I had stood the previous day, we found the streets filled with people in holiday mood, and flags were breaking out of windows all along the streets. Our jeep, with siren screaming, was slowed to a snail's pace, but with an Italian boy riding the hood to show us the way, we managed to press through crowds tossing flowers, offering glasses and bottles of wine, fruit, bread, and embraces, to arrive at Capitoline Hill. The square was empty, and the buildings seemingly deserted. We wondered if we were in the right place but we were assured by our Italian guide that it was the Capitoline Hill where Mussolini used to stand on the balcony and make his speeches. We thought the conference might be taking place inside, where there were only Italian officials, and clerks, all obviously very much frightened. From one, we learned there were a large number of American cars about the Excelsior Hotel and that the American Commander was thought to be there. So we started off for the Excelsior Hotel. Halfway, we met the official party forcing its way through the ever increasing crowds. Jeep after jeep—Clark, Keyes, Juin, dozens of staff officers, and hundreds of newspaper correspondents and photographers. We turned into the column and followed them to the Capitoline Hill, which we had just left, and which was still deserted, although a few of the natives were beginning to straggle in. We gathered with Clark on the balcony. Bulbs flashed, and correspondents milled about, asking: "How do you feel about capturing Rome," and similar questions. Clark made a speech which began: "This is a great day for the Fifth Army—" And I reckon it was, but I was anxious to get out of this posturing and on with the business of war.

The following morning we learned by radio that the long awaited cross-channel invasion was under way at last. The same day my Command Post moved north of the Tiber.

I had known for some time that I was to command the assault forces in the invasion of southern France which was to take place as soon as naval vessels and craft could be made available from the Normandy landings. The original plan was that General Clark was to command the Seventh Army for this invasion and that it was to consist of my VI Corps and a French Corps. Recently, it had been decided that General Clark was to remain with the Fifth Army in Italy. I had selected the 3rd Infantry Division, and the 45th and 36th Infantry Divisions for this assault. The arrangement now was for the IV Corps to relieve the VI Corps as soon after the capture of Rome as possible. On June 7th, General Clark informed me that the relief would take place at noon on June 11th.

Meanwhile, we had continued the pursuit north of Rome, with the 34th Infantry Division and the 1st Armored Division carrying the burden in our sector. We pushed on past Civitavecchia, where we captured the "Anzio Express" that had caused us so much trouble. two huge railway guns, 280 mm caliber, 65 feet in length, firing a projectile that weighed nearly 700 pounds. Our airplanes had destroyed bridges and prevented the Germans from withdrawing them.

Major General Willis D. Crittenberger and his Corps staff arrived on June 10th and were briefed. That afternoon I journeyed along Highway 7 to our farthest point of advance—a destroyed bridge where troops were waiting for engineers to make ready a by-pass. There at marker 136, 85 miles north of Rome, I bade good-bye to the Italian campaign—or so I thought.

It had been an adventurous nine months.

CHAPTER SEVEN

THE INVASION OF SOUTHERN FRANCE

1. *ANVIL Planning Problems*

At first light on the morning of August 15th, 1944, huge formations of transport and fighter aircraft passed over the coast of southern France and released clouds of parachutes and gliders into the dim valleys below. Almost simultaneously, hundreds of heavy, medium and fighter bombers were blasting the beaches and coast defenses along a twenty-five mile strip of coast line east of Toulon. While the debris and smoke thickened the soft morning haze, dozens of war ships offshore opened an intense bombardment of this same terrain, and three veteran American infantry divisions borne in assault landing craft ploughed their way ashore and rolled over the German defenders, to be followed some days later by three French divisions, all transported in the vast armada of more than 1100 ships then deployed off shore. The invasion of Southern France was on. More French divisions were to come after. Less than a month hence, this American Corps and its French comrades had destroyed a German Army, taken more than 100,000 prisoners, liberated all of southern and eastern France, and had joined hands with the Normandy invasion more than 450 miles north of its landing beaches.

This was the secondary attack to assist the cross-channel invasion, OVERLORD. Few secondary attacks in history have achieved such startling results. ANVIL was the code name first given to this operation. It was changed to DRAGOON shortly before the invasion when the name ANVIL had been compromised.

My VI Corps was withdrawn from the campaign in Italy after the capture of Rome to prepare for the invasion of southern France. At the time, I knew little more. During the last days of December, while the Anzio decision was still hanging fire, General Clark had told me that there was to be an invasion of southern France in conjunction with OVERLORD, then planned for the following May, and that General Eisenhower had selected him to command this invasion. The assault would be made by American troops and Clark wanted me to command it. At a later date he told me Seventh Army

Headquarters was to plan the operation and that he was to command both the Seventh and Fifth Armies until after the capture of Rome. General Patton, he said, was still under a cloud from the "slapping incident", but General Eisenhower was taking him to England for a command during the cross-channel invasion.

After the Anzio landing, and about the time that I was placed in command of the Corps, Clark told me General Wilson had recommended to the Combined Chiefs that Clark remain with the Fifth Army in Italy. He did not know what the outcome would be, but he wanted to remain with the Fifth Army until the capture of Rome in any case. Early in March he was relieved of responsibility for planning the invasion of southern France, but I was still to command the assault and would be allowed to select the divisions that were to constitute my corps.

Three days after the capture of Rome, Clark said my Headquarters would be relieved on June 11th, and the troops would be released as required to begin preparations. General Alexander had just recommended to the Combined Chiefs that the VI Corps remain with the Fifth Army in order to clear the Germans from the Italian peninsula and open a road to the Balkans. Clark favored this recommendation although he thought that there was little likelihood it would be approved by our own Chiefs of Staff.

The selection of the 3rd and 45th Infantry Divisions for the proposed assault was an obvious one since they were the most experienced of the American divisions and both of them had had training and experience in landing operations. I designated the 36th Infantry Division as the third element because of its outstanding performance during the action following the breakout from the beachhead. I believed this recent success would erase in large measure the setbacks of Salerno and the Rapido. Having tasted of the bitter cup on two occasions, and having more recently eaten of the fruits of victory, the Division could be expected to equal and keep pace with its more experienced team mates.

My VI Corps Headquarters moved to Rome during the afternoon of June 11th, for what we thought would be a week or ten days' well-earned rest. But on June 15th, the inevitable order came:

Commanding General VI Corps (TRUSCOTT)   Bigot-Anvil

Desired that General and not to exceed five key staff officers report to CG Force 163 Ecole Normale, Algiers, for ANVIL briefing at earliest convenience. Not contemplated that visit exceed three days.

PATCH, to CG VI Corps.

Carleton, Langevin, Harrel, Conway, O'Neill, Wilson (my aide) and I reached Algiers early the next afternoon after a four hour flight in General Joe Cannon's C-47 that took us over Sardinia.

At AFHQ I found Major Generals David G. Barr and Thomas B. Larkin, both old friends. I learned that General Marshall was to arrive in Algiers the following morning, and Barr requested my presence at Maison Blanche when his plane arrived. At Force 163, I met General Patch. After some introductory remarks, we drove out to his villa in the country where I was to be his guest.

It was the first time Patch and I had met. I was fully aware of his fine reputation and knew he was highly esteemed. He was thin and wiry, simple in dress and forthright in manner—obviously keenly intelligent with a dry Scottish humor. His quick and almost jerky speech and movement gave me the impression he was nervous and found some difficulty in expressing himself. Our conversation during the evening concerned our war experiences. Patch had served in the Pacific. He had commanded the division that relieved the Marines on Guadalcanal. He and his staff were new to the European Theater and this was to be their first assault landing operation. This, I think, influenced both of us in our early associations. I had no occasion to change my views about General Patch; I came to regard him highly as a man of outstanding integrity, a courageous and competent leader, and an unselfish comrade-in-arms.

General Marshall was surprised to find me in Algiers. He asked me to accompany him on the half-hour ride from Maison Blanche into town. During the ride he questioned me at great length about my experiences at Anzio and elsewhere, particularly with reference to the performance of our weapons and equipment, and the fighting quality of our American soldiers.

He began the conversation by inquiring whether Clark had mentioned that General Eisenhower had asked for me for the cross-channel assault. I replied that I had heard nothing of it. He went on to say it had been decided I could not be spared from the beachhead command. He regretted it on my account for the assignment in England would have meant an Army command. He felt I should know Eisenhower had asked for me, and be aware that my services at Anzio had been well understood and were fully appreciated. I could only answer that I was perfectly satisfied to do the best I could wherever he thought my services were best employed. I was deeply touched, for there was no call upon General Marshall to tell me this. It was one of those generous and thoughtful things that always distinguished him in his dealings with his subordinates.

All of June 17th at Force 163, my staff talked to various members of Headquarters in search of information. I joined them there in the afternoon. My aide's journal records our reactions:

> Back to Force 163 at 1330 for session on plans.
> Poor briefing at 1600 at which Patch is absent. An acute disappointment to all present. Plans are far behind. VI Corps conclave on porch to discuss lines of action. Decision to tackle AFHQ in A.M.

I had spent two hours or so with General Patch before the briefing. Patch explained that my Corps was to make a three-division assault on beaches east of Toulon, after which the French Corps would land behind us, and they would be followed by three or four additional French divisions as shipping became available. My Corps was to hold the beachhead and to protect the right flank while the French Corps captured Toulon. Then we were to drive westward and capture Mar-

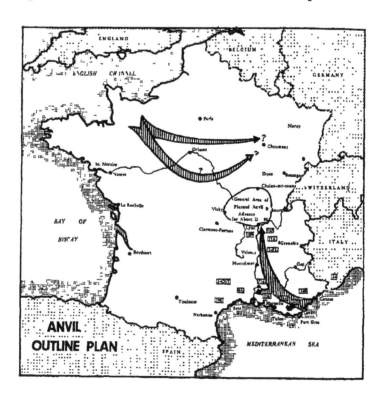

seilles, the primary objective of the assault. His staff was working out the ramifications of the plan.

I described the VI Corps and brought General Patch up to date on the experience and competence of the divisions, the division commanders and their staffs, and my own staff. I explained my own views on assault landings. In particular, I emphasized the importance of undivided command responsibility during the initial phase, the necessity for assembling Army, Navy and Air planners as soon as possible to allow them to work together in developing the detailed plans, the importance of rigorous training, and the necessity for moving our own headquarters to Naples without delay in order to coordinate our preparations. We seemed to be in accord on every detail.

The briefing by Patch's staff on the 17th described the landing areas, summarized the disposition of the enemy in southern France, discussed the outlying beaches, giving reasons for the selection of those designated for our use, and indicated the beachhead objective for three simultaneous division assaults. The troop list was far from complete. There was an estimate of craft which would be needed, but no account of any allocations, neither were there details of Naval or Air support although it was assumed this would be adequate. Administrative and logistical planning was very much behind.

We were provided with original reports and outlines on which the operation had been based, intelligence and terrain studies more up to date, some copies of British ISIS Reports, and a draft of the Army strategy. These were to be used as a basis for our own work. I thought I might learn something more about ANVIL from AFHQ so I decided upon a visit.

Brigadier General Reuben E. Jenkins had been a classmate of mine at the Command and General Staff School and was head of the planning staff at AFHQ. From him I gathered something of the history of ANVIL. Jenkins had been present at the SEXTANT conference, supervised the writing of the original appreciation and outline when the ANVIL decision was made—allegedly by Stalin at the Teheran conference. He had gone on to London and Washington to present the material to the Chiefs of Staff and the Combined Chiefs of Staff respectively.

The outline envisaged an assault by an American Corps of two divisions, or three if shipping was available, assisted by an airborne landing of one Regimental Combat Team, on beaches in the Rade de Hyeres and Cavalaire Bay east of Toulon to establish a beachhead. Beginning about D plus three, two French corps totalling about seven divisions would come ashore. The initial objective was the capture of Toulon and the major port of Marseilles, after which, with the force built up to some ten divisions, exploitation northward toward Lyon and Vichy, to join with General Eisenhower's forces, was to follow.

Jenkins insisted that a US Army should control the landing and subsequent operations until the juncture with General Eisenhower's forces had been effected, whereupon the US Corps would revert to SHAEF while the French Army took over its two Corps and carried on. Jenkins maintained the French would be insufferable if given command of the US Corps, and opinion at AFHQ was unanimous that the French should not, in any case, be entrusted with the assault landing.

In January AFHQ established Force 163 to carry on ANVIL planning. At the start, the staff comprised members from the Seventh Army who had not accompanied General Patton to England, with some remnants of Force 141 staff that had participated in the HUSKY project. Studies by Force 163 resulted in shifting the assault area eastward to avoid the off shore islands and to utilize better beaches.

For the first two months, no French were brought into the Force 163 staff, though General de Gaulle insisted that, with the invasion of France on, French troops could not be employed anywhere but in their own country and that French "honor" demanded that Frenchmen serve only under French command. He even suggested they be given command of the entire ANVIL undertaking. When this was refused they held out for a deputy commander on the AFHQ model, but General Clark, who was then commanding Force 163 as well as the Fifth Army in Italy, refused to accept one. When General Patch took over in March, however, it was decided to integrate a French staff on the opposite-number system throughout all sections. The fact that the French had seven of the ten divisions involved, coupled with General de Gaulle's complete ascendancy, weighed heavily in all discussions of command during the rest of the planning period. Colonel Conway of my staff, who was then a member of Jenkins' group, held that de Gaulle was appeased only by the promise to infiltrate a French armored division into France over the Normandy beachhead—which, incidentally, was kept, for Le Clerc's 2nd Armored Division participated in the liberation of Paris and the drive across his homeland.

When General Patch joined Force 163 early in March, he brought with him key members of his IV Corps staff. OVERLORD had now been postponed until about the first of June. Planning continued on the assumption that the ANVIL forces would invade southern France in conjunction with the Normandy invasion. While no troops could be assigned until the situation in Italy was clear, Force 163 made ready to submit the outline plans to General Wilson, the Supreme Allied Command Mediterranean (SACMED), for approval on March 29th. Shortly before, however, General Wilson announced that Naval and other resources would not permit the launching of ANVIL before late July. But at the end of May General Wilson was advised by the Combined Chiefs of Staff that ANVIL would have priority over all operations outside of Italy, and it was then that my VI Corps Headquarters was withdrawn from the Italian campaign.

Yet, it was still not certain that ANVIL would take place as arranged. Both General Alexander and General Wilson believed the delay in launching ANVIL would prevent it from directly assisting OVERLORD. They were urging the Combined Chiefs of Staff to continue the pursuit to clear the Germans from Italy, and to utilize the ANVIL resources later in a landing operation in the northern part of the Adriatic for a drive into southern Hungary. But General Eisenhower stood out for ANVIL, saying that he required the port of Marseilles and that he did not believe the Allied resources were sufficient to maintain two major theaters inside the European theater, both with decisive missions. General Eisenhower won the argument.

Major General Thomas B. Larkin, with whom I had been associated in TORCH planning in London, was now commanding the Service of Supply, NATOUSA, and was responsible for stocking the supplies for ANVIL. Practically all of a ninety-day reserve and maintenance supply for the ten-division ANVIL force had to come from the United States, which took months to assemble.

However, the requisitions, based at this early stage on close approximation, had been made, and supplies were either piling up in depots, being loaded, or on the high seas. My talks with Larkin were reassuring.

General Patch and I attended a demonstration at Salerno on June 20th, planned for the Navy to show some of the support techniques which had been used in Normandy and which would be available to support our daylight assault. My aide's journal recorded this:

> Board LCT at Salerno and sail down to beaches. On board Admirals Hewitt, Lowry, Rogers; Gens. Patch, Truscott, O'Daniels, Wilson, Wolfe, etc; Colonels, Captains, etc. Opportunity for considerable conversation between events of demonstration. Beach bombing by 12 B-26's shore bombardment by Brooklyn and two DD's, lunch aboard. Whoofus Apex 40,000 lbs. TNT, rockets, landings after each event in knee deep water. DUKW all the way in to airport with Gen. O'Daniels, and home late by Cub again. Late supper and long bull session.

I had been associated with Admiral Hewitt in the TORCH and HUSKY operations, and we held similar views about the conduct and supervision of them. Lowry and Rogers were to command the Naval sub task forces for the 3rd and 45th Infantry Division assaults. Admiral Moon had not yet arrived from England, where he had supported the Normandy invasion. Lowry, of course, had landed my division at

Anzio, and the "considerable conversation" to which my aide refers was related to it.

Admiral Hewitt, General Patch, and I reviewed the subject in detail. Once more I emphasized the importance of undivided command responsibility during the assault phase, the necessity for assembling Army, Navy and Air Force planners as soon as possible, the importance of rigorous training founded on actual operational plans, and the necessity for both Admiral Hewitt and General Patch moving to Naples without delay to facilitate and integrate our preparations. That afternoon, we were in accord on every detail, and I undertook to establish headquarters in Naples.

The next day, Carleton selected the location, and within forty-eight hours the Corps Planning Staff was established. Carleton had picked out a former Italian barracks, not far from the water-front in downtown Naples, which had recently been used as a rest center for the American troops. The "Block House" was a huge quadrangle with an interior courtyard, surrounded by a high wall in which there were only two entrance gates. Inside, two floors provided ample office space for the Army, Navy, and Air Force staffs, in addition to living accomodations for some officers and all of the enlisted personnel. Security was relatively simple, and the arrangement almost an ideal one for a headquarters. The Corps HQ, except for the Planning Staff, was established at Bagnoli, a suburb on the outskirts of the city.

By June 26th, we had drafted a tentative plan for the landing. I sent off this message to General Patch:

> After a study of the outline plans and knowing the characteristics of the three divisions assigned to me, I have decided to employ them from left to right as follows: 3rd Division on beaches south of 262; 45 Division in center on beaches south of Argens River; 36 Division on beaches north of Argens River. This does not conform with certain information that has reached me through Naval sources that Naval plans are based upon a slightly different arrangement. Also I believe that to be successful assault units each Division must be mounted in LSTs and not more than one regiment from each division combat loaded on AP ships. Admiral Lowry informs me that this is entirely practicable. Believe Naval plan loading one entire division on AP ships will jeopardize assault in this situation. Urgently request your concurrence my basic plan so that training here can go on along that line.

That same afternoon a revised plan arrived from Force 163 with an accompanying letter from General White addressed to Carleton. These letters and the changes in the Army plan were disturbing. General Patch wrote:

My dear Truscott:

   Attached is a tentative Army ANVIL plan. It has not as yet had the approval of the Supreme Allied Commander, and therefore is subject to change. However, it will at least give you and your staff a basis for planning.

Admiral Hewitt is anxious to learn the dispositions of your divisions under your plan in order that he can assign his Naval Sub Task Force Commanders and place them in contact with the Division with whom they are to operate. While I do not wish to hamper you in any way, it is essential from a Naval point of view that the 45th (ship to shore) Division attacks in the center. Further, we have assumed for planning purposes that you will probably place the 3rd Division on the right, since that is the hardest task and the enemy defenses are strongest in that area.

Please submit any changes you may wish to suggest as early as convenient and feel utterly free to comment.

General White's letter was more disturbing. He wrote:

The Navy will not have a planning staff at Corps level.
Their command echelon corresponds to Army and Division.
However, the Navy now plans to have a planning staff arrive in Naples about July 10 and are prepared to coordinate closely on all matters of mutual concern.

It is now planned that Special Service Force and the Airborne force will operate directly under Army. You will be kept fully informed of their plans as they develop. Planners from the Twelfth Tactical Air Command will be made available to you as soon as MATAF has completed their preliminary planning.

The new Army plan prescribed a new beachhead line which was far beyond the capability of the three assault divisions to gain and hold, should they encounter heavy opposition. It also contained several other features I did not consider sound. Furthermore, it left the command authority for the assault in a most uncertain and confused state. The following day I sent off a long letter to General Patch indicating my fears that an indeterminate command relationship during the assault phase might jeopardize the operation, and listed my objections to parts of the revised Army plan. In connection with command relationships, I wrote:

As I see it, this assault is a one-Corps assault. The planning and command of of the assault troops should be vested in the assault force commander. Naturally, the Army commander should exercise any control he desires, but this should be exercised through the assault force commander. It is, in my opinion, absolutely essential that Army and Navy assault force commanders be aboard the same ship during the assault operation, otherwise, the Army assault commander will be merely a spectator. He can exercise no influence on the conduct of the operation. Since the detailed planning must be done on Corps level, it seems perfectly obvious to me that there should be a Naval component to coordinate in all matters involving this assault, which, in its early stages, is largely of Naval concern. In my opinion, that Naval planning staff should be here now.

There is a parallel here in the command organization to that which existed at Salerno. The Army commander in that operation actually exercised command of the assault divisions. I was informed by the then Commanding General VI Corps that his skeletonized Headquarters was brought along on the operation to be landed later and to assume command after the beachhead had been established He was landed earlier without communications or transportation and placed in command. I have no doubt that much of the difficulty that attended the Salerno landing was due to the confused command organization during the assault phase. I sincerely hope that we will not repeat that mistake.

I went on to comment on five specific features of the Army's tentative plan. I did not concur in the Army plan to land the 1st Special Service Force on the off shore islands immediately after dark on the night before the assault, because it would alert the entire coast and obviously bring about a stronger reaction to our landing. Moreover, I thought that this mission might require more than the 1,200 officers and men allotted. I agreed that the Airborne Force should land under Army Control and pass to Corps Control when contact was made on shore, but pointed out that Airborne planners should work with the Corps and division staffs. I pointed out the extension of the beachhead line in the Army plan ran the grave risk of repeating the error of Anzio. We would be so extended that we would not be able to mass sufficient strength for the advance to the west, which was the primary purpose of the operation. I objected to landing the 45th Infantry Division astride the Golfe de St. Tropez since that placed the portion of the command landing on the western beach almost a day behind the remainder of the division, and greatly complicated communications. I was in entire disagreement with the Navy plan to allocate all XAP's to the 45th Infantry Division for a ship-to-shore assault.

This letter was obviously none too well received at Army Headquarters for it brought forth a prompt response from General Patch on June 28th:

Sixth Corps
Attention Major General Truscott

Evident that you have not made detailed study of problem reference your radio message and letter June 27. Urgent that you and selected planning officers your staff including artillery officer report this headquarters without delay. Not practicable for my staff to arrive there earlier than planned.

(Signed) PATCH

My aide's journal for Friday, June 29th records our second trip to Algiers.

> Party to Force Hq at 0830. General spends morning with General Patch, emerging with complete agreement on all points in plan and letter, except for control of 1st SSF. Navy Force evidently misconstrued plans as outlined, but now in complete agreement. Beach briefing in war Room. Intelligence reports only two beaches with underwater obstacles. Otherwise no new dope. General to St. George at 1500 for meeting with Adm. Hewitt. Navy points ironed out except for planning Hq and move to Naples. Agree to splitting XAPS with three divisions. Also see Adm. Moon, just in from UK, and Gen. Rooks. Short conference with Gen. Patch. Army and Navy seem to be getting together better. Back to villa for cocktails and General dines with Gen. Rooks.

We returned to Naples the following day in much better spirits than when we had come. While I had not been able to have all of the planning headquarters assembled in Naples as soon as we would have liked, we had obtained agreement upon all other essential items. Moreover, we had cleared the atmosphere and had a firm basis for mutual understanding.

Our plans were based upon a thorough knowledge of terrain and beaches in southern France, particularly of the assault area, and on an unusually complete intelligence concerning enemy strength and dispositions. Not even the Normandy invasion had better advance information. Basic intelligence as represented by the British ISIS and similar studies was as complete and detailed as for any area in the world. Superior maps were available. Aerial reconnaissance was continuous and there was no dearth of expert photographic interpreters. And the French underground, the Maquis, in continuous communication with AFHQ in Algiers, kept us informed of every German movement and change in disposition.

About twenty miles west of Cannes—often regarded as the most select spot on the beautiful Cote d' Azur—lies the town of Frejus where Napoleon landed from Elba to begin his last one hundred days as Emperor of the French. The ANVIL invasion area extended from Theoule sur Mer, midway between Cannes and Frejus, southwest to Cap Benat, sixteen miles east of Toulon. The Argens River, which empties into the sea a few miles south of Frejus, and the Golfe de St. Tropez, a dozen miles to the southwest, divided the assault area into approximately three equal sectors.

The coast here is rugged with huge red rocks, rather wildly beautiful, but there are occasional sandy beaches which were suitable for our purposes. Beaches were numbered and those selected in the eastern sector were: 264B, a small beach near Agay a few miles east of Frejus, and

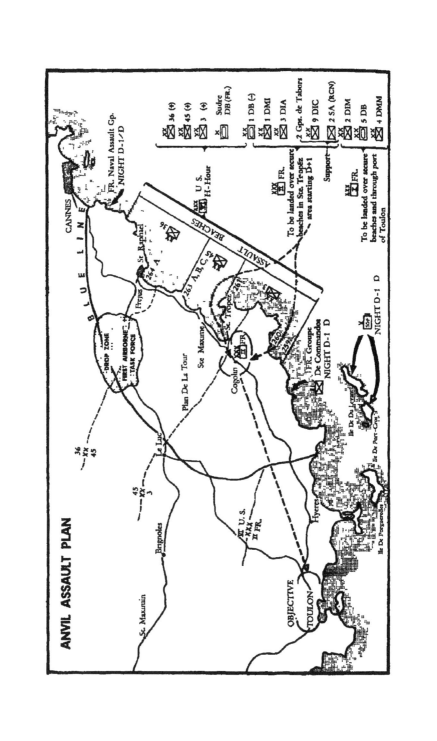

ANVIL ASSAULT PLAN

264A, a long sandy beach immediately south of Frejus; in the central sector, three small beaches, 263 A, B and C, near St. Maxime in the Golfe de St. Tropez; and in the western sector, 259 in Cavalaire Bay, and 261 on the peninsula of St. Tropez and immediately south of the town.

Inland, the hills of the Esterel, to the east of the Argens River, and the rugged Chaines des Maures, to the west, rose steeply behind the shore to a height of nearly 2,000 feet, parallel to the coast. They were heavily forested with maritime pines and cork oaks, with vineyards and cultivated fields in the valleys and along the lower slopes. Across these ranges there were two principal roads, the Route Napoleon in the Argens River Valley from Frejus to Le Muy, and a steeper one leading from Cogolin at the head of the Golfe de St. Tropez to Le Luc and Vidauban. There were several other unimproved mountain roads which troops could use. An excellent road followed the coast line from Cannes westward to Toulon and Marseilles. Another left the Route Napoleon at Le Muy and continued westward through Le Luc, Brignolles, and Aix en Provence to Avignon on the Rhone.

When we began preparing for ANVIL, German Naval power in the Mediterranean had been reduced to a single destroyer, a dozen escort vessels, some twenty MAS boats (submarine chasers), and a dozen submarines, which were capable of harassing Allied shipping, but posed no real threat to the ANVIL operation. Nor was the Luftwaffe much better off, for Allied air power dominated the skies over France and Italy. However, the Luftwaffe did have bases in the western Mediterranean region, with 110 long range bombers, 25 bomber reconnaissance aircraft, and 120 fighters and fighter bombers. While these aircraft were primarily intended for attacking Allied shipping in the Mediterranean, they posed a real threat to any attack force, a danger that could be increased by transfer of additional aircraft from Italy or from northern France.

In outline, the Army plan provided for a daylight assault on the coast of southern France to establish a beachhead, leading to the capture of Toulon. The night before the landing, the 1st Special Service Force was to clear enemy coastal batteries from the islands of Port Cros and Levant, and a French Commando was to destroy an enemy coastal battery at Cap Negre west of Cavalaire Bay so that shipping could approach the beaches. Also, a French Naval demolition party was to block the roads leading from Cannes toward the landing area. Then, at first light, about 0400, the Airborne Task Force, a provisional division of American and British airborne troops, was to land in the vicinity of Le Muy to assist the landing forces by attacking the defenses about Frejus from the rear. At 0800, following a massive Air and Naval bombardment, the VI Corps would land with three divisions abreast to establish the beachhead. Once this was done, the French Corps would come ashore, pass through our left flank, whereupon both Corps would advance westward to capture Toulon and Marseilles.

The German XIX Army with headquarters in Avignon was responsible for the enemy's defense of southern France. Deployed along the coast and at strategic points in the interior, it had a total of twelve divisions at its disposal. After the cross-channel invasion on June 6th, three divisions were sent from the Mediterranean coast to join the fighting in Normandy. They were replaced by two divisions which had suffered heavily in early fighting and needed time for rest and refitting. In the early part of July, when we began intensive planning, the XIX Army consisted of two Panzer divisions, nine infantry divisions, and a large number of coastal defense units, battle groups, and separate battalions. By the end of July, most of the 9th Panzer Division was sent to northern France, but it was replaced by the 11th Panzer Division from the Bordeaux area, which was in movement toward Lyon on the day we landed.

These German divisions varied in strength and combat efficiency. The 157th Reserve Division and the 148th Infantry Division were rated as first class. The 242nd and 244th Infantry Divisions were known to be about 15 per cent under strength in personnel and equipment, but they were thought to be good combat divisions. West of the Rhone were two veteran divisions, but reduced in strength.

German defenses made wide use of artillery, including coastal defense guns, railway artillery, French and Italian Naval guns, medium and light field artillery, self-propelled guns and tanks. All beaches were mined, and obstructions were protected by machine guns, self-propelled guns and tanks. Intelligence showed underwater obstacles on three of the assault beaches and indicated that the Germans were expanding these measures as rapidly as possible. Their defenses, however, were not organized in depth. It seemed to me the enemy would probably follow the tactics which Kesselring had found effective against our landing at Anzio: delay the landing forces and gain time to assemble reserves for counterattack when our main effort could be determined.

In the invasion area we expected to find at least 10 infantry battalions, 50 tanks, 84 fixed coast defense guns and 14 self-propelled guns immediately available to oppose us. We estimated that the enemy could confront us with at least a division and a half, on D Day, more than two divisions by the morning of D plus 1, more than three divisions on D plus 3 including half of a Panzer division with 80 or more tanks, more than five divisions on D plus 4 including an entire Panzer division with some 200 tanks. We expected the enemy to counterattack locally with whatever forces were available, but we did not envision a major blow to fall until the enemy could concentrate a material superiority of force. Our aim was to prevent his ever attaining that degree of force.

My instructions were contained in a directive from General Patch; which was confirmed in final form on July 18th. The relevant portions read:

2. The VI Corps has been selected as the assault corps for Operation AN-VIL. Under the direction of this Headquarters you will be responsible for planning and executing the assault on the mainland with the forces placed at your disposal, and will supervise the equipping, training, and mounting of such forces.

3. The units under your command are listed in Annex #2 to ANVIL Outline Plan.

4. *a.* Shipping and craft are allotted to you on the basis of an assault with an immediate follow-up of an armored combat command.

b. The II French Corps has been allotted shipping to provide for landing the equivalent of two divisions in the beachhead, starting on D plus 1 as soon as beaches are made available to them by the assault force.

5. *a.* The Eighth Amphibious Force has been designated to conduct the amphibious portion of training for the operation.

b. The Invasion Training Center has been attached to the VI Corps for the period of your training.

c. In your planning and training, consideration must be given to the following:

(1) That the assault will be made in daylight.

(2) That officers and men travel light, and vehicles and equipment are reduced to the minimum.

(3) That the maintenance of your force will have to be continued indefinitely over beaches and through small ports.

d. A final exercise will be conducted on or about D minus 10 for assault divisions in which Army, Navy, and Air Forces will participate in as realistic a manner as time and facilities will permit.

In such a daylight assault supported by a massive Air and Naval bombardment, our first aim was to land the three infantry divisions in the greatest possible strength and in the shortest possible period of time to overwhelm the German defenses before resistance could become effective. Our next endeavor was to land the essential supporting weapons, fighting vehicles and supplies as rapidly as possible to permit early reorganization of the Corps for the advance to the northwest. Since the LST's were the quickest and most effective way of landing assault troops with supporting weapons, vehicles and supplies, I wanted to use them to land the echelons of each division. We chose a Corps Beachhead Line—the Blue Line, we called it in orders—just far enough inland to protect our beaches from enemy artillery fire and to give us control of the northern exits from the coastal ranges, leading into the Argens River valley.

Frejus was a critical area. Our best route inland followed the Argens River valley northwest from Frejus. Our fighter aircraft would fly from Corsica and Sardinia until we had captured and cleared the airfield at Frejus, the only airfield within the locality. The beach and port of Frejus were of vital importance for maintenance of the Army. It was also the most heavily fortified and defended region. The Provisional Airborne Division was to be dropped in the vicinity of Le Muy to assist in capturing Frejus by attacking the defenders in the rear. At first we contemplated a direct assault at H Hour on Beach 264A at Frejus but it became increasingly clear the attacking force would be exposed to enfilade fire from its right flank during the last several miles of its approach, which would almost certainly result in heavy casualties and might even jeopardize the whole operation. Yet it was vitally necessary the beach be cleared, and Frejus and the airport captured on D Day; this could not be accomplished by troops landed on any other available beaches. Accordingly, we decided to land over the Agay beaches, the 141st RCT of the 36th Division to clear resistance and protect the right flank. This would be followed without delay by the 143rd RCT which would free the area toward St. Raphael and attack Frejus from the south and east. At H plus 6 hours, the 142nd RCT was to assault Beach 264A at Frejus following a massive Air and Naval bombardment. By dark, the enemy would be eliminated so that weapons, vehicles and supplies could roll ashore, with the port and airfield in our hands.

The 45th Infantry Division in the center would land with the 180th and 157th RCT abreast on the beaches east of St. Maxime, the first with two battalions in assault, the other with one, and with the remainder in Regimental reserve. Their orders were to clear the beach area, seize the high ground overlooking the Argens River, assist the 36th Division in clearing Beach 264A, and advance rapidly to Blue Line to gain contact with the Provisional Airborne Division. The 179th RCT was to disembark promptly behind the assault echelon, but was not to be employed without Corps authority.

On the left, the 3rd Infantry Division would go ashore with two regiments abreast, the 15th and 7th RCT, the 15th with one battalion in the assault wave, the 7th RCT with two. The 30th RCT in reserve was to land immediately behind the 15th RCT over Beach 261. This Division was to destroy enemy resistance on the beach, capture St. Tropez, drive to the Blue Line within its sector, and protect the left flank of the Corps.

Combat Command 1, 1st Armored Division (French), which we called CC Sudre after its commander, was attached to the Corps. I hoped to land it over at Frejus as soon as Beach 264A was neutralized. CC Sudre was to assemble in that vicinity prepared for offensive action to the northwest. I thought there might be an opportunity for an armored drive northward along the Route Napoleon; if not, there would be need for the armor in the western drive to Toulon and Marseilles.

To each division was attached a tank battalion, a tank destroyer battalion, three antiaircraft and artillery battalions, a barrage balloon battery, and three battalions of corps artillery, as well as a long list of engineers, hospitals, supply and maintenance troops. Each division would reorganize on the Blue Line and the advance from there would begin on Corps order.

Such, in broad outline, was the plan as it finally evolved, and—with one exception, which I will mention later on—as it was ultimately carried out. But its evolution was by no means easy. Many problems and misunderstandings were to plague us before all was resolved and agreed upon.

The 3rd Infantry Division moved to Pozzuoli, where we had trained for Anzio, on June 19th. Three days later the 45th Infantry Division reached Salerno where it was to go through its paces at the Invasion Training Center. On July 4th, the 36th Infantry Division returned to its first battlefield on the Paestum beaches at Salerno, where the Division had landed, and where it would be adjacent to the Invasion Training Center for exercises. June 27th, Corps and Division planning staffs were established in the Block House. Admiral Lowry's men joined the 3rd Division planners there on June 28th, and two days later, Admirals Moon and Rodgers and their staffs joined those of the 45th and 36th Divisions. It was an ideal arrangement for joint representation, particularly after the arrival of Seventh Army Headquarters in Naples on July 11th, Admiral Hewitt's Headquarters on the following day, and Air planners some days later.

Almost at once we found that the troop lists furnished by Force 163 contained some units we did not need and omitted others we did need. After it had been analyzed, I submitted a revised list to General Patch with specific requests for additional units we considered essential. After

General Patch's approval AFHQ promptly made these units available. The first few weeks our arrangements were in a constant state of flux, each change complicating our loading allocations.

ANVIL was based on the assumption that its forces would be supplied and maintained over beaches until the capture of Toulon, which we thought might be about D plus 20. The beach groups were attached to the VI Corps and were to be responsible for the beach organization and maintenance during the assault phase—that is, until the beachhead was established and the Seventh Army Headquarters could assume its normal responsibility for supply. A beach group, in our plans, was essentially an engineer regiment with attachments of service troops and Naval personnel especially trained to organize beaches, facilitate the landing and movement of personnel, supplies, equipment and vehicles, unload cargo ships, establish and operate supply dumps, evacuate casualties and prisoners of war, and similar functions. One beach group battalion lands with each RCT; a beach group organizes the beach maintenance area for a division landing.

Over-the-beach maintenance was largely a theoretical subject with the Army planners, whereas Colonel E. J. O'Neill and other members of my staff had not only theoretical knowledge but also a vast background of practical experience in Africa, Sicily, Salerno, and most recently over an extended period at Anzio. We had found in practice that we had always been able to handle more supplies over beaches than had ever been contemplated. We urged the use of beaches near St. Maxime for a maintenance center. We were not able to convince the Army planners, nor when I appealed to General Patch on July 11th, was I able to persuade him. General Patch agreed to my landing the 45th Infantry Division over beaches 263 A, B and C; otherwise he demurred on the supply problem. That same day he sent me a memorandum of which the second paragraph outlined a complicated program for disembarking the beach battalions in the 45th Infantry Division area, and assembling them around Cogolin to develop a supply depot for that division. It called for an intricate loading and landing arrangement for the 3rd and 45th Infantry Divisions, which events were to prove unnecessary, for the beaches around St. Maxime turned out to be far better than we had hoped, and much of the command was actually unloaded over them.

After an encouraging letter from Brigadier-General Gordon P. Saville of the Twelfth Tactical Air Command, we were hopeful of obtaining close air support based in part on the use of forward controllers on the ground, and observers in cub airplanes. But we could never obtain agreement from the Air planners that this was a practical approach. Accordingly, our Air support plan was based upon previous procedures, where the experience of the Corps staff with Air support at Anzio stood us in good stead.

Overall Air support provided for continuous large-scale bombing of targets in southern France for more than thirty-five days preceeding the actual invasion. There was to be an intensive bombing of the Marseilles area shortly before D Day to lead the Germans into believing the assault might fall there. The pre-D Day air program was the responsibility of the Seventh Army and Headquarters Mediterranean Allied Air Forces. We applied ourselves to the Air and Naval gunfire support plans for the D Day assault, and the Air program to assist our operations thereafter.

After careful study and analysis, every possible target in the invasion area was listed, and complete data, including photographs, were prepared for each one. The combined forces determined which targets would be dealt with by air attack, by naval gunfire, or by both.

The final air offensive provided for bombing attacks beginning at first light on D Day and continuing until thirty minutes before H Hour (0800), the time of landing, by more than 300 fighter bombers in flights of 4, 6, or 8, on more than 72 targets in, or adjacent to, the division assault areas. At H minus 30, 450 medium and heavy bombers were to blast the landing beaches—40 heavy bombers, or 120 medium bombers, to each 1,000 yards of beach, using 500- and 100-pound fragmentation and incendiary bombs. At H Hour—long enough after the bombing for dust and smoke to settle and permit observation of fire—battle ships, cruisers and destroyers would blast the beaches as the landing flotillas approached. Fighter bombers would be overhead at H Hour, and all through the landing, to attack enemy guns that might still be firing. Others would range inland on armed reconnaissance to attack troops that might be moving toward the assault areas or bridges and other defiles to interrupt such movements. To insure coordination, areas recognizable from the air were designated within which no air attack was permitted except on pre-briefed or controlled missions. Sixteen Navy dive bombers and a like number of fighter bombers would be on call on carriers and bases.

All details of Air and Naval gunfire support were completed and approved by the end of July.

Early in July, Frederick—recently promoted to Major General—was relieved from command of the 1st Special Service Force, and assigned to organize and command the Provisional Airborne Division which comprised the British 2nd Independent Parachute Brigade, the 517th and 551st Parachute Infantry Regiments, the 509th Parachute Infantry Battalions, the 550th Glider Infantry Battalion, the 460th and 463rd Parachute Field Artillery Battalions, the 602nd Glider Pack

Howitzer Battalion, and a number of service troops attached from Army elements. All these contingents had to receive airborne training in the limited time available. This force, trained on airfields near Lido di Roma not far from Rome, was transported in 535 C-47's and C-53's, and 465 gliders of the Provisional Troop Carrier Wing, commanded by my old friend Brigadier General P. L. Williams.

We went over all details of the Corps assault plan with Frederick, and from them he developed his plans for the airborne mission which was to be dropped in the Argens valley near Le Muy to block roads leading toward the beachhead and then to attack the defenses of Frejus from the rear. The troops were to parachute into three drop zones at first light about 0430 and eliminate resistance before the glider-borne troops were brought in on scheduled flights beginning about 0930.

Frederick's feat in organizing and training this composite force and perfecting the operation within a period of less than one month is one of the remarkable exploits of the war. It was one of the most successful airborne drops.

We had begun to devise a training program while we were in Rome, immediately after we were withdrawn from the Italian campaign. On our return from our first visit to Algiers we issued two letters of instruction. The first outlined the scope of individual and unit training objectives and methods, and emphasized physical and psychological preparation with special reference to speed marching and individual combat, as a way of attaining it; a thorough working knowledge of all weapons; a thorough acquaintanceship with the techniques of combat; an understanding of life under combat conditions; and the development of leadership in all ranks. The second directive dealt with the utilization of the Invasion Training Center.

This Center, which General O'Daniels had organized under the Fifth Army at Port aux Poules and where the 3rd Infantry Division had begun its assault training for Sicily, had been moved to Salerno and attached to the VI Corps. The time element was such that we were able to use the facilities of the ITC for only the 45th and 36th Infantry Divisions, which trained there between June 27th and July 22nd. The 3rd Infantry Division, far more experienced in amphibious operations, conducted its own exercises at Pozzuoli between June 24th and July 14th.

The ITC, commanded by Brigadier General Henry C. Wolfe, was composed of a staff with special engineer troops and equipment for amphibious training. A special Naval staff cooperated with their opposite members of the staff throughout. Here troops familiarized themselves with all types of shipping, landing craft, and special vehicles. They were thoroughly instructed in the techniques of loading and unloading personnel and vehicles, and the tactics of beach assault. Troops were drilled in mock-ups on dry land, witnessed demonstrations by experienced troops, and then participated in actual landing exercises by platoon, company and battalion. Artillery units were trained in loading and unloading artillery pieces from DUKW's, in firing from DUKW's both on land and water, and in using DUKW's as prime movers until artillery vehicles could come ashore.

The ITC conducted special courses to assist the divisions. There were waterproofing schools to teach the art of waterproofing vehicles to permit landing in water much deeper than wading depth; "obstacle gapping" to teach infantry assault waves methods of clearing beach obstacles by pole charges and bangalore torpedoes, and the employment of armored "gapping" teams for breaching walls, bridging anti-tank ditches and the like, and training in the employment of DD tanks. The DD (Duplex Drive) was a system of floating medium tanks with a canvas screen attached to the hull which could be raised and held in place mechanically. When raised, it floated the tank. In the water, the tank was driven by a propeller powered by a standard truck transmission attached to the sprocket hub. For use in assault landings, DD tanks entered the water from an LCT with a specially designed ramp extension. The DD flotation equipment was extremely vulnerable to fire, mines, and underwater obstacles. Crews were provided with and trained in the use of Momsen lungs used by crews to escape from sunken submarines. Each division actually employed about one company of DD tanks in the assault.

The graduation exercise in the training of each division was a full-scale rehearsal planned to simulate actual conditions in every possible instance. The 3rd Infantry Division had theirs on July 31st, and the 36th and 45th Infantry Divisions on August 7th.

We constructed obstacles similar to those which intelligence indicated we could expect, and used every aid to reproduce battle conditions and to make the rehearsals entirely realistic: live ammunition, naval gunfire with reduced charges, rockets, bangalore torpedoes, mines with simulated charges, smoke, and the like. "Gapping" teams cleared paths through obstacles. Beach groups organized beaches, and sufficient vehicles were unloaded to test our plans. Few divisions have ever been better prepared for the task which lay ahead when we had done with our invasion training.

On July 5th, soon after we had published the tentative Corps assault plan, Brigadier General Sudre, who commanded the attached 1st Combat Command of the 1st Armored Division (French), called upon me to discuss the employment of his command, the CC Sudre, which was stationed in North Africa not far from Port aux Poules. CC Sudre was to be mounted in Oran and join the convoy for landing on D plus 1 following the initial assault.

I discussed with General Sudre our invasion plans and outlined the various missions for which we might wish to employ his command. The Argens River valley was the most suitable terrain for the use of armor. We hoped, therefore, to land the CC Sudre over Beach 264A at Frejus, to surge to the northwest, or drive northward along the Route Napoleon if the assault went as we planned and hoped. Otherwise, it would be utilized to the west to assist in removing the enemy south of the Durance River while the attack on Toulon and Marseilles was underway. General Sudre departed wholly cooperative and most enthusiastic and extended to me an invitation to visit his command near Oran at an early date.

On July 14th, General Sudre sent a staff officer to present his plans for carrying out the missions we had assigned him. This officer also brought an invitation from General du Vigier, Commanding General 1st Armored Division (French), to visit Sudre's command on July 17th. I accepted and, with members of my staff, made arrangements for the visit. My aide's journal reports.

Monday, July 17th, 1944

Family up between 0500 and 0530. Campodichino by 0700 and take-off in C-47 at 0720. Party consists of CG, Aides, CS, Gens Stack and Shepard, Cols Harrel, O'Neill, Johnson, Martin, de Shazo, Lt. Cols Conway, Sladen, Reichman, Asp de Pierres. Land La Senia 1300, met by Gens Sudre and Koenig and staff officers. Party billeted in Grand Hotel, Oran. Conf in Gens room with Gen Koenig on loading and supplying French. Joined by Gen Sudre, Maj. Laurent, Cols Harrel, O'Neill, Conway, C/S. Troop list, loading, maintenance Col O'Neill will relay grievances. 1800 party to 1st DB (Armored Division.) Guard of honor and salutes. Assi ben Okra. Dinner with Gen du Vigier, Gen Sudre and staff officers. Gay affair with usual toasts and speeches. Back to Oran and waffle with C/S and Col Harrel until 2300.

Tuesday, 18 July, 1944

Party up for 0730 breakfast at hotel. 0900 motor to CC1, 1st DB for inspection of brigade. Met by Gens du Vigier and Sudre and staffs. Brigade looks very good indeed. Men alert, and new equipment. Proceed to Div CP in St Cloud for further conference on combat command needs. Luncheon with Gen du Vigier. Present: CG, C/S, Aides, Gens Stack and Shepard, Col Martin, Col Lehr and Maj Johnson. Party to La Senia at 1245. Take off 1330. Gen. Sudre and Lt. Fournier also along. Arrive Naples 1830. Home to villa for drinks and dinner. Bed early.

I had taken along on the trip the Assistant Division Commanders and the Chiefs of Staff and G-3's of both the 3rd and 36th Infantry Divisions, because the contemplated employment of CC Sudre would probably bring the combat command into close relations with one division or the other. Sudre returned with us to "button up" final details, and to obtain the solution to some of his administrative and logistical problems. All went well for the next few days, and French participation seemed to be well in hand.

About half-past ten, the morning of July 20th, Colonel Conway brought a French staff officer who represented General de Lattre du Tassigny in to see me. General de Lattre du Tassigny—who was to command the French Corps landing behind us, subsequently to expand into French Armee B—had just returned to Naples. General de Lattre apologized for the lateness of the invitation, but he hoped that I would have luncheon with him to meet his staff and the division commanders of the French forces. Cancelling a previous engagement, I accepted.

At half-past twelve, Conway and I presented ourselves at the swank villa where General de Lattre resided. There we found a party of about twenty of his staff, and division commanders, to whom we were introduced. Both du Vigier and Sudre were present. De Lattre was a man of about my own age, with thin hair graying around the temples, a square open face with cold eyes, medium height, trim, neat and very soldierly, in appearance. Even his greeting was cold and reserved, wholly lacking in the warmth I had found in previous contacts with Frenchmen such as Juin, du Vigier, Sudre, and others. Both Conway and I were impressed with the stiff and formal air that enshrouded the gathering, for every officer present followed de Lattre's lead.

After introductions aperitifs were served and I endeavored to hold a conversation with de Lattre, Conway acting as interpreter. A few minutes to finish the drink and we sat down to luncheon—a long, stiff affair, typically French in the number of courses and order of serving. American rations were supplemented by fish and fruit obtained locally, and accompanied by an ordinary local Italian red wine. Conversation lagged during the luncheon. Everyone attended to the business of eating, the sounds of mastication dominating the scene. It finally came to a close and we soon learned the reason for the cool reception. De Lattre was in a towering rage, and the Frenchmen present had felt the lash of his tongue before we arrived.

We adjoined to the drawing room where de Lattre launched into a tirade in French directed toward me. As translated by Conway, I found I had violated the normal niceties of military and diplomatic protocol by inspecting one of his units without his permission and without his presence. It was a slight to him and to the honor of France.

But I stopped him. I had no intention of slighting anyone. I was commanding soldiers who were to assist in liberating France. My visit was not only entirely appropriate for inspection of troops that were to serve under my command; it was made at the specific request of the French commanders concerned, and it was essential preparation for the forthcoming operations. If that was all that he had to discuss, we were wasting our time.

De Lattre then proposed to discuss plans with me privately. He, his Chief of Staff, Conway and I adjoined to another room, leaving the group of Frenchmen speechless behind us. The Chief of Staff laid out a map upon a table, and de Lattre began by saying that there were obviously certain misunderstandings that should be eliminated and that he chose to present these directly to me in all frankness knowing that as a soldier I would understand this approach. He went on to outline his conception of the operation. He explained that he and General de Gaulle had consented to the loan of this armored Combat Command to serve under an American command only with the understanding it would be available to him when and where he wanted it and in no case later than D plus 3. De Lattre was indignant that changes had been made in the assault plan without consulting him, specifically in reducing the perimeter of the beachhead line. In general, he would allow me to use the Combat Command subject to these restrictions, but he would want to know in advance what employment I might propose.

I listened to General de Lattre calmly. I described to him the various missions which might fall to the French Combat Command attached to the VI Corps, all of which had been discussed with the French commanders involved. I was perfectly willing for him to know the orders I might issue to the Combat Command during action, but any idea he should review and approve or disapprove them was of course entirely unacceptable. If there was any question as to the status of the French Armored Command attached to the VI Corps, it was a matter for the Army Commander to pass judgment on.

I left General de Lattre, and reported at once to General Patch exactly what had taken place. He was angry because de Lattre had not consulted him about these problems first, and he assured me that I would be free to employ CC Sudre as the situation warranted. He pointed out that so far as the assault was concerned, de Lattre commanded the French II Corps consisting of three French colonial divisions, some Goums, and the 1st Armored Division (less CC Sudre). The Army plan mentioned nothing about CC Sudre reverting to de Lattre's command on D plus 3. On the contrary, it said that CC Sudre would revert to Army reserve when released by VI Corps.

My conversation with de Lattre I reported in writing the following day with my own recommendations.

That should have settled the matter but it did not. Both du Vigier and Sudre were in dutch with de Lattre. That night following my conference with de Lattre, Sudre came to Conway, who described the subject of their conversation:

> General du Vigier and Sudre are strongly behind you. The latter made a point of calling in person last night to apologize for his chief's bad manners. He was as much up in the air as you about the employment of his CCI after D plus 2. But he did protest vehemently against the tirade in which de Lattre chose to plunge over the matter of the inspection. Sudre says that he invited you with du Vigier's concurrence and that's all there is to that. Incidentally, he (Sudre) was pretty well eaten out himself and has been ordered to stay at the Army Commander's villa until this matter is straightened out. He asks that no misunderstanding be allowed to arise between you and him. And he directed me to assure you that if he were privileged to go ashore under your command, you need have no worries or doubts about his doing his job until you released him.
>
> The lack of cooperation between de Lattre and Patch leads me to believe that you should try to get a complete analysis of that whole situation at your earliest convenience. If General Patch won't indicate the trouble, I'm sure General Jenkins would. In any event, you should know about it.

A recommendation I made, for the substitution of an American armored combat command, was turned down as being impracticable for political and other reasons. Nevertheless, the Army staff continued to exhibit undue interest in my plans for employing CC Sudre, and I was never able to obtain any assurance from General Patch as to how long I might be able to retain control over this armored command. General Patch's noncommittal attitude disturbed me. Eventually I came to the conclusion that he was reluctant to admit he was up against an insoluble problem which he hoped would solve itself once the beachhead was established. Since he was either unable or unwilling to pass judgment in favor of the VI Corps before the invasion, I could foresee that once we were ashore in France, political considerations would dominate any decision with respect to CC Sudre and that they were not likely to be propitious to the smooth operations of the VI Corps. Thus, when we had gotten the command ashore and needed it most, it was more than likely it would be removed from my control regardless of the tactical situation of my command.

The Navy used Apex and Drone boats, Reddy Foxes, Naval Demolition Teams, Rocket Craft and Naval gunfire, to remove underwater obstacles and insure the safe delivery of troops ashore, which was their responsibiltiy. The Apex boat was a landing craft which towed two others, called Drones, at an angle behind them, each Drone loaded with ten tons or more of high explosives. At an appropriate time the Apex boats released the Drones and directed them by radio control toward the obstructions and exploded them. Reddy Fox was a Naval version of the bangalore torpedo—a long pipe filled with explosives, towed or pushed into position over the obstacles and exploded. Rocket craft, or Whoofus, as the soldiers called them, were landing vessels equipped with banks of up to 1000 rockets which could be fired in salvos or discharged simultaneously. Naval Demolition Teams were specialists trained in destruction of underwater obstacles by handplaced charges and similar methods.

Intelligence revealed underwater obstructions off at least three of the assault beaches, but there was much conflicting opinion as to the nature of them, and even as to the actual existence of some. Each of the Navy Sub Task Force Commanders had a different solution. I thought we should have reconnaissance to determine whether or not the obstacles did exist, just as Admiral Conolly had done for us on the Licata beaches in Sicily. Accordingly, on August 1st, I sent a memorandum to Admiral Hewitt, to which he replied: " I believe that the menace of underwater obstacles has been somewhat exaggerated." He thought that "studied reports from OVERLORD have lent undue emphasis to a subject new in this theater for the most part." He went on to describe the nature of some of the obstacles as determined from aerial photographs and said that vertical photographic coverage would be continued to the last minute, and he was not in favor of any other preliminary reconnaissance, saying, "I know of no preliminary reconnaissance other than actually running boats through obstacles which will ensure that boats can beach." He was not in favor of using pontoon causeways to ram through underwater obstacles, although he did agree that the LCT's would be used to smash through them, adding, " I believe that LCT's will do the job—coupled with hand demolitions as necessary after the initial waves have landed."

I sent another memorandum:

Without exception every Navy officer with whom I have discussed the subject has expressed the opinion that underwater obstacles constitute a more serious problem for us than was the case in the Channel where the tidal range allowed assault craft to beach and allowed demolition parties to work on dry land. The available information on the nature of the obstacles in our area does not indicate that these obstacles are exceedingly formidable; however, I think we must assume that these obstacles do have the capability of interfering with the approach of landing craft to the beaches to some degree at least, and certainly the accomplishment of the troops' mission on the shore depends upon their reaching the beach.

I went on to point out that both Admiral Lowry and Admiral

Rogers proposed to make an early reconnaissance by speed boat several hours in advance of H Hour if I had no objection and the Admiral approved.

This appeal was more fruitful. The Admiral finally agreed to leave the solution of the problem to his Naval Sub Task Force Commanders in consultation with the assault division commanders.

Our need for armor was vital and would become increasingly important as we expanded the beachhead. Obviously the initial plans should have included an American armored command in the assault corps, but that was now impossible for logistical reasons, even had it been practicable in a political sense. I finally came to the conclusion we would have to improvise an armored combat command to be assured of possessing one after the first few days.

On August 1st, the day after the 3rd Division rehearsal, I called a meeting of my planning staff, informing them of my decision to organize a provisional armored group to be commanded by Brigadier General Fred W. Butler, my assistant Corps commander, and to be designated Task Force Butler. His staff, and essential communications, were to be provided by the Corps Headquarters. The group was to consist of the Corps Cavalry Squadron, the 117th Reconnaissance Squadron, one armored field artillery battalion, one tank battalion less one company, one tank destroyer company, one infantry battalion in motors, an engineer battalion and the necessary service troops. It was to be ready to mass in the vicinity of Le Muy on Corps' order at any time after D Day. Since loading and landing arrangements were already complete and could not be changed—in fact some elements had already loaded—these units were to be taken from those most easily accessible when the time came for the group to assemble. Butler was to form his staff at once, and assisted by the Corps staff, complete the organization plans for three lines of action after assembly of the Force: First, an advance to the Durance River in the vicinity of St. Paul to seize crossings there and to the west; second, an advance to the Durance River at Manosque to seize crossings in that area; and third, an advance to the north toward Grenoble to block roads east of the Rhone in the vicinity of Montelimar.

During the next four days, all facets of organization were completed, and every element included as well as the divisions from which they would be drawn was warned of this possible assignment. While this force lacked the strength of an armored combat command, and it had no opportunity to train together for its mission, we were at least assured we would not be left without some armored contingent should CC Sudre be suddenly removed from my control.

Most of the misunderstandings pertaining to ANVIL planning occured early, before General Patch and Admiral Hewitt moved their headquarters to Naples. Afterwards our relations were very close, misunderstandings rare, and planning proceeded without any major difficulty. Any differences of opinion were always adjusted without rancor or reserve. Few operations of such magnitude have been planned more cooperatively or mounted more efficiently than ANVIL.

During the planning period visitors included King George VI, who reviewed the fleet in the Bay of Naples and for whom Sir Henry Maitland Wilson entertained at a luncheon in the Palace at Caserta attended by all the senior British, French and American commanders in the Italian theater. Secretary Stimson visited us, accompanied by my old friend Major General A. D. Surles. He was greatly reassured over the prospects of ANVIL's success after General Patch and I had spent an evening discussing the operation with him.

On August 1st, the code name ANVIL was changed to DRAGOON by direction of the Combined Chiefs of Staff, since it was feared the name ANVIL had been compromised. As an old cavalryman, I took this change of name to be of good omen.

Final orders—Army, Navy, and Corps—were completed by August 1st, and the Sub Task Force orders were packaged for distribution on board ships and craft—not to be opened until we were well out to sea. This may seem surprising, but no one outside commanders and their staffs knew where we were going. Most men understood we were to make an assault landing somewhere, but few had any inkling it was to be southern France. Even the enemy expected it to take place somewhere in northern Italy, probably around Genoa.

July 28th General Patch and his staff had briefed Sir Henry Maitland Wilson (SACMED) and General Devers on the final Army plans for the invasion; and on August 3rd, Admiral Hewitt, the Naval Sub Task Force Commanders, and their staffs presented a similar brief on Navy operations. August 8th, the day after the rehearsals of the 36th and 45th Divisions, General O'Daniels, Eagles, Dahlquist and I presented the final briefing on the Corps assault plans.

We reviewed the divisions—the 3rd Division on the same ground and in the same formation in which I had reviewed them just before sailing for Anzio. It was a magnificent and inspiring sight. I addressed the officers of each division to impress upon them their individual responsibilities for the success of our forthcoming venture, and to offer them words of advice from my own experience.

August 12th, the whole command was finally loaded. At nine o'clock that night, I was piped on board the *Catoctin*, the Headquarters ship, where I was greeted by Hewitt. General Patch, with a few members of the Seventh Army staff, was there, and I went at once to find him. Both of us were glad that the long period of preparation was ended, and we now looked forward to some action. I will never forget Patch's last words to me that night: "Truscott, I am coming along on the *Catoctin*, but I want you to know I do not want to embarrass you in any way. I am not going to interfere with the way you fight your battle. I want you to know it." I thanked General Patch, and assured him that I had no desire but to work in the closest possible cooperation with him, and that I would always be glad to have his advice.

2. *DRAGOON Assault*

My aide's journal describes the *Catoctin* voyage as follows:

Sunday, 13 August, 1944
A rather sleepless night for all in the hot staterooms. General and C/S up for leisurely breakfast at 0800. Gen. H. M. Wilson aboard to wish party good luck, with Adm Morris, RN, Secty of Navy and Adm Hewitt aboard. General on deck to watch proceedings as ship pulls out of harbor at 1100. Anchor out in bay, and Prime Minister by in speed boat with Adm Morris to wave good-bye and good luck. Ship finally under way after lunch, and Gen. spends afternoon reading. Heat still most oppressive, with ventilating system broken. General is eating at Flag Mess. Waffle with C/S and all in for night cap early.

Monday, 14 August, 1944
Another bad night in oven like cabin. Day quiet and almost uneventful, with ship passing through Sardinia-Corsica strait at noon and skirting western coast of Corsica all afternoon. Gen. Saville in during morning to straighten out question of bombing enemy CPs. Destroyer alongside. Gen. Somerville, Secty Patterson request permission to come aboard tomorrow. Msgs from Gen. H. M. Wilson and Adm. Cunningham wishing all good luck. In late evening begin to pass through LCIs. Some 1001 ships making this invasion. Largest in history. Jitters cooling off a little, and General writes letter to wife before starting to bed.

Only a small portion of the invasion fleet was visible. The whole Corps and many Army troops had loaded in Naples, and in small ports from Pozzuoli to Salerno. For days, the Bay of Naples had been filled with ships and craft of every description, but when the *Catoctin* weighed anchor and headed out to sea, most of the shipping had already disappeared. The slower moving LCT's, LCI's and LST's with their Naval escorts had sailed the previous afternoon. Our headquarters ship was a part of the convoy of speedier vessels.

Most of the French II Corps had loaded in the ports of Taranto and Brindisi in the heel of Italy. CC Sudre of the 1st Armored Division and other elements of the French Corps were en route from Oran in North

Africa. Ships were loading and under way from these ports and from Palermo in Sicily and the ports in Sardinia and Corsica.

Routes for all convoys converged off the west coast of Corsica, and then flowed northward during the night, like a mighty river, toward the transport areas where the troops would disembark and head ashore. Nothing was visible from the decks as the *Catoctin* ploughed its way through the quiet waters, except an occasional hull silhouetted against the horizon. I slept little, because I wanted to be on hand for news. At last a signal reported all convoys were on time and in their proper places.

Charts and maps in the War Room below deck showed the dispositions of the vast armada, and our imaginations pictured the activities we could not see. On the left, the transport area of the 3rd Infantry Division. Nearest shore, 22 LST's and 38 LCT's with the three assault battalions and their supporting weapons; then, 47 LCI's which would land the support battalions, and to sea, the six combat loaders with the reserve regiment and ten MT's and one personnel ship filled with the reserve supplies and additional personnel. All told, there were 124 ships and craft carrying 29,432 men and 3,337 vehicles. Farther out still, in readiness to provide artillery support during the approach to the beach and the early hours on shore, would be the Fire Support Group: one battleship, six cruisers, seven destroyers; ten LCTR, each with a thousand rockets, and two LCG's would accompany the landing waves, while two LCF would increase protection against enemy air attack.

In the center, off the Golfe de St. Tropez—the transport area of the 45th Infantry Division—were ships and craft arranged in similar order: 22 LST's and 50 LCT's with the assault battalions and their supporting weapons; 38 LCI's with the support battalions; six combat loaders with the reserve regiment; 15 MT's and four personnel ships loaded with reserve supplies and additional personnel, in all 135 ships and craft carrying 30,926 men and 3,477 vehicles. And in the Fire Support Area: two battleships, three cruisers, 11 destroyers, with six LCTR and two LCG's and two LCF to accompany the landing waves.

On the right, off the Agay and Frejus beaches—the transport area of the 36th Infantry Division—were 23 LST's, 22 LCT's, 30 LCI's, seven combat loaders, ten MT's and two personnel ships carrying 29,820 men and 3,597 vehicles of the 36th Infantry Division, also six LST's, five MT's and one personnel ship carrying 4,600 men and 960 vehicles of Combat Command Sudre. In the Fire Support Area: one battleship, six cruisers, 11 destroyers, with 14 LCTR's, two LCG's, and two LCF to accompany the landing waves.

Four hundred and fifty ships and craft carried on their decks and at their davits the hundreds of LCVP's and LCM's which would carry

DRAGOON ASSAULT Map 5

the assault battalions shoreward and aid in unloading men, supplies and equipment—94,578 men and 11,371 vehicles to be landed within a matter of hours. And this was only the assault force. Eastward a smaller Naval force was landing the French Naval Demolition Group. To the west, ten transports escorted by six cruisers, three torpedo boats, and 15 smaller craft were landing 2,100 men of the 1st Special Service Force on the off shore islands and a French Commando of a thousand men on the coast west of the assault area. From every port, troops, equipment and supplies which were to follow the assault were already loading and under way.

Organizing this vast armada, planning and directing its routes, coordinating and protecting its movements so that each of a thousand pieces fell into place at the exact time, fully prepared for its manifold duties, was something of a gigantic jig-saw puzzle—or a chess game of the gods with the broad Mediterranean as a board. Our admiration for the professional ability of our Naval comrades was boundless, and our respect for their achievement in this complicated operation was profound.

Dawn came at last, but the mountains on the distant coast were barely visible through the morning haze. Then flight after flight of bombers appeared against the morning sky like birds flying shoreward. Bright flashes and towering clouds of smoke and dust marked distant locations, as the rumble of the bombardment drifted out to sea. Minutes passed, and guns from battleships, destroyers and cruisers, and a host of lesser craft, poured a hail of steel onto the landing beaches.

We could picture the landing craft heading ashore with wave after wave of LCVP's loaded wth grave and intent soldiers. The Apex boats, with Drones in tow, were leading to blast through underwater and beach obstacles. Stub-nosed LCT's with long ramps sloped skyward would disembark the clumsy DD tanks into the water. Others would put tanks and vehicles on shore. DUKW's loaded with division artillery. And an hour or so later the LCI's driving ashore to land 250 men of the support battalions. And following them, the LCVP's from the combat loaders with the reserve regiment of each division with the exception of the reserve of the 36th Infantry Division which was to make the delayed landing to clear Beach 264A and Frejus.

Then came the first messages: "Landings on time . . . opposition light . . . scattered artillery, mortars and small arms . . . operation going well." There was an indirect report that the airborne landing near Le Muy had been successful. But the 1st Special Service Force, although they had landed on the off shore islands, was having trouble.

About the middle of the morning far off to the east, a huge flight of aircraft moved towards the shore. The first wave of glider troops! Then the *Catoctin* stood in near the beaches of the 3rd Infantry Division in Cavalaire Bay. All seemed to be going well on shore with less confusion on the beaches and in the waters off shore than was to be expected. Air alerts, but no enemy bombers. Looking eastward: off St. Tropez peninsula and into Golfe de St. Tropez toward the beaches of the 45th Infantry Division, we saw steady progress of craft toward shore—no disorder—no confusion. It was now near noon. We stood over toward Beach 264A near Frejus to watch the delayed landing of the 142nd RCT of the 36th Infantry Division. A few thousand yards off shore, we had a grandstand seat.

Exactly on schedule, nearly a hundred B-24's in close formation blasted the beach defenses in a magnificent exhibition of precision bombing. Then they were gone, and the debris and smoke began to settle. Once more the guns of the fleet pounded the beach defenses. Could anything live under such a bombardment? Seaward, landing craft pressed their way to the coast, the white waves curling back beneath their stubby bows, behind the minesweepers clearing a channel for their approach. A few shots echoed from an 88 on shore near St. Raphael south of Frejus. The minesweepers continued on to within a few hundred yards off shore and then turned back. Occasional shells were now falling in front of the leading craft. Then the Apex boats released their Drones which continued on toward the shore and detonated with tremendous explosions and huge clouds of black smoke— all but one, which went out of control, dashed wildly up and down the beach, turned out to sea to our consternation, then turned about again. It finally grounded in the mouth of the Argens River without exploding. These were exciting moments to those of us who watched from the deck of the *Catoctin*. But suddenly, the whole flotilla of landing craft halted just a few thousand yards from the beach. What was wrong? Were they waiting for the maverick Drone to settle? Admiral Hewitt endeavored to communicate with Admiral Lewis. Then, while we watched, helplessly, to our profound astonishment the whole flotilla turned about and headed to sea again. Hewitt, Patch, and I were furious. The Admiral promised an investigation. But an intercepted message from Admiral Lewis, reported that, owing to beach opposition, they were landing RCT 142 over the Agay beaches in accordance with the alternate landing plan.

The Admiral lowered an LCVP for me. Accompanied by Carleton and Wilson, I set off for beach 264B to find Dahlquist. It appeared he had not been consulted in the change of plan. It had been a Naval decision, caused by failure to breach the underwater obstacles. The RCT was now landing on Beach 264B. Dahlquist's landings otherwise had gone off satisfactorily and the opposition had not been heavy. The French Naval party to the east had been unsuccessful, and his troops had gathered in the remnants and taken over the mission. He was confident he would be on the Blue Line and would have Beach 264A cleared by morning.

Afterwards I learned that Dahlquist sent a message to Admiral Lewis congratulating him for his prompt action in changing the plan of landing when the obstacles could not be overcome. I made known to Dahlquist my complete displeasure with this procedure. It was in fact almost the only flaw in an otherwise perfect landing. Failure to carry out this delayed landing as arranged was to hold up the clearing of Beach 264A by more than a day. It was to necessitate a change in the landing of CC Sudre and ground echelons of the Tactical Air Force. It was to delay the seizure and occupation of air fields near Frejus, and in the Argens valley, which in turn were to prevent our having close air support east of the Rhone when we began our drive to the north a few days later. It was in my opinion a grave error which merited reprimand at least, and most certainly no congratulation. Except for the otherwise astounding success of the assault, it might have had even graver consequences.

I returned to the *Catoctin*, reported to Patch and Hewitt, and arranged for CC Sudre to disembark over 45th Infantry Beaches during the night. Then, with the remainder of my command group, I set off for the St. Maxime beaches to join the forward echelon of my Command Post which had now landed. I was also accompanied by Colonel Jean Petit, my French liaison officer—the same who had opposed my landing at Port Lyautey in North Africa. Going ashore, I scooped up a handful of sand from the beach, turned to Petit and asked: "Well, Jean, how does the soil of France feel to an exile?" His eyes were filled with tears. He could not answer.

I found Eagles at his Command Post not far from St. Maxime. His reconnaissance elements had made contact with part of Frederick's Airborne Task Force near Le Muy, although we were not yet in communication with Frederick's Command Post on shore. Eagles had taken all of his D Day objectives and was pushing on to the Blue Line in his zone. I directed him to have the 180th Infantry proceed on through St. Aygulf during the night and assist the 36th Infantry Division in clearing Beach 264A at Frejus.

Back at the Post, I reviewed our program with the staff, who now had complete reports from both the 3rd and 36th Infantry Divisions. Except for Frejus and Beach 264A, which Dahlquist expected to take during the night, all initial objectives for the assault had been taken, and both divisions were pushing on to the Blue Line where some elements had already arrived. While we would not be secure on the Blue Line before the next day, the assault mission had been successfully accomplished. It was, I thought, a fitting celebration of the twenty-seventh anniversary of my original commission as an officer in the United States Army.

We estimated that we had broken the power of two German divisions. We could not estimate the number of enemy killed and wounded, but 2,129 prisoners of war had passed through our cages. Our own casualties had been light—much lighter than we anticipated—183 killed and wounded; 479 non-battle casualties. Speed and power, thorough planning, training, and preparations, had paid off. It was time to exploit our advantage.

In an offensive battle, the object is to destroy the enemy. Every military leader on the offensive seeks to attack the enemy in flank and rear where he is most vulnerable. In my own campaigns in Africa, Sicily and Italy, this had always been our purpose. We had trained men for superhuman efforts, and had then driven them to the limits of human endurance in an effort to attain it. But our aim had never been fully achieved primarily because the enemy was just as mobile as we were, which permitted him to escape before we could close the trap. Also, the forces which we placed in the enemy's rear had not been strong enough to effect such an end, as was seen in our landings on the north coast of Sicily and at Anzio. Every military leader dreams of the battle in which he can trap the enemy without any avenues or means for escape and in which his destruction can be assured. My study of the terrain of eastern France, and of the many possible ways the battle might develop, led me to dream of creating such a maneuver.

The vital area lay between the Italian and Swiss borders, marked by the Maritime and High Alps on the east, and the Rhone River on the west. The Rhone, a broad, deep river with an unusually swift current, rising amid the glaciers and lakes of the Swiss Alps, passes through Lake Geneva, tumbles on southwest to Lyon, and turns south toward the Mediterranean about one hundred seventy-five miles away. If all bridges were destroyed, which was well within the capabilities of our Air Forces, German forces to the east and west of the Rhone would be effectively isolated from each other. Their forces east of the Rhone could only escape northward by roads east of the river.

Another stream had an important bearing on our plans. The Durance River rises in the High Alps near Briançon midway between the Swiss border and the sea, flows southwest for about sixty-five miles, turns south parallel to the Rhone for another forty miles, and then sweeps westward in a wide loop for another forty-five miles to join the Rhone at Avignon. Army plans envisaged an advance to the west

once the beachhead was established with the two Corps abreast to clear
the enemy from the region between the lower reaches of the Durance
and the sea, capturing Toulon and Marseilles—which was, of course,
our first concern.

North, between the Durance Rivers and the Rhone, are, for the
most part, rolling farmlands and vineyards with occasional wooded
hills. It is traversed by an excellent network of roads going in all directions. East of the Durance are the Lower Alps, and farther to the north,
the High Alps—rugged country with limited road facilities.

Two main roads led westward from the assault area—the coast highway through Toulon and Marseilles, and farther to the north, Highway 7 through Brignolles, St. Maximin, Aix en Provence and Salon
where it turned northwest to Avignon. Two other principal routes led
north. The main one from Cannes and Nice joins Route Napoleon, at
Castellane, continues northwest to Chateau Arnoux on the Durance
River, where it meets a main road leading north from Marseilles, and
carries on through Gap and Aspres to Grenoble. The other, follows
close along the east bank of the Rhone.

About one hundred miles from the coast, one of the principal roads
that connect these two major routes leads west from Aspres through
Die and Crest, and joins Highway 7 at Livron, a distance of some seventy miles. Crest, which lies fifteen miles from the Rhone, marks the
exit from the foothills on the north bank of the Drome; and to the
north lies the open farmland of the valley of the Rhone. South of the
Drome, the foothills extend westward almost to the Rhone, terminating in ridges that parallel the Rhone closely for a distance of about
fifteen miles. These ridges, averaging in elevation 1,000 to 1,500 feet,
with precipitous western slopes, dominate Highway 7 at their base
along the east bank of the Rhone, as well as a secondary road that leads
northward through Crest.

Several miles north of Montelimar, the Rhone passes through a narrow defile—the Cruas Gorge, where there is barely room between the
foot of the precipitous ridge and the east bank of the Rhone for the
highway and railroad. North of this gorge, the Rhone bends westward
leaving a flat plain some two miles wide at its northern end along the
Drome.

This high ground immediately north of Montelimar was a vital factor for blocking any German withdrawal up the east bank of the
Rhone, and the key terrain was the southern terminus of these foothills, where a long ridge several miles long, with an elevation of about
1,000 feet, lay close against the east bank of the Rhone with the road
and railroad close against its precipitous western slopes. Just to the east,
another parallel ridge dominated the valley of the Rubion and the sec-

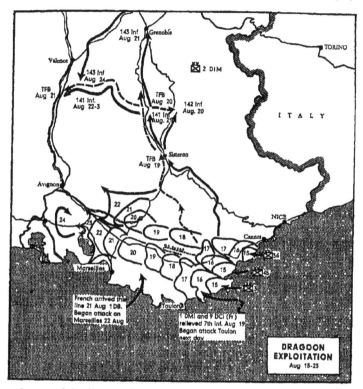

143 Inf
Aug 21

Grenoble

TORINO

Valence

2 DIM

143 Inf
Aug 24

TFB
Aug 21

141 Inf.
Aug 22-3

TFB
Aug 20

142 Inf
Aug. 20

141 Inf
Aug. 21

I T A L Y

TFB
Aug 19

Sisteron

Avignon

22

21

24

20

22

21

19

18

20

19

NICE

17

17

16

15

36

Cannes

Marseilles

18

16

14

15

17

16

15

45

3

French arrived the
line 21 Aug 1 DB.
Began attack on
Marseilles 22 Aug

Toulon

1 DMI and 9 DCI (Fr)
relieved 7th Inf. Aug 19
Began attack Toulon
next day

**DRAGOON
EXPLOITATION**
Aug 15-23

ondary roads leading north to the east of Crest. The ridges to the north and the foothills south of Crest were next in importance. If the fortunes of war permitted us to seize this terrain, we could block the retreat of enemy forces to the north along the east bank of the Rhone. If the enemy gained this terrain, we would be confronted by an enormously strong position which would be difficult to turn, and which the enemy could hold long enough to make good his escape.

If we should succeed in breaking through the German coast defenses quickly, we could expect the enemy to concentrate, in order to oppose our drive to the west. During this period, there might be an opportunity to thrust northward toward Sisteron and Grenoble, and possibly to block the German withdrawal by seizing the high ground north of Montelimar. Should this occur, we should most assuredly grasp it. No Army plan or terrain study had considered the possibility of such an early exploitation, and I was never able to obtain assurance from General Patch that the French Armored Combat Command would be available for me to strike home this advantage should the occasion lend itself.

My aide's journal records my movements during our second day on shore.

Wednesday, 16 August 1944

2d Bn 180 Inf under way only at daylight. 36th held up outside Frejus. CG up at 0630, goes to office in chateau. Gen. Sudre in. Problem of supplies for force. To move out NW from St. Maxime. No news from ABTF, but 45 Rcn in contact with 509 and Yarborough. Staff meeting, and CG off to 1 Bn 180 Inf, now fighting in St. Aygulf. Meets Col Duvall in center of town. Back to CP for further checking with staff and off to 3d Div CP N of Cogolin. Meets Adms. Hewitt, Lemmonier, Gen. Patch and Col. Guthrie on road near beach, having taken 15 prisoners. Entire party to 3d, stopping for celebration in Cogolin. Meet Gen O'Daniels and Shepard; instructions to continue advance to W and NW. Party to Cavalaire Beach. Talk to Col. Boatner at Beach CP, where CG leaves party and proceeds down coast road to 3d bn 7th Inf, talks to lead company commander Capt. Blakie. Snipers and fire fight. Meets Gen. Butler again on road back to CP; he is off to Le Muy to reconnoiter. Light lunch and talks with Gen. Baehr, Col. Langevin, and Harrel on scheme of maneuver. Orders out to divisions to continue rapid pushes in zone. Gen Frederick breezes in. 2/3 ABTF collected in vicinity Le Muy. Situation there well under control. Change in plan to relieve ABTF with 36th, group 45th around Vidauban for push to NW. Bulk 3d Div to move W on Axis Highway 7, with 45th N and NW. Air raids at dusk; and quiet evening with late supper and CG to bed immediately afterward.

Since we could not land Sudre's command over the beach at Frejus, we could not mass the command in the vicinity of the Argens valley for employment to the northwest or north as we had planned. I decided therefore to assemble his force at Le Muy in the gap between the 3rd and 45th Infantry Divisions for the drive to clear the area between the Durance River and the sea coast. I thought General Patch would leave Sudre under my command for this phase, but I did not expect that CC Sudre would be available to drive north of the Durance River. However, we had organized Task Force Butler and had formulated plans for its employment. Consequently, I warned Butler and the Corps staff to prepare for its assembly. Butler was en route to Le Muy to survey the location when I encountered him on the road.

General Patch agreed that I should push on to the northwest without waiting until the French Corps was ready to begin its advance. My idea was to have the 3rd Infantry Division use the 7th RCT to hold the general Carnoulles-Hyeres line until relieved by the French, who were to begin landing the following day, and then to drive westward with the remainder of the Division on Route 7 through Brignolles and St. Maximin to the south, cutting all roads leading into Toulon from the north. Eagles' 45th Infantry Division would keep pace on the north, following the line of Vidauban-Salernes-Barjols-Rian to the bend in the Durance River at Peyrolles. I hoped to move CC Sudre by road between these two main routes. Frederick's ABTF would take over the mission of protecting the east flank to free the stronger 36th Infantry Division. The latter would assemble in the area between Draguignan and Le Muy in readiness for employment in the advance to the west if needed, or for an advance northward through Digne. Task Force Butler was to assemble at Le Muy the following day.

Dahlquist had finally cleared Frejus and by nightfall on our second day ashore, we were everywhere beyond the Blue Line and were pressing the advance against ineffective opposition. More than 2,600 prisoners of war had been added to our bag, and our own losses continued to be light—115 killed and wounded, 417 non-battle casualties.

My aide's record of the third day reads:

Thursday, 17 August.

> Gen. Patch in 0730 with secret intelligence of 11 Panzer Divisions moving to block advance at Brignolles. Staff meeting in War Room, and Gen. off to 3d CP at Collobrieres. Gen. O'Daniels ordered to push advance to Brignolles. Up to Gonfaron on tortuous road and CG stops there at 30th CP (Maj. Parker). On to CP CCl between Gonfaron and Le Luc. Gen. Sudre instructed to push N and NW through Cabasse and Le Val to cut Brignolles from north. His force now in Le Luc. CG off to 45th CP vicinity Vidauban (Gen. Eagles and Paschal). They cleaning out pocket east of Le Luc. 45th axis now Vidauban-Salernes. Jeep through Vidauban, Le Muy, Frejus. Bridge not fixed there. Back by long detour to CP at 1630. Work on reports, orders, scan War Room Journals. Gen. Butler in for instructions. Will strike N toward Digne in AM. Gen. Frederick in with captured kraut major general. His area defined for assembling forces. Gen. du Vigier and Col. Lehr in. Would like Corps help in getting their Hq ashore. Col. O'Neill does job. Back to empty villa for cocktails and drive in rain to new Corps CP S of Vidauban. Attack coordinated for 0500, with Butler moving at 0600, but 3d to keep going during night. Very late supper followed by bed.

The secret intelligence about the move of the 11th Panzer Division did not alarm me, for even if it were true, the Corps dispositions were more than adequate to deal with it. Air reconnaissance had reported German divisions west of the Rhone moving eastward, but there were no indications of enemy movements from Toulon, Marseilles or elsewhere east of the Rhone to oppose us. The cause of this delay in enemy reaction became apparent during the day.

Frederick's Airborne Task Force had dropped all around German Headquarters LXII Reserve Corps at Draguignan and had completely dispersed it, capturing several hundred prisoners. The Corps Commander, Lieutenant General Neuling, and several of his staff escaped that day, but were taken two days later by Task Force Butler. Another important development was the capture by the 45th Infantry Division of the signal center which controlled German communications along the south coast. Thus, at the most crucial hour of battle, the German command was deprived both of its directing head and any effective means of transmitting information or instructions.

We issued few written field orders during the operations following the assault. The divisions were kept fully informed, and each element had a broad general mission. I controlled our strategy, for the most part, by oral orders to the commanders; thus, my instructions were based as near as possible, upon personal up to date knowledge and information, which was collected by the staff for dissemination to the commanders, and for the record. The system worked well in this campaign.

When Butler joined me late in the afternoon, he reported that his force was now gathered at Le Muy except for two units which were expected during the night. We adopted the plan, which Butler and his staff had prepared at my direction back in the Block House in Naples, for an advance northwest to the Durance River and then north toward Grenoble or west to seize the high ground north of Montelimar to block a German withdrawal through the Montelimar Gap east of the Rhone. I directed Butler to march at 0600 the following morning on the general axis Draguignan-Riez-Digne, with Digne as his first objective, reconnoitering roads paralleling his main axis on both flanks. How far he would be able to advance northward would depend upon the resistance that he encountered and other eventualities. He had been my assistant Corps Commander since Anzio. He was thoroughly familiar with all my views, and he was one of the most fearless men I ever met.

The Maquis, or French Forces of the Interior, as General de Gaulle had named them, were numerous in eastern France and were especially active in the mountainous areas of the border regions. One German division, the 157th Reserve Division, had been operating against them in the area around Grenoble for some weeks. So effective were the Maquis that the Germans moved only in large numbers. The Maquis were well provided with arms and explosives by the Allies, and Allied officers with communications had parachuted in to assist them in coordinating their operations. We had expected a good deal of assistance from them, and we were not disappointed. Their knowledge of the country, of enemy dispositions and movements, was invaluable, and their fighting ability was extraordinary.

Against this background, these orders to Butler were to lead to one of the most gallant exploits of the entire war. While no one in Army

Headquarters had anything whatever to do with the organization of this special Force, the preparation of plans for its employment, the orders for its assembly, or assignments for its initial mission, General Patch invariably approved when I informed him of my actions.

On the fourth day early reports indicated the 3rd Infantry Division was fighting at Brignolles, but that other forces were moving with only scattered opposition. I set off with Jimmie Wilson for Brignolles, and I found O'Daniels, with McGarr of the 30th RCT, on the outskirts. Two battalions were fighting in the town and O'Daniels expected to have the situation cleared up soon. His 15th RCT had already blocked the roads leading into Toulon from the north. Leaving him to push on through Brignolles, I made my way back through a great snarl of traffic caused by the mix up of the 3rd Infantry Division and CC Sudre on Highway 7.

I found Sudre in the village of Cabasse a few kilometers east of La Val. He had established his Command Post in the restaurant of a local hotel. There, the proprietor and his help were scrambling to serve *petit dejeuner*, wines and liquors, while the mayor, leader of the local resistance forces, and mobs of towns people were throwing flowers, making speeches of welcome, and offering toasts to the French troops and their American allies. It was quite an experience in the midst of battle—one that was repeated in almost every village and town.

Sudre was a happy man. He had the flush of victory. His command had met the enemy—their first battle. They had in fact come off extremely well, destroying several German tanks and capturing a number of artillery pieces and vehicles, as well as several score of German prisoners. Even more important from my point of view, Sudre had captured Le Val thus cutting the road north of Brignolles. I told Sudre to press his advance westward to St. Maximin west of Brignolles as soon as he could escape from the welcoming committees. Then, in response to a radio message from Carleton, I returned to the Command Post for a conference with General Patch, arriving there shortly after noon.

General Patch, whose headquarters was now established on shore at St. Tropez, was concerned about de Lattre's delay in beginning the attack to take Toulon. Unloading of the French Corps was progressing; they had one division on shore and most of another, although they were having some trouble discharging equipment. Patch was urging de Lattre to begin operations but de Lattre insisted on waiting until his whole command was ashore and he could organize the full scale attack he had planned. Patch was afraid the delay would make Toulon more difficult to capture.

I did not think the Germans were in any great strength in Toulon—just some disorganized elements of the 242nd Division along with some coast defense and service troops. I was confident the 3rd Infantry Division could take the city within forty-eight hours and offered to undertake the operation if Patch wished me to do so. Patch was tempted, but only for a moment. Both of us realized it would be a mistake to divert the 3rd Infantry Division for this purpose. French troops were available for the operation, and such a change in plans would have grave political repercussions and make de Lattre even more recalcitrant than he was.

Accordingly, we agreed I would drive on to the west and isolate both Toulon and Marseilles, leaving them to be captured by the French. Patch would endeavor to have de Lattre relieve the 3rd Infantry Division north of Hyeres and begin the attack on Toulon as soon as possible —without waiting until D plus 6 as de Lattre was currently planning.

At nightfall, things looked very good. Our forces were past Brignolles, Bras and Barjols, and Task Force Butler was at Riez with reconnaissance north of Digne.

On the fifth day, D plus 4, at my staff meeting I was informed that the French were starting relief of the 7th RCT north of Hyeres, and concluded that General Patch had been able to influence General de Lattre. General Saville came in during the meeting to discuss means of providing close air support during our operations. As our planes were still flying from Corsica and we had no forward ground control, we asked Saville to knock the Rhone ferries and bridges out as a principal mission.

Then Generals Devers, Eaker, and Persons joined us and were briefed on the progress we had made, after which I took them to visit the front. O'Daniels we found west of Brignolles. He was to remain east of St. Maximin keeping the roads leading into Toulon blocked until Sudre passed through St. Maximin heading southwest to cut the coast road. At Le Val we found Sudre, who was to continue through St. Maximin to Aubagne, where he would cut the coast road and he prepared to attack Toulon from the west in conjunction with the French forces. We reached Eagles' Command Post in time for lunch; he was to continue on the Durance and establish a bridgehead across the river.

While we were with Eagles, Carleton relayed a message from the Seventh Army. CC Sudre would be moved at once to Flassans where it would be relieved from attachment to the VI Corps and pass to control of French II Corps at 2100. I was prepared to lose Sudre's command, and I had ordered them to Aubagne with that thought in mind. However, I did object to turning the command about and countermarching it some twenty miles against the flow of Corps' traffic on Route 7. I sent a message to Carleton asking him to explain this to

Army and to recommend that Sudre pass to French control at St. Maximin or Aubagne. I left General Devers and party, and returned to Le Val to warn Sudre. While I was still with him a message from Carleton informed me that Army disapproved my recommendation. Sudre and I were most unhappy; Sudre in fact had tears in his eyes.

I could not believe that my recommendation had been brought to the attention of General Patch. I thought that it must have been disapproved by a staff officer who was not familiar with the situation, and who did not comprehend the confusion that would result from countermarching this command some twenty miles. I set off for Army Headquarters.

I reached St. Tropez in the middle of the afternoon, found General Patch, and stated my case. He said he was fully aware of the confusion that this movement would cause, and he had passed on my recommendation to General de Lattre. But de Lattre had refused. Convinced that the capture of Toulon was going to be very difficult, he had demanded Sudre's command. Patch felt for political reasons he had to agree, otherwise de Lattre would be increasingly difficult to work with and would almost certainly delay, still more, the attack on Toulon. While I thought that General Patch's decision was wrong, I accepted it without further question and returned to the Command Post to begin the movement.

Thus Sudre's command turned east at St. Maximin and Brignolles, crossing the column of the 3rd Division which was moving west on Route 7, and returned to the vicinity of Flassans. Traffic congestion and confusion on that road all through the night and much of the following morning was almost indescribable, for there was neither time to plan, nor facilities for, strict control. And then, no sooner had Sudre reached the Flassans locality than he was turned around and sent back again over the same road towards the same objective that I had proposed to give him.

When I returned to my Command Post near Vidauban after my conference with General Patch, all but the rear echelon of the command group was in movement to Le Val. Lieutenant Preeble from Butler's staff was waiting for me. Butler was at Sisteron! He had dispersed several enemy detachments and had captured more than a thousand prisoners. Maquis with whom Butler was in contact reported German detachments scattered over a wide area from Briançon to Grenoble, and the Maquis were eager to have Butler's support. I decided that the time had come to start the 36th Infantry Division north behind Butler.

I sent for Dahlquist. His 143rd Infantry was now at Draguignan. His 142nd RCT was in the Argens valley east of Carces. The 141st

RCT had not yet been relieved by Frederick's ABTF, and had been heavily engaged during the day at Fayence on the eastern flank. I told Dahlquist to start one RCT north the following day to join Butler at Sisteron, and to prepare to follow with the rest of the division as rapidly as he could. Lieutenant Preeble returned to Butler with instructions for him to remain at Sisteron the following day to allow elements of the 36th Division to join him, and to push reconnaissance to the southwest, west, and northwest to determine the practicability of seizing the high ground north of Montelimar.

Sunday, August 20th, D plus 5, it seemed to me was the day for decision. My aide's journal records:

> 45th now on river line and 3d west of St. Maximin heading for Aix. French attacking Toulon. Staff meeting. Projected swing of main effort to N with 3d holding river line N of Marseilles. Major Hansen in from General Butler. Gen. Patch on phone OKs move of 36th behind Butler. Gen. Saville in —finding difficulty locating airfields inland. Stays for lunch. CG off after lunch to 3d Div. Up road short of Aix to see Gen. O'Daniels. 3d to go on through Aix and block roads leading out of Marseilles. Back to St. Maximun, up to Barjols, Tavernes and 45th CP Gen. Paschal. Meet Gen. Eagles on road to river. He will have two regiments across tonight. 179th to move N up river. Back to Cp 1830. CG outlines his idea of operation. Push to N contingent on how long it will take for French to clear Toulon-Marseilles, releasing 3d Division. Col. Petit in; believes French will take Toulon tomorrow. Lt. Col. Conway sent off with orders for Butler to move to Montelimar.

Air reconnaissance reported German columns withdrawing north along the west bank of the Rhone, and indicated that all bridges were destroyed south of Lyon. There had been no movement across the Rhone in either direction. We did not know how much of the German XIX Army still faced us east of the Rhone, but no general movements to the north had been observed. In fact, the 11th Panzer Division, one of the Germans' best, had moved southward in that area since our landing. It seemed likely that at least three full divisions with parts of four or five others as well as numerous Corps, Army, and coastal defense troops, were still south of Montelimar. We did not know what portion would be isolated in Toulon and Marseilles, but I thought most of the mobile elements would have withdrawn from these cities. In view of our overwhelming air support, I doubted the Germans could now concentrate for a major counterattack.

Concentrating the Corps in the north would require several days in view of the difficult terrain and road conditions for troop supply and transportation, and the necessity for protecting the French right flank. When Colonel Petit informed me that he thought the French would take Toulon the following day, I decided to act.

At 2045, the evening of August 20th, I sent an urgent message to Butler:

> You will move at first light 21 August with all possible speed to Montelimar. Block enemy routes of withdrawal up the Rhone valley in that vicinity. 36th Division follows you.

In the letter of instructions, which sent Colonel Conway off on a hundred mile drive in the darkness, I told Butler to seize the high ground north of Montelimar, informing him that Dahlquist had orders to support him with one RCT, Corps Artillery Long Toms, the 155th battalion from the 36th Division, and that the bulk of the Division would follow as rapidly as conditions permitted. Butler would be attached to the 36th Infantry Division as soon as Dahlquist arrived in the area and could assume control.

My aide's journal records a hectic day:

Seventh Day on Shore, Monday, 21 August. (D plus 6)

3d jumps off at 0600 against Aix. Gen. Dahlquist in by Cub at 0815. He will join Butler at Montelimar, bulk of his force blocking there and lesser blocks east of Durance and north of Aspres. Command of Butler Task Force to 36th. Supply difficulties large, but Division should be in Sisteron area by tonight. Staff meeting. Colonel Harrel to go to 7th Inf, Lt. Col. Conway new G-3, Lt. Col. Doleman to come up as Asst. G-2. C/S reports telephone message from Gen. White—more secret intelligence—11th Panzer across river. Move 179th N is halted. CG to 3d CP after lunch. Talked to Gen. Shepard, Lt. Col. Connor at CP, continues on to Aix for roadside meeting with Gen. O'Daniels. 3d ordered to hold line Le Puys-Etang le Berre, push reconnaissance forward. Long trip around to Rian, St. Paul and pontoon bridge at Meyrargues to 45th. Gen. Eagles to hold present position and leave 179th where they are. Back to new CP at Rian. Gen. Baehr in. 36th fouled up. Not moving infantry and artillery as ordered. Baehr back to straighten them out. Lt. Col. Conway in with some info. Will Lang is dinner guest. Col. Petit in for coffee. French want to take over Aix line, which suits us fine if they hurry.

Dahlquist's 143rd RCT (less 2nd Battalion with Butler Task Force) had reached Sisteron late the afternoon before, and was in contact with Butler Task Force. Dahlquist's 142nd RCT had reached Castellane and was shuttling north to the Montelimar Gap. The 141st RCT had been relieved by Frederick's ABTF on the east flank and was assembling in the vicinity of Draguignan. Dahlquist was concerned with the problems of movement and supply, which were enormous because all units were still at assault scale of transport. We discussed the problem with Colonel O'Neill, my good G-4, who was confident that by careful use of available transport, he could supply ammunition, gasoline, and rations for two divisions as far north as Grenoble.

Dahlquist thought the whole division would be in the Gap-Aspres-Sisteron area by nightfall. He was to join Butler at Montelimar and employ the bulk of his force for blocking there, with lesser blockades east of the Durance River and north of Aspres to prevent interference from those directions. He would have to decide upon his troop dispositions when he had familiarized himself with existing conditions; but blocking the Montelimar Gap was to be the important mission.

Dahlquist had not been gone very long before the telephone call from General White informed us that "secret" intelligence indicated that the 11th Panzer Division was south of the Durance River.

While I did not believe that Germans were in any position to launch a major counterattack, a sudden thrust against either the 3rd or 45th Infantry Divisions might be somewhat embarrassing since my only reserve division was now advancing north from Draguignan to join the Butler Task Force at Sisteron. As a result, I stopped the movement of the 179th RCT northward, told Eagles to hold where he was, and told O'Daniels to hold a line west of Aix extending from Pertuis to Etang de Berre.

We were attempting to set the stage for a classic—a "Cannae"—in which we would encircle the enemy against an impassable barrier or obstacle and destroy him. There was some question as to how many of the enemy we would trap, and more debate about whether or not we could build up sufficient strength in the enemy's rear to prevent his escape. We did not have precise information on the enemy's activities in the wide northern area; but I had gone over this problem with both Butler and Dahlquist and had given them specific missions to execute, leaving to their own discretion the methods to be used. Immediately, after my staff meeting on the morning of August 24th, Jimmie Wilson and I set off by Cub for Aspres to check with Dahlquist.

We landed there shortly after eleven o'clock. Dahlquist was absent at the Gap. From Colonel Vincent, his Chief of Staff, I learned to my profound dismay that both RCT 141 and the Corps artillery battalion, which should have been with Butler at Montelimar, were still in bivouac. Dahlquist, Colonel Vincent said, had been alarmed over early reports that the enemy was advancing in strength from both Grenoble and the Gap. He had delayed the movement until he could determine whether or not these units could be spared. The reports had been inaccurate and exaggerated. Colonel Vincent had information that the 143rd RCT had reached Grenoble where General Stack had allowed one battalion to enter the town; and a report that some 4,000 Germans had surrendered to the 142nd RCT near the Gap to avoid surrendering to Maquis who had them surrounded.

I was angry, and I soon had Colonel Harmony and his command on the way to join Butler. I also left distinct orders with Colonel Vincent for Dahlquist to proceed to the Montelimar area forthwith with the bulk of his Division, and informed him I would attach the 179th RCT of the 45th Infantry Division to him for employment at Grenoble. While I did not feel that I could tell Dahlquist how to deploy his command for battle in the Montelimar area, I thought that he should have some guidance, as this was his first division command in battle. So on my return to the Command Post, I wrote Dahlquist, elaborating upon the orders I had given him.

Dear John:

I visited your Command Post this morning and, as your Chief of Staff has probably informed you, was considerably upset because my original instructions covered in subsequent messages had not been carried out. Apparently, I failed to make your mission clear to you. The primary mission of the 36th Infantry Division is to block the Rhone Valley in the Gap immediately north of the Montelimar. For this purpose you must be prepared to employ the bulk of your Division. If this operation develops as seems probable, all of your Division will be none too much in the Rhone valley area.

I am moving the 179th Infantry of the 45th Infantry Division north from the vicinity of Montfort without delay. When this regiment reaches Aspres, it is attached to you to employ in the vicinity of Grenoble. The elements of your Division now in Grenoble should be moved without delay to the area now occupied by the Butler Force, unless there is a radical change in the situation prior to the hour of such movement. In such case, you will of course consult me before employing them somewhere else. On the roads in the vicinity of Gap and east thereof, I desire that you employ blocking forces only. Keep in mind that your primary mission is to block the Rhone Valley. I will move the remainder of the 45th Division less one regiment to the Grenoble area as soon as possible. At that time, I will make the 45th Division responsible for the area east of the Grenoble-Sisteron road.

In connection with the Butler Force, keep in mind that that Force has enemy both in front and rear and the necessity for all-around defense is obvious. Extend reconnaissance toward Bourge le Peage and Valence. Likewise, push reconnaissance to the south to gain contact with enemy forces. You can expect, as the enemy advances northward and comes in contact with the Butler Force, that he will continually work to outflank to the east. Therefore, every road between Montelimar and Highway 94 (Nyons-Serres) must be blocked and roads south thereof covered by reconnaissance, either by motor or Cub plane, and you must be prepared to counter this capability. For that reason you should shift the bulk of the 142nd Infantry to the west of Aspres without delay.

On the following day, August 23rd, I was not able to visit Dahlquist as I had planned to do, as this journal note records:

179th sent to Grenoble after all and 143d down by Bourg le Peage to join Division. 3d pushing on ahead with no resistance to speak of. Colonel Harrel in to say good-bye. Staff meeting and CG cancels visit to 36th in favor of morning on plans. Off at 1030 to see Gen. Eagles at 45th CP at Mirabeau.

45th now N of river. Relieved by 3d and 180th to go to Gap area relieving 142d. 157th to remain separate command under Gen. Church until relieved by 3d. Return to CP via Peyrolles at 1230 to see Gen. Patch who does not show up. More work on plans. Archbishop Spellman, Ambassador Murphy, Gen. Noce for visit. Former holds Mass. Gen. Patch appears at end of service, and guests on to the 3d at Aix. Conference with Army commander, and CG off to 3d to get Gen. O'Daniels moving faster. No sign of relief by French although they are in Marseilles.

I had released Colonel Harrel, my old G-3, to command the 7th Infantry, at General O'Daniels' request. I was sorry to lose Harrel, and only agreed to do so to give him command experience and on O'Daniels' promise that he would release him without question if I should require his services in the future for any important assignment.

Renewing associations with Archbishop Spellman, Ambassador Murphy, and General Dan Noce was a very pleasant interlude. Archbishop Spellman's Mass under the warm August skies in my Command Post will always be one of my treasured memories. I know of no churchman who made greater personal contributions to the prosecution of the war—none who appreciated more keenly the problems of the men who were fighting it.

General Patch approved the actions I had taken, and once more promised to expedite the relief of the 3rd Infantry Division by the French.

Late in the afternoon I had a handwritten message from Butler which reported his situation north of Montelimar during the morning:

Gen Truscott—

We have a much improved position today. Have gained more high ground north of Montelimar and are getting into position to clean up the latter place this afternoon.

Column of about 50-60 vehicles, including a few tanks (reported Mark VI's), hit us at Cleon (0660) this morning. Road block and reconnaissance held, artillery did its stuff, and now the reserve (1 tank Co and 1 Inf Co) are pursuing. Apparently Jerry is hurt plenty. Yesterday over 100 vehicles destroyed and two trains were hit and badly messed up. TD's and tanks have direct fire positions on road north of Montelimar.

About 30 missing in yesterday's mix up at Puy St. Martin, lost one tank, one light tank, and two armored vehicles. K and W about 10. Jerry took a polishing.

A Panzer officer captured today has a fund of information, summary of which is going back by plane herewith.

FBB

2 Bns of 141 now in. Third reported en route. 142 is headed for Nyons and I have a plane out hunting for them. 131 artillery is here.

The next morning, air reports showed that German columns were still moving north on both sides of the Rhone, despite the establishment of our blockade north of Montelimar. Columns moving northward on the east bank of the Rhone indicated that Butler's blockade was not as effective as we had hoped. Immediately after our morning staff conference, Wilson and I set off to visit Dahlquist at his Command Post in Marsanne, a few miles north of Montelimar. There I conferred at length with Dahlquist, Butler, and Stack.

Butler had reached the vicinity of Marsanne late the afternoon of August 21st, and had placed artillery in position to fire on Highway 7. Patrols during the night established a road block at Coucourde but had been driven out by superior forces. When the 141st RCT arrived in the area the following day, Butler had tried to capture the town of Montelimar, but had been repulsed. He had overlooked the vital importance of the high ground just north of Montelimar, particularly the long ridge just to the east of and parallel to Highway 7 between Montelimar and Coucourde. The Germans had seized this vital terrain. Butler had then occupied a defensive position extending eastward from the Condillac pass to Puy St. Martin on the road between Montelimar and Crest.

Dahlquist had arrived the morning of August 23rd. As other elements of the Division took up positions, Task Force Butler was intermingled with them over a wide area. Dahlquist had then disbanded the Task Force and returned elements to their parent units. Then he had made another effort to take the town, but it, too, had been repulsed. There were mistakes, as I pointed out to Butler and Dahlquist, but it was water under the bridge. The essential task was to occupy the long ridge overlooking Highway 7 north of Montelimar. Dahlquist assured me he had launched an attack to capture the ridge that morning and his troops were now on the northern end. He was so confident of his ability to hold his position and block any enemy withdrawal up the Rhone that he wished to divert the 143rd RCT which had reached Bourg le Peage to occupy Valence, in order to avoid trouble in capturing the place later. I was by no means as optimistic as he was. I had no objection to his occupying Valence if he could do so without becoming involved in a battle which would delay the arrival of the 143rd RCT in the Montelimar area. I directed him to reassemble Task Force Butler by dark that day so as to have strong striking force in Division reserve.

Leaving Dahlquist, I stopped at Aspres to see Eagles. His 179th RCT was now in the Grenoble area, the 180th in the Gap area, both with reconnaissance and road blocks over a wide range, and in scattered contact with light enemy forces. The 157th Infantry had been relieved north of the Durance by the 3rd Infantry Division and was to move north during the night, to the vicinity of Serres, where I directed that reconnaissance be pushed out to the west. Eagles was having his troubles with the Maquis who were active in all the border towns, and badgering Eagles to send American troops to support them.

When I returned to my Command Post near Rian about midafternoon, I had another conference with General Patch to bring him up to date. The French were still engaged in Toulon and Marseilles, and had made no move to relieve elements of the 3rd Infantry Division south of the Durance. We now had information the 11th Panzer Division was north of the Durance which indicated the German withdrawal was underway. Patch agreed that I could start the 3rd Infantry Division north without waiting longer for relief by the French.

Late in the afternoon there was a report from Dahlquist that the 143rd RCT had by-passed Valence and had arrived at Crest, and that he had beaten off another German attack northwest of Montelimar.

Friday, August 25th, was D plus 10. My aide's journal records the day:

> 3d on move. 7th relieves 157th and reconnaissance at Carpentras. 15th in position by 0230, ready to push on N flank followed by 30th. 157th at Serres. No attack on 36th. CG works on plans after staff meeting. Gen. O'Daniels in. Assigned objective Nyons-Orange line. 3d to form bottom of nutcracker. Light lunch 1130 and CG off to 3d by jeep W of Pertuis. They are still moving ahead. News of enemy advance E to Grane from Loriol Situation there could be much better. Off to new CP, stopping at Laragne (2d Bn 179th Captain Snyder) and Serres (157th Gen. Church). Latter off with regiment minus tanks and 1 Bn to Crest. New CP at Aspres. Army FO and plans for further advance to N and NW. 36th having trouble, but announced road blocked at La Coucorde. TF Butler sent through Grane to clear Loriol situation. Col. Langevin in with brief information. Supper and early bed.

The following morning I was most unhappy about the situation at Montelimar. Air reconnaissance made the previous day had reported that Germans were continuing to withdraw to the north. In spite of assurances, our block on Highway 7 was not effective. During the afternoon, the Germans had even launched an attack eastward from Loriol toward Crest, which was stopped by Task Force Butler. When I reached Dahlquist's Command Post, now located south of Crest, that morning, I left him in no doubt as to my state of mind: "John, I have come here with the full intention of relieving you from your command. You have reported to me that you held the high ground north of Montelimar and that you had blocked Highway 7. You have not done so. You have failed to carry out my orders. You have just five minutes in which to convince me that you are not at fault."

Dahlquist said he had believed, from reports sent to him, that his troops were on the hill along Highway 7 north of Montelimar. He had not discovered the error until the day after, when he visited the regiment and found them on the hill to the east of the ridge in dispute. He had during the preceding day bent every effort to make the block effective, but the enemy had been too strong. He had been threatened by an enemy attack east from Loriol in the direction of Crest which had actually cut his supply road south of Crest, and by a strong armored attack north from Puy St. Martin toward Crest. Nevertheless, he now had a block at Coucourde and had four battalions of artillery emplaced where they could interrupt the road. Except for his initial mistake, Dahlquist thought he had done as well as could be expected. I did not fully concur, but I decided against relieving him.

General Patch joined us as I was about to leave the Command Post, and we reviewed the situation. When he departed, I set off by jeep to visit the various front line units. I found Butler at Condillac with his

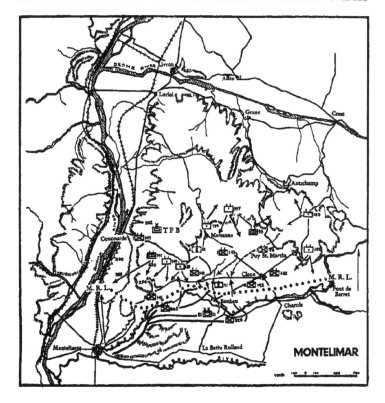

Task Force, a battalion of the 143rd Infantry, and elements of the 141st Infantry. Heavy fighting was in progress on the ridge parallel to Highway 7 and at Coucourde. From the ridge just north of Condillac I had my first look at Highway 7 in this area and could see some of the damage inflicted by our guns. I found the 141st RCT on the bridge south of Marsanne, the 143rd RCT near the town of Marsanne, and the 142nd near Puy St. Martin. Fighting was general all along the front, with the heaviest fighting in the Coucourde area where Butler was seeking to reestablish the block on Highway 7. I returned late in the afternoon to Aspres by jeep in a driving mountain storm.

August 25th, the 3rd Infantry Division had started its drive from the south hard on the heels of the retreating Germans, and by the evening of August 27th, had reached a point within five miles of Montelimar. In the Montelimar sector, and also to the northwest of the town, at Coucourde to the north, and about Loriol on the Drome, heavy fighting continued during the days of August 27th and 28th. I spent most of these two days flying by Cub from the Corps Command Post at Aspres to the 3rd Infantry Division coming up from the south, and then to Dahlquist's Command Post in the battle area. On both days we flew over the front and could see much of the damage we were inflicting upon the enemy. "Carnage compounded," Wilson called it. The Corp's "After Action Report" aptly describes the scene along Highway 7 during these two days: "The 142nd Infantry maintained its commanding positions overlooking Highway 7 from the vicinity of Coucourde while the Division artillery, using direct and tank fire, ranged up and down the highway delivering a steady stream of fire on the completely disorganized, bumper to bumper column of vehicles which included armor and horsedrawn guns and equipment. 36th Division Artillery continued to hammer away at the motionless enemy vehicles which continued to jam up bumper to bumper along Highway 7 between Montelimar and Loriol, as fighter bombers in direct support of VI Corps pounded the escape routes of the northward German retreat. South of Montelimar, two battalions 15th Infantry surrounded and captured a double banked column of approximately 350 German guns and vehicles which were stretched along the highway over a distance of two kilometers."

I was disappointed because most of the 11th Panzer Division and much of the 198th Reserve Division had broken through our block. In fact, I was disappointed that any Germans on the east bank of the Rhone had escaped our trap. However, when I later flew over the entire area at low elevation and at slow speed to examine the battle field, I found that we had done better than I had thought while the battle continued. From Montelimar north to Loriol, road and railroad were lined with tanks, trucks, guns, and vehicles of every description. Hundreds of railway cars loaded with guns and equipment, including no less than seven of the long range railway guns like the "Anzio Express" which had tormented us so much at Anzio. Hundreds of dead horses and dead bodies littered the plain south of Loriol. Engineers cleared the roads with bulldozers before our own transport could use them. And the sight and smell of this section is an experience I have no wish to repeat.

I know of no place where more damage was inflicted upon troops in the field; and it is rather interesting to note that it was done almost entirely by ground weapons, artillery, tanks, tank destroyers and demolitions. Our air support, because of the lack of forward ground control, was employed only on briefed missions or armed reconnaissance north of the Drome River, the northern edge of the battle area, and west of the Rhone. Montelimar netted some 5,000 prisoners, destroyed more than 4,000 German vehicles, and eliminated the 338th and 189th German Divisions.

In fourteen days, at a cost of 1,331 killed and wounded, the VI Corps had encircled Toulon and Marseilles, almost destroyed the German XIX Army east of the Rhone, captured 23,000 prisoners, and was more than a hundred miles north of the beaches with elements still another hundred miles farther on. Even if Montelimar had not been a perfect battle, we could still view the record with some degree of satisfaction.

On August 25th, while the battle of Montelimar was still in progress, General Patch issued orders outlining plans for continuing the advance to the north with the object of joining up with General Patton's Third Army, then advancing eastward across France. North of Montelimar, Lyon was the assembly point for German forces escaping northward on both banks of the Rhone, and General Patch expected the Germans to defend there. French Army B was still engaged in Toulon and Marseilles, while the VI Corps was on the east bank of the Rhone a hundred miles to the north. Therefore, General Patch decided to have the VI Corps continue the advance, through Grenoble and Valence, on Lyon. Elements of the French Army B were to cross the Rhone at Avignon, take up the pursuit west of the Rhone, and assist the VI Corps in capturing Lyon. After the capture of Lyon, the VI Corps was to cross to the west bank of the Saone and drive northward on the axis Autun-Beaune-Langres. The French Army B, after capturing Marseilles, was to advance northward on the axis Sisteron-Grenoble-Bourg-Besançon, relieving all elements of the VI Corps in the mountain passes north of Briançon.

On August 29th, we began the move northward from Montelimar.

The 157th RCT struck north through Aspres and Grenoble to rejoin the 45th Infantry Division which was approaching the Rhone River twenty-five miles east of Lyon, while the 36th Infantry Division drove along the east bank of the Rhone. The 3rd Infantry Division, after policing the battle field, was to move north to Voiron. The advance continued against light and scattered resistance, for the Germans fought only to make good their escape. By the morning of September 1st, the 36th Division was on the eastern outskirts of Lyon. The 45th Division was south of Bourg approaching the road leading northeast from Lyon, and in contact with the 11th Panzer Division. The 3rd Division was at Voiron northwest of Grenoble. French forces west of the Rhone were approaching Lyon from the southwest.

I had had a message from General Patch during the afternoon of August 30th saying that French Forces of the Interior—the Maquis—wished to seize Lyon by an uprising within the city, but had been ordered not to attempt it except in coordination with the main American and French forces. Subsequently, he advised me that, for political reasons, it would be desirable to permit the French forces to enter Lyon first.

On the morning of September 2nd, Dahlquist sent an officer's patrol into the city to investigate Maquis reports and found the city clear of the enemy. September 3rd, the French 1st Infantry Division entered the city from west of the Rhone.

I had been concerned over continuing the pursuit, for if the VI Corps crossed to the west of the Saone we would lose all contact. Late the afternoon of September 2nd, I started Jimmie Wilson with Sergeant Barna on a two hundred mile drive in the pouring rain back to the Army Command Post at Brignolles to deliver this letter to General Patch.

Dear General:

At the present time, the 45th Division is attacking Bourg astride the Bourg-Amberieu Road, making favorable progress, having reached a point four or five miles off the town against light opposition. My reconnaissance squadron is north of Bourg, reconnoitering west toward Macon. The 36th Division with its left near the Rhone River, has advanced to the outskirts of Lyon. I expect the combined action of the FFI and General du Vigier's division to have Lyon in our hands today. The 3rd Division is assembled near Amberieu immediately in rear of the 45th Division.

It is apparent that elements of the 85th Corps which escaped the Montelimar pocket have withdrawn through Lyon to the north. The German 4th Corps has of course been west of the Rhone all of the time and we have had no contact with them. We are in contact with elements of the 11th Panzer Division in the Bourg area, and reports indicate that we destroyed at least

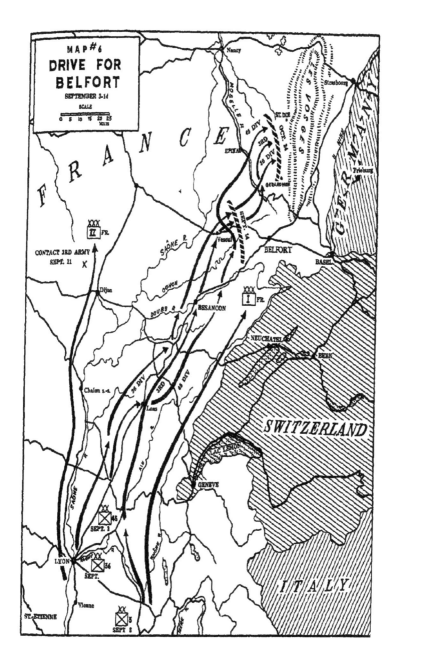

MAP #6

DRIVE FOR BELFORT

SEPTEMBER 3-14

SCALE

0 5 10 15 20 25
MILES

Nancy

MOSELLE R.

Strasbourg

ST. DIE

45 DIV

OCT. 24

EPINAL

3RD

DIV

36 DIV

Friebarg

GERARDMER

GERMANY

VOSGES

R. RHINE

F R A N C E

SAONE R.

Vesoul

SEPT. 14

BELFORT

BASEL

XXX
II FR.

CONTACT 3RD ARMY
SEPT. 11 X

OGNON

Dijon

DOUBS R.

BESANCON

XXX
I FR.

NEUCHATEL

BERN

36 DIV

3RD

45 DIV

Chalon s.-s.

Lons

SWITZERLAND

SAONE R.

AIN R.

LAC LEMAN

GENEVE

ITALY

48
SEPT. 3

LYON

36
SEPT.

Rhone R.

ST. ETIENNE

Vienne

3
SEPT. 8

15 of their tanks yesterday. It seems to me that the enemy is making every possible effort to withdraw along the west bank of the Saone, utilizing the river as an obstacle to protect him from pursuit.

If I continue direct pursuit up the west bank of the Saone, I shall have no opportunity to interrupt his main column. I believe that the enemy is so disorganized that we are justified in taking calculated risks with the hope of interrupting his retreat, preventing his escape to Germany, and inflicting more losses upon him.

I recommend that the pursuit continue at once on the axis Lons le Saunier-Besançon-Belfort, for the following reasons:

(1) If the VI Corps crosses to the west bank of the Saone, as at present contemplated, it is not only in direct pursuit of the enemy's only intact force, the 4th Corps, but will lose so much time in crossing, that contact is certain to be lost. The Belfort Gap is a military objective of the utmost importance, and the advantage of intercepting the enemy there is obvious.

(2) The axis of pursuit which I have indicated follows the grain of the Jura Mountains and is, therefore, less subject to demolitions than any other route in the Saone valley. Further, this route offers a shorter route to the Belfort pass than any route available to the enemy following the Saone valley. We can expect more assistance from the Maquis in the mountainous area than in the valley of the Saone, and we can expect to encounter fewer obstacles and defensive positions, judging from past experiences.

(3) From present indications, the enemy is thinner in this area than any other at this time.

Under the present Army order, this pursuit would be a logical one for French Army B; however, it does not seems that French Army B could be in position to initiate this pursuit for several days at least. Therefore, I recommend that the VI Corps be permitted to continue the pursuit along the axis I have indicated. I am prepared to initiate the operation with one regiment in motors supported by armor and mechanized reconnaissance elements tomorrow, and to follow with the remainder of one division as rapidly as necessary. Utilizing the rail line north of Sisteron to this area, and with maximum assistance from Army and Base Sections, I am certain that I can supply the essential combat elements for this operation. I believe that time is the essential and that the pursuit should be initiated no later than tomorrow.

If you approve this plan and will advise me, I will get it under way at once. If you disapprove, then I shall shift to the west bank of the Saone as rapidly as possible, prepared to carry out my present instructions.
With best regards, I am,
Sincerely

Wilson arrived at the Army Command Post at Brignolles just at midnight. General Patch had a short conference with several members of his staff, then telephoned me at ten minutes of one in the morning. Our connection over the French telephone lines was far from perfect. Patch's voice was faint and indistinct. I finally made out the words: "Your plan is approved. Go ahead." Then there were some words about the French I could not understand—but that could come later.

Logistical problems resulting from shortage in transportation, use of transport for troop movements, and the enormous distances between troops and supply bases were more difficult to overcome than enemy opposition. On the evening of August 22nd, when the vitally important movement of the 36th Infantry Division to join Butler at Montelimar was only beginning, we were forced to take 10,000 gallons of gasoline from the 45th Infantry Division to enable it to move. At the time there was no gasoline in the beach dumps and none was to be unloaded over the beaches the following day. It was a matter requiring a drastic solution, and I sent Colonel O'Neill to solve it. He found a beachmaster who agreed to unload a ship if he could bring one in. He obtained a landing craft and headed seaward to the fleet, going from ship to ship until he found an M/T ship loaded with gasoline. On board, he explained our dire situation to the skipper and persuaded him to move his ship in to the beach for unloading on the condition that O'Neill would square his action with Admiral Hewitt, which O'Neill did. By daylight gasoline was being unloaded on the beach so that our operations could continue unabated. Had O'Neill attempted to solve this problem through the Army G-4, delay in unloading would have had serious implications on the battle at Montelimar and elsewhere.

The Germans had destroyed a railroad bridge at Sisteron. From there through Grenoble and northward, this rail line was in good condition with sufficient rolling stock and engines to run eight or ten trains daily. By commandeering this line to haul supplies north of Sisteron, the Corps was able to free many trucks for the long haul from the beaches to Sisteron.

After Lyon, our rate of advance depended entirely upon our ability to supply the Corps with gasoline, ammunition, and rations. Army Headquarters had taken over operation of the beaches a few days after the assault, and was bending every effort toward rehabilitating rail lines and establishing supply dumps as far north as possible. However, the Army was hampered by delay in arrival of Army transportation, service troops, and difficulties in obtaining labor. On September 1st, supply dumps were all south of the Durance River, although the Army was planning to open a supply base at Montelimar within the next few days. At this time, the 45th Division at Amberieu was 213 miles from the gasoline, ration and ammunition supply point at St. Maximin; the 3rd Division at Voiron, 165 miles away, and the 36th Division at Bonchert, 158 miles away. While the Army moved supply depots forward as quickly as possible, our rate of advance necessitated extended lines of communication. Hauls of 400 miles for ammunition, gasoline, and rations were common.

Every supply vehicle in the Corps was fully engaged night and day hauling gasoline, ammunition and rations from the distant dumps to the troops. These trucks could not be spared for troop movements as would likely have been the case under normal conditions. For troop movements going northeast from Lyon, we organized three provisional truck companies—one for each division—from among the allocated vehicles of the divisions and Corps troops.

The supply situation of the VI Corps was precarious but it was intensified by the appeals for help of French commanders. On September 3rd, du Vigier was in Lyon without gasoline to move. I almost broke O'Neill's heart by giving du Vigier 10,000 gallons from our slender stocks. After this we had almost daily requests from French commanders for gasoline and ammunition. Even though we were fully aware that de Lattre's troops were better off than ourselves with respect to organic transport, we helped whenever we could. On September 8th, I wrote General Patch:

Dear General Patch:

I have just received a note from General Duval, 3rd DIA, in which he states: "My General: I am hard pressed by the Boche north of St. Hippolyte. My artillery has no more ammunition. I beg you instantly to send me as rapidly as possible 30 truck loads of ammunition via Le Russey. It is a capital question and very urgent. I will be infinitely obliged if you will help me. (Signed) Duval". I will send General Duval some ammunition. As you know, my supply at the moment is strictly limited; however, I will do what I can to help him out.

I am informed that he has only five trucks with which to haul ammunition from their dump in Grenoble. I cannot vouch for this statement but I do know that we have daily appeals for both ammunition and gasoline. While I am only too glad to help in any way, I do not have the means to answer these constant appeals. At the same time, since they elected to go into that area Montbeliard, I am dependent upon them to protect my flank south of Doubs River if I am to have any freedom of maneuver to the north of that stream.

I am wondering if there is anything that you can do to improve Duval's supply situation. My ability to assist would be greatly increased if I had the two truck companies that I requested.

I will greatly appreciate your doing whatever you can, either directly or through French Army B, to alleviate this situation.

General Marshall visited the French and American troops in early October. He told me later that when he had visited de Lattre's Headquarters, de Lattre had launched into a bitter denunciation of me, saying the VI Corps had shown to advantage because I had stolen the gasoline allocated to French troops.

In the drive for the Belfort Gap we were preoccupied with logistics more than tactics, but the Germans did make a determined effort to stop our advances along the Doubs River, particularly in the Besançon area. In these actions, the 157th Reserve Divison, which had been west of the Rhone and had not previously been engaged, joined with the remnants of the 11th Panzer Division in the effort to hold us south of the Doubs River until mid-September in order to permit German forces farther to the west to complete their withdrawal through the Belfort Gap and passes farther to the north.

After General Patch telephoned his approval, we lost no time in putting the new plan into effect. My aide's journal records our activities:

Monday September 3, 1944

Corps CP moves to Amberieu after morning briefing. New order to all division commanders under changed plan. 3d to shuttle NE with all possible speed, with 36th continuing push to N. 45th to clean up situation at Bourg and assemble behind 3d. General to 3d CP SW of Lagnieu. New scheme explained to Gen. O'Daniels. They will start immediately. Lunch back at CP. Off to 45th CP at 1500 where plan is explained to Gen. Eagles. Up to I Co, 180th Inf. Observed tank and small arms fire SE Bourg. Back to CP 1800, meeting Gen. O'Daniels on road. 7th Inf already on move and making time. Debacle at Montrevel when 1½ companies 117th Cav. go to sleep and are surrounded and captured. C/S goes to find out what happened. Gen. talks to Maj. McGeary Exec of 117th in War Room after dinner. Still no explanation, but remnants pulled out and sent north.

This incident was almost the only mistake this gallant 117th Calvary Squadron made during the entire campaign. I had ordered Colonel Hodge to gain the rear of the 11th Panzer Division, which was opposing the 45th Infantry Division at Bourg, and he had done so. This detachment had obviously grown somewhat careless, because when the 11th Panzer Division withdrew during the night, these two companies were surprised and overrun, and most of one and a half companies were captured. It was a sad blow to me, even though many of these men rejoined us within the next few weeks. It is a testimonial to the "Cavalry spirit" and to the attitude of the American soldiers that this blow only spurred the squadron on to greater efforts.

Monday, 4 September, 1944

Gen. Dahlquist in at 0330 to be briefed on new mission. 7 RCT to Poligny. 45th collecting itself with patrols in Bourg, reporting no contact. 36th pushing rapidly north with Lyon clear. Morning briefing and meeting with G's and Generals, where plan of action is outlined. General spends rest of morning going over it and talks briefly to Col. Guthrie. Gen. Patch flies in from Grenoble after lunch. Gets tactical picture—approves execution of plan—discusses various administrative and supply matters. Secret intelligence that 11th Panzer Division has orders to attack. All divisions report progress. CG off 1300 for 45th CP at Bourg. Gen. Eagles reports excellent progress assembling division around Lons le Saunier. On to 36th CP at St. Trivier.

Gen. Dahlquist able to move division farther ahead than expected. Back to CP at 2030, Col. Langevin and Lt. Col Conway in to discuss projected moves. Late dinner and bed.

General Patch informed me that de Lattre insisted on deploying Bethouart's French I Corps up on my right in the narrow corridor between the Doubs River and the Swiss border. Duval's 3rd Algerian Infantry Division was already moving north of Grenoble. I had not expected this but I made no objection even though it would restrict my approach to the Belfort Gap and to the area north of the Doubs River.

Tuesday, 6 September, 1944

3d Div. occupies high ground S of Besançon; 45th moving toward Baume, 36th at Mouchard. Regular briefing and CG spends morning in CP on plans; decision to let 3d Div take Besançon and cross Corps center there. CP moves 1400 to vicinity Salin les Bains. Traffic discipline enforced as CG drives up. Maps future moves in War Room after arrival. Gen. Patch in unexpectedly. Still pleased with operation and goes off with Capt. Wilson to 45th and 3d CP's, spending night at 3d. Gen. Bethouart (I Fr Corps) and Duval 3d DIA in. Amicable agreement on boundary question, their chief concern being boundary N of Doubs. Coffee and cocktails to cement agreement. Will Lang and Maj. Barkin are dinner guests at late meal. Bed immediately afterward.

General Patch and I had agreed that, after Besançon, I would cross to the north of the Doubs and approach Belfort on the axis Vesoul-Lure-Belfort, leaving the road just north of the river to the French corps.

Besançon is a city of 75,000 population astride the Doubs River, dominated by heights, and surrounded by fortifications of past ages, built for the most part to protect the city against invasions from the east. It was an unusually strong place, and the German garrison showed every intention of defending it. I told O'Daniels to look the place over carefully, but if he thought he could seize it without additional help, to go ahead; otherwise, he was to occupy the heights and wait for instructions. The 3rd Infantry Division cleared the city on September 7th after some heavy fighting and some spectacular assaults upon the numerous fortifications. Some 700 prisoners were taken.

During the next four days against increasing opposition, the 3rd and 36th Divisions turned northward, captured Rioz and Vesoul, while the 45th Divisions cleared Villersexel and L'Isle sur Doubs. September 12th the Corps was disposed with the 45th Infantry Division on the line L'Isle sur Doubs-Villersexel; the 3rd Infantry Division advancing on Lure; and the 36th Infantry Division in the area between Vesoul and Luxeil. We were in contact with Bothouart's I Corps south of L'Isle sur Doubs, and our plan was to continue the advance on Belfort. We had captured a German map the previous day which did much to clarify the enemy situation and gave us reason to hope that German strength in the Belfort Gap was not too formidable.

General Patch flew in to see me again September 12th. General Devers' newly organized VI Army Group was to become operational on September 15th on which date it was to assume command of the Seventh Army and French Armee B. SHAEF was pressing for a junction of the forces, after which the Seventh Army would have the VI Corps and a corps from General Eisenhower's forces under its command. This meant that our operations against the Belfort Gap would now have to be coordinated with higher headquarters. My plan was to turn the 3rd Infantry Division eastward through Lure while Dahlquist turned eastward through Luxeil, advancing against Belfort on the front Villersexel-Lure-Giromagny, with the three divisions abreast, each one holding one RCT in reserve. General Patch approved this plan and added: "The Belfort Gap is the Gateway to Germany."

Even with our supply difficulties, inclement weather, and increasing enemy opposition, we made good progress during the following day. Then, on the morning of September 14th, we received the Army plan. My aide's journal records my reactions:

Colonel Conway presents Seventh Army plan. Army to have VI and XV Corps; axis of attack: Luxell-Remiremont-Strassbourg-Karlsruhe. General both surprised and disappointed, plan being entirely contrary to his conversation with General Patch on 12th. Plan sacrifices valuable time in Belfort attack, relegates Army to minor role with possibility of complete bogging down in Vosges during the winter. CG spends morning stewing over it.

I summarized my objections in a letter to General Patch on September 15th, although I had no hope that it could have any effect upon the decision.

Dear General:

I have received a copy of FO 5 and plans are under way to effect the necessary relief and carry out the maneuver indicated therein. I was somewhat surprised that the maneuver of the VI Corps is at such variance from that I understood in my conversation with you the other day. I am certain that you have considered the problem carefully but I would like to present my views for your consideration.

At the present time, the Corps holds the line L'Isle-Lure-Luxeil. The last two points are not actually in our possession but should be by tomorrow morning. To the south of the Doubs River, the 1st French Corps, with one division and one RCT of another division, is disposed. The remainder of the 9th DIC is to arrive in the near future but the date is not fixed so far as I know. General Bethouart informed me yesterday that he would not be ready to attack before the 19th. To the west and north, scattered remnants of the retreating German forces are still endeavoring to escape.

As you stated the other day, the Belfort Gap is the Gateway to Germany. It is obvious that the Boche is making strenuous efforts to strengthen the defense of this area and that he expects to hold that area as long as possible. While the permanent fortifications face generally eastward, the natural defensive strength of the area needs little comment. Given sufficient time, the Boche can increase the defenses and make the reduction of this area a slow and costly process, even against our superior power. Every consideration points to the fact that time available to him should be reduced to the minimum. Consequently, the assault on the Belfort Gap should begin at the earliest moment that sufficient troops can be made available and sufficient supplies can be built up.

At the moment, three American and one-plus French divisions are in position to continue the advance toward Belfort. In three days, additional French divisions will be available and at least one French armored division could be available. Subsequently, additional French divisions will become available. It is to be noted that the force now available or to become so within the next two or three days is equal to all that will be at the disposal of French Armee B for such an assault when the entire French force has arrived. Even if the landing schedule is advanced from D plus 60 to D plus 40, it is most unlikely that French Armee B can begin effective operations against the Belfort area much before early October, by which time the Boche will have had considerable time to strengthen his defenses.

The axis prescribed in FO 5 leads through the Vosges Mountains, where roads are limited, terrain rugged and easily defended. With the approach of weather in which rain and snow are to be expected, operations will be most difficult. As demonstrated in Italy during last winter, the Boche can limit progress to a snail's pace and even stop it entirely, even against superior strength. With the SHAEF main effort in the direction Aachen-Bonn-Berlin, this mountainous area has little value if the Belfort Gap is breached, and operations therein can contribute little to the success of SHAEF's main effort. It would seem wasteful to employ the three most veteran divisions in the American Army in an operation where they can be contained by a fraction of their strength and where their demonstrated ability to maneuver is so strictly limited.

Our supply situation as you know is already precarious. Our supply problem has been difficult and, of course, will become more so when heavy fighting incident to the reduction of the Belfort Gap requires enormous ammunition expenditures. However, I have no doubt that, by strenuous effort, solutions can be found and adequate supplies for the operation can be provided.

The Italian front seems to have bogged down in the face of determined German opposition on the Gothic Line. An approach from the Nice area toward Genoa is a feasible operation, especially if supported by sufficient landing craft to permit "end runs" such as contributed to the success on the north coast of Sicily. The appearance of this veteran Corps in the Genoa area would almost certainly break the stalemate in Italy and might bring results as decisive as those which have characterized the operation throughout France. If French Army B is considered sufficient to break through the Belfort Gap, I believe that this operation for the VI Corps might contribute more to the German defeat than the operation ordered through the Vosges Mountains. It could be supplied from bases in the Marseilles area and would considerably alleviate the supply situation for troops in this area.

It seems to me that the following conclusions are justified:

(a) The greatest assistance to the SHAEF main effort by troops in this area is through the Belfort Gap.

(b) If the gap is to be breached, the operation should begin at the earliest practicable time permitted by available troops and logistical considerations.

(c) French Army B will not dispose more resources than are available now or will be within the next few days.

(d) VI Corps is already engaged in the operation of driving in the German covering forces and is well disposed to assist the assault on Belfort.

(e) The operation prescribed in FO 5 for VI Corps can have little effect on the Belfort operation or on the SHAEF main effort and may bog down in winter warfare in the mountains.

(f) An operation toward Genoa and the PO Valley would break the Gothic Line and might insure the destruction of German forces in Italy. This would probably be the most valuable use that could be made of these three veteran divisions.

Therefore, I recommend that the VI Corps: (1) Be employed in opening the Belfort Gap; or (2) That it be employed to capture Genoa and assist in the destruction of the German forces in Italy. It is requested that this latter proposal be submitted to the Army Group Commander for consideration.

General Patch was not overly impressed with my letter. The evening of September 16th, he called me by telephone. Transcription of our conversation was about like this:

Gen. Patch: I don't think that letter of yours was advisable. A less sensitive man than I—and I'm not sensitive at all—would see a lack of confidence shown in your leaders. I think I should tell you that it wasn't a very creditable letter.

Gen. T.: I wrote that letter only because it was something I believe. I don't know the full picture of course.

Gen. P.: I know that, but when I have something on my chest, I just have to say it to that person—that's the way I am.

Gen. T.: So far as I am concerned, you have my complete and whole-hearted support, once the decision is made. If you think someone else can do this job better than I, it is all right with me—but I don't think you can.

Gen. P.: I know that.

Gen. T.: I have gotten into position and the orders are issued on that plan of yours. Everything is ready I have both Luxeil and Lure under attack, and we feel that we can't stop right now.

Gen. P.: Don't stop, keep right on moving, but don't carry out that order until I get it approved.

Gen. T.: I did not understand that. I thought we could go ahead with your order.

Gen. P.: No, I must get it approved first, but I'll get word to you as soon as I can.

Gen. T.: If I go ahead the way I'm going, I will be up against the Belfort defenses the day after tomorrow. If I do, I'm out of the zone prescribed in the Army order.

Gen. P.: I can't see any good holding your people up and not keep pressing the enemy.

Gen. T.: The point is, we are going in two directions—one toward Belfort, the other in the direction I am ordered to advance by the Army order.

Gen. P.: If you follow them, you'll be following the Army order all right.

Gen. T.: I'm in a quandary as to how things will develop if I am going in two directions.

Gen. P.: I'll talk to you when I see you. I may come up and spend the night tomorrow night. In the meantime, don't lose any sleep over it.

Colonel John F. Cassidy, my deputy chief of staff, came in with word that day that my name and Carleton's had been sent to the Senate for confirmation of promotion to Lieutenant General and Brigadier General respectively. Even this news and a mild promotion party did little toward raising my spirits.

I saw General Patch on September 17th. He was now enthusiastic about the sweep to the north though the Strasbourg Gap, but it had not yet been approved by SHAEF. He thought we had no alternative but to suspend our attack, and wait for two or three days in our present positions. Meanwhile, the French forces were to relieve the 45th Infantry Division south of Lure so that Eagles would be available for the advance to the north. It was not until September 21st that we were able to begin crossing the Moselle, with the 36h Infantry Division crossing in the vicinity of Remiremont and the 45th Division crossing about Epinal. Because of delays by the French in taking over from the 3rd

Division in the Lure Area, O'Daniels did not begin crossing in the vicinity of Rupt until September 24th.

I met General Patch again on September 23rd. He had just returned from Versailles where he had conferred with General Eisenhower. His news was depressing. He brought word that the British were to make the SHAEF main effort on the north flank of the Allied armies, and that the logistical position was such that only the British forces could be supplied; the supply situation in the north was much worse than ours. The American forces would be compelled to go on the defensive along the entire front. It looked more than ever like a winter in the Vosges.

General Patch and General Devers visited my Command Post again on September 27th. The "big picture" was unchanged, but Devers and Patch thought there were signs the resistance we were encountering was a light shell only, with no reserves behind, and that the Germans were in a state of complete confusion. The plan outlined was to have the VI Corps advance on Strasbourg through the St. Die pass through the Vosges Mountains, while the XV Corps, which was to come under Seventh Army Command the following day, took the route leading eastward from Baccarat and Raon l' Etape. Army Field Orders No. 6 issued the following day committed the VI Corps to the St. Die route.

Operations made slow progress during the first two weeks in October. Rain was almost incessant and vastly increased the hardships of moving and fighting. Cold caused acute discomfort, and the losses and exertions of preceding weeks were having their effect. All units were under strength, and officers and men were in need of rest. North of the Moselle, rugged foothills covered with dense forests made operations most arduous. Thick woods required greater concentrations of troops to wipe out the enemy, while the Corps was extended on such a wide front that any concentration was difficult. Our supply situation became more critical with the additional maintenance needed for XV Corps.

On October 15th, we launched an attack to capture Bruyeres and break through the German defenses in the direction of St. Die. The plan was to have the 45th Infantry Division attack from the west, while the 36th Division, with the attached 442nd RCT made up of Japanese-Americans, who had been guarding the Franco-Italian border, were to drive from the south. If we succeeded in breaking through the German positions, we were to use the 3rd Infantry Division to exploit the break-through toward St. Die. This attack was well under way on October 17th and was making good, although relatively slow, progress. That morning I was called to the Army Command Post at Epinal to confer with General Patch and General Eisenhower.

General Eisenhower greeted me warmly, and made some complimentary remarks about our previous operations. There was some discussion of the current situation on our front, and then General Eisenhower said: "Lucian, I am going to relieve you from the VI Corps. You are an embarrassment to me now that you have been made a lieutenant general. All of my Corps commanders now want to be made lieutenant generals. I am going to assign you to organize the Fifteenth Army. You won't like it, because this Army is not going to be operational. It will be an administrative and training command, and you won't get into the fighting."

I replied that I would much prefer to remain with the VI Corps and was perfectly willing to remain as a major general since I had not asked to be promoted, that is, if General Patch was willing for me to do so. General Patch said that he would like to have me remain. However, General Eisenhower said it was not practicable to have me remain with the Corps, and that he needed me for organizing the new Army. Major General E. H. (Ted) Brooks was to replace me in command of the VI Corps, and he was already on his way. I was to remain while the present assault was under way and until Brooks had affairs well in hand. Then I was to come to SHAEF, stopping off on the way to discuss the organization of the new Army with General Bradley under whose command I would be. He would send me home for a short leave. When I returned, I would take up my new command.

That was almost the end of the campaign in southern France for me. We captured Bruyeres. Brooks joined the Corps and was thoroughly briefed. The attack was pressing ahead and there seemed to be good prospects of achieving the break-through. On October 24th, Carleton, the aides, and I went the rounds of the divisions to say good-bye to the commanders and staffs with whom we had been comrades-in-arms for so long. The following morning, we said good-bye to General Patch and the Army staff and departed for Vittel for a visit with General Devers and the Army Group staff.

We spent two nights with General Devers, a night with General Patton at Third Army Headquarters in Nancy, and then on to General Bradley's Headquarters in Luxembourg, and General Courtney Hodges' First Army Headquarters in Spa. On October 30th, I checked in with my good friend Bedell Smith at SHAEF. We spent a few days on preliminary planning for organizing the Fifteenth Army. Then I left Carleton to assemble the staff officers whom we were bringing with us from VI Corps and to collect the elements which were then waiting in England. On November 4th, accompanied by Wilson and Bartash, Sergeants Barna and Hong, I departed for my first visit home in more than two years.

•

CHAPTER EIGHT

AN ARMY COMMAND

1. *Return to Italy*

Mrs. Truscott and I spent the last few days of my leave in Washington where I was engaged in final conferences with various officials prior to my return to Europe. One day I spent flying to West Point to visit my son Lucian, and enjoyed a long visit with him and his "wives"—as roommates were called. My party was scheduled to leave Washington the afternoon of November 21st. That morning I went in to pay my final call on General Marshall.

While I was with General Marshall, General Handy, Deputy Chief of Staff, General Hull, Chief of the Operations Division, and others came in for the usual morning presentation of the military situation, for which I remained at General Marshall's request. It was intensely interesting, covering briefly, concisely, and in detail the military deployment of our forces in all parts of the world. The briefing ended, members of the staff presented problems for General Marshall's decision. Ed Hull presented one that was to affect me.

Hull referred to the recent death of Sir John Dill, chief of the British military mission in Washington. He reported that the British planned to bring Sir Henry Maitland Wilson from the Mediterranean Theater to replace Sir John Dill and to have General Alexander replace General Wilson as Supreme Allied Commander Mediterranean. Hull remarked that he supposed General Clark would replace General Alexander as Commanding General Allied Armies in Italy, which would leave the Fifth Army command vacant. The problem was: did General Marshall wish General Keyes to command the Fifth Army as General Clark would doubtless recommend, or did he wish to assign someone else?

General Marshall turned to me. "How do you feel about going back to Italy?"

I was taken aback, but I answered, "Sir, I will do the best I can wherever you wish to send me."

"I know that," General Marshall remarked shortly. "That is not what I asked you. How do you feel about going back to Italy?"

"Well, sir," I replied, "if the choice were left with me I would prefer to remain in France. I have looked forward to serving with General Eisenhower again."

"I suppose you prefer France because you think France is the decisive theater," General Marshall said. "You think that is where the war will be won."

"Yes, sir. Something like that," I explained, and then added: "Of course you know that both Corps Commanders in the Fifth Army have always been senior to me."

General Marshall made no reply. Turning to Hull, he said, "Query General Eisenhower on this subject."

So the conference ended.

I was to leave from La Guardia Field for the transatlantic flight late that afternoon. I thought that if I could see General Eisenhower before he replied to Hull's cable, he might make it possible for me to remain in France. But delays in departure and while enroute prevented my arriving in Paris earlier than November 24th.

I went at once to see "Beetle" Smith at Versailles. When I entered his office, he looked up at me and said with mock severity: "Well, you are a nice one. No sooner do we get you back under our command than off you go and find yourself a new assignment." I remarked that I had hoped General Eisenhower would reply to Hull's cable saying he had need of my services. "Beetle" replied: "Not a chance. The PM personally asked for you." He handed me a cable which was lying on his desk in which General Eisenhower had said that because of my previous experiences in Italy, my familiarity with conditions there, and my good relations with the British, I was the logical choice for the Italian assignment and that he was glad to release me for it.

We left Orly Air Field near Paris on the afternoon of December 5th, and reached Caserta later the same day. The last ten days I had spent visiting various American Headquarters in France, and collecting those who were to return with me. General Eisenhower authorized me to take back with me the officers whom I had brought on from the VI Corps for the Fifteenth Army, for we realized that the principal staff officers of the Fifth Army would accompany General Clark to his new command. My party included Carleton, Cassidy, Conway, Harrel, O'Neill, Myers, Barkin, Daniels, my aides Wilson and Bartash, Sergeants Barna and Hong and several other enlisted men.

We reached Florence on December 7th, and were met by Don Brann, the Army G-3. The following morning, we proceeded to the Army Command Post in Futa Pass about twenty miles north of Florence, where we found Generals Clark, Gruenther, and many other old friends, and learned that General Alexander had fixed December 16th as the date for the changes in command. For a week, we familiarized ourselves with the situation and with conditions existing in the Fifth Army.

The Army Command Post was located near the miniscule village of

Traversa on Highway 65 just on the north side of Futa Pass, at an elevation of about 2700 feet. Here Highway 65 ran along the steep mountainside by the crest of the divide which separated the headwaters of four or five streams dividing a vast area to the north. There were a few scattered trees but for the most part the mountain slopes were steep, barren and rocky. In a few comparatively level regions the Commanding General, Chief of Staff, each of the General Staff Sections, one or two of the Special Staff sections, along with clerical, administrative, and communications personnel, were housed in trailers, tents, and a few prefabricated buildings. The rest of the Army staff was located with the Rear Headquarters in Florence.

In a cleared part at the northern end, there was a prefabricated building—"The Hut"—which General Clark used as a sort of club room for some members of his staff and for conferences. Off to one side, was Clark's rather luxurious trailer. In rear of The Hut stood a small wall tent which was the Army Commander's mess with the kitchen tent nearby. Beyond that, the Chief of Staff's Office and then the various staff sections were located. I placed my van, which we had brought on from the VI Corps, not far from Clark's, and later on erected office tents for my personal staff. Here, in ice, snow, mud, and fog we spent the winter.

Departure of the VI Corps and the French divisions for the invasion of southern France had left the Fifth Army with only five divisions under its command—the 1st Armored and the 34th, 85th, 88th, and 91st Infantry Divisions. The Eighth Army had some sixteen divisions. Both Armies had pressed the pursuit of the retreating Germans and by mid-August had reached the general line Ancona-Perugia-Arezzo-Arno River. There, it had been necessary to rest, regroup, and reorganize the extended supply lines.

In September, General Alexander had launched a major offensive to break through the Gothic Line and destroy the German armies in Italy. The Eighth Army began the attack during the last week in August and by the first week in September had broken through the Line south of Rimini. The Fifth Army then crossed the Arno River and by September 22nd, after bitter fighting in some of the most difficult terrain yet encountered, Keyes' II Corps had pierced the Gothic Line at Il Giogio and Futa Passes.

Meanwhile, the Eighth Army, retarded by torrential rains, was lagging behind. General Clark changed the direction of his main effort toward Faenza and Imola in an effort to break through into the Po plain and assist the advance of the Eighth Army. This attack spent its forces by the end of September with the 88th Infantry Division on Mt.

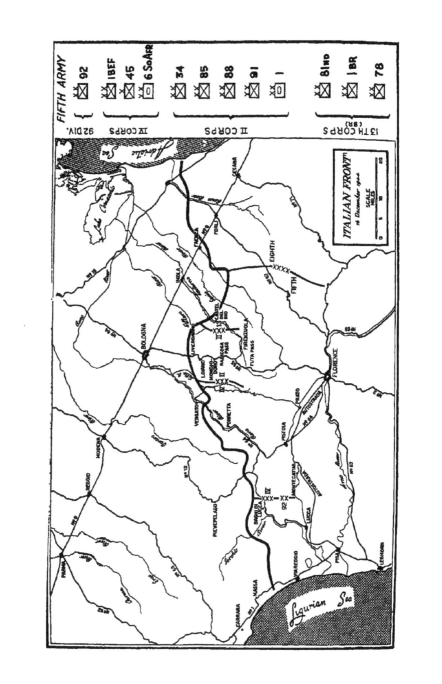

Battiglia some ten miles from Imola and with the British XIII Corps even farther away from Faenza.

General Clark then shifted the pressure back to Highway 65 for the drive toward Bologna. Under unfavorable conditions of weather and against increasing enemy opposition, it made slow progress, and was brought to a halt by mid-October with the II Corps still south of Pianoro and ten miles away from Bologna. In a final desperate effort during the last two weeks in October, Clark turned to the northwest again. The 88th Infantry Division captured Mt. Grande almost on the edge of the Po valley near Castel San Pietro. There, with success almost within their grasp, torrential rains, physical exhaustion, and supply troubles brought the advance to a heart-breaking halt. So the lines had remained.

Field Marshal Kesselring still commanded the German forces opposing the Allied Armies in Italy. His Army Group Southwest comprised the same two Army commands we had known the previous winter—the Fourteenth commanded by General Lemelsen generally opposite the Fifth Army, and the Tenth Army commanded by Lieutenant General Herr on the Eighth Army front for the most part. At the end of October, Kesselring's command included thirty-three divisions—twenty-seven German and six Fascist Italian—as compared with some twenty-seven British and American divisions. Actual infantry strength of the opposing forces was not disproportionate, although the Allies had the advantage because of the larger size of their divisions, particularly the American divisions, and the depleted strength of some German formations. The great advantage in combat strength which the Allies possessed lay in their overwhelming air power.

General Alexander renewed the offensive at the end of November to prevent the withdrawal of any German forces from Italy to oppose the Allied armies on other fronts. The plan was to have the Eighth Army begin the attack in the Adriatic plain and drive the Germans west of the Santerno River. When the Eighth Army reached the Santerno, which it was expected to do about December 7th, it was to turn northward to outflank Bologna from the east, while the Fifth Army joined in the attack making its main effort with the II Corps astride Highway 65. The attack of the Eighth Army got off to a good start, but was soon slowed down by rains and floods. When we joined the Fifth Army on December 8th, the Eighth Army had not yet reached the Santerno. However, all preparations had been made for the Fifth Army attack, and the II Corps stood by on seventy-two hours notice. In familiarizing myself with the strategy of this attack—the PIANORO Plan as it was known—I became acquainted with the existing conditions of the front. I also came to learn that General Clark was very sensitive to any criticisms or suggestions pertaining to the PIANORO plan.

The Northern Apennines extend from the Mediterranean coast near Genoa southeast across the Italian peninsula toward Rimini on the Adriatic, parallel the coast for some distance, and then turn inland to become the Central Apennines which form the backbone ridge for the Italian boot. The Northern Apennines are barren and rugged. Many peaks exceed 6,000 feet in height. At the narrowest point between Florence and Bologna, the range is about sixty miles in width. The crest line is not well defined, but lies nearer the Arno River valley than the Po valley so that the more important streams flow northeast toward the Po. The most important of these mountain streams, the Reno River, rises near Pistoia on the edge of the Arno River valley and cuts almost entirely across the range to enter the Po plain at Bologna. From Futa Pass, where the Army Command Post was located, the principal streams fanned out like fingers on a wide-spread hand—the Sillaro toward Castel San Pietro, then the Idice, the Zena, the Savena, and the Setta, the latter joining the Reno River a few miles south of Bologna. The main roads followed these valleys, in many places hewn from the steep mountain sides, with steep grades and many loops and turns. There were few roads connecting the valleys so that cross-communication was most difficult.

The British XIII Corps, commanded by Lieutenant General S. C. Kirkman, which had been under Fifth Army command during the fall offensive, held the eastern sector of the Fifth Army front, facing Highway 9 generally between Faenza and Castel San Pietro. This Corps had three divisions and a Guards Brigade in line, the 8th Indian, 1st British (which had been with me at Anzio), 1st Guards Brigade, and 78th Division. The II Corps front extended from Mt. Grande overlooking the Po valley near Castel San Pietro west across the rugged ridges to Setta Creek west of Highway 65. Major General W. H. E. Poole's 6th South African Division faced Mt. Sole in the angle between Setta Creek and the Reno River. West of the Reno River to the Serchio valley, the IV Corps under Major General W. D. Crittenberger held a wide but inactive sector with the 1st Brazilian Division and Task Force 45, composed of antiaircraft troops employed as infantry. The 92nd Infantry Division occupied the coastal sector north of Leghorn. The 92nd Infantry Division and the Brazilian Expeditionary Force had arrived in the theater during the fall offensive. Both were inexperienced. All others were veteran divisions.

For the PIANORO operation, the II Corps had available the 34th, 85th, 88th, and 91st Infantry Divisions and the 1st Armored Division. The plan envisaged an attack along Highway 65 with Mts. Monterumici, Adone and dei Frati—enormously rugged features southwest of Pianoro—as initial objectives for the II Corps and with Mt. Sole as the objective for the 6th South African Division. Then there would be a drive north to capture Bologna.

This was the most heavily fortified area along the entire front—held by German forces not materially inferior in strength to those which would be attacking. Under unfavorable conditions of weather and terrain, it seemed to me an appalling undertaking. Even with overwhelming support of our air forces, I thought it would be a difficult and costly venture even if it could succeed. When Clark asked my opinion, I mentioned these reservations and suggested a maneuver west of Highway 64 might be much easier going and perhaps accomplish the same purpose more quickly at less cost. Clark disagreed, and he was always thereafter sensitive to any criticism of this PIANORO plan.

Beginning the day after our arrival, I spent my days visiting the various parts of the front, familiarizing myself with conditions among the troops, renewing acquaintances with many commanders and staffs, and becoming acquainted with others. Rain, snow, and cold, particularly disagreeable in the high mountains, continued to delay the attack. Keyes and Crittenberger were cavalry men, as was I. Keyes had been my instructor at Training Camp during World War I; he had been my superior as General Patton's deputy in Africa, in the Provisional Corps in Sicily, and in the II Corps for a brief period before I sailed for Anzio. Crittenberger had been an instructor at the Cavalry School when I was a student. Both these officers had always been senior to me, and now our positions were reversed. It was a difficult situation for them, I know, but neither ever showed it by word or deed. No commander ever had more loyal support than these able officers gave to me.

The change in command took place on December 16th, following a farewell ceremony for General Clark at the Army CP. The following day, we were honored by a visit by the Military Affairs Committee of the House of Representatives, my first function as an Army Commander, which my aide's journal describes:

Scattered clouds today. Still very muddy. Situation on front quiet. Family up for breakfast usual hour. Influx of brass hats of various denominations, waiting for arrival of Congressional party (House Military Affairs Committee) which is brought over Altuzzo Pass by General Clark, arriving at approximately 1000. Congressional party and hangers on are briefed in hut by General Clark, where subordinate commanders are introduced, followed by coffee and doughnuts. Also present, Generals Keyes, Cannon, and Chidlaw. Entire party off in procession of 30 jeeps to Monghidoro for brief church service and K ration lunch in wrecked church. They meet Gens. Bolte and Williamson. Under way again in mud to Loiano, making a loop there and returning by Highway 65 to 8th Evac Hospital for inspection tour. Gen. Truscott makes entire trip with Representative Costello, Acting Committee

Chairman. From 8th Evac Hospital back to PRO office for discussion and more coffee and doughnuts, Gen. Clark having left partly at 8th Evac. Gen. Truscott says good-bye at 1600, returns to CP with Bill Mauldin, talks over Mauldin's new book with him in the van until 1700. Cocktails in hut, dinner, and early bed.

In the staff changes that took place following the departure of Clark and the officers who accompanied him to 15th Army Group, Carleton became Chief of Staff, Cassidy Deputy Chief of Staff supervising administration, Daniels, G-1; Harrel, G-3 with Conway as Executive and Chief of the Planning Syndicate; and O'Neill, G-4. Brig. Gen. E. B. Howard did not accompany Clark to 15th Army Group but remained as Army G-2. Myers and Barkin became principal assistants to the Signal Officer and Headquarters Commandant, respectively. My principal staff officers, therefore, were those who had been closely associated with me for a long period.

We began each day with a staff meeting in which each section reviewed its problems and activities. Once a week, we assembled all of the special staff officers from the Rear Headquarters in conference with the staff at the Forward Command Post, to keep them completely informed. These meetings proved most effective.

I spent December 22nd with the 6th South African Division in the rugged terrain facing Mt. Sole in the angle between Setta Creek and the Reno River. Late in the afternoon, I proceeded to Florence after a message from General Clark requested me to meet him there. He had intelligence that indicated a strong build-up of enemy forces in the Serchio Valley. Our front in the Serchio Valley was about twenty miles north of Lucca and only about forty-five miles north of our principal port and supply base at Leghorn. It had been an inactive front and was held by colored troops—the 370th Infantry of the 92nd Infantry Division, and part of the all-colored 366th Infantry Regiment. No Army reserves were there—in fact, all of the combat divisions were either in the front lines or in the II Corps sector in readiness to begin PIANORO, on three days' notice.

The German counteroffensive in France—the Battle of the Bulge—had started on December 16th, and it was still rolling on unchecked. Clark was fearful the German command might be preparing a similar unpleasant surprise for us. We knew that elements of the 148th Grenadier Division and an Italian division were already in the area. And there were signs that the 157th Mountain Division, and possibly the 16th SS Panzer Grenadier Division, were moving up. Clark's G-2 thought the Germans might be able to free at least two other divisions, even though they were severely restricted and handicapped to undertake any large scale rapid movements. In view of our weakness on the coastal sector, a strong German attack in the Serchio Valley sector would be a grave threat to our vital supply base at Leghorn. Nor was it pleasing to contemplate what might happen if German armor suddenly appeared in rear of the 92nd Infantry Division along the coast. Clark thought we should take adequate precautionary measures, and I was in complete agreement.

Two brigade groups of the 8th Indian Division were being withdrawn from the line and moved to the vicinity of Lucca for rest and refitting. We decided to use them in the Serchio Valley in case of need. In addition, we moved two Regimental Combat Teams of the 85th Infantry Division, which was in Corps reserve for the PIANORO plan, as well as some additional artillery and tank battalions, over to the coast. Since the 1st Armored Division was in the II Corps sector where terrain and weather conditions made the employment of armor impracticable, I ordered it to Lucca in Army reserve. These movements got under way during the next two or three days, but they had not been completed when the enemy struck.

On the morning of December 26th, the Germans launched several limited-objective attacks in the Serchio valley, with forces involving some five or six battalions, which struck the 1st Battalion 370th Infantry and the 2nd Battalion 366th Infantry, both of which "melted away" —a term which was to be frequently used in describing action of colored troops. General Crittenberger, whom I had made responsible for operations in the coastal sector, moved the Indian brigades forward to stop the German advance, which they did very promptly. Then with strong air support by the XXII Tactical Air Command, the Indians advanced. By December 30th, they had retaken the towns of Gallicani and Barga and had completely restored the situation. Meanwhile, commanders, staff officers, and military police had rounded up stragglers and had reorganized the dispersed battalions.

It was fortunate the Germans did not make any greater effort in the Serchio valley than they did. Elements of four German divisions had been identified in these actions, but none of them involved more than combat groups with limited objectives. It seems likely the Germans were making a reconnaissance in force which they might have exploited if additional troops had not been encountered there. We were relieved that this was so, for a major attack could have been embarrassing or even gravely dangerous.

The high command was concerned because in spite of our efforts one German division had been withdrawn from Italy in November and another had departed during December. On December 29th, General Clark was still bent upon carrying out the PIANORO attack, even though we would now require seven days in which to complete preparations because of the Serchio valley flap. However, flood conditions had brought the advance of the Eighth Army to a standstill in the Adriatic plain; and snow and ice blanketed the mountains on the Fifth Army front so that the movement of men, not to mention weapons and vehicles, over the precipitous and rugged slopes would be extremely difficult. Then an examination of our ammunition reserve during the latter part of December showed there was only enough to support fifteen days of offensive operations, and no more would be available until the end of January.

I thought there was almost no chance the PIANORO attack could be successful under the existing conditions. General Keyes was more optimistic, but his most cheerful estimates did not envisage reaching the Po plain within fifteen days. I recommended that the PIANORO attack be cancelled, and that we contain the enemy on our front with limited-objective attacks involving not more than a division at any one time. After conferring with General McCreery and me on December 30th, General Clark reluctantly agreed to postponement of any major offensive until the ammunition situation improved. The following day, I was called to Florence to confer further with Field Marshal Alexander and General Clark. Field Marshal Alexander agreed the PIANORO plan was out of the question and said that definite plans for resuming the offensive would have to await adjustments on the front of both Armies.

There was another conference at Fifteenth Army Group—as General Clark's Headquarters was now known—on January 4th at which it was decided we would hold our defensive positions and build up ammunition reserves for a spring offensive with a target date of April 1st. In readjusting the front, the British XIII Corps would revert to Eighth Army control, but the 6th South African Division would remain under Fifth Army command. Owing to the necessity for economy in ammunition in order to build up the thirty-day reserve, the Fifth Army was authorized to undertake only two limited-objective attacks in division strength: one by the 92nd Infantry Division in the coastal sector to test further the battleworthiness of the colored troops, the other in the IV Corps sector to capture Mt. Belvedere and improve our positions west of Highway 64.

To hold our defensive positions, we reorganized and arranged a schedule of reliefs so that each division would have a period of four weeks for rest, rehabilitation of equipment, reception of replacements, training and conditioning for offensive operations. On the front, we followed the procedure we had found effective at Anzio. Each division employed two regiments in its forward areas, holding one in reserve for training and to facilitate rotation of regiments in the more rigorous front line duties. Similarly, each regiment usually employed two battalions in its forward sectors, holding one in reserve to facilitate similar rotation of duties and training among the battalions of the regiment.

The period of stalemate did not mean a cessation of fighting. So far as the front line was concerned, combat followed the normal pattern of warfare when both sides are gathering their strength for a major effort. German artillery was far more forceful than it had been during the preceding winter, even during the defensive period at Anzio. Our own artillery was active within the restrictions placed upon it and we made extensive use of smoke screens to limit German observation and reduce the effectiveness of their artillery fires. Patrol activities were continuous, and the Germans were quick to exploit any carelessness in any of our forward positions. On our own side, we sought to obtain identifications and other information of opposing enemy forces, to eliminate troublesome enemy posts, to deceive the enemy as to our own intentions, and to improve our own techniques—all of which, carried on in bitter weather, in rugged mountains sheathed in snow and ice, saw some of the most gallant and heroic actions of the campaign.

For the service echelons—and only about one-fourth of the Army's strength was in the infantry combat companies—the period of stalemates was a period of even increased labors. Consumption of most supplies continued at normal rates, and reserves had to be built up. Battle casualties continued, though less in number. But the rigorous conditions to which troops were exposed resulted in more injuries and illness—respiratory ailments and jaundice in particular. And rehabilitation and replacement of worn out and broken equipment and the maintenance of serviceable equipment is always an increased burden during a lull in activities.

Nearly all of our supplies came from the United States. They were unloaded at Naples and Leghorn and delivered by rail and truck to Army depots near Florence, Pistoia, Lucca and Pisa, from where they were carried forward by truck over difficult, winding mountain roads with steep grades to Army dumps in the forward areas. From there they were trucked, as far as roads permitted, to the Army units. Supply of the forward elements was by jeep and mule train over tortuous mountain trails. The Army utilized fifteen Italian packtrains with a strength of nearly 4,000 mules. Every veteran of this winter in the Apennines will always remember their loyal and courageous service under arduous conditions and often under fire. Without them, the campaign would hardly have been possible.

All roads in the Army area were taxed far beyond their normal capacity, besides suffering still more damage from the severe weather conditions. Road maintenance and repair imposed enormous burdens upon Army engineers. Floods washed away temporary repairs and bridges. Landslides frequently blocked roads. Snow plows were in almost continuous use. Engineer assistance was required to move stalled vehicles. Traffic congestion made road maintenance extremely difficult. Nevertheless, in the face of all of these obstacles, Brigadier General Frank Bowman and his engineers, employing all available road building and maintenance equipment, the labor of hundreds of soldiers, and thousands of Italian laborers, kept the roads open and steadily improved them in preparation for the spring offensive. No troops in the Army performed more valiant work than the engineers.

Highway 65 north of Florence was an especially difficult problem. It was the supply route for four infantry divisions and numerous Army troops in addition to normal communications and other travel. The traffic became so heavy—continuous streams in both directions—that rigid traffic control and discipline was necessary to prevent jams comparable to those of rush hours in an American city. Control was based upon convoy speeds permitted by road conditions. Control points were established and the highway was patrolled constantly. Trucks were required to maintain prescribed speeds, and one was not to pass another while it was moving. Passenger vehicles, messengers, and smaller individual cars were permitted to thread their way. But once this system became effective, we eliminated the traffic jams that had often halted movement for hours.

Throughout the Italian campaign, the supply situation had always been difficult. Limited in the early days by lack of shipping and production, it was now rendered even more critical by the low priority of the Italian theater with respect to others. As a result, the Fifth Army, more than any other, developed economical supply methods and superior techniques for conservation and utilization of all available resources. Combat areas are always littered with materiel and equipment, damaged or abandoned during and after battles. So this materiel—guns, vehicles, clothing, equipment items of every description—when there was a lull in action, was collected at Army dumps at the front and returned to the supply services. In addition to their normal supply and maintenance services, the Army Quartermaster and the Army Ordnance Services, under the direction of their respective chiefs, Brigadier Generals Joseph Sullivan and Urban Niblo, ran extensive salvage and reclamation facilities, far beyond that normally expected of a field Army. Sullivan operated a factory employing hundreds of Italian workers for reconditioning salvageable clothing and for manufacturing special winter clothes and other articles not then available in the Italian theater. Niblo's "Willow Run" was a huge repair shop for the complete rebuilding of trucks and jeeps by assembly line methods, utilizing hundreds of Italian mechanics under the supervision of American ordnance personnel. These installations were the show centers of the service areas during this winter. Similar shops rehabilitated other items of equipment. These activities not only furnished the Army with equipment and supplies otherwise unobtainable; they also provided useful employment for thousands of Italians who would have been an onerous responsibility, and in addition saved millions of dollars for the United States Government.

At this time it should also be stressed that the Medical Service directed by Brigadier General Joseph I. Martin, the Army Surgeon, made an enormous contribution to the welfare of the command. Besides the normal care for casualties, sick and injured, it cooperated with commanders in carefully watching over everyone's health. In spite of the rigorous conditions under which men served, there was less than a third of the trench foot cases of the previous winter, and the rate for respiratory diseases was even lower. Typhoid, which was prevalent in the Arno Valley, left the command untouched.

No one has better summed up the morale factor in Army life than Napoleon, who is reputed to have said than in war the morale is to the physical as three is to one. Morale is a personal concern for every military leader, for no Army in battle is ever any better than the spirit that animates it. The Fifth Army gave a great deal of consideration to the welfare of its troops and morale building activities all throughout the Italian campaign. Yet, in my first few weeks, I found commanders gravely concerned over morale problems.

It is not hard to maintain morale when troops are advancing and winning victories. Then it is always high; and spirits soar in spite of the worst privations, physical exertions, and dangers. The end of December found the Fifth Army about as it had been at the end of October —when some confidence existed that the end of the war was in sight. For two months preparations for the offensive had given the men a renewed purpose. Now those who had suffered the rigors of a campaign in the mountains during the previous winter could only look to another winter campaign in higher and more rugged mountains under worse conditions of cold, rain, and snow. It was not a pleasing prospect —and it was made less palatable because the attention of the world was focused upon the eastern and western fronts in Europe. The Italian theater was on a low priority in comparison to other theaters for men, supplies, and equipment and the public had all but forgotten that there was an Italian front. This fact was reflected in that greatest of all morale factors among American troops—the mail from home.

Conditions that affected morale of American soldiers during this second winter in Italy were not new, nor, except in one or two instances, were they even peculiar to the Italian theater. Men long subjected to the restrictions of military control and the tensions of battle longed for the individual freedom they had known in civil life. American soldiers were homesick. Prolonged absence brought personal problems—usually family distress, business or financial troubles, or affairs of the heart. Most men dreaded the relative inactivity, hardships, and indecisiveness of another winter campaign in the mountains. The public press and mail brought almost daily reminders from people who wondered why these soldiers were not fighting in Europe. Some individuals and units who had been overseas a long time even held the belief that they had already done their part toward winning the war, and that their places should be taken by others with less overseas service.

The War Department had established, during the previous year, a policy which permitted the rotation of a limited number of men from the Italian theater for assignment within the United States. While the numbers involved were comparatively small, this rotation was important for morale since it held out some hope to the homesick soldier that his return might not have to wait the end of the war. Returning veterans were of the utmost value in training soldiers who had not yet seen combat.

But sound discipline is also the fundamental basis for good morale, and the Fifth Army laid great stress upon leadership in all ranks, intensive training in every echelon, thorough preparation for all missions, as well as provision of the best possible food, clothing and equipment. Adequate periods for rest and relaxation, facilities for entertainment and amusement, and intelligent information programs with newspapers, radio, and magazines were all measures utilized to sustain and build morale. But perhaps no single activity contributed more in this respect than our rest center program.

Only those who have experienced war can fully appreciate the continuous strains under which men live in battle. There is no eight-hour day—no overtime—no Sundays off—few week-ends. In no profession are occasional leave periods so important for reasons of health, both physical and mental, as among combat troops. During the First World War, men were granted occasional leaves which they spent in Paris, other places in France, or in England. But it was not practical for soldiers to take furloughs in Italian towns owing to the devastated state of the country's economy. Accordingly, the Fifth Army initiated a rest program in November, 1943, and the first center was established in Naples, under direction of the Special Services Officer, 3rd Infantry Division, which I was then commanding. Others were subsequently established at Sorrento, Capri, Rome, Florence, and elsewhere.

Men and units who believed they had already done more than their share toward winning the war presented a more difficult problem, which General Keyes described in a letter addressed to the Commanding General, Fifth Army, on November 28th. He brought it to my attention several days after I assumed command.

General Keyes began:

> After an exhaustive study of the disciplinary and morale status of the 34th Infantry Division I am led to the conclusion that certain personnel of this division should be withdrawn from combat and returned to the United States, if this division is to continue in combat. The division has maintained a consistently high AWOL and Courts Martial rate for some time. An inordinately large percentage of the Courts Martial cases have been for misbehavior before the enemy, disobedience of orders, aggravated AWOL, and related offenses. The division has a high "exhaustion" rate. Investigation discloses that all of these conditions are traceable, either directly or indirectly, to a common, motivating influence: a deep conviction by the older, or original, officers and men of the 34th Division, that they have done their part in this war, that they should be permitted to return to the United States and the struggle left to those who have not been absent from home for two years. After periods of rest, rehabilitation, and reorganization in rear areas, the unit displays little, if any, increased efficiency when again committed to action. The attitude of the men would seem to stem, not from "combat" weariness, but from general "war" weariness.

General Keyes pointed out that at the rate of about one per cent a month, which the division was permitted to send home under the existing War Department rotation policy, more than three years would be required to return to the United States the thirty-five per cent, or 5,000 men, remaining who came over with the division, and then remarked:

> The American public, through the press, has been led to believe that families may expect the return of the soldier who has been overseas 18 months. The families thus affected by the present rotation policy are so few as to be negligible in the over-all picture. A feeling of discontent and unjustified imposition is manifesting itself in the families of the original members of this division and is being transmitted to the soldier overseas by the very mediums most affecting his state of mind.

Keyes considered three possible solutions: returning the division to the United States; redistributing personnel among other divisions in the theater, or, and this he recommended, setting a time limit beyond which men would not be required to serve overseas. Specifically, he thought no member of the United States Army should be required to serve overseas longer than three years, and that every member of the Army so desiring should be returned to the United States within thirty to thirty-six months of his departure therefrom, except that disciplinary cases would be required to serve three full years and make up any bad time accruing to them overseas.

In my reply to General Keyes on December 21st, informing him that I was forwarding his letter to higher authority, I remarked:

> I do not believe that the replacement machinery within the Army could stand the strain of replacing all members of the U. S. Army as they reach their 30 months service. However, I do not see why combat troops could not be so replaced at the end of 30 or 36 months and men in other categories taken care of by normal rotation. So far in my travels I have gained a definite impression that there is no real problem in the rear area troops.
>
> As for the 34th Division specifically, I cannot but feel that their difficulty is entirely one of discipline and command responsibility. The 3rd, 1st and 9th Divisions have had the same service under very similar combat conditions. The morale in all these units is excellent to superior. If there are officers in the 34th Division who have lost their usefulness and their efficiency and feel that they have done their part in the war, I think General Bolte should take immediate corrective measures. As you well know, that is the purpose of the reclassification boards and it is only by the stern and impassive use of reclassification boards that units like this can be maintained at a high standard of efficiency and morale.

I sent General Keyes' letter on to General McNarney, pointing out that it indicated conditions in the 34th Division as General Keyes saw them, but of which I had no personal knowledge as yet. While I was aware that any change in War Department policy would have many ramifications, I thought there was a need for determining a length of time after which men who had served in combat should be returned to the United States, and I thought the time might well be set at about three years, but I added:

> The later disposition of any personnel returned under any such policy would obviously have to be determined by the over-all manpower position, and any announcement would have to be phrased carefully to prevent any individual affected by it from falling into the belief that his participation in the actual fighting had ended.

McNarney's lengthy reply to me was interesting in several respects. In his capacity as Deputy Chief of Staff to General Marshall, he had been thoroughly familiar with manpower problems and with War Department policies. He pointed out that there was no possibility that either of Keyes' suggestions would even be considered by the War Department. The build-up overseas in 1942 had been so rapid that rotation at the end of three years would soon effect several hundred thousand men. To rotate one man a month required a troop basis of usually six. To rotate 12,000 men a month would require a troop basis of 72,000—the number we would have to do without to implement such a policy. Under Keyes' plan, we would soon be rotating 100,000 men monthly from the European theater, and would require a troop basis of more than half a million men. Even if shipping permitted, this was so impractical that it would be useless to make such a recommendation to the War Department.

McNarney went on to point out that the 34th Division deserved no special consideration over many others: the 1st, 3rd, and 9th in our own theater had all entered combat at the same time. The 5th Division had gone to Iceland in 1941. Another National Guard division, the 41st, had gone to the South Pacific early in 1942 and had been in combat since. The 24th and 25th Divisions had been stationed in Hawaii when the war began and had many men who had already been overseas two or three years. He thought that Keyes' letter gave "definite indications of command failure particularly in the lower echelons." He wrote:

> The situation is no doubt further aggravated by the fact that almost a year ago some misguided individual introduced a bill in Congress to require the 34th Division to be returned to the United States. Although I believe the bill never received consideration by either of the military committees, it did receive some publicity. It was evidently backed by relatives of the original members of the division, and their attitude is without doubt reflected in their letters to the soldiers, which further convinces the men that they are being mistreated.
>
> I am forwarding General Keyes' communication, together with a copy of your letter and a copy of this letter to the War Department in the hope that by proper public relations activities they can in some way convey to the home areas of the 34th Division, and to the public at large, the inestimable damage that is done by this over-sympathetic and pitying attitude.

This interchange illustrates a fact too little recognized. Commanders in the field who are trained men and who are striving to solve such personnel problems cannot know the ramifications of what seem to them to be reasonable and effective solutions. Yet, newspaper correspondents, congressmen, relatives, and friends with no military background whatever agitate for solutions which are not only impossible or impracticable, but which would also jeopardize the war effort, and in any case would only be detrimental to the individuals and units concerned.

One point in General McNarney's letter with which I did not agree was the reference to command failure "particularly in the lower echelons". I had noted all throughout my career a tendency on the part of senior officers to explain all deficiencies away by placing the blame on the junior officers, which I believe is wrong, as I have stated earlier. Command failures do not stem from the lower ranks, although they may exist there. Usually they originate among the higher echelons and are merely reflected downward.

I might note here that after my first inspection of this Division, where I renewed acquaintance with General Bolte, his Assistant Division Commander General Braun, the regimental commanders, and most of the battalion commanders, I was convinced there was nothing organically wrong, and nothing we could not correct. If the Division was made to feel that only the best was expected of it, as with other divisions, it would not fail us in the test. General Bolte shared these views; his confidence and my own were to be fully justified during the final campaign.

The problem of the "forgotten front" was more intangible. The situation was made known to the War Department in the hope that Public Relations would be able to present a true picture to the American public which in turn would be reflected in the soldiers' mail. It was a matter of continuing concern to Public Relations officials of both the theater and the Army, and every effort was made to provide correspondents with suitable material. But many correspondents had little liking for spending uncomfortable days in the mountains seeking stories of small actions which would have limited news value. Rome not only offered far more in the way of physical comforts; also, there was always the chance for an important news story in a capital city of that size under existing conditions. News of the Army front could be culled from the day to day releases by the Theater Public Relations officials.

The Fifth Army Public Relations and Historical Sections collaborated on a program that had important repercussions. Press releases were prepared describing actions of various units and gallant exploits of many individuals; they contained names of individuals, and identified units, where regulations permitted. They were mailed to newspapers in the home towns, counties or states of units and individuals. Their publication produced an immediate and excellent reaction in the mail from home. And soldiers felt less forgotten when they or their units were mentioned in the home papers.

The Fifth Army received the 10th Mountain Division by way of reinforcement during the winter of 1944. It was not allocated to the Fifth Army, however, until other theaters had declined it because of its relatively small size and its specialized mountain training and equipment, and mule transport. This was fortunate for the Fifth Army since it was one of the best combat divisions I knew during the war.

It had been formed at Camp Hale, Colorado, in the summer of 1943 with the 85th, 86th and 87th Mountain Regiments and other necessary division troops. Formation of these specialized regiments had begun in 1942. They had attracted an unusually large number of men who were winter sports enthusiasts, members of mountain climbing and ski clubs, and who lived in our western mountains. The Division contained within its ranks an unusually large percentage of college men.

Major General George P. Hays, brought from the 2nd Division Artillery then in action in France, had been assigned to command the 10th Mountain Division on the eve of its departure for Italy—a fortuitous turn of fortune because Hays, one of the ablest battle leaders I ever knew, fitted the Division like a well-worn and well-loved glove. Brigadier General Robinson E. Duff was the Assistant Division Commander. Brigadier General David L. Ruffner, the Division Artillery Commander, I had known at Fort Lewis Washington where he commanded a battalion of pack artillery while I was a member of the IX Army Corps staff.

General Duff and the 87th Mountain Infantry arrived in Naples just before Christmas, and moved immediately into the quiet sector between Mt. Belvedere and the Serchio Valley which was held by Task Force 45. The other two regiments, the 85th and 86th, reached Naples on January 13th, and the remainder of the Division five days later.

We knew that these regiments had received long and thorough basic training, and that one—the 87th—had participated in the unopposed landings on Kiska in the Aleutian Islands. The thirty-mile front between Mt. Belvedere and the Serchio valley passed through some of the highest and most rugged terrain of the Northern Apennines. It was not practicable for any large scale assault, and was, in consequence lightly held by both sides. It was a sector where the specialized mountain and winter warfare training of this Division could be used to advantage, and it was ideal for acclimating men to conditions of combat.

By January 26th, the Division had relieved Task Force 45 which had been made up of antiaircraft troops employed as infantry, now withdrawn to be reorganized to form the 473rd Infantry Regiment. When I visited the 10th Mountain's various regiments and talked to officers on practical aspects of mountain fighting, I was deeply impressed. And almost at once, this inactive sector became one of the most active on the entire Army front as their patrols probed into the enemy lines.

I had told General Hays he would have an attack mission just as soon as his Division could gain some experience and was ready for a limited-objective attack to capture Mt. Belvedere for which plans had now been completed by the Army staff.

Highway 64 is one of the two principal roads through the Apennines leading toward Bologna. During the fall offensive, General Clark had concentrated all available strength in the main effort northward along Highway 65, with the 6th South African Division on Highway 6620 leading north from Prato. The IV Corps, responsible for all of the Army front from Highway 64 to the coast, was left with barely enough troops to protect the port of Leghorn and the line of communications in the Arno valley, and could only follow up the Germans as they withdrew When the drive was stopped at the end of October, the 6th South African Division faced Mt. Sole in the angle between the Reno River and Setta Creek. In the IV Corps sector, the German front followed the long rugged ridge west of the Reno River and north of Silla Creek and then cut across the mountains to the Serchio valley.

Highway 64 was therefore open to use only as far north as the point where Silla Creek joined the Reno River. It was desirable to clear the enemy from this ridge west of the Reno to permit the use of Highway 64 and to reduce the exposed flank of the 6th South African Division, and, more particularly, to provide a more favorable avenue of approach to the Po valley than the heavily defended route along Highway 65. General Clark had made a belated attempt to open Highway 64 when Task Force 45 attacked and captured Mt. Belvedere in late November. However, the Germans counterattacked and recaptured the peak, and Task Force 45 failed in another effort to take it. The last attempt had been made against Mt. Costello by the Brazilians on December 12th, and this, too, had failed completely.

The German 114th Mountain Divison held the sector. Our plan was to launch an attack in two phases, the first to capture Mts. Belvedere, Toraccio, and Castello. Then if the German reaction was not too strong, in the second phase we would clear the ridge as far north as Vergato. By the middle of February, Crittenberger and Hays with their staffs and subordinate commanders had completed their detailed plans which I had approved.

This operation began on the night of February 18th when one battalion scaled a 1,500 foot cliff leading to the Serrasiccia-Campiano ridge to protect the left flank. The following night, five battalions launched a bold night attack without preparatory or supporting fires, and took their initial objectives with bayonets and grenades. The attack continued during the next three days with strong air support as well as artillery, with the Brazilians joining in to capture Mt. Castello on their right flank. Every objective was taken and held against strong counter-

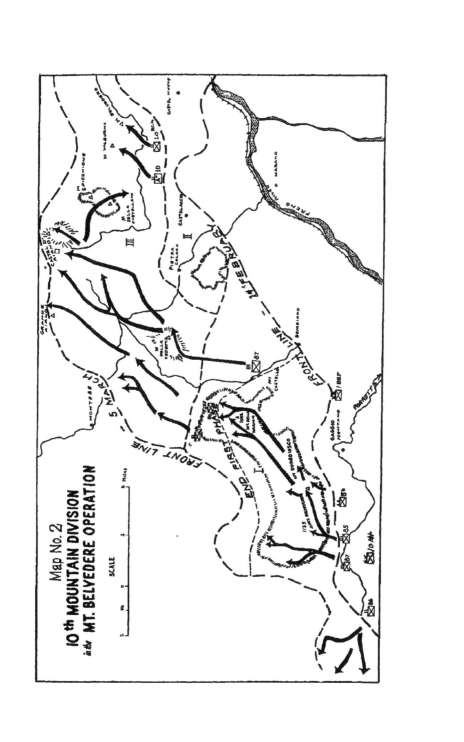

Map No. 2
10th MOUNTAIN DIVISION
in the MT. BELVEDERE OPERATION

attacks in which the Germans suffered heavy losses. By February 24th, the first phase was completed.

While Hays reorganized and prepared for the next step, we watched the German reaction. There was some movement of reserves, but no more than we expected. On March 3rd, the second phase got under way, this time following an artillery barrage and strongly supported by our tactical air command. In two days, the Division had cleared the enemy from the ridges to a point just south of Vergato and had taken Castel d'Aino, and had beaten off repeated counterattacks by the 29th Panzer Division which the German command had rushed to support the crumbling front. Then, since the Germans showed signs of moving other troops into the area, I called a halt. With another month to wait before the spring offensive, I had no wish to attract German reserves into the area or to cause them to increase the defenses by further fortifications.

The performance of this 10th Mountain Division in its first battle was impressive; they performed like veterans. Heavy losses had been inflicted upon the Germans and more than 1,200 prisoners had been taken. It had been a noteworthy lesson for the Brazilians and they had profited by it, by taking Mt. Castello which had previously defied them during the last of the first phase, and they had continued with increased confidence. The operation also aroused the admiration of the whole Army. Better still we had set the stage for a main effort in the spring offensive west of Highway 64.

Most officers who served during World War I and who remained in the Army afterwards came to know in one way or another of the unsatisfactory combat record of the colored troops, although the story was never publicized so far as I know. During my twelve years as student and instructor in service schools, we examined many failures of troops in combat but I do not recall that any of these dealt with colored troops. The problem was not new, for there had been colored troops in the Army since the Civil War. But it was not serious, however, until total mobilization brought a pinch in manpower.

When I was ordered back to Italy to command the Fifth Army, I was aware that the 92nd Infantry Division had joined the Fifth Army. Just before leaving France for Italy, I saw General Devers who had been Deputy Supreme Allied Commander Mediterranean and Commanding General Mediterranean Theatre of Operation (US), before organizing the VI Army Group in September. He told me General Clark had already reported that the Division was wholly unreliable in combat. Devers remarked that he was convinced colored troops had not yet had a fair chance. He was confident the Division would fight if it was properly indoctrinated and given an opportunity to gain some self assurance. He was sure I would be able to employ the Division effectively.

As a matter of fact, I agreed with General Devers. I had never been assigned to either of the two colored cavalry regiments during my service, but I had been connected with both of them for considerable periods. I knew many fine soldiers among them, men whom I was proud to number among my friends. I had been closely associated with colored people since infancy. I liked them, believed in them, and symphathized with their problems. I was confident that if this Division was assigned objectives well within its capabilities and was properly instructed it would gain confidence and develop a pride which would insure good results in combat. It was, after all, a procedure which had worked well with other units; there was no reason why it should not work equally well with colored troops.

My first visit to the 92nd Infantry Division front took place on December 19th and 20th, soon after I assumed command of the Fifth Army, and less than a week before the Serchio valley flap which I have already mentioned. I was favorably impressed with all that I saw. Personnel presented a smart appearance. Units were well-equipped, went about their work in a professional manner, and gave every indication of being highly trained. In spite of some earlier unsatisfactory performances, a spirit of optimism pervaded throughout. My visit was the occasion for a ceremony in which some forty bronze stars and combat infantry badges were awarded to members of the Division. A platoon from each company assembled in one of the most colorful ceremonials I had ever witnessed.

The 92nd Infantry Division was commanded by Major General E. M. (Ned) Almond; the Assistant Division Commander was Brigadier General John E. Wood, the Artillery Commander, Brigadier General Williams H. (Red) Colbern, an old friend from Fort Riley days. At the time of my visit, there were 774 officers in the Division, of whom 538 were colored in grades ranging from second lieutenant to lieutenant colonel. In the attached 366th Infantry, all officers were colored. In addition to the division commander, assistant division commanders, artillery officer, chief of staff and the three regimental commanders, most of the infantry battalions were commanded by white officers. However, two of the four artillery battalions and several of the infantry battalions were commanded by colored officers, as were most of the companies and platoons.

The Division had been activated in mid-October, 1942, at four stations: Fort McClellan, Alabama; Camp Atterbury, Indiana; Camp Breckenridge, Kentucky, and Camp Robinson, Arkansas. By April,

1943, it was assembled at Fort Huachuca, Arizona, for its divisional training. The first element of the Division sailed for Italy in July, 1944, and entered combat during the latter part of August in an inactive sector along the Arno River. By mid-November, 1944, the complete Division was in Italy, and responsible for the inactive front in the Serchio valley and coastal sectors. It had had almost two full years of training, including fifteen months as a unit at Fort Huachuca, under the able direction of General Almond and his subordinate commanders.

During my visit, I discussed the employment of the Division in a limited-objective attack well within the capabilities of its troops. Almond was enthusiastic, and set about his planning, which was interrupted by the Serchio valley flap between Christmas and New Year. However, when the major offensive was postponed, attack by the 92nd Infantry Division was one of the two operations authorized for the Fifth Army during the winter months.

The Apuan Alps parallel the Ligurian coast, and north of Lucca, separate the Serchio valley from the coastal sector. This area of rugged mountains, rising to heights of nearly 6,000 feet, traversed by no roads, and impracticable for military operations, was a mass of sharp peaks with precipitous slopes, deep gorges, and sheer rocky cliffs. Between the mountains and the sea lay a flat coastal plain about four miles wide, cut by canals and drainage lines, densely populated and intensely cultivated. This was the area selected for the limited-objective attack.

The first week in February, the 365th Infantry held the Serchio valley area. In the coastal sector, General Almond had available two regiments of the 92nd Infantry Division, the 370th and 371st and the attached 366th Infantry Regiment including the battalion which had not been returned to the Serchio valley after the December flap. German forces opposing the Division there consisted of the 281st Regiment of the 148th Grenadier Division with one battalion holding spurs of Mt. Folgorito which overlooked the coastal plain, another in the series of low hills along the edge of the plain, and a third along the Cinquale Canal. For the limited-objective attack, General Almond selected these spurs of Mt. Folgorito and the low hills which would require an advance of little more than a thousand yards. We estimated that each of the objectives in this area was well within the capabilities of one experienced infantry battalion with the support which would be available. Each was assigned to a regiment. There was to be a secondary attack near the coast to seize a bridgehead across the Cinquale Canal. This was assigned to one battalion, 366th Infantry. Planning got under way before the middle of January and the finished draft was successively approved by the IV Corps and Army Headquarters.

The attack got off to a good start the morning of February 8th with powerful artillery and air support, and we were optimistic about its success. However, no further progress was made and the third day found the command back on its starting line with a heavy loss of weapons and equipment together with some 560 killed and wounded. In a report which I sent to General Clark subsequently, I made the following comments:

I was present from 0900 to 1700 on the 8th and could observe a great deal of that day's operations; thereafter, I followed the course of the operation by reports from the Commanding General IV Corps. During the first day, the 3rd Battalion 366th Infantry reached its objective north of the canal, where it remained throughout the day. Several tanks, perhaps 6 or 8, were disabled by mines. This battalion was subjected to considerable shelling and mortar fire during the day. Apparently, during the night of the 8th, much of the infantry, perhaps 200, "melted away" and were collected as stragglers on the south bank of the stream and returned to their units. The 370th Infantry, during the day of the 8th, cleared the area—an advance of about 1000 yards. This progress was satisfactory and about as much as could be expected during this day. At nightfall, two companies were in possession of a prominent hill east of Porta, but about dark a heavy mortar barrage caused these companies to withdraw. The 371st Infantry advanced several hundred yards up the very steep hill "Georgia" but made little further progress during the day. It is to be noted that the day of the 8th was clear and the air support by the XXII Tactical Air Command was continuous and excellent.

During the 9th, the weather changed; rain fell during most of the day; there was no flying. During this day General Almond reinforced the battalion of the 366th north of the Cinquale Canal with at least two companies of a reserve battalion. This battalion held its position throughout the day, but during the night, straggling occurred as before. Men are reported to have abandoned equipment and clothing, returning to the south bank of the canal stripped. Again they were collected, reequipped, and returned to their units. During the day of the 9th, the 370th Infantry was able to reoccupy the area from which the companies had been driven during the night previous. The remainder of the day was spent in reorganizing and assembling units preparatory to continuing the attack on the 10th. The 371st Infantry made little progress during the day, but reorganized preparatory to continuing the attack on the 10th. The Division commander requested permission to continue the attack on the 10th, which I granted; however, stiffening enemy resistance resulted in no progress. Enemy attacks with mortars and artillery caused elements north of the Cinquale Canal to withdraw. Again they were collected south of the canal and reorganized there to hold that position During the night, the companies of the 370 Infantry again withdrew from the high ground back to their starting point. During this day, the 371st Infantry is reported to have taken the hill "Georgia" representing an advance of about

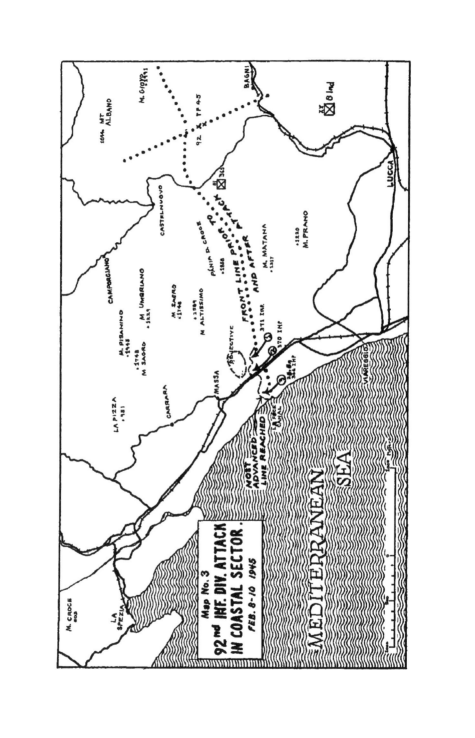

Map No. 3
92nd INF. DIV. ATTACK
IN COASTAL SECTOR.
FEB. 8-10 1945

MEDITERRANEAN SEA

800 yards from positions which they have been holding for some time. This is a rough outline of what happened.

Of the tanks moved north of the Cinquale Canal, 12 medium and 4 light are reported to have been lost, for the most part by mines; however, several were knocked out by artillery and one is reported to have been knocked out by a bazooka.

General Almond's attack was, in my opinion, well planned, well organized, and well supported. The failure is due entirely to the unreliability of infantry units. During the day of the 8th, while I was present, the opposition appeared to be extremely light. There was relatively little artillery, mortar fire was light, and I heard only occasional and light small arms fire.

There were many colored service units in the theater rendering satisfactory service—truck companies, engineers, bridge companies, ordnance and quartermaster units, and the like. We made exhaustive investigations of these operations to determine the reasons for the failure, in search of ways to help this Division. It is interesting to note that all reports were unanimous that supporting arms and services of the Division had functioned effectively, and this was confirmed by my own observations. Artillery support was all that could be asked for. Except for failure to bridge the Cinquale Canal, the Division engineers had performed satisfactorily. Communications had been effective throughout except for some failures in the infantry battalions. All of the supply services had functioned smoothly. The Division had been satisfactory in every respect except the one element which justified its existence—the combat infantry.

The 370th Infantry Regiment, which made the main effort, was well organized, completely equipped, and had been trained intensively in a rear training area for more than a month in preparation for this attack. It was also the regiment with more combat experience than others in the Division. Its commander, Colonel Raymond G. Sherman, was a superior officer in every respect, and his staff was well organized and trained. This regiment had shown to better advantage than the 366th Infantry, but nevertheless the attack had been a complete debacle. Failure had occurred "when the mission involved standing fast under enemy counterattack or mortar or artillery fire." The men "exhibited an unwillingness to close for hand-to-hand combat with the enemy and when such combat seemed imminent individuals in numbers and sometimes organizations had withdrawn from combat in disorder." All commented on the apparent fear of darkness and of the unknown, which caused units to "melt away", and upon the tendency to panic and hysteria. Reports emphasized the lack of mutual confidence and trust among men and a gross inclination to exaggerate danger. Commanders down to the battalion level exercised close personal supervision, which was reflected in the casualty rate among senior officers. Lack of control by company-grade officers was shown up by the disorganization of units, lack of cohesiveness in smaller units, and by the excessive amounts of equipment and materiel lost. It was the general consensus that personnel exhibited no pride of race and little pride in accomplishment.

Reports conceded that the fighting capabilities of the Division justified its employment only in a relatively quiet and unimportant defensive sector until more stamina and dependability could be developed. To my mind the operation had clearly demonstrated that in spite of excellent and long training, tiptop physical condition, and superior support by artillery and air, the infantry was devoid of the emotional and mental stability necessary for combat. I did not believe that further training under the present conditions would make the Division capable of offensive action.

There were many brave and competent colored officers and men in this infantry division. By no means all were prone to terror and fright; not all "melted away" in the face of danger and the unknown. I decorated some and commissioned or promoted others who were worthy members of the fraternity of gallant soldiers and who would have been a credit to any organization. It was a matter of deep regret to all officers who were concerned with the employment of this Divison that the proportion of those who failed to measure up was so large. But it was to the credit of colored Americans that many did, for the social and economic system under which they had lived and labored had hardly been conducive to the development of pride of race, love of country, the sense of individual responsibility, and qualities of leadership.

Our colored soldiers were the product of heredity, environment, education, economic and social ills beyond their control—and beyond the sphere of military leaders. This background is brought out in a comparison of personnel under general classifications tests with those of the average in other combat divisions made at that time: Class i, 1.1 vs 3.2; Class II, 10.2 vs 16.3; Class III, 16.3 vs 35.1; Class IV, 44.1 vs 35.2; Class V, 27.2 vs 10.2. The Division therefore contained an unduly large percentage of men in the lower classifications. The Division had been activated with more than 2,000 illiterates, although this number had been reduced to a few hundred. During its two years of existence nearly 1,500 men had been transferred to limited service, more than 1,200 discharged for physical disability.

There was no segregation of races in the Mediterranean theater. White and colored personnel intermingled on duties, in clubs, rest centers, Red Cross facilities, casual depots, and elsewhere without undue friction and without any serious disturbance of any kind. On many occasions colored officers and men expressed to me their personal satisfaction with their treatment in rest areas; a number of colored junior officers wrote me letters of appreciation.

We were still, however, faced with the problem of utilizing these colored troops to the best advantage. It was finally decided that one further test was desirable. We would concentrate in one infantry regiment all men who had been decorated, all who wore the combat infantry badge, all who won battlefield promotions, and all of the best personnel of the three infantry regiments. The other regiments would be withdrawn during the spring offensive and employed on inactive parts of the front. To replace them, the 442nd Infantry Regiment (Japanese-Americans) would be brought back from France, and the 473rd Infantry Regiment, which we had just formed from converted antiaircraft artillery battalions, would be attached. The 366th Infantry was withdrawn from the lines, deactivated, and its personnel used to form two engineer general service regiments which discharged their duties efficiently.

The new division gave a good account of themselves in the spring offensive, although the performance of the colored regiment with selected personnel was disappointing. The rest worked steadily and with perseverance.

In considering the future employment of colored troops, there was general agreement that segregation in units of division size had proven unsatisfactory because of the inability to develop strong and compelling leadership. There was wide belief, although not unanimous, that complete integration was impracticable and would lower the standards of combat divisions. Some recommended including colored regiments in divisions; others advised including colored battalions in infantry battalions, or even colored platoons in infantry companies. I think experience has demonstrated such solutions are practicable in combat zones, at least with smaller units. However, it does not, in my opinion, solve the problem. I would integrate colored personnel into units according to the ratio of colored population to white. Association with other soldiers would result in no undue friction, and would do much toward developing individual pride, loyalty, sense of responsibility and a spirit of cooperation.

When the ammunition shortage compelled postponement of a major winter offensive our thoughts turned to preparations for the spring offensive. Conway and his assistants from other staff sections were some of the busiest individuals on the Army staff about this time. By January 17th, we had investigated the possibility of taking the offensive at an earlier date—in January or February—and we were developing studies and outline plans for the two limited-objective attacks which we were allowed and held to by the curtailment of ammunition. On January 19th, Clark told me he had discussed the spring offensive strategy with McCreery. Since the British had three time as many divisions in Italy as did the Americans at the time, McCreery wanted Clark to concentrate his whole effort on the Eighth Army front in the Adriatic plain. Clark, however, did not agree, and contended the Fifth Army should make a strong effort west of Highway 65 while the Eighth made its main effort along Highway 9. I suggested to Clark we should consider throwing the weight of the Fifth Army west of Highway 64 because the German defense was much less fortified there than on the front of the II Corps along Highway 65 south of Bologna. Clark replied that he would never agree to a main attack west of Highway 64.

On January 24th, General Clark confirmed these previous instructions in a letter to the Army commanders in which he wrote:

> The instructions contained in this letter are issued at this time in order to enable you to plan your rest and reorganization period so that your troops will be in the best possible condition to resume extensive offensive operations in the spring. While it is not practicable now to determine the date for launching this offensive, you will plan your reliefs, reorganization and training so that they can be concluded by 31 March 1945.
>
> There are no indications that the enemy intends to withdraw forces from Italy for employment elsewhere. We know from experience that it is contrary to his habit to give up valuable terrain until forced to do so. It is possible, however, that he may be obliged to execute a major withdrawal from Italy as a result of developments on other fronts. In such an event, 15th Army Group would attack as soon as possible following the basic plan contained in this directive. Army commanders must be prepared to launch such an attack on short notice. The present strength and disposition of enemy forces south of the Po River are such that a hostile offensive is a capability. It is considered that the two most probable areas are in the Po valley against Eighth Army on Rimini, or against Fifth Army's left directed against Leghorn. Both Armies will prepare and keep current plans rapidly to meet such attacks.

The letter mentioned that the 10th Mountain Division would be ready for combat by mid-February, as well as the probable arrival of three additional British infantry divisions in time for the offensive. The Eighth Army was to strike first supported by the whole weight of Allied Air Forces in Italy, and when it reached the line of the Sillaro River, the Fifth Army was to join in, making its major onslaught west of Highway 65, to capture Bologna. Both Armies would re-group around Bologna and move up supplies to press the drive, unless the enemy was already beaten, in which case we would "continue to destroy him."

Almost at once, however, the high command became excited over the possibility of a German withdrawal from Italy. One division had left Italy in November and another had departed in December. About this time we learned the 16th SS Panzer Grenadier Division was being withdrawn, and there were indications that a general withdrawal might be a possibility. On January 28th, Army Group demanded we be prepared to implement the PIANORO plan on short notice. Fortunately, we were never ordered to do so for the steep mountain slopes were sheathed in ice which would have handicapped the movement of infantry enormously, and made the movement of supporting weapons all but impossible. An attack through the most heavily defended portion of the German lines under such oppressive conditions of weather and terrain would have been an appalling undertaking, and one which would have had little prospect of success.

Then, a few days later, there was even more depressing news. On February 4th, General Clark called General McCreery and me to Florence for an urgent conference. There he informed us he had just been advised that the Combined Chiefs of Staff had decided to send five divisions from the Eighth Army to reinforce Montgomery's 21st Army Group in France, beginning at once with the Canadian Corps. Moreover most of the American fighter bombers were to go to France, beginning at once with two groups. The Combined Chiefs had said that the 15th Army Group mission would be to prevent any German advance south of their present positions and to attack at once in case of a German withdrawal from Italy. It was a sad blow to our hopes!

Clark went on to say that he did not think we would be required to attack before April 1st. Since the loss of these divisions would restrict the Eighth Army, he proposed to have the Fifth make the main effort of the spring offensive west of Highway 65, while the Eighth Army would relieve the Fifth Army on Mt. Grande and make as strong an effort in the Po valley as would be possible. Several Italian groups, armed and trained by the British, were to become available soon. Clark indicated one would be made available to the Fifth Army for employment on defense west of Mt. Grande. He invited our comments on this strategy.

My reply on February 7th summarized my views on offensive operations by the Fifth Army, which governed our actions thereafter:

> I believe that your intention to have the Fifth Army make the main effort is eminently sound. After careful study of all possible plans, I am convinced that the area indicated for the main effort, west of Highway 65, promises

greatest chances of success. Owing to the greatly increased defenses in the area immediately south of Bologna between Highways 64 and 65, I consider that in developing the operation, we should clear the area up to the general line: Pianoro-Praduro-Mt. Mantino and establish a firm base for subsequent operations. Since prepared defenses west of Highway 64 are a great deal thinner than to the east of that road, we should be prepared in attacking from that line to make our main effort west of Highway 64, isolating Bologna from the north and northwest, preparatory to the final stage. In such case, a strong holding attack east of Route 64 would, of course, be necessary. Of course, if operations draw great strength to the west of Highway 64 and it appears when we reach the Praduro area that the main effort between Highways 64 and 65 is more suitable, then our plans should be sufficiently flexible to permit such disposition.

In preparation for an attack in this area, we would, of course, be in a much better position if we held the general line Mt. Pero-Villa d' Aino-Mt. Belvedere when the attack is launched. As you know, we are prepared to clear the Mt. Belvedere-Caistelnuevo area with the 10th Mountain Division, beginning 20 February, in two phases of limited-objective attacks, the first being the seizure of Mt. Belvedere-Mt. della Torraccia area. It would be most undesirable for operations in this area to attract divisions from the Eighth Army front or reserve divisions, reserves to be reconstituted from withdrawals from the Eighth Army front However, I believe that we should pursue these limited-objective operations beginning with Mt. Belvedere as far toward the Mt. Pero-Mt. Mantino-Villa d'Aino line as possible without bringing about an undesirable concentration on the enemy's part in that area. This, I believe, may be accomplished if we avoid undue concentration in the area and proceed step by step. I have the IV Corps working on detailed plans for such an operation at the present time and will submit them to you within the next few days.

I am not prepared to express a firm opinion on the area selected for the Eighth Army effort in the spring offensive. I suggest that an operation from Mt. Grande might be considered, and that such an operation would have the advantage of closer association with the main effort of the Fifth Army and possibly a more immedate threat to Highway 9 and the envelopment of German forces disposed along the Senio River farther to the south.

On February 11th, Clark replied that he was pleased I was in accord with the general plan he had outlined and he agreed with my comments on preliminary operations. But he added a significant reminder· "However, as I have explained to you previously, I cannot agree to a main attack generally along the high ground west of Highway 64."

I had come to the conclusion that this section west of Highway 64 was most promising for breaking through the German positions and into the Po valley. The success of the limited-objective attacks in the Mt. Belvedere area during the latter part of February and the first few days in March confirmed this. I was determined to retain this concept in our final plans, and I did not want Clark, because of his predilection for PIANORO, to interpose a restriction which would make it

impossible. I had not forgotten the change of direction in the breakout from Anzio.

In March, prior to making our final arrangements, there were, opposing the Allied Armies in Italy 24 German and five Italian Fascist Divisions. Of these, 16 German divisions and one Italian division were in
the line; two German divisions were in reserve south of the Po River;
two German and three Italian divisions were in northwest Italy; and
four German divisions and one Italian were in northeast Italy. The
Germans had steadily increased their fortifications of the Genghis Khan
Line where they faced us during these months, and it had become evident that they would not withdraw from Italy until compelled to do
so. Their implementation of new defense lines along the Po River and
north of the Adige River between Lake Garda and the Adriatic Sea
made this even more obvious.

The Fifth Army had nine divisions at this time (American six Infantry and one Armored, one South African Armored, and one Brazilian
Infantry), one Italian Group, two separate colored infantry regiments,
and several tank and tank destroyer battalions. The Eighth Army had
ten infantry divisions and one armored division, five armored brigades,
several separate brigades and detachments, and three Italian groups.
There was therefore no great disparity in the ground strength of the
opposing forces.

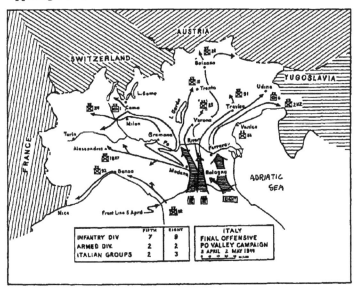

Our great advantage lay in our air superiority with its complete domination of the skies, in addition to our superiority in armor, in material resources of every kind, and in morale, for German armies were now reeling in defeat on both the eastern and western frontiers of Germany.

In line opposing the Fifth Army were eight German divisions and one Italian, supported by some 367 pieces of light artillery, 75 pieces of medium artillery, 138 antitank guns, 160 self-propelled guns, and some 47 tanks employed as artillery, or a total of some 789 guns. The two German divisions in reserve south of the Po River could easily intervene on the front of the Fifth Army. G-2 estimates showed two German divisions from northwest Italy and two from northeast Italy might also be moved to oppose our advance. But the G-2 Estimate added:

> Due to the increasing shortage of motor fuel and to the interdiction of road and rail nets by our Air Force, movements of reserve forces are expected to be somewhat slower than in the past. Examples of this are the approximately 8 days travel time required to move the 114th Division from the Lake Commachio area to the Mt. Belvedere area. Other indications of enemy transport difficulties are the recent reports of the practice of one truck pulling two others, oxen being employed to move artillery pieces, and the extensive use of hand carts for supply. However, during the attack adequate fuel may be initially available to make tactical moves, fuel having been saved by the economy indicated.

Generally, Clark's plan followed the same pattern that General Alexander had prescribed for the fall offensive. The purpose was to debouch into the Po valley, and drive north across the Po River to the Brenner Pass, thus isolating northwest Italy which would then fall of its own weight. In phase one, the Eighth Army was to cross the Santerno River and the Fifth Army was to emerge into the Po valley and capture Bologna. In phase two, either or both Armies were to break through German defenses and surround the Germans south of the Po River. In phase three, both Armies were to cross the Po River, advance northward, capture Verona, and develop the Adige position. D Day was to be April 9th.

Four days before, the Fifth Army would prepare for the spring offensive by an attack in the coastal sector with the 92nd Infantry Division, which had now been reorganized to include the 442d and 473d Infantry Regiments retaining only one of its original colored regiments. This assault would seize Massa and the small port of La Spezia. It was not expected to draw reserves to the coastal sector, but it was hoped that it would confuse the enemy and prevent his moving troops from

On April 9th, the Eighth Army, supported by the full weight of the Allied Air Forces in Italy, was to begin its main offensive, breach the Senio and Santerno Rivers, and continue the attack in the direction of Bastia and Budrio. If conditions were then favorable, the Eighth Army attack was to develop toward Ferrara. Three days later, on April 12th, the Fifth Army, also supported by the weight of the Allied Air Forces, was to launch its attack, debouch into the Po valley, and capture or isolate Bologna.

As finally published in orders on April 1st, the Fifth Army was to attack with Corps abreast generally astride of Highway 64, to overrun the line of the Panaro and capture or isolate Bologna. The attack would begin with a preliminary operation by the IV Corps to capture an objective west of the Reno River—the Green Line—which would bring it abreast of the 6th South African Division on the left of the II Corps. Both Corps would then forge ahead and penetrate the Brown Line, which would take them through the main enemy positions and onto the Black Line, where they would reorganize and coordinate for the final drive into the Po valley.

The IV Corps was to loose the onslaught with the 1st Armored Division on the right near Highway 64, the 10th Mountain Division on the left along the main divide between the Reno River and Samoggia Creek, with the 1st Brazilian Division to protect the left flank. The II Corps was to move when the IV Corps reached the Green Line. It would have the Legnano Group to hold the front west of Mt. Grande, while the 34th, 91st and 88th Infantry Divisions and the 6th South African Division made the assault. General Keyes' plan provided for two regiments of the 34th and two of the 88th Infantry Divisions to be in Corps reserve initially.

Coulters' 85th Infantry Division, in Army reserve, was to transfer from the region of Lucca to Vergato immediately after D Day, prepared to relieve the 1st Armored Division on the Brown Line to press and follow up the attack.

Orders emphasized speed of execution and boldness in the exploitation of successes. Plans were developed for continuing operations beyond the Black Line to take care of every eventuality; for instance, where the IV Corps had reached the Black Line, but II Corps was still on Brown and advancing with difficulty; or where the II Corps had reached the Black Line without much trouble but IV Corps had encountered strong opposition and had not advanced beyond Green Line. Each Corps delineated alternative arrangements for keeping up the offensive in either event, whether with or without the 85th Infantry Division under its control, in order to carry out the missions of seizing the line of the Panaro River and sending strong mobile columns to take the crossing sites over the Po River. The II Corps had the extra mission of capturing or isolating Bologna and making contact with the Eighth Army; the IV Corps, the protection of the Army's flank.

The modified PIANORO was quite different from the original, which had envisioned a frontal assault by all of our available strength against the most heavily defended part of the German lines—the area south of Bologna along Highway 65 extending westward to the Reno River.

To insure surprise for the Fifth Army assault, we initiated a cover plan or ruse called BIG GAME to create the illusion that the American II Corps with the 85th and 88th Divisions was moving from the Fifth to Eighth Army front. The fiction or "mock-up" was carefully carried out, reconnaissance made, simulated command posts established, and fictional assumption of command of the II Corps sector by the IV Corps completed. Full use was made of camouflage, activity in supply dumps shrewdly controlled, radio activity limited, traffic restricted, artillery support reduced and then gradually built up again. Small preliminary stabs were made to pin down and confuse the enemy, and add to the illusion. And limited enemy air activity contributed to making BIG GAME very effective.

When we rejoined the Fifth Army in December, Carleton and I and other members of my staff were delighted to find that much progress had been made in providing direct air support for ground troops. The XXII Tactical Air Command had finally adopted the system of forward ground control which we had long recommended. It provided for Air officers and communications, and utilized jeeps and Cub aircraft, as well as ground troops to direct fighter bombers on selected targets. In the Fifth Army, the system was called "Rover Joe" and "Rover Pete." The one factor which brought the system to perfection was added when Brigadier General Thomas R. Darcy established his forward Command Post with my own at Traversa in Futa Pass before the final attack. Darcy, an outstanding Air officer, entered enthusiastically into all details of our planning, as did his staff. This close and intimate relationship produced the most effective air-ground cooperation that I ever experienced during the war.

Normally, the fighter bombers of the XXII Tactical Air Command provided a few aircraft for missions in support of ground forces on the front; the Desert Air Force did likewise for the Eighth Army. Normally, however, most of their effort was concentrated on interdicting enemy rail and road communications, destroying bridges, tactical reconnaissance, and armed reconnaissance against enemy road and rail movements. Medium bombers concentrated upon enemy communica-

tion through the Brenner Pass, important industrial and supply installations, and similar targets. The heavy bombers of the Strategic
Air Forces bombed distant targets from the Brenner Pass far into German territory, from Rumania almost to the Baltic Coast. This disruption was very effective and caused grave difficulties for the German
command in both supply and movements. But even with little or no
German air opposition this "Operation Strangle" was never able to
completely immobilize German troops and supply movements even
across the Po River.

In general, the air support program for the spring offensive provided
about 160 fighter-bomber sorties to support the 92nd Infantry Division
in the coastal sector on April 5th and 6th, and medium bombers to bomb
the heavy guns at La Spezia, while other operations followed the
normal pattern. On April 9th and 10th the maximum effort of the
XXII Tactical Air Command, Desert Air Force, 57th Bombardment
Wing's medium bombers, and the Strategic Air Force was to be concentrated on the front of the Eighth Army as troops began their assault
to break through the German defenses along the Senio River. This
maximum effort would be transferred to the Fifth Army front as
our attack got under way. Thereafter the fighter bombers of the XXII
Tactical Air Command were to give close air support cover for ground
troops, fly tactical reconnaissance, armed reconnaissance and other
missions. The Desert Air Force would furnish the Eighth Army with
similiar protection. Medium and heavy bombers returned to their
long-range strategic missions.

In developing our own air plan we allocated the fighter bombers
of the XXII Tactical Air Command to the IV Corps during the first two
days, while the effort of the Desert Air Force, the medium and heavy
bombers, was centered on the strong enemy defenses south of Bologna
on the front of the II Corps. Hundreds of targets were selected, data
prepared, and air crews briefed upon them. All fighter bombers in close
support were briefed on alternate targets in case "Rover Joe" had none
for them when they checked in with him over the battlefield.

Attempts to employ medium and heavy bombers in close support of
ground troops had resulted in stray bombs falling among our own
ground forces at Cassino, Anzio, and elsewhere. But by establishing a
Bomb Release Line—antiaircraft smoke shells set to burst in line at a
prescribed altitude for the guidance of aircraft in flight—we effected a
solution.

2. *The Final Campaign*

As reorganized for the spring offensive, the 92d Infantry Division
consisted of the 370th Infantry, the 442nd Infantry (Japanese-Amer-

icans), and the 473rd Infantry, the white regiment recently converted from antiaircraft artillery. The 370th Infantry had been strengthened with selected personnel from the other two organic regiments of the Division, the 365th and 371st Infantry Regiments. These two colored regiments were to screen the front until the attack began, and then be withdrawn from the Division and employed in the inactive mountainous sector of the IV Corps front west of Mt. Belvedere.

General Almond's plan was to strike with two regiments abreast, the 442nd Infantry, commanded by Lieutenant Colonel Virgil R. Miller, along the mountains overlooking the coastal plain, with the 370th Infantry on its left attacking through the lower hills along its edge. It was similiar to the unsuccessful February attack, except that the objectives were not so limited. The 473rd Infantry held the Serchio valley with one battalion in division reserve in the coastal sector; the 473rd was commanded by Colonel William P. Yarborough who had been in charge of the 509th Parachute Battalion under me at Anzio. There was to be an intense artillery preparation by some eight battalions of artillery and tanks.

The attack began on the morning of April 5th when the two regiments passed through the front lines and advanced on their first objectives. The 442nd Infantry very quickly captured them—the same objectives which the Division had failed to take in the February attack —and pressed on through the mountains. By dark they had taken Mt. Fragolito, well on the way to the high ground overlooking Massa. The 370th Infantry started well, pushed about two miles through the low hills along the edge of the coastal plain, but had then withdrawn in some disorder in the face of German counterattacks. General Almond ordered renewal of the attack for the following morning.

When I visited the division on April 6th, the 442nd Infantry was still making progress in the difficult mountain terrain, but the lag of the other regiment on their left was causing concern. I visited Colonel Miller at his Command Post near Azzano, with General Almond, and then we conferred with Colonel Sherman. An attack ordered for the morning had not come off because the battalions could not be reorganized in time. Another scheduled for the afternoon was cancelled, since straggling had reduced the infantry battalion to overall strength of less than one hundred men. Accordingly, I authorized General Almond to employ the 473rd Infantry in the coastal sector, replacing it in the Serchio valley with the 365th and 370th Infantry Regiments.

The following day, the 442nd Infantry captured the heights overlooking Massa, and was then confronted with the hazards of mountainous terrain, unfavorable weather conditions, and delay in the attack on its left flank. However, the 473rd Infantry entered action on the 8th and by the 9th had fought its way through mine fields and pill boxes to the outskirts of Massa.

My aide's journal records my visit to the front the following day:

> 92nd is all around Massa. 0930 General off with Maj Wilson by L-5. Beautiful morning. Arrive 92d Div air strip 1015, drive up to new Div CP in vicinity of Montignosa Confer with Gen Almond and staff briefly. In jeep with Gen Almond to Massa. Party is well shot at on road. Arrive at Town Hall and discuss situation with Col Yarborough. Much flag waving and excitement on the part of the citizens of Massa. Party returns to Div CP and goes up to 442d Regt where Col Miller gives his situation. Return to air strip and take off 1140, arriving at ski jump at 1210.

The advance continued against stiffening enemy resistance. Carrara was taken on April 11th. Then there was some delay while the Massa-Carrara road was repaired sufficiently to permit the maintenance and supply of the 442nd in the mountains, which then was causing some anxiety. On the 14th, as the major offensive of the Fifth Army started to roll, the 92nd Infantry Division was confronting a strong defensive position defended by all available German troops in the coastal sector, including the 148th Grenadier Division and at least one battalion of the 90th Grenadier Division—one of the reserve divisons available to the German high command.

With the Fifth Army surging across the Po plain, the 92nd Infantry Division, with the 442nd and 473rd Infantry Regiments sparking the advance, captured La Spezia and occupied Genoa. As a diversionary measure it was wholly successful, the success being due to the courage, endurance and heroism of these two regiments. As a test of the fighting ability of colored infantry units, the operation had merely confirmed our previous experience.

There had been a welter and scurry of activity in the last days before our final offensive. My days were filled with conferences with the Army staff and with subordinate commanders and their staffs. There were last minute details to verify, changes to discuss and approve or disapprove, arguments to resolve, ceremonies to attend, future plans to deal with. All the while our preparations were continuing apace. The Eighth Army attack got under way the afternoon of April 9th, and there was increasing tension and exhilaration as our own time drew near. We were fearful the enemy might have some notion of our plans, and a captured enemy appreciation disclosed that the Germans were anticipating an attack. However, his estimate revealed that he expected our major effort along Highway 65 south of Bologna.

By the morning of April 12th, the Eighth Army attack was making good progress, and the eastern and western fronts were both rolling along. Our troops were in position and ready to move off. However, weather prevented flying, and I was determined the IV Corps should not begin without the planned air support. Accordingly, the attack was postponed for a day. On the morning of April 13th—the day the radio announced the death of President Roosevelt—every fighter base in the coastal sector was again fogged in so that no aircraft could fly. Again there was another day's postponement. No damage was done, however, except to fray some nerves, for the front remained quiet. The IV Corps had restricted activity to a minimum. Weather reports late in the afternoon indicated unfavorable weather for the following morning, but we decided to wait until morning before putting off the attack again.

Time: 0500, the morning of April 14th. Place: My small mess tent at Army Command Post at Traversa. Present: General Darcy and I, Carleton and Wilson, my aide; Sergeant Hong serving coffee. Other equipment: A battery of telephones. One rings. Darcy answers. "Grossetto fogged in, visibility zero." One after another, each fighter base reports "Fogged in. Visibility zero." The attack is set for 0800. I telephone Crittenberger and give him the bad news. He is to hold troops in readiness to attack on one hour's notice, and I will keep him informed. More coffee. Darcy with a telephone in each hand, frequently talking into both, checks the bases. Still fogged in. More coffee. A telephone to Crittenberger. Darcy again checks the bases. Still fogged in. Airplanes are waiting with engines warmed up and pilots in the cockpits. More coffee. Another report to Darcy—a glimmer of hope— "Grossetto—fog may be thinning—visibility now nearly one quarter mile." Telephone to Crittenberger. More coffee. Darcy again checks bases. An interruption: Grossetto. "Can see end of runway. They're taking off." Minutes pass as flight after flight is reported airborne. We can almost hear the motors seventy-five miles away. We cheer. Telephone Crittenberger: "The attack is on 0900." It had been a strenuous three hours, for the fighter group from Grossetto which was airborne at 0800.

Fortunately, other fields cleared and the air support was assured for this first day at least.

Well, the die was cast. The attack was finally under way. There was the usual staff meeting at 0900. The Eighth Army was still making good progress. The Russians had entered Vienna and were approaching Berlin. The Allies were racing across Germany from the Rhine. Afterwards, I spent an hour with the Army Judge Advocate reviewing records of General Courts Martial. Another one of the administrative details of Army housekeeping which I had neglected during the past few days. A hasty lunch, then off with Wilson by L-5 to the IV Corps front. From an OP on Mt Castellana, we watched Hays' 10th Mountain Division scale and capture Mt. Rocco Roffino. Fighting was heavy, opposition was intense in spite of the bombing and artillery barrages, with high explosive and fire bombs. But we watched the Mountaineers reach and clear the top. The 10th Mountain Division were forging ahead and the drive of the 1st Armored Division soon got under way.

The 10th Mountain Division was to attack down the crest of the divide between the Reno and Samoggia Rivers—a series of rugged peaks heavily defended, by the 94th and 334th Panzer Grenadier Divisions, and strongly mined all the way to the Black Line. On the right, the 1st Armored Division, with its three infantry battalions, was to keep pace on a narrow front, until the capture of Mt. Pero on the Brown Line. There, I hoped to pass the 85th Division through to press home the advantage and to assemble the 1st Armored for employment on the left flank of the IV Corps as the Corps broke out into the Po valley. The Brazilians were to follow and protect the left flank and to take over the ground as it was captured. The 10th Mountain Division would carry the brunt of the attack to the Po valley—and beyond.

The next morning the IV Corps was near the Green Line. Weather was spotty but flyable. At noon, the entire headquarters assembled in a natural amphitheatre for a memorial service for President Roosevelt. Immediately afterward, I departed by L-5 for the airport in Florence. General Darcy had modified his P-51 to carry a passenger "piggy back." We climbed up over the Alps to an elevation of nearly 20,000 feet to watch the strategic bombers "clobber" the area south of Bologna on the front of the II Corps. At that elevation the sky seemed strangely bright and empty. The earth below, where thousands of men and guns were waiting, looked like a miniature relief map, a patchwork quilt in dull, neutral colors. Darcy jiggled his wings and pointed. Below us was a black line and as I watched the regular flashes and black puffs I realized I was looking at the Bomb Release Line marked by bursting antiaircraft shells. Then off to the south, with the sun glinting on silvery sides and wings, came the bombers. Flight after flight, more than 800 heavy and 250 medium bombers, in a steady formation gliding on below us to the north. Another jiggle of wings, and Darcy was calling my attention to the bombs dropping below. Then the whole earth was carpeted in flashes and towering columns of smoke. Among the bombers as they made their way steadily to the north, there were flashes and puffs that marked the effort of the German antiaircraft artillery. It was the first bombardment I had ever watched from above. It was a breathtaking sight and an unforgettable experience.

In just a few minutes the show was over. The whole area between Highway 65 and Highway 64 south of Bologna was concealed from our view in a shroud of dust and smoke. I had wanted to look over the Po valley in the rear of the German lines, so Darcy, dropping down to an altitude of some 10,000 feet, headed there. We followed the Panaro River, which was to be our first objective on breaking out of the mountains, nearly to the sea, turned west and followed the Po River almost to Milan. Darcy, whenever I wanted to look over a possible crossing site or some other feature, turned in tight circles so that the airplane seemed almost to stand on one wing tip. Up and down the principal roads and water courses we flew, and almost the only sign of enemy activity was an occasional burst of German ack-ack that traced our course. There was not a bridge on the Po between Milan and its mouth, and the valley looked like good armored terrain. We flew back over the section where the IV Corps was advancing. Here Darcy checked in with "Rover Joe" and then directed a flight of fighter bombers on German artillery which our ground observers could not see. A beautiful sight! Then back to the base. It had been a valuable reconnaissance, one of a number I made with Darcy far in the rear of the enemy lines. However, I was careful never to let the fact be known among the higher echelons, for I had some doubt that these activities would be viewed with favor.

By dark of April 15th, the 10th Mountain Division was beyond the Green Line and the 1st Armored Division had taken Mt. Pero. Except for the fighter bombers of the XXII Tactical Air Command which were supporting the IV Corps, the whole weight of the Mediterranean Air Forces had been concentrated on the German defenses south of Bologna on the front of the II Corps during both days of the attack. It was the second massive raid of the strategic bombers that Darcy and I had witnessed from aloft during the afternoon of April 15th. At dawn, April 16th, the II Corps began its assault.

General Keyes' plan was to have the South African Division capture Mt. Sole, Mt. Caprara and Mt. Abelle and clear the angle between the Reno River and Setta Creek. On its right, Kendall's 88th Division was to capture Mt. Monterumici, assist Livesay's 91st Division to capture Mt. Adone, and drive northward east of Setta Creek. The 91st Division was to capture Mt. Adone and then drive northward between Highway 65 and the Reno River. Bolte's 34th Infantry Division was to capture Pianoro and drive north along Highway 65. To the east, the Legnano Group held the front and was to follow up any German withdrawal. These rugged mountains, with their natural strength vastly fortified by German defenses, had confronted the II Corps since the end of the previous October.

During the day of April 16th, General W. H. E. Poole's 6th South African Division captured Mts. Sole, Caprara, and Abelle in a series of well-organized attacks but with heavy losses, against heavy opposition. I found elsewhere, as I visited General Keyes and each of the Division commanders, progress was slow against heavy opposition, and gains were small. Keyes and his division commanders, however, were optimistic.

The following morning, reports revealed that the 10th Mountain Division was well beyond the Brown Line, through the worst of the German defenses, and still moving, while the II Corps was still experiencing heavy going. I set off for the IV Corps to be on hand to review the situation. By midday, the 10th Mountain Division was attacking its Black Line objectives and the 1st Armored Division was on Mt. D'Avigo, well in advance of the Brown Line. Between the Reno and Samoggia Rivers, German opposition was disorganized; west of the Samoggia, the Germans were fighting stubbornly in a desperate effort to plug the gap we had torn in their lines, and had thrown in a reserve division. In view of the limited infantry strength of the 1st Armored Division, the desirability of employing armor in the Samoggia valley to assist the advance of the 10th Mountain Division, and the slow progress of the II Corps east of the Reno River, I came to the conclusion that the time had come to employ the 85th Infantry Division, which was completing its movement in the vicinity of Vergato. It was to relieve the 1st Armored without delay and advance northward, west of the Reno River on the right of the 10th Mountain Division. One combat command of the 1st Armored Division was to be moved across the rear of the 10th Mountain Division to advance down the Samoggia valley on the left of the 10th Mountain Division. Accordingly, I released the 85th Infantry Division to the IV Corps and made Crittenberger responsible for operations west of Highway 64. Coulter began the relief of the 1st Armored Division the same afternoon.

The following morning, Hays' Mountaineers were continuing their advance. One regiment of the 85th had relieved the 1st Armored Division and was now going up on the right of the 10th Mountain Division. The II Corps front reported little progress against stubborn opposition. About half-past nine that morning, General Keyes and his G-3, Colonel Bob Porter, came to see me. The 88th Division had taken Mt. Monterumici, but that had not affected Mt. Adone and other parts of the front as had been expected. In view of the progress of the IV Corps west of the Reno River, Keyes wanted to withdraw the 88th Infantry Division, move it to the west, and send it up the east bank of the Reno River, on the right of the South Africans. I agreed with Keyes' proposal, and he proceeded at once to implement it.

General McNarney had spent the previous night with me. When Keyes left, we set off by Cub to visit the IV Corps front. We were met at the Corps' air strip and taken to the Command Post where we went over the situation with Crittenberger and his staff. Hays' Mountaineers were still advancing as was Coulter's 85th; the 1st Armored was just beginning its movement across the rear of the 10th Mountain to the west flank, an enormously difficult movement because of the restricted road net of second class roads rendered even more precarious by enemy demolitions. We found General Coulter at Riola and then turned west to find Hays' Command Post. After trying several roads blocked by demolitions, we finally made our way through traffic jams on through Tole and found Hays well up toward Mt. Moscoso, with his troops still advancing. On our way back we encountered General Prichard of the 1st Armored Division whose leading combat team was now fighting over in the Samoggia valley, and a little later, General Crittenberger who informed us that Air Force reports disclosed the Germans were beginning to withdraw on the front of the II Corps.

Just before General McNarney left my Command Post that afternoon to depart for Caserta, he asked me when I expected to reach Highway 9 in the Po Valley. I replied that we would be across Highway 9 by one o'clock of the 20th. McNarney said: "I'll bet you a quart of Scotch that you are not." I accepted his wager but as things turned out, I lost by about an hour. I wrote this to General McNarney and sent on the prize. A few days later, it was returned by him with the request that it be presented to the first soldier of the 10th Mountain Division who actually crossed Highway 9. I complied with his wishes and dispatched it to General Hays, doubting that the soldier would ever be found. General Hays surprised me. Later he sent me a photograph showing him presenting the Scotch to Private First Class B. L. Lessmeister, the lead scout of Company A 86th Mountain Infantry, whose home town was Montrose, Missouri.

By the afternoon of the 19th, the 10th Mountain was on the spurs overlooking the Po valley, with the 85th Infantry Division moving up on its right. On the front of the II Corps, the enemy had begun to withdraw. Adone, dei Frati, Pianora had all been taken and the Corps was advancing against stubborn enemy delaying detachments. The 6th South African Division had reached Praduro and was continuing the advance northward along Highway 64. Most of the 20th, I spent in the IV Corps sector travelling by jeep. Finally I commandeered a Cub of the 10th Mountain Division artillery for a reconnaissance over the battle lines. This was when I determined that our troops were definitely across Highway 9. Returning to the 85th Infantry Division, I directed Coulter to swing eastward with his leading elements across the sectors of the

88th and 6th South African Divisions to seize the road center at Castel-
lechio in the hope of cutting off the retreat of German forces withdrawing in front of the II Corps. All three divisions of the IV Corps
were now well out of the mountains and across Highway 9. Both the
10th Mountain and the 1st Armored were already on their way to their
next objectives.

Early, the morning of April 21st, tanks and infantry of the 34th
Infantry Division rolled up Highway 65 and into Bologna, and elements of the Polish Corps of the Eighth Army entered from Route 9
almost simultaneously. Bologna was taken. We were now out of the
mountains—at last!

On April 19th, when the advance of the IV Corps had caused the
German withdrawal on the front of the II Corps, I had issued orders
for continuing the pursuit to the Po River as soon as Bologna was
isolated or in our hands. The two Corps, each with one armored and
two infantry divisions, were to press on boldly and rapidly, seize the
line of the Panaro River, and then press on to the Po to secure crossing
sites and cut off German forces still south of the river. This plan was
put into effect on April 21st.

The Allies had organized an extensive Partisan underground movement in northern Italy. These anti-Fascist Partisans were organized
into guerilla bands, armed and equipped by air drop, and directed by
Allied officers who parachuted in to join them. They had been active in
some sectors during the winter, but had reserved their principal effort
to coincide with the spring offensive. They were of invaluable assistance, not only for their knowledge of the country and enemy dispositions, but also for important assistance in clearing out snipers and enemy
opposition in some of the towns and cities. Bologna was the first place
where they distinguished themselves during the campaign, but their
assistance thereafter was widespread. In fact, Partisans took over some
of the cities before our arrival, on the heels of the departing Germans.

Crittenberger continued the advance of the IV Corps with the divisions in the same order as they had debouched into the plain—the 85th
on the right, 10th Mountain in the center, and the 1st Armored Division
on the left, with the Brazilians following the latter to protect the left
flank and rear. Keyes started with the 6th South African Armored Division leading the Corps' advance with the 91st and 88th Infantry Divisions following abreast.

Hays organized a Task Force with armor, infantry, engineers, and
artillery under his assistant division commander, General Duff, which
seized the crossing over the Panaro twenty miles northwest of Bolonga,
on the 21st, then pressed on to the Po River at San Benedetto on the
morning of April 22nd. By midnight, Hays had most of his Mountain

Division assembled in that area; but both the 85th Infantry Division and the 6th South Africans in the II Corps zone were still engaged along the Panaro River north of Bologna.

That same afternoon, Keyes, Crittenberger, and I, with the division commanders of the II Corps, General Anders and a group of Polish generals, and others, were required to join General Clark for a triumphal entry into Bologna. We assembled at Bolte's Command Post in the Zoological Gardens on the southern outskirts, stood around while photographers recorded the event for posterity, and then Clark led a procession of jeeps, escorted by military police with wailing sirens, on a tour of downtown streets. What we were supposed to accomplish, I do not know. There were few Bolognese about and these did not seem overly enthusiastic. It was a far cry from the tumultuous reception in Rome the previous year.

At my morning staff conference April 23rd, reports indicated that Hays was making preparations to cross the Po at San Benedetto, and that other elements of the IV Corps were now approaching the river. The II Corps seemed to be moving more slowly. Prisoners were now flowing into our cages by thousands, and we were still hopeful of cutting off most of the German forces south of the river. Immediately after the conference, General Darcy and I flew by Cub to Florence, transferred to Darcy's P-51, and set off for another reconnaissance over the battle area.

Some fighting was in progress on the II Corps' front and on the left flank of the IV Corps west of Modena. Occasionally we were greeted by bursts of flak. However, the German forces were now in a state of confusion and disorder. Columns were moving in opposite directions on adjacent roads, others were crossing routes. Hundreds of vehicles were streaming toward the river in a desperate effort to escape. A short distance west of San Benedetto where the 10th Mountain Division was making preparations to cross, Darcy circled, pointed downward toward a column of troops moving eastward, and shouted: "Boche!" I nodded agreement. The next I knew, we were plunging earthward in a steep dive and Darcy was strafing the Germans. In several attacks, he set a number of vehicles on fire and dispersed the German column; then we turned eastward. Below Ostiglia, we found several other German columns approaching the river with none of our own troops in the vicinity. We circled over these, making one or two strafing passes to keep them halted and dispersed, while Darcy called other fighter bombers to the area and directed them onto the target. While some of the German forces had escaped to the north bank, vast quantities of weapons and equipment had been abandoned on the south bank, for there was no means of conveying it across.

Darcy and I returned from the P-51 reconnaissance and then we flew on by Cub to San Benedetto where Hays was crossing. Darcy cracked up the Cub, landing in a small wheatfield, but neither of us was hurt. At Hays' Command Post near the river bank, I learned he had brought up assault boats during the morning and shortly after noon had made an assault crossing under fire, which had been wholly successful. Two regiments were now across, with a bridgehead safely established. Our success in breaching this major obstacle had exceeded our wildest hopes. The problem now was to get bridges across and to continue the pursuit relentlessly, for it was now obvious that victory was almost within our hands.

We were joined by my old friend from Ranger days, Colonel William O. Darby. On duty in the War Department's Operations Division at the time, he was accompanying General Arnold and other dignitaries on a visit to the theater, and had come up to the front to visit General Hays who was an old friend. A few hours before, General Duff had been seriously wounded by a mine, leaving Hays without an assistant division commander. Hays asked me if I could arrange to have Darby assigned in Duff's place. I thought I could, and told Darby to consider himself assigned until he heard from me. When I returned to my Command Post, I sent a message to Clark and McNarney and asked them to arrange with the War Department for Darby's assignment as assistant division commander, which was done without any trouble. But it was a sad blow to me when this gallant officer was killed on the last day of April near the northern end of Lake Garda. Darby was one of the outstanding leaders whom I knew during the war. It was fitting that the War Department should promote him posthumously to the rank of brigadier general.

Our bridge trains were still south of Bologna. Although I ordered them forward that night, there was so much congestion on roads, and such upheaval in the Po valley, that there was delay in getting the bridging material to the sites. However, at noon April 25th, Hays and I crossed the first completed bridge and a few hours later another was completed in the IV Corps sector. The II Corps reached the river on April 24th, and began crossing by ferry while its bridge was under construction. By the morning of April 26th, a third bridge was completed at Ostiglia.

The general plan of operations of the 15th Army Group envisaged that both Armies, after crossing the Po, would force the Adige position, and drive through northeast Italy. General Clark had thought that, when this phase began, it might be necessary to leave Crittenberger's IV Corps Headquarters as occupation troops in the northwest.

On April 24th, when we began crossing the Po River, our battle was all but won, although, besides the battered remnants fleeing before us, there were still some important German forces to the northwest. Our first task was to seize Verona and seal off the Brenner Pass. Then we could turn east with part of the command, mop up, and assist the Eighth Army in capturing Padova. At the same time, it was desirable to prevent the escape of the German forces to the northwest as well as those still south of the Po River to the west of our crossing sites. Accordingly, the next week the Fifth Army fanned out in all directions ostensibly in confusion, but it could be better described as "controlled dispersion." As soon as the 10th Mountain Division, the 85th and 88th Infantry Divisions were across the Po, all three pressed on at top speed toward Verona which was in our hands by April 25th. Hays then continued north along the eastern edge of Lake Garda. Coulter cleared the Adige position near Verona and reverted to Army reserve. Keyes' II Corps with the 88th and 91st Divisions abreast forced crossings over the Adige River, and pushed on eastward toward Vicenza, then Treviso, while the Eighth Army drove on along the Adriatic coast.

Meanwhile, the 1st Armored Division crossed behind the 10th Mountain Division at San Benedetto and drove northwest to block all roads leading from the Po valley into the Alps as far west as the Swiss border at Lake Como. South of the Po River, there were considerable German forces still trying to escape from the mountains west of Modena. On April 24th, I had left the Legnano Group to garrison Bologna and had started the 34th Infantry Division west on Highway 9 with the Brazilians. The 34th drove westward to Piacenza—seventy-five miles in three days against scattered but stubborn opposition—and destroyed two German divisions in the area between the Po and Highway 9. April 28th, I ordered Bolte and his Division on a long move to the north of Milan to join the 1st Armored Division in operations against the last intact German forces in north Italy, the German LXXV Corps, leaving the Brazilians to clear up the area south of the Po River.

The Brazilians debouched from the mountains on the 23rd and Mascarhenas, their commander, turned westward between Highway 9 and the mountains on the south, blocking the escape route of the remaining German forces. There was some brisk fighting during this advance in which the Brazilians acquitted themselves well. Action ended on April 29th when the 148th Panzer Grenadiers and the Italian Bersaglieri Division surrendered to Mascarhenas. Mascarhenas was justifiably proud, for the take included some 15,000 prisoners of war and vast quantities of supplies and equipment. Mascarhenas then pushed on west to Alessandra and made contact with Almond and the 92nd Division, which had taken Genoa on April 29th.

Mussolini's headquarters had been located on the western shores of Lake Garda. The 10th Mountain Division staged an amphibious operation in DUKW's across the lake in an effort to take him and other Fascist officials. Unfortunately, they were already in flight toward Switzerland. We made strenuous efforts to intercept and rescue him from Partisans after they had captured him, but without success. Mussolini and his mistress were shot by the Partisans and then hanged in the most gruesome fashion by an immense mob in Milan on April 29th.

Major Marinelli and I came close to disaster on this date. We were flying over the II Corps and had marked leading elements of the 88th Division near Bassano, and the 91st Infantry Division toward Treviso. Turning southward, we looked for the 6th South African Armored Division. At a place where we thought they were, we were welcomed by several batteries of German flak. Marinelli twisted and turned his way earthward through a hail of lead to tree-top level, and we made our escape with no more damage than a few holes through wings and fuselage of the L-5.

April 30th, I was called to Florence to confer with General Clark. He told me arrangements had been made for the surrender of the German forces, effective noon, May 2nd. Until then, we were to keep up our advance; but at that hour, hostilities would cease, and we would halt in place. German emissaries would enter our lines at the north end of Lake Garda and meet General Alexander's representatives to complete the arrangements.

My aide's journal records our last day of combat, May 2nd:

A clear morning. Usual 0830 briefing, IV Corps reporting no change. Still pockets remaining. 88th Division continuing north into the Alps, collecting many prisoners. Counted total is now over 80,000. Gen. Howard in 0930 with latest intelligence, followed by Col. Harrel for discussion of plans. Gen. Osborne, MTO I&E Officer and Lt. Col. Worthington come in briefly to discuss projected I&E program. Army commander stays in CP all morning waiting confirmation of the surrender. Col. Johnson in at 1045 with latest court martial cases. General spends his time on papers and letters before lunch. Chief of Staff and Col. Ladue in to discuss surrender plans. Rain after lunch. Gen. talks with Gen. Clark by phone after PRO come in with AHQ news release announcing surrender. Some confusion but surrender official at 1400. Chief of Staff in with Col. Cassidy. Latter directed to draft Army Order of the Day. Mike Chinigo arrives from Rome. Gen. and Maj. Wilson leave 1500 by Cub in rain flying to II Corps CP at Bassano. Weather completely foul and unable to land. Returned to wrecked Vicenza Airport. Stop

at II Corps rear where Gen. talks to Gen. Willems by phone. Weather clearing at Bassano, so Gen drives back to airport and takes off for II Corps again,
landing without incident at 1705. Met by Gen. Willems and driven to Corps
CP. Gen. goes over situation. Gen. Keyes arrives at 1730. General informs
him of surrender. Army commander returns to CP in olive grove south of
Verona at 1845. Chinigo in to offer his congratulation on the surrender, followed by Chief of Staff, Cols. Lloyd and Cassidy, Gen. Howard, Cols. Harrel, O'Neill, Conway. Few magnums of champagne are cracked open to celebrate the victory News is broadcast to troops in the area and there is a great
deal of noise, fireworks, and so on from all Army and civil personnel in the
Verona area. Gen. Darcy joins celebration at 2100, Col. Daniels later. Very
late dinner and bed.

When the surrender came, the Fifth Army held the major portion
of north Italy from the Austrian border on the east to the Swiss and
French borders on the west. The II Corps was assembling the 91st
Infantry Division at Treviso, which together with the road leading
north was to become part of the Eighth Army zone. The 85th Infantry
Division was advancing up the valley of the Piave, the 88th Division
up the Brenta valley into the Alps, driving north toward the Brenner
Pass. The 10th Mountain Division under Army control was five miles
north of Lake Garda. In the IV Corps Sector, the 1st Armored Division
had blocked all passes into the mountains to the Swiss border at Lake
Como, and was assisting the 34th Infantry Division which, on May
2nd, reached Novara and Biella, whereupon the German LXXV Corps
surrendered. South of the Po, the Brazilians had reached Alessandra;
the 92nd Infantry Division at Genoa had pushed detachments out
toward the French border toward Turin and Cuneo. The 365th and
371st Infantry Regiments were both guarding prisoner of war enclosures which were now bulging with nearly a hundred thousand men.
It had been an eventful period—this "19 Days from the Apennines to
the Alps."

As the Germans withdrew in Italy, Fascist civil officials usually fled
with them and left communities without normal governmental functions or means of maintaining law and order. Public utilities were disrupted by war. Transport was almost non-existent for civilian use. Food
was extremely scarce, and distribution of the low food stocks was almost impossible. Communities were torn with dissension—pro-Ally
against pro-Fascist—royalists against republicans—town against country—land owners against peasants—capital against labor. Throughout
northern Italy, particularly, there was a strong communist party ready
to fan the flames of dissension and to exploit every opportunity for
subversion. In the Partisan movement, there had been an uneasy truce

among the conflicting elements while all concentrated against the common enemy. The withdrawal of the Germans, however, was followed by a bitter struggle for power among the dissident factions which verged at times on civil war.

Allied Military Government, or AMG as it was familiarly known, controlled occupied territory by establishing and supervising civil administrations. It was composed of specially selected or trained officers and men of all branches of the service of both the United States and Great Britain. The Allied Control Commission supervised execution of the armistice terms by the Provisional Italian Government and directed the military government except in areas where the Allied Armies were operating, in which case the establishment and supervision of military government was a responsibility of the Army commanders. In the Fifth Army, this task fell to the G-5 or Civil Affairs Officer of the Army staff assisted by AMG personnel attached to the Fifth Army.

Brigadier General Erskine E. Hume, G-5, Fifth Army, was the staff officer responsible for the establishment and supervision of Allied Military Government in areas occupied by the Fifth Army. Hume and his assistants followed closely behind the troops. In each community, they organized the civil administration promptly. They appointed mayors, judges and police officials. They restored public utilities—power, telephone, telegraph. They opened banks and supervised the currency; they established schools, opened factories, supervised labor, and provided for collection of food available in the localities. One of their most important functions was the distribution of food, and a very large part of the food to sustain the civilian populations was obtained from Allied sources. The value of their work can hardly be overestimated.

When the Germans surrendered on May 2nd, we had, with Partisan help, liberated all of northern Italy east of Milan and Genoa. Crittenberger had the 1st Armored Division and the 34th Infantry Division rounding up the German LXXV Corps northwest of Turin, and the 92nd Infantry Division extending control westward from Genoa. Allied Military Government officials accompanied these troops and established military government as rapidly as possible. On May 4th, however, we were still clearing out pockets of enemy resistance, corralling thousands of prisoners, and trying to inaugurate effective control over the Partisan bands to prevent excesses all too common among untrained and undisciplined guerilla troops. We had not yet extended our authority to the Swiss and French borders except in a few places, and we had not yet completed the establishment of military government throughout the region which was an important part of my mission. As a matter of fact, in attempting to carry it out, we were soon involved in a ridiculous international situation, one that was both amusing and annoying. A French general commanding troops armed and equipped with American uniforms for the most part, and supplied almost entirely from American sources, was threatening to fire upon American troops performing their duty.

During our invasion of southern France, the tide of war had rolled on northward, leaving German forces in the Maritime Alps along the Franco-Italian border. Part of de Lattre's French Armee B, the Detachment Army of the Alps, was left here to protect the line of communications of the Sixth Army Group in the valley of the Rhone. It was in contact with German forces, some of which still held a narrow strip of French soil, when the Allies in Italy were preparing for their final offensive. General Clark thought a demonstration by these French troops would aid the spring offensive, so early in the year, he requested Sixth Army Group to arrange one. Although the Army group was willing enough, the French were not; they did not wish to be limited to a mere demonstration.

The French had felt very keenly the Italian "stab in the back" of June, 1940, in which they had been compelled to accede to an ignominious armistice in Turin. In November, 1942, the Germans and Italians had extended their occupaton over all of southern France, and the Italians had set about preparations to annex some areas of French territory. Like most contiguous areas of Europe, the border population was mixed, and there were ample grounds on both sides for boundary disputes. However, northern Italy was territory of a government which Allied policy had supported since the Armistice of 1943. It had just been liberated from German domination, but it was filled with many contending factions, none of which could be characterized as pro-French. In fact, these factions were almost unanimous in their anti-French sentiments. The Allied High Command therefore had no desire to complicate the already delicate situation in northern Italy by interjecting French troops. Accordingly, when the French demanded greater participation in the spring offensive than a mere demonstration on the French side of the frontier, a fixed limit generally along the eastern exits from the mountain passes was indicated as the line beyond which French troops would not advance.

French troops began operations on this border on April 9th, simultaneously with the attack of the Eighth Army in the spring offensive. On April 27th, when we had already crossed the Po River, captured Verona, and broken through the Adige line, it was obvious that the French advance could have no further effect upon operations in Italy. Accordingly, General Clark asked the Sixth Army Group to halt the

French troops and withdraw into France any elements that might have crossed the boundary. A week later, on May 4th, two days after the German surrender, General Clark informed me that the order had not been obeyed and the French commander would not retire without the consent of his government. He also mentioned that affairs on the border were confused and that the French were making unreasonable demands upon the Italians. We were not to encourage the French in any way, but were to make every effort to get them to withdraw beyond the frontier. Meanwhile, we were to establish Allied Military Government up to the Franco-Italian border.

In an effort to obtain accurate information, I sent Colonel Conway to Nice to confer with the French commander. He informed General Doyen, commanding the Detachment Army of the Alps, of our mission. General Doyen said he had halted his advance as he had been directed, but he would not withdraw into France without orders from his government. He proposed that our troops proceed to seal the border and establish military government as we had been ordered to do, either allowing French troops to remain in place with freedom of movement or else agreeing upon a line of demarcation between the French and American forces.

Meanwhile, General Alexander had appealed to General Eisenhower saying that the presence of French troops in Italy was undesirable. On May 8th, I was advised that SHAEF had requested the French government to have General Doyen coordinate his withdrawal into France with arrival of my troops at the Franco-Italian border. I was also instructed to establish Allied Military Government in northwest Italy up to the Franco-Italian border as rapidly as possible, but to avoid any armed clash with the French at all costs.

Crittenberger, in Milan, was pushing troop detachments into northwest Italy as soon as they became available, and AMG officers were moving in with the troops and establishing military government. We had already established patrols at several points along the border. I invited Doyen to visit me at Verona to talk over the problem, which he did on May 15th. We gave him plush treatment—a ceremony at the airport and an escort to the Command Post, a guard of honor and a review, an elaborate luncheon, and so on—but to no avail. He asserted French claims to reparations and some regions along the border. He would not withdraw into France without the agreement of his government; he did not believe that any French officer could do so. He was cordial and wished to be cooperative, but it was evident that the French had no intention of retiring. A week later I returned his visit; he was still waiting orders from Paris.

We continued our extension of military government and troop

movements into northwest Italy, and the French became increasingly annoyed. The last week in May, General Doyen wrote me saying France would not consent to any modification of the existing state of affairs, and that he had been directed to occupy and administer territory in Italy. Any insistence upon establishment of Allied military government would be considered a hostile act which would have grave consequences.

Doyen went so far as to remove the AMG administration which had been established in several places, and threatened to employ French troops to prevent our operating there. By this time French and Americans had become quite thoroughly intermingled. While we had avoided any incident, the condition was most unsatisfactory. Since the French had refused to accede to the AFHQ and SHAEF requests, General Alexander submitted the problem to the Combined Chiefs of Staff for decision.

I returned to the United States during June on one of the "homecoming celebrations." On my way back I stopped in Washington to see Tom Handy—General Marshall was absent—and others in the War Department. I asked him what had happened about the Franco-Italian border dispute. Handy said it was settled. When the matter was presented to the President, he had simply said: "Cut off their supplies." On my return to Italy, I learned that the Allied High Command had begun by stopping the supply of gasoline. One morning, French officials, including even the French Ambassador in Rome, found that no gasoline was available for French Forces. Confronted with this situation, the French quickly came to terms, and agreed to withdraw. Following joint Franco-American ceremonies in Turin during the last week of July, the last of the French forces cleared out of Italy.

When hostilities ceased on May 2nd, the Fifth Army already had taken more than 80,000 prisoners. These were under guard in PW enclosures south of the Po River around Modena and Bologna. The German surrender involved all other German forces in Italy—several hundred thousand—who had so far escaped our troops and were scattered around in great disorder through the Alps short of the Austrian and Swiss borders.

On May 3rd, the representatives of General Von Vietinghoff (the German commander in Italy who had succeeded Kesselring) arrived at our lines north of Lake Garda. They were met by General Hays and a party from the 10th Mountain Division and escorted to my Command Post in the olive grove south of Verna. We housed them in tents overnight—Lieutenant General Schlemmer, Commanding General XIV Panzer Corps, five officers and six enlisted men—but I would not see any of them. I had never had any wish to exchange civilities with any of the numerous enemy generals who passed through my headquarters during the war; and I had no curiosity about them that the usual G-2 PW interrogation could not satisfy. The following morning we sent them on to 15th Army Group in Florence.

That afternoon, Carleton and I were ordered to Florence to be present with General McCreery of the Eighth Army and his chief of staff, and members of the 15th Army Group, while Clark staged a "surrender" meeting with General Schlemmer. Clark's remarks and Schlemmer's reply had obviously been prepared in advance. The meeting struck me as pointless, for the only purpose was a photographic record in Hollywood tradition.

Following the visit of General Schlemmer, General Clark sent a large group of staff officers headed by a brigadier general from 15th Army Group to Von Vietinghoff's headquarters in Bolzano to supervise the execution of surrender terms. Meanwhile, the Fifth Army, standing pat in accordance with the cease fire terms, had no immediate responsibilities. Days passed. Clark's group found the Germans somewhat recalcitrant and increasingly more difficult to deal with. Almost every question had to be referred to higher headquarters for decision. Progress was correspondingly slow. Then there was a blast of publicity which I summarized in messages to Crittenberger and Keyes on May 18th:

> An article in Stars and Stripes Friday 18 May by staff correspondent charges that during days following VE day (1) armored and arrogant Germans, wearing SS Death's Head, still roamed the streets of Bolzano in freedom; (2) 88 Division forced to ask General Wolf for permission to set up a CP, (3) All billeting done through SS; (4) Germans showed defiance by billeting five American Red Cross girls next to PRO station; (5) SS men had been driving powerful cars through streets, fraternizing with civilian girls, eating in restaurants from which Italian civilians barred; (6) German newspaper continued publication for days after American troops came in.

> You will complete a thorough inspection with the least practicable delay to insure that no such conditions as those alleged now exist in areas for which you are responsible, and that all instructions relative to the treatment of surrendered forces are being carried out to the letter and in strict accordance with the terms of the surrender agreement. I desire a report of compliance at the earliest practicable period.

Clark immediately passed on to us responsibility for enforcing the surrender terms and collecting the German forces in PW enclosures—more than two weeks after the surrender. The terms provided that German units would move to the concentration camps under their own officers who would be permitted to retain their sidearms until they became prisoners of war. We gave the German command written instructions for this movement and I directed Keyes with the II Corps to enforce strict control. Von Vietinghoff's protest at moving from the mountains to the summer heat of the supposedly malarial Po Valley, I disregarded. The collection and movement of 250,000 Germans in the Fifth Army area was carried out smoothly, effectively, and without incident. At the PW enclosure south of Brescia, the 442d Infantry —the Japanese-Americans—disarmed them, separated the senior officers, and sent the general officers on to a special camp south of Florence.

We had no difficulty whatever with the German prisoners. They were well disciplined and their attitudes were usually correct in every respect. In fact, we found them to be cooperative and willing workers.

As redeployment took away the maintenance and service units' repair shops, engineer troops and the like which had supported the Fifth Army in Italy, they were replaced by service units organized from among the German prisoners of war. Dozens of truck companies, ordnance companies, quartermaster companies, engineer units, labor service units, and others all helped to reduce the problem of guarding prisoners; and maintenance in the American army in Italy was never at a higher level.

While we were planning and carrying out our final campaign in northern Italy, those responsible for directing the war effort were already formulating plans for the next phase after the destruction of the Nazi armies, that is, the prosecution of the war against the remaining Axis partner, Japan, and the policies to be followed with respect to Germany and the nations that had, willingly or not, been allied with her. At the time of the Yalta conference in February, 1945, at which the heads of states agreed upon policies with respect to these matters, it was thought that the war against Japan might continue for another year and require most of the manpower then deployed in Europe. Based upon this assumption, the War Department had evolved plans for redeploying troop units and individuals from the European Theater to the Pacific as rapidly as possible after the defeat of Germany. In general, units were to be selected according to need and type. Personnel would be chosen according to points based on length of service, time in combat, and other factors.

General McNarney and his theater staff, working closely with the Fifth Army staff, developed careful redeployment plans. Units for transfer to the Pacific were designated. Those to remain on occupation duty in Europe were earmarked. Others were to be transferred to the

United States at appropriate intervals as shipping became available for inactivation. All personnel were classified according to a point score. Plans were made for mass transfers among units, low score personnel to units for early redeployment to the Pacific, high score personnel for early transfer to the United States, and so on. Staging areas were selected and organized for processing of individuals and units. Carefully prepared training programs were devised to fit units and individuals for combat conditions in the Pacific. Those redeployed were completely reequipped with the best equipment obtainable in the theater. Huge shops were established to overhaul and prepare for shipment weapons, tanks, trucks, and other equipment.

Because of shipping limitations and other curtailments, it would take months to carry out this program. Meanwhile many men not slated for the Pacific would be waiting transfer home. Occupation duties would absorb comparatively few of these. There was no longer the need for the intensive training which had heretofore filled their days. For the men who would remain in Italy for longer periods, an extensive educational system was organized, in which they could resume studies interrupted by the war, or they could learn a trade. Arrangements were made for attendance at Italian universities for a certain number. And a university was organized in Florence from among the instructors found in the command who were fully qualified, whereby hundreds of men acquired college credits.

Our rest centers were enlarged, and leaves encouraged. The whole of the Italian Riviera became a rest center for enlisted men. Visits to historic places in Italy were promoted. One of the most popular furloughs was the five-day trip through Switzerland which thousands of American soldiers enjoyed.

There were few complaints concerning the redeployment program in Italy, and it was completed efficiently. Much credit is due to General McNarney and his staff for their conception and support of the problem, to the Fifth Army staff for implementing and supervising the program, and to the division, regimental, battalion and company commanders who permitted no relaxation in discipline, but held their commands to the high standards which should be expected of American soldiers.

At Yalta, the chiefs of state had decided upon the treatment to be accorded Germany and Austria. Germany was to be treated as a defeated nation, Austria as a liberated one. Allied occupation forces for Germany were to be provided by SHAEF; those for Austria, from Italy. Both Germany and Austria were to be occupied by the four powers, each of which would have an occupation zone, including a sector in the capital city. Original plans for FREEBORN, the occupation of Austria, made the Fifth Army responsible for organizing the Group Control Council and the Austrian occupation forces. We began work on these plans during March.

By the end of April, Seventh Army troops had reached Austria. It was then proposed to utilize SHAEF troops, but to transfer the Fifth Headquarters to Austria after the end of hostilities. We had been developing the redeployment program simultaneously with FREE-BORN. However, I came to the conclusion that Fifth Army Headquarters should be retained in Italy to manage redeployment, and that General Clark's 15th Army Group, for which there would be no further need, should be charged with the Austrian occupation. I must admit, too, I had little liking for occupation duties and entertained some hope we might be used in the war against Japan. On May 3rd, the day after VI (Victory in Italy) Day, I wrote to General Mc-Narney, setting forth my views and recommending that the Fifth Army not be sent to Austria.

General McNarney, I suppose, consulted the War Department. At any rate he notified me on May 6th that he approved my recommendation that Clark's Headquarters get the Austrian assignment. General Clark telephoned me the next day to give me the news, obviously delighted with the assignment. I never told him that I had any part in securing it for him.

In June, I visited several key cities in the United States especially chosen to honor and fete representative groups of senior officers, and enlisted men of all ranks and grades from the various theaters. On my way back to Italy, I stopped off in Washington and intimated to General Handy that I desired to serve in the war against Japan if there should be an opportunity. On July 29th, there came a message from General Marshall reminding me of that conversation and suggesting I take a few key members of my staff and visit China to confer with General Wedemeyer and the Generalissimo concerning a combat assignment in China.

Carleton, O'Neill, Harrel, Conway, Wilson, Bartash, and Sergeants Barna and Hong made up my party. We left on August 8th, and were waiting plane connections in Cairo when there came the first news of Japan's willingness to surrender. I called Washington and was told to proceed with the trip to China. I will always be glad we were given the opportunity.

Cairo . . . the pyramids. The flight from Cairo to Abadan over the cradles of civilization, now desert wastes. Abadan to Karachi . . . sand . . . heat . . . filth . . . poverty. Karachi over Agra—where we could not land because of buzzards on the air fields, where we circled round and round for an aerial view of the Taj Mahal. Calcutta . . . heat and humidity . . . teeming population . . . docks cluttered with vast quantities of supplies for China only a fraction of which could be delivered. Flying the Hump, Calcutta to Kunming . . . wild and rugged mountains . . . Chungking. Wedemeyer and his comparatively small headquarters . . . the Generalissimo. Chungking and Chiang Kai Shek . . . symbols of resistance to Japanese aggression.

I encountered many old friends in China. Wedemeyer and I had been classmates at Fort Leavenworth. Ray Maddocks, his Chief of Staff, and I had been instructors together at Fort Riley. There were others from my Fort Leavenworth days and many old cavalry friends in the Chinese Combat Command, commanded by Major General B. Robert McClure at Kunming. It was not a large command, only a few score American officers. Their task had been to assist in the organization, training, and direction of the Chinese "armies"—little more than divisions—with American arms and equipment. This had been a grim and austere task, for all land communication had been severed by the Japanese. All supplies had to be flown in over the "Hump"—one of the most amazing supply feats of the war. These officers were up against other problems besides supply shortages—the differences between Chinese and western cultures, language barriers, and the Chinese predilection for what we would call graft. No American officers and men contributed more to the war effort with less to work with than these gallant and dauntless individuals of the China Combat Command.

The plan had been for me to command a group of Chinese Armies in northern China while General Simpson took charge of a similar group in southern China. These were to take part in the fight against Japanese forces on the mainland of China while the Allied forces were making the assault upon the Japanese home islands. I was glad that the fortunes of war decided otherwise.

Carleton and I were in Chih Kiang (Yuan Chow) when the Japanese envoys arrived to negotiate surrender with the Chinese command, assisted by General McClure's representatives. Having seen what we could of China, there was nothing further to hold us. We packed up and returned, detouring to spend one day in Ceylon visiting Admiral Mountbatten, who was now Supreme Allied Commander in Southeast Asia. We were back in Italy on August 30th.

When we got back, redeployment was so far along that the end was almost in sight. The Fifth Army Headquarters became inoperative in Italy on September 9th, the second anniversary of its first battle at Salerno. Most of the personnel had already been transferred elsewhere. Those remaining packed records and prepared the Headquarters for shipment to the United States for inactivation. On September 20th, personnel embarked on the *Hagerstown Victory* at Leghorn. There, I said good-bye to the remnants of the staff that had served me so well and promised to meet them when they landed in Boston for inactivation. Carleton, the two aides, Sergeant Barna and I were going by motor through the Brenner Pass to visit General Patton, General Eisenhower and others in Germany before returning to the United States and home by air. At least, so we thought.

.

CHAPTER NINE

THE GERMAN OCCUPATION

When Carleton, the aides, and I left Italy and headed north through the Brenner Pass to visit Germany, we intended to leave Paris by air for the United States the following week. We expected to be present for the final inactivation of the Fifth Army Headquarters when it arrived on the *Hagerstown Victory*. In fact, all of our baggage, except clothes enough for one week of travel, was aboard. But a new Army command was to come as a complete surprise.

We spent September 22nd with General Patton at Third Army Headquarters in Bal Tolz a few miles north of the Austrian border, and September 23rd with General Keyes who was now commanding the Seventh Army with Headquarters in Heidelberg. Then we went on to Frankfurt where I was put up by my good friend "Beetle" Smith. The following morning, I went in to pay my respects to General Eisenhower. He greeted me in his usual warm manner, then said: "Lucian, you are just the man I need. Unless you have some objection, I think I will send you down to relieve George Patton."

General Eisenhower went on to say that General Patton had caused a storm of criticism by a press conference in which he had justified utilizing Nazis in civil government offices and had likened the German political scene to the struggle between Democrats and Republicans in our own country. He had also shown a lack of sympathy in caring for Jewish displaced persons whom high level policy had accorded special privileges and accommodations. Since ill-considered words and actions could only embarrass the administration and jeopardize the occupation, he thought that General Patton should be replaced by someone not as inclined to intemperate outbursts.

General Eisenhower knew, of course, that General Patton was my close personal friend. I explained that I had no desire to supersede him, but that I wished to be of service. If General Patton had to depart, I thought he would probably prefer being replaced by me than by someone who might be less sympathetic. General Eisenhower said he would consult with General Marshall. Meanwhile, I was to go on to Berlin and Paris, but I was not to leave for the United States until he authorized me to do so. I had two days in Berlin, another day in Frankfurt, and two days in Paris. Then I was called back to Frankfurt to relieve

General Patton as Commanding General, Third Army and Eastern Military District (Bavaria).

At Frankfurt I spent some time reviewing background material and files and discussing occupation problems with members of General Eisenhower's United States Forces European Theatre (USFET) staff and their civilian political advisers. Besides matters of Allied Military Government, and prisoners of war, which had concerned us in Italy, here there were the displaced persons, repatriation of Soviet nationals, and the prosecution of war criminals to contend with. The story of these problems is the story of my connection with the German occupation.

October 4th, I had a final conference with General Eisenhower before leaving for Bavaria and the new assignment. He repeated that the most acute and important problems with which we had to deal in Germany at that time were those involving denazification and the handling of those unfortunate persons who had been the victims of Nazi persecution. Unfavorable publicity in either case would embarrass the administration and would have extremely ill effects upon occupation policies. We were to adopt a stern course toward the Nazis. We were to be ruthless, in eliminating them from all positions in government and industry, and in the seizure of Nazi properties. Also, he had prescribed preferential treatment for Jewish displaced persons in allowances of food, clothing, housing, and supplies, and had directed that no restrictions whatever were to be placed upon them.

I went to Bad Tolz that night and stopped again with General Patton, whose welcome was just as warm as it had ever been. We spent most of two days reviewing occupation procedures. The only sign he ever gave of the blow which he must have felt came when he said: "Lucian, if you have no objection, I want to have a big formal ceremony and turn over the command to you with considerable fanfare and publicity. I don't want Ike or anyone else to get the idea that I am leaving here with my tail between my legs." I assured him I was perfectly willing to participate in any ceremony he wished to arrange.

The occasion, which took place on Sunday, October 7th, turned out to be quite simple but very moving. Because of inclement weather, it was held in the huge gymnasium of the SS *Kaserne* where the Third Army Headquarters was located. General Patton and I, with the four Corps commanders and the principal members of the Army staff, took our positions on the stage which had been appropriately decorated. We faced the rest of Third Army Headquarters and all of the Army troops available in the Bad Tolz sector. Honors were rendered and the command presented. Then General Patton made an appropriately emotional farewell address and handed over to me the Third Army flag to symbolize the transfer of command. I replied briefly. A final rendering of the honors and the National Anthem terminated the ceremony. After a farewell luncheon with the Corps commanders and Army staff, we escorted General Patton to the station and saw him off on his private train for Bad Nauheim. His new assignment was Commanding General Fifteenth Army—the same headquarters which I had been slated to organize almost a year earlier and which was now performing the function of a theater Board. That is, the headquarters was engaged in evaluating the lessons learned during the war and making recommendations as to changes in our tables of organization.

Two months later, the whole theater was to be thrown into deep mourning when General Patton was badly hurt in an automobile accident, and a few days later died from his injuries. He was perhaps the most colorful, as he was certainly the most outstanding, battle leader of World War II.

Third Army Headquarters was divided between Munich and Bad Tolz, some twenty miles to the south near the Austrian border. The rear echelon and most of the administrative services were located in Munich. General Patton had established the forward echelon or Command Post at Bad Tolz in a splendid modern *kaserne* which had been the SS academy under the Hitler regime. This *kaserne* consisted of a huge quadrangle which housed the offices and most of the enlisted personnel, a dozen or so houses which had sheltered some of the academy staff, a riding hall, stables, and various shops and other installations. Most of our staff were billeted in hotels and requisitioned houses in the town of Bad Tolz, a former health and pleasure resort.

Just a few miles from the Austrian border and almost in the shadow of the Alps, this part of Bavaria is of surpassing beauty. It was not, however, a convenient location for an Army headquarters. And it was just about as far from the theater headquarters in Frankfurt as it was possible to be and remain in Bavaria. I considered moving it to Munich. However, we finally established the Office of Military Government for Bavaria there, and assembled the rest of the Army Headquarters in Bad Tolz, where it remained until we moved to Heidelberg the following spring when the Zone was reorganized.

General Patton himself had taken up residence on Tegernsee, a beautiful lake some miles east of Bad Tolz, and a resort spot where a number of the top Nazis had built some very fine villas. He had selected the finest of these, a swank, modern and rather luxurious home with a fine view of lake and mountains. There were game rooms, a bowling alley, an indoor target range, squash courts, and every possible convenience for pleasant living. It had belonged to the publisher of "*Mein Kampf*," and quotations from the book were molded in relief in the plaster on the ceiling of the drawing room as part of the decorative scheme. The place had escaped damage during the war although some fighting had flared up nearby. Luckily, unlike other buildings it had not suffered from looting. Carleton, the aides, and I lived here during our stay at Bad Tolz, and it was a rare week when we did not have guests from among the many persons who visited the Army Headquarters for one reason or another.

The Crimean conference resulted in the so-called Yalta agreement in which the British, Americans, and Russians declared their intentions with respect to defeated Nazi Germany and agreed upon zones of occupation where each of the Allies would enforce their prerogatives. At the Potsdam conference, in July, 1945, the same powers agreed upon the political and economic principles of a coordinated Allied policy with regard to Germany during the period of Allied control. This declaration reads:

The purposes of the occupation of Germany by which the Control Council shall be guided are:

1. The complete disarmament and demilitarization of Germany and the elimination or control of all German industry that could be used for military production. To these ends:

(a) All German land, naval, and air forces, the S.S., S.A., S.D., and Gestapo, with all their organizations, staffs, and institutions, including the General Staff, the Officers' Corps, Reserve Corps, military schools, war veterans' organizations and all other military or quasi-military organizations, together with all clubs and associations which serve to keep alive the military tradition in Germany, shall be completely and finally abolished in such manner as permanently to prevent the revival or reorganization of German militarism and Nazism.

(b) All arms, ammunition, and implements of war and all specialized facilities for their production shall be held at the disposal of the Allies or destroyed. The maintenance and production of all aircraft and all arms, ammunition, and implements of war shall be prevented.

2. To convince the German people that they have suffered a total military defeat and that they cannot escape responsibility for what they have brought upon themselves, since their own ruthless warfare and the fanatical Nazi resistance have destroyed German economy and made chaos and suffering inevitable.

3. To destroy the National Socialist Party and its affiliated and supervised organizations, to dissolve all Nazi institutions, to ensure that they are not revived in any form, and to prevent all Nazi and militarist activity or propaganda.

4. To prepare for the eventual reconstruction of German political life on democratic basis and for eventual peaceful cooperation in international life by Germany.

These agreements listed in some detail the political and economic principles and policies which were to govern the treatment of Germany and which were to be implemented by the Allied authorities. The German government had been totally destroyed so that there was no central authority capable of maintaining order, administering the country, and complying with Allied demands. The Allied Commanders in Chief in the declaration of June 5th, 1945, assumed supreme authority over all powers possessed by the German government, the High Command, and any state, municipal or local authority. Allied policy was directed toward decentralization of the political structure and the development of local autonomy. Local self-government and responsibility was to be restored, but no central government was to be established for the time being. The Allied Control Council would be the supreme authority, although certain central administrative establishments were to be inaugurated.

We had already found that occupation problems were far more numerous and perplexing than we had known in Italy. This was due, in part, to the different status accorded the two countries by the Allies, and in part to their divergent economic and political orders. The Allies had accorded Italy the status of co-belligerent. The aim of Allied Military Government had been to return control of government to the Italians as soon as possible, to sustain the established government pending post-war elections, and to restore the economic system. Allied Military Government in Italy was well organized, and staffed with qualified British and American officers and men. Huge funds and enormous quantities of supplies had been poured into Italy. Except for the more important party members, no great effort was made to eliminate Fascists from positions in government and industry.

In Germany, where the entire structure of government had been destroyed, the country was divided among the four conquering armies, and the quadripartite Allied Control Commission was the sole governing authority. While the economic structure had greater potential assets than the Italian, greater demands were placed upon it, and almost no assistance extended to it. In reorganizing government and industry, great emphasis was laid upon the complete elimination of Nazi party members from any position whatever in government and industry. General Patton's mistake had not been in remarking that denazification removed all of the best trained individuals from government, but in failing to appreciate that the fundamental objective of the occupation necessarily had to be the training of more democratic-minded officials to take their places.

In the United States Zone General Clay, as Deputy, usually represented the Military Governor—first General Eisenhower and then General McNarney—on the Allied Control Council. Initially, control of the German administration was exercised through the tactical chain of command and administered by the G-5's, or Civil Affairs officers, on Theater and Army staffs. For the first few months there was no central German administration at either national or state level so that Military Government officers were the ruling authority at every government level.

In order to coordinate the Military Government in the United States Zone more closely with German administrative departmental supervision which was being developed, and to prepare for the ultimate transfer of military government to U.S. civilian agencies, a further step in reorganization was effected October 1st, 1945, whereby the U.S. Group, Control Council (Germany), became the Office of Military Government for Germany (U.S.). The G-5 Division, Headquarters U.S. Forces, European Theater, became the Office of Military Government (U.S. Zone). In Bavaria, the Eastern Military District (the regional military government detachment) and the Third Army G-5 Section became the Office of Military Government for Bavaria. Other Offices of Military Government in the U.S. Zone were Western District, Banden-Wurtemberg, Greater Hessen, and Bremen. Military government detachments at lower levels were designated as Offices of Military Government for Regierungsbezirke, Stadtkreise, and Landkreise respectively.

When I relieved General Patton, my authority extended to all of Bavaria and a part of Czechoslovakia. Although redeployment was well advanced, the Third Army still included four Corps Headquarters: the XV Corps, under Major General W. M. Robertson in northern Bavaria; the XII Corps, under Major General Fay B. Prickett, in eastern Bavaria; the XX Corps, under Major General Horace L. McBride in southern Bavaria; and the XXII Corps, under Major General E. N. Harmon, in Czechoslovakia. There were a dozen or more Divisions and numerous Army and Corps troops, but the complexion of these was changing daily under mass redeployment transfers. Corps and Division commanders were responsible for the security of their respective areas, for supervision of displaced persons camps, and for execution of redeployment plans.

The office of Military Government for Bavaria was directed by Colonel Roy. L. Dalferes, the G-5 or Civil Affairs Officer of the Third

Army. However, he was due to return to the United States shortly. Recognizing that supply problems would be the most difficult the Military Government in Bavaria would have to face—collection and distribution of food, and other supplies, from various sources for displaced persons and the civil population—I decided it would be an advantage to have someone experienced in administration and supply as Director of Military Government for Bavaria. For this reason, I selected Brigadier General Walter M. Muller, who had been General Patton's G-4, for the post. It was a fortunate selection, for he served with distinction during the rest of the time Military Government remained.

A Theater Commanders' meeting, attended by Army Commanders and their principal staff advisers from both military and Military Government staffs, was convened once each month in Frankfurt to discuss occupation problems.

General Eisenhower earlier had expressed the opinion that a civilian agency should assume responsibility for administering the occupation as soon as possible. While neither the State Department nor any other civil agency in the government had trained personnel for the task, it seemed rather obvious that Military Government would be dissolved eventually. To prepare for this, the Military Government administration was separated from the tactical chain of command. It is noteworthy, I think, that when the State Department finally assumed responsibility for the administration of Germany, most of the Military Government officers who had been trained by the Army were absorbed into the civil organization.

The first Minister President of Bavaria was Dr. William Hoegner, who had spent most of the years of the Hitler regime as a refugee in Switzerland. In October he completed the selection of his ministers who were to head the various governmental departments in Bavaria when they were approved by our Military Government authorities. By the end of the year, the Bavarian Government was sufficiently well integrated to assume almost full responsibility for the administration of the civil affairs in accordance with the occupation edicts.

Redeployment was a more difficult problem than in Italy because more troops were involved, the population was unfriendly, and Allied relationships—especially the attitude of the Russians—were a complicating factor. On the other hand, there were many more educational, cultural, rest, and recreational facilities than were available in Italy, although they were still not being used to maximum advantage even in October. Suspension by Theater order of all military drills and training for individuals and units awaiting redeployment, no adequate program of informing men of redeployment problems, a factious editorial policy followed by the European edition of the "Stars and Stripes" — all contributed, during these months, to lowering morale and discipline and stirring up dissatisfaction and discontent.

Officers and men were transferred wholesale and without regard to individual preference to units designated for return to the United States as shipping space became available. This procedure completely destroyed the close and intimate relationship which existed normally between officers, non-commissioned officers and men which is the fundamental basis for discipline and control in any military organization. Since the availability of shipping was never known accurately, plans were continually changing. It was not unusual for men to be transferred several times in the course of a week or ten days. Soldiers are habitually loyal to the division with which they trained and served in combat; consequently these mass transfers had an adverse effect upon morale and were even worse upon discipline.

However, we devoted ourselves to improving the educational and vocational training opportunities and increasing rest and recreational facilities, so that towards the end of the year, when the bulk of the redeployment had been accomplished, conditions reached a satisfactory state with regard to discipline and morale.

There has probably never been in all history a comparable destruction of a fighting force by the people to whom the force belonged. The hysterical demand of the American people to "bring the boys home" wrought greater demoralization in a few weeks than a major defeat in battle would have done. What had been a magnificent fighting force became little more than a rabble — an undisciplined mob. The damage to American prestige was incalculable. Effects upon American policy have been far reaching. Evils engendered during these months have continued to plague us. While this condition had its origin in the thoughtless demands of the American people and the Congress, I am of the opinion that military authorities cannot escape some measure of responsibility. Had our high military authorities taken a strong and positive stand in opposition to such hasty dissolution of the forces, it is likely the American people could have been made to understand the logic of their position and would have supported them. There is no doubt, whatever, that the soldiers would have done so.

At the Yalta Conference, the three governments, America, Britain, and the U.S.S.R., had agreed to cooperate in repatriating the nationals of various countries who had been displaced from their native lands by German conquest or employment, and to exchange repatriation commissions to facilitate and expedite the work. The Western nations, having few of their own nationals involved, except as prisoners of war, apparently did not comprehend the magnitude of this problem nor the complications which were to be encountered in carrying out this agreement. Hundreds of thousands of people were involved, and most of them had their origin in lands now dominated by the U.S.S.R. However, most of them hated and feared the Russians even more than they hated the Germans. This was to make repatriation impossible in a vast number of cases, and was to complicate the displaced persons problem enormously.

When American troops entered Germany, they found more than a million of these unfortunate persons in the American Zone, a major portion of them in Bavaria. They represented almost every European and Asiatic nationality with whom the Germans had come in contact during the war. Some of them had come to Germany of their own accord to work on farms and in factories. Others had been imported as forced labor. Still others had been Russian or Polish prisoners of war. Some of these, such as Vlassov's Army, had changed sides and fought with the Germans, and many thousands had been inmates of Nazi concentration camps.

These hundreds of thousands of refugees, liberated by the advance of Allied troops, constituted a serious hazard to military movements, to health and to the maintenance of order. Immediately after the cessation of hostilities, they had been collected, sorted out by nationality as far as practicable, and placed in camps where they could be fed, clothed, and cared for, until disposition could be made of them. Full use was made of German *kasernes* or permanent military posts, labor camps, hotels, schools, other public buildings, and private dwellings. Scores of camps, varying in size from those housing a hundred or so, to thousands of persons, were scattered all over Bavaria.

Initially the camps had been administered and supervised by military personnel. For food and supplies, they were a charge upon the German economy — as they had been prior to our arrival. However, the German allowances had never been sufficient by our standards, and further, the German economy had all but collapsed. Continued assistance from military sources had been essential. General Eisenhower had accepted the offer of the United Nations Repatriation and Rehabilitation Administration (UNRAA) to assist the armed forces in caring for these displaced persons in the American Zone. When I assumed command of the Third Army, UNRRA Headquarters had recently been established in Frankfurt, and UNRRA teams had already taken responsibility for administration in a number of camps. Others were being taken over as rapidly as personnel became available and arrangements could be completed. However, extensive support, both logistical and administrative, continued to be required from military sources.

In one of my first moves I undertook to inspect all troop installations and displaced persons camps in the Army area. In the weeks that followed, I visited scores of camps, and saw several hundred thousand displaced persons in every part of Bavaria. Many were from the Baltic states — persons who had been sympathetic to the Germans and had cooperated with them during the Nazi attacks on Russia. Many had willingly come to Germany to work; others had fled as the Russians advanced into their homelands. Hatred and fear of the Russians were the distinguishing characteristics of these people. Although the Russian annexation of the Baltic states was not recognized by the United States, few of these Balts ever expected to return to their native lands. Most of them preferred to emigrate to the United States or elsewhere in the Western Hemisphere. The Baltic camps were by far the cleanest, and best administered of all.

Displaced persons of Russian nationality fell into three main groups, the Ukrainians, White Russians, and Vlassov's Army, although there were smaller numbers of Caucasians, Mongols, and other Asiatics. The Ukrainians, intensely nationalistic, had welcomed the Germans as liberators and had collaborated with them. They had come to Germany of their own accord, or had fled in front of the advancing Russians. The hatred of these people for the Soviets and their fear of them was almost without parallel. Their burning desire was for the liberty of their country. They would die before returning to it while it was under Soviet domination. The Ukrainian camps were all well managed and gave no trouble.

Another large group of Russians had been prisoners of war. Some of them had worked for the Germans voluntarily, others not so freely. Vlassov was a Russian general who had rendered valiant service to the Russians during the German invasion. He was eventually captured by the Germans with most of his Army, and went over to the other side. He organized several divisions from among the Russian prisoners of war. For obvious reasons, these persons had no intention of ever returning to Russia.

A small group that presented a unique and special problem was a Jugoslav division which had been captured by the Germans and held as prisoners of war. At the time of their capture they had been fighting under Mihailovich who was then recognized and supported by the Allies. They considered themselves allies of the Americans, but they were bitter enemies of the Tito regime which was now formally recognized by the Allied Governments. As such they could not be repatriated to Yugoslavia.

French and Italian workers who had been employed in Germany had been repatriated immediately after the cessation of hostilities as had been all Allied prisoners of war remaining there. UNRRA and other agencies carried on an extensive campaign to persuade the Poles and others from eastern Europe to return to their homelands. With the Poles it was fairly successful, but the campaign made no impression whatever among the Balts, Ukranians, and Jugoslavs. The Jews carried on a program of clandestine emigration to Palestine, exfiltrating groups from Bavaria to Italy or southern France, where they embarked on ships chartered by some of the Jewish committees. This illegal traffic only served to complicate matters.

Many factors contributed to making the problem of dealing with Jewish displaced persons a thorny one. In the first place, world-wide sympathy for these luckless people, and the deep and almost universal desire to make some recompense for the trials which this pitiful remnant had survived, created an emotional atmosphere that influenced every decision and action with respect to them. The Jewish displaced persons were quick to realize this fact, which they did not fail to exploit to their own not always unselfish ends.

The problem had political implications both national and international. Jewish leaders were determined to exploit the world-wide sympathy for the Jews to obtain the refuge in Palestine which had long been their aim. Britain — mindful of the Arabs, — and sensitive to the oil and other crucial affairs of the Middle East — was reluctant to admit further Jewish immigration even though it was financed by American money. Jewish leaders were also aware of the Jewish influence in American political life, and this movement was largely directed by American Jews. In fact, nearly all of the Jewish displaced persons were concentrated in the American Zone, with the vast majority of them in Bavaria. Munich became the center of Jewish activities, which occupied so much of the UNRRA time and effort that UNRRA headquarters was moved there from Frankfurt early in December.

Another hindering factor was the number of agencies and individuals who were active in the Jewish field. Besides the military authorities, Military Government officials, and UNRRA personnel, there were others non-official or quasi-official in nature. Perhaps the most important was the American Joint Distribution Committee representing various Jewish congregations and welfare organizations. It maintained an extensive network of activities not all by any means limited to welfare and charitable work. The Committee had political objectives; it sought to control and direct the Jewish displaced persons movement and to influence government policy with respect to it. To complicate matters further, the Committee was torn by internal strife. Orthodox Jews did not get on with their Reformed brethren, and there was no general agreement even among the liberals. Nor did the Committee escape the effect of the national and international jealousies and controveries which existed among the Jews. Dissension was sometimes bitter.

Federal Judge Samuel F. Rifkind of New York was Special Adviser on Jewish Affairs on General Eisenhower's staff. There were important American and British Jews in an almost continuous stream to add their criticism and advice. Since few of them were familiar with local problems and responsibilities, the advice and efforts of these visitors often merely stirred emotions and caused further disagreement. UN-RRA teams in Jewish camps were composed entirely of selected Jewish personnel, Americans mostly, who represented an exceptionally high professional standard and included doctors, nurses, college professors, vocational training experts, and professional welfare workers.

My first visits were to the Jewish displaced persons camps at Landsberg, Feldafing, and Wolfratshausen, in the Munich area which were rather typical of scores to be found throughout the zone. Landsberg and Feldafing had brought criticism down upon General Patton. Landsberg had been the permanent station of a German artillery brigade with accommodations for five or six thousand troops. The *kaserne* consisted of modern stone barracks, administration buildings, warehouses and shops, with a few wooden barracks of typical temporary wartime construction. Within the *kaserne*, there were several dwellings which had once housed some of the German staff, and adjacent to it, a number of private dwellings had been requisitioned.

The camp had been organized and administered by a young Army officer; an UNRRA team was just taking over when first I visited it. This young officer, a Jew himself, had shown great imagination, initiative, and organizational ability in obtaining materials and establishing educational and vocational training courses, as well as in teaching the rudiments of self-government. Shops included metal, wood, and leather work and other trades for men; cooking and sewing, and similar activities for women. However, these facilities were rarely used to full capacity. I was always rather astonished, in every camp I inspected, by the large number of idle persons.

Each camp was governed by a Citizens' Committee, elected by popular vote, which usually made the camp rules, appointed the guards, and made other camp details. Great emphasis was placed upon these elections for they were the introduction to democratic methods and procedures.

Young men and women were housed in separate barracks usually three or four to a squad room intended for six or eight soldiers. Families were kept together, and those cared for in requisitioned dwellings were allowed to run their own messes. Most of the camp population, however, were fed in central dining rooms. Needless to say, the differences in food habits among the various Jewish sects occasioned much difficulty in feeding.

These accommodations were equal to those provided for our own soldiers in peace time, on the whole, and they were in fact more nearly adequate than many then occupied by American troops in Bavaria. They were not, however, as clean, sanitary, and well ordered as were the military installations. These displaced persons were well clothed and well fed, and, as I have noted, recreational as well as vocational training opportunities had been provided them. This camp life was no more than a temporary measure, and any permanent solution required governmental action by more than one country, which was far beyond the scope of responsibility of military authorities in Germany. Since members of the American-Jewish Joint Distribution Committee, the UNRRA teams, Camp Committees and many others were fully cognizant of this fact, one would have thought that these unfortunate individuals would have displayed a more cooperative spirit toward the military authorities than was ever actually the case.

It was soon evident that there was a concerted plan afoot to obtain publicity which would keep world sympathy stirred up on behalf of these destitute refugees. To this end, there was a series of efforts to embarrass military authorities by publicity alleging military responsibility for crowded and unsatisfactory conditions, for mistreatment of individual displaced persons, for unfavorable treatment in comparison with Germans, and similar unfounded accusations. For example, early in December, General Smith called me from Frankfurt to say that a member of the UNRRA team in the Landsberg camp, an American college professor, had resigned in a bitter letter which denounced the Army for maladministration and lack of care in this camp. Instead of sending the protest to Mr. Whiting, the UNRRA Director in the U.S. Zone whose headquarters was then in Munich, or to my headquarters in Bad Tolz, or even making known to us his specific complaints, this man sent his letter to a Jewish newspaper correspondent in Frankfurt who had called on General Smith for comments before making it public. I suggested that General Smith come down for a personal investigation of conditions, which I had seen only a few days before, and that he bring with him the correspondents who were then in Frankfurt. General Smith arrived the next morning by train accompanied by numerous correspondents.

After a conference in which the UNRRA team and the Camp Committee aired their complaints, the group made a thorough inspection of the camp. Most of the grievances were either minor items of crowding and supply, which the camp officials could easily have corrected, or they dealt with matters of rehabilitation and resettlement which were far beyond the power of authorities in Germany to correct. The day was well spent, however, for there was no unfavorable publicity since the charges could not be sustained. We heard no more of the letter of resignation. Such incidents did not make the problem of Jewish displaced persons an easy one.

Since we could impose no restrictions whatever on these victims of Nazi persecution, they were able to move freely from one camp to another as their whims dictated. New Jewish arrivals from eastern Europe, which it was American policy to receive, usually descended upon the camps chosen by their guides even though they might be crowded and more space available elsewhere. Once established in a camp, these unfortunates resisted all attempts to move them to other more suitable camps.

Most of the Jewish camps were hotbeds of black market activities. Munich and Landsberg perhaps being the worst offenders in this respect. Food and other supplies provided for the camps found its way into the black market. Evidence gathered by our investigating agencies showed that the Jews dominated the black market in Bavaria and were involved in nearly all illegal money transactions.

At Yalta, Stalin had obtained the agreement of the President and Prime Minister to repatriate displaced persons as rapidly as possible after the cessation of hostilities. I do not suppose it ever occurred to Mr. Roosevelt and Mr. Churchill that there might be appreciable numbers of these persons who would have no desire to return to their native lands while under Soviet domination, and who would actually die rather than go back. What a surprise it must have been to our officials when they learned that the majority of the displaced persons in Germany belonged in this category! There is little doubt, however, that Mr. Stalin anticipated just such a reaction, for the Russians were ready with a large Repatriation Commission to work in the Allied Zones, and with a detailed plan for effecting the repatriation of these persons whether they wished to return or not.

When it was discovered few Russian nationals, other than prisoners of war, were going to return willingly, the Russians demanded that the Americans compel their return. Some time before I assumed command of the Third Army, an effort had been made to repatriate some two or three hundred Ukrainians who did not wish it. When soldiers entered the camp to escort these persons to the waiting trucks, there was wild hysteria. The group — men, women, and children — took refuge around the altar in a building used for church services, where they clung to each other as they chanted prayers. Some half dozen or more attempted suicide by slashing their wrists with knives. Since it was soon apparent that any coercion would have dire results, the attempt was quickly abandoned. One of my first acts was to obtain USFET interpretation of the Yalta agreement. Armed with this analysis, we undertook to encourage persons to go back to their native lands and offered to facilitate the return of all who wished to do so. We would not, however, compel any other than criminals and lawbreakers to return against their will.

The Russian Repatriation Commission in the American Zone was headed by a Major General Davidoff with headquarters in Frankfurt. During my first weeks in command, I learned it was very active in Bavaria, visiting displaced persons camps, demanding lists of Russian nationals, and endeavoring to interrogate persons in those camps. These visits were causing hysterical outbreaks and near riots in some places, so we issued orders that no Soviet representative could enter any displaced persons camp without being accompanied by an American officer. We would not provide the Soviet Commission with rosters of persons residing in the various camps, but we would permit them to interview any who were willing to listen, although these interviews were to take place with an American officer present to prevent intimidation, and to insure that the displaced person would be informed of our policies regarding repatriation.

The Yalta agreement stipulated that Russians would be permitted to maintain collection centers administered by Russian personnel in the Allied Zones to speed repatriation. I was astounded to find out that the Russians had acquired, without reference to American authorities, a number of estates lying near some of the larger displaced persons camps where they proposed to collect persons for repatriation. Reports indicated that Russian agents had already kidnapped a number of individuals. Over the protest of General Davidoff, I immediately closed all of these centers in Bavaria except one. Over that one, we posted a guard ostensibly to prevent interference with its operations, but primarily to make certain that the Russians did not violate American policies. These precautions eliminated most of the difficulties in dealing with the Russian Repatriation Commission.

The men of Vlassov's "Army" represented a special case. Some had actually been engaged in Czechoslovakia at the war's end. Vlassov's "Army" had of course disintegrated; the remnants had lost their identity and were scattered among the displaced persons camps. For obvious reasons, the Soviets were anxious to obtain custody of these persons, and the Yalta agreement had specifically provided for the return of criminals and those guilty of crimes against the state. We had no wish to protect these individuals but we were not willing to permit the Soviets to compel the repatriation of innocent persons under this cover.

Though we refused to give Russian officials a list of all displaced persons, and permitted them visits only when accompanied by an American officer, we did agree, however, that if the Soviet Commission would provide us with a list of the persons sought together with a description of the offense with which they were charged, we would ourselves make a thorough search for them. If found and the claim appeared justified, we would turn these persons over to Russian authorities at the border between the Russian and American zones.

Eventually, the Soviet Commission furnished us with lists of several thousand names including a number of general officers and numerous officers of lesser rank. Thorough search of camps and records located about 1,500 of these persons. The cases were reviewed by a board of American officers to determine whether or not their return was justified under this category. We anticipated serious trouble when we undertook to remove these persons. Accordingly, careful plans were drawn up, provision made for truck and rail transport; then at an appointed hour, a large force of troops moved into the area, sorted out the individuals, moved them to the railroad, loaded them, and transported them under guard to the border where they were turned over to Soviet officials. The entire proceeding was carried out without serious disorder, and only one or two attempted suicides.

The hatred of the Baltic nationals, the Ukrainians, and the Poles for the Soviets was an amazing phenomenon. I was never able to understand why the Soviets were so determined to repatriate them whether they wished to return or not. General Davidoff and other Russian officers of whom I asked the question invariably gave evasive replies, generalizing that these people belonged in Russia and that the Russian government wished to welcome them back to their homes. Personally, I suspected the Soviets wished to eliminate a dissident element which would be active in opposition to the Soviet regime as long as it remained without the Soviet Union. Possibly another reason was the need for labor to rebuild the devastated country, for needless to say most of those who did return would find themselves in slave labor camps.

Little progress was made in repatriation and practically none in resettlement of displaced persons during the time I remained in command of the Third Army, which was up until May, 1946. In the following six years, UNRRA and its successor, the International Relief Organization, resettled many hundreds of thousands of persons. This period saw most of the Jews resettled in Palestine or the United States, most of the Poles returned to Poland, and most of the other nationalities resettled in various countries all over the world. Nevertheless, six years after the time of which I write, there still remained more than a hundred thousand displaced persons awaiting resettlement. Few problems have been more difficult to solve and few have ever caused more human misery than this one.

The trial of war criminals was a major objective of Allied policy after the defeat of Germany. During the months that followed the Allied victory, many agencies were involved in arresting and confining those accused for war crimes, in locating witnesses and assembling evidence, and in making other arrangements for the trials. When I joined the Third Army, preparations were under way to conduct trials of war criminals at two places in the Army area — Nürnberg and Dachau.

At Nürnberg, it was decided to try those major war criminals whose crimes under the Moscow Declaration of October, 1943, had "no particular geographic allocalization." Representatives of the governments of Great Britain, the United States, the Soviet Union, and France had reached agreement during the summer on the method of trial before a Quadripartite Tribunal. Each nation was to be represented on the Tribunal and on the prosecution staff. Mr. Robert H. Jackson, Associate Justice, United States Supreme Court, had been designated as Chief of Counsel and had been charged by Executive Order with making preparations for the trials. Theater Headquarters had been directed to give whatever assistance Mr. Jackson might require, and consequently assumed full responsibility for all liaison and contact with Mr. Jackson and the Office of the Chief of Counsel. The Third Army would merely offer supplies, labor, and give other assistance as specifically directed by the Theater Headquarters.

The Palace of Justice in Nürnberg had been selected as the site for the trial of the Nazi bigwigs, presumably because of its past associations with the rise of Naziism and for the effect which it was supposed to have upon the German people. There may have been poetic justice in this selection, but it had many disadvantages from a practical point of view. The Court Room had been bombed out and required extensive remodeling, which had to be done by Army engineers. Materials were scarce. Equipment was inadequate. The engineers had lost many of their best men by redeployment. Nürnberg had suffered much war damage. The city was overcrowded. Housing and facilities were overtaxed. It was not centrally located and it was not easily accessible by rail, road, or air.

As the target date for the opening of the trials approached, there seemed to be some doubt that preparations would be completed in time to permit it to begin on time or that the arrangements would be adequate. Members of the press were violent in their criticism of conditions in the press camp and elsewhere, and both Mr. Jackson's office and the Theater Headquarters were extremely sensitive to this unfavorable publicity.

Some friction had developed between members of the staffs of the Tribunal and the Office of the Chief of Counsel over accommodations and other administrative details. Nürnberg was filled with personnel of many nationalities, some assigned to duties with the trials, others on a more temporary status. All had to be taken care of, and most of them were becoming increasingly captious. The German civil administration was little more than embryonic. Law enforcement was a serious problem.

A week before the trials were scheduled to begin, on November 14th, Theater Headquarters advised me that the Third Army would be held accountable for the administration and maintenance of the Nürnberg trials, a procedure which should have been adopted in the beginning. With that, I made a detailed inspection assisted by members of the Third Army staff. We found the administrative side wholly inadequate with authority divided among several agencies. The office of the Chief of Counsel had concerned itself with managerial details with which it was not familiar, and which interfered with its primary legal function for conducting the trials. We established Nürnberg as a separate area command under Brigadier General LeRoy Watson, gave him an adequate staff, and placed all necessary Army resources at his disposal. This able officer won the high regard of everyone connected with the trials. Under his able leadership, the support of the Nürnberg trials caused no further trouble.

On my visits to Nurnberg, I had many discussions with officials connected with the trials. I was present on the opening day and heard the reading of the indictments. At various times, I heard the presentation of testimony. I saw the accused in their cells, at exercise in the prison yard, in conference with their counsel, and before the Tribunal in the Court Room. The Court Room scene has been described by many persons. It was one of imposing dignity, but it was not one to fill me with the pride I have felt in American court rooms. I believed that these major Nazis were guilty of waging aggressive war and other crimes against humanity for which they should be brought to the bar of justice. But when I looked down upon the Court Room scene I was never able to escape the impression that I was witnessing a conquerors' triumph, for it was only the totality of the conquerors' victory that made this impressive spectacle possible.

At Dachau, preparations were made for the trial of those war criminals whose crimes had a "particular geographic allocalization" for American forces, that is, for crimes against American personnel, or ones committed in areas allocated to American forces. These persons, of whom there were a great many, were charged with offenses recognized as crimes under the laws of war established in various treaties and conventions. In the United States Zones, they were brought to trial under our military laws before military courts.

Dachau was selected as the site in the Third Army Zone because it was conveniently placed near the former Nazi concentration camp now holding the accused, and because there were ample accommodations there for the Court and personnel. The first of these trials, involving thirty-eight persons, was scheduled to begin on November 15th, under the able direction of Colonel James C. Cheever, Judge Advocate, Third Army. Prosecution and defense counsel were represented by officers with legal training detailed by Army order, four trial judge advocates, and a similar number of defense counsel. Several German lawyers were associated with the defense. These officers spent many weeks preparing these cases for trial.

These trials seemed especially important to me, because they involved lesser fry of the Nazi regime whose crimes were recognized by existing treaties and conventions. They would afford us an opportunity of giving the Germans an object lesson in the Western method of administering justice. Fairness, impartiality, and strict application of laws and rules of procedure were therefore essential. Some of these thoughts I expressed to the members of the Court, trial judge advocates, and defense counsel when I addressed them a few days before the trial began.

I was in attendance at the opening, and at other times during the course of the trial. The setting was simpler than at Nürnberg, but it was fully as dignified and effective. A low rail divided the almost square Court Room into approximately equal parts, the rear portion with seats for about one hundred fifty spectators, the fore part for Court officials. The nine-man Court—Brigadier General John M. Lenz was president, Lieutenant Colonel W. M. Denson, Trial Judge Advocate—sat in a row behind a desk on a raised platform facing the spectators. To the left of the Court was the dock in which the thirty-eight accused were arranged in four or five tiers. Immediately in front were the tables for the trial judge advocates and defense counsel, with the defense counsel immediately in front of the prisoners. Between the counsel and the Court were chairs for witness and interpreter. Opposite the prisoners was the press box. When the trial opened, every seat was filled, and all followed the proceedings with a quiet but intense interest.

The first trial lasted just a month. Since public interest was centered in the more important and spectacular Nürnberg trials, the accomplishment at Dachau was not generally well understood. It was a hard fought legal battle in the best American tradition, with the defense counsel under the able leadership of Lieutenant Colonel Douglas T. Bates, stubbornly contesting every legal point just as he would have done had the accused been Americans like himself. The Court distinguished itself by its fairness, and impartial jurisprudence. The trial resulted in convictions for all but one or two of the accused. Sentences ranged from relatively short prison sentences to death by hanging.

When it ended there was a most unusual demonstration. The thirty-eight prisoners left the dock in a body and almost mobbed the defense counsel in thanking them for the efforts that counsel had made in their behalf. Colonel Bates and others of the defense staff told me later that prisoner after prisoner told them that no German lawyer would ever have made such a fight in their behalf even before a German Court; they felt that their trial had been fair and impartial.

This first Dachau trial set the standard for those that followed. As a matter of interest, the only death warrant I have ever had to sign was for the execution of several convicted in this first trial. It occurred some months later after the trial record had been reviewed and approved by both Army and Theater Commanders.

The Third Army—and, in fact, the whole United States Zone of Occupation—was in a continual state of reorganization during my stay in Germany. Redeployment was continuing at the maximum rate until well after the end of the year, and caused almost endless shifts in personnel from one unit to another, necessitating continual readjustment of areas of control as one organization after another was ordered home. As the number of divisions and other units in the Army area declined, Corps Headquarters became less and less necessary. Corps Headquarters were reduced successively from four to two, then to one, and finally to none at all. The only complete elimination of responsibility came when American forces withdrew from Czechoslovakia, simultaneously with the withdrawal of Russian troops, as the government of President Benes was restored to full sovereignty.

I had occasion to visit Czechoslovakia and Prague several times prior to our withdrawal. American troops had occupied the western part of Czechoslovakia since the end of hostilities in May. Russians occupied the remainder of the country, and the line which separated Russians and Americans was even then an Iron Curtain, Russian style. Russian and American outposts faced each other at points on every road that crossed the boundary line, and no contact was permitted between the two armies. This was not because the American forces desired such restrictions but because they were imposed by the Russian command to prevent Russian soldiers coming into contact with American soldiers. General Harmon quite appropriately enforced similar control measures in retaliation; in consequence, his relations with General Zadov of the Fifth Guards Army were quite good and were carried on with mutual respect. British, Russian, French, and American troops joined units of the newly organized Czech Army in a parade honoring Czechoslovakian Independence Day on October 27th. Russian officers were courteous during the official functions in connection with the ceremonies, but there was no fraternizing between Russian and other troops.

I was much interested in the attitude of the Czechs toward the Russians and Americans. The fear and hatred of the Czechs for the Russians was evident on all sides during my visits. Reports of pillaging and mistreatment of the civil population by Russian soldiers were numerous. On the other hand, the Czechs liked and admired the Americans. Wherever I went on my inspections of the American garrisons, I was welcomed by crowds of Czechs in colorful native costumes with the traditional friendship ceremony of bread, salt, and flowers, which were offered in succession.

At the Potsdam conference, the three governments, Britain, the United States, and Russia, had recognized that the transfer to Germany of German populations or elements thereof remaining in Poland, Czechoslovakia, and Hungary would have to be undertaken and all had agreed that any transfers would take place in an orderly and humane manner. The Allied Control Council had been directed to submit an estimate as to the time and rate at which such transfers could be carried out, having regard to the present situation in Germany, and the Czechoslovak government had been requested to suspend expulsions pending the report of the Control Council.

It was in Czechoslovakia that I first came in contract with this problem which added to the burdens of our Military Government in Bavaria. Czech hatred of the Nazis was acrimonious and intense and it was centered upon the Sudeten Germans who had lived among the Czechs for many generations, but who were now paying the price for supporting the Nazi conquest. They were required to wear identifying arm bands. Their properties were being expropriated. Many were tried and imprisoned. Severe restrictions were placed upon others. And all of these preparations for expulsion were carried out with a ruthlessness and brutality which was reminiscent of the Nazis, which cost the Czechs much sympathy among American troops. The expulsion began during the winter months, vastly increasing the occupation problems in Bavaria, because even those destined for other parts of Germany had to pass through Bavaria.

None of the Declarations of Allied Intentions with respect to Germany had fixed any period during which the occupation was to continue. There was necessarily much speculation on this score during the months that followed victory. Many persons concerned with the occupation thought that many years, possibly a generation, might be required to convince the German people of their war guilt, to extirpate Nazism and militarism, and to prepare the German people for the reconstruction of their political life on a democratic basis that would permit peaceful cooperation with others in international life. These were the purposes of the occupation, and to realize them the presence of American and other Allied troops might be required for many years.

Theater Headquarters estimated that the equivalent of at least one reinforced Corps of three or four divisions would be required for occupation duties in the American Zone. However, with the complete demobilization of the Army and with the traditional attitude of the American people toward standing armies when the nation is not at war, it would be difficult to maintain such a regular force abroad. To provide for this contingency and to insure the success of the occupation, it was decided to organize a specially selected and trained force of about 30,000 officers and men into a constabulary especially designed for carrying out the occupation tasks, gradually taking over full responsibility as Army divisions were withdrawn.

It was to be known as the United States Constabulary. It would consist of a headquarters, certain service elements, and two brigades. Each brigade would have a headquarters and two regiments; each regiment, three squadrons each of three companies, along with some other elements. While the organization was to utilize the framework of the mechanized Cavalry regiments, it would be specially designed for police and constabulary work and was to be exceptionally mobile for patrolling the entire zone.

Reorganization plans provided for the inactivation of the Seventh Army Headquarters, and for Third Army to command all troops in the United States Zone. Accordingly, I was directed in December to get on with forming the Constabulary and was asked to designate the officer whom I wished to have assigned to command it. I selected Major General Ernest N. Harmon who had recently returned to the United States with the inactivation of the XXII Corps.

Soon after the first of the year, Harmon began selecting his staff and proceeded with organizing and training the Constabulary in close cooperation with the Army staff. Our objective was to have the Constabulary established so that it could assume full responsibility for occupation duties by July 1st, 1946. This work was carried out with conspicuous success during the first part of the year. When I left the Army command at the end of April, elements had already begun to function and were attracting very favorable attention by their effectiveness and their high standards of appearance, training, morale, and discipline.

The soundness of the decision to organize the Constabulary is fully justified when one considers that the occupation force was eventually reduced to the Constabulary and one infantry division. It was not until the cold war strained relations and threatened hostilities between former allies that it became desirable to transform Constabulary units once more into regular military organizations.

The early months of 1946 were a repetition of the fall of 1945 so far as I was concerned. My days were filled with a variety of activities. And one of these, receiving close attention from the press, was the difficult problem of denazification. All who had been more than nominal participants in the rise to power of the Nazi party were to be removed from public and semi-public office and from positions of responsibility in important private undertakings. Every individual employed by the civil administration, the military forces, in schools, business, or elsewhere, had to prove that he or she had never been a member of the Nazi party. A vast number of government and party officials, military commanders, staff officers, and others were placed upon an automatic arrest list. That is, these persons were sought out and when found were confined in concentration camps pending eventual disposition. The Counter-intelligence Corps (CIC) was the principal agency for searching out and arresting these individuals. Denazification remained one of our serious problems, all the more so because the correspondents were always more than ready to pounce upon any oversight. One wave of publicity which investigation proved to be entirely without foundation was based upon a report that the wives of high-ranking Nazi officials were entertaining American officers in their homes just across Tegernsee from where I was then living.

Another problem, a favorite with correspondents, was demilitarization. Occupation authorities were widely criticized because of the slow progress in destroying German military installations and war potential. Few of these criticisms were justified because the correspondents failed to realize the magnitude of the problem or the inadequate means which were available. In order to allay some of this faultfinding, Theater Headquarters directed me to lay on at least one good demolition which the correspondents could witness. We selected the huge I. G. Farben powder plants at Kaufburen. Late in October, I flew over to Kaufburen where one of the enormous Farben plants had been prepared for demolition. There in the presence of most of the correspondents in the American Zone I pressed the buttons that set off two tremendous explosions which obliterated this huge installation.

One important division of Military Government was the Information Services Control Commission. In Bavaria it was familiarly known as

DISCC and was under the direction of Colonel B. B. McMahon. It was responsible for investigating individuals and companies and institutions concerned with publications of newspapers and periodicals, the operation of radios, schools and other means of public information. When these media were found to be free from the taint of Nazism and met other democratic standards, they were authorized to resume their labors under the supervision of Allied authorities. Except for Nazi and military propaganda and matters prejudicial to the occupation forces, DISCC encouraged free speech and political activity. During these months I visited many towns in the American Zone to award licenses for opening of newspapers, periodicals, and radio stations, and had occasion to address most of the editors and publishers licensed in Bavaria. This work made an important contribution toward the reconstruction of German political life along democratic lines.

On the whole, relations between the occupation forces and the vanquished civil population were as satisfactory as could be expected. Most German men of military age were still prisoners of war, although the Americans were freeing those who were not Nazis, nor members of affiliated Nazi organizations, nor war criminals. This was one reason, perhaps, why there were relatively few offenses against occupation personnel. The attitude of our own soldiers toward the Germans caused little trouble. Strange to say, those who were most arrogant and overbearing in their attitude toward the Germans were those who had not fought during the war but who had joined since the war ended. There was some friction over hunting and fishing, since Bavaria is a hunters' paradise. The forests abounded in game of all kinds, the streams with trout and bass. American soldiers, if they thought at all, considered that the game belonged to them by right of conquest, and proceeded to take what they wished without reference to conservation procedures or regulations, and often with wanton carelessness. I remember one incident that caused much unhappiness among the Bavarian game keepers. Two soldiers in a jeep opened fire on a herd of deer with a machine gun and drove away leaving eight of them lying dead. This friction diminished as control over our own soldiers improved during the process of reorganization.

Changes in the United States Zone proceeded according to schedule. The Seventh Army Headquarters was inactivated the first of April, when Third Army Headquarters moved to Heidelberg in order to be in a more central location and closer to Theater Headquarters in Frankfurt.

Immediately after this I had word that my wife was seriously ill in Walter Reed General Hospital. General McNarney lent me his B-17. Accompanied by my aide, Captain Lloyd K. Jensen, I returned at once to Washington. (Bartash and Wilson had returned to civil life in December and January.) I spent ten days with Mrs. Truscott and then returned to Germany expecting that she would join me there during the summer when the movement of dependents to Germany was authorized.

During the return trip, I caught a severe chest cold and was hospitalized soon after my arrival in Heidelberg. When I had recovered from the chest infection, the Army surgeon informed me that electrocardiagraphic examination showed that I had suffered a coronary occlusion and that the only known way to repair the damage was complete rest in bed for a period of six weeks. General Keyes was recalled from a visit that he was making to Italy during the last days of April to take over the command of the Third Army. That ended my second Army command and my last wartime mission.

I returned to the United States in July, where I spent six months under observation at Walter Reed Hospital and another six months on duty with Personnel Boards in the War Department. At the end of the second six months period I was reexamined. Since the cardiac condition had not improved I was retired from active duty on September 30th, 1947, just six weeks after completing thirty years of active service.

So ended a career.

CHAPTER TEN

AFTERTHOUGHTS

My CAREER prior to World War II was not unlike that of many other Regular Army officers of my own age group and background. Prior to World War I, I had been a country schoolteacher in Oklahoma. Later, I enrolled at the First Officers' Training Camp, and entered the Army as a cavalry officer, but saw no overseas service during World War I. From 1919 to 1925, I commanded a cavalry troop stationed for the most part along the Mexican border. There followed six years at the Cavalry School, two years as a student and four years as an instructor. From 1931 to 1934, I commanded another troop of cavalry, stationed this time at Fort Myer, Virginia. From 1934 to 1936, I was a member of the last two-year class at the Command and General Staff School at Fort Leavenworth, and was held there for the next four years as an instructor. In the period between June, 1940, and the spring of 1942, I spent six months in an armored regiment in the 1st Armored Division, nine months on the General Staff of the IX Army Corps, and six months commanding the 5th Cavalry Regiment in the 1st Cavalry Division, leaving that assignment for my first wartime mission to London in May, 1942.

For one who was by nature rather serious and studious, these assignments provided exceptional opportunities for professional development, and it is only fair to say that I did not neglect them. My opportunities for study were better than average. At the beginning of World War II, I was about as well trained and prepared as any officer of my own age group. However, I had had no actual battle experience. I had never heard a shot fired in anger.

Each phase of my war experience was an important step in my own military education and my development as a battle leader. Each phase contained new lessons or modified or altered the emphasis on others. It is probable that this must always be the case. While we can approximate the physical conditions of battle including the extreme of fatigue, discomfort, and sound effects, we cannot create in peace time all of the psychological conditions and tensions that result from the fear, uncertainty, loneliness, and horror incident to war. Nor can we foresee in peace time the conditions under which future battles will be fought. While any future war will begin with weapons currently available, which is to say, those left over from the last war or developed in peacetime, scientific developments in weapons, transportation and other fields will affect the nature of battle as will political, sociological, and geographic factors that cannot be foreseen. No greater mistake can be made in military leadership than that of clinging to outmoded concepts, outmoded methods, and outmoded equipment. To a very high degree the measure of success in battle leadership is the ability to profit by the lessons of battle experience.

In London, I learned much from my British associates, especially in the preparation of staff papers and the technique of planning. Somewhat to my surprise, I found that British staff papers were far more thorough and much better expressed than corresponding American papers which I had known in my own experience. British planning technique through the phases of initial concept, appreciation, outline plan, and detailed planning was more specialized and involved far more conference and committee work—in which the British excelled—than I had been accustomed to. Their method was also far more thorough and secure than any I had known. A knowledge of British planning, organization, staff procedures, and tactical methods, not to mention some knowledge of British personalities, was invaluable to me throughout the war.

As a cavalry officer, I had long been imbued with the value of speed in military operations. I had, in schools, urged that our own infantry should equal the marching and endurance standards of Roman legions or Stonewall Jackson's "foot cavalry" of Civil War fame, but with little or no effect upon those charged with development of infantry doctrines who held that infantry marched two and a half miles an hour and twelve miles a day. My experience with British Commando training in England confirmed my long held opinions, and led me to believe that such a performance was practicable with modern American soldiers, and furthermore I was to prove to my own, and others, satisfaction that it was one of the best forms of training for battle.

Finally, during my London sojourn, I had my first battle experience, heard my first shot fired in anger. Dieppe showed me something of the fear and uncertainty of battle, something of how well laid plans can go astray, and something of the dangers and difficulties incident to daylight withdrawal—to entering battle looking over one's shoulder so to speak. Most important, Dieppe, popularly rated as a costly failure, proved the practicability and feasibility of the amphibious invasions we were then planning. I was convinced that the force engaged at Dieppe could have captured the place and established a beachhead had

the operation been undertaken with that in mind rather than as a raid
with an immediate withdrawal.

GOALPOST was my first battle command. This three-day battle
corroborated the general soundness of our training methods, but it also
disclosed some features for which my previous military education and
training had not fully prepared me.

It had never occurred to me that naval gunfire passing over the heads
of an infantry battalion could cause such panic that the battalion would
take to its heels and disperse so that it required most of two days to
collect the stragglers. Yet no shell fell within a thousand yards of the
battalion, and no enemy was firing upon it. Subsequent investigation
disclosed two causes for this sudden abandonment of duty. The battalion was not familiar with the characteristic sound of naval gunfire
passing overhead. Having just landed on a strange and hostile shore, advancing in darkness on a dangerous mission, and entering battle for the
first time, the battalion was keyed to a high pitch of nervous tension.
It broke completely under a new and terrifying sound. Our training
had been at fault for we had failed to accustom men to all of the unfamiliar sounds of battle, and we had failed to instill the rigorous discipline and control to prevent these panics.

I was astounded by the relatively large number of American soldiers
who surrendered to our French opponents when they still possessed
means of continuing the fight or who could have withdrawn to continue the fight elsewhere. And again post-mortems showed that our
peace time training was at fault. These men were doing what our peace
time maneuvers had taught them to do, for then when the opposing Red
and Blue sides approached contact, umpires had ruled one or the other
side captured. I remembered an incident in the 1941 Louisiana maneuvers when a force of two or three companies had surprised an entire
regiment in dense woods and the umpires had ruled the entire regiment
captured. Instead of instructing men to fight to the bitter end we had
actually taught them to surrender whenever they were caught at a disadvantage. We should have taught them that so long as there is any
possibility whatever of continuing the fight, surrender is disgraceful.

I was surprised to find what a relatively small proportion of individual weapons available in any unit were ever employed in action.
One would think that every unit engaged in combat would employ
every possible weapon, for battles are won by destroying or threatening
to destroy the enemy. But this had not been so in the actions in which
our infantry and armored battalions had been engaged. Our investigation revealed that the battle had been waged with a series of small unit

actions and that each of them had been won by a fraction of the unit with the assistance of supporting arms—artillery, naval gunfire, machine guns, bombers, tanks. And each of these small unit actions had been sparked by some courageous and energetic spirit who was not necessarily the designated leader. It seemed evident that this was a normal condition of warfare. Therefore, the proportion of weapons which any unit employed in action would be a test of its training and a measure of its combat leadership.

I found most officers and men lacked confidence in themselves and were hesitant and uncertain in battle. They were inclined to wait for a superior to tell them just what to do. Even though the action may have been perfectly obvious or even already specified in orders, they were reluctant to assume responsibility. This feature was so general that I came to the conclusion these men were not wholly to blame, and that there had been two grave defects in their training. First, although our peacetime doctrines taught that fighting was a simple process and preached simplicity in all its aspects, we had actually made combat a difficult and complicated subject. Perfection in drill was almost impossible to attain, and even the best of efforts usually met with scathing criticism. Every field exercise and maneuver was followed by a critique in which criticism and ridicule were general. Few who passed through the service schools in the competitive days between the two World Wars would say that their courses were either simple or easy. Second, instead of encouraging initiative in junior officers and men, we had actually discouraged it in them. Senior officers had lectured endlessly on initiative as a quality which everyone should possess, or develop, and "Use your initiative" was a phrase dinned at men morning, noon, and night. Yet, in fact, no junior officer or man could deviate one iota from the text or regulations or orders without risking harsh criticism. "What the school teaches" was the definitive answer to almost all military discussions and questions. Far from encouraging junior officers and men to try things — to "stick their necks out" — we had concentrated on a strict uniformity within a pattern which was not always fully understood. Viewed in this light, it was hardly surprising that junior echelons had lacked confidence to act boldly in the uncertain conditions of their first battle.

Another surprising factor was the inaccuracy of reports during battle and the difficulty of appraising any given situation. After being completely misled or misinformed on several occasions, I concluded that few reports in battle could be accepted as true without verification. It was not that those reporting had deliberately intended to deceive, although there was a natural tendency to tell a superior what he would like to hear and to put one's self and one's unit in the best possible light.

I found that a report limited to what the reporting officer actually saw, or experienced, or had verified, could be accepted provided that accuracy of orientation could be established. Beyond that, reports were subject to errors of observation, interpretation, and exaggeration, and could only be accepted with caution. But the best means for evaluation was an on-the-spot inspection since there was no substitute for personal reconnaissance in battle command.

One other important lesson was impressed upon me by the progress of our GOALPOST operation. Our operational plans were far too optimistic with respect to the time required to accomplish the operation; it required three days to accomplish what we had anticipated would take one. This is often the case in war. Ability to carry the plans out without change is a mark of sound planning always to be strived for in war.

One must actually experience the hardships of war to understand the awful strain, both mental and physical, which battle imposes upon men, the dreadful fatigue and fear which destroys the will and poisons every fiber. I had seen much of it during these three days. And I had observed a tendency on the part of commanders and comrades to sympathize and pity. I felt little of these sentiments during battle, and moreover felt we could not permit them to deflect men from their duty. We could not give way to weariness for that would only give the enemy an advantage. We could not allow able-bodied men to take care of wounded or sick comrades until the battle was won. This drive is an important function of command.

In Tunisia, as a staff officer for General Eisenhower, I was closely associated with the operations which brought American soldiers into collision with the German veterans for the first time. While the results were not calculated to fill American hearts with pride, the experience taught our soldiers a great deal about the art of fighting, and was important in my own emergence as a battle leader. Among soldiers entering combat for the first time, we observed the same hesitation and uncertainty which we had noted at Port Lyautey. There was the same mental and physical fear, the same reaction to battle and battlefield leadership, the same failure to utilize all available weapons, the same unreal attitude of being "on maneuvers", the same inaccuracy of reporting. There were other lessons that derived from the dissimilar situation in Tunisia, particularly in the Allied organization, the extent and nature of the area involved, and the character of the enemy force. It was impressive to watch, however, the speed with which American soldiers profited by their battle experience. Within the few weeks covering my association with the Tunisian campaign, these men became veterans capable of meeting the Germans on better than even terms.

Reviewing these events, there was one serious and conspicuous short-coming in the lack of mutual understanding and confidence between British and Americans which actually imperiled the Allied forces. Few British officers understood American organization, tactical methods, and command and staff procedures. A similar condition existed among American officers with respect to the British forces. British commanders and staff officers impressed Americans as being supercilious, conceited, and arrogant. British officers considered the Americans to be loud, boastful, and inexperienced. The nature of British organization and tactical methods caused their commanders to employ American bat-talions and small units under their command with little regard for the integrity of units to which Americans were accustomed. This piecemeal employment to "plug holes in the dike" on the British and French fronts caused bitterness and misunderstanding, and was a contributing factor in setting the stage for subsequent American reverses. Relations be-tween British and American commanders and staffs during this period showed clearly that in any Allied command each nationality must be employed in accordance with its own direction, manner and procedure and that these prerequisites must be appreciated by responsible Allied commanders.

Faulty interpretation of intelligence – radio interception – led offi-cers at AFHQ and British First Army Headquarters at Constantine to believe that the main German attack was to strike farther north than it did. Although reconnaissance showed no German preparation in the area, preoccupation with this interpretation caused General Anderson to hold Robinette's Combat Command B at Maktar until Rommel had overrun McQuillin's Combat Command A at Sidi bou Zid and was actu-ally knocking at the doors of Kasserine Pass. The failure to verify this intelligence was an error, and a check should have been sought by every possible means. While General Anderson's decision set the stage for the attack on McQuillin at Sidi bou Zid, it was not responsible for the disaster which befell him on Valentine's Day. The responsibility for that debacle can be fairly laid upon the Corps Commander, General Fredendall, and upon Combat Command A itself. General Fredendall had prescribed detailed dispositions for McQuillin's command which were not in accord with what the conditions and the terrain demanded, although he had never been within many miles of the area in question. Only a few hours before disaster struck, I was present with General Eisenhower at McQuillin's Command Post. There was nothing to indi-cate that an attack was imminent, although the German forces must have been in movement just a few miles away at the time. Adequate reconnaissance would have discovered the German movements; good security measures would have prevented surprise and destruction of the command. General Anderson shares the responsibility for the disaster that followed. His release of only one tank battalion from Combat Command B to take part in the counterattack to relieve the beleaguered infantry battalions on the djebels at Sidi bou Zid prevented the force from being strong enough to accomplish the mission. General Anderson, however was not responsible for the counterattack force blundering into an ambush in which an entire tank battalion was destroyed. This must be charged to lack of reconnaissance, poor security, and inadequate combat leadership.

One contributing factor to American reverses was the command method of most of the American commanders, who conducted their battles from a command post which they seldom left, and Fredendall's, for example, was hidden in a deep canyon more than fifty miles from any part of the front. Robinette told me that he never went forward during actual fighting because it was essential for him to view the situation objectively. Few commanders in the higher echelons ever spent much time in personal reconnaissance, visiting troops, or inspecting disposition. No higher commander reconnoitered the defensive position at Kasserine Pass, none ever checked the defensive deployments there. As a result these commanders had a wholly unrealistic concept of battle for they saw battle as symbols on a map — as a map problem, which led to faulty orders and dispositions. Every commander owes it to himself and those under him to be fully informed and acquainted with the terrain and conditions confronting his command, and this necessitates a personal reconnaissance. Once orders are issued, a commander's primary responsibility is to insure that they are carried out, which makes personal visits of inspection imperative. No one can overcome the inertia of uncertainty and hesitation as effectively as the commander himself.

One encouraging sign in these American reverses was the reaction of our own soldiers to defeat. The British were inclined to consider battle as something of a game and to adopt a sporting attitude toward the German enemy even in defeat. American soldiers had none of this attitude. Americans play games to win; they fight battles in the same spirit. Our soldiers knew they had taken a licking, but they did not like it. Defeat did not depress them, nor affect their natural conceit; they felt only a burning anger. Fortunately, the loss in life among the armored units was much less than we had expected in proportion to the loss in armored vehicles. Wherever I went while we were trying to reequip these armored units, officers and men said to me: "Give us tanks and equipment. We can lick these Germans. We know how to do it now."

My Tunisian experience also provided me with an outstanding example of how American soldiers can be indoctrinated in training. Our tank destroyer battalions, organized only a few months previous, with no historical prototype, equipped with an improvised weapon — an almost unarmored half-track mounting an entirely inadequate 75 mm gun — had been taught during their training that it was their duty to seek out and destroy enemy tanks. The number of half-tracks which these gallant units left on the Tunisian deserts was mute testimony to the superiority of German armor, and antitank guns. It was also evidence of the efficacy of their indoctrination, a mark that I was to note among these units throughout the war.

AFHQ planners, in preparing the SATIN plan, had estimated that no more than one armored division and one Regimental Combat Team could be supplied to the Tebessa area over the single road and narrow gauge railway leading south from Constantine. As operations actually developed, four American divisions and numerous other troops were eventually supplied and maintained there. We learned two important lessons from this erroneous calculation. First, logistical planners were usually conservative and allowed large safety factors for unforeseen contingencies — which was particularly true of the British planners who dominated the AFHQ logistical planning. Second, British administrative services were not as experienced in the organization of transportation systems or in the maintenance and utilization of transport as were their American comrades. Furthermore, British trucks lacked the power, speed and capability of American trucks. These considerations weighed heavily in every operation in which British and American forces were associated.

However, the outstanding lesson that I learned in Tunisia had to do with personal relationships, for here lay the great weakness which was, in my opinion, responsible for most of the difficulties of that troubled period. One could sympathize with the lack of understanding and mutual regard between British and American commanders however one might deplore it. Yet the bitterness, personal and professional jealousy, the complete lack of understanding, and even hatred, which existed among some of the American commanders and staffs, I could never condone. If similar feelings existed among the British, their natural reserve prevented it from ever coming to my attention. It seemed obvious to me that no force could ever be successful hampered by such dissension.

This period of observation was especially valuable to me. It was my firm conviction that our troubles in our early battles resulted from the inadequacy of training and leadership, due in large measure to our own lack of experience. Nevertheless, I felt that American soldiers properly trained, conditioned, disciplined, and led, would be more than a match for the regimented Germans.

My year's campaigning with the 3rd Infantry Division in Africa, Sicily, southern Italy and at Anzio was one of the most instructive and interesting periods of my career. It gave me invaluable experience. We had more than three months in which to prepare for the invasion of Sicily, and to put many of my theories concerning infantry training to the test. My principal objectives were to attain the highest possible marching and physical standards and to develop initiative and leadership among officers and non-commissioned officers.

I found it was possible to approximate standards of Commando and Ranger training with an entire infantry division, and I noted that the mental determination this required was conducive to the best psychological training. As men reached increasingly difficult standards, self-confidence grew. And with the weeding out of those who could not meet the demands of such rigorous training there developed a pride among those who could.

In promoting initiative and leadership among junior officers and men, I insisted that battle was a simple business when conducted by common sense methods, and by soldiers who were physically fit and knew how to use their weapons, were capable of working and living together in the field as a team, and were disciplined to withstand hardship and danger in attaining the objective. I would not permit any junior officer to be punished for any mistake when he was acting on his own initiative. On the other hand, I insisted that all commanders deal harshly with failure to act boldly when the situation required it. The change was gradual, but the development of leadership in the 3rd Infantry Division was marked and a cause for intense satisfaction.

Speed marching was another practical advantage of this high state of training, especially noticeable when divisions entered action in Sicily. All battalions had been psychologically prepared to expect hard fighting and heavy losses. And during the campaign they moved so rapidly that opposition was often overcome before it could become fully effective. Speed of execution often made difficult operations seem simple and easy.

Every successful commander adopts some means of making himself known to his command and impressing his own personality upon it. I had worn a russet or red leather jacket during my first nights ashore in North Africa. I adopted this as a personal uniform along with a shiny lacquered helmet so that every soldier in the Division would be able to recognize me at any distance. No orders were issued forbidding others to wear similar articles, but no one did.

One innovation which became a recognized part of our uniform came about through an allergy of mine. Choking dust and exhaust fumes from tanks and trucks irritated my sensitive nose and throat as we made our way along the moving columns, during the second day on shore in Sicily. Tears streamed from my eyes, and I was soon in a paroxysm of sneezing and coughing, which caused me to seek some means of protecting my face. I took from my pocket a handkerchief – it was a cloth map of Sicily which the "Escape Team" from AFHQ had given me back in Jemmapes. I tied this map around my neck as a scarf and drew it over my face like a mask, just as cowmen in the Southwest use bandannas. I continued to wear it about my neck throughout the campaign, ready for instant use.

As days passed, I discovered that more and more men in the Division were using handkerchiefs in the same way. I was glad, for a scarf could protect not only the face but the neck itself, and the shirt collar, from sweat and dirt. And as a symbol it would enhance esprit. Among other things, it could be a favorable element in *causerie de bivouac* and afford a degree of interest and amusement as well as fill a practical need. I would wear the white map – no one else would be permitted to do so. Anyone who commanded anything from squad to division could wear a white scarf. All others would have to select some other color, but each unit would be encouraged to select a distinctive one. No orders were to be published in writing; it would all be done by word of mouth – by suggestion.

The idea soon caught on in the 3rd Infantry Division and stirred up much interest, for the silk scarf became a recognized part of the uniform. It was not many months before salvaged parachutes and captured silk were at a premium for almost every unit in the theater wore a distinctive scarf of some kind. As a matter of fact, a bandanna-like scarf should be part of the combat uniform of every soldier.

The control and direction of men is a fundamental problem of command. It is easy enough to issue orders – and far too many commanders solve every problem by issuing an order – but it is not always easy to determine how orders are being carried out. Yet every commander is concerned with the discipline of his command, which, in the last analysis, means the degree to, and the manner in which, orders are executed. Nothing undermines respect for command more quickly than orders which are not enforced, or which can be evaded easily, or which were never expected to be enforced. Such orders should never be initiated.

Most commanders hit upon some object which for them is a ready and obvious test of how the orders are carried out within their commands. One of my first colonels, "Sunny Jim" Hornbrook, always inspected incinerators just before reveille, and woe betide the hapless mess sergeant and cook who did not have the swill boiling merrily over a roaring fire. With others, it was the shape of the campaign hat, or the color of cotton clothing, or polished brass and buttons, or other recognized features.

For my part, I selected two points which seemed reasonable; violations of them were easily observed since I could note them as far as I could see a man. First, helmets would be worn at all times in the combat zone, which was certainly reasonable, for helmets were a protection in case of sudden air attack, artillery, or mortar fire. Second, no vehicle would carry more than its authorized passenger load, and in the case of jeeps, this was four persons. Since we were always short of transport and maintenance, this was a fair request, for when a vehicle was broken down or destroyed, we never knew when a replacement would be available.

Naturally enough, in the heat of action, I found both these orders flagrantly violated. At the start, I reprimanded individual offenders and reminded regimental commanders of the orders, but found I was accomplishing nothing. When next I found a group without helmets, I requested that the platoon leader be brought before me. I asked him if he was aware that my orders required all officers and men to wear helmets in the combat zone. He admitted that he was. In the presence of his platoon, I reprimanded him for his neglect of duty and fined him $50 for failure to carry out my orders. Five times I repeated this action with different groups for violations of the helmet or vehicle order, and in each case sent a memorandum to the regimental commander informing him of my action. This policy eliminated such misdemeanors in the 3rd Infantry Division, and in the process I had learned that the American soldier was willing to accept punishment for his own dereliction, but was unwilling to have a platoon leader or company commander suffer for him, which accounts for the fact that my instructions were carried out. It wasn't made known that the fines were never collected.

When an American speaks of traffic control, the congestion of the rush hour in a large city comes to mind, along with the harassed and not always too polite traffic police and motorcycle cops. The degree of congestion is worked out scientifically by traffic engineers, and is directed with an efficiency that is generally recognized. I wondered sometimes in Sicily just how specialists would have dealt with the traffic problems that were suddenly thrust upon us, after the capture of Palermo when we started east toward Messina. It was soon obvious that traffic congestion could hinder our operations as much as the enemy. Our one road forward was always a dead-end road, made so by German demolitions, and made dangerous during the last half-dozen miles or so by German fire. Every bridge was blown, and by-passes were always one-way roads. There were all too few turn-arounds of any kind, and none at the forward end. Likewise there was a dearth of places where vehicles could park off roads. Three regiments of infantry, seven or eight battalions of artillery, several signal battalions, two regiments of engineers, two or three battalions of tanks and tank destroyers, and the hundreds of vehicles for supply, administration, and command, all had to use the single road — 20,000 men or more.

During the battle of San Fratello there was a traffic jam on the road immediately in front of the German position, which took most of the night to clear. In daylight, this would have been disastrous, so it was never allowed to recur. We established a control point at a turn-around just short of the battle zone, under Division military police. Beyond this, we allowed only essential communications, command, artillery, and supply vehicles. For the infantry regiments, in action, we permitted ten jeeps or weapons carriers for each battalion to transport weapons, supply ammunition, water and rations. All other vehicles were held in guarded motor parks under supervision of the Division G-4, and all motor movements were controlled by G-3 Troop Movement Section. This assault scale transport worked well, and was thenceforth to be normal practice when we were faced with similar problems on restricted roads. Under such road conditions strict traffic control is essential for mobility.

In the rugged terrain of Sicily and southern Italy, we had need for a greater degree of mobility than even my fast-marching infantry battalions could attain, and to this end we organized a provisional cavalry troop, pack train, and pack artillery battery, utilizing captured and requisitioned animals and equipment. We had no trained personnel and had to draw men from units within the division. Few individuals, even those from farms, had any real experience with horses and mules. None had had any training with pack animals, and there was almost total ignorance of the care and maintenance needed. Moreover, since we created these units while we were still advancing, there was no opportunity for basic training. Yet without them, we could not have carried out our operations as we did and our losses would have been heavier. These units were reorganized at the end of the Sicilian campaign and given a brief period of intensive training before entering the Italian campaign at Salerno. Although never authorized by AFHQ, they rendered valuable service to the Division until we disbanded them during the defensive period at Anzio.

I was convinced in Sicily that if we had had a cavalry division when we started east from Palermo, we could have prevented the escape of the Germans across the Straits of Messina. I also believe that with the help of one good cavalry regiment after we crossed the Volturno in October, 1943, the battles for Cassino and Anzio might never have been necessary. The increased mobility would have enabled us to gain the German rear, which could not be done successfully on foot. General Patton shared these views with me.

The 3rd Infantry Division entered action in Sicily with 184 officers and men over the Table of Organization strength of 15,523. Every element in the Division was at a peak of condition as a result of nearly four months intensive training and preparation. Limited service personnel had been eliminated and all battalions were capable of marching five miles in one hour, eight miles in two hours, and long distances at three and a half miles an hour. I think it is safe to say that few divisions have ever entered action in a higher state of combat efficiency. Thirty-eight days later, after thirty days of actual campaigning, combat efficiency was somewhere near the peak in every respect except the infantry. We had suffered 1,925 battle and 2,983 non-battle casualties — a total of 4,908 men, or a third of our strength. Infantry companies were at little more than half strength, although it had not seemed from day to day that losses were excessive. I endeavored to make an analysis of casualties in order to determine just what had happened to my Division, but I discovered that I lacked essential data for an authoritative study. I set about establishing the necessary administrative organization within my Headquarters to provide this information for me after the next campaign.

The 3rd Infantry Division entered combat in Italy on September 18th, 1943, at slightly below T/O strength and at a high state of combat efficiency. The Division was relieved from action on November 17th after fifty-nine consecutive days of offensive action against German forces employing delaying and defensive tactics. During this period, the Division sustained 3,144 battle and 5,446 non-battle casualties, a total of 8,590 men. In the the same period, the Division received 4,118 replacements and 2,213 assigned personnel returned to duty from hospitals. Thus, when relieved, the Division was still short some 2,200 officers and men. This mere statement of casualties gives no full indication of the reduction of combat effectiveness, which could only be done by a careful analysis of casualties by branch unit, and military classifications. So I started an examination which disclosed some rather startling facts.

Division infantry suffered battle casualties at a rate of seven times that of other elements. The trend of effective combat strength in the infantry regiments was downward from the first day of combat. The greatest losses were riflemen, automatic riflemen, squad leaders, machine gunners, platoon sergeants, and second lieutenants. The rate of loss among second lieutenants was twice that of first lieutenants, three times that of captains, one and a half times that of majors, and seven times that of lieutenant colonels. The high loss of second lieutenants (152 per cent in 59 days, 66 per cent by battle casualties) suggested the high standard of junior leadership, but it also suggested a lesser degree of training and experience as well as a greater risk. The ratio of leader loss showed a gradual decline in combat efficiency, due to the reduction of experienced leaders and the lack of opportunity to train and indoctrinate replacements. The survey indicated that members of small combat units underwent the greater risk, exposure and hardship, and that infantry elements bore the brunt of battle. For instance, infantry combat casualties were seven times that of field artillery, non-battle losses only one-half that of field artillery. Ninety-three per cent of all losses were infantry. Eighty-six per cent of losses were in the infantry battalions. Thirty-five per cent of losses in battle casualties were riflemen; 12 per cent were squad leaders and the same figure applied to ammunition handlers. The direct relationship between battle and non-battle casualties indicated that the greater exposure and hardship incident to active operations cause increased rates of disease and non-battle injuries. In my final recommendation in this report I said: "The prestige of the infantry soldier must be enhanced in proportion to the hazard, exposure, and hardship required of him. Pay based on hazard and exposure, plus distinctive insignia for hazardous combat duty would contribute to this end."

Anzio contributed little that was wholly new in the field of military knowledge, but it was a sort of post graduate course for those who served there. When we were ordered on the defensive at the beginning of February, I had not trained the 3rd Infantry Division in the organization and conduct of defense, for we had concentrated on the offensive. Since there was no terrain that offered special advantages for defense forward of the Mussolini Canal — the Corps Beachhead Line — and it seemed unlikely that we could hold any position forward of that line against a strong German attack, I undertook to have each regiment occupy and organize the front line, an intermediate position, and the Corps Beachhead Line simultaneously. The enemy soon taught me that in this deployment I had made a grave error. The first small attack rolled back one front line battalion upon the intermediate position, and this resulted in such confusion that only the enemy's failure to follow up his advantage saved us from serious trouble. I saw then that no unit can defend while looking over its shoulder, and reorganized our defense to hold the front line, leaving the Division reserve and the Division engineers to organize the Corps Beachhead Line. I never made that mistake again; nor did the 3rd Infantry Division thereafter ever give up any ground that it held.

Technically, observers at Anzio were always impressed with the organization of artillery fires and the antiaircraft defense, both of which reached a state of perfection which few had ever seen. However, the technical specialists were not solely responsible for these developments. Our success was due in part to my command insistence upon original and unorthodox methods, and perhaps even more on the close cooperation between every command and staff echelon throughout the beachhead. Our visitors were always impressed by our confident, optimistic, and offensive spirit.

Looking back upon my experience in command at Anzio, I think I made my greatest contribution in restoring confidence and morale among all elements of the beachhead. I suspect this is, psychologically, always a fundamental principle of command. The successful commander must display a spirit of confidence regardless of the dark outlook in any grim situation, and he must be positive and stern in the application of measures which will impress this confidence upon his command.

Some command posts at Anzio were located in deep caverns or deep shelters insulated even from the sounds of battle. These shelters had an unfortunate psychological effect on men who worked in them. Since they depended on situation maps plotted from reports in visualizing any situation, situations often looked much worse than was the case. There was almost a claustrophobia that magnified unseen dangers and tended toward panic. Visits to the front by these men, however, usually restored the spirit of optimism. This psychological characteristic also affected the defense at Anzio. Except in a few areas, the water level at Anzio precluded the digging of deep trenches in the defense areas of World War I type, although the defense was similar in many other respects. A much more alert, energetic, and elastic defense materialized than would have been the case had we employed extensive trench perimeters engendering a Maginot Line psychology.

Some of the more important lessons at Anzio were those involving personalities, for the military art is a most personal one. General Alexander I had met first in Tunisia. I had encountered him on several occasions during the drive north from Salerno when he had visited my Command Post. We had conferred several times at Anzio. Almost invariably he arrived with a single aide. His quiet, unassuming, and dignified manner always put the staff completely at ease. His instant comprehension of complicated and difficult situations always surprised them. General Alexander had an unusual eye for terrain, and his determination to examine key localities in person was sometimes embarrassing.

During our effort to capture Cisterna at the end of January, General

Alexander came to my Command Post at Conca. After we had explained the situation, he wished to see the terrain about Cisterna. I was almost immobilized from a wound in my left leg which I had received a few days earlier. Accordingly, I sent General O'Daniels to escort General Alexander, having first endeavored unsuccessfully to persuade General Alexander to exchange his red-banded cap for my helmet. To avoid unnecessary exposure, I had given O'Daniels explicit instructions as to where he was to take General Alexander—an observation post from which he could obtain a fair, though somewhat distant, view of Cisterna with a minimum of risk.

When I returned from a conference late that afternoon, Carleton informed me that a company commander in a battalion then engaged just south of Cisterna had telephoned saying: "By God, Colonel, you tell General O'Daniels and that guy with the red hat-band that if they want to prove how brave they are, please to do it some place else. They walked over my front line, and as soon as they left the Boche shelled the hell out of us."

Later, when I upbraided O'Daniels for disobeying my instructions and taking Alexander to this distant and exposed part of the front, O'Daniels replied: "Say, General, did you ever try to give orders to the Army Group Commander?" He had all of the personality and drive of Patton and Montgomery, without any of their flamboyance. He had the intellect and astute diplomatic skill of Eisenhower. Alexander was, in my opinion, outstanding among the allied leaders.

Clark was wholly different from Alexander. He had been an able staff officer, and he was an unusually able executive and administrator. However, he lacked Alexander's training and experience in high command, his first major command having been Salerno — a rough lesson. When Clark visited my Command Post, he usually arrived with an entourage including correspondents and photographers. His public relations officer required all press dispatches, even from Anzio, to include the phrase "Lieutenant General Mark W. Clark's Fifth Army". His concern for personal publicity was his greatest weakness. I have sometimes thought it may have prevented him from acquiring that "feel of battle" that marks all top-flight battle leaders, though extensive publicity did not seem to have that effect on Patton and Montgomery. Few men had greater personal charm than Clark, and no superior commander ever made greater efforts to support subordinates in their tasks. I cannot recall that Clark ever disapproved of any request I made, and he was always untiring in his efforts to immediately expedite any logistical or tactical problem.

Among the division commanders at Anzio, Harmon, O'Daniels, and Frederick were outstanding battle leaders. Harmon and O'Daniels were both rugged, down to earth physical types, with boundless energy. Both had keen minds, vivid imaginations, and plenty of initiative. They were well-trained, with a thorough knowledge of the business of fighting. Harmon had specialized in logistics and American armor. A classmate of Clark's, he was disappointed because he had not been selected to replace Lucas, but no one could have been more loyal to me than Harmon. I consider him to be one of the superior battle leaders that I knew during the war. O'Daniels had been my assistant division commander. He was a rugged, gruff-voiced Irishman, who thoroughly enjoyed fighting, and had no equal in bull-dog tenacity or as a fighting infantry division commander. He well merited the sobriquet "Iron Mike" by which the division knew him.

Frederick was another type. He was slight in build, with an almost unhealthy pallor, but rather dignified in appearance. He wore a somewhat inconsequential mustache and this combined with a gentle manner, gave him more the look of a haberdashery clerk than the first-class fighting man which he was. His fearless disregard of danger, indicated by nearly a dozen wounds, won him the admiration and respect of everyone, especially of the fine group of fighting men that he commanded. Frederick had that "feel of battle", and excelled as a battle leader.

Eagles, Ryder, and Walker were all intelligent, well-trained and professionally competent division commanders. All were personable and well liked by their divisions and by those with whom they came in contact. They were not, however, outstanding battle leaders.

It is rather difficult to compare British and American commanders at the division and lower levels because of the differences in organization, tactical doctrines, command methods and other factors. Templar was conspicuous among the British commanders. He was intelligent, energetic, and colorful, with a keen sense of humor. At the time, I thought that he was the only British division commander who would have done well with an American division. Penney had been a signal officer. He was a fine-looking man, with a personality that was pleasing to superiors and equals in rank, but rather forbidding to those who served under him. Penney lacked confidence in himself, I think, for he was invariably pessimistic in his approach to every problem, and rather inflexible in adjusting himself to changing situations. Gregson-Ellis I had known in England. He had a first-class mind and was one of the ablest staff officers I knew. He was fearless. His gaunt figure clad in shorts, his hawklike features topped by a rather silly looking (on him) tin hat, stalking about the front lines with a long staff reminiscent of a shepherd's crook in hand, always brought Ichabod Crane to my mind.

Armchair strategists have criticized both the strategic concept and the conduct of the Anzio operation and have alleged "intelligence failure", "poor leadership", "lack of aggressiveness", "too much transportation", and like reasons for its so-called failure. Such criticism is normal when military operations fall short of preconceived hopes and expectations. But what are the facts? Did Anzio accomplish the purpose for which it was undertaken? Was it worth the cost?

The specific mission assigned in General Clark's Field Order No. 5, January 12th, 1944, was: "*a*. To seize and secure a beachhead in the vicinity of Anzio. *b*. Advance on Colli Laziali." The purpose of the operation was not stated in this order, but was given in General Alexander's Operations Instructions No. 32, January 2nd, 1944, addressed to General Clark and to General Leese commanding the Eighth Army: "The objects of this operation will be to cut the enemy's main communications in the COLLI LAZIALI area southeast of Rome, and to threaten the rear of the 14 German Corps." The initial landing force in SHINGLE carried out only part of this mission; it was not fully accomplished until four months had passed, when the landing force had almost quadrupled in size.

Few military operations have ever had a better intelligence than that upon which SHINGLE was based. Knowledge of a German division's withdrawal from the area of the landings — which would have been discovered by our intelligence if the landing had been delayed — would not have enabled us to establish a secure beachhead any more rapidly than we did. In all ranks of the Corps landed at Anzio, leaders were as well trained and competent as any in the Allied forces, and they were fresh from extensive experiences in Sicily and southern Italy. More than twenty per cent loss in battle casualties during the first thirty days of battle does not indicate any lack of aggressiveness or willingness to fight. No Corps or Division ever had abler staffs than those that planned SHINGLE, and few operations ever have been more carefully planned or been under such difficult conditions.

One must admit, I think, the initial strategic concept erred in two respects: overestimating the effect that the landings would have upon the German high command; and underrating the German capacity for countering this move. Our own high command expected — or at least hoped — the landings would cause a hasty German withdrawal from the southern Front. None of the commanders who landed at Anzio held any such belief, and we had learned through experience to respect the resourcefulness of our German opponent. Any reckless advance to the Colli Laziali without first establishing a firm base to protect our beaches would have been sheer madness and would almost certainly have resulted in the eventual destruction of the landing forces. Field Marshal Kesselring, the German commander in Italy, remarked to AP correspondent, Daniel De Luce, in an interview in January, 1946: "It would have been the Anglo-American doom to over-extend themselves. The landing force was initially weak, only a division or so of infantry, and without armor. It was a half-way measure as an offensive that was your basic error."

Our own high command eventually realized the initial effort had been a "half-way measure as an offensive" and regrouped the Allied Armies in Italy accordingly. With both the Eighth and Fifth Armies reinforced and massed on the western part of the southern front, and with the beachhead forces increased to more than seven and one-half divisions, there was reason to hope that the original object for which the Anzio operation was undertaken might be attained. General Alexander's instructions to General Clark for the breakout operation were: "Launch an attack from the ANZIO bridgehead on the general axis: CORI-VALMONTONE to cut Highway 6 in the VALMONTONE area, and thereby prevent the supply and withdrawal of the German Tenth Army opposing the advance of the Eighth and Fifth Armies." However, once again a "half-way measure" was to prevent us from fully achieving our purpose, for changing the direction of the attack from the beachhead and leaving only the 3rd Infantry Division and the 1st Special Service Force to block the Valmontone Gap was even less than a "half-away measure as an offensive." There has never been any doubt in my mind that had General Clark held loyally to General Alexander's instructions, had he not changed the direction of my attack to the northwest on May 26th, the strategic objective of Anzio would have been accomplished in full. To be first in Rome was poor compensation for this lost opportunity.

Battle casualties at Anzio amounted to some 7,000 killed and 36,000 wounded and missing in action. 44,000 received hospital care for sickness and injury. Seven and one-half divisions and dozens of supporting units were concentrated in the beachhead for the final effort. More than a half-million tons of supplies were unloaded there to support them. One cruiser, a hospital ship, several other war vessels, Liberty ships, and smaller craft were sunk and destroyed. Was Anzio worth this cost?

The Germans concentrated more than a dozen divisions in the effort to destroy the beachhead, and their losses were even heavier than our own. Until the final attack, there were never fewer than seven German divisions in the beachhead area and others were held in readiness not far away. These divisions would have been available for use on the Russian front, in the Balkans, to oppose the Normandy landing, or elsewhere. For four long months, the beachhead was, as Kesselring put it, a "festering wound south of Rome", posing a continual threat to the enemy forces in Italy and affecting every German plan. It cost the

Germans some 50,000 casualties, and took a toll of aircraft, artillery, tanks, and supplies which they could ill afford. While the beachhead did not prevent the escape of the German Tenth Army, it speeded the German withdrawal and made impossible any defense south of Rome. Though no one who spent four bitter months at Anzio would ever willingly repeat the experience, none of them — and few who study the Italian campaigns — will ever doubt that Anzio was worth the cost in "blood, toil, sweat, and tears".

The invasion of southern France was characterized by the coordinated violence of the initial assault and by the speed and energy with which success was exploited. These are essentials for victory in any military operation, which commanders and staffs do not always recognize. DRAGOON was fortunate in this respect because the Corps and division commanders and staffs had wide experience in assault landings. They had been thoroughly indoctrinated with the value of speed in military operations and the divisions had attained high standards in speed techniques.

At Anzio, the VI Corps for the assault landing was composed of one British and one American division. These divisions were organized differently, trained under different tactical curriculums, methods, command and staff procedures, employed different weapons, and even ate different rations. These diversities complicated routines and operations and necessitated almost duplicate administrative and logistical establishments. The DRAGOON assault, composed entirely of American divisions, demonstrated the value of a homogeneous assault force. The fact that the French forces which followed the assault were equipped and organized on an American scale, and used American equipment, weapons, and supplies, made the command and logistical problems in southern France far simpler than they had ever been in Italy.

Besides the careful and thorough assault planning on the part of the Corps and division staffs, DRAGOON clearly illustrated the value of anticipatory planning to exploit enemy weaknesses with speed in execution. Had we not planned the organization, assembly, and employment of Butler Task Force before we sailed from Naples, we would not have been able to gain the rear of the German XIX Army at Montelimar. That Army might then have been able to develop an effective withdrawal and our exploitation would then have been far less rapid and extensive. Our assault divisions had been thoroughly trained in rapid movement, and their close pursuit prevented the enemy's withdrawal to even a new defense line. There have been few operations in which the speed of execution has paid greater dividends than in the

invasion of southern France. An essential difference between the landings at Anzio and in southern France might be noted. In southern France
the landing was made in sufficient strength; it was not a "half-way
measure as an offensive".

At the time of the capture of Rome, both General Alexander and
General Wilson recommended to the Combined Chiefs of Staff that
troops should not be withdrawn from Italy to invade southern France.
They did not believe that an invasion coming so long after the Normandy landing would be of major assistance to OVERLORD. They
were in favor of shortening the war by utilizing these resources to clear
the Germans out of Italy and to thrust into the Balkans toward the
Hungarian plains, thus leaving the Allies in a much stronger political
position when the war ended. Looking back over the post-war years,
there is little doubt that the Western Allies would have profited, politically, had this recommendation been adopted. However, it was disapproved because General Eisenhower considered ANVIL-DRA-
GOON essential to the success of OVERLORD, and only in this light
can its ultimate value and significance be judged.

In one month, American and French forces of the Seventh Army had
almost completely destroyed the German XIX Army, captured some
80,000 prisoners and inflicted other heavy losses in personnel, equipment and supplies. The Allied Armies had driven nearly five hundred
miles north from the beaches to the Vosges Mountains and had joined
hands with General Patton's Third Army on the right flank of the
OVERLORD forces. This junction of DRAGOON and OVER-
LORD cut off many additional thousands of German troops in southwest France, and caused them to surrender without further resistance.
DRAGOON was therefore responsible for clearing the Germans from
all of southern and southwestern France south of the advancing flank
of General Eisenhower's OVERLORD forces, already extended over
a large area and on supply lines of extreme length. Moreover, DRA-
GOON held down large German forces which would have posed a
serious threat to the OVERLORD forces and compelled General
Eisenhower to counter them. No secondary attack in history ever
attained greater results. And from a political point of view, the question
as to whether or not DRAGOON was a mistake involves the strategy
of the Italian campaign and the overall strategy of the conduct of the
war in Europe.

One other possibility might have been considered: leaving the VI
Corps in Italy while the seven French divisions undertook DRA-
GOON, thus enabling the Allied Armies to clear the Germans from
Italy and thrust into the Balkans during the fall of 1944. There is every
reason to believe that the French forces could have established a beach-

head in southern France and captured the ports of Toulon and Marseilles. But it is highly debatable whether they would have been able to exploit northward as the VI Corps was able to do, because they lacked the experience in assault landings and the technical and practical skill to utilize transport, which was essential. The existence of these French divisions in the Rhone Valley would have served to protect the flank of OVERLORD, but certainly they would have inflicted less damage on the enemy. In this event it might have been possible, by the early months of 1945, to have cleared Italy of the enemy, and established Allied forces in the Balkans without jeopardizing OVERLORD in any material way. While the decision to undertake DRAGOON was undoubtedly sound under the circumstances, the course of postwar events makes one wish that some Balkan thrust had been attempted.

Except for the few months in southern France, my experience spanned the whole of the bitter and costly Italian campaign. Fifth Army losses, including the British, French, Brazilian and Italian troops that served under Fifth Army command in Italy, amounted to some 32,000 killed, 134,000 wounded and 22,000 missing. Nearly one quarter million German prisoners of war passed through Fifth Army cages, and it is likely that the German losses in killed and wounded exceeded our own. Figures for the British Eighth Army, always the stronger of the two armies, are no doubt comparable, for it was burdened by and exposed to the same bitter fighting.

Despite the armchair strategists both in and out of uniform who began to question the strategy that placed the Allied Armies in Italy, there is no question that the Italian campaign made an important contribution to the Allied victory in World War II. It eliminated the Axis menace in the Mediterranean; from its inception removed one Axis partner from effective participation in the war; occupied thirty-five or forty divisions which the Germans desperately needed elsewhere, inflicted heavy losses in men and materiel and imposed enormous strains upon an already overburdened economy; and provided bases from which the Allied Air Forces carried the air war over all of German-held territory from Rumania to Poland.

Few persons would question that it was sound strategy to invade Sicily in order to free the British "life line" through the Mediterranean, or to invade the Italian mainland after Mussolini's downfall to complete knocking Italy out of the war, and obtain bases there to prosecute the air war. Committed so far, continuation of the campaign to capture Rome was essential for political and strategic reasons. Perhaps the principal reservation or objection to the Italian campaign centers upon whether or not it should have received more or less weight in Allied war councils in comparison with the Normandy invasion, and, therefore, either a larger or lesser allocation of armament and power.

Those who view post-war relations today will be convinced that the campaign in Italy should have received a far greater consideration in Allied war councils, for had Allied troops occupied portions of southeastern Europe or the Balkans, the present political situation could hardly have come about. But military concentration to gain the maximum effort is one of the first principles of war, and a prerequisite on the road to victory. Secondary fronts are given the minimum of assistance to enable them to accomplish their essential tasks and complement the main effort. Thus, considered militarily, rather than politically, the overall strategy was entirely sound.

When General Alexander urged cancelling the invasion of southern France in favor of clearing the Germans out of Italy and driving through the Balkans, General Eisenhower told the Combined Chiefs of Staff that he did not believe Allied resources were sufficient to support two theaters in Europe, both with decisive missions.

It may be worthy of note that the Italian campaign was essentially mountain warfare, and was fought on, and for, the steep, barren, and rugged chains of mountain peaks and ranges that dominated the few roads that ran north and south. The divisions that made up the Fifth Army—and the Eighth Army, too, for that matter—were ordinary infantry and armored divisions, which had to acquire training, modify organization, and improvise equipment and methods as the campaign progressed, for until the arrival of the 10th Mountain Division, no division in the Fifth Army had been specially organized, equipped and trained for mountain warfare.

Until the final campaign in northern Italy, close air support for ground troops was never as effective as it should have been and was often entirely missing. This is not to say that ground forces did not derive some advantage from the interruption of enemy communications and the blasting of industrial targets hundreds of miles away, for these air missions did have a vital effect upon the course of the war. They did not, however, help the ground soldiers much in overcoming serious obstacles on their immediate front. It was not until the Air Force accepted the principle of control by a forward ground controller and the Tactical Air Commander established his headquarters with the Army commander that close air support became truly effective. This is, in my opinion, a minimum requirement for effective air support for ground forces.

The Fifth Army, like other American forces, was actually a highly mechanized force with many tanks and tank destroyers, much motorized artillery and antiaircraft artillery, and trucks and other vehicles in profusion. Traffic control became a vital problem. Our two and a half ton truck and our jeep made us far more mobile even in mountain warfare than our British Allies, for these vehicles had far greater cross-country mobility than any of the British vehicles.

Yet, with all of the support made possible by mechanization both in the air and on the ground, it was the infantryman who bore the brunt of the Italian campaign. It was the infantryman who scaled the heights and stormed the German positions. The whole campaign depended upon the physical and mental condition, the state of training, and the morale of the individual soldier, and, particularly, of the individual infantryman.

The British soldier was the product of a far more rigorous discipline, of the Prussian type, than was the American soldier. This was due to British military traditions and in part to the social structure of British life. This stricter discipline may have made the British soldier appear more phlegmatic than his American comrade, lacking the American's ingenuity and resourcefulness. British soldiers always seemed to me more suited for defense than for attack, while with American soldiers the reverse was true. Although the American could distinguish himself on defense when occasion required, the British soldier could always be expected to hold to the last man whenever he was told to do so. British and American soldiers invariably got on well together, and it was only among the high echelons that friction developed between the Allies. All in all, British and Americans held each other in mutual respect; they were worthy Allies who fought well together.

French troops in Italy and southern France, colonials for the most part, performed well and merited the high regard in which they were held by the American troops. In both areas, French troops were perhaps more volatile than Americans, but they displayed considerable dash. There was never the close relationship between American and French soldiers that existed between American and British soldiers, one reason being the language barrier.

When American soldiers first came in contact with the German soldier, the latter was already a veteran with a long military tradition, the product of long and thorough military training, led by experienced and capable officers, and equipped with the most modern weapons. The German was then better trained especially for operations in small units, and the quality of his leadership was superior. German soldiers displayed an ingenuity and resourcefulness more American than British. The American quickly adapted himself and learned much from the German. Sicily and southern Italy proved that he had mastered his lessons well. From Anzio on there was never a question of the superiority of American soldiers.

The American soldier did not like war. He dreaded the uncertainty, danger, and hardship. He was rather resentful of military discipline and its interference with his individual liberties. He hated the monotony of military training and the physical effort it required. When asked why he was fighting, the answer was as often as not, "because I have to." He may not have known just why he was in Africa, or Italy, or elsewhere, but he appreciated well enough why he was fighting. War had been forced on the country at Pearl Harbor; like others, he had to do his part toward winning it. Disliking war, discipline, training, discomfort, and hardship, the American soldier accepted them philosophically as aspects of a disagreeable task to which he applied his native ingenuity and resourcefulness. The American soldier demonstrated that, properly equipped, trained and led, he has no superior among all of the armies in the world.

•

INDEX

INDEX

A

Acerno, 257, 258-259, 260
Ackworth, Lt. Comdr., 54, 63
Adige Line, 479, 498
"Adolf Hitler Line," 370
Advanced Command Post, North Africa, 130-138, 141, 150, 151, 153, 156, 157, 159, 160, 172
Africa, campaign in, 124-173
Agrigento, 218, 219-222
Air Force, U.S.A., 278-279, 353, 354, 356, 398, 455, 471, 482, 483, 488, 554-559
Air Task Force, 79
Airborne Force, 390, 393, 399-400, 419-420
Akers, Lt. Col. R.F., 154, 155
Aleutian Islands, 465
Alexander, General Sir Harold R., 133-134, 150-151, 159, 167-170, 173, 174, 187-188, 195, 214-215, 221, 222, 262, 280-281, 287-288, 290, 291, 294-296, 298, 332, 344, 351, 364, 366, 368-369, 382, 387, 447, 448, 449, 451, 456, 495, 499-500, 546-547, 549, 552, 554
Alger, Colonel, 157, 159
Algiers, 57, 58-59, 61, 72-73, 124, 127-129, 246
Allen, Henry T., U.S.S., 85, 88, 93, 96, 97, 109
Allen, Maj. Gen. Terry, 73, 142, 170, 190
Allied Air Forces, 205, 289, 290, 306, 321, 324, 335, 337, 349, 346, 347, 349, 353-356, 399, 476, 481, 482, 488
Allied Control Commission, 497
Allied Control Council, 510-512, 527
Allied Force Headquarters, Algiers, 124, 129-132, 151, 152, 158, 163, 173, 174, 180, 193, 199-200, 383, 385-386, 537, 539
Allied Military Government, 497, 499-500, 508, 511-512

Almond, Maj. Gen. E.M., 469-470, 471, 473, 484
Ancon, U.S.S., 246, 247, 249-250
Anders, General, 370, 492
Anderson, Lt. Gen. Sir Kenneth A.N., 125, 126, 129, 131, 133-142, 144, 147-159, 162, 164, 167-169, 173, 537-538
ANVIL campaign, 381-409
Anzio, 9, 286-380, 545-546, 550-551
"Anzio Express," 337-338, 339, 380, 433
Apennines Mountains, 465-466
Apex boats, 405-406, 412, 413
Apuan Alps, 470
Archibald, Colonel, 26, 35, 38, 56
Armies
  First Army (British), 125, 129, 130, 131, 134, 140, 142, 150
  Second Army, 15
  Third Army, 57, 433, 508-509, 512, 523-524, 526-531
  Fifth Army, 9, 245, 246, 262, 280, 283, 286, 288, 290, 291, 304-306, 328-330, 351, 364, 366, 380, 382, 448, 451, 456, 458, 459-461, 464-465, 468, 476, 477, 479-480, 482-485, 494, 496, 500, 504, 505, 550, 555
  Sixth Army (Italian), 198
  Seventh Army, 195, 218, 222, 380, 381-382, 398, 399, 441, 445, 504, 528
  Eighth Army (British), 128, 133-134, 150, 153, 195, 245, 246, 249, 252, 254, 262, 288, 351, 364, 365, 366, 370, 449, 451, 456, 476-477, 479-481, 483, 485, 498, 550
Army Groups
  VI Army Group, 468, 498-499
  XV Army Group, 249, 262, 280, 454, 456, 476, 477, 493, 501, 504
Armored Force, 15
Army War College, Washington, D.C., 18

Milton Keynes UK
Ingram Content Group UK Ltd.
UKHW022158260324
440183UK00017B/778